TEACHING LAW IN THE TRENCHES

TEACHING LAW *in the* TRENCHES

The Essential Features of Clinical and Externship Teaching

Wallace J. Mlyniec
LUPO-RICCI PROFESSOR OF LAW EMERITUS
GEORGETOWN LAW CENTER

CAROLINA ACADEMIC PRESS
Durham, North Carolina

LIBRARY OF CONGRESS CATALOGING-IN-PUBLICATION DATA

Names: Mlyniec, Wallace J. author
Title: Teaching law in the trenches : the essential features of clinical and externship teaching / Wallace J. Mlyniec.
Description: Durham, North Carolina : Carolina Academic Press, 2026. | Includes bibliographical references and index.
Identifiers: LCCN 2026013505 | ISBN 9781531018122 paperback | ISBN 9781531018139 ebook
Subjects: LCSH: Law—Study and teaching (Clinical education)—United States | Education—Study and teaching
Classification: LCC KF282 .M597 2026
LC record available at https://lccn.loc.gov/2026013505

CAROLINA ACADEMIC PRESS
700 Kent Street
Durham, North Carolina 27701
(919) 489-7486
www.cap-press.com

Printed in the United States of America

This book is dedicated to the
hundreds of students and fellows I have taught
and to the hundreds of clinical teachers who have enriched
my understanding of clinical pedagogy and
brought joy to my life.

CONTENTS

PREFACE

This book has been many years in the making. It is the product of my own thinking and experimenting with different teaching modalities and the product of the ideas and theories developed by teachers in the nationwide clinical community. When I started as a clinical teacher, there were very few of us. Indeed, it was not unusual for schools to have one staff attorney or teacher with very little support. Now there are close to two thousand members of the clinical section. This growth demonstrates the significance of experiential teaching in the legal academy.

Today, many of the first generation of clinical teachers are retiring. They are being replaced by new teachers who may not find other clinical teachers with a great deal of experience on their faculties. Thus, they may not find mentors to help them understand and navigate the complexity of clinical pedagogy. Several years ago, I began wondering how they would learn the essential features of experiential pedagogy. The amount written about clinical teaching is vast, perhaps too vast for the new teachers to ever have the time to find the older articles let alone read the best of them. There are several books written that try to synthesize the pedagogy and collect it in one place. Nonetheless, "Where do I begin?" remains a critical question for new teachers. As I complete my teaching career, I thought it was time for another attempt at answering that question while offering suggestions to more seasoned clinical teachers.

I chose the title *Teaching in the Trenches* because it often felt like we were in an actual battle for the heart of legal education during the early years of the clinical movement. At times, it still feels like that. We not only have to struggle against our adversaries and judges in the court room, we also have to battle the non-clinical faculty in our own schools who continue to think we do not belong in the academic world. While that adversarial environment has tempered to some extent, it has not disappeared. Thus, teaching in the trenches remains an apt metaphor.

This book is a collection of fifteen essays in which I try to explain what I believe are the essential features of clinical and externship teaching. Excerpts from other important articles written by talented clinical teachers follow each of my essays. Some are old but still important while some discuss novel issues in our evolving endeavor. Some amplify my understanding of clinical pedagogy while others take a different tack.

The book can be read as a complete unit when a teacher begins a new semester. Individual chapters can also be read when a teacher confronts a difficult teaching question concerning one of the essential elements. In either case, I hope the essays and excerpts assist both new and seasoned teachers as they continue to explore the wonders of experiential pedagogy.

ACKNOWLEDGMENTS

In some sense, I have been writing this book for more than 50 years. Thus, it is impossible to name all the people who have influenced my thinking about clinical pedagogy. I will try to remember them all and apologize to those who I neglect to mention. Mentioned or not, I thank them for all they have contributed to this book and to my development as a clinical teacher.

I will start with my colleagues at Georgetown. We have been fortunate to have had successful deans at Georgetown for more than 70 years. All have valued experiential education, and all supported me throughout my career. Paul Dean helped create the E. Barrett Prettyman Fellowship Program in 1950. Adrian Fisher secured a level of independence from the university in 1971 which created the financial foundation that allowed the future expansion of clinical programs. In the 1970s and 1980s, David McCarthy and Robert Pitofsky transferred experiential education from soft money funding to hard money funding. They also created faculty status for clinicians, first on a contract track status and then on the tenure track. Judith Areen created the first Associate Dean for Clinical Education in 1990 and began the large expansion of our clinics throughout that decade and a half. Alex Aleinikoff continued that expansion during the early 2000s and William Treanor also continued the expansion of the clinical faculty during his fifteen years as dean. Bill also coordinated the transition of our retiring first-generation clinical faculty to a new cohort of tenure track clinical faculty.

Several members of the Georgetown faculty were critical to my developing understanding of clinical teaching. Kris Henning and Eduardo Ferrer, both extraordinary teachers, collaborated with me in the Juvenile Justice Clinic for decades. For many years, John Copacino, Robert Stumberg, Rachael Camp, and Jane Aiken shared much of the teaching in our Elements of Clinical Pedagogy class along with members of our Legal Research and Writing faculty, Vicki Girard and now Erin Carroll. I learned many of the supervision techniques noted in this book from them. Many other members of our faculty also taught in the class from time to time and shared their knowledge with me as well. I am grateful to all of them.

Deborah Epstein has been my closest partner in this endeavor. We have talked about clinical teaching for decades and jointly established the Georgetown Summer Institute. We wrote two books together and shared the leadership of the clinical pedagogy course we teach to the Georgetown clinical fellows. I learn something from Deborah every time I watch her teach or read her articles.

There have been teachers from other schools who have contributed to my development as a teacher and thus to this book. Everyone who presented at an AALS or CLEA conference added to my conception of clinical pedagogy. My friend of a lifetime Elliott Milstein, and his colleagues Ann Shalleck and Robert Dinerstein from American Law School, have been especially supportive. Catherine Klein from Catholic University was one of our early collaborators in the Georgetown Summer Institute. Other members of our Pincus Village gang, Susan Bryant (my research assistant before she became famous) from CUNY Law School; fellow Chicago guys Steven Wizner and Jay Pottenger from Yale; Conrad Johnson and Jane Spinak from Columbia; Claudia Angelos from NYU; Dean Rivkin from the University of Tennessee; Kate Kruse from Mitchell-Hamline; and Elizabth Cooper from Fordham all learned as much from each other at dinners with fine wine, joyous camaraderie, and serious conversation as we did at the clinical conferences. And Brad Colbert from Mitchell Hamline and David Santacroce from the University of Michigan always managed to make me laugh as they challenged my ideas and offered theirs. Finally, all of the law teacher-authors who graciously consented to my use of excerpts from their articles have had a profound impact on this book.

I cannot ever thank my Georgetown colleagues and my friends from other schools enough for the influence they have had on the ideas that have gone into this book.

Many Georgetown law students contributed to this project. Being a law student research assistant can be both a joyful and tedious undertaking. We all know that Bluebooking is the scourge that every RA must endure. Yet the joy flowing between students and writers when the RA finds a perfect excerpt to include in the book or when the writer chooses the RA's language for inclusion in the book is thrilling. Moreover, the conversations that ensue about why those ideas fit well are often remembered long after the book is in print. Sometimes it may launch a change in career plans. So it was with the first RA who worked on the book, Katie Kronic, now a law professor herself at the University of Baltimore. Other talented students joined me as the years passed. Jennifer Legvengood, Jasmine Sola, Elana Bauer, Haley Etchison, Meghan Strong, Matt Rawson, and Geoff Kozens worked on related projects that provided additional background to some of the concepts incorporated in this project.

Because of other intervening projects, the book took much longer to write than I thought it would. Thus, the RAs who worked on the books for the past few years deserve a great deal of credit. Janelle Sampana, Heather Hu, Conor O'Shea, Marie Laplante, and Ian Elliott spent hours tracking down articles, editing my work, and often suggesting and sometimes writing first drafts of ideas derived from non-legal sources that improved the content of the book. Of course, they cleaned up endnotes to ensure accurate Bluebook citation form and cross-referencing citations for accuracy. I am deeply indebted to them for all of their contributions.

I am grateful to the production staff for this book. My first reader is always my wife and favorite librarian, Abby Yochelson. Abby is a gentle critic who can spot written gibberish better than anyone I know. Along with Abby, Jennifer Lane from Georgetown and Susan Beal from Portland, Oregon, were my primary editors. Susan is a good friend who has edited another of my books. Betsy Kuhn and her Georgetown team edited and formatted many of the articles that supplement my essays. My librarian Rachel Jorgenson trained my research assistants and was always available for whatever research request I or my RAs made. Yelena Rodriguez tracked down articles and printed them out since I still don't like to read substantive information from a computer screen. Jennifer also drove the copyright consent process, a nightmare task for any book project, while the Director of the Georgetown Library, Austin Williams, answered the challenging questions about copyright law issues. Jennifer was also the person who maintained order during the production process.

Finally, this book would not exist without the staff at Carolina Academic Press. Senior Acquisitions Editor Carol McGeehan saw merit in the project early in its development and had great patience while waiting for me to develop the proposal. Managing Editor Ryland Bowman made helpful suggestions throughout the book's development and, like Carol, had great patience with my continued requests for submission extensions. Steve Oliva, the book designer at CAP, corrected my editing mistakes and helped bring the the manuscript to print.

TEACHING LAW IN THE TRENCHES

One

INTRODUCTION

The Evolution of Clinical Pedagogy

The concept of experiential education, as embodied in classical in-house clinical courses, externship courses, and hybrid courses has, after a long, sporadic, and difficult history, become an accepted part of the legal academy.[1] Teaching the merger of theory and practice as part of a student's legal education is rooted in the early experiments that brought law practice into the curriculum at the University of Denver law school in 1904.[2] This merger was also promoted as the theoretical basis for experiential education outlined in the academic writings of Jerome Frank in the 1930s,[3] Gary Bellow and Bea Moulton in the 1970s,[4] and Anthony Amsterdam in the 1980s.[5] William Pincus, who provided funding for new experiments in clinical education in the 1960s and 1970s through the Ford Foundation and the Council on Legal Education for Profession Responsibility,[6] helped to enhance and expand experiential learning. Ultimately, the American Bar Association (ABA) adopted law school accreditation standards mandating that experiential education be a significant aspect of a student's legal education. These standards led to the grudging acceptance of clinical education's academic legitimacy by the Association of American Law Schools (AALS).[7]

"Clinicians are typically full-time legal educators who teach and or supervise law students with an experiential learning process designed to help students develop critical, analytical, and reflective thinking, and the judgment necessary for the actual day-to-day effective and ethical practice of law. Most clinical professors supervise student cases or projects and/or teach in either in-house clinics in the law school or in externships (also known as field placement programs). Clinical faculty may be designated as tenured or tenure-track faculty, clinical faculty, lecturers in law, supervising attorneys, adjunct faculty, or some other classification system adopted by a particular institution...."[8] These variously titled educators have been dedicated to perfecting the art of clinical pedagogy since its tenuous and controversial reemergence in the 1960s.

The pedagogy has continued to evolve ever since.[9] Hundreds of articles and several books have been written[10] about the various tasks students must learn and lawyers must perform. Clinical faculty must also master these lawyering tasks if they are to teach students not just to perform them, but to understand the reasons why they are essential to effective lawyering. Many of these authors have addressed how to work with students to develop a method for approaching client representation, how to understand the relationship between theory and practice, how to execute lawyering tasks once they are understood, and how to transfer the lessons learned in one task to others, both similar and disparate. They also addressed how students can develop methods to enhance a lifetime of learning new tasks as they themselves mature as lawyers after graduation and their practices develop.

By creating this vast bibliography, the early authors also created a vocabulary for clinical pedagogy that is often misunderstood by non-clinical teachers. It is also sometimes unclear to, or misused by, those beginning their clinical teaching careers. Even faculty who have some familiarity with the foundational terms of clinical pedagogy sometimes use the terms imprecisely. The lexicon includes some relatively easy-to-understand terms like in-house clinics and externships, reflection, critique, and feedback. Others, like transference, backward design, scaffolding, context, intentionality, and intervention, have specific meanings in the clinical lexicon that transcend their ordinary understanding.

In addition, other terms that were created in the early days of clinical education, such as directive and non-directive supervision,[11] stubbornly remain in the lexicon out of habit, even when their use can reinforce a false dichotomy about intervening in a student's work. All interventions are, in a sense, directive, whether we are leading students to arrive at a correct analysis or strategy or telling them the correct analysis or strategy. But context and goals determine the type of intervention a faculty member uses. There is now fairly clear evidence that students learn better and retain more when teachers use active learning methods rather than lecturing, or merely telling students what to do and how to do it.[12] On the other hand, there are times when we do give students an answer, or tell them where to find an answer, because of the context in which the intervention takes place. We also do it when there is no pedagogical reason to withhold the answer, or when the answer itself will lead them to a higher level of inquiry. As a result, experienced clinical teachers try to avoid the terms directive and non-directive because the words inaccurately describe the pedagogical intervention methods we actually use in the clinic. Nonetheless, the traditional words die hard, and most clinical teachers continue to use them as a shorthand description of what they are doing. When appropriately used in the proper context, both kinds of interventions can successfully help students learn. But in some instances, using those terms to describe the faculty member's action may lead to less than exemplary or inaccurate instruction.

The Emerging New Generation of Clinical Teachers

The modern clinical education model is now more than sixty years old. The founding generation of clinical teachers is quickly disappearing because of happy retirements and inevitable deaths. New teachers, many of whom have little grounding in clinical pedagogy, are now replacing the pioneers. Few (though thankfully an increasing number) have had prior training in clinical pedagogy in fellowships attached to law clinics or as visiting faculty members in well-established clinical programs. Those without prior training are nonetheless often expected to immediately take on the supervision of several students working on cases or projects and classroom teaching assignments when they arrive.

Many of the new clinical teachers are coming to academia straight from practice. When these "practice-trained" clinical teachers remember their own law school experience, they rely on traditional academic teaching methods or reference their own clinical experience. Traditional law school podium teaching has little in common with clinical pedagogy. Nor does participating as a student in a clinical course in law school adequately prepare a person to actually be a clinical teacher. A former law student's knowledge of clinical teaching comes from learning rather than teaching. Some law school clinical and externship programs merely move cases through the clinic, the way a public interest organization moves a case through a judicial and legislative forum, rather than treating clinical courses as academic programs. This is especially true of clinics outside of the United States where bar and court rules or university policies constrain the students' experience. Faculty in those programs often see themselves and their clinic as extensions of a legal aid office, rather than as an integral part of an academic institution. Thus, a former clinic student, even one from a well-run law school clinic, seldom understands the knowledge, techniques, or the craft that experienced clinical professors bring to educating students to become competent lawyers.

New faculty who come from an active law practice background are equally unprepared to establish a well-run clinical course, even if they were training directors at their prior firms or public interest organizations. Training supervisors perform very different tasks from those of a clinical supervisor. Those new teachers generally rely on their experiences as training supervisors, having only a vague understanding of clinical pedagogy or the scholarship requirements of the academy. Often, they also may find themselves floundering or merely teaching skills. Although law schools recognize the vocational aspects of their mission, teaching the theory of practice in an academic setting transcends the training new lawyers receive in a law firm or public interest office.

Resources for Experiential Teachers

New teachers may look for help in the hundreds of articles and the several books that have been written about clinical teaching. When they do, they may find that recent articles often assume the reader has more than a basic knowledge of clinical pedagogy. Older articles are often rich sources of information for new and mid-level teachers; however, new teachers may leave them unread, thinking they are too outdated to be of much use. Hence, new teachers and even those approaching mid-level experience may ask, "Where should I begin to find answers to the complicated teaching and learning challenges arising in my work?" They may also wonder, "Why can't I find everything I need to consider in one place?"

The same questions are now asked around the world. Clinical education has grown dramatically, both in terms of the number of law schools supporting clinical courses and in the number of faculty members teaching in them.[13] Although clinical education has its roots in the United States,[14] grants from the Ford, Soros, and other foundations have awakened legal academies around the world to the importance of clinical pedagogy. The challenging work of the Global Alliance for Justice Education (GAJE), a worldwide organization dedicated to promoting justice through education, has inspired legal academics around the world to emulate or adapt the clinical method used in the United States, or to develop wholly new methods more relevant to their own nations.[15]

There is now a worldwide need for a book to help these new teachers answer the question "Where do I begin?" Experienced clinical teachers may also need a book to reenergize their teaching methods and to stay aware of both the historical roots of clinical pedagogy and its evolving nature as the movement matures. As noted above, the dedication of clinical educators to create a distinct pedagogy has resulted in an abundance of articles being written about lawyering, teaching methods, supervision techniques, grading, and a host of other topics related to teaching the reflective practice of law. There are articles about the role of lawyers and the place of lawyers in a democracy where the rule of law is applied unequally or is diminishing. Several authors have provided guidelines for the structure and operation of a clinic; others have collected excerpts from various law review articles focusing on specific topics that arise in a clinical course. That academic discourse, oral and written, has created a pedagogy that is rich and sophisticated, but still eludes new teachers. It is also often overlooked by more senior teachers in the time-crush of their daily teaching and supervision activities. In addition, the majority of newer articles do not answer the basic questions about the foundational pedagogic elements of experiential teaching, or how one prepares for their first few years of teaching in a clinic or externship. Moreover, the articles seldom cut across the boundaries of the various kinds of clinics and other experiential courses as they focus on specific areas of law or fora.

Genesis of This Book

This book is different from the books and articles that preceded it. The goals and content come from a course I designed, Elements of Clinical Pedagogy, to train our graduate clinical fellows. I have now co-taught the course with Professor Deborah Epstein for many years, along with the assistance of other members of Georgetown Law Center's clinical faculty. I learned and developed ideas set forth in the course and in this book during my long career as a clinical teacher. Many of my experienced colleagues and those from other law schools also contributed ideas and techniques, which we integrated into our thinking and in the way we designed and teach the pedagogy course. We prepare our clinical teaching fellows to become our co-teachers and case and project supervisors, and to enter into the legal academy as full-time clinical teachers after they complete their fellowships. Unlike most other clinical fellowships, Georgetown's fellowship is a degree-granting program.[16] Therefore, the Elements of Clinical Pedagogy course is more than just a primer on how to practice law, or an instruction manual on how to supervise law student cases and projects in a specific clinical program. Our course is a comprehensive introduction to teaching law students about the interrelationship between theory and practice using the clinical pedagogical method. It also helps them become lifelong learners.

Our work in the pedagogy course was the basis of two articles that I wrote in 2012, and two books I later co-wrote with Deborah Epstein and Jane Aiken. The articles "Where to Begin? Training New Teachers in the Art of Clinical Pedagogy"[17] and "Developing a Teacher Training Program for New Clinical Teachers"[18] were published in the CLINICAL LAW REVIEW in 2012. Our books, THE CLINIC SEMINAR[19] and TEACHING THE CLINIC SEMINAR,[20] were published in 2014 by West Academic. These articles and books set forth some of the critical questions that new and mid-career clinical teachers must address concerning the goals and content of a clinic, its supervision techniques, and its seminar content and execution. They also address how the goals and content inform the execution of the faculty member's methodology. The books and articles remain relevant today, but there is good reason to write a comprehensive book now for new and mid-career clinical teachers.

Many changes have occurred within the legal academy and in clinical education theory during the last decade that make this book especially timely. The design and structure of the Elements of Clinical Pedagogy course has evolved since we first wrote the articles and books. Many of the current readings for the course were never mentioned in the earlier syllabus. As we learned more from the fellows and new teachers about what was most important to them, we added new topics to the course. Moreover, we reexamined and refined the teaching methods that we use. As the pedagogy grew more sophisticated, we consolidated what we learned as we taught, incorporated effective new ideas from other teachers, and revised the goals of both the course and the individual classes. We learned from our clinical colleagues from across the globe through our participation in GAJE, and from our own training offered to clinical professors in the United States and around the world. We also learned new methods from the yearly sessions during the AALS Clinical Education Conferences.

The ABA has also been instrumental in recognizing the value of clinical and other forms of experiential education as necessary for educating law students. In 2014, the ABA adopted new accreditation standards for US law schools, mandating that students receive at least six credits of experiential education in their coursework.[21] Because of these recent ABA requirements, US law schools are increasing their experiential course offerings and seeking additional faculty members to staff them. The need for additional members of the experiential faculty is occurring at the same time as the so-called "founding generation" of American clinical teachers are leaving their faculty positions. The new teachers are losing the benefit that experienced teachers could provide.

Because of the change in accreditation standards, experiential education in the US legal academy now seems less fragile and more firmly ensconced in law schools, and the number of new clinical teachers in the United States increases every year. However, law school deans and most non-clinical faculty now expect their clinical colleagues to teach students more than how to move a case or project from start to finish. They want students to study theory as well as practice skills in their clinical courses—and to learn how theory and practice merge in an ethical and competent legal practice. Predictably, the expectations of deans and non-clinical faculty will only grow stronger as the ABA accreditation standards require schools to expand their experiential offerings and the size of their clinical faculties.

Experiential education is also gaining acceptance and expanding in law schools outside of the United States, as educators and lawyers begin to recognize a student's need to understand how good theory informs good practice, and how lessons from practice can strengthen theory. As a result, law professors around the world are developing courses that teach students how to integrate practical experience with sound theoretical foundations while pursuing their academic studies.

The number of new clinical teachers throughout the world increases every year, thanks to the work of GAJE and other international regional conferences, as well as the conferences sponsored by the Clinical Legal Education Association (CLEA) and the AALS Section on Clinical Education in the United States. The new teachers need a book that not only brings together the foundational aspects of experiential education but one that guides them toward success.

What to Expect in This Book

New clinical teachers, whether they are field-trained in legal services offices, apprentices working with other clinical faculty as visiting professors from practice, or as clinical fellows, cannot intuitively understand the core tenets of the clinical pedagogical method. Those entering the profession in other countries with limited exposure to the U.S. clinical education practices may find it even harder. After more than sixty years of development, the abundance of articles and books published to guide clinical professors—the canon of clinical education—is both a blessing and a curse. It can be daunting to newcomers and even to mid-level clinicians and may even perplex seasoned experiential teachers.

It is not easy for clinical teachers to locate and read the large number of articles and books available as they prepare for their classes, while also maintaining their active case and project supervision loads. Indeed, trying to keep up can be overwhelming. In addition, these materials are often compartmentalized to specific topics in experiential education. The authors of topical articles, for example, those discussing ethical questions in clinical education or client-centered interviewing methods, often presume that the reader already has a basic knowledge of clinical pedagogy upon which to graft the article's more sophisticated techniques.

Retiring clinical education pioneers take with them a wealth of accumulated knowledge concerning clinical pedagogy, leaving behind less experienced and very busy colleagues to guide the newcomers. Hence, the new teacher often wonders where to even begin. One obligation of the founding generation of clinical teachers is to ensure that newcomers are trained for their current and future teaching and supervision duties as they gain actual teaching experience. It is also imperative that mid-level teachers appreciate that their jobs are more than just supervising cases or projects. These experiential teachers are responsible for safeguarding and preserving the rich legacy of the clinical education movement, learning and practicing the core elements of clinical teaching, and further developing clinical pedagogy theory within the academic community.

Becoming a successful teacher is not intuitive.[22] Indeed, intuition may be thought of only as an immediate act of cognition, based on the sum total of all the lessons one has learned about a subject, that springs to mind based on prior acts of metacognition and experiences.[23] Nor are most teachers just born to be teachers. Successful teaching results from preparation, acquired knowledge and experience, failure, conversations with experienced teachers about successful and unsuccessful moments in the classroom and supervision sessions, and reflection.[24] Teaching requires certain attributes that can be learned. Preparation, passion, and presence are the necessary attributes of any teacher.[25] But the stakes are even higher given the unique teaching relationship between experiential teachers and their students and the formidable process of representing clients in the process.

A Path for Clinical Teachers

I have several goals for this book. The first is to guide new teachers on a path to excellence in an academic rather than a simply practice environment. The second is to remind seasoned teachers of the academic nature of our work, even as they endeavor to serve the clinic's clients effectively. The third is to evoke the evolving contextual complexity of clinical pedagogy in both new and seasoned teachers—who then periodically reevaluate their methods to reinvigorate the pedagogy as the complexity evolves.

Therefore, I present some of the critical questions about clinical pedagogy that teachers will need to confront and answer as they move through their careers. The ideas and teaching methods discussed in this book are based upon six fundamental beliefs embodied in the clinical pedagogical movement.

1) Clinical teaching is different from, and more expansive than, doctrinal teaching or professional legal practice.
2) Clinical teaching is goal-driven and based on a backward design process.
3) Faculty intervention into a student's work is intentional and based on making choices that simultaneously advance a student's education and a clients' interests.
4) Clinical education is based on an expansive theory of justice.
5) Client and student needs are equally important in a clinical program, and the needs and interests of one do not have to be sacrificed for the other.
6) Clinical teaching is contingent on the teacher's personal investment in individual students and accepting students where they are on their path to knowledge and professionalism. Thus, each teaching activity should be planned in a

way that maximizes the student's learning potential in the clinic and in their future careers.

These six principles are the foundation of this book and of lifetime learning. They form the basis for any experiential course and are a guide for all clinical and other experiential teachers. Moreover, they provide a method to monitor and advance a student's academic success and personal well-being while in the clinic.

For all these reasons, a book-length treatment of the topics we introduced to new experiential education teachers more than a decade ago in other books and articles seems critical now. I hope this book serves that purpose. I have gathered tenets of my earlier work, along with significant contributions accumulated during the last five decades from other clinical scholars, to explain the pedagogy to new teachers. I want to not only share the foundational contributions from early clinicians but introduce newer concepts teachers have been developing as our pedagogy matures. Thus, it is a primer offering valuable lessons to ease the new clinician's entry into the profession and help them to become career legal academics as they nurture students' learning and preserve clients' interests.

This book will also enable more senior clinical teachers to reimagine how the interrelationship of theory and practice affect clinic design. It provides insights into how students' relationships with their peers, with their teacher, and with their clients can affect clinic design. I hope this book will help teachers understand the importance of articulating goals as the first step in planning supervision sessions and seminar classes. It explains why the original notions of directive and non-directive supervision are antiquated and unhelpful, and how an adaptive notion of intervention better describes clinical supervision methods. Finally, it suggests how a clinic's classroom component can affect and ultimately improve student supervision and client representation.

A Note on Vocabulary

Several forms of experiential education have developed since the reemergence of clinical education in the mid-to-late 1960s. The term in-house clinic refers to those programs housed within the law school where a full-time faculty member supervises the students' cases and projects. Externships are those programs where lawyers in organizations unrelated to the law school itself supervise the students' case or project work. Classroom instruction and reflection taught by full-time or adjunct faculty usually accompany those programs. Hybrid clinics or practica combine elements of both models. Depending on the law school, the terms used above to define programs may differ from these more generally accepted definitions. A school may define any kind of experiential program as a clinic. So, hybrid courses or externships in some law schools may be called clinics for administrative reasons. Conversely, a school may choose to drop all of those distinctions and merely operate a broad-based experiential program with separate courses defined by their subject matter and method of instruction. Notwithstanding their nomenclature, all involve many aspects of true clinical pedagogy.

For consistency in this book, I use the words "clinical" and "experiential" going forward to encompass all forms of experiential legal education involving clients. I recognize that there are differences in the goals and methods used in each, and that the literature about in-house clinical courses, externships, and other forms of experiential courses reflect those differences. Nonetheless, except when noted, a reader can assume that experiential and clinical can be treated as synonymous with all forms of experiential education that use students to represent real clients, recognizes the importance of theory as it relates to practice, and uses the clinical pedagogical method.

Similarly, faculty are often given different titles or are described by the role the faculty member is assuming in the moment. Thus, a faculty member may be referred to as a teacher in the classroom, but as a supervisor when working on the case or project. Clinical faculty may be on a unified tenure track or a separate clinical tenure track, on a contract track with governance responsibilities, or be employed on a series of term contracts without a role in faculty governance. Some are called adjunct or practice faculty or visitors from practice. Some will be called fellows whether or not they are pursuing an advanced degree at the law school. Going forward in this book, the terms faculty member, teacher, and supervisor will be used interchangeably and refer to anyone teaching in an experiential course using clinical pedagogy because they all assume the role of leading students on their journey to becoming civic-minded professionals skilled in the tasks of lawyering.

A Note on Content

Some content in this book is derived from two articles I wrote for the Clinical Law Review. Since we hold the copyright together, it is not always specifically cited for ideas I have explained in earlier work. I am grateful that the Review published the articles and have also allowed me to use those ideas without constant attribution. Some content also comes from my book Teaching the Clinic Seminar, which I co-wrote with Deborah Epstein and Jane Aiken. I am grateful that West Academic not only chose to publish the books, but that they and my co-authors agreed that I may use ideas without specific attribution, since we jointly hold the copyright.

A Note on the Accompanying Articles

Each of my chapters are followed by a subchapter called Other Voices. As the history of clinical education shows, we are a collaborative community in which ideas are shared and incorporated into our own work. I am grateful to the clinicians and their publishers who allowed me to use their scholarship to further explain the topics of the main chapter.

The text of the articles accompanying the main chapters of this book are excerpts rather than full text with omitted portions noted with ellipses. The original footnotes have also been omitted with the permission of the authors and their publishers. I have included the excerpts for those readers who wish to delve deeper into the subject of the main chapter. Full citations are also included for those who wish to read the entire article. I encourage all readers to explore at least the excerpts if not the entire article.

A Closing Note

My goal in writing the essays which comprise this book was to introduce new teachers to the vocabulary and the tools they will need to bring a new generation to the excellence of a movement we all treasure. I also hope the book encourages more senior teachers, those who were thrust into their teaching and supervision roles without much prior training, to explore the roots of clinical pedagogy and to continue to develop our unique pedagogy, reimagine it, and advance our mission within their own law schools. I also hope that it reenergizes them and serves to enhance their skills as they move into their maturing years. Finally, I hope that by the time teachers finish reading this book, they will have gained a new or renewed understanding of the complexity of our work and its importance to our communities, our students, and to academia. The past is prologue; but the future of clinical education is now, and it is in the hands of a new generation of teachers. I wish them well.

Other Voices

Clinical Legal Education Association, *A Taxonomy of Clinical Program Design*

HANDBOOK FOR NEW CLINICAL TEACHERS (5th ed. 2009)*

This document provides an overview of some of the common types of clinics, and some of the fundamental design questions facing most clinical programs. It does no more than to introduce basic ideas, and to distinguish different approaches one from the other....

Types of Clinics

Clinicians and law schools have generated an enormous diversity in clinical programs, responding to many influences: social justice, client need, clinician interest and motivation, funding, teaching goals and more. This section provides some points of distinction between various programs, organized:

By relationship of student, client & supervisor:

A. Direct service ("live client"): Students form lawyer-client relationships directly with clients, in law practices engaged exclusively in clinical practice, under the supervision of law school clinicians.

B. Externship: Students in law offices engaged primarily in non-clinical practice, under the supervision of both attorneys engaged in that practice and law school clinicians.

C. Hybrid: Programs which combine and vary elements of the others, including vary either the nature of the law practice, its relationship to the law school, and the degree to which the clinician engages in specific case supervision and active practice in the underlying practice.

By lawyering activity:

A. Litigation: Students represent clients in formal advocacy to authoritative decision makers, typically in courts or administrative agencies and in trial or appellate advocacy.

B. Transactional: Students represent clients in planning, negotiating and drafting of transactions from individual planning through community organizing, to regulatory and legislative rule-making.

C. Dispute resolution/neutral practice: Students engage in either informal negotiation or in practice as neutral mediators or arbitrators.

D. Judicial: Students work as clerks in judicial chambers, both trial and appellate, typically in an externship model.

---

* Excerpts are reprinted with the permission of the Clinical Legal Education Association.

E. Community organizing: Students work with community groups to advocate for group issues and concerns, including economic development and/or social justice.

F. Legislative advocacy: Students accept legislative drafting and advocacy projects on behalf of clients seeking redress through legislative action. Related to both transactional and community organizing clinics.

G. Ombudsman/informal advocacy: Students advocate on behalf of clients towards informal, non-litigation solutions to individual or community problems.

H. "Unbundled" clinics: Students engage in lawyering tasks seen (and taught) as a sub-set of "full lawyering, such as counseling pro-se assistance or negotiation.

By relationship to law school and funding sources:

A. In-house vs. external:

1. In-house clinics function exclusively as clinical practices within the law school, in which clinicians work with students to provide the chosen legal services.

2. External clinics function as law practices outside the law school, with attorneys hired to practice in the chosen field, and with clinical training as an accepted, not primary feature.

B. Hard money, soft money, direct state support:

1. Clinics funded with hard money operate as part of the law school's internal budget, based on sources of support for the entire institution, including alumni giving and state support. Seen as institutionally secure, but within administrative discretion.

2. Clinics funded with soft money operate on funds from temporary sources, including grants, foundations and governmental programs. Seen as unstable and provisional, but providing a measure of independence from decanal control.

3. Clinics funded with direct state support operate on funds from state or local government to provide a designated legal service.

Association of American Law Schools, *Glossary for Experiential Education**

The ABA Standards for Approval of Law Schools now require that law students take at least six credits in "experiential courses." ABA Standard 303(a)(3). These standards also define three different kinds of courses that satisfy this requirement: I) "law clinics," II) "externships," or "field placements;" and III) "simulations." ABA Standard 304. While most law schools have each of these kinds of courses, some have also created

* Excerpts are reprinted with the permission of the AALS Section on Clinical Education.

other courses that do not fit neatly within these definitions, in an effort to diversify student opportunities for experiential education.

These changes have created a confusing welter of names and labels. In some cases, the same name refers to very different courses; in others, different names refer to the same kind of course. Any one course can have features that overlap with but are not identical to the features of similar courses. No one set of terms defines these courses precisely and usefully.

With this document, the Section on Clinical Legal Education of the Association of American Law Schools offers a uniform set of terms and descriptions for the more common forms of experiential education including clinical legal education. The Clinical Section intends this glossary to encourage the development of experiential teaching in law schools and to identify the elements of course design characteristic to the different kinds of experiential courses.

...

The Clinical Section acknowledges the range of different kinds of experiential education offered throughout our community. The Section is also sensitive to the issues underlying the use of certain terms, in particular "clinical" and "experiential," which historically has meant in-house clinics and externships or field placements, and simulations, respectively. In developing this taxonomy, the Section draws from the expertise of members of the Section and specifically from two sources: Alliance for Experiential Learning in Law, *Experience the Future: Papers from the Second Annual Symposium on Experiential Education in Law*, 7 Elon L. Rev. 1(2015) (hereinafter "Alliance Article"); and Deborah A. Maranville, et al., Building on Best Practices: Transforming Legal Education in a Changing World (Lexis Nexis 2015) (hereinafter, "Building on Best Practices"). The authors of these two sources compiled and analyzed a list of terms, using similar vocabulary and similar definitions. The Alliance article included more terms, including those that described programs taught by our colleagues in non-clinical programs.

...

Terms Referring to Experiential Education Generally

Experiential Learning:

> Experiential learning is what happens when we learn from experience. It is nature's way of learning. Humans depend on experiences, or observations of the experiences of others, to understand the world. We learn from experience on our own, and sometimes, we enlist teachers to help us engage in more directed learning from experience. Another way to describe experiential learning is "incidental learning": the learning that comes to us as we experience life, with no particular focus or structure.

...

Experiential Education:

Experiential education is an active method of teaching that integrates theory and practice by combining academic inquiry with actual experience. It encompasses many methodologies in which educators purposefully engage with learners in direct experience and focused reflection in order to increase knowledge, develop skills, clarify values, and develop people's capacity to contribute to their communities. Experiential education methods in legal education include both simulated practice experiences, in which students assume the role of a lawyer in a simulated setting, and clinical legal education experiences, in which students assume the role of a lawyer, either in support of others as a mentee or as a student lawyer with a high level of direct responsibility as lead counsel or member of a lawyer team.

An experiential course is a credited course in which experiential education occurs.

ABA Standard 303(a)(3) defines an experiential course as follows:

"An experiential course must be a simulation course, a law clinic, or a field placement. To satisfy this requirement, a course must be primarily experiential in nature and must:

1. Integrate doctrine, theory, skills, and legal ethics, and engage students in performance of one or more of the professional skills identified in Standard 302;

[The skills in Standard 302 are:

(a) Knowledge and understanding of substantive and procedural law;

(b) Legal analysis and reasoning, legal research, problem-solving, and written and oral communication in the legal context;

(c) Exercise of proper professional and ethical responsibilities to clients and the legal system; and

(d) Other professional skills needed for competent and ethical participation as a member of the legal profession.]

2. Develop the concepts underlying the professional skills being taught;

3. Provide multiple opportunities for performance; and

4. Provide opportunities for self-evaluation."

In this document, experiential education includes law clinics [and] externships ... addressed more fully in the sections that follow. The term does not include pro bono opportunities, which are often uncredited activities in which experiential or incidental learning may occur.

Clinical Legal Education:

Clinical legal education is a particular form of experiential education that engages students in addressing real-world legal matters in interaction with others through supervised practice experience. Under the supervision of either a faculty member or a field supervisor who is accountable to the law school, students assume the role of a lawyer either in support of others as a mentee or as a student lawyer with a high level of direct responsibility as lead counsel or a member of a lawyer team.

A clinical legal education program is a collection of courses offered by a school in which a significant part of the learning involves supervised practice experiences in which students assume the role of a lawyer, either in support of others as a mentee or as a student lawyer with a high level of direct responsibility as lead counsel or a member of a lawyer team. The shape and size of these programs vary greatly in response to many influences: social justice, client and community need, clinical faculty interest and motivation, funding, and teaching goals. Some law schools mandate clinical education for students and others guarantee a clinical experience for any student who wants one....

Self-Evaluation:

The ABA's new definitions of experiential courses, law clinics [and] externships... require that each include "opportunities for self-evaluation." The ABA has not yet provided guidance on the meaning of "self-evaluation" nor is there a commonly accepted definition of the term. We recommend that the term "self-evaluation" be read to include two inter-related aspects: the capacity to assess a specific lawyering performance and make appropriate changes; and the capacity to reflect on experience more generally so as to improve insight, broaden understanding, and develop decision making ability.

I. Law Clinics

Law Clinic:

A course in which a significant part of the learning involves students assuming the role of a lawyer representing actual clients, or performing other lawyering roles, under the supervision of an attorney who is a member of the law school faculty member (full-time, part-time, or adjunct), fellow, or staff attorney. Law clinics have a low student to faculty ratio in order to allow faculty to rigorously supervise legal work, provide on-going and cumulative opportunities for student self-evaluation and provide on-going, individualized feedback to students on their performance, both distinguishing features of law school clinics. Law clinic courses include a classroom seminar that may address substantive or procedural areas of law, ethical rules, lawyering skills and theory, and case rounds. The law clinic seminar employs signature pedagogies such as simulations, role plays, case rounds and opportunities for students to reflect on the larger social and political context in which they practice. Law clinics also require students to engage in self-evaluation and other reflection, through individual supervision, journals, and other formats. Many law clinics also incorporate social justice concepts.

Law clinics may operate within the law school or in the community, with or without community partners. Students typically work part-time in a law clinic and receive credit for the casework and seminar while taking other law school courses. In some cases, a school might offer a full-time clinic experience, where students work longer in a clinic and thus receive a higher number of credit hours.

The ABA defines a law clinic in Standard 304(b):

> A law clinic provides substantial lawyering experience that (1) involves advising or representing one or more actual clients or serving as a third-party neutral, and (2) includes the following:
>
> (a) direct supervision of the student's performance by a faculty member;
>
> (b) opportunities for performance, feedback from a faculty member, and self evaluation; and
>
> (c) a classroom instructional component.

For ABA purposes, to qualify as an experiential course, a law clinic must meet the requirements of *both* Standard 303(a)(3) and Standard 304(b).

In-House Clinic:

A law clinic operated by the law school in which faculty members supervise students to provide law related services. An in-house clinic need not be physically located within the law school building.

II. Externships/Field Placements

Externship or Field Placement:

A course in which a significant part of the learning relies on students either representing clients or performing other lawyering roles under the supervision of practicing lawyers or other qualified legal professionals who are not members of the law school faculty, in practices outside the law school. Common kinds of practices include governmental, judicial, non-profit, and for-profit placements; site supervisors can include attorneys, judges, mediators, and legislators. Site supervisors share supervision of students with a faculty member. Site supervisors agree to provide direct feedback and guidance to the students and maintain ultimate responsibility for the client or legal matter. Faculty have overall responsibility for assuring the educational value of the learning on site and the academic inquiry at the law school. In particular, faculty prompt students to engage in the guided reflection that is a defining characteristic of externships, often but not necessarily through a seminar associated with the course.

Externship courses usually involve students working part-time at the placement, while taking a related seminar and other courses at the law school. However, semester-in-practice or immersion externships have become increasingly common. In these courses, students work close to full-time and may also take a related seminar and a more limited pool of other courses.

The ABA Standards refer to these programs as "field placements" (See e.g., Standard 303(a)(3), Standard 303(b)(2) and Standard 304(c). The term "externships" is not used by the ABA in Standard 303 but represents the nearly universal label for these courses in law schools and the national community of clinicians. This document uses the terms interchangeably.

An externship program refers to the collection of externship courses within a law school's clinical legal education program. Many externship programs organize externships into specialties, which then may have topic-specific companion courses, such as criminal, civil, and judicial practice.

ABA Standard 304(c) defines a field placement course as follows:

> "A field placement course provides substantial lawyering experience that (1) is reasonably similar to the experience of a lawyer advising or representing a client or engaging in other lawyering tasks in a setting outside a law clinic under the supervision of a licensed attorney or an individual otherwise qualified to supervise, and (2) includes the following:
>
> (a) direct supervision of the student's performance by a faculty member or site supervisor;
>
> (b) opportunities for performance, feedback from either a faculty member or a site supervisor, and self-evaluation;
>
> (c)a written understanding among the student, faculty member, and a person in authority at the field placement that describes both (A) the substantial lawyering experience and opportunities for performance, feedback and self-evaluation; and (B) the respective roles of faculty and any site supervisor in supervising the student and in assuring the educational quality of the experience for the student, including a clearly articulated method of evaluating the student's academic performance;
>
> (d) a method for selecting, training, evaluating, and communicating with site supervisors, including regular contact between the faculty and site supervisors through in-person visits or other methods of communication that will assure the quality of the student educational experience. When appropriate, a school may use faculty members from other law schools to supervise or assist in the supervision or review of a field placement program;
>
> (e) a classroom instructional component, regularly scheduled tutorials, or other means of ongoing, contemporaneous, faculty-guided reflection; and
>
> (f) evaluation of each student's educational achievement by a faculty member; and

> (g) sufficient control of the student experience to ensure that the requirements of the Standard are met. The law school must maintain records to document the steps taken to ensure compliance with the Standard, which shall include, but is not necessarily limited to, the written understandings described in Standard 304(c)(iii) [sic]"

For ABA purposes, to qualify as an experiential course, an externship course must meet the requirements of *both* Standard 303(a)(3) and Standard 304(c).

Cooperative Education Program:

A structured educational strategy integrating classroom studies with learning through work experiences in a field related to a student's academic or career goals. Unlike in an externship, students in a Cooperative Education Program, also called Co-op Program, typically do not receive academic credit for the fieldwork. Law schools enhance learning from fieldwork in Co-op Programs in a variety of ways, such as course/fieldwork sequencing, vetting of field supervisors, assessments of student work, student journals, and pre- or co-requisite companion courses. *Compare* "semester-in-practice" or "immersion" courses, in which students receive credit.

Internships:

The term "internships" is often used interchangeably with "externships" or "field placements." We suggest that term should be read to refer only to experiences in outside law practices, paid or unpaid, for which students do not receive credit.

III. Emerging Experiential Models

The terms "law clinic" and "externships" refer to long-standing models of clinical course design that the definitions in the previous two sections describe. At the same time, emerging models of clinical education have arisen that combine aspects of law clinics, externships, and other courses in new ways. For ABA purposes, to qualify as an experiential course, any of these emerging clinical models must meet the requirements of *both* Standard 303(a)(3) and Standard 304(b).

Given the diversity of forms these clinical models take, there is no one set of widely recognized terms that describe each model or the differences between the models.

...

V. Other Experiential Education Terms

The inclusion of these terms in this section does not indicate that all of these models would satisfy the ABA requirements for being considered an experiential course. For each of these models, the requirements of ABA Standard 303(a)(3) would have to be met before the course could be counted as an experiential course.

Service Learning:

Service learning is a teaching and learning strategy that integrates meaningful community service with instruction and reflection to enrich the learning experience, teach civic responsibility, and strengthen communities. In law schools, service learning can include law clinics and externships. The term does not encompass simulations, which typically do not include community service.

Social Justice Education:

Social justice education teaches students how the laws, policies, and practices of institutions and communities further injustices in society at large. Within experiential education, social justice education incorporates the development of skills necessary for students to challenge subordination of, and create systemic change for, underserved populations, often in partnership with the affected communities. A significant number of law clinics and externships use social justice education methods, either explicitly or implicitly. Simulation courses may also be designed to use social justice education methods.

Pro Bono Program:

A program designed to inspire and to enable students to engage in pro bono service, while in law school. The primary purpose of these programs is to teach students why pro bono service is an important professional value and to introduce them to the ways in which they can contribute in their practice as attorneys.

Traditionally, this term has referred to legal work uncompensated by credit or pay. The term now includes for-credit clinical opportunities, where explicit education and reflection teach why pro bono service is an important professional value. This definition comports with both the ABA rules and new requirements implemented by the New York Bar. *See*, Interpretation 303-3 of ABA Standard 303(b)(2); New York Bar. N.Y. Comp. Codes R. & Regs. tit. 22, § 520.16 (2012).

. . .

Endnotes

1. *See* Roy Stuckey, *Power and Politics in the Founding Era of Clinical Education* (2021), https://repository.library.georgetown.edu/handle/10822/1062764.

2. "... Denver Law has led the way since 1904, when we founded the first legal aid dispensary in the nation." University of Denver Sturm College of Law, *Clinical Programs: Student Law Office*, https://www.law.du.edu/academics/practical-experience/clinical-programs.

3. *See generally* Jerome Frank, *Why Not a Clinical Lawyer-School?*, 81 U. Pa. L. Rev. 907 (1933).

4. Gary Bellow & Bea Moulton, The Lawyering Process: Materials for Clinical Instruction in Advocacy (1978).

5. *See generally* Anthony G. Amsterdam, *Clinical Legal Education—A 21st-Century Perspective*, 34 J. L Edu. 612 (1984).

6. Council on Legal Education for Professional Responsibility. Inc., First Biennial Report (1970) (hereinafter First Biennial Report).

7. American Bar Association Standard 303) (a)(3); Robert Dinerstein, *Report of the Committee on the Future of the In-House Clinic*, 42 J. L. Educ. 508 (1992).

8. AALS Section on Clinical Legal Education Membership, Outreach, and Training Committee in consultation with the AALS Section on Clinical Legal Education Executive Committee, Clinicians' Desk Reference, (2018) at 2. The terms "clinical teacher," "externship teacher," "clinical supervisor," and "experiential teacher" all define faculty members who endorse the nature of clinical pedagogy. While the structure of the courses and the modalities and goals of teaching of the various courses are often different, they are similar enough that the terms will be used interchangeably throughout this book to describe the courses and the people who teach them. It does not include those who teach purely simulation courses since all experiential courses require an actual client.

9. Georgetown University Law Library, Special Collections, *Transcription of Oral History with Paul Bergman*, National Archive of Clinical Legal Education Collection (Jan. 5, 2001), at 7, https://repository.library.georgetown.edu/handle/10822/1060857.

10. *See*, J.P. Ogilvy, *Clinical Legal Education: An Annotated Bibliography* (2005), https://scholarship.law.edu/cgi/viewcontent.cgi?article=1994&context=scholar.

11. *See generally* James H. Stark, Jon Bauer & James Papillo, *Directiveness in Clinical Supervision*, 3 B. U. Pub. Int. L.J. 35 (1993).

12. Becky Supiano, *It's Not About the Evidence Anymore*. Chronicle of Higher Education, (June 22, 2022). interviewing Scott Freeman, emeritus lecturer at the University of Washington.

13. The AALS Section on Clinical Education had 1,857 members as of November 2024. Email from Julia Hub, Section Services and Meetings Coordinator, American Association of Law School, to Wallace Mlyniec, (Nov 11, 2024). GAJE has 550 active members as of November 2024. Email from Frank Bloch, Professor Emeritus at Vanderbilt Law School to Wallace Mlyniec (Nov 11, 2024). There is also a European Network for Clinical Legal Education, https://www.encle.org/.

14. First Biennial Report, *id* note 6, at 36–37.

15. Global Alliance for Justice Education, *Welcome to GAJE*, GAJE.org, https://www.gaje.org.

16. Georgetown Law, *Graduate Teaching Fellowships*, https://www.law.georgetown.edu/experiential-learning/clinics/clinical-teaching-fellowships/ (2024).

17. Wallace J. Mlyniec, *Where to Begin? Training New Teachers in the Art of Clinical Pedagogy*, 18 Clinical L. Rev. 505 (2012).

18. Wallace J. Mlyniec, *Developing a Teacher Training Program for New Clinical Teachers*, 19 Clinical L. Rev. 327 (2012).

19. Deborah Epstein, Jane Aiken & Wallace J. Mlyniec, The Clinic Seminar (2014).

20. Deborah Epstein, Jane Aiken & Wallace J. Mlyniec, Teaching the Clinic Seminar (2014).

21. American Bar Association Standard (303) (a)(3).

22. Beth McMurtrie, *The Damaging Myth of the Natural Teacher*, The Chronicle of Higher Education (2021).

23. Maryellen Weimer, *Understanding the Role of Intuition in Teaching*, Faculty Focus, Higher Ed Teaching Strategies From Magna Publications (May 29, 2013), https://www.facultyfocus.com/articles/academic-leadership/understanding-the-role-of-intuition-in-teaching/.

24. Rob Jenkins, *The 4 Properties of Powerful Teachers*, Chronicle of Higher Education (March 16, 2015), https://www.chronicle.com/article/the-4-properties-of-powerful-teachers/.

25. *Id.*

Two

THE NATURE OF CLINICAL PEDAGOGY

The literature regarding clinical pedagogy today is often described in terms of its goals, teaching modalities, and methods, and its sites of instruction. A clear definition itself, however, is often missing from those articles and books, or the authors assume that the readers already know what clinical pedagogy is. In the vast literature concerning clinical pedagogy, one of the best definitions of the field still comes from the Association of American Law Schools (AALS) Section on Clinical Legal Education's 1992 *Report of the Committee on the Future of the In-House Clinic*.[1] The Committee defined clinical pedagogy as

> first and foremost a method of teaching. Among the principal aspects of that method are these features: students are confronted with problem situations of the sort that lawyers confront in practice; the students deal with the problem in role; the students are required to interact with others in attempts to identify and solve the problem; and, perhaps most critically, the student performance is subjected to intensive critical review.
>
> If these characteristics define clinical teaching, then the live-client clinic adds to the definition the requirement that at least some of the interaction in role be in real situations rather than in make-believe ones. That is, the interaction with others in role occurs with real clients and participants in the legal system rather than with other students and actors. The nature of the real issues and cases in the live-client clinic provides both concreteness and complexity to the student's learning experience.[2]

The Limitations of Law School Teaching

For decades prior to the advent of the modern clinical education movement, teaching generally followed the Socratic method initiated by Christopher Columbus Langdell.[3] Because the method was static, and because law teachers of that era thought of themselves primarily as scholars, teaching was always a secondary concern of the legal academy. Even though law schools expect faculty to carry a teaching load as part of their responsibilities, the combination of research and scholarship has always been the coin of the academic realm.

Legal educators and the legal academy in general have mistakenly assumed that new teachers have an intuitive grasp of teaching methodology based on their experiences as law students or law clerks. Moreover, while students evaluate a faculty member's teaching via course evaluations at most law schools, a negative evaluation raises little concern unless it indicates serious and recurring pedagogical shortcomings. Teaching loads and evaluations are a factor when law school deans determine salary increases, but the production of scholarly articles notably outweighs other factors. Moreover, schools base tenure decisions largely on scholarly productivity, so tenure is seldom denied based on poor teaching ability unless scholarly productivity is also substandard. All these factors contribute to the secondary role that teaching has occupied in most law schools.

Few law schools offer specific pedagogical training to new teachers because many legal academics believe it is not needed. The basis for that notion is that new teachers can begin and continue teaching throughout their careers without any formal instruction on teaching methodology, learning objectives, or learning theory. Serious conversations about the science of teaching seldom take place in law schools or other post-college academic departments.[4] Because traditional law-school teaching methods are relatively similar regardless of which school one attended, and because the extent of one's teaching load is more often discussed than teacher training and quality, new faculty members may reasonably assume that teaching is simply the price they must pay in order to produce scholarship. Ultimately, law teachers may ignore or even disparage the study of pedagogical methodology. Hence, they often fail to connect closely with their students as they begin teaching and seldom recognize their students'—or their own—deficiencies until late in their academic careers. Even when they connect with their students, most law professors teach only doctrinal analysis, and not the other skills necessary for the practice of law. In addition, traditional law school exam courses assess students based almost exclusively on what they remember from the course readings and the lectures they heard. Students then answer the exam questions in one several-hours-long period of rapid-fire typing. The exam process reveals little about the student's growth as a learner, and even less about the teacher's ability to assess what a student learned in the course or whether the teacher advanced a student's learning and growth. For a host of personal and contextual issues, it may not even reflect all that a student actually knows. Nor does it reflect what lawyers actually do in practice.

Evidence suggests that law faculty are finally beginning to engage in training sessions to improve their teaching methods. The Covid-19 pandemic produced new and greater awareness and concern about pedagogical methodology. The almost overnight shift to teaching via Zoom during the pandemic and the need to plan for an uncertain period of time away from the standard norms and methods of in-class teaching showed how essential the knowledge of pedagogical theory and practices are. Teachers were forced to rethink their methods as they abandoned in-person teaching and quickly pivoted to online instruction. Moreover, a greater awareness and solicitousness of students' feelings of exclusion from a healthy classroom environment (with race, class, religion, politics, disability, sexual orientation, and gender identity as contributing factors) forced faculty to recognize how crucially teaching methods create and sustain an atmosphere that enhances student learning. These concerns have led to adaptations of the traditional methods of instruction used to convey substantive law in the legal curriculum. Nonetheless, this focus on teaching methods may be diminishing since the return to in-person education.[5] On the other hand, the advent of artificial intelligence is already generating conversations about its impact on teaching so the focus may remain.

Unlike traditional law faculty, clinical faculty have been discussing teaching theory and methods and how best to convey content since the early 1970s. That conversation continues today through the Association of American Law Schools (AALS) and the Clinical Legal Education Association (CLEA) national conferences, the many regional conferences that now occur each year, and the international conferences sponsored by the Global Alliance for Justice Education (GAJE) and other international groups. Prior to the development of clinical pedagogy, the dialogue that occurred between faculty and students in classes of one hundred or more and the strict hierarchy that existed between professors and students formed the basis for the Socratic method. Indeed, the displeasure with the exclusive and sometimes perverse use of this method helped create the clinical pedagogical movement in the late 1960s and early 1970s.[6] Despite the greater awareness of teaching methods that exists among all law teachers today, clinical faculty members face more and different challenges than their non-clinical colleagues. The challenges relate to class goals, seminar structure, the presence of clients in the academic enterprise, the influence of state bar rules, and to case and project supervisory methods. Challenges also arise concerning student feedback and critique, formative assessment, summative assessment (grading), and the unique teaching modalities inherent in clinical pedagogy.

Clinical teaching modalities are seldom used in traditional law school courses, although some non-clinical teachers are beginning to find them useful in traditional classroom settings. Clinical courses are different from traditional courses because clinical students are responsible for the interests and sometimes freedom of real clients. Client representation is the essential feature of all experiential courses. The various modalities also feature an element of uncertainty and indeterminacy. Clinic students may appear in court expecting to start a trial but instead have to pivot quickly to first argue about a newly revealed discovery violation or a new settlement offer. Facts are often muddled and uncertain. Two people who witness an event may have different interpretations of what occurred. Additionally, real clients, who possess and exhibit the full spectrum of human emotion within the inherent unpredictability of real law practice, force clinic students to confront and possibly abandon the seeming certainty that is inherent in judicial opinions.

The Essence of Clinical Pedagogy

Simulations and other clinical teaching modalities that sometimes occur in non-clinical courses are different from those used in experiential education. They typically have static (and fictional) case facts in an artificial context. Faculty design them to operate within a universe of relatively clearly applicable legal rules that forecast a central issue, with relatively well-balanced cases on both sides of the argument. In addition, the fictional and neatly defined nature of this work means that the whole enterprise generally lacks the emotional content that accompanies representing real clients.

Clients, however, bring uniquely high stakes, uncertainty, fluidity, and the range of human emotions into each teaching modality used in a clinic. Clients come to the clinic with various legal and individual problems and other difficulties in their personal lives which are often manifestations of the existing legal structures and dynamics in society. Hence, teaching challenges exist beyond the law and procedural aspects of the case that can become magnified by human personality. Several factors can compound the complexity of clinical teaching, rupture lawyer-client relations, and alter the personal and professional interactions of all participants. For example, the students' own worldviews and personal challenges may conflict with the personal and professional experiences of their supervisors. The same dynamic can occur between students and their clients. Because clinical pedagogy is so multifaceted, with so many variables affecting every mode of instruction, mastering it is not easy. It draws on antecedents from more formal traditional academic teaching, shares some kinship with other non-doctrinal learning in the legal academy (like first-year legal research and writing courses), and, to some extent, reflects methods derived from lawyer training in law offices and public-interest organizations. Moreover, it operates within the unpredictable behavior of not just students and clients, but other lawyers, witnesses, and judges. Thus, clinical teaching exists as a unique form of pedagogy with its own goals, methods, and challenges.

New clinical law school faculty seldom learn how to work within this framework before they begin to teach. Those who do may have gained some experience as a clinical fellow, a practitioner-in-residence, or a visiting professor in a law school clinical program. In serving in such positions, new teachers might have absorbed the basics of the pedagogy by watching the work of more experienced clinical teachers as they supervised student cases and projects. Others are lucky enough to participate in one of the few clinical master's degree programs, where they learn the theory behind the art and science of clinical pedagogy in a structured training program, working with experienced clinical faculty members as they supervise their own students. These structured programs often provide classes in the theory and practice of clinical pedagogy and conduct supervision rounds about simple or difficult teaching and supervision issues arising with their own students. There, they can learn and challenge that theory and practice and reflect on it as it arises in new contexts. They can also experiment with new methods under the tutelage of the experienced faculty.

For the most part, however, new clinical teachers continue to come from practice without formal clinical teaching training. They come from legal aid and public defender positions and tend to bring the methods they used or learned in those organizations' new lawyer training programs and on-the-job observation. They often assume that the methods used by clinical teachers and those used by legal services training directors are equivalent, and that their training in prior employment positions can provide the basis for their work in the academic setting. This misconception fails to acknowledge the differences between the goals of new lawyer training in high-volume legal services offices and those of law student training in an academic setting. Todd Edelman, once a training director at the Public Defender Service for the District of Columbia, later a clinical professor and then a judge in DC Superior Court, aptly described those differing goals in a conversation that I related in one of my earlier articles.[7] He noted that legal-services training supervisors work with lawyers who often have large caseloads and who will quickly become solely responsible for their cases. A training supervisor's goal is to provide those new attorneys with the tools they need to succeed on their own in a specific area of practice. The tools they teach are the lawyering skills the new lawyer will use every day in a specific type of practice. The supervision is thus less intensive and narrower than that which occurs in a clinic. It is less intensive because the goal in a public-interest law office is to train the lawyer to move a client's case through the system expeditiously and successfully and then move on to the next case. The acquisition of specific lawyering tasks and efficiency are the major goals of the training. It is also less intensive because larger questions regarding mission and values are already clear to someone who joins the organization, and there is little concern for how the skills learned might apply in other areas of law. The new lawyers have already made life choices about values and goals, so training directors do not need to discuss uncertain values or emerging learning or professional goals. Public interest lawyers, unlike students, are unburdened with typical student anxieties regarding competence, failing to protect their first clients, future employment, education debt, bar exams, and final exams. Moreover, the students may still be engaging in self-dialogue about their values, their role as lawyers, and whether they made the wrong choice when they enrolled in law school. These differences require a method of teaching lawyers-in-training that is different from the methods of training new lawyers.

Clinical Pedagogical Goals and Needs

The norm in a clinic is to make every aspect of the case a potential subject of academic examination and growth for the student. The pedagogical goals are to integrate theory and practice, and to demonstrate the transference of skills learned in one aspect of practice to other aspects of that practice and, perhaps most importantly, to dissimilar areas of practice as well. I have said on many occasions that it takes me much more time to prepare a student's case in a clinic than it would if I just represented the client myself. But that is precisely the point: this "inefficiency" is the necessary and worthwhile cost of learning. For that reason, clinic caseloads, unlike those in public-interest law offices, remain small.

We accept the inefficiency because clinical goals include an understanding of how theory informs practice and how practice, in turn, becomes the basis for theory. Clinical faculty want to teach students not just how to *do* something, but also the *why* of something—the theory behind the action. The clinical inquiry asks students what alternatives other than their current choice of action may exist. It demonstrates a process for making good choices from among the alternatives and explores why the action ultimately chosen is the best way to proceed. Clinical teachers want their students to become skilled lawyers with a robust sense of professionalism, regardless of the kind of legal practice they ultimately pursue. They want students to learn the art and science of transference so that tools developed in one situation have utility in completely different contexts later in their current case or project, and even later in their professional and personal lives. Clinical education also provides a laboratory to study jurisprudence. Faculty want students to use their cases and projects to consider the history of our legal system and to understand how our current laws and methods for dispute resolution are applied and enforced in practice. Moreover, we want them to leave law school knowing who benefits—and who suffers—from the systems we have created.

It is true that supervision in both clinics and legal services offices focuses on broad questions concerning strategy and case theory, on fine-tuning trial and legislative hearing performance, on document and transaction preparation, and on the use of advanced techniques specific to the type of representation provided. In legal service training, however, there is much less need to discuss theory or the overall values and work ethics with lawyers who have already chosen a specific field of practice. Nor will legal-service supervisors usually focus on larger systemic and societal questions that arise, the legal settings in which they are resolved, or in the personal (as distinct from professional) development of their lawyers. That would be inefficient for practitioners in high case volume offices. In a clinical course, however, those questions are at the heart of the experience. Practicing lawyers will inevitably encounter injustices within the legal system. One role of clinical education is to expose students to these injustices before they enter practice so they can reflect on how and whether they want to contribute to this system, reform it, or even abolish it.[8]

A Jurisprudential Laboratory

Clinic is an *academic* experience, not a Continuing Legal Education or an on-the-job training experience. The "why" of something is just as important as, and perhaps more important than, the "what" or "how" of something. Students come to a clinical course knowing little about real-world lawyering. They come to learn, and it is the weaker students, rather than the most outstanding, who most need the clinical experience. Clinics live within an academic institution, not a public-service organization. By exploring lawyering role and experiences, faculty encourage students to reflect on, analyze, and criticize, when necessary, the models of representation and societal constructs, and the law, lawyers, and judges involved in a case or project. It is a laboratory where students and faculty openly and critically discuss unstated assumptions about who has power in such systems, and who does not. It is a place to explore whether seemingly rational practices produce irrational and unfair results. It is a place where faculty ask students to challenge their own actions and assumptions about the law, democratic societies, and human behavior, and then develop their own path forward as ethical lawyers and civic leaders.

The clinic supervisor not only teaches students the art and craft of lawyering, but also guides students to ask how institutional structures, social forces, and the political landscape affects a client's life and a case as it develops.[9] However, experiential faculty also prompt students to challenge themselves and their assumptions to look beyond the specific skills that lawyering requires. They help students find "the opportunity and space for thinking differently or critically about a legal issue, for stretching or reorienting a standard narrative within and about the law, and for persuading a court to adopt that view."[10]

Clinical Teaching Requirements

As will be noted throughout this book, clinical teaching is demanding work. Whether they are new to the academy or whether they have been teaching for a long time, teachers need to answer three main questions. They must be answered in relation to the academic nature of clinical pedagogy, the personal aspects of the students they will teach, the academic and professional goals of the clinic, and the personal aspects of the clients they will serve. The questions are;

(1) Why do I teach?

(2) What do I teach?

(3) How do I teach?[11]

To answer those questions teachers must remember that clinical education is goal-driven, intentional, and reflective. The three questions listed above require reflection and intentional choice; and they must be answered in relation to the goals to which one's clinical course will adhere.

Why Do I Teach?

The answer to the first question, "Why do I teach?" has two parts. The answer to the first part asks a purely personal reflection about a teacher's life choice to change their career path. The impetus to leave the active practice of law and come to the academy can be based on any number of personal reasons. Some may wish to impart the knowledge they amassed during a successful career as a lawyer to a younger generation of students. One may wish not only to teach but to publish articles and books, so the knowledge can be widely disseminated. One may see the clinic as a better way to represent clients, perhaps with greater institutional resources and a smaller caseload.

That smaller caseload, and diverse set of responsibilities and pressures, may help a practitioner transition into a new season of their personal or family life. One may just have a curious and scholarly mind and assume the academy will provide a better space to pursue theory and philosophy within the realm of the legal profession. Surely, these are not the only possible reasons for a redirection in one's career. There probably are almost as many reasons as there are clinical teachers.

Once clinical teachers make that personal choice, however, they must accept that they are no longer involved in merely representing clients but have chosen to be part of an academic community. Their major task is teaching students using this unique pedagogical model. But joining the academic mission involves the acceptance of many new tasks. Clinic directors now spend only 54% of their time (on average) teaching the clinic course itself. Their remaining time is spent on a variety of endeavors, including managing the administrative operations of their clinic, creating new knowledge through research and academic writing, attending faculty meetings, serving on committees, reading the scholarly work of their colleagues, and becoming academic leaders who manage other law school programs.[12] All these roles have to be considered when answering the question "Why do I teach?"

The second part of the answer is driven by the goals of the clinic. Many things can be taught in a clinical course. No teacher can hope to select all the possible goals of experiential education, because our time with the students is seldom more than one year and generally limited to one semester. Thus, teachers must make intentional choices from the various possible clinic goals and have a clear understanding of whether the institutional goals of the law school are consonant with the teacher's own personal goals. If they are, the "why" question is answered satisfactorily. If they are not, teachers will be unable to advance their goals through the teaching mission.

What Do I Teach?

The second question, "What do I teach?" is equally important. Although the first generation of clinics focused on trial skills, the maturation of clinical pedagogy has demonstrated that almost any type of practice could be explored with clinical pedagogy. If one has been a general practitioner, almost any kind of case could be the subject of the clinic's practice. In addition to trial court litigation, appellate litigation, agency practice, domestic and international policy work, and transactional practice can all be explored using clinical pedagogy. Some lawyers will come to clinical education knowing the type of law they want to practice with their students. Others, especially those coming from the legislative or policy side of practice, will have to choose which of the many causes they could support through their clinic work is most compatible with what students need to learn. Finally, those choosing to make social justice instruction a specific goal of the clinic need to determine which legal and non-legal material will be required.

Once the teacher makes an intentional choice to design a clinic focused on the topic to teach, they must then examine the possible goals of experiential pedagogy and choose those clearly relating to that subject matter. They must familiarize themselves with the jurisdiction's student practice rules to determine whether the court and the bar rules permit client representation in the kind of case that will be the subject of the clinic, and whether the rules require students to take specific courses like ethics or criminal and civil procedure prior to enrolling in the clinic.

After they determine their students meet the court and bar rules, they can formulate their educational goals and work backwards to design a course to meet those goals. That design includes choosing cases, classroom activities, and supervision structures using different generally accepted teaching modalities. The design process includes determining the kind of readings and classroom activities that will advance the faculty member's learning goals for all clinic students and the personal learning goals of each student. It also includes what, if any, self-directed activities the students can be expected to perform and whether those activities will take place before or after they have had classroom or supervision discussions about the activity. Once those "what" questions are answered, the teacher can move onto the final question.

How Do I Teach?

The third question, "How do I teach?" is also driven not just by goals, but also by the subject matter of the clinic. There are many modalities and styles of teaching that lend themselves to helping students learn about the chosen goals. Supervision, reflective critique, and self-evaluation are the hallmarks of any clinical course. However, there are many ways to impart knowledge. Small group discussions, independent reading and research, in-person or online discussion groups, quick-writes before or during a class, post-class memos, case rounds, demonstrations, role-playing, modeling, and even lectures based on the Socratic method are all usable teaching and learning techniques. But they must be intentionally chosen for the specific purpose of furthering learning goals and competent client representation. While modeling and lectures have value, they cannot be the core teaching modality of a clinical course. Studies have shown that active rather than passive learning results in deeper understanding and greater retention of the lessons learned.[13] Clinical and other experiential learning is based on active learning and real-life experiences. That is why it has become so successful.

Clinical Pedagogy Fundamental Beliefs

As noted in the Chapter One of this book, clinical pedagogy is grounded in six fundamental beliefs:

(1) Clinical teaching is different from, and more expansive than, doctrinal teaching or professional legal practice.

(2) Clinical courses are goal-driven and structured using backward design.

(3) Faculty intervention is intentional and based on making choices that simultaneously advance a student's education and a clients' interests.

(4) Clinical education is based on an expansive theory of justice.

(5) Client and student needs are equally important in a clinical program, and the needs and interests of one do not have to be sacrificed for the other.

(6) Clinical teaching is contingent on the teacher's personal investment in individual students and accepting students where they are on their path to knowledge and professionalism. Thus, each teaching activity should be planned in a way that maximizes the student's learning potential in the clinic and in their future careers.

These fundamental beliefs explain why a clinic is an academic and professional laboratory, with client service as a critical aspect of the student's development as a professional and a person.

Common Features to Enhance Metacognitive Learning

Clinical pedagogy requires that students learn not just how to do a legal task, but to master how to accomplish those tasks when teachers are no longer there to guide them. Clinical and other experiential faculty want students to be active rather than passive learners who know how to approach new challenges on their own in a systematic and productive way. This permits knowledge to be transferred from one situation to another. It is common for students to not recognize that the knowledge and skills they learn in performing one task can be applied to another, similar task—or to a related or even completely different task in the future. They often think learning is intuitive and that the supervisors just know how to do something they cannot understand. They need to reject that notion of intuition and develop the ability to apply lessons learned systematically in other contexts. Learning how to move from knowing how to accomplish a task to a comprehensive understanding of the process of arriving at the proper decision and the theory behind the task is the hallmark of learning for transfer and is an essential element if the students are to become lifelong learners.

Just as students sometimes think that learning is intuitive, some faculty members also think that teaching is intuitive. In reality, neither teaching[14] nor learning[15] is intuitive. What we call intuition is a mental model born of experience that teachers can overlay on particular instructional problems to detect a timely solution.[16] It is based on years of demanding work and establishing patterns of thought and action that permit one to respond to an unfamiliar situation with a teaching technique adapted from techniques we ourselves have learned over time. Just as we ask our students to reflect on their lawyering actions, teachers must also reflect on their teaching practices, seeing which work and why, and then discarding those that do not. Thus, our repertoire of teaching techniques grows and improves from year to year.[17] We then employ the new and revised techniques intentionally after reflecting on a student's level of learning.

It is not that clinical teachers intuitively know how to teach. Becoming a good teacher requires the same metacognitive process that we wish to inculcate in our students. This process of engaging and reengaging with subject matter and the method used while teaching has a dual benefit. It can reignite passion for the subject matter in the teacher, who can then pass that same passion along to the students.[18] Certain common features of clinical pedagogy permit students to develop metacognitive learning and gain the ability to transfer knowledge from one event to another.

Real Clients

From their beginnings, clinical and other forms of experiential education have been based on real cases, not simulated ones. Students are confronted with the problems real lawyers face in real practice.[19] Thus, the first and most recognizable common feature of experiential pedagogy is that students have real clients. Students interact with others to identify a client's legal problems and interests and resolve them while acting in the role of a lawyer, not a student. These real-life consequences require students to act in the realm of uncertainty and indeterminacy. Accepting substantive law and theory at face value may serve to answer questions on an examination, but it seldom leads to a clear problem resolution in actual legal practice. Nuances in human behavior seldom permit immutable, one-size-fits-all applications of legal theory in the context of a client's case. Representing real clients requires students to see the relationship between theory and practice; it forces them to consider assumptions, both theirs and those of others, which have led to the interpretations of that theory, and to evaluate and consider alternatives to expected actions and outcomes. There are choices to be made based on judgments that require not just an understanding of law, but a knowledge of legal procedure and all the ethical rules that govern them. Moreover, law, procedure, and legal rules operate within the context of people's lives. The economic, social, and psychological traits of our clients, decision-makers, lawyers, and ourselves drive resolutions of legal problems as much as the law. These practical problems relating to clients are all layered upon the educational needs of our students and the learning goals that faculty establish for the clinic. Reflecting on the process of reaching the solution amidst all of these variables helps students gain a deeper understanding of the issues in context. When guided through that process by the case or project supervisor, students begin to see how the lessons learned in this one action can be used in similar or even disparate situations.

Goal-Driven Coursework

A second common feature of clinical and experiential pedagogy is that courses are goal-driven. Teachers establish goals for the clinic and then make every design choice for the course—drafting a syllabus, selecting materials and class activities, selecting clients, and choosing strategies to secure client interests—in accordance with those goals. In 1992, the AALS *Report on the Future of the In-House Clinic* listed a series of possible goals for clinical courses. They included developing modes of planning and analysis for dealing with unstructured situations; providing professional skills instruction; teaching a means of learning from experiences; instructing students on professional responsibility; exposing students to the demands and methods of acting in role; providing opportunities for collaborative learning; imparting the obligation of service to indigent clients; informing students about how to engage in such representation; providing knowledge concerning the impact of the legal system on poor people; providing the opportunity for examining the impact of doctrine in real life; providing a laboratory in which students and faculty study particular areas of law; and critiquing the capacities and limitations of lawyers and the legal system.[20]

These and other goals provide a mission for the clinic.[21] They permit the faculty member to choose from among the many possible goals of a clinical course to create a clear message of and expectation for both learning and practice. They clarify the framework in which a student will be qualitatively assessed during the planning and performance of legal tasks as their knowledge grows. They also provide the bases for the formative and the summative assessment or grade at the end of the term. This goal-oriented approach fills the gap in traditional law school teaching identified early in the development of experiential legal education by Anthony Amsterdam in *Clinical Legal Education—A 21st Century Perspective.*[22] Law schools have traditionally struggled to establish goals which are the basis for exploration and reflection. That exploration, however, goes beyond legal training. The goals form the basis for academic and personal inquiry into students' values, professional identity, and life choices as they begin to mature into their professional role in society. Without educational goals, the clinic becomes a simple job-training program.

The Backward Design Process

Backward design of clinical courses is the feature of clinical pedagogy. It is used to ensure that teachers actually accomplish the goals they set for the course. Backward design begins by first clearly defining the program's goals and then working backward, so that every choice made in the design of the clinic supports those end goals.[23] The backward design process, developed by Professor Grant Wiggins, asks teachers to begin with what they want students to understand and what tasks they want the student to be able to perform at the end of the term. It does not begin with deciding what the syllabus will direct the students to read, what specific classes the faculty member will teach, and what activities to perform. Teachers first decide what they want the students to learn before they develop the theoretical content of a course and the performance elements of the clinic that enable them to achieve the clinic's earning goals. Once those goals are set, the faculty member intentionally chooses what course content and materials and which learning activities enable a student to achieve those goals within the time allotted for the course.

Intentionality

The backward design process implicates the fourth feature of clinical pedagogy: intentionality. Actions and judgments in a clinical course must be intentional, and choices must be made with regard to representation and instruction that align with both the course goals and the clients' interests. Structuring a course to create independent students and student-driven learning involves many judgments and choices. For example, teachers must decide what factors will guide the topics of the clinic seminar and how to balance the structure of the fieldwork, the classroom activities and supervision sessions, and periods of reflection into the course structure. They must intentionally choose the skills students need to learn to represent clients in clinic cases or projects and choose the non-fieldwork activities that best prepare students for their legal work. The design of the clinic and the nature and structure of individual learning opportunities begin to emerge once the teacher decides what they want students to learn. They then begin working backwards to intentionally create the course content, activities, readings and every other aspect of the clinic that will permit the students to learn and achieve the learning goals the faculty has set for the clinic.

Clinical educators balance their ethical responsibility toward the client with their responsibility to foster the most fulfilling learning experience possible for the student.[24] If what faculty are teaching does not foster the clinic's learning goals, a disconnect will exist between the clients' actual needs and interests and the students' individual learning goals. That disconnect will create random or haphazard judgments, choices, and actions that are inefficient and ineffective, both for the client and the student. Faculty must intentionally make those judgments and choices and create the activities in the experiential course based on sound theory merged with as much practical knowledge as possible. When the right balance is struck, faculty can intentionally deliver exemplary student learning and strategic and ethically sound client representation.[25]

The intentionality of clinical teaching requires an understanding of which teaching techniques best suit the faculty member's goals within the context of the events that are occurring in the case or project. We use many modalities in the clinic and classroom: lectures, small and large group discussions, case rounds, role-plays, moots, quick-writes, critical incident questionnaires, and simulations. We choose a modality intentionally to ensure the content furthers learning and assists with the client's representation.

Faculty should also conduct their supervision sessions with the same intentionality. For example, do the questions faculty ask, or the information they provide, enhance the student's learning? Does a role-play used to convey the nuance of a cross-examination enhance the students' ability to understand its purpose and improve their ability to achieve their clients' interests? When students appear to be developing a task based on false assumptions, teachers must ask themselves whether the student is ready to confront the false assumption on which a judgment is being made in the moment, or whether it can instead await a more propitious time without harming the clients' interests. Another important question is whether the delay will negatively affect the client's interest or damage the lawyer-client relationship. When a student is planning to perform a task, such as the production of a written document, framing questions for a direct- or cross-examination, developing arguments for trial or an appeal, preparing testimony before a legislative body, or creating strategies to execute a negotiation, faculty can decide how much liberty they will give to the student to perform that task. The clinic's goals drive these choices, activities, and techniques that will convey knowledge to facilitate a student's learning and ensure their client's needs are served. However, each choice a teacher makes demands an understanding of which techniques best convey the knowledge and the insights they seek to impart to ensure that students learn and that clients receive the services that they need.

As must now be clear, many forms of intervention exist and may occur at various points in the life of a case or project. It is important, though, to be wary of excessive intervention, as it can be detrimental to the learning process.[26] Supervision can shift the decision-making responsibilities from the student to the teacher, which runs counter to the goals of clinical education.[27] Some interventions must be taken immediately to avoid breaking the law or violating an ethical obligation. In those cases, a supervisor should restrict the student's ownership of the case or project and take over. But that extreme intervention should only take place when it is absolutely necessary "to expedite resolution of the legal problem and save time, money and anxiety for the client and others[,]"[28] or when the workload requires shared responsibility.

The Reflection Processes

Intentional and systematic reflection is the fifth common feature of clinical pedagogy. According to Professor Carolyn Grose, reflection is "the method that guides students' extraction of theory from practice and the application of practice to theory; and it pushes students to generalize from the specific and transfer their learning beyond the specific."[29] As Professor Donald Schön pointed out, we and our students can reflect on our thinking and our actions at various stages of a case or project.[30] We can reflect on our actions while planning a case theory, a set of direct- or cross-examination questions, or any other course of action, and apply new insights while we are planning without interrupting our work to reshape what we are doing. We can reflect on judgments and choices that students made after they have performed a task. We even reflect on a reflection the student made contemporaneously with an action taken. Reflection reinforces successful actions and demonstrates how they can be used in other circumstances. This demonstrates the importance of reflection when transferring the knowledge gained in one circumstance to a new circumstance. Students and faculty can—actually must—reflect about a performance that did not work well to determine if it was an ineffective strategic choice, poor execution of the task, or an unanticipated action by another participant in the case or project.

These reflection sessions occur during feedback supervision sessions about single actions, judgments, or decisions, and during periodic formative assessments when an entire body of work is analyzed. Reflections such as these are formative and designed to enhance learning rather than summative when applied to rank the student's performance and assign a grade. Indeed, ranking the performance in terms of grades has no place in most reflection sessions. The goal is to advance individual learning, not to rank the student qualitatively against others. Using reflection to enhance learning makes students more willing to confront errors and even failures, learn from them, and avoid them in the future.

Although clinic faculty members and students usually think about reflection in terms of case or project performance, it also plays a role in a student's personal development. When students reflect on their emotional and cognitive reactions toward their clients, opposing lawyers and their clients, judges, or even the entire legal system, students are able to consider how their personal and professional values are evolving and how they have grown as lawyers and as people. The same can be said for reflecting about collaborative learning and clinical methodology. Focusing on more than the student's individual casework also provides a forum for a deeper engagement with a student's professional identity. Such conversations help hone skills and values that they can apply in varying contexts throughout their lives.[31]

Faculty use students' self-reflection reports and formal reflection sessions to monitor their progress. Reflection can identify students' strengths and challenges to determine what lessons they have learned regarding client representation, and to assess their personal goals and clinic goals. Reflection also suggests the direction students need to take to increase their knowledge, awareness of lawyering roles and ethics, and to improve their performance. Clinical pedagogy requires students to self-reflect prior to formal supervisorial sessions and formative assessment reviews to better facilitate student-driven learning.

Faculty also use reflection sessions to confirm that students have mastered the knowledge and tasks associated with client representation. They allow students to assess their educational growth and personal development, ensuring that students have learned how to learn. The legal profession requires lawyers to evaluate and address new tasks throughout their careers, all as part of the trans-substantive[32] "process of lawyering."[33] Reflection sessions encourage lifelong learning and develop individual methods that help students increase their knowledge as the demands of their work change.

Teaching and Learning for Transfer

The sixth common feature of clinical pedagogy is teaching to transfer.[34] Teaching to transfer, a central goal of clinical education, gives students "the ability to generalize from lessons and skills gathered in one set of circumstances and transfer the knowledge gained from such lessons and skills to a different set of circumstances."[35] More concretely, there are actually two types of transfer.[36] "Near transfer" occurs when the lessons learned in one context are easily applied to an analogous situation.[37] "Far transfer" occurs when the two situations are different. The latter is more challenging for students and teachers to facilitate.[38] Students often forget that their knowledge in one context can also be applicable in another. They must come to recognize that lessons learned in prior, and perhaps completely different contexts, may also be useful in the new one.

Educational research shows that transfer across contexts is especially difficult when a subject is taught in only a single context, rather than in multiple contexts.[39] Far transfer occurs when students begin to see the correlations between seemingly dissimilar situations.[40] Students learn the relevant aspects of transference when it is taught in multiple contexts with accompanying examples, not just its specific use in a particular action. For example, learning to develop the theory of a case for trial aligns with methods used during witness interviews and discovery sessions. Advocacy strategies developed for court can also be useful in negotiations with opposing counsel or in the legislative arena.[41] Clinicians help their students learn the lessons emphasized in a particular class or case by identifying other points in the clinic curriculum where the same or similar understandings apply, and then connecting those lessons to the broader lawyering process.[42] We do so by naming underlying connections, so that students can more clearly see the applicability of their learning across different contexts in their clinic work. As a result, students learn to transfer that knowledge to different contexts, thereby developing their "ends-means thinking."[43] The transfer process facilitates the ease with which students retain and enhance their repertoire in their post-graduate professional lives.

Cultural Awareness

The seventh feature of clinical pedagogy is cultural awareness. Students' cultural understanding is frequently different from (and more immediately necessary than) what traditional classroom teachers usually encounter. Clinic clients, though often poor and receiving services free of charge, deserve respect and understanding. They are not laboratory specimens students examine for their own educational benefit.[44] The freedom, resources, and welfare of clients are at stake whenever students undertake representation. The weight of that responsibility can create impediments to learning and performance that do not occur in traditional classroom-based courses or in learning-by-doing courses that use fictional cases. On the other hand, learning about people whose lives are different from the students representing them creates an opportunity for life-changing perspectives. As such, clinical teachers pay close attention to the human interactions that occur between students and clients, constantly attuned to the psychological and sociological impediments that such interactions can produce.[45]

Race, class, wealth, national origin, gender identification, sexual orientations, and political and religious beliefs seem to exist in stark contrast among the citizens of the United States. Simple discourse, let alone mutual understanding, often seems impossible. As Eduardo R. Ferrer and Kristin N. Henning note in *Critical Clinical Frames: Centering Adolescence, Race, Trauma and Gender in Practice Pedagogy*, this discord is so stark that it led them to develop a distinct pedagogical framework for their juvenile justice clinic. They write that "given the demographics and common experiences of our clients, we have adopted four primary pedagogical frames for our clinic: 1) Adolescence; 2) Race; 3) Trauma; and 4) Sexual Orientation, Gender Identity, and Gender Expression ('SOGIE')."[46] Different ideas and beliefs about how these issues exist in the country permeate law schools as much as any other institution. Not confronting them is nearly impossible in a clinical course. In addition, clinical teachers must be acutely aware of the educational hierarchy that exists between students and clients. They must also recognize the strange hierarchy that exists when the professor acts simultaneously as a partner in strategizing about a case or project, a mentor and perhaps a friend in day-to-day interactions, and also the ultimate source of all power in the class. "These [dynamics] need to be examined in the same manner as any legal issues in the matter."[47]

There are many ways to guide students through this process during their clinic term. One way to guide them is to formulate the clinic goals with the use of pedagogical frames.[48] A pedagogical frame has a specific theme used to analyze new information, such as personal characteristics or socio-economic status.[49] Framing theory can both facilitate learning and enhance client representation because it expands how students interpret information and challenges them to apply the schemas to each client or case.[50] Using specific schemas, and clearly naming them, also gives students agency earlier in the life of a case or project, allowing them to be the drivers of their own learning process.[51] It provides a way to raise social justice issues, whether or not those issues are a specific goal of the clinic.

Engaging in this kind of reflection on the life students have chosen is not only encouraged but required in a clinic course. If reflection and critique do not occur, there is no reason a clinic should be part of an academic institution. Universities exist to create and disseminate knowledge and to challenge assumptions of the status quo. Failure to do so is to abandon the academic mission. That is why a clinic cannot be a public legal services agency where students eschew the larger academic questions to serve the largest number of clients, and why the best clinics and other experiential courses do not serve as de facto legal services offices.

Each semester or year in a clinic, clinical teachers ask a new group of students to learn how to engage with clients' legal issues, the personal issues surrounding the clients' legal problems, and the cultural environment in which the client resides and the law operates. They are asked to do all of this with often little prior exposure to the lived experiences of their clients. At the same time, clinical teachers are learning to engage with each new student on topics as diverse as the substantive and procedural law, legal ethics, legal institutions, legal practice skills, cultural mores, professional identity, and personal values. By the time most students come to the clinic, they should have learned in other classes that the law, legal ethics, and skills of legal practice are not immutable, and that neutral principles may be neutral in theory but are seldom in practice. Because students seldom share the same life experiences as their clients, faculty have to learn how to weave the students' personal life experiences into the cultural, social, personal, and economic lives of their clients to determine how legal principles and practices work outside of the accepted cultural and political norm. The students' experiences are energizing and daunting at the same time because, from the moment they begin their clinic work, they are asked to undertake a huge level of responsibility for the lives, needs, and interests of other people, many of whom are often older than they are and few of whom share similar life stories. Few students have ever encountered that level of responsibility in any area of their own lives before. Similarly, some new faculty have never been responsible for guiding students through those kinds of professional and often personal challenges.

A Method Greater Than the Sum of Its Parts[52]

All clinical programs have key goals related to the practice of law. Clinical faculty teach the students about the role of a lawyer, the relationship between theory and practice, relationships with clients, the substantive law, procedure, strategy, tactics, and the ethics of the legal profession that help to move a case or project along to secure a client's interest. However, there are also goals that are more personal to the student. Clinical courses help students determine their suitability for the kind of work the clinic does. Students will not always view the subject matter of their clinic as their potential life's work, though some or even many will seek out a clinic for precisely that reason. Students come to the clinic to learn about lawyering, but they also come to learn how to learn once they leave the academy and begin to practice on their own. Thus, clinical education is more than the sum of its strictly traditional legal professional goals. Successful clinics integrate the technical goal of lawyering with the student's need to establish a professional identity, integrated with other personal life goals.

Students come to a clinical course with hopes and fears and expect that their faculty member will help them face these new responsibilities. They trust their teachers and rely on them to guide them through this difficult transition from student to professional. This nuanced process creates a greater level of academic responsibility that is substantially more difficult to navigate than the challenges faced by their non-clinical colleagues. Clinical faculty are ethically responsible for both the clients' interests and well-being and for the students' learning and well-being as they traverse these new and sometimes difficult challenges. Clinic faculty have two clients in every case or project: the actual client in need of representation, and the student client in need of a guide to becoming a professional and a participant in the civic order.[53] Given the complexity of the cognitive and emotional experiences that often accompany the students' time in the clinical course, faculty become responsible for their students' personal well-being, as well as their academic and professional education.[54]

A goal of any clinical program, and perhaps all academic programs, should be what we at Georgetown call *cura personalis*, a Latin term meaning "care for the whole person." It is a foundational goal of Jesuit education,[55] but is also a signature part of clinical pedagogy. It connotes attending to the individual needs of our students with as much care as we have for our clients. Because clinical teachers have an equal duty to students and clinic clients, they need to meet students where they are at that moment. Clinical pedagogy asks the faculty member to focus on the students' personal learning in several ways. In each case, supervisors should start from a place of generosity.[56] This student-centered approach can be created in several ways.

- Faculty should create the space, time, trust, and other support necessary to ensure that students retain control over their work product and succeed in their client representation.
- If a student fails to meet a client's needs or to preserve a client's interests, teachers should not immediately assume the student is at fault. Instead, they should first reflect on how they can alter their supervisory methods to help the student overcome the causes of the shortcoming and, in future cases, strive to avoid such shortcomings altogether.
- When a student struggles with organization, timeliness, or basic competence, teachers should see this as an opportunity to help the student develop and sharpen those skills themselves.
- Faculty should resist the natural instinct to intervene in the moment or take over a client's representation unless a client's interest is truly in jeopardy. Instead, they should find a way to improve the students' performance on behalf of the client.
- Teachers should not blame a student when an intervention is necessary. Instead teachers should first reflect on what they can learn from the experience, focusing on why the intervention occurred and how they, as supervisors, can help the student reach a better learning outcome.
- When negative assessments occur, faculty should offer students a path that permits them to improve their performance without feelings of guilt, shame, or ineptitude.
- Students should be encouraged to take calculated risks. However, when their efforts come up short, faculty do not penalize their failure harshly or personalize it. Instead, teachers should create a growth mindset that encourages students to enthusiastically try to master the task again.

The faulty role in a learned and learning academy is to help students become competent lawyers and ethical members of their communities. The goal is to help them become more than they appear to be in any given moment. In this way, *cura personalis* is not just a slogan signaling Jesuit affiliation for a school like Georgetown—it is the lifeblood of all clinical pedagogy, and a North Star for clinical faculty everywhere.

This student-teacher relationship is very different from what non-clinical faculty members experience. The trust that emerges from working through difficult professional and personal experiences in clinic creates a level of trust and affection that is usually greater than that of a podium faculty member's mentor-mentee relationship with a student. Indeed, clinical teachers often speak about the familial intimacy of clinical teaching.[57] That intimacy develops because of the intensity of shared experiences and emotions between faculty and students brought on by the clients' victories and defeats. The emotional ups and downs students face in their daily lives coping with the stress of job searches, personal relationships, debt, and the demands of other courses and extracurricular activities that they share with their clinic supervisors add to that intimacy. Students today are living in a world fraught with domestic and international political strife, as well as climate and international uncertainty. The personal contact and the information that clients, faculty, and students share with one another exceeds that in any other law course. Clinical faculty spend as much time with their students as they spend with their families, and students spend much of their academic and even personal time in their clinic offices with their student and faculty colleagues. Clinic student friendships often last a lifetime, and clinic alumni retain a special relationship with and memories of their clinic supervisors as they themselves mature into practicing lawyers. Some even find themselves returning to clinic as teachers one day. All these factors help shape a pedagogy in clinic that is unique in legal education.

As noted earlier, law schools have seldom encouraged faculty members to study the science of teaching. There has long been an assumption in legal education that since new teachers were once law students, they intuitively understand how to conduct lectures, plan and direct seminar activities, engage students in problem-based classes and simulations, and perform traditional Socratic exercises. Although experience reveals that this is a false assumption, that attitude continues to exist, even though there is some evidence it is changing.

One would think that clinical teachers would know that teaching is not simple, but that is also not always the case. Clinical fellows and new teachers often tell me that clinical teaching is harder than they thought it would be. Teaching, especially in a clinical setting, is extremely challenging, and teaching in a clinic requires a deep understanding of multiple needs. Teachers must be aware of educational motivators; recognize the role of empathy; have an appreciation for different learning styles and teaching methods; be able to loosen hierarchical boundaries; have a thorough knowledge of legal theory, ethics, and practice; and convey that knowledge in an understandable fashion to students. All of these factors affect a teacher's work with students and clients. Supervisors must accomplish all of this while ensuring that the students protect client interests. The work also requires compassion, empathy, and humility. These are the traits that teachers bring to their students that create a familial intimacy and a relationship unlike that of a traditional law professor in a doctrinal class.

The articles following this and other chapters of this book explore the sometimes overwhelming feelings that new, and even seasoned, teachers have when teaching an experiential course. They will lead to some interesting questions for teachers to consider after reading them.

Other Voices

Anthony G. Amsterdam, *Clinical Legal Education—A 21st Century Perspective**

34 J. Legal Educ. 612 (1984)

I. Introduction

Since the theme of this conference is "Approaching the 21st Century," I mean to talk about legal education in the twenty-first century, not the twentieth.

...

I speak for twenty-first century ears, not twentieth.

II. Summary of Points

First, I want to specify one of the principal ways in which legal education at the end of the twentieth century was too narrow. In those days the criticism was often voiced that legal education was too narrow[.] ... Legal education in those days was too narrow because it failed to develop in students ways of thinking within and about the role of lawyers-methods of critical analysis, planning, and decision making which are not themselves practical skills but rather the conceptual foundations for practical skills and for much else, just as case reading and doctrinal analysis are foundations for practical skills and for much else.

Second, ... [there] was the assumption that the job of law schools was to impart to students a self-contained body of instruction in the law. In the twenty-first century we realize, of course, that a major function of law schools is to give students systematic training in effective techniques for learning law from the experience of practicing law.

Third, I want to describe briefly a pedagogic method-sometimes called the clinical method of legal instruction-which was developed in the last quarter of the twentieth century to broaden legal education in all of these dimensions.

Fourth, I want to point out-and this is what would have been political dynamite at the end of the twentieth century—that the only way in which the law schools could have afforded to utilize this new technique of legal instruction effectively was to cut back substantially on teaching what they used to teach in the way they used to teach it.

III. Discussion

Point One: Divers Analytic Modes

The best way to develop my first point is to itemize three kinds of analytic thinking that were traditionally taught in law schools and three that were not.

---

* Excerpts are reprinted with the permission of the author and the Association of American Law Schools which owns the copyright for articles published by the Journal of Legal Education.

1. *Case reading and interpretation.* Law schools traditionally taught students how to interpret judicial opinions, to examine their implications and the limits of their implications, to reason from them and predict their applications in other hypothesized factual situations. (This involves comprehension of the basic *stare decisis* principle, such concepts as "holdings" and "dicta" and notions of why and how the procedural posture of litigation frames the "issues" for decision, the idea of "distinctions" and "analogies," and how and when distinctions and analogies can be drawn.) Through this mode of reasoning, a student or a lawyer can predict or argue that a decided case will or will not, should or should not, control legal consequences in different factual situations subsequently arising.

2. *Doctrinal analysis and application.* Law schools traditionally taught students how to synthesize whole bodies of decided cases, how to discern patterns in them, identify and reconcile potential contradictions, isolate and compose the strands of reasoning reflected in them, so as to distill principles or rules or doctrines which can then be applied to predict or argue the legal consequences that will or should attach to given fact situations. In this mode of reasoning, techniques of classification and characterization are developed which are the lawyer's (and the judge's) tools for determining whether, for example, one precedent or another more strongly attracts a given situation.

3. *Logical conceptualization and criticism.* Law schools traditionally taught students-to some extent-how to array legal authorities and principles in some sort of logical system, so as to criticize the symmetry or asymmetry of its parts, trace out their relationships, and discern or propose explanatory principles that might account for the whole system, improve its harmony, perhaps increase its serviceability for one or another purpose.

...

Now let me itemize three of perhaps fifteen or twenty that were not:

1. *Ends-means thinking.* This is the process by which one starts with a factual situation presenting a problem or an opportunity and figures out the ways in which the problem might be solved or the opportunity might be realized. What is involved is making a thorough, systematic, and creative canvass of all of the possible goals or objectives in the situation—the "end points" to which movement from the present state of affairs might be made-then making an equally systematic and creative inventory of the possible means or routes to each goal, then analyzing the ways in which and the extent to which the various means and goals are compatible or incompatible with one another, seeking means to reconcile them or to prioritize them to the extent that they are irreconcilable. This includes estimating the probabilities that certain means will lead to certain goals: it may utilize such analytic techniques as best-case/worst-case analyses, and such strategic principles as keeping options open. In any event, by reasoning backward from goals, by mapping the various roads that might be taken to each goal, by proceeding backward step by step along each road and asking what steps have to be taken before each following step can be taken, one comes at last to have

some well-advised basis for answering the question "how on earth do I get started in dealing with this situation? (What are the implications of the various first steps that I could take?)"

...

2. *Hypothesis formulation and testing in information acquisition.* This is a matter of devising methods for acquiring the information needed to make decisions when one starts with less than all of the necessary information. It is seldom practicable and almost never efficient to begin to deal with any situation by gathering every piece of information that might conceivably be remotely relevant. Hypotheses about what is really relevant are the precondition of effective information gathering. The trouble is that these hypotheses must necessarily be framed before the acquisition of information that could generate alternative and perhaps better hypotheses. Are there modes of thinking that enable one to select better rather than worse initial hypotheses for the purpose of guiding one's information gathering, then to test and to modify or refine the hypotheses progressively as additional information is acquired? Certainly there are.

...

3. *Decisionmaking in situations where options involve differing and often uncertain degrees of risks and promises of different sorts.* When I was in law school, I spent virtually all of my time learning analytic techniques for predicting or arguing what was the legal result, or what should be the legal result, *in a given fact situation.* Since I got out of law school, I have spent virtually all of my time dealing with situations in which the facts were not given, in which there were options as to what fact situation should be created—situations in which I had the choice whether to present evidence on certain aspects of the facts in a litigation or to leave the record silent on those aspects, whether to draft a contract or a release that was more or less specific on a particular subject, whether to counsel a client to follow one or another course of conduct. In these situations, the real question concerned the relative probability that various legal results would obtain under alternative states of facts; the task was to decide which state of facts should be created in view of the relative costs and benefits of each including the comparative risks of the best, worst, and intermediate legal results that might obtain under each state of facts. To perform this task, it was not enough to identify each state of facts and ask "what result?" or even to recognize that, for many states of facts, the result was uncertain. It was necessary to specify and compare degrees of uncertainty, and to identify the considerations that made particular degrees of uncertainty less acceptable in the case of some legal results than in the case of others.

...

I have described these six kinds of analytic thinking to make a single basic point. By no means all of us so-called clinical teachers who began in the twentieth century to teach such things as counseling and negotiation and trial advocacy thought of ourselves as doing something properly described as skills training. We thought that what we were doing was no more or less skills training than what traditional classroom teachers of contracts and torts and criminal law had done when they taught students to read and interpret cases and to analyze legal doctrines. Case reading seemed to us to be skills training in the double sense that it required certain skills and was the precondition of still other skills. In exactly the same sense we were doing skills training when we taught ends-means thinking, information acquisition analyses, contingency planning, comparative risk evaluation in decisionmaking, and the like. These subjects seemed to us no less conceptual or academically rigorous than case reading and doctrinal analysis. We therefore could not see the issue of the 1970s and 1980s as being whether the law schools should go on teaching legal analysis or should conduct skills training. We rather saw the issue as *which* legal analyses and skills the law schools should teach, and *how much* of each.

Here, we did differ from some of the traditionalists. Looking back on our own student days, we felt that we had spent too much time on too few legal analyses and skills. We had learned case reading and doctrinal analysis *sub nom.* torts, contracts, criminal law, property, civil procedure, admiralty, antitrust, and twenty-two other substantive titles. The substantive law we learned in these courses was interesting, but it was nothing that we could not have learned equally well, to the extent we wanted or needed it, by independent reading in law school or on-the-job research after we got out. Having learned to interpret cases and to analyze doctrine in a half a dozen courses, we had no trouble at all reading cases and analyzing doctrine in any new substantive area we encountered.

...

Point Two: Learning to Learn from Experience

When we were students, law school did absolutely nothing to prepare us to learn from our experience in practice after graduation. Law school was conceived as a wholly self-contained and terminal educational episode. Practice after graduation was either ignored as a potential source of education or viewed as an entirely different kind of education—the school of hard knocks—having no institutional affiliation or functional connection with the school of law.

In the twenty-first century we realize what a misguided and pedagogically unproductive view that was. We realize that law schools cannot hope to begin to teach their students "law" in a scam three years. The students who spend three years in law school will spend the next thirty or fifty years in practice. These thirty or fifty years in practice will provide by far the major part of the student's legal education, whether the law schools like it or not. They can be a purblind, blundering, inefficient, hit-or-miss learning experience in the school of hard knocks. Or they can be a reflective, organized, systematic learning experience—if the law schools undertake as a part of their curricula to teach students effective techniques of learning from experience.

Point Three: The Method of Clinical Legal Instruction

Toward the end of the twentieth century, techniques of legal education became widespread which were designed precisely to teach students how to learn systematically from experience, and simultaneously to educate them in a broader range of legal analyses and skills than had theretofore been taught in law schools.

This development was called "clinical legal education." It took numerous forms, but the basic technique was this:

1. Students were confronted with problem situations of the sort that lawyers encounter in practice. The situations might be simulated—roleplaying exercises in which some students played the role of legal counselors and others played the role of clients, for example—or they might be real—students might be assigned to represent actual clients and to counsel those clients under the close supervision of clinical faculty members, for example.

2. The problem situations were: (a) concrete, that is, textured by specific factual detail; (b) complex, that is, they required the consideration of interacting factors in a number of dimensions—legal, practical, institutional, personal; and (c) unrefined, that is, they were not predigested for the student through the medium of appellate opinions or coursebooks, but were unstructured, requiring the student to identify "the problem[s]" or "the issue[s]."

The students dealt with the problem *in role*. They bore the responsibility for decision and action to solve the problem. They had to: (a) identify the problem; (b) analyze it; (c) consider, formulate, and evaluate possible responses to it; (d) plan a course of action; and (e) execute that course of action. In all of these activities, the students were required to interact with other people. They were thus required to work through the relationships between legal analysis, communication, and interpersonal dynamics.

3. The students' performance was subjected to intensive and rigorous *post mortem* critical review. With faculty and other students, the performing students sat down, re-created, and criticized every step of their planning, decisionmaking, and action. Sometimes this was done by replaying videotapes or audiotapes of their performance, sometimes by reviewing notes and memoranda that they had made during the performance stage, often by both. The students' own thinking and behavior in role were thus made the central subject of study, just as, in a traditional classroom course, a judicial opinion or a statute would have been the subject of study.

4. This critical review focused upon the development of models of analysis for understanding past experience and for predicting and planning future conduct. It identified and explored the questions to be asked following any experience-a meeting with a client, a negotiation with another lawyer, a conference with a government official, a trial, the closure of a case-in order to draw from that experience the maximum of learning it can provide. The students learned to ask, for example: "What were my objectives in that performance? How did I define them? Might I have defined them differently? Why did

I define them as I did? What were the means available to me to achieve my objectives? Did I consider the full range of them? If not, why not? What modes of thinking would have broadened my options? How did I expect other people to behave? How did they behave? Might I have anticipated their behavior—their goals, their needs, their expectations, their reactions to me—more accurately than I did? What clues to these things did I overlook, and why did I overlook them? Through what kind of thinking, analysis, planning, perceptivity, might I see them better next time?" These questions are, of course, the points of entry to examination of the kinds of reasoning I've mentioned ends-means thinking, contingency planning, and the rest. They are also the beginning of the students' development of conscious, rigorous self-evaluative methodologies for learning from experience—the kind of learning that makes law school the beginning, not the end, of a lawyer's legal education.

...

Association of American Law Schools, Section on Clinical Legal Education, *Report of the Committee on the Future of the In-House Clinic**

Principal Editor: Robert Dinerstein

42 J. Legal Educ. 508 (1992)

...

II. The Principal Goals of In-House, Live-Client Clinics

...

... [T]he Committee has identified nine teaching goals present, to a greater or lesser degree, in most clinics.

A. Developing Modes of Planning and Analysis for Dealing with Unstructured Situations

Anthony Amsterdam has described these modes of learning as "conceptual foundations for practical skills" and analogized them to the foundations provided by case reading and doctrinal analysis taught in first-year classes. These analytical methods differ from case reading and doctrinal analysis, among other reasons, because they are prospective as well as retrospective, and because their context is not bound by the pre-digested world of the appellate case.

One of the modes of planning and analysis that Amsterdam has identified is "ends-means thinking." That skill involves starting with a fact situation presenting a problem or opportunity and figuring out the ways in which the problem might be solved. The

* Excerpts are reprinted with the permission of the authors and the Association of American Law Schools which owns the copyright for articles published by the Journal of Legal Education.

skill requires a thorough canvass of one's goals and an equally thorough study of the ways in which those goals might be accomplished.

A second kind of analytical mode requires structuring and applying doc trine to situations where the facts are unclear or developing. Thus, while in the classroom doctrinal analysis is usually confined to analysis of what will happen in a given fact situation, the student in a clinical program is required to grapple with the impact of doctrine when there is no "given" fact situation.

The clinic is an ideal vehicle for imparting these skills. First, the problems presented to students have all the difficulty, texture, and chance that occur in the world of practice. Students must consider this range of issues while problem solving. Second, the in-house clinic possesses the resources to develop these skills. Many clinical teachers who convey these skills begin with lecture and simulation discussing problem-solving models. Most then follow with intensive discussion during student supervision. While time-consuming, that individual supervision is a powerful means to focus student attention on these skills.

B. Providing Professional Skills Instruction

This goal is so well established that, as noted above, it is often taken as a synonym for clinical education. For years, clinics have been providing training in interviewing, counseling, fact investigation, oral advocacy, and brief writing. For many clinicians, a critical component of that teaching is to provide models for the exercise of these skills, rather than simply focusing on how-to-do-it. At present, there is no serious dispute within the academy that law schools must provide opportunities for such instruction. Indeed, ABA accreditation standards require law schools to offer courses in professional skills instruction.

The Committee recognizes that this goal of clinical education may be conveyed efficiently by simulation. Indeed, most clinicians recognize the utility of simulations by using them to teach lawyering skills in their classroom components, complementing that instruction with the one-on-one supervision in actual cases. Even so, there may be some unique advantages to skills instruction in the live-client setting. Clinics require students to apply practice skills in situations of unpredictability and stress that are unlikely to occur in the same way in simulated performance. Moreover, the live-client experience provides strong motivation for students to learn and apply their nascent professional skills.

C. Teaching Means of Learning from Experience

One of the primary goals in teaching modes of analysis and professional skills is to provide means by which students can learn from experience. Most of us recognize that most of our learning about the law occurred after graduation. Law school cannot possibly teach even most of the "law" in three years. For better or worse, that learning will occur in practice. Because the student's performance in role is the heart of the clinical experience, many clinicians recognize as an explicit goal the inculcation of methods by which the student can learn from experience. By critiquing student performance and by encouraging students to engage in self- and peer-critique, clinicians seek to provide their students with the tools to enable them to engage in analysis of their performance when they are in practice. To that end, most clinicians not only engage in extensive post-performance critique, but do so with the use of analysis or models that can be adapted by the student for use in future performance.

D. Instructing Students in Professional Responsibility

For many years, clinicians have been attempting to use live-client instruction as a vehicle to train students in professional responsibility and professional self-awareness. By professional responsibility, we refer to more than an awareness of the rules of the Code of Professional Responsibility. For many clinicians, the teaching of professional responsibility also includes the development of the student's ethical understanding. That understanding requires that the individual interpret her performance in light of the rules and values of the profession. As David Barnhizer has written, this notion of professional responsibility comprehends a series of judgments and value orientations that become both an explicit and implicit part of the individual's decision making and professional behavior. The achieving of this level of understanding demands education experiences that are capable of providing a source and kind of involvement penetrating enough to cultivate the clarification of values, and flexible enough to allow the instructor to guide the experience into a functional structure. This level of understanding is developed not in sole relation to intellectual theories of ethical behavior, but in response to the kinds of actual forces that will confront, challenge, and tend to seduce the person as a lawyer.

Most clinicians believe that it is part of their charge to teach this kind of professional responsibility. In the clinic, students are provided with firsthand exposure to the actual mores of the profession. They are also required to respond in role to ethical dilemmas, with real-life consequences attached to their decisions. Students are able to judge their ethical standards not just by their ideals, but by their actual deeds. All of us have had the experience of student behavior diverging radically from not only the norm the student may have been taught, but the norm the student actually articulated prior to the performance. The in-house aspect of clinics is critical to this goal, because it allows student performance to be observed and critiqued by a faculty member on the scene. Moreover, the students are able to observe the faculty member modeling how she would address the professional responsibility issue in question, and to learn that competent professionals take ethical responsibilities seriously.

E. Exposing Students to the Demands and Methods of Acting in Role

Clinics also may have as a goal the analysis of role-based behavior. While related to the professional responsibility concerns just discussed, the analysis of role implicates the interpersonal side of lawyering and can have foci beyond ethics or responsibility. Mark Spiegel and Carrie Menkel-Meadow have identified two different dimensions of inquiry.

First, because lawyers do their work through others, lawyering can be conceptualized according to the psychological aspects of the transaction. Clinical work may use theories developed in social psychology to explain lawyering behavior. Thus, students may attempt to analyze the effects of partisan role on behavior and the effects of role in communicating with persons who have different interests.

A second component is sociological in nature and looks to the impact of socially generated role-expectations on behavior. Thus, a student may use the clinical experience as data for determining "what is expected" in a given situation. That analysis, in turn, can provide insight into issues such as problems of authority relationships, lawyer dominance of clients, and relationships with adversaries. This inquiry, as Menkel-Meadow has argued, can be "simultaneously procedural, instrumental, and evaluative."

In-house clinics thus provide students with an opportunity to learn about critical relationships, such as the lawyer-client relationship, from a variety of perspectives that can inform their understanding of the legal system and their role within it.

F. Providing Opportunities for Collaborative Learning

Although related to a number of goals already discussed, an additional feature of the in-house clinic is the opportunity it provides to engage in collaborative learning. Most of law school learning is intensely individual. Legal practice, in contrast, is replete with situations in which preparation and performance occur in a collaborative environment. The in-house clinic provides a setting where this collaborative learning can occur. Moreover, in many clinics, an examination of the process of student-student or student-faculty interaction is an explicit focus of the experience.

G. Imparting the Obligation for Service to Indigent Clients, Information About How to Engage in Such Representation, and Knowledge Concerning the Impact of the Legal System on Poor People

In addition to providing the opportunity for students to engage in service, clinics may seek to teach students how to accomplish such representation and to expose students to the effect of our legal system on poor people. This goal, somewhat de-emphasized in recent years, was one of the original justifications for clinical education and has recently been rearticulated by Gary Palm, who urged clinical education to provide students with instruction that they will never otherwise receive. This instruction includes learning about poverty.... They should confront the failure of our government to provide equal justice and fair legal procedures for the poor. We should help them structure their careers to include pro bono work through community group representation, litigation, and legislative advocacy.

Nurturing the student's ability to engage in representation of indigent clients ought to be an important part of the training of ethical lawyers. The clinic can provide both the experience of representing indigent clients and the opportunity for reflection on and discussion of such representation.

H. Providing the Opportunity for Examining the Impact of Doctrine in Real Life and Providing a Laboratory in which Students and Faculty Study Particular Areas of the Law

Stephen Wizner and Dennis Curtis described the purpose of their clinical teaching as attempting "through a sustained and comprehensive combination of practice and research to develop a profound understanding of the legal theory, economic implications and social dynamics of a given segment of the legal system." This goal of the in-house clinic can be analogized to a "seminar plus." Many of our nonclinical colleagues frequently offer seminars in which students engage in a thorough examination of an area of law or of legal institutions. In-house clinical programs can provide all of what seminars provide and a good deal more. By examining and understanding the impact of doctrine on individual lives, students deepen their understanding of that doctrine. That understanding may also lead to sophisticated student involvement in law reform efforts infrequently attempted by seminars. Thus, clinical students may involve themselves in presenting comments to administrative agencies, filing amicus curiae briefs, or even presenting testimony before legislative agencies.

I. Critiquing the Capacities and Limitations of Lawyers and the Legal System

This critique is intertwined with and builds upon the goals already discussed. Robert Condlin has described the critique of lawyering as requiring analyzing and evaluating the patterns and theories immanent in the methods lawyers use to perform and think about skill practices against conceptions of what would be better, for the purpose of resolving perceived contradictions between theory and practice. This analysis presupposes a critical theory, which in turn presupposes worked out views on the nature of a fair and just legal system and the role of lawyer practices in operating and improving it.

In addition to analyzing legal practices, clinical programs can provide the opportunity for examining the functioning of legal institutions as a whole, analyzing how such institutions are operating currently and how they might be changed to work more effectively. While a clinic alone probably cannot accomplish this function, it is a critical complement to other areas of the curriculum in which such issues are or ought to be addressed. The clinic provides data about the reality of practice and the legal system that the student cannot obtain in class. The clinic further requires the student to examine her own performance in light of this data. Finally, the clinic provides an opportunity for dialogue on these questions that is difficult to achieve in the classroom, even in those classes organized in seminar fashion.

J. Conclusion: Integration or, The Whole Is Greater than the Sum of Its Parts

Clinics provide the best opportunity in the curriculum to integrate these manifold teaching goals. The goals, of course, state educational objectives. We believe they also state lawyering qualities that we would like ourselves and our students to possess. Many of us would like to have the opportunity to teach our students all of the goals listed above. All of us would also hope that we and our students possessed the qualities that would result from taking those goals to heart—analytical planning abilities, proficient legal performance skills, an understanding of the rules of professional responsibility and the implication of ethical issues, an ability to learn from experience, a deep understanding of role and the impact of doctrine, a commitment to and knowledge about service, and an ability to challenge prevailing notions of acceptable lawyer behavior and legitimate institutional functioning.

None of us can be perfect exemplars of all of these qualities, and none can teach all of these goals in our clinic with perfect emphasis. But the Committee believes that the in-house clinic provides the optimal means of integrating the theoretical, analytical, skills, and ethical goals we have identified. Moreover, an important concomitant of the development of these goals is the opportunity for personal growth that the clinic affords to students. No other learning experience in law school combines the extraordinarily varied and dramatic context of real cases and problems with the opportunity for intensive teaching, supervision, growth, and reflection.

...

Carolyn Gross, *Beyond Skills Training, Revisited: The Clinical Education Spiral**

19 Clin. L. Rev 489 (2013)

...

I. What Is Clinical Pedagogy?

A. Introduction

Despite my 12 years of teaching experience, many of them in the clinic; and my two years of clinical experience as a student in law school, I felt the need to delve deeply into the annals of clinical pedagogy and scholarship in order to excavate a dear description of the goals and methods of clinical pedagogy. As the footnotes attest, I read a lot, from Jerome Frank to Gary Bellow to Margaret Johnson.

I combed the pages of the Clinical Bibliography and reread the old classics. Not surprisingly, this research—fun and educational as it was—resulted in no such "clear description" of the goals and methods of clinical pedagogy. Instead, I gathered a rather diffuse consensus.

In describing this consensus in the sections below, I differentiate between what I call clinical "goals"—that is what the clinic is trying to do/accomplish/achieve; and clinical "methods"—how the clinic or clinical teacher reaches those goals. Obviously, this can be an arbitrary line, and often goals become methods and vice-versa. Particularly in light of the recent focus on "backward design" and outcomes-based education, and

* Excerpts are reprinted with the permission of the author and the Clinical Law Review.

because I tend to organize my teaching in this way, I find the distinction a useful one in analyzing the questions I have raised.

B. Goals

Reflecting on the scholarship of and about clinicians written over the past decades, I offer the following in response to the question, "What do we do that transcends skills training for lawyers?" The bottom line is that clinical pedagogy aims to teach students to approach lawyering as a theory-driven practice, framing each activity with intentionality and reflection.

More specifically, clinical education has three broad goals: providing learning for transfer; exposing students to issues of social justice; and offering opportunities to practice lawyering skills. I discuss each of these goals below.

1. Learning for Transfer

Clinical pedagogy aims to teach students how to learn. This is distinct from teaching students how to "think like a lawyer"—which is, for many, the goal of most first-year courses. Bill Quigley, for example, contrasts clinical education to passive teaching methods, such as the "'banking' concept of education" where students are seen as empty vessels into which teachers pour their knowledge. Put another way, Kim O'Leary describes the goal of a clinical course as "engag[ing] the student in the process of learning and understanding how the learning process takes place." The result is that "students transform into self-learners [and) teachers become reflective self-evaluating transformative agents of education...."

Embedded in this goal is what has come to be called "learning for transfer;" the ability to generalize from lessons and skills gathered in one place and circumstances and transfer such lessons and skills to a different set of circumstances. Many suggest that this is the heart of clinical pedagogy. It is certainly the theoretical base of what we now call clinical pedagogy.

Elliott Milstein and Bob Dinerstein describe this task as helping students to "see the connection between their lawyering experiences in clinic and those they will encounter throughout their careers, to treat each insight they have as a lesson potentially generalizable to other lawyering situations...." Clinical teachers guide their students to reflect on how one interview, for example, is similar to other interviews, and, therefore, what theory about this particular lawyering skill they can extract and apply to other interviews in the future.

One of the most important applications of this goal of teaching students how to learn is to guide them to recognize choice moments and to be able to make intentional choices in the face of uncertainty. Simply put, again by Milstein and Dinerstein: "[I]f we are not teaching our students to recognize other choices, we have failed."

2. Social Justice/Critical Thinking

The second broad goal of traditional clinical pedagogy is to teach, or at least expose students to, concepts of social justice. Some might see this goal as one to indoctrinate students into liberal ideas about helping the poor and saving the planet—and indeed some clinics do have some version of these values as their goals. But in fact, the "social justice goal" is much more complex and less doctrinaire than that.

I like to think of the social justice mission of the clinic as twofold: first, to expose students to the underbelly of the legal system, and its place and role in society; and second, to challenge them to think critically about that system and their place in it. Thus, "clinicians attempt to destabilize the law school curriculum and legal practice by inculcating a set of skills and values that will permit their graduates to appreciate the benefits of the legal system and law practice while remaining critical of their shortcomings."

Or, as Shalleck and Ahmad theorize, "Clinical thought has provided ways to identify, discuss and debate the work of the lawyer in its technical and social aspects." Clinicians "have sought in their work on pedagogy, on lawyering, on social justice to reconstruct. They have acted to create new pedagogical structures, theories and practices within legal education."

Of course, in addition to the critical thinking piece, the social justice goal might also include a commitment on the part of the clinic to providing legal services to those whose access to such services is limited. And certainly, clinical education emerged in part "from a desire to re-connect students to social justice...." Some scholars go so far as to say that clinical teachers and lawyers have a duty to ensure that law students are exposed to injustice and understand the role that they may play in either working for or against injustice.

This duty is by no means universally accepted, however. Indeed, many teachers and clinical scholars question the efficacy of using the clinic primarily as a way to provide legal services to the poor, suggesting that "[a] service orientation by clinical programs can too easily become a rationale for permitting law teaching to slip into vocational, how-to-do-it instruction. "This emphasis risks undermining the theory-based goals of critical thinking and learning for transfer.

3. Skills and Lawyering Process

The third broad goal of clinical pedagogy is to expose students to and encourage them to deconstruct the work and role of the lawyer, and the lawyering process. This goal has both a skills component and a professional development/values component. Some who write about this merge the two, others treat them as distinct.

Gary Bellow described clinical pedagogy as "a departure from a primary focus in legal education on broadening perspectives and on developing judgment, discipline and intellect." More recently, Mil stein and Dinerstein describe the work of clinical teachers to "map out the lawyering process into its component parts and then to propose ideas and theories about what constituted high quality performance of that component." Thus, clinical teachers· expand on the idea that lawyering is a process made up of distinct and related skills and they encourage their students to dig deeper and to recognize "the process that lawyers use of finding the opportunity and space for thinking differently or critically about a legal issue, for stretching or reorienting a standard narrative within and about the law, and for persuading a court to adopt that view."

Shalleck and Ahmad describe how clinical pedagogy challenges students to "identify, question and inquire deeply into the complex, embedded practices through which legal rules and doctrines take on meaning in the world through the interpretive activities of lawyers as they engage with clients in understanding their stories and in shaping for and presenting them to the world."

4. A Loose Consensus

Running through all of these goals—teaching students to learn, engaging them in social justice work, challenging them to deconstruct lawyering process and role—is the thread of critical self-reflection and reflection about the legal system and lawyer. Also woven throughout is the shimmering indeterminacy of facts, law, client, student, teacher, relationship.

Thus, clinical pedagogy not only offers students the opportunity, but in fact requires them to engage in critical self-reflection and thinking about these issues; whether they are practicing a lawyering skill or struggling with an ethical question or reporting on their client issues. This is what Phyllis Goldfarb describes as the "practice-theory spiral." It is the essence of clinical pedagogy.

C. Methods

There is as much consensus about a description of "clinical methods" as there is about "clinical goals."

My understanding of that consensus is that clinical methods consist broadly of three themes: (1) grounding the teaching in the students' case/client work; (2) teaching lawyering as "process" composed of various themes; and (3) giving students multiple opportunities to reflect on their experiences. These three themes are intertwined in the "practice-theory" spiral, with (1) as the practice and (3) as the theory. I see number 2 as the heart of "clinical method," comprised as it is of both theory and practice. The themes—comfort with uncertainty, client-centeredness, professional judgment, etc.—are the theory. The practice is the methods we use to teach those themes through examination of the work of the lawyer.

This move from skills to theory and theory to skills is an attempt to prepare students for a future that is not certain; the challenge for all teachers is to transcend the day to day in an attempt to teach more broadly. That is my clinical scholarship as well: I teach about what I write and write about what I teach; my ideas get tested in the classroom. And the beginning point—of the teaching and the scholarship—is always the student's individual frame of reference and his/her own perceptions of the world.

I describe, below, how the three themes—of teaching grounded in casework, examining lawyering as a process, and reflecting on both theory and practice—translate into teaching methods through three concrete techniques/practices: role assumption, advocacy for live clients, and reflection.

1. Role Assumption and the Situated Student

There is much written on the value of experiential learning particularly for adult learners. And clinics certainly use hands-on experience by students as the basis for their learning: "The single most critical defining element of clinical education is that it is experience-based learning." In most clinics, the context in which this experience takes place is the lawyer-client relationship, and the representation of clients by the students, acting in role as the clients' attorney.

Students are given responsibility for their client matters, with the professors providing a range of supervision and guidance. In many clinics, students are told in no uncertain terms that these cases and clients are "theirs," not the supervisors'. Students thus act as lawyers, often for the first time in their law school careers.

Indeed, Barry, Dubin, and Joy note that early clinicians saw the clinic as "a 'case book'—not, however, of dead letters descriptive of past controversies, but always of living issues in the throbbing life of the day, the life the student is now living." Gary Bellow describes the "central feature of the clinical method [as] its conscious use, both conceptually and operationally, of the dynamics of role adjustment in social life." In the clinical experience, the student assumes a role, learns the obligations of the role, recognizes certain cues involved in assuming that role, and ultimately acquires the aptitudes required to perform the role.

More than simply embodying the role of a lawyer representing clients, however, the clinical method helps students reflect on and learn from that role assumption. Milstein describes the ideal of supervision, for example, as to "[h]elp students extract theory from experience, apply theory to solve real-world problems, and rev se theory in light of experience...." Thus, clinical teachers and the clinic program aim to start where students are, using their experience in the world as the starting point and reference point.

2. Advocating for Situated Clients

But clinics take the concept of experiential learning even farther by teaching the situated student through advocacy for the situated client. As a method, the clinic "allows legal educators to examine the dynamics of the lawyer-client relationship from within the relationship itself." The student begins to inhabit a new status: " In performing specific legal tasks, students experience feelings of responsibility to others, independence, competency, immediacy, and contribution as members of a professional community." But they achieve that new status in the context of representing "live" clients. They receive supervised responsibility in the real world to solve real problems. This new personal responsibility and the necessarily accompanying choices about how to use it contextualizes the students' assumption of the lawyering role and makes it more complicated.

Thus, clinicians work to meet the pedagogical goal of deconstructing and understanding the work of the lawyer by placing students in that role, in the context of representing live clients. They challenge students to extract theory from their practice, and to look to theory to guide their decisions about how to represent their clients. Clinical teachers ask their students to consider what lawyering skills "mean" in the context of their lawyering practice: What is problem solving? What are its components? How does an effective lawyer respond 1n the context of this particular client's situation?

This clinical method is the inverse of the traditional case method, which dissects problems presented from casebooks. In clinic, students and teachers build problems together, from facts of clients' situations, and law and policy and other considerations that situations call forth.

3. Reflection

The third method of clinical pedagogy, which weaves its way through the other two methods is deliberate and systematic reflection. Reflection is the method that guides students' extraction of theory from practice, and the application of practice to theory; and it pushes students to generalize from the specific and transfer their learning beyond that specific.

The role of the clinical teacher is "to enlist the motivations, impressions, and relationships of role performance in efforts to enhance self-reflection, self-consciousness and a more encompassing understanding of those phenomena of the legal order which are the focus of pedagogic inquiry."

Part of this method involves transparency on the part of the teacher—making her goals and methods explicit to her students. In this way, she models reflection: "We also reinforce the importance of 'naming' our activities and techniques for students so that they are clearly identified for later use. Naming involves giving students frameworks within which they can fit the teachers' questions."

Marc Feldman suggests that student reflection on the clinical experience and its components leads the student to greater "self-consciousness, responsibility, and perceived status." Such self-awareness prepares students for the realities of practice, where they might not have a supervisor, senior partner, or mentor to assist with reflection on performance and practice. Using reflection as a teaching method thus serves the clinical goal of teaching students how to fish.

4. What Clinicians Do and Why

As with clinical goals, all three of these methods—role assumption, advocating for live clients, and reflection—weave among each other, and with the goals they serve. Embedded in all three of these methods are the jurisprudential and pedagogical themes of the clinical movement: indeterminacy, uncertainty, the necessity of making choices about professional role and behavior, the idea that law is made through the interactions of client and lawyer, through interactions of fact and law.

Thus, deconstructing clinical goals and methods helps us understand what clinicians do. We give names to the things we do in order to understand what we do and why we do it. We give names to things in order to make them exist and capable of analysis: a vocabulary that provides definition.

...

Endnotes

1. *See generally,* Association of American Law Schools, Section on Clinical Legal Education, *Report of the Committee on the Future of the In-House Clinic,* 42 J. LEGAL EDUC. 508 (1992) [hereinafter, AALS Committee Report].

2. *Id.* at 511.

3. *See, e.g.*, Beth Hirschfelder Wilensky, *Dethroning Langdell,* 107 MINN. L. REV. 2701, 2707–10 (2023).

4. *E.g.*, Beth McMurtrie, *Why the Science of Teaching is Often Ignored,* CHRON. HIGHER EDUC. (Jan. 3, 2022), https://www.chronicle.com/article/why-the-science-of-teaching-is-often-ignored.

5. *See* Richard Badenhausen, *Everything About How We Evaluate Teaching Needs a Makeover,* CHRON. HIGHER EDUC. (June 8, 2022), https://www.chronicle.com/article/everything-about-how-we-evaluate-teaching-needs-a-makeover (discussing how attitudes toward teaching must change).

6. Wallace J. Mlyniec & Meghan Strong, *The Role of Law School Clinics in Implementing the* Gault *Decision*, in RIGHTS, RACE, AND REFORM: 50 YEARS OF CHILD ADVOCACY IN THE JUVENILE JUSTICE SYSTEM 128–53 (Kristin Henning, Laura Cohen & Ellen Marrus eds., 2018). Critiques of the rigid law school classroom also arose in the Critical Legal Studies movement. *See, e.g.*, Duncan Kennedy, *Legal Education and the Reproduction of Hierarchy*, 32 J. LEGAL EDUC. 591 (1982). And law professors today have continued honing the critique even today. *See generally, e.g.*, Wilensky, *supra* note 3.

7. Wallace J. Mlyniec, *Developing a Teacher Training Program for New Clinical Teachers*, 19 CLINICAL L. REV. 327, 333 n.21 (2012).

8. Carolyn Grose, *Beyond Skills Training, Revisited*, 19 CLINICAL L. REV. 489, 495 (2013).

9. Ann Shalleck, *Clinical Contexts: Theory and Practice in Law and Supervision*, 21 N.Y.U. REV. L. SOC. CHANGE 109, 181 (1993–1994).

10. Grose, *supra* note 8, at 497.

11. The process of asking and answering these three questions first emerged at the Georgetown Summer Institute where Georgetown Professors Deborah Epstein, Jane Aiken, and I, American University Law Professors Ann Shalleck and Elliott Milstein, Columbia Law Professor Conrad Johnson, Catholic Law Professor Catherine Klein, and CUNY Law Professor Susan Bryant explored these questions with new clinical teachers from many different law schools.

12. Robert R. Kuehn & David A. Santacroce, *An Empirical Analysis of Clinical Legal Education at Middle Age*, 71 J. LEGAL EDUC. 622, 651 (2022).

13. Becky Supiano, *It's Not About the Evidence Anymore*, CHRON. HIGHER EDUC. (June 22, 2022), https://www.chronicle.com/article/its-not-about-the-evidence-anymore. (interviewing Scott Freeman, emeritus lecturer at the University of Washington).

14. Maryellen Weimer, *Understanding the Role of Intuition in Teaching*, FACULTY FOCUS (May 29, 2013), https://www.facultyfocus.com/articles/academic-leadership/understanding-the-role-of-intuition-in-teaching/.

15. Anne M. Cleary, *Learning Is Not Intuitive: What This Means for How We Learn*, PSYCH. TODAY (Sept. 10, 2018), https://www.psychologytoday.com/us/blog/quirks-memory/201809/learning-is-not-intuitive-what-means-how-we-learn).

16. *See* Weimer, *supra* note 14.

17. Rob Jenkins, *The 4 Properties of Powerful Teachers*, CHRON. HIGHER EDUC. (March 16, 2015), https://www.chronicle.com/article/the-4-properties-of-powerful-teachers/.

18. *Id.*

19. *See generally* CLINICAL EDUCATION FOR THE LAW STUDENT: LEGAL EDUCATION IN A SERVICE SETTING, CLEPR NAT'L CONF. PROC., BUCK HILL FALLS (1973).

20. *See generally* AALS Committee Report, *supra* note 1.

21. *See* Susan Bryant, Elliott S. Milstein & Ann C. Shalleck, Transforming the Education of Lawyers: The Theory and Practice of Clinical Pedagogy (2014) (adding the additional goals of building a lifelong commitment and skills to learn in professional settings and developing skills associated with the human dimensions of practice).

22. Anthony Amsterdam, *Clinical Legal Education—A 21st Century Perspective*, 34 J. Legal Educ, 612 (1984).

23. Professor Grant Wiggins developed the concept of backward design. *See, e.g.*, Grant Wiggins & Jay McTighe, The Understanding by Design: Guide to Creating High Quality Units (2011).

24. William Quigley, *Introduction to Clinical Teaching to the New Clinical law Professor: A View from the First Floor*, 28 Akron L. Rev. 463, 485 (1995).

25. Deborah Epstein, Jane Aiken & Wallace Mlyniec, Teaching the Clinic Seminar, 1–17 (2014).

26. George Critchlow, *Professional Responsibility, Student Practice, and the Clinical Teacher's Duty to Intervene*, 26 Gonz. L. Rev. 415, 419 (1990).

27. *Id.*

28. *Id.* at 436–37.

29. Grose, *supra* note 8, at 500.

30. Donald Schön, The Reflective Practitioner: How Professionals Think In Action (1984).

31. Alistair E. Newbern & Emily F. Suski, *Translating the Values of Clinical Pedagogy across Generations*, 20 Clinical L. Rev. 181 (2013).

32. Trans-substantively refers to the same rules being applied to cases regardless of the underlying substantive rights. Suzette Malveaux, *A Diamond in The Rough: Trans-Substantivity of The Federal Rules of Civil Procedure and Its Detrimental Impact on Civil Rights*, 92 Wash. U. L. Rev. 455 (2014) at 456 n.1.

33. Bryant, Milstein & Shalleck, *supra* note 21, at 28. "The term 'lawyering process,' first used by Bellow and Moulton in their book, The Lawyering Process, describes the work that dominates the life of a practicing lawyer and articulates the collection of theories, skills, and values that lawyers employ." *Id.* at 36–38 (typographical error corrected) (internal citation omitted).

34. Epstein, Aiken & Mlyniec, *supra* note 25, at 16–17.

35. Grose, *supra* note 8, at 494.

36. *See, e.g.*, David A. Binder & Paul Bergman, *Taking Lawyering Skills Training Seriously*, 10 Clinical L. Rev. 191, 197–98 (2003); Susan M. Barnett & Stephen J. Ceci, *When and Where Do We Apply What We Learn? A Taxonomy for Far Transfer*, 128 Psych. Bull. 612, 613 (2002) (explaining the theoretical and practical importance of transfer); *id.* at 614–15 (tracing history of psychological research into transfer); Tonya Kowalski, *True North: Navigating for the Transfer of Learning in Legal Education*, 34 Seattle U.L. Rev. 51, 52 (2010) ("'Transfer of learning' is at the very essence of what lawyers do every day. The most classic example comes from formal legal analysis, where attorneys take concrete rules and analogies from precedent and apply them to new legal problems.").

37. *See, e.g.*, Binder & Bergman, *supra* note 36, at 198 & n.29 (explaining, and collecting sources on, near transfer); Kowalski, *supra* note 36, at 61–63 (similar); Barnett & Ceci, *supra* note 366, at 619–20 (similar).

38. *See, e.g.*, Binder & Bergman, *supra* note 366, at 198 & n.28 (explaining, and collecting sources on, far transfer); Kowalski, *supra* note 36, at 62–63 (similar); Barnett & Ceci, *supra* note 366, at 619–20 (similar).

39. *See* National Research Council, How People Learn: Brain, Mind, Experience, and School, 8–9, 65, 260 (John D. Bransford, Ann L. Brown & Rodney R. Cocking eds., expanded ed. 2000); Mary Nicol Bowman & Lisa Brodoff, *Cracking Student Silos: Linking Legal Writing and Clinical*

Learning Through Transference, 25 CLINICAL L. REV. 269, 278–79 (2019); David A. Binder, Albert J. Moore & Paul Bergman, *A Depositions Course: Tackling the Challenge of Teaching for Professional Skills Transfer*, 13 CLINICAL L. REV. 871, 884–86 (2007).

40. The difference between near and far transfer turns on similarity. *See* Barnett & Ceci, *supra* note 36, at 621. Similarity, however, is multidimensional—including knowledge base, modality of transferring (e.g., written vs. oral), and the physical, temporal, functional, and social contexts involved. *See id.* at 621–24 (proposing taxonomy of transfer along those dimensions); *see also* Binder, Moore & Bergman, *supra* note 39, at 882–84 (discussing near and far transfer).

41. *See, e.g.*, Bryant, Milstein & Shalleck, *supra* note 21, at 28–29.

42. *See id.* at 36–38 (highlighting importance of clinical faculty focusing on the lawyering process and explaining strategies for doing so effectively).

43. *Id.*

44. Quigley, *supra* note 244, at 493.

45. *See* Deborah N. Archer, *Open to Justice: The Importance of Student Selection Decisions in Law School Clinics*, 24 Clinical L. Rev. 1 (2017) (discussing students' learning of skills important to cultural competency, like rapport-building, as opportunities for near and far transfer); Bowman & Brodoff, *supra* note 399, at 280–90 (emphasizing importance of teaching to transfer in first year legal writing classes to bolster student success in clinics).

46. Eduardo R. Ferrer & Kristin N. Henning, *Critical Clinical Frames: Centering Adolescence, Race, Trauma, and Gender in Practice-Based Pedagogy*, 30 CLINICAL L. REV. 113 (2023)

47. Quigley, *supra* note 24, at 492.

48. Ferrer & Henning, *supra* note 46, (defining a "pedagogical frame" as "an explicit schema through which students are encouraged to intentionally and critically examine and interpret everything they encounter in furtherance of their representation of their clients' expressed interests").

49. *Id.*

50. *Id.*

51. *Id.*

52. AALS Committee Report, *supra* note 1, at 517.

53. By civic order, I mean not just the functions of government and public authorities, but also "private or enterprise sector (for example, business enterprises) as well as voluntary and non-profit organizations such as neighborhoods, sports clubs, peak industry associations, think tanks, service clubs, churches, mosques, synagogues, centers for the performing arts, museums and other cultural resources—indeed, all the things voluntary associations do." See Word Reference Language Forums, https://forum.wordreference.com/threads/civic-order.2885136/.

54. *See generally, e.g.*, Jennifer Howard, *Learning to Think Like a Lawyer*, 2 CLINICAL L. REV. 167 (1995–1996).

55. In Jesuit education, *cura personalis* refers to the process of educating the whole student—mind, body, and spirit—and to instill a passion for learning, reflection, service, and the greater good of humankind. Its objective is to assist in the fullest possible development of all the God-given talents of each individual person as a member of the human community. Peter-Hans Kolvenbach, *Go Forth and Teach: The Characteristics of Jesuit Education*, JESUIT SECONDARY EDUC. ASS'N FOUNDS., 7 (2005), https://jesuitschoolsnetwork.org/wp-content/uploads/2018/08/GoForthAndTeach.pdf.

56. The phrase, "starting from a place of generosity" was coined by Professor Kris Henning during one of our Elements of Clinical Pedagogy classes on supervising students.

57. *See generally, e.g.*, Kathleen Sullivan, *Self-Disclosure, Separation, and Students: Intimacy in the Clinical Relationship*, 27 IND. L. REV. 115 (1993).

Three

A SHORT HISTORY OF CLINICAL PEDAGOGY

Beginnings are always important. Although new teachers are eager to undertake their new responsibilities with their new students and colleagues, they often come with little knowledge of the history of clinical pedagogy or why that history remains relevant today. Even mid-level clinical teachers, who began their career long after the battles to establish a place for clinical education in the legal academy, often ignore the history and do not appreciate how the early battles to gain acceptance shaped their current methods and status. As William Faulkner once wrote, "The past is never dead. It's not even past."[1] Clinical education's past and those who fought to have it accepted into the legal academy imbue the evolution of clinical pedagogy and remain relevant today. Foundational stories may evolve into myths, but most myths always reflect the reality that spawned them. The foundational stories of clinical education reflect the birth and evolution of a remarkable pedagogy and should be a source of inspiration to new generations of clinical teachers.

It is hard to imagine a modern law school curriculum that does not include an in-house clinical program and other experiential courses, but that was not always the case. The roots of clinical education can be traced back to the legal dispensaries developed in some law schools during the late 19th and early 20th centuries. Dispensaries were developed first at the University of Denver Law School in 1904,[2] and later at the University of Cincinnati College of Law, George Washington University Law School, Harvard Law School, University of Minnesota Law School, Northwestern University School of Law, University of Pennsylvania Law School, University of Tennessee College of Law, and Yale Law School throughout the 1890s and early 1900s.[3] These dispensaries were in some sense remnants of the law-office training that new lawyers received before university-based legal training became the norm.

The Langdellian Method

As university-based training replaced law-office training, Christopher Columbus Langdell, the Dean of Harvard Law School from 1870 to 1895, introduced the Langdellian method of legal training. His method spread to most of the then-existing law schools and came to dominate U.S. legal education after 1870.[4] Langdell believed that law was a science best learned by studying previous case law via the Socratic method. In Langdell's universe, practical training would and should be gained in a law office after the "science" was mastered in the university. Lectures and the Socratic method of questioning students about a judge's reasoning set out in appellate cases were the main teaching methods used to instill knowledge of the science of the law into the minds of future lawyers. As the Langdellian method became embedded in university-based legal education, most academics did not see the dispensaries as integral to a sound legal education. The dispensaries were peripheral to the essential work of university-based legal training and would remain so for the next hundred years. To be sure, there were efforts to introduce actual case work into the academy. For example, Yale professor and later judge Jerome Frank, a proponent of the Legal Realism movement, debunked the myth of rule certainty underpinning Langdell's conception of the law.[5] Frank attempted to resurrect live-case legal practice as a requirement of formal law school training and authored several articles in the early 20th century defending his thesis.[6] Nevertheless, the Langdellian method prevailed.

The Cultural and Political Roots of Clinical Education

The Due Process Revolution

Although several universities developed proto-clinics in the early- to mid-20th century, the modern clinical movement began in earnest in the mid-1960s. This development owes its existence to three completely different academic and social movements that began in the 1960s and early 1970s.[7] The first movement was the development of the Supreme Court's jurisprudence concerning the incorporation doctrine and the due process clause, which constitutionalized criminal and some civil law and procedure.[8] Under the leadership of Chief Justice Earl Warren,[9] various cases decided during this period applied many of the procedural guarantees contained in the Bill of Rights and the due process clause of the 14th Amendment of the Constitution to state court proceedings. Most importantly, landmark rulings expanded the Constitutional right to counsel in criminal[10] and other kinds of cases.[11] These cases helped launch the creation of legal services offices and the need for lawyers to staff them.

Social and Cultural Awakening in the 1960s and 1970s

The second movement, a great awakening of concern for civil rights and the evil of racial discrimination, crystallized during the late 1960s and early 1970s. The Vietnam War was also raging and political turmoil was spreading across the nation as Americans began to question the truth about the war effort. Civil rights and anti-war activists found common ground in social justice theory and animosity to governmental acts, laws, and regulations enforced by actors who seemed unconcerned or violently opposed to those who sought to expand citizens' rights and protections. Protestors against the war and those in favor of civil rights also employed similar tactics, taking to the streets to oppose the war and fight discrimination. Sit-ins, marches, picketing, and other types of protests occurred throughout the South and in urban areas throughout the country. These civil rights demonstrators and anti-war protestors were often brutally beaten by police and mobs, arrested, and jailed. The resulting arrests required a cadre of lawyers to defend the sizeable number of protestors being incarcerated.[12] Police crackdowns on demonstrators resulted in more attention to both First Amendment Constitutional guarantees, and to laws that seemed to endorse discrimination and permit the violence occurring in the streets.

Atrocities occurring in Vietnam brought new attention to human rights violations, more protests and demonstrations, and more arrests, as did voter registration movements to end discrimination. A new awareness of the danger of unchecked government power emerged and the clash of social justice principles and state power could not be avoided. As this awareness grew, citizens and some elected officials began to recognize the need to eliminate all types of discriminatory laws, to create specific protections for voting and other legitimate citizen actions to end the continuing vestiges of Jim Crow laws' brutality, and to adopt policies to end the slaughter in Vietnam.

This awakening generated a heightened interest in other rights-based movements related to the cultural upheavals of the time. A new women's rights movement[13] and a children's rights movement[14] found their roots in the aspirations of those seeking to create racial equality and restrictions on unfettered government action in the United States. At the same time, student- activists noticed the absence of any serious academic inquiry into these legal and cultural upheavals in undergraduate political science and history departments or at law schools where future government leaders were being trained. Legal activists and scholars recognized existing laws often underpinned the resistance to these movements but also saw law as a means to reverse these policies. This spurred a growing interest in legal methods that would completely change the legal culture and landscape of the country. The clash between the principles of power and the principles of justice demanded a response from law schools. Slowly, new courses found their way into the curriculum.

The political ferment and energy of the era encouraged teachers to create new substantive law courses concerning the rights of various groups and individuals. Scholars began writing casebooks and journal articles which enabled discrete courses that had never been part of the legal academic canon to emerge within law school curricula. Prior to this era, children's rights were often relegated to a single class session or two within a criminal law course or a domestic relations course. As the dialogue about children's rights expanded, teachers began to develop courses specifically related to children's rights in schools and courts, and challenge laws that did not provide due process to litigants in juvenile delinquency and child welfare cases.[15] As more women joined the ranks of the overwhelmingly male population in law schools, and as a few women began to populate law faculties, courses regarding gender discrimination law against women began to emerge.[16] Traditional property law teachers began spending more class time on landlord-tenant issues alongside the historical property law traditions emanating from common-law principles. Rights developed in President Lyndon Johnson's Great Society programs encouraged teachers to create courses addressing the expanding rights of poor people.[17] Additionally, atrocities in Vietnam resulted in courses concerning human rights and other international obligations.

Changes in the Legal Academy

During the same period, the legal academy's new Socratic discourse about the expansion of civil rights and the awakening of the country's cultural and social conscience was joined by a third critical academic and social movement called clinical legal education. The modern idea of clinical legal education was modeled roughly on medical school training and financed by the legendary William Pincus, a program officer at the Ford Foundation and later director of the Council on Legal Education for Professional Responsibility (CLEPR).[18] As other foundations also began to provide seed money, legal clinics devoted to representing marginalized Americans began to proliferate in the nation's law schools. By 1965, the Ford Foundation had given almost two million dollars for experimental legal education.[19] Between 1965 and 1968, CLEPR provided $290,000 to twenty-one law schools for summer and in-term experiential programs.[20] By the end of 1972, CLEPR had made 116 grants totaling more than four million dollars.[21] Schools that accepted the money had to adhere to Pincus' definition of clinical education. He defined it as "lawyer-client work by a law student, under law school supervision, for credit toward the law degree."[22]

The early clinical teachers funded by Pincus wanted to combat the institutionalized injustices concerning racial and other forms of discrimination, poverty, and the war that permeated that period of American history.[23] They were also on a mission to transform legal education to make it the vehicle that would achieve their first goal. They believed existing governmental policies were either intentionally created to restrict equality, economic justice, and peaceful solutions to international problems, or were managed ineptly in ways that preserved them. They also believed that training the law students who would later assume positions of responsibility in the government would bend the arc of the moral universe toward justice.[24] As the nation's law schools' clinical courses increased in number, the law teachers funded by Pincus were joined by like-minded students seeking more relevance in their legal education. At the time, few courses explored social justice-related issues or lawyers' pro bono responsibilities. The new clinics filled this unfilled niche.[25]

The American Bar Association (ABA), state bar associations, and courts advanced the clinical education movement by recognizing that law students could provide an inexpensive way to fulfill the new unfunded mandates, like the mandatory appointment of free counsel in various cases that the Supreme Court and other courts were establishing.[26] In addition, providing student-attorneys for clients who did not have a constitutional right to a lawyer could ease the judges' burdens.[27] Soon special student practice rules were developed to avoid the unauthorized practice of law.[28] Clinical education brought the practice skills students were learning while working in law offices directly into the legal academy. But rather than seeing practice as merely a set of skills, clinicians integrated practice into the purely doctrinal and theoretical education students were receiving from their other professors to complete their education.

To be sure, most clinics espoused the goals elucidated by William Pincus when he defined clinical education. They also served the more practical requirements of the courts. However, the goals set forth by both the Pincus/CLEPR grants and the new student practice rules were mostly structural, rather than pedagogical. The practice rules usually dealt with course credit, permission to represent clients, supervision by lawyers who were integrated into the academy in some way, the proper variety and number of cases students could manage, and the indigency of the clinic's clients. Nonetheless, the pedagogical goals of reinforcing problem-solving as a legal skill while exposing students to other common legal practice skills that complement doctrinal and theoretical understanding were implicit in the rule structure.

There can be no doubt that Pincus, like the clinicians he enabled, wanted to change the face of legal education. That battle was not easy. Most law deans and traditional faculty at the time resisted expanding clinical courses into the curriculum. They also resisted the possibility of allowing clinicians to join the permanent tenure-track law faculty. This resistance was so widespread and entrenched that in 1980 the ABA adopted a specific interpretation of their accreditation standards that included recognizing clinical teachers as part of the faculty. After harsh pushbacks from law school deans and faculty, this interpretation was swiftly suspended. This act would turn out to be the opening salvo in years of battles about the academic status of clinical faculty.[29] The resistance increased when law schools were asked to pay for the clinical programs from their own revenue streams as private foundation and government funding for clinics diminished.[30] The common position of many traditional law faculty was that "clinical programs have weak intellectual content and unqualified teachers, and [they are] teaching incorrect values and ideas."[31]

It is true that most early clinical professors did not pay much attention to the nature of clinical pedagogy, and that the quality of clinical teaching was mixed in the 1970s.[32] Many teachers were public interest lawyers who were hired for their practice experience. Some came to represent as many clients as they could. In my own school, the early leader of clinical education referred to it as "tennis shoe law," meaning that students should run from courtroom to courtroom to help as many clients as possible.

Most early clinical teachers arrived with little or no experience as clinical teachers. Indeed, there was no collective understanding of clinical education goals or the methodology to achieve them. The goals and methods of clinical pedagogy had yet to be developed.[33] Many of the new teachers merely brought the practice of law out of their prior offices and reestablished it in the law schools. They thought they could use students to expand the number of lawyers trained to represent poor and politically motivated clients. Often, serving these clients was their central focus and their scholarship, if any, evolved downstream of this distinctive client-centered perspective.[34]

Caseloads in the first clinics were intentionally high, and faculty assumed that students would learn to practice law merely by engaging in the actual practice of law under their tutelage. But that was the flaw of law-office training prior to the ascendency of academic legal training. Pincus understood this and used CLEPR funds to support his belief that law schools would become better centers of learning if Carl Llewellyn's and Jerome Frank's ideas were finally adopted. Frank and Llewellyn understood that the merger of theory and practice strengthened both. They believed that students would learn the law and the theory behind those laws and practices better when they applied theory to practice with real clients.

Pincus intuitively knew that as well. His goals, however, did not directly or precisely include using pedagogical methods and legal theory to understand practice. He did expect students would develop a professional identity using real cases, and that their ability to think like a lawyer rather than a judge would improve. He thought those traits would flow from well-directed legal practice. The modern pedagogical goals of exercising judgment in the face of uncertainty, developing interpersonal and cultural competency, understanding social justice, or engaging in intentional self-reflection and lifelong learning were seldom discussed by most early clinical teachers. The academic nature of the clinical education was not there at the beginning. That would come later,[35] and as the modern pioneers explored the intricacies of clinical teaching, they recognized that clinical pedagogy "was more than the sum of its parts."[36]

The Growth and Development of Clinical Pedagogy

As early as 1979, Professor Joseph Harbaugh, later a dean at three law schools, listed the needs of the new clinical education movement as (1) training for new and experienced teachers; (2) materials to develop the pedagogy to train the teachers and a vehicle to widely distribute them; and (3) research into the nature of law, lawyering, and the teaching of lawyering skills and professional responsibility.[37]

This three-pronged combination that gave rise to clinical education—the due process revolution, the social upheaval that led to the expansion of the various civil rights movements in the 1960s and 1970s, and the creation of clinical education through William Pincus' funding—gave rise to what has become the most significant change in legal education since the creation of the Langdellian case method. This movement has grown to the point where more than seventeen hundred law professors self-identify as clinical teachers within the AALS.[38] The AALS Clinical Section supports seventeen committees and has its own newsletter.[39] We continue to see the growth of clinical education and the development of other forms of experiential education in the academy today. We have navigated an evolution in clinic design and pedagogy, built over a half-century of experimentation and development. This exploration occurred because clinical teachers shared their emerging pedagogical theories within an inclusive community at multiple conferences, sponsored by many national, regional, and international organizations. We see the methods of clinical education once decried by traditional law teachers now being adopted by them. And we see a body of scholarship that is equal to the intellectual power of the best articles and books written by any law teachers.

One would have thought that the battles fought years ago about ABA accreditation standards were the beginning of a universal recognition that clinical education has academic value and that it and its faculty had earned a place in the legal academy. And to a great extent, it has. Yet even today, as ABA accreditation standards mandate experiential courses across the curriculum, battles continue as deans still try to contain the spread of clinical education for financial and philosophical reasons. They fight to limit the academic freedom and security of position protections that at least some clinical teachers gained years ago. Non-clinical faculty continue to treat scholarship about the theory of practice and about clinical pedagogy itself as insufficiently rigorous. University and law school tenure committees seldom understand how the demands of running a law practice within a scholarly academic enterprise necessarily results in less and different scholarly production by clinical faculty when compared to faculty who teach three or four lecture or seminar courses a year. The fact that non-clinical faculty are otherwise free to read, research, write, and publish, while clinical faculty are meeting with students and constantly attending court or other hearings throughout the work week seems to have no relevance when tenure decisions are made.

History always informs the present. Studying the early debates concerning experiential pedagogy and the strategies used by the clinicians to secure the passage of the ABA accreditation standards remains important today. Those standards established the status, security, and the path from contract to tenure status, and redefined the standing of clinical teachers in the legal academy. Moreover, the standards guaranteed academic freedom to and a role for clinical faculty in law school governance.

These battles are far from over, but they take different forms today. Remembering and using the lessons of our history will help expand the number of experiential courses throughout the curriculum. Using the lessons will also help the next generation of clinical law teachers expand the theories and methods underpinning experiential pedagogy, fight the new battles over the quality of clinical scholarship and the productivity of its adherents, and continue the debates about status and curricular design. Moreover, the early clinicians' writings still resonate as we continue to enhance and adapt our teaching methods and produce scholarship that is as rigorous as that of our non-clinical colleagues. Finally, an understanding of the foundational theory of clinical pedagogy is essential to developing professionalism and instilling the characteristics of lifelong learning among law students.

The readings that follow this chapter more fully describe the evolution of our movement.

Other Voices

Jerome Frank, *Why Not a Clinical Lawyer-School?*

81 U. Pa. L. Rev. 907 (1933)

I

The method of teaching still used in some university law schools (and accepted by them as more or less sacrosanct) is founded upon the ideas of Christopher Columbus Langdell. It may be said, indeed, to be the expression of that man's peculiar temperament.

Langdell unequivocally stated as the fundamental tenet of his system of teaching "*that all the available materials ... are contained in printed books*". The printed opinions of judges are, he maintained, the *exclusive* repositories of the wisdom which law students must acquire to make them lawyers.

Now it is important to observe the manner of man who impressed those notions on American legal pedagogy for more than half a century.

When Langdell was himself a law student, he was almost constantly in the law library. His fellow students said of him that he slept on the library table. At that time, he served for several years as an assistant librarian. One of his friends found him one day in an alcove of the library absorbed in a black-letter folio, one of the year books. "As he drew near", we are told, "Langdell looked up and said, in a tone of mingled exhilaration and regret, and with an emphatic gesture, 'Oh, if only I could have lived in the time of the Plantaganets!'"

He practiced law in New York City for sixteen years. But he seldom tried a case. He spent most of his time in the library of the New York Law Institute. He led a peculiarly secluded life. His biographer says of him: "*the almost inaccessible retirement of his office, and in the library of the Law Institute, he did the greater part of his work. He went little into company.*" His clients were mostly other lawyers for whom, after much lucubration, he wrote briefs or prepared pleadings.

Is it any wonder that such a man had an obsessive and almost exclusive interest in books? The raw material of law, he devoutly believed, was to be discovered in a library and nowhere else; it consisted, as he himself said, solely of what could be found in the pages of law reports. One of his biographers praises him because he sought "*the living founts*" of law in the works on the library shelves! Practicing law to Langdell meant the writing of briefs, examination of printed authorities. he lawyer-client relation, the numerous non-rational factors involved in persuasion of a judge at a trial, the face-to-face appeals to the emotions of juries, the elements that go to make up what is loosely known as the "atmosphere" of a case,—everything that is undisclosed in judicial opinions—was virtually unknown (and was therefore meaningless) to Langdell. A great part of the realities of the life of the average lawyer were unreal to him.

What was almost exclusively real to him was he translated into the lawschool curriculum when, in 1870, at the age of forty-four, he became a law teacher at Harvard. The so-called case system (the "Harvard system" which the university law schools adopted and by which some of them are still largely dominated) was the expression of the strange character of a cloistered, retiring bookish man. Due to Langdell's idiosyncrasies, *law school law came to mean "library-law."*

...

A brief outline of the history of legal education in American universities is helpful as a preliminary to some tentative suggestions for changes:

It began with the apprentice system. The prospective lawyer "read law" in the office of a practicing lawyer. He saw daily what courts were doing. The first American law school, founded by Judge Reeves, in the 1780s was merely the apprentice system on a group basis. The students were still in intimate daily contact with the courts. Then (about 1830) came the college law school with teaching on the college pattern of lectures and text-books. This step is ordinarily pictured as progress. For the student now devoted fulltime to his books and lectures and the distractions of office and court work were removed. A more unpleasant story could be told: The student was cloistered; he learned of court doings from books and lectures only; the *false* aspects of theory could no longer be compared by him with the actualities of practice.

There followed the period when the leading law schools were dominated by the great systematic text-book writers, the makers of so-called (American) "substantive law", substantive law which was divorced and living apart from procedure. The rift widened between theory and practice.

Then came Langdell. Noting his plea for induction, his efforts to avoid the glib generalities of text-books, one cannot help feeling that he was seeking obliquely and fumblingly to return to some limited extent to court-room actualities. But he was patently thinking of the lawyer as brief-writer and nothing more. Consequently, the material on which he based his so-called "induction" was hopelessly limited.

Ostensibly, the students were to study cases. But they did not and they *do not study cases.* They do not even study the printed records of cases (although that would be little enough), let alone cases as living processes. Their attention is restricted to judicial *opinions. But an opinion is not a decision.* A decision is a specific judgment, or order or decree entered after a trial of a specific lawsuit between specific litigants. There are a multitude of factors which induce a jury to return a verdict, or a judge to enter a decree. Of those numerous factors, but few are set forth in judicial opinions. And those factors, not expressed in the opinions, frequently are the most important in the real causal explanation of the decisions.

...

The trouble with much law school teaching is that, confining its attention to a study of upper court opinions, it is hopelessly oversimplified. Some thing important and of immense worth was given up when the legal apprentice system was abandoned as the basis of teaching in the leading American law schools. This does not mean that we should return to the old system in its old form, that we want mere apprentice-trained lawyers or law schools which are merely "expanded law offices". But is it not plain that, without giving up entirely the case-book system or the growing and valuable alliance with the so-called social sciences, the law schools should once more get in intimate contact with what clients need and with what courts and lawyers actually do? Must we not execute an about-face and return to Judge Reeves' 18th century apprentice method, but on a higher, more sophisticated level?

II

To be more specific, the following ideas are recommended for consideration:

...

Suppose, however, that there were in each law school a legal clinic or dispensary. As before indicated, a considerable part of the teaching staff of a law school should consist of lawyers who already had varied experience in practice.

...

The work of these clinics would be done for little or no charge. The teacher-clinicians would devote their full time to their teaching, including such clinical work, and would not engage in private practice.

The law school clinics would not confine their activities to such as are now undertaken by the Legal Aid Society. They could take on important work for governmental agencies or other quasi-public bodies. The professional work they would do would include virtually every kind of service rendered by law offices.

In this way, the students would learn to observe the true relation between the contents of upper court opinions and the work of the practicing lawyers and the courts. *The student would be made to see, among other things, the human side of the administration of justice,* including the following:

(a) How juries decide cases. The factors that count in jury trials. The slight effect of the judges' instructions on verdicts. The hazards of a jury trial.

(b) The uncertain character of the "facts" of a case when it is "contested", *i.e.*, when conflicting testimony is introduced. The difference between what actually happened between the parties to the suit and the way those actual happenings can be made to appear to a judge or jury. The transcendent importance of the "facts" of a case. The inherent subjectivity of those "facts" in "contested cases." The inability to guess future decisions (even when the "legal rules" seem clear) because it is impossible to guess, before a suit has been begun, whether there will be an issue of fact, and, if so, whether conflicting testimony will be introduced, what judge or jury will try the case and what the reaction of that unknown judge or jury will be to that unknown testimony.

The student should learn that "legal rights and duties" are inextricably intertwined with litigation, that, for instance, there is no such thing as "the law of torts" as distinguished from decisions in lawsuits, and that the so called rules and principles of torts are only some among the many implements employed by lawyers in their efforts to win lawsuits.

(c) How legal rights often turn on the faulty memory of witnesses, the bias of witnesses, the perjury of witnesses.

(d) The effects of fatigue, alertness, political pull, graft, laziness, conscientiousness, patience, impatience, prejudice and open-mindedness of judges. How legal rights may vary with the judge who tries the case and with that judge's varying and often unpredictable reactions to various kinds of cases and diverse kinds of witnesses.

(e) The methods used in negotiating contracts and settlements of controversies.

(f) The nature of draftsmanship: How the lawyer tries to translate the wishes of a client (often inadequately expressed by the client) into wills, contracts or corporate instruments.

What is intended is not that (as a scoffing neo-Langdellian recently suggested) the student should in his law-school days learn "the way to the post-office" or "the mechanics of the short-trial list". What is intended is that, almost at the beginning of and during his law-school days, the student should learn the very limited (although real) importance in the actual legal world of so-called substantive law and of so-called legal rules and principles. He should learn that "legal rights" and "duties" mean merely what may someday happen at the end of specific lawsuits. And that all so-called legal rules—including the so-called rules of substantive law—are "procedural"; *i.e.*, among the many implements to be used in the kind of fight, conducted in a court room, which we call "litigation". He should learn that judges are fallible human beings and that legal rights often depend on the unpredictable reactions of those fallible human beings to a multitude of stimuli, including the rules, but also including the fallible testimony of other human beings called witnesses. The student should become aware of the slippery character of "the facts" of a case, when there is conflicting testimony, and of the marked importance of what happens in trial courts.

…

Margaret Martin Barry, Jon C. Dubin & Peter A. Joy, *Clinical Education for This Millennium: The Third Wave**

7 CLIN. L. REV. 1 (2000)

...

I. THE CHALLENGES OF THE PAST: BUILDING THE CLINICAL ENTERPRISE

A. The Search for a Coherent Pedagogical Clinical Enterprise

1. The Birth of the Modem Law School and the First Wave of Clinical Legal Education

The first wave of clinical legal education in the United States began in the early part of the twentieth century, shortly after the casebook method emerged in the late 1890s as a popular route to preparing for a career in law. The casebook method's emphases on appellate judicial decisions and the Socratic method as the means to teach the skill of legal analysis were a departure from the three prevailing methods of American legal education in the nineteenth century: the applied skills training method inherent in the apprenticeship system; the general education approach of the prevailing European legal educational model, which was adopted by some colleges and universities in the United States; and an analytical and systematized approach to the law as interconnected rational principles, taught primarily through lectures at proprietary law schools. The single focus on legal analysis in the casebook method became "the objective" and "the structure" of early legal education in the United States and represented early legal educators' "narrow view of legal education." Even though the casebook method was growing to become the dominant pedagogy in law schools, there were critics of this method from the start.

While the casebook method was gaining wide acceptance, law students at several law schools in the late 1890s and early 1900s established volunteer, non-credit "legal dispensaries" or legal aid bureaus to provide hands-on opportunities to learn and practice lawyering skills and legal analysis, and also to serve a social justice mission by providing legal assistance to those unable to hire attorneys. As early as 1917, one commentator—William Rowe—published a law review article advocating law school based clinical legal education as the best way to train law students to become competent lawyers. Prior to writing this groundbreaking law review article, Rowe was the proponent of a resolution adopted by the New York State Bar Association in 1916 that provided: "*every law school shall make earnest clinical work, through legal aid societies or other agencies, a part of its curriculum for its full course.*"

In his 1917 article, Rowe discussed law student volunteer affiliations with legal aid efforts, and he argued that these arrangements should be formalized and transformed

---

* Excerpts are reprinted with the permission of the authors and the Clinical Law Review.

into a feature of the law school curriculum with faculty involvement. The law schools, he observed, were lagging behind medicine, architecture, engineering, and other disciplines in providing such clinical experiences to students. Most law schools offered only a two-year course of instruction at the time that Rowe was writing, and he foreshadowed some efforts to integrate clinical education throughout a student's law school experience when he wrote: "*One year of the clinic is not enough*. Indeed, eventually, the clinic may be made *a principal medium of instruction in all years for all subjects*. That will be the natural and logical development." Rowe advocated a system of clinical legal education in which students would take their clinic cases "to the classroom of the professor dealing with the subject under which the case logically falls. The clinic thus becomes a 'case book' not, however, of dead letters descriptive of past controversies, but always of living issues in the throbbing life of the day, the life the student is now living."

The type of clinical legal education that Rowe promoted most closely resembles a modern externship or perhaps hybrid clinic, in which students are placed with an off-site legal aid office, prosecutor, or public defender, combined with "general classroom work, with *'demonstrations' of current clinical problems*, as well as individual instruction and guidance in each case in hand." Rowe also anticipated that the clinic would be overseen by a faculty member "fully prepared to devote himself permanently to the work, [and] who can, with his assistants, agreeably to all concerned, associate himself, if necessary for temporary purposes, as counsel or otherwise, with any lawyer whose office or business may become connected with the clinic."

In 1921, the Carnegie Foundation for the Advancement of Teaching funded a study on legal education, commonly called the "Reed Report" after its nonlawyer author, Alfred Z. Reed. The Reed Report identified three components necessary to prepare students for the practice of law: general education, theoretical knowledge of the law, and practical skills training. The emphasis on legal analysis in the casebook method fulfilled only one of these three objectives by providing students with a theoretical knowledge of the law. To satisfy the requirement of a general education component, the Reed Report called for at least two years of pre-law college training—a proposal the ABA promoted, starting in 1921. At that time, not a single state required a university-based law school degree as a precondition for admission to the bar, proprietary law schools were still prevalent, and apprenticeships still provided the basic legal training for many entering the legal profession. In the midst of this highly unregulated climate for entry to the legal profession, the Reed Report's recommendation of practical skills training was not vigorously pursued by law schools.

In the wake of Rowe's early efforts to integrate clinical education into the law school curriculum, and the Reed Report's call for practical skills training, John Bradway and Jerome Frank pioneered the cause of clinical legal education methodology in the 1920s through the 1940s, advocating an in-house clinic as an essential component of sound legal education. Yet, despite the efforts of Bradway and Frank, only a handful of law schools instituted in-house clinical courses through the first half of the 1900s.

The dearth of clinical legal education programs in the first half of the twentieth century reflects several conditions that law schools faced in that era. First, law schools were distinguishing themselves from apprenticeships, and clinical legal education efforts to create "model law offices" as part of law school education did not further this market differentiation. Second, law schools of this era were terribly underfunded and clinical legal education courses with intensive faculty supervision were not as economical as large classes employing the casebook Socratic method. Third, law school teachers of this era disagreed about the value and feasibility of teaching lawyering skills other than legal analysis. For example, a 1944 Report of the Association of American Law Schools (AALS) Curriculum Committee, primarily authored by Karl Llewellyn, noted that the "current case instruction is somehow failing to do the job of producing *reliable professional competence* on the by-product side in *half or more of our end-product, our graduates*." Fourth, the period from the 1920s to the 1940s was marked by ABA and AALS efforts to create and raise standards for law schools, and none of these standards focused on encouraging or requiring clinical legal education experiences. These four factors combined not only to limit the number of clinical programs but also to stunt the growth of clinical pedagogy by limiting the number of law faculty teaching clinical courses.

By 1951, the value of "legal aid clinics" affiliated with or operated by law schools had become "[o]ne of the current controversies in legal education...." Robert Storey, then the Dean of Southern Methodist University School of Law, summed up the feeling of some legal educators when he lauded the "clinical method" for exposing "the student to actual problems confronting him with actual people who are in actual trouble" and for furthering "equality of justice" by helping to set up "an adequate system of legal aid offices." Yet, in spite of Dean Storey and others who promoted clinical legal education in the 1950s, clinical legal education was in a holding pattern.

In the 1950s, there was no single vision of clinical legal education and the concept of a law school "legal aid clinic" encompassed any "law school sponsored program for law student work on legal aid cases." A 1951 study of clinical programs identified twenty-eight clinics run by law schools, independent legal societies, or public defender offices. At five schools, a clinical legal education experience was mandated, but most schools offered clinics as electives or extra curricular activities. The work assigned to students varied among programs, but typically included client and witness interviews, drafting pleadings, and preparation of legal documents. Some programs gave students the opportunity to negotiate matters with clients' creditors, and at least nine law school clinics provided opportunities for trials and other court appearances. Most clinics attempted to have students work on cases from beginning to end. Student supervision was cited as a "major problem," and the task of supervision was often delegated to experienced students, who supervised less experienced students. At ten of the twenty-eight law schools with some form of clinical program in 1951, students did not earn any academic credit for their work. At four schools, clinic credit was available as part of a student's credits for a general course on legal practice. At the remaining fourteen schools, students only earned between one and three hours of credit for clinic work.

By the end of the 1950s, thirty-five law schools reported "some form of legal aid clinic." In thirteen of these law schools, legal aid clinics were located inside the schools. In a few law schools, all or most law students were required to do some legal aid work. In fifteen law schools, students were able to earn limited academic credit for clinic work. In only five law schools, supervising faculty were able to receive teaching credit for their clinical courses.

Although the number of clinical legal education programs increased slightly from the late 1940s to the early 1950s, the late 1950s ended on a note of relative stagnation for the nascent clinical legal education movement. There were several different models of clinical programs, and no generally accepted definition or description. Schools defined "clinical" programs to include both credit-earning and non-credit-earning real-life experiences for law students either in programs located within the law school or offsite at legal aid or public defender offices. The level of faculty involvement and supervision varied greatly, and clinical experiences existed on the fringes of the law school curriculum.

The limited growth of clinical programs during this decade may reflect the fact that clinical instruction was only one of several experiments under way to address perceived deficiencies of the casebook method. Some of the other "experiments" included simulated trial practice courses, legal research and writing courses, drafting courses, and subject matter seminars based on simulated problems. Notwithstanding these "experiments"—many of which are now standard fare in virtually all law schools—the 1960s witnessed continued complaints by law students and some law faculty about large classes, the dominance of the casebook method, and the lack of writing opportunities. Of all the curricular experiments since the introduction of the casebook method in the late nineteenth century, "the concept of clinical legal education was to prove the most important." In fact, clinical legal education is "so often called the most significant change in how law was taught since the invention of the case method that it now sounds trite."

2. *The Maturing of the Modern Law School and the Second Wave of Clinical Legal Education*

During the second wave of clinical legal education—a period spanning from the 1960s through the late 1990s—clinical legal education solidified and expanded its foothold in the academy. The factors that contributed to this transformation included demands for social relevance in law school, the development of clinical teaching methodology, the emergence of external funding to start and expand clinical programs, and an increase in the number of faculty capable of and interested in teaching clinical courses. Perhaps the most powerful of these factors was the zeitgeist of the 60s, which produced "student demands for relevance." In reflecting on the growth and direction of clinical legal education, Professor Dean Hill Rivkin has noted: "It was the societal legacy of the sixties ... that most shaped clinical legal education. The fervor of the sixties penetrated law schools quite passionately."

a. The Social Justice Dimension of Clinical Legal Education

The earliest forms of clinical legal education embraced the dual goals of hands-on training in lawyering skills and provision of access to justice for traditionally unrepresented clients. Initially, the legal realism movement of the 1920s and 1930s provided support for the goal of teaching lawyering skills and professional values in law school legal aid dispensaries. Legal realists like Llewellyn and Frank advanced the view that students must learn about law as a means to an end rather than as an end itself. Thus, it is no surprise that Llewellyn and Frank were early advocates of clinical legal education.

In 1965, a proponent of clinical experiences in law school noted the demands for relevance in legal education and "a desire on the part of a significant number of law students to help make the law serve the needs of the poor." This sentiment, present since the earliest law student volunteer "legal aid dispensaries," blossomed in the design of most clinical programs during the 1960s and 70s. These clinical programs provided representation to indigent clients with a myriad of legal problems. Many of these programs also responded to the call of Professor Arthur Kinoy to "tak[e] on major cases and situations involving the relationship of the processes of the law to the fundamental problems of contemporary society ... [so as to] provide a fascinating teaching tool for probing into the most fundamental theoretical, substantive, and conceptual problems, all within the context of the throbbing excitement of reality."

In building upon the earlier clinical programs, clinical faculty during the second wave expanded clinics to demystify law for students and to represent client communities with claims that thrust clinical programs into the civil rights, consumer rights, environmental rights, and poverty rights movements. During this same period, the Critical Legal Studies (CLS) movement grew out of the earlier legal realism movement in legal education. While clinical teachers were working with law students to use the law as an instrument for social justice and change, proponents of CLS were using the classroom to demystify the law and to teach students that "political conviction plays an important role in adjudication and that the shape of the law at any time reflects ideology and power as well as what is wrongly called 'logic.'" However, unlike some CLS adherents whose critique of law and the legal system leads them to skepticism or nihilism, clinical faculty struggled to maximize law's potential for remedying injustice and inequity.

Professor Martin Guggenheim points out that this focus on social justice is important "not only because of its effect upon clients but also because of its effect upon students." Clinical courses expose students not only to lawyering skills but also the essential values of the legal profession: provision of competent representation; promotion of justice, fairness, and morality; continuing improvement of the profession; and professional self-development. These professional values are taught and at the same time thousands of clients receive access to justice through clinical programs. In this way, clinical programs meld legal theory with lawyering skills, and students learn lawyering values by providing legal assistance to clients who would otherwise lack access to justice. As Professors Philip Schrag and Michael Meltsner observed:

> [H]undreds of thousands of low-income clients have been well served by clinic students. Although this magnitude of assistance is very low compared to the need of indigent people for legal services, in most cases the value of the service to clients has been incomparable: avoiding homelessness, avoiding or reducing time in prison, obtaining disability benefits, securing the right to remain in the United States, obtaining safety from a threatening spouse.

The social justice dimension of the practice of law and other professional values can find expression in other parts of the curriculum as well. Yet, too few traditional courses explored social justice issues in the latter part of the twentieth century, and those that did rarely explored the relationship between lawyers' pro bono responsibility and their obligation to improve the legal system. Rarer yet were law schools in which the curriculum as a whole reinforced these professional values. In these respects, law school curricula even at the start of the twenty-first century generally fell short of the ABA Standard that law schools "should encourage and provide opportunities for student participation in pro bono activities."

The approach many lawyers continue to take toward their professional duties reflects the general lack of emphasis on social justice and public service in their law school experience. The legal profession perpetually struggled with its obligation to respond to the unmet need for legal representation throughout the twentieth century. Some called for mandatory pro bono service while others objected to it as forced labor or because they simply were afraid that the time demands would be too onerous. The pro bono debate was replayed for several years, with the most recent ABA iteration coming in the form of its Ethics 2000 recommendation that the matter required further study. Current competitive demands, evidenced in part by the high salaries paid by many large law firms, suggest that mandatory pro bono service will lose even more ground as existing pro bono service, such as it is, gives way to the pressure to increase billing.

As we enter the third wave of clinical legal education, law school clinics continue to play an important role in making access to justice a reality for many low-income people. They do so not only by exposing law students to the legal problems that the poor face but also by allowing students to experience what amounts to a "tactile" connection with the obligation to find substantive and creative ways to respond to unmet legal needs. The result should, at a minimum, lead to greater commitment by clinic graduates to work toward a resolution of the legal services problem. The goal of educating students to this responsibility for assuring access to justice is best met if such education permeates the curriculum. Each law school course should raise issues of access to justice with clinical courses exposing students to the reality of how these issues play out in the lives of indigent clients and the systems currently used to address their needs. If law schools are truly committed to professional values, then these values must be discussed in every class and not simply relegated to clinical courses.

b. The Development of Clinical Teaching Methodology

While student demands for relevance in the law school curriculum and the social ferment of the 1960s played an important role in spurring the growth of clinical programs, it was the development of a clinical teaching methodology that was critical in solidifying the place of clinical legal education in the law school curriculum during the period running from the 1970s through the present.

Clinical scholarship started to burgeon in the second wave of clinical legal education during the 1970s and early 1980s. The clinical scholarship of this era broke new ground by exploring lawyering skills and clinical teaching methodology, thereby moving the dialogue far beyond the earlier scholarship of Bradway, Frank, and others who primarily focused on the general concept of using real cases to teach law students. Until the mid-1970s, there was no common understanding of what was meant by clinical legal education and no serious effort to construct a vocabulary for discourse. As Professor Gary Bellow observed, the term clinical legal education applied "to any law-related activities in which students engage outside the classroom, as well as a number of traditional law school activities, i.e., legal research, moot court, even appellate case analysis.' Without a commonly understood pedagogy, clinical legal education was too amorphous to take firm root and spread to every law school.

In the 1970s and 1980s, Bellow and others started to construct a "common vocabulary of discourse on educational issues." By focusing on clinical education as a method, clinicians began to explore what clinical teachers were and should be doing, how clinical teaching methodology could be infused throughout the law school curriculum, and what the purposes and goals of clinical teaching should be. Important early examples of clinical scholarship focused on clinical methodology, what it meant for students to assume and perform the lawyer's role in the legal system, how to identify and teach the elements of various lawyering skills, how to develop and explain theories of lawyering, how to refine and improve the supervisory process, and how to incorporate experiential learning theory into clinical law teaching.

Clinical scholars explained that the primary goal of clinical legal education should be to teach students how to learn from experience. Clinical faculty began to focus on how they could "learn from their experiences as lawyer-teachers and as lawyer-scholars." They began to work with their students to explore the theoretical underpinnings and practical dimensions of lawyering skills and professional values. To help students develop the skill of self-reflection, clinical faculty critiqued them and encouraged them to employ self-critique, "a process described by Donald Schon as 'reflective practice' or 'reflection in action.'" As a result, by the late 1980s, there was general agreement with the observations in the *Report of the Committee on the Future of the In-House Clinic* that:

> Clinical education is first and foremost a method of teaching. Among the principal aspects of that method are these features: students are confronted with problem situations of the sort that lawyers confront in practice; the students deal with the problems in role; the students are required to interact with others in attempts to identify and solve the problems; and, perhaps most critically, the student performance is subjected to intensive critical review.

Equipped with a "common vocabulary" and a generally accepted definition of a methodology, scholarship about clinical teaching blossomed in the latter part of the

1980s and throughout the 1990s. During this period, and in large part because of this scholarship, clinical legal education gained a more permanent place in law schools. The emergence of a critical mass of teachers interested in thinking and writing about clinical methodology also led to the founding in 1994 of the CLINICAL LAW REVIEW under the auspices of the Clinical Legal Education Association (CLEA), the AALS, and New York University School of Law (serving as the host school). Building upon the theoretical bases explored by clinical scholarship and the social justice and skills bases of client representation, clinical programs are thriving and moving forward into the future. Still, clinical programs continue to· face some questions about their financial viability that have persisted since the emergence of clinical legal education.

B. The Search for Financial Viability

It is impossible to imagine the future of clinical legal education without discussing the financial costs, and that issue cannot be intelligently discussed without reference to the history of funding for clinical programs, the different types of clinical courses, and the larger subject of the overall cost of legal education. Any such discussion also necessarily implicates questions concerning the goals of legal education, the quality of the educational experience, and the role of the law schools in preparing graduates for the practice of law. It is beyond the scope of this article to explore all of these aspects in depth. The following discussion will focus on those dimensions of funding that are particularly relevant to our vision of the third wave of clinical education—which we regard as including an in-house clinical experience for every student.

1. *Funding the Growth of Clinical Programs and the Transformation of Legal Education*

During the early part of the second wave of clinical legal education, funds from the Ford Foundation fanned the flames of calls for law school programs to serve the needs of the poor. From 1959 to 1965, the Ford Foundation provided intermittent grants totaling $500,000 to nineteen law schools through a program headed by William Pincus and entitled the National Council on Legal Clinics (NCLC). The Ford Foundation made an additional grant of $950,000 in 1965, and NCLC was renamed the Council on Education in Professional Responsibility (COEPR), and then later renamed the Council on Legal Education for Professional Responsibility (CLEPR) in 1968. From 1968–1978, the Ford Foundation granted an additional $11 million to CLEPR to provide support for clinical legal education programs. CLEPR awarded 209 grants to 107 ABA-approved law schools totaling approximately $7 million.

...

C. The Search for Institutional Legitimacy

Although some commentators predicted that the loss of significant soft money support in the 1980's and 1990's would result in a decline in clinical education—with the greatest anticipated reductions coming from resource intensive real-client, in-house clinics—the data reveal that reports of this demise have been premature. Indeed, during the 1990's, the raw number of persons teaching in clinical programs increased steadily as did law school commitments to in-house programs and to job security and status for all clinical faculty. While precise figures are not available due to less systematic record keeping before 1995, the AALS Directories of Law Teachers for 1989–90 and 1999–2000 reflect an increase from approximately 800 Clinical Legal Education Section members in 1989–90 to 1300 a decade later.

By the end of 1999, there were 183 U.S. law schools with clinical programs in the database maintained by Professor David Chavkin on behalf of the AALS Section on Clinical Legal Education and CLEA. The total database includes 1736 persons who self-identified themselves as clinicians. Of this number, 849 persons indicated that they regularly teach in-house clinics, and 234 persons indicated that they regularly teach in externship clinics. Thus, approximately 80% of reporting clinicians indicate that they regularly teach in-house clinics. A little over a decade earlier, only 33% of all law schools reported that they had in-house, live-client clinics and the total number of clinicians in the Section was less than the number who now self-identify as in-house clinicians.

...

Minna J. Kotkin & Dean Hill Rivkin, *Clinical Legal Education at a Generational Crossroads: Reflections from Two Boomers**

7 Clin. L. Rev. 197 (2010)

...

In this essay, two long-time clinical teachers discuss the impulses present in the formative years of modern clinical education that made the field challenging and fertile for lawyers with public interest lawyering backgrounds and the reform agenda that was robustly pursued by clinicians in these early decades. The essay laments the decline of an explicit systemic reform focus among newer clinicians—directed both at legal education and poverty law—and calls for a renewed dialogue about the future directions of the clinical enterprise.

I. Introduction

The enterprise that we entered into with Steve Reed, Karla McKanders, Praveen Kosuri, and Bridgette Carr at the 2009 Association of American Law Schools ("AALS") Clinical Conference, a simulated conversation about generational differences in our work, began as an effort to understand our students better: the so-called "Millennial Generation." To prepare for the session, we read current assessments of this generation and its proclivities, attitudes, and outlooks. There is a whole industry (driven by marketing and advertising people) devoted to understanding the latest trends affecting this generation, just as the Gen-X cohort and our affinity group, the Baby Boomers,

* Excerpts are reprinted with the permission of the authors and the Clinical Law Review.

were similarly (and still are) analyzed. As lawyers, all of us were skeptical of the kind of sweeping generalizations that characterize this literature.

Instead, as good clinicians, we sought to draw on our own experiences in crafting the dialogue for the simulation that we performed at the Clinical Conference. But something happened. Our focus on students transformed into a focus on ourselves. This exploration of generational differences among clinical teachers is a topic that has not explicitly surfaced much in clinical writings, although it has been a sub-text of many conversations about our field.

Clinical education is a relatively new development in the overall scheme of legal education. Nevertheless, in the three markedly different essays that follow, Gen-X and Millennial clinicians analyze how they arrived at their careers via distinct paths and how those paths influenced their approaches to clinical legal education. In their essays, our collaborators show that they have incredibly varied life experiences and expectations and that how they relate to each other and their students will be determinative of the future of clinical legal education. Praveen Kosuri challenges the presumption of social justice as the driving force behind clinical legal education and argues for greater inclusion of his generation—Gen-X—in the determination of what the future of clinical education will look like. Steve Reed, also a Gen Xer, describes how his large firm, private practice background has informed his approach to clinical teaching and his interactions with Baby Boomer colleagues and Millennial students. And Karla McKanders, a Millennial herself, describes her pathway to clinical legal education and challenges the perception that Millennials can be generically categorized as she reflects upon the challenges of working with Gen-X and Baby Boomer colleagues.

In this introduction, our goal is to explore the contours of these differences. We begin by explaining our own professional trajectories. We then consider how our experiences shaped our vision of clinical education and explore similarities and differences in the visions expressed by our collaborators.

II. Career Arcs

Most of us who formed the vanguard of clinical education in the 1970s and 1980s came to law school teaching from public interest/legal services/public defender backgrounds. We represented poor people in welfare hearings, public housing evictions, consumer matters, and other arenas of inequality. We also worked in the proverbial "community." We represented disempowered groups who were striving for economic and social justice. The idea of law reform was real, whether through "individual" cases or through "law reform." It was an era where the possibilities of generating tangible social change through law seemed real.

Clients were central to our practices. It was not uncommon for clinical teachers to say that the greatest fulfillment in their work was serving clients. It was clients from whom we drew our strength and satisfaction, more so than students. And what's more, we were able to do this work in an environment that was more refined and less vulnerable than public interest practices in the field without teaching components. Our focus on clients led us to theorize about client-centered lawyering and what that ideal meant.

Despite the relative superiority of our practice settings when compared to public interest work "in the real world," we found ourselves in the basement of legal education, literally and figuratively. One President of the AALS called our field a "side show." The "main action" was under "another tent." Our colleagues did not know what to make of us. They appreciated our ability to deflect from them the demands of students for more practice-oriented courses, and many admired us for our insistence that social justice and public service was an integral part of legal education. Students agitated for more "relevant" instruction. It was an exciting time; a lot was up for grabs.

Despite our presence in the lofty heights of the academy (even from the basement), we continued to define ourselves as public interest and poverty lawyers. Clinical education was an extension of these movements. Our clinics gave committed students a home, a safe space to pursue their causes and their values. We supported their aspirations and goals, unlike many of our non-clinical colleagues.

Then subtle changes appeared. We started to become what we were: law professors. Law professors write, get involved in the work of the profession, participate in governance (though often as second-class citizens), and do public service (almost anything seems to count in this subordinated category). We began to measure our worth and value by these traditional academic metrics. This was a double-edged sword. To succeed in the academy, we had to distance ourselves from practice, our long-time sustenance, although this gave us time and room to research and write. The growth of clinical scholarship could not have happened if clinical teachers had continued to immerse themselves in the day-to-day nitty-gritty of practice. The shift to "supervision" gave clinicians a distinctive pedagogy and breathing space away from the corpuscular nature of law practice. We let our students attend to the details, while we drifted further away from being practitioners.

Were we co-opted by the allure of the academy? Maybe. Did we lose our critical edge because of this? Maybe. Did anybody really care as long as our students clamored for what we had to offer: practice skills, a bit of passion, a lot of personal attention, and mentoring? As we became more ensconced in our roles as law professors, we had to make certain compromises. Despite this, we did not abandon our values altogether. Our DNA still compelled us to challenge mindless hierarchy, and our democratic values led us to insist loudly that our voices be heard in decisions that affected us. We also believed, like most of our colleagues, that we had something genuinely important to say. And we did.

Our scholarship still drew on our insights from practice. The Lawyering Process book by Gary Bellow and Bea Moulton, both former legal services lawyers, is the apotheosis of this approach. Its exegesis of the then-existing interviewing and counseling literature, for example, grew from a political consciousness about empowering poor people. Most of this early scholarship was not a disembodied skill set but grounded in models from practice.

We also genuinely believed that our ideas about legal education were superior to the received pedagogy in raising issues of values. Was this a form of hubris? Rebellion?

An inexorable changing of the guard? A generation shift? To further our agendas, we drew on our skills as educators *and* organizers. We created a national community to push our ideas both in the academy and the profession. In the process, though, did the "Great Clinicians" become dinosaurs, unable to confront change; unable to adapt to the changing values, attitudes, and skills of our students, but especially our younger colleagues?

III. A Newer Paradigm

Are the newer clinicians cut from a different cloth? It would be easy to stereotype them as so. As our colleagues' essays show, in varying degrees, modern clinicians seem more careerist and intentional. The notion of having a "career" has long struck us as an unhelpful, indeed counterproductive concept. Professional roles are restrictive enough, without labelling them "careers." The image of rising on the career ladder implies an intentional step-by-step progression in worn footsteps. In our colleagues' essays, we discerned three distinct themes: more intentional career arcs; a turn away from the ferment of reforming legal education; and a marked shift in emphasis from clients to students.

In their essays, each of our collaborators devotes thick space to discussions of their professional arcs. In varying degrees, each thoughtfully planned the paths to their current work. They consulted knowledgeable people about life in academia and did due diligence about what life as a clinician would be like. Only then did they decide to take the leap.

This intentionality contrasts with our more serendipitous entry into clinical education. At the outset of our lives in legal education, there was little history of how to become a successful and satisfied member of the academy. We knew that our practice backgrounds were critical, but how to capitalize on these skills and experiences in our new positions was terra incognita. We improvised, organized, and shared our successes and travails with the then-small number of colleagues across the country. We engaged in this community-building because we were largely isolated in our own institutions. Our colleagues did not know what to make of us.

As evidenced by our collaborators' essays, today's landscape is vastly different. The number of clinical teachers has risen dramatically. At many schools, there is now a critical mass of colleagues. They occupy positions that are, more or less, secure. The need to tap into a national community to foster change in legal education, and to enhance the influence of clinical teaching in the academy, is less pressing. This inward turn contrasts with our long-standing efforts to empower the voices of clinicians by equalizing their faculty status. Our bedrock belief is that only through full participation of clinical faculty can true reform be realized.

Our collaborators evince an inward turn in the movement to reform legal education. The national efforts to reform legal education, that so occupied our energies, seem remote to our collaborators. Those battles have been fought and, for them at least, have been fragilely resolved. None of their essays reflect the same importance that we attach to these national efforts. Their chief focus is on their teaching lives. We do not denigrate this focus, but, to us, it is short-sighted and a bit politically naive, especially now when efforts are ardently afoot to negate the begrudgingly granted gains that clinicians have made in solidifying security of position and its perquisites. This is not a call for job security for the sake of feathering the nests of clinicians, but rather to recognize the pivotal importance of job status to the furtherance of educational reform.

Finally, our collaborators' essays also reveal a shift in emphasis from clients to students. They labor over how to handle the Millennial generation's espoused desire to build their skill sets. They largely recognize that other goals, such as the promotion of social justice, may be part of the clinical curriculum, but, unlike many of us, they do not rank this goal as their highest priority. They respond more to the expressed desires of this generation of students—a consumer-driven orientation. Many of us, on the other hand, aspired to build a cadre of public interest lawyers in our own image. In the end, did we succeed in this endeavor? Hardly, but the efforts brought their own rewards and pushed back against the forces in legal education that sought to subordinate progressive change through law.

Our collaborators often view clients as fungible. Rich or poor, clients provide the text from which to teach skills. Public service is a by-product of clinical work, not a central part of the teaching mission. To us, the turn to "public service" and also *pro bono* work should not be viewed in these instrumental terms. There should be an ideology at play here—social change through client-centered initiative—but this phenomenon goes substantially unacknowledged by these essays.

IV. Conclusion

The paucity of writing about intergenerational issues among clinicians is understandable. These are sensitive issues that call into question deeply held values about how we conduct our professional lives. Each of our collaborators expresses "passion" about his or her work. Our differences are rooted in our histories. This is not unexpected. It is inexorable that a newer generation will strike out on its own course. Our collaborators are developing their own visions, while expressing respect for our historical struggles.

We urge them to hone their reflectiveness, to pursue their passions, but not to forget that clinical education must maintain and expand its critical edge. Clinical education is rooted in notions of transformative service to clients and communities. This commitment accounts for much of its richness. It is ignored at the peril of losing the soul of the movement. The short-term gains from adopting the myopic horizons of the Millennial generation of students may be illusory. We recognize that this may sound paternalistic and preachy. But we hope that a fruitful dialogue will be initiated by this set of essays. By conceiving this project, our collaborators are building the future of the field.

Endnotes

1. William Faulkner, Requiem for a Nun, (Act 1, Scene 3) (1951).

2. "... Denver Law has led the way since 1904, when we founded the first legal aid dispensary in the nation." *Clinical Programs: Student Law Office*, University or Denver Sturm College of Law, https://www.law.du.edu/academics/practical-experience/clinical-programs.

3. Wallace J. Mlyniec & Haley Etchison, *Conceptualizing Student Practice for the 21st Century: Educational and Ethical Considerations in Modernizing the District of Columbia Student Practice Rule*, 28 Geo. J. Legal Ethics 207, 210–11 (2015) (citing Margaret Martin Barry, Jon C. Dubin & Peter A. Joy, *Clinical Education for This Millennium: The Third Wave*, 7 Clinical L. Rev. 1, 6 (2000)).

4. Russell L. Weaver, *Langdell's Legacy: Living with the Case Method*, 36 Vill. L. Rev. 517 (1991).

5. Julius Paul, *Jerome Frank's Contributions to the Philosophy of American Legal Realism*, 11 Vand. L. Rev. 753 (1958); Neil Duxbury, *Jerome Frank and the Legacy of Legal Realism*, 18 J. L. & Soc'y 175 (1991).

6. *See, e.g.*, Jerome Frank, *Why Not a Clinical Lawyer-School?*, 81 U. Pa. L. Rev. 907 (1933).

7. Wallace J. Mlyniec & Meghan Strong, *The Role of Law School Clinics in Implementing the* Gault *Decision, in* Rights, Race, and Reform: 50 Years of Child Advocacy in the Juvenile Justice System 128–53 (Kristin Henning, Laura Cohen & Ellen Marrus eds., 2018); Wallace J. Mlyniec, *The Evolving Design of a First Generation Clinic, in* Transforming the Education of Lawyers: The Theory and Practice of Clinical Pedagogy 320–26 (Susan Bryant, Elliott S. Milstein & Ann C. Shalleck eds., 2014).

8. The incorporation doctrine is a constitutional doctrine by which portions of the Bill of Rights are made applicable to the states through the Due Process Clause of the Fourteenth Amendment. *See e.g.*, Chicago Burlington & Quincy R.R. Co. v. City of Chicago, 166 U.S. 226 (1897) (incorporating the protection against taking property without due compensation); In re Oliver, 333 U.S. 257 (1948) (incorporating the right to a public trial); Klopfer v. North Carolina, 386 U.S. 213 (1967) (incorporating the right to a speedy trial); Mapp v. Ohio, 367 U.S. 643 (1961) (incorporating the protection against unreasonable search and seizure).

9. Earl Warren served as Chief Justice between October 5, 1953, and June 23, 1969. *See, e.g.*, *Earl Warren*, Oyez, https://www.oyez.org/justices/earl_warren (last visited Oct. 2, 2022).

10. *See, e.g.*, Gideon v. Wainwright, 372 U.S. 335 (1963); In re Gault, 387 U.S. 1 (1967); Argersinger v. Hamlin, 407 U.S. 25 (1972).

11. *See e.g.*, Santosky v. Kramer, 455 U.S. 745 (1982) (termination of parental rights); Goldberg v. Kelly, 397 U.S. 254 (1970) (termination of public benefits).

12. *See e.g.*, Taylor Branch, Parting the Waters: America in the King Years, 1954–1963 (1988); Jack Greenberg, Crusaders in the Courts: How a Dedicated Band of Lawyers Fought for the Civil Rights Revolution (1994); Michael Harrington, The Other America: Poverty in the United States (1962).

13. The Women's Rights Movement marks its beginning to a tea party on July 13, 1848, when Elizabeth Cady Stanton and several other women met and began to devise a large-scale movement. A second wave of activism began in the 1960s spurred on by writings by Betty Freidan, the creation of a Presidential Commission on the Status of Women, and the enactment of Title VII of the 1964 Civil Rights Act, which banned discrimination on the basis of sex. *See, e.g.*, Bonnie Eisenberg & Mary Ruthsdotter, *History of the Women's Rights Movement*, Nat'l Women's History All, https://nationalwomenshistoryalliance.org/history-of-the-womens-rights-movement/ (last visited Oct. 2, 2022).

14. The Children's Rights Movement can trace its source into the early 19th century in Europe and to the horrors children faced during World War I. The Progressive Movement and the advent of juvenile courts in the early 20th century are generally thought of as the beginning of a consciousness of children's right in the United States. In reality, this movement and the courts were more about protecting children than establishing independent rights for children. Two events are considered

significant in the development of children's rights. The first is the Supreme Court's decision in In re Gault, 387 U.S. 1 (1967), establishing the right to counsel and other due process guarantees in U.S. juvenile courts. *See generally* RIGHTS, RACE, AND REFORM: 50 YEARS OF CHILD ADVOCACY IN THE JUVENILE JUSTICE SYSTEM (Kristin Henning, Laura Cohen & Ellen Marrus, eds., 2018). The second is the United Nations Convention on the Rights of the Child adopted by the U.N. General Assembly in 1989 which guaranteed positive rights for children. *Children's Rights History, Historical Overview of the Children's Rights Evolution*, HUMANIUM, https://www.humanium.org/en/childrens-rights-history/ (last visited Oct. 2, 2022). As of this writing, the United States is the only country that has not ratified the treaty. *Frequently Asked Questions on the Convention on the Rights of the Child*, UNICEF, https://www.unicef.org/child-rights-convention/frequently-asked-questions (last visited Oct. 2, 2022) ("More countries have ratified the Convention than any other human rights treaty in America has not ratified the Convention.")

15. The first true Juvenile Justice Clinical courses were established at Georgetown Law Center and New York University School of Law in 1973. Mlyniec & Strong, *supra* note 7, at 136.

16. The first courses in Women and the Law were taught at New York University Law School in the fall of 1969 and at Yale Law School in the spring of 1970. Both Georgetown and George Washington University's National Law Center initiated their Women and the Law class in the fall of 1970. Professor Cunnea, *A Timeline of Women's Legal History in the United States and at Georgetown University*, http://wlh.law.stanford.edu/wp-content/uploads/2011/01/cunnea-timeline2.pdf.

17. *See* Jack Bell, THE JOHNSON TREATMENT: HOW LYNDON B. JOHNSON TOOK OVER THE PRESIDENCY AND MADE IT HIS OWN, 280–81, 283 (1965); Mark I. Gelfand, *The War on Poverty*, *in* EXPLORING THE JOHNSON YEARS 126, 132–34 (Robert A. Devine ed., 1981); Hugh Davis Graham, *The Transformation of Federal Education Policy*, *in* EXPLORING THE JOHNSON YEARS 155 (Robert A. Devine ed., 1981).

18. William Pincus and the Council on Legal Education and Professional Responsibility (CLEPR) helped create the model for early clinical courses and funded a great many of them. *See, e.g.*, *CLEPR's 40th Anniversary: Papers and Speeches from the AALS-ABA-CLEA Celebration of CLEPR*, 16 CLINICAL L. REV. 23, 35–38 (2009).

19. Orison S. Marden, *CLEPR: Origins and Program*, *in* CLINICAL EDUCATION FOR THE LAW STUDENT: LEGAL EDUCATION IN A SERVICE SETTING 5–6 (Working papers prepared for CLEPR National Conference, Buck Hills, Pa. (June 6–9, 1973).

20. *Id.* at 6–7.

21. *Id.* at 9.

22. William Pincus, *Legal Education in a Service Setting*, *in* CLINICAL EDUCATION FOR THE LAW STUDENT 1973 27–39 (Working Papers Prepared for CLEPR Nat'l Conference, 1973).

23. Marden, *supra* note 19, *passim*.

24. Martin Luther King Jr. spoke the words "... the arc of the moral universe is long, but it bends toward justice" in a speech entitled "*Remaining Awake Through a Great Revolution*" given at the National Cathedral in Washington D.C. on March 31, 1968.

25. *See generally* Margaret Martin Barry, Jon C. Dubin & Peter A. Joy, *Clinical Education for This Millennium: The Third Wave*, 7 CLINICAL L. REV. 1 (2000).

26. ABA Model Rule (1969), *reprinted in* BAR ADMISSION RULES AND STUDENT PRACTICE RULES 993–95 (Fannie J. Klem, Steven H. Leleiko & Jan H. Mavity eds., 1978).

27. As Justice Brennan noted in Argersinger v. Hamlin, 407 U.S. 25, 44 (1972) (Brennan, J., concurring).

> [l]aw students as well as practicing attorneys may provide an important source of legal representation for the indigent. The Council on Legal Education for Professional Responsibility (CLEPR) informs us that more than 125 of the country's 147 accredited law schools have established clinical programs in which faculty-supervised students aid clients in a variety of civil and criminal matters. These programs supplement practice rules enacted in 38 States

authorizing students to practice law under prescribed conditions. Like the American Bar Association's Model Student Practice Rule (1969), most of these regulations permit students to make supervised court appearances in criminal cases.

28. Mlyniec & Etchison, *supra* note 3, at 218–220.

29. Peter A. Joy & Robert R. Kuehn, *The Evolution of ABA Standards for Clinical Faculty*, 75 TENN. L. REV. 183 (2008).

30. CLEPR "went out of business" in 1980. *E.g.*, Minna J. Kotkin, *Reconsidering Role Assumption in Clinical Education*, N.M. L. REV. 185, 191 n. 28 (1989).

31. Roy Stuckey, Power and Politics in the Founding Era of Clinical Education, 21–22 (2021) (unpublished manuscript) (on file with the Georgetown Law Library) (paraphrasing David Barnhizer, Speech at The National Conference on Title IX Funding at American University (Mar. 13, 1981).

32. *Id.* at 3.

33. *Id.*

34. *See* Minna J. Kotkin & Dean Hill Rivkin, *Clinical Legal Education at a Generational Crossroads: Reflections from Two Boomers*, 17 CLINICAL L. REV. 197 (2010).

35. *See e.g.*, Gary Bellow & Bea Moulton, THE LAWYERING PROCESS: MATERIALS FOR CLINICAL INSTRUCTION IN ADVOCACY (1978); Anthony G. Amsterdam, *Clinical Legal Education—A 21st-Century Perspective*, 34 J. LEGAL EDUC. 612 (1984).

36. Robert Dinerstein, *Report of the Committee on the Future of the In-House Clinic*, 42 J. LEGAL EDUC. 511, 516 (1992).

37. Stuckey, *supra* note 31, at 11.

38. Jean Waterman & Judith Areen, THE FIRST 125 YEARS, AN ILLUSTRATED HISTORY OF THE ASSOCIATION OF AMERICAN LAW SCHOOLS 125 (2024).

39. *Id.*

Four

SUPERVISING CASES AND PROJECTS

Close faculty supervision of students working on real cases and projects is the central tenet of clinical and other experiential education pedagogy, and the faculty-led supervision session is its primary teaching modality. Because it is so central to learning and client representation, specific and intentionally planned feedback about a student's planning and performance of lawyering tasks forms the basis for most supervision sessions. Faculty design these sessions to help students accomplish the specific legal tasks needed to move a case or project forward. Successfully advancing the client's interests in the case satisfies the representational goals of the clinical course. However, much more occurs in a well-structured supervision session. Because these activities take place in an academic setting, teachers meld the concepts of theory and practice into every action, judgment, and decision students make. Faculty-led supervision sessions also demonstrate a process that fosters a student's ability to transfer knowledge from one circumstance to another, a process that helps inform the practice of lifelong learning. This academic mission underlies all case and project supervision in a clinical setting. That is what distinguishes it from the training that takes place in a typical public-interest law office.

A quote often attributed to Aristotle explains that "Excellence is never an accident. It is always the result of high intention, sincere effort, and intelligent execution; it represents the wise choice among many alternatives—choice, not chance, determines your destiny."[1] A more modern statement of the theory-practice synergy is that theory informs practice, and practice enhances theory. Placing the concept squarely within the nature of clinical pedagogy, Professor Phyllis Goldfarb describes this union of theory and practice as the "practice-theory spiral."[2]

Three central goals of clinical pedagogy emanate from this spiral. The first is to ensure that students know how to perform a legal task. This is the practice dimension. The second is to know why they choose to perform a particular task in a particular way in a particular context. This is the theory dimension. The third is to ensure that students understand the strategic reasons behind the choices they make, and how to transfer that knowledge and reasoning to other activities—both similar and disparate—that call for the same or similar strategic conceptions. This is the spiral dimension that moves theory integrated with practice into similar or dissimilar tasks in the future.

Faculty members who teach in clinics and other experiential courses generally think of supervision as the conversations that take place in scheduled meetings about a specific topic between a supervisor and an individual student (or student team) during the life of the case or project. Although the majority of student supervision occurs during those sessions, learning and supervision also takes place during other clinic activities. Supervision—understood broadly and within the context of an integrated clinical learning program—can, does, and should occur in many places.[3] It occurs in seminar discussions; case-rounds sessions; email conversations; phone calls and video chats; and written feedback on student drafts of motions, policy papers, briefs, and other student case or project written documents. It also occurs in reflection sessions at the completion of a task in the case or project and during formative assessment meetings. It may take place when the student pops their head into the supervisor's office and says, "I have a quick question," or when the supervisor sees the student informally and says, "I have been thinking about your case. See what you can find out about this and then let's talk." Many acts of supervision also occur in the in-between spaces inherent in the practice of law, while having a casual lunch with a student or walking back and forth from court. For reasons discussed later, however, these quick or unplanned interventions pose the danger of being less well-thought-out than an intentionally planned session can be.

Supervision does not always involve the case or project. Indeed, it often takes place during conversations about the student's anxieties, personal growth, career plans, or personal or family issues unrelated to "clinic work."[4] As Professor Robert Dinerstein once wrote about clinical education, "The whole is greater than the sum of its parts."[5] That is because clinical teachers are not constrained the way a training director is. Unlike training directors in firms or public interest organizations, clinical teachers do not need to move a case or project along efficiently. Nor are they limited to merely being the provider of substantive or procedural legal content. They are more than the gatekeepers between the student and the body of knowledge the student needs to competently represent a client. The learning universe of clinical education is both broader and deeper than training for a new job. Teachers today are beginning to understand that their "job is to counsel students as they grow and mature—helping them integrate their social, emotional, and intellectual growth—so the union of these sometimes separate dimensions yields the ability to seek, understand, and use knowledge to make better decisions in their personal lives and to value contributing to society."[6]

Law school clinical teachers are in the vanguard of this teaching concept, and supervision, in its largest sense, serves this mission by integrating students' personal lives with their formal educational endeavors. Creating a professional identity within the contours of their personal identity is a major goal of legal education. The intensity of the clinical education experience allows faculty to play a significant role in their students' ascertainment of that identity. Because supervision is at the core of the pedagogy, all experiential teachers need to learn appropriate intervention techniques that maximize both student learning and growth as well as client interests and satisfaction.[7] Some experiential teachers see tension between a clinical course's pedagogical purposes and its representational purposes. Those two purposes, however, do not reside in a dichotomy and do not present a zero-sum experience. On the contrary, they are, or at least should ideally be, symbiotic. If a teacher plans the pedagogical experience well and executes it effectively, the student's education and the client's representation will both have the best possible outcomes.

Clinical pedagogy is goal-oriented, intentional, reflective, and dependent upon the experiential context of the interactions among faculty, students, clients, opponents, and decision makers. Because clinic is experiential,[8] the concepts discussed in the articles and books about supervision only begin to make sense when teachers understand the theoretical and practical aspects of the supervision methodology, reflect upon their use in context, and learn how to transfer the three-step method of "think, plan, and execute" to the students. What is clear, however, is that supervision of or intervention into a student's work can happen in many ways and at many places in the life of a case or project, all depending on the context in which the intervention occurs.

This chapter and the readings that follow focus on the *methods* of intervention—not the substantive issues such as law and broad legal theory, personal and institutional values, cultural differences, legal skills, and ethics that often *prompt* an intervention. Later chapters of this book address the specific substantive topics that give meaning to the methods and outcomes of interventions. This chapter, other chapters that discuss supervision of particular legal tasks, and the readings that follow them all discuss the purpose of intervening into student performances on projects and cases, and the various methods a teacher can use when supervising students. They explore the so-called directive and non-directive methods of intervention, modeling, and other intervention techniques that teachers use when students are developing case theories, investigation strategies, arguments and presentations, negotiations, policy alternatives, and other lawyering tasks such as planning and performing witness interviews, client counseling sessions, and witness examinations and arguments at hearings. The specific methods supervisors can use when students are researching and drafting various legal and policy documents will be discussed in the next chapter.

Scaffolding and the Zone of Proximal Development

Generally speaking, an intervention is "an act of interfering with the outcome or course especially of a condition or process (as to prevent harm or improve functioning)."[9] As clinical teachers, we have, in a sense, two clients: (1) our students, and (2) the clinic clients whom the students represent. Some might think that while one of our goals is to improve the students' legal knowledge and practice skills, our primary goal in this educational model is to prevent harm to our clients and to maximize their interests. They might also think that our ethical duty to our clients and our desire to protect our own law licenses[10] would both require that student learning be subservient to the needs of our clients. While providing sound representation to clients and maximizing their interests are true and laudable goals, they must accompany the learning goals that infuse the students' academic enterprise.

Determining the primary method of intervention was one of the major debates among experiential teachers in the early days of clinical teaching. Historically, clinical teachers debated the merits of two forms of intervention: telling the student how to do something (the so-called "directive" method of intervention) and leading the student to arrive at the correct resolution through discussion (the so-called "indirect" or "non-directive" method of intervention). How one resolved that debate affected how the early generation of clinical teachers performed their supervising duties. The debate assumed that a supervisor had to choose only one way or the other, and that one method was superior to the other in accomplishing our teaching goals while protecting clients.[11] Under this framework, "discussions about adherence to the principle of non-directiveness often impl[ied], if not directly state[d], that non-directiveness is a goal in and of itself."[12]

To some extent, the debate continues today; but experienced clinical teachers have largely abandoned the direct-versus-indirect supervision battle. What they now recognize is that a teacher's goals, the student's capabilities, the client's needs, and the context in which an intervention takes place all dictate the appropriate supervision method a teacher will use. Picking the "correct" side in the supposed dichotomy, therefore, is no longer an all-or-nothing existential philosophy to which a teacher must forever adhere. Instead, context determines the appropriate method of intervention.[13] Experienced teachers use both methods, depending on which is appropriate in the specific context, and may use them interchangeably depending on the learning goal involved. After all, as renowned educator Stephen Brookfield has written, echoing other prominent educators, "Education always has a directive nature we cannot deny."[14] The result is a more holistic approach to teaching and intervention—one that is more sensitive to the particular facts and circumstances of each opportunity to intervene. It also makes the decision to intervene or not more intentional. Frankly, this result more honestly describes what teachers have really been doing since the early days of clinical education when the intervention dichotomy was framed more rigidly.

This context-dependent approach is especially important because clinical teachers provide feedback about the lawyering process during many stages in the life of a case or project. Supervisors have several goals when giving feedback, and not every intervention is the same. Ideally, teachers seek to improve the students' performances of specific tasks and reflect on the process leading to the execution of a task before the student performs it. They do so to further the students' learning and to improve clients' chances of achieving their goals. Conversely, if supervisors observe the students practicing the task and believe the students can improve their performance, they may intervene directly in the moment if it is necessary, or afterward if the error is not critical.

Rather than debating the value of directive and nondirective interventions, modern clinical teachers now choose the appropriate method of intervention based on the principle of scaffolding. "Scaffolding consists of the activities provided by the educator, or more competent peer, to support the student as he or she is led through the zone of proximal development. Support is tapered off (i.e., withdrawn) as it becomes unnecessary, much as a scaffold is removed from a building during construction. The student will then be able to complete the task again independently."[15] Scaffolding theory is a derivative of Lev Vygotsky's Zone of Proximal Development.[16] "Vygotsky believed that when a student is in the zone of proximal development for a particular task, providing the appropriate assistance will give the student enough of a "boost" to achieve the task. To assist a person to move through the zone of proximal development, educators are encouraged to focus on three important components which aid the learning process: the presence of someone with knowledge and skills beyond that of the learner (a more knowledgeable other); the social interactions with a skillful tutor that allow the learner to observe and practice their skills; and scaffolding, or supportive activities provided by the educator, or more competent peer, to support the student as he or she is led through the zone."[17]

It is remarkable that as early clinicians developed and debated methods of intervention, they seldom referred to educational theory. If they had, they would have realized that their debate about the value of direct or indirect supervision failed to realize the integration of methods to promote learning. Perhaps it was the existence of a client that made the clinicians unwilling to adopt educational theory. More likely, it was not something many of them were familiar with. Educational theory was not applied to law school teaching in the early years of clinical theory, and it is seldom used today. Early clinicians often did not distinguish one context from another when deciding to intervene. But the notion of context reflects the stages of client representation and adds it to the mix. Today, clinical teachers use both direct and indirect methods of intervention based on a student's current knowledge and capabilities within the context of the current status of the case or project. Doing so permits the student to master the task based on what they are able to do and move forward to a higher level of understanding or performance with the appropriate assistance of the teacher. Hence, the student grows as a learner as the student-supervisor team protects the interests of the client.

The dual methods of feedback can be used when the students base their contemplated action or strategy on inadequate knowledge, faulty assumptions, or conflicting values, or when the student's strategic or tactical choices implicate complicated ethical issues beyond the ken of novice lawyers. In supervisory sessions, teachers consider the student's learning goals and the client's legal goals, report what they have observed, and discuss the student's motivation for making a choice or taking an action. They then ask the student to reassess the possible choices and contemplate actions, suggest and discuss different performance techniques, analyze the pros and cons of each, and then determine whether their choices are the best among the options. Some might say that asking for pros and cons is directive supervision, while asking the student to determine which option is the best is non-directive. Both observations are correct and reflect the iterative conversation between student and teacher along the spectrum of interventions. That is because supervisors use the various methods discussed in this and other chapters of this book to provide intentional, well-thought-out feedback. The goal of feedback is not just to provide a basis for understanding rules and techniques for the contemplated task. It is also used to reflect on how lessons learned in previous situations are transferable to the current situation and to other parts of the lawyering process that may arise in the future. Thus, student learning goals and client interest goals do more than just coexist. They mutually reinforce one another in a positive and productive way.

Stages of Supervision

Students come to their first supervision session with little understanding of how to accomplish all the lawyering tasks that clinic will require of them during the next semester or two. Nor will they know much about the clinical method and their role in it. Most law school classes remain heavy on theory and perspectives and on the analysis of statutory meaning and judicial interpretation. Even civil and criminal procedure courses are more about substantive law than the actions lawyers use to comply with the law and procedure. Client behavior and interests, if considered at all, are static as reported in the judicial opinions and rules discussed in class. The answers professors give to student questions about client behaviors and interests are often hazy because they are seldom reported in judicial opinions.

Despite the lack of discussion about these critical factors, students and faculty often assume there is a certainty to the law. That is because the facts presented in appellate opinions, unlike those in an ongoing case, are static. The judicial reasoning may be clear to the opinion drafters and even to some teachers, but absence of the human elements of the case can leave students wondering how the result actually affects the people involved in the case.[18] The uncertainty is greater if there are dissenting or concurring opinions. "The very presence of dissents challenges the myth of legal decision-making as objective and straightforward; in speaking back to court opinions, dissents lay bare the complexities and reveal points of ambiguity in cases"[19] All too often, students do not engage with this uncertainty in large classes. Seminars permit more engagement, but the students are not expected to assume a responsibility to act except during an occasional simulated hearing.

Consideration of case law and court rules are different in the clinic because cases are frequently about client interests more than about the meaning of the law. Clients are not static. They are people with strengths and weaknesses who often come to lawyers because they are in trouble. Clinic is also different because the student is responsible for the client's legal welfare and for the execution of meaningful actions to secure the client's goals. The goals and interests are often incompatible with the law or exist in the interstitial space between the law's rigidity and the human conditions clients bring to the lawyer. While law exudes certainty, practice exists in the realm of uncertainty. In clinics, unlike other courses, the elusiveness of the law in real time and the unpredictability of the actors in the case or project require that students act in a world of indeterminacy.

Confronting this level of responsibility can be daunting for students. A student's uncertainty about the law or their fear of making errors can create anxiety and feelings of incompetence. They will ask many questions seeking the correct answers until they become comfortable with uncertainty. Only when they are comfortable and begin to fully engage in the clinical method can they truly construct knowledge in context, begin to transfer knowledge from one aspect of practice to another, and begin to understand how the law works in society. Their learning processes will improve as the semester progresses. The relationship between supervisor and student can, and should, "var[y] through time" because what may have been "effective supervision at one point may result in an undesirable learning consequence at a later point."[20] For example, a "close, structured form of supervision [may be appropriate early in the student's clinical experience, but over time may] become stifling and overly restrictive"[21] once the student has found their bearings and develop[s] more independence later in the semester. Indeed, getting this balance just right—"[d]ivining the appropriate mix of freedom and direction and control in the teacher-student relationship is one of the ongoing challenges of clinical educators."[22]

An early writer about clinical methodology, Professor Peter Hoffman, provided a framework for understanding why striking this balance at any point is challenging, and why it can and must evolve throughout the student's time in clinic.[23] The framework has evolved but nonetheless remains basic today. Interestingly, it echoes the concept clinicians call scaffolding and the concept educational theorists call the zone of proximal development. Hoffman suggests it helps to chart the general arc of progression for students in clinic through three stages: beginning, middle, and final.[24] In the beginning stage, students typically find stepping into the role of a student-*lawyer* to be unfamiliar, uncomfortable, and nerve-wracking. In this stage, students know little of the substantive law and procedure they need to use and are even more inexperienced in applying that knowledge to novel factual scenarios. They do not have experience exercising the judgment needed to confidently counsel clients amid the uncertainty of their claims or to make difficult strategic choices to achieve client goals.[25] Even making decisions that an experienced practitioner wouldn't give a second thought to—like the wording of a simple email to a prosecutor when attaching a form discovery letter, or knowing the first step to take upon receiving a new case—can feel overwhelmingly difficult, imbuing the student with the fear of messing it up. The uncertainty of not knowing what one doesn't know can be almost paralyzing.[26] As a result, supervisors will take a more hands-on role in helping the student get and stay on track at this beginning stage. Teachers will even provide detailed initial instructions along with the reasons for those instructions when necessary. They will also set clear expectations for how the supervision will unfold.[27] For example, supervisors will clarify which tasks require supervisory approval before completion and which do not.[28] And perhaps most importantly, the supervisor will begin building a supportive relationship with the student that will further the student's learning.[29]

In the middle stage, the training wheels start to come off. This happens gradually and intentionally, but the two stages remain distinct.[30] In the middle stage, students "become capable of taking more responsibility and initiative for their cases."[31] Whereas beginning-stage students may receive instructions (the so-called direct method of supervision) and just execute the needed actions, middle-stage students work with the supervisor to determine next steps (the so-called indirect method of supervision). Supervision in this stage becomes a collaborative and dynamic conversation more akin to that of senior and junior colleagues in a law firm than the rigid hierarchy that often exists between traditional teachers and students.[32] To be sure, intervention is not directionless at this stage. However, the supervisor begins to cede authority to the student commensurate with the students' capabilities, controlled by the context in which plans are selected, judgments and decisions are made, and actions are taken. Supervisors become more of a "sounding board and corrective" as students propose their own choices for working up a case or project and explaining their thought process. Supervisors encourage them to flesh out alternative options, weigh pros and cons, and think through other strategic considerations.[33] As students grow more confident and capable of handling the day-to-day maintenance of their cases, more of their time and energy becomes available to discuss and reflect on a broader range of topics, including values and ethics, the role of lawyers in the legal profession, and the functioning and legitimacy of the legal system.[34] Embedded in these conversations is not just the mastering of certain lawyering tasks. The process introduces students to metacognition and learning for transfer—the practice-theory spiral. Because all of these actions are intentionally integrated into the supervisory sessions, the clients' interests and the students' learning are accommodated.

In the final stage, students are "sufficiently secure and competent to act, in effect, as lawyers in their own right."[35] Of course, students still require supervision in this stage, but it will be more deferential, with the faculty member sometimes opting for the student's choice of action among multiple reasonable alternatives.[36] The supervisor's role has transformed from giving many instructions in the beginning stage, to being sounding board in the middle stage, and finally to being "a confirmer and guider" in the final stage. The supervisor becomes a "safeguard against serious error," and a "safety net" for checking decisions the student initiated.[37] Learning continues in this stage, but within a more sophisticated, secondary zone of proximal development.

Planning the Supervision Session

Irrespective of the student's stage of development, or their level of comfort with the clinical method, they will always have questions. A student's question about their cases and projects will generally fall into five categories: (1) task performance, such as how to conduct an interview, cross-examination, or other task that may have many acceptable approaches and a few specific approaches to avoid; (2) procedural questions that may or may not have one correct answer; (3) substantive legal questions that may or may not have one correct answer; (4) ethical or values-based questions that may or may not be clearly answerable by reference to the rules of professional conduct, or may not involve ethics at all; and (5) strategic questions that seldom if ever have one "correct" answer.[38]

Because clinical methodology requires intentional interventions, it helps to have the students create an agenda for the supervision session in advance so that the students' concerns can be accommodated along with the teacher's plan for the session. In planning the session, the supervisor has many things to consider. Considering the learning goals involved is critical, but so too are the complexity of the issue, the context in which the issue arises, the level of the student's development at this point in the semester, and the effect that delaying a decision will have on the client. Other considerations include what the student has done alone to answer relevant questions; whether other students will likely have the same questions; whether the question needs an immediate answer; and whether there are other pressing issues that are more important to resolve at this point. There may also be other factors relating to the client, the opponent or their lawyers, or the tribunal to consider that may be as important to the learning or representational goals.

Supervision should never be a random activity based on a serendipitous agenda with little or no preparation. The supervisor-student sessions should be intentionally planned and follow an agenda proposed either by the student or the faculty member. Notwithstanding the importance of well-planned intentional intervention, teachers will sometimes give feedback on the run if a one-off question arises during a chance encounter with a student. Teachers provide such quick advice when the context demands it, or when learning is incidental to the advice needed. They are often tempted to give feedback immediately after an action, fearful that if they do not respond immediately both the student's and the teacher's memory will slip, and an important teaching moment will be lost. While years of experience will give a faculty member a toolbox to address these chance encounters intentionally, off-the-cuff supervision runs the risk of being based on inaccurate or biased assessments of an observation, or a factual misunderstanding of the context or the student's purpose when initiating the action. When that occurs, it may lead to an incomplete or inappropriate response and to faulty decisions based on inaccurate or misperceived information, false assumptions, or implicit biases. Consequently, teachers should postpone most feedback conversations to avoid premature critique and advice. Instead, the supervisor should take notes about the observation and use them during a later discussion when a well-thought-out formal supervision session occurs.

While supervisors sometimes compare actions a student takes to prior actions the student has performed in other cases, feedback primarily focuses on the current client's case or project. At the same time, however, supervisors note how the students sought to accomplish their goals. A student's overall performance in the clinic course is seldom, if ever, discussed in these supervision sessions, other than to refer back to similar actions the student may have successfully taken in another case. Nor should teachers evaluate actions in the sense of grading the student on each action taken. Overall performance is part of the formative (qualitative) assessment that comes after the supervisor has acquired more data from other cases or projects.[39] Of course, formative assessments can occur after the completion of an individual case or project, but it is difficult to spot patterns of behavior from a single example. Hence, supervision sessions are focused on the case or project at hand, and more formal formative assessments take place either mid-semester or at the end of a student's enrollment in the clinic. No matter when the formative assessment takes place, its success depends on the copious notes supervisors have taken during supervision sessions and during observations of actions executed throughout the course of the semester. Those notes ensure that the formative assessments and later summative assessment (grading) are based on accurate recollections of the student's performance and not on a faulty memory, subjective impressions, implicit biases, or other thought processes that cannot be explained or justified.

The post-event supervision sessions may also provide time to reflect on issues that may not be specifically case- or project-related, but which arose because of the nature of the work the student has been doing or the judgments and assumptions the student may have made. Students may have perceived value clashes between themselves and their clients or among team members. Events during the case or project may have caused a disorienting moment,[40] forcing a student to question long-held beliefs. The student may have gained some new understanding about the role of a lawyer, or the legitimacy of the systems that purport to deliver fair and just results. These conversations are often difficult for both the student and the supervisor. Clinical teachers cannot inspire a student's deep reflection of these difficult issues without first engaging in their own self-awareness. Clinicians, like all others, are subject to conscious and implicit biases which can undermine the giving and receiving of feedback. If teachers have not analyzed these issues for themselves, their comments may leave students, particularly those traditionally underrepresented in law schools or those already feeling marginalized for other reasons, feeling more unwelcome.[41]

To maximize the effectiveness of feedback, teachers should preempt the detrimental impact of biases on interpersonal interactions. They can do this through training, exposure to diversity, cultivating growth mindsets, and rejuvenating habits. Lack of sufficient sleep and low blood glucose levels can cause cognitive fatigue, which increases the likelihood of biased thoughts or actions.[42] Students who are not physically fit, alert, and mentally present during a supervision session will seldom benefit from the lessons discussed. Those who are will be better able to transfer the knowledge gained into practice. Fitness and presence are, however, a two-way street. Faculty need to take stock of their own decision fatigue and general fitness. Some difficult conversations should only occur when the faculty is well-rested, clear-headed, and mentally alert. Finally, supervisors must be "honest with [them]selves—and with [their] students—about [their] own limitations"[43] when planning these difficult conversations.

There are many ways to plan a supervision session after considering the factors discussed above. One planning method that we teach our graduate clinical teaching fellows involves five stages: (1) naming and framing the issue, (2) option generation,

(3) option analysis, (4) decision making, and (5) reflection.[44] The first, naming and framing, is done by the supervisor after the student presents the issue. (As the semester progresses, we can ask the students to name the issue.). "Naming" is simply placing a label on what the student has raised. It can be as simple as stating that the student's presentation raises a client counseling issue, an ethical issue, a strategic issue, or something else. Once the issue is named and framed, students can focus on the one needing resolution rather than the peripheral issues surrounding it. When supervisors ask questions about how the resolution for the named issue can be used or has been used in other situations, naming and framing begins the process of learning for transfer. It helps students place the issue in context and encourages them to apply their learning from previous discussions of similar issues.

The second stage, option generation, asks the students to delay judgment on the path forward until multiple possible approaches or resolutions have been identified and considered. We encourage the students to suggest at least three options. Early in the semester, we contribute additional options if they get stuck. Option analysis, the focus of the third stage, is just what it sounds like. It requires the student to consider the pros and cons of each option in turn by identifying short- and long-term legal and nonlegal consequences of each option as it relates to advancing the client's goals. We take notes, on paper or a whiteboard, so we can analyze the options in the next stage. The fourth stage, decision-making, occurs after the pros and cons are compared and weighed. The supervisor encourages the student to think about the consequences of each choice, both on the case and in non-legal areas. The final stage of supervision is reflection. Here, we review the process we used to analyze the issue, the decision we reached, whether the student is comfortable with the resolution, and what questions they still have.

At each stage, supervisors vary their interventions between the so-called directive and nondirective methods depending upon the factors the supervisor considered while planning the session. At the end of the structured analysis, students will not only have a proper resolution of the issue they raised, but they will have also learned a method for making judgments, mastering a new legal skill, and transferring that method of decision-making to other aspects of the cases or projects. This process can also be helpful when confronting nonlegal personal issues. It is through this intentional process that the supervisor curates the symbiotic relationship between the clinic's pedagogical goals of teaching students and its representational goals of advancing clients' interests.

Notwithstanding adequate planning, supervision sessions can go awry. No one is infallible, and the uncertainty of human relations can move the best planned supervision session in unexpected directions. Deviations may be necessary. But a supervisor should always consider in advance what might be lurking around the edges of this session that will require a different supervision strategy. Faculty must keep track of the students' work, their personal health, and the circumstances of all of the people involved in the case when developing the plan. Unforeseen events with clients and opponents may occur. Teachers will be better able to respond to those in the moment as they mature in their craft. Interpersonal issues may also arise and affect the students' perspective on the nature of the case or their own ability to move forward. The latter will be discussed further later in this chapter.

Metacognition and Transference

In most instances and where time permits, a proper intervention resembles the best of the Socratic method. The Socratic method carries a somewhat frightening reputation for many law students and lawyers based on their own bad experiences with it. But the Socratic method, properly conceived and executed, is not the thinly veiled hazing ritual depicted in *The Paper Chase*.[45] Instead, when used correctly, and with patience, kindness, and respect, teachers lead students to determine, though their own thought processes, a preferred course of action by asking them to respond to a set of intentionally designed questions. Those questions, however, do not necessarily lead to the teacher's forgone conclusion. Nor is it a twist on "hiding the ball." On the contrary, it is an inquiry into the complexity of the material being discussed, and the uncertainty that accompanies most judgments or courses of action that a lawyer might develop. Indirect intervention developed through questions does more than lead to a satisfactory resolution of the issue. It also demonstrates a path for resolving complex questions that has transsubstantive utility, whether in other similar situations or in unrelated legal actions. This method also gives priority to the notion of metacognition and leads to teaching for transference.

Teaching for transference is a hallmark of clinical teaching. Its purpose is to instill in students the ability to perform a task and use the knowledge and process in solving other kinds of problems. It is driven not just by cognition, but also by metacognition. Cognition involves possessing "the skills needed to perform a task."[46] Those skills are generally task-specific, and "deal primarily with the direct application, manipulation, or transformation of given learning material."[47] Unlike cognitive skills, metacognitive skills are not task-specific, and often encompass a variety of different subject areas.[48] Metacognition is a process by which a person gains an awareness and control over their own learning and thinking.[49]

Metacognition, in turn, consists of two components: "knowledge of cognition" and "regulation of cognition."[50] Knowledge of cognition is "an awareness of which knowledge and skills a person brings to the learning task, an awareness of what the new task requires, and matching the knowledge and skills to the new task."[51] Regulation of cognition refers to control over a person's learning process and entails three steps: "[1] planning for the task, [2] monitoring the learning process involved in the task, and [3] evaluating the final outcome of the task."[52] Together, those two components—both the knowledge and the regulation of cognition—create a cognitive regulatory loop through which a person monitors and controls the learning process.[53]

Through that continuous loop of knowledge and regulation of cognition, one develops metacognitive knowledge.[54]

There are three categories of metacognitive knowledge: (1) declarative knowledge, (2) procedural knowledge, and (3) conditional knowledge.[55] "Declarative knowledge" is what a person knows.[56] In the metacognitive context, it is information a person consults while processing different cognitive tasks.[57] This includes knowing what factors contribute to performing a cognitive task well, such as a good memory being helpful in learning.[58] "Metacognitive procedural knowledge" refers to strategies for how to perform different cognitive tasks.[59] People with advanced levels of procedural knowledge perform tasks more automatically and often possess a wider variety of strategies to solve problems.[60] Finally, "metacognitive conditional knowledge" requires applying these strategies correctly, or at the correct time, and for the correct reason.[61] Conditional knowledge is especially important because it "enables people to adapt to the situational demands of each individual task."[62] To once again use Professor Goldfarb's words, that is what produces the "practice-theory spiral."[63]

Metacognition incorporates the concept of learning for transfer. "Transfer has been defined as the use of knowledge and skills acquired in an earlier context when confronting a new task or context. It occurs when a person's learning in one situation influences that person's learning and performance in other situations."[64] "A student who can apply a concept in new and varied settings, without being shown exactly how to do so by a supervisor, has fully understood the idea in question."[65] Clinical faculty teach to transfer knowledge because

> there is too much for anyone to learn. [G]iven that unpredictability is inevitable; [and] given that being flexible and adaptive with one's repertoire is key to any future success, it stands to reason that we should focus our [teaching] efforts on the goal of transfer.... The point of school is not to get good at school[,] but to effectively parlay what we learned in school in other learning and in life.[66]

Students demonstrate that they have successfully learned how to transfer knowledge when after achieving an understanding of some substantive information and its application to a task, they can apply that understanding independently and in a variety of different contexts.[67]

Students can develop the skills of transfer if supervisor interventions slowly explore an issue through questions that help the student understand and solve the problems involved. The more direct method of telling students how to resolve an issue will solve the immediate problem but will not help students transfer that knowledge to other issues or contexts. These metacognitive strategies promote active learning and give students a clearer understanding of the substantive material studied in law school. They also prepare students to be better lawyers in their careers that follow.[68] The active learning of experiential education accomplishes this by showing students how their cognitive understanding of the rule of the case, the content of a statute, or the availability of a specific strategy can be used for tasks other than the one at hand, which in turn furthers a client's interest. Indeed, a student's ability to accurately self-assess throughout the learning process is an essential part of being an independent, lifelong learner.[69] That is why understanding what metacognition is and why it matters and effectively integrating metacognitive strategies into the curriculum are necessary to best teach students how to learn.[70] That is why they are so important to clinical pedagogy.

The road to metacognition is arguably not an efficient way to provide legal representation to real clients. Although it may be more efficient to merely show the student how to do something, for example, demonstrating during a supervision session a set of interview or cross-examination questions that have been successful in the past, little transferable or metacognitive learning will come from that kind of session. Certainly, a teacher's ability to perform the act is greater than that of the student and is a crucial factor as the teacher leads the student through the conversation. Clinical teaching, however, offers more than the ability to execute the act under discussion. A proper intervention seeks to create a method of thinking based on an understanding of the purpose of the act, the theory underlying the act, the strategy behind the act in the context of the relief the client seeks, and the status of the case or project. Learning the thought process behind the task is what separates clinical pedagogy from a skills program. That intentional intervention into the theory supporting the skill and the process for analyzing it produces life-long transferable learning.

Using the examples above, if all the students learn in a clinic is that a lawyer uses leading questions in the course of a cross-examination, or asks a prescribed set of questions during an interview in a particular kind of case or project, they will not understand how or why a lawyer arrived at those particular cross-examination questions, or how and why the process can be used in other lawyering tasks. The same is true for developing interview questions, or any other lawyering task. Teachers need to name the learned transferable knowledge and process for arriving at the knowledge so that the process becomes a foundational element of the students' lifelong learning about legal practice. Students will need to replicate that process on their own or with colleagues after they leave law school as they develop and expand their abilities throughout their legal careers. That is why it is so critical to clinical pedagogy.

Intervention Methods While Providing Feedback

Almost every action a student takes during the course of representation can form the basis for an intervention. There are many ways to intervene when a student is learning to practice law. It is easy to assume that supervision sessions precede momentous events in the life of a case. For example, students practice opening statements before conducting a trial or delivering moot oral arguments before arguing a case on appeal. Similar acts occur prior to interviewing clients and witnesses. However, an intervention can and must occasionally immediately occur concerning many different actions—some simple, some complex—in the life of a case or project. Indeed, even simple tasks will often benefit from an intervention. For example, it is not uncommon for teachers to conduct a supervision session just prior to, or while, a student makes a routine phone call or sends an email. The choice of which words and tone to use and what information to include or omit not only affects the current act but may also affect later conversations the student will have with a witness, client, or opposing counsel. These conversations may also affect subsequent letters or legal documents the student might prepare. Feedback may also occur after the fact as the results of the action taken are analyzed. Teachers need to understand when and which pedagogical method to use when an intervention is necessary. This will not always be intuitive. Although clinical teachers develop a greater sensitivity to the need for and type of intervention as their teaching experience grows, they should try in every instance to use the deliberative, intentional, and reflective method of intervention.

Clinic teachers provide feedback at many stages of the lawyering process, and with many different methods. Most of this feedback is task-focused and not student-focused. It is intentional, objective, detailed, immediate, forward-looking, nonjudgmental, and sometimes, but not always, reflective. Supervisors prepare the feedback concerning the student's choices in advance, making intentional choices about the various issues to discuss because there will most likely not be time to discuss all of the possible issues in a single session. Supervisors should prepare the discussion as a reflective exercise unless immediate action is necessary to protect the client or the student. In which case, the reflection will occur after the harm is avoided.

These interventions are non-judgmental in the sense that teachers critique the proposed or completed action, but do not criticize the student personally. Teachers encourage, praise when appropriate, and guide students to better outcomes rather than undermining the student's confidence with stern personal critique. Indeed, "[h]arsh feedback does not help people thrive and excel."[71] Rather, criticism must be "delivered with respect and care" to be effective.[72] This is especially true when providing feedback to law students who are in a less personally powerful position than those already practicing law. Supervisors, by virtue of grading and writing letters of recommendation, are gatekeepers to future employment.[73] These moments of feedback are critical to moving a case or project along and to helping the student develop a growth mindset. Growth mindset is "an implicit theory that intelligence can expand in response to challenges. Those who [adopt] such a mindset may persist longer and achieve more.... [R]ecent research reveals that such mindsets are not immutable personality characteristics, but rather can themselves be changed and shaped by cultures and social contexts, including law school environments."[74]

Sometimes, the student needs more information before a deep intervention can take place. For example, consider potential interventions in the construction of a cross-examination script. There may be antecedent legal questions that require additional research before the student and supervisor can decide whether a certain line of questioning or the admissibility of a document into evidence are even permissible. Additional factual investigation may be necessary to gather statements to be used to set up an impeachment or draft questions for a cross-examination. Students may need additional conversations to be clear about the client's goals before discussing theories of the case or project. With issues like these unresolved, intervention into the theory of the case or the execution of a task can come too soon. The premature timing of the intervention may frustrate the purpose of intervening at all.

The planning section of this chapter listed the five topics that are most often the basis of the supervision session. Four stages of the decision-making process were also discussed in this chapter. Once the issue is named and framed, the student and supervisor work through the stages leading to a decision. Teachers provide feedback on the interim choices the student is making by asking questions about possible decisions or about the simulated performances of the task. While giving feedback, teachers often suggest that students consider different case theories, multiple other approaches to interviewing or examining witnesses, alternate approaches to researching arguments, and different strategies for delivering legal arguments. Teachers supervising transactions or projects, rather than cases, make similar suggestions regarding other options and choices when students prepare policy papers and written submissions to agencies, legislative bodies, or clients, or when they prepare testimony. Supervisors will also ask questions to help students determine the need for better legal citations, whether there are cases that support or are contrary to their client's position, or if there are strategic moves that might change their case theory or improve their reasoning about the project. The pros and cons of each option are explored, as supervisors probe to ensure that the student fully understands a client's goals before choosing the best strategy to achieve a satisfactory outcome.

Supervisors seldom tell students what to do outright. Instead, their questions help the student become aware of different strategies and options for achieving their clients' goals and correct improper performance techniques. This is not to say that teachers should always avoid providing a clear answer or demonstrating an activity for the student. Some students actually learn best by watching an activity and then practicing it until it becomes part of their repertoire. Role and task demonstrations surely have their place. But even when the teacher does intentionally resort to role demonstration for a proper pedagogical purpose, the mere demonstration of the task as an example is not, by itself, enough. That merely shows what students can glean from any Interviewing or Trial Advocacy handbook. Instead, the teacher must go one step further. A reflective conversation must accompany the teacher's demonstration to achieve the metacognitive goal of helping the student understand how the faculty member determined that the demonstrated option was the best or most effective way to perform the task. The dialogue should also explore what other options were available, and why the option demonstrated is preferred in the context of the client's case or project. That dialogue and reflection should then explore how the method that was used to choose the solution is transferable to other lawyering activities.

Although interventions generally occur in formal supervision sessions, there are other clinic venues and ways other than the semi-Socratic dialogue to impart the needed lessons. Supervisors often engage the student in role-plays. These role-plays can work in two ways; first, to see if the contemplated execution of an action actually works as well as expected, and second, if it doesn't work as anticipated, to help the student see, hear, and feel what doesn't work about it. Teachers can use classroom discussions or case rounds[75] when similar issues seem to be arising in the cases of multiple students. Supervisors sometimes intervene and give feedback on the run as single questions arise through chance encounters with a student. However, interventions may also occur during the actual performance of an interview, a deposition, or a court or legislation hearing. Notes may be passed between the teacher and the student, and short breaks in the action may occur to confer about a proper question or argument. No matter where the intervention occurs or what teaching modality is used, teaching metacognition and transfer can occur as long as the intervention is intentional, contextual, and planned.

Supervising Interpersonal Aspects of Role

Other observations of the student's actions require a more nuanced intervention because the issues the teacher notices are as personal to the student as they are relevant to the case or project. Interventions about legal or strategic issues can be fraught with interpersonal issues that students may be reluctant to address.[76] The supervisor may need more time or even more examples of what they have just witnessed to formulate the precise reasons for intervening, and the proper method to use when doing so. Intervention for these purposes becomes far more sensitive and must be conducted with great care. Nonetheless, the method and stages of the intervention will be the same. The conversation still must be goal-oriented, intentionally planned, reflective, and directed toward the student's growth.

When these intertwined personal and case-related issues arise, teachers will be intervening into actions and ideas that may be fundamental to a student's values and life experiences. For example, students who have never worked with underserved populations may make assumptions about how easy it is to find services on one's own. Students who have never experienced poverty may not realize how hard it is to survive on limited funds. Others may assume America has entered a post-racial epoch, not realizing the extent to which people of color are subtly or overtly discriminated against. Still others may have succumbed to the false social media postings that claim most immigrants are criminals. The fundamentality of those beliefs does not exclude them from critique when the student's values affect the lawyer-client relationship. It may also be critical when students prepare to confront a "disorienting event"[77] that challenges assumptions that are part of their life schema.[78] Assumptions and issues of ethics, values, and personal beliefs affect how one practices law and thus are appropriate subjects for an intervention. When raised, however, they can have tremendous interpersonal consequences. As such, teachers must be very careful to speak about the action or the assumption in a non-threatening manner and without malice toward the student. These interpersonal role issues can be based on observed actions or voiced assumptions which then generate conversations and reflections about how they affect strategic choices that the student made or is about to make. Students must understand whether their personal beliefs became the basis for the choices made, and whether the execution of the action to be taken is to advance the client's interests or the student's notions about what is best for the client. If the latter, students must confront whether their perspective is based on inaccurate or biased value judgments.

Often, the time pressures that all clinical teachers experience do not permit more than corrective suggestions to achieve the client's goals. Finding time for deep conversations about the effect of personal values on lawyering choices is not always easy. This is especially true when there is more to say in terms of assessment and reflection. Although Donald Schön[79] would have us be reflective within all of our actions, other demands posed by the case, the student, and the other cases and students in the clinic often limit the time for deeper conversations. When teachers have the time and when students begin to challenge and reject inaccurate assumptions, or when they recognize the basis for the differing values between lawyer and client, faculty celebrate the student's growth. The supervisor then returns to feedback to help the student determine how the false assumptions or differing values led to the judgments the student made, and how they can use the reflective process to recognize values and assumptions to make better choices in future actions. The teacher also uses the process to help students understand what they learned in terms of judgment and decision-making. If the actions taken in the current case do not seem to advance the client's interest because of the false assumptions or value differences, the supervision session turns to why it may fail to achieve the client's goals and how the goals can be enhanced using a different technique or strategy.

Given that differences in race, class, gender, and education often exist between students and clinic clients, clinic faculty often begin supervision on values and assumptions prior to the time cases are assigned to students. These can occur during orientation sessions or seminar classes early in the semester about differences and similarities between students and clients. The issues can be raised in specific classes or structured rounds using simulated conversations or videos about recognizing and challenging assumptions before judgments are made. Values and assumptions permeate the practice of law, and they cannot be avoided. Because they are so deeply ingrained in our life schemas, they are likely to arise in case work as the semester unfolds. Hence, starting the conversations early will make these later case-related conversations about a student's values and assumptions easier to conduct.

Taking Control

The existence of clients and the nature of representation do not always permit teaching for transfer. In some, albeit rare instances, the context in which an issue arises may be such that the supervisor must intervene immediately and simply tell the student or team what to do. Teachers should seldom take that action, should do so reluctantly, and do it only when the client's interests demand it. Legal actions often have time-based rules, and judges, legislators, and project clients often set timetables that lawyers cannot ignore. A student's learning curve may develop slower than the teacher had anticipated, making it impossible to meet a timetable unless immediate action is taken to delay or expand the deadline. If the student cannot complete the work to meet that deadline, the supervisor must take control.

Emergencies sometimes arise, creating situations that the student has never faced before. If the emergency involves an action beyond the student's current knowledge, the supervisor must take control. Ethical issues sometimes arise that demand immediate action to avoid or appropriately remedy an ethical breach before harm comes to a client, or before the supervisor's or student's standing with the Bar is jeopardized. An unforeseen question may arise during a presentation or hearing that only the supervisor can resolve. Some actions must be taken, and some arguments must be made before a certain juncture, lest they be deemed waived or forfeited at a subsequent time. In each of these situations, the supervisor may have to take control to protect both the client and the student. When that occurs, the leisurely learning conversations that lead to transfer lessons cannot precede the intervention. Supervisors must intervene by telling the student how to proceed, or by taking over the performance themselves to protect the client or the student.

Losing control can affect the student's perception of their ability. They come to the clinic with certain assumptions about what they know and what they believe they can accomplish without much help. At the same time, even successful students know that they are in a clinic to improve. Nonetheless, they do not expect to have supervisors take control of an action. When that happens, a student's confidence may be severely shaken. Because teachers know that they may have to take control, students should not be surprised when it occurs. They should be primed for the possibility of such an event early in the semester through orientation exercises and discussions, or in early case rounds classes. This will ease, although probably not eliminate, a sense of failure.

All clinical teachers will face this inevitable, albeit uncomfortable, moment during their careers. Ultimately, context and intentionality define the proper form of intervention. Once the student or supervisor remedies the immediate situation, both the student and teacher should analyze how the jeopardizing circumstances or events originated, why they presented a crisis, whether and how the crisis was resolved, if other paths existed to resolve the issue differently, and how the precipitating event could have been avoided in the first place. In essence, the supervisor engages the student in a reflective after-the-fact intervention that resembles the pre-event supervision session that would have occurred if the issue had been anticipated or if time permitted that kind of supervisory session prior to the event.

Understanding Failure in Context

Students will experience various forms of failure during their clinic experience. Failure, it should be noted, is used here without the shameful valence that most aspects of law school often graft onto it, thereby causing failure to be "treated like the other F-word."[80] Those experiences, whether major or minor, whether related to their client's case or solely to themselves, often take a great toll on the student's self-esteem. The failure they experience, however, is often not even a failure. It may merely be a mistake that causes little consequence to a case, but one that causes embarrassment or self-doubt to the student.

Failure is a strange word in the learning process.[81] When mistakes or failure occur, they are seldom as damaging as they may seem in the moment.[82] Rarely is it the case that mistakes or failures reflect the student's character or overall potential to be an effective and successful lawyer. On the contrary, mistakes are just a part of the learning and growth process. We all make mistakes. Indeed, most mistakes do not always lead to real failure; some are simple and easily corrected. Students and even some lawyers sometimes miss a recent case opinion while in the preliminary stages of research on an issue. Many of us have shown up at a clerk's office with some part of a pleading missing—perhaps a certificate of service—causing the clerk to reject the filing. These are surely mistakes, but they can usually be rectified to avoid true failure. Nonetheless, students may view any mistake as a failure on their part.

Other mistakes are often caused by carelessness or recklessness. It is not uncommon for students to mishandle a piece of evidence or speak to an opposing party without opposing counsel's permission, especially in multiparty litigation. Their overeagerness may result in a misstatement during a discovery conference, or even in court. These, of course, are serious errors that can affect both the client's case and the student's and the supervisor's standing with the court or the Bar. Those need to be acknowledged and corrected quickly to avoid the filing of ethics complaints, and to minimize the harm to the client's case.

Clinical teachers encourage students to take risks in a world of uncertainty. They assume that clinic faculty are experienced enough in their subject matter and practice that most mistakes, especially the serious ones, can be avoided. But in a world of uncertainty, the possibility of failure always exists. Students and supervisors make choices about strategy that may turn out wrong, despite a diligent and effective representation of the client. When students lose a case, everyone will recognize that some form of failure exists. The clients have failed to win their case; but perhaps that was the "just" decision and no amount of excellent lawyering could have changed that result. On the other hand, the supervisor's and student's strategic choices may have failed to sway the judge or legislators. That "failure" could have been caused by their choices. But it could have been caused by erratic juries, incorrect judicial rulings, or testimony by a witness who they had no reason to believe existed. Moreover, it will be impossible to evaluate choices they could have made against the ones they chose. We seldom know the destination of the road not taken.

When mistakes occur, embarrassment can lead people to minimize their complicity in the error or worse, conceal it from others. They may hide it from their supervisor who needs to know what the student actually did or did not do in order to protect the client, the student, and themselves. Being honest about an error usually makes rectifying it easier, thus avoiding a true failure. Being honest with clients about errors that may affect them also adds to the trust relationship between student-lawyer and client. Trust can be reclaimed as clinic staff attempt to devise a strategy that lessens the harm of the error.

Failure is something students and teachers need to accept and learn from—not just because it is an inevitable and important part of leaning and growth, but also because leaning into its inevitability and normalizing it "minimizes its power" to demoralize and derail us.[83] Lawyers live with a great amount of uncertainty in their professional lives. There are so many variables and so many players in most legal disputes and in most collaborative legal activities. Although mistakes are inevitable, they should not become the default. Good planning with deep consideration of the pros and cons of every action should precede a decision or an action. But growth can happen from mistakes and even true failure, as well as from success. The absence of excellence occurs only when the same mistake is made repeatedly without reflection. That is why the manner with which a teacher deals with failure is so important. This does not mean teachers should minimize the gravity of the mistake or excuse the student's role in the action or judgment. Even when the mistake is solely based on the student's performance, teachers need to own it as much as the student. Student practice rules make the supervisor responsible for the student's mistakes. The unwritten teaching code demands that supervisors work to ensure that mistakes seldom occur. Honest conversations are necessary, but accusations are not helpful. Teachers must explain the error or failure, why they intervened in the moment, what error might have occurred without intervention, and why they chose such a dramatic form of intervention. Throughout the conversation, the supervisor must be mindful of the student's feelings of guilt, and remind the student that learning is often a difficult journey, especially when another person's interests are at stake. If some of the fault lies with the teacher, they must model how to accept mistakes and the occasional true failure that will accompany the life of a lawyer. Supervisors need to show students how to cope with mistakes and failure, and how students can use the reflective learning process to eliminate their recurrence. As Aristotle told us, "Excellence, then, is not an act but a habit. Excellence is never an accident."[84] Using a reflective process will ensure that metacognition occurs and learning for transfer is reinforced, both of which lead to the habit of excellence and the minimalization of error.

Post-Event Feedback

There will be differences in the way pre- and post-event feedback and reflection sessions take place. Students may approach pre-event reflection sessions with an understandable dose of anxiety. They will worry about whether they can anticipate the teacher's questions, whether they have prepared enough, and whether they will be able to respond on the fly to unexpected questions. Nonetheless, the pre-event supervision sessions are often more relaxed and collaborative than post-event sessions. Preparation sessions can create an atmosphere where a student's excitement about planning and strategizing are palpable. Post-event sessions can be relaxed and exciting when the client prevails and the student's performance has been exemplary. But when students know or feel that they made a mistake and that their "failure" caused the supervisor to remedy the situation, a different atmosphere may exist as they arrive for a post-event supervision session. Students will often come to these sessions self-chastised and apologetic, sometimes even mortified, and expecting to hear hurtful criticism. No one wants to feel like they have failed. But learning is a journey that often runs through error,[85] even though students may not realize it yet. Even when they do, the general atmosphere of law school makes that realization disappear before the session begins.

The existence of these feelings of fear and self-disappointment require that teachers resist centering fault immediately with the student during the conversation. The fault may in fact lie with the supervisor, or some person or event not particularly related to the case or clinic process. Focusing on the student's actions first prevents teachers from considering the possibility that fault lies elsewhere. The mistake may have been caused by the supervisor, the judge, the client, or some unanticipated actor or event. Whenever teachers begin to sense that lessons are not being understood by students, whether in a classroom or during some other learning event, teachers should first look at their own actions and then look at external factors before focusing on potential student errors. Of course, teachers are not always at fault when learning does not progress the way it should. Nonetheless, teachers should determine before the post-event supervision session begins what they could have done differently to help the student resolve the unanticipated issue, the ethical quandary, or the inability to accept an unfavorable outcome.

As noted earlier, clinical teachers' jobs are to counsel students as they grow and mature. They seek to help students integrate their social, emotional, and intellectual growth in ways that permit these sometimes separate dimensions of life and work to operate. Life requires integration of its many facets rather than a balance; balance indicates a zero-sum game. An integrated life is one where students seek, understand, and use knowledge in unison with their values and emotions to make better decisions in both their professional and personal lives and to make valuable contributions to society.[86] Teachers need to ensure that the critique of any error during feedback or formative assessments[87] is one that leads to growth and the elimination (or at least the minimization) of factors that impede growth. Consequently, clinical supervisors must choose their words carefully, use an appropriate tone during the conversation, and have a sense of empathy with students as they move along the path to integration and growth. They must help students understand that making a wrong choice, or not succeeding in a task, is a normal and expected outcome in one's legal career. It is an inevitable step on the path to learning. Indeed, it is one that every person the student admires or considers a mentor has experienced when they were in the student's shoes.[88]

Supervising Students' Personal Issues

Practicing law can be stressful. The work is often arduous, requiring long hours wrestling with difficult legal issues, difficult opposing counsel, difficult judges, and difficult clients. The stress in public interest work can be even greater, given the poverty, health issues, and traumatic experiences that often accompany the claims students are pursuing for their clients. Studies of practicing lawyers routinely document many stress-related behaviors that plague their personal lives.[89] Stress issues are also common among law students[90] and often arise in clinical settings.[91] When clinical teachers and fellows gather for supervision rounds sessions,[92] students' personal issues are a routine topic of conversation. Some of the problems, like organizational confusion or research blocks, may seem at first to be issues of cognitive knowledge or simple time management skills. But more often than not, the "problem" is not simply cognitive or skills-based. There are always other events going on in students' lives that affect their learning and client representation.

There are many personal issues that can affect the students' academic progress and their actions related to their cases or projects. First and foremost, the methods used in clinical pedagogy create a new learning experience for many students. Most of their education has been based on receiving content from experienced teachers which they have been asked to absorb and retain and then demonstrate their retention of the "correct" answers when they draft their papers and exams. Because uncertainty and ambiguity are inherent in the practice of law, "correct" answers are often elusive, and sometimes illusive. This uncertainty can result in several different impediments to learning. Some students can grow resistant to the pedagogical method, constantly seeking the "correct" answer from the supervisor rather than engaging in an exploration of the topic in ways that enable them to discover the best choice among many feasible options. On the other hand, students may begin to think that given the uncertainty, their solutions are sufficient even when untested or insufficiently explored. Those students then reject feedback on their work and thus never reach the point of metacognitive understanding. Third, some students suffer from imposter syndrome, believing they will never get the right answer because they do not belong in law school in the first place. For reasons inherent in the clinical method or because of external experiences, those students continually lack confidence and constantly work in fear of making mistakes.

Students are also often overwhelmed by the sheer amount of work they are asked to perform, or the nature and amount of responsibility they are asked to assume when representing a client's interest. Even a lawyering task as simple as a routine status hearing in a misdemeanor criminal case or landlord-tenant case where the student will only speak for a few seconds to pick a next court date, may involve multiple rounds of edits and supervision sessions before the student's court appearance. Students are also tasked with telling clients disappointing news about their case, often with few answers to the questions their clients pose and far less certainty about their answers. They then imagine a practicing attorney knows more and could have answered all of the client's questions confidently. Some students are also confronted with the vicarious trauma that accompanies working in indigent legal services.[93] Client stories are often filled with violence, health issues, poverty, housing and food insecurity, racial insults, death, and other forms of trauma. Hearing those stories daily can take a toll on students working with marginalized clients.

These new responsibilities may lead to boundary issues between clinic partners or between students and their clients. Although practicing attorneys face similar boundary issues, clinic students can feel them especially acutely. Clinic students are often experiencing these issues for the first time in their legal careers. Moreover, the boundary issues are slightly different because of clinic design. Clinic students have very few cases, so they can dedicate what would otherwise be an inordinate amount of time and energy to a particular client's case. Practicing attorneys establish their own boundaries as they mature in their practice. Some lawyers will turn down an unhoused client's request for money or food after being released from arraignment because they cannot afford to feed and house all their hundreds of clients. Others will gladly part with a dollar or two. Some lawyers have no difficulty letting after-hours calls go to voicemail, while others answer every phone call after they get home from the office. Some lawyers try to accommodate all of a client's social needs while others triage client demands. Law students, however, may feel especially guilty turning down client requests, knowing that they, in theory, *could* afford to buy their one and only client a sandwich or have the time to talk to their client on the phone, even at odd hours. The line between professional and personal relationships can become a fine one in any lawyer-client relationship. But when students see themselves as "saviors" for clients in distress, or become a friend as well as lawyer for their client, they may absorb feelings that detract from the independent judgments that one expects in a professional relationship.

Relationship factors within the clinic can also affect students' learning. Students are often paired to work on cases, and those pairings do not always work out well. Gender and race issues among partners, or even between students and supervisors, can be the most difficult to confront and resolve.[94] Whether erroneously perceived or real, unequal effort between partners and overbearing behavior or undue deference within the team not only affects their personal relationship, but can affect the quality of client representation. Relational issues outside the clinic also can impede student learning in the clinic. Domestic partner breakups, sick or dying parents or other relatives, undisclosed disabilities, and negative physical and mental health episodes can all create challenges to a student's performance. Poverty, poor housing situations, or indebtedness can also affect students' performances.

Finally, especially for upper-level students, a common topic of conversation and resulting stress throughout their time in clinic will likely include their post-graduate job searches as they balance clinic work and other classes alongside traveling for interviews, contemplating a hiring-committee's difficult hypothetical questions, and navigating the ups and downs inherent in finding a first legal position. Supervisors have to be mindful of these professional development and personal demands on students' time and attention, and the stress that it produces. Because supervisors themselves are lawyers and may have practiced in the field(s) their students are considering, they are uniquely well-positioned to offer advice and guidance, and to be a sounding board for these kinds of issues in their students' lives.

When these and other personal events arise, some students may completely disengage from clinic work. Document drafts arrive consistently late, meetings are missed or postponed, and deadlines for any number of clinic-related activities are routinely ignored. Classroom work suffers and supervision sessions become truncated because necessary preliminary work has not been completed. When such events occur, the reasons for them may perplex the teachers. Most law students feel the pressure to succeed, so how can the work become so unprofessional?

Attributing reasons for the behavior is difficult when there appears to be no knowledge deficit. It is easy to think laziness or some other personal trait as the cause of any of these negative behaviors. But intentional neglect is seldom the problem. Thus, ascribing negative character traits should not be the starting point of a supervision session to discuss what we are observing. Throughout this book, I have stressed the importance of meeting students where they are, searching for the root cause of a learning impediment, working with the student to recognize those causes, and then working together to create a path to the remedy. Although choosing to do less-than-adequate work might be a possible cause, I have only rarely confronted such cases in my career. Law students are generally people driven with ambition. They did not come to law school, nor did they sign up for clinic, to fail.

Professor Robert Stumberg of Georgetown created a method for analyzing difficult supervision issues for the class we teach to new teachers and fellows. Naming the model was difficult because we did not want to name it in a way that would predict an anticipated resolution or pathologize the student. We settled on "Adaptive Supervision" to signal that the issue the supervisor is confronting may be uncommon, in need of some more expansive thinking, or require a novel approach. The Adaptive Supervision method is similar to the supervision rounds method, but it begins with the premise that our typical methods do not seem to be addressing the learning or case-related issue.[95]

The Adaptive Supervision method involves three stages. Supervisors first consider the behavior they are observing, which can fall under the categories of Productivity/Role, Cognition, Relationships, or Emotions. In stage two, the supervisor then seeks to ascertain the possible factors that could be contributing to the observed behavior, which include the supervisor, the clinic structure, the client, external actors like opposing lawyers, judges, or other external influences. Supervisors should begin by analyzing their own possible contributions to the difficulties to avoid focusing on the fault of the student to determine whether the supervisor has caused the lack of progress. The supervisor then analyzes the other potential contributing factors in terms of the observed behavior to determine the potential causes of the unproductive behavior. Only when the potential causes are clear in the supervisor's mind can they and the student begin to evaluate which of the possible contributing factors is causing the underlying issue and consider one or more ways to adapt the supervision. That conversation hopefully leads to a mutual understanding of the causes of the unproductive behavior, and an open discussion of what measures can be taken to adapt the supervision to remove the learning impediment. Those measures may require a change in the way the supervisor oversees the student's work; a change in the clinic structure to adapt to the student's learning pattern; a recognition of the external factors and an allowance for those factors; or changes in the student's approach to the clinic work.

It is possible that the resolution will be too difficult or so far out of the ordinary that success is jeopardized. The difficulty the supervisor may have noticed could have been caused by the student's reluctance to divulge the cause of the behavior, by the supervisors erroneous analysis of the contributing factors, or by a misplaced assumption about what was really going on behind the scenes. Of course, learning can be impeded by factors beyond the immediate control of the supervisor. There has been an increase in the number of students suffering from anxiety disorders and depression in recent years.[96] The Covid-19 pandemic brought many of these issues to the fore and exacerbated them.[97] Supervisors do not have the ability to resolve issues that are beyond their professional expertise. Nonetheless, they need to be aware that these issues affect learning and can affect the students' work on their cases or projects.[98]

Some students' learning impediments will require the services of the school's Office of Accessibility Services. Some students' schedules or workloads may have to be adjusted because of sick partners or other close relatives or because of difficult-to-resolve childcare issues. Some students need time or counseling to come to terms with separation from their emotional partners. Serious personal issues like financial distress, food insecurity, or concern about limited post-law school employment opportunities and mounting student debt will require other law school personnel to help remedy or counsel the student about the issue. Professional counseling or mental health services may be necessary, but that usually requires a student to be proactive in seeking such services. However, the severity of depression may be preventing the student from acting. Some schools do not have the capacity to serve the sheer number of students in need. That raises the question of how far faculty should be prepared to go beyond the university's available resources. This is particularly thorny when the student has already sought psychiatric services which may not be adequate to improve performance in legal practice. Nonetheless, faculty must be aware of the range of student services provided by the school and be prepared to help the students obtain the necessary support. In some cases, students may need to take an administrative withdrawal from the clinic if they cannot meet their professional obligations to cover their cases or projects. In some cases, the issues may reach beyond the clinic, forcing the student to withdraw from school.

Because classes are small, clinic supervisors may be the first to notice the personal factors affecting the student's behavior. It is hard for nonclinical teachers to notice these issues because their classes have far more students. In addition, clinic students usually trust their supervisors and are more willing to discuss personal issues with them. The tools faculty use for reflective conversations about legal work are often adaptable to issues of a personal nature. Intervening into personal issues, like case-related issues, will benefit from planning, intentional choices, and reflective interactions.

How Can a Supervisor Do It All?

The pedagogy described above may seem demanding, daunting, and a rather inefficient way of completing work on a client's case or project. It is demanding and inefficient because it almost always takes more time to prepare a case or project with a student than it would take a faculty member to represent the client alone. In addition, faculty usually work with seven to ten students in the clinic. It is true that the pedagogical method is inefficient, but it is inefficient on purpose. Clinical education is designed this way because our job is to do more than work a case to completion. It is more than teaching the skills required as the case or project develops. It is to develop students' ability to become lifelong learners in a profession designed to improve the common good and strengthen democracy. As such, clinical education offers an experience that cannot be reproduced elsewhere, either in other law school classes, or in the professional world.

Notwithstanding this intentional inefficiency, structural problems within the clinic sometimes compromise the implementation of this pedagogical approach. Student demand and other demands on the law school's budget can affect the number of students enrolling in a clinic. As a result, clinical courses at many law schools enroll more students than a well-structured clinical course should have. In addition, teachers cannot always predict the complexity of a case or project before representation is undertaken. Seemingly simple cases sometimes evolve and become more time-consuming than anticipated. Students come to the clinic with other demands of law school and the demands of their personal lives weighing on them. Finally, students come with various levels of competence, often with strengths in different areas of practice.[99] When these factors interfere with their clinic work, supervisors still have to carry the load to ensure competent client representation.

There is also a steep learning curve that comes with even predictable stages of learning. At the start of the course, all students need intensive supervision because everything is new. As their ability and confidence improves, they begin to exercise more control over their cases and the supervisor begins to react to their initiative rather than creating the path for their work. Towards the end of the term, supervisors expect the students to be the equivalent of first chair or co-equals on the case or project and will intervene only when necessary to avoid error. But not everyone improves at the same pace. All of these issues increase the time a faculty member spends on the teaching mission of the clinic. Hence, the demands on the teacher increase and the inefficiency remains.

In most schools, supervisors must balance their teaching time with other institutional commitments and the demands of scholarship. The shortage of time that all clinical teachers experience often permits little more than corrective suggestions to help students move a task forward. This is unfortunately true even when there is more to say in terms of feedback and reflection. Although Professor Donald Schön[100] minimized the constraints on the teaching mission and highlighted reflection as "the core of practice,"[101] some demands posed by clinic caseloads, project size and forum-filing rules, can restrict the amount of time that a teacher spends with each student in the clinic. The needs of other students in the clinic and the demands of teachers' own personal lives do not always permit teachers to fulfill the "core of practice" for every student every time the opportunity presents itself. On the other hand, because the academy's purpose is to create civic-minded lawyers with a high sense of integrity and purpose, teachers must find the time to explore personal, professional, and systemic values with each student. They also must find time to discuss their students' life choices and the struggles that a student might be having with respect to the law school or within their own personal lives.

As stated in the introductory chapter of this book, clinical teaching is most effective when it is based on the teacher's personal investment in individual students, designed to accept students where they are, and planned in a way that maximizes a student's learning potential in the clinic and in their careers thereafter. Reflection can occur in many places during a student's tenure in the clinic, and feedback is the way a faculty member can help the student understand their place in the legal profession and their place in the world. But integrating all the demands that the pedagogy and the institutional commitments place on clinical teachers is never easy.

The readings that follow this chapter and later chapters about supervision will explore more of the basics of experiential pedagogy and specific issues arising in particular supervision situations.

Other Voices

Ann Shalleck, *Clinical Contexts: Theory and Practice in Law and Supervision**

21 N.Y.U. Rev. L. & Soc. Change 109 (1994)

Introduction: Genesis and Method

Nowhere is the intersection of legal theory and legal practice more intense than in supervising students representing real clients on real cases. Supervision is an ongoing dialogue between student and teacher about that representation. The teacher gives shape to the dialogue through each decision about what to include in, and how to conduct, the discussion. The student's practice is the focus of the supervisory discussion, but the teacher frames how that practice is understood. In shaping the dialogue, the teacher conveys both explicitly and implicitly a vision of law, legal institutions, and lawyering.

. . .

Students in clinical courses have a unique opportunity to combine analysis of their own experience with critical, systemic analysis. Seeing, participating in, and, most importantly, reflecting upon the law in action provides the student with an opportunity for engaging in self-conscious critical analysis of legal institutions, rules, and procedures that is rooted in, yet transcends, the student's own experience. At the same time that they engage in critical, systemic analysis, however, the students act as advocates for a particular client. They are learning to confront another person's desires, fears, and idiosyncrasies while undertaking strategic action on that person's behalf. They must master the modes of thought and skills necessary for those tasks.

. . .

A Vision of Supervision

. . .

The issues that the teacher frames as the most important for supervision (the decisions) and the ways that she chooses to view those issues (the contexts) create a complex and constantly shifting scheme requiring the teacher's constant attention to the fundamental assumptions underlying each choice she makes. This scheme permits the supervisor to shift "back and forth between the concrete and the abstract, the practical and the reflective, the specific and the general. By engaging in this process, the teacher constructs a concept of supervision out of the material presented by the cases and the students, the dynamics of the educational enterprise, and the self-conscious application of critical perspectives to daily work in the clinic.

* Excerpts are reprinted with the permission of the author and the New York University Review of Law and Social Change.

The particular characteristics of supervision will, therefore, constantly change. Identifying these characteristics at any particular time helps us to see the themes and concerns we have made central to the supervisory project. In [any] case, at least eight characteristics of supervision [may] emerge. First, the teacher is very active in defining the content and structure of the supervisory experience. Although a student may be very involved in shaping a particular dialogue, the teacher initiates and directs the inquiries into particular topics....

Second, the teacher engages in a very self-conscious decision-making process in shaping supervision.... In making each decision, [teachers] look to the overall structure of the clinical course, the flow of case-related experiences, the knowledge developed through case activities, the relationship between the students and their clients, the particular qualities of individual students, and the dynamics of the relationship between the students and herself. While any given interaction between teacher and student may become very nondirective—either in the sense of being very free flowing, without a structured or predefined agenda, or in the sense of not leading to a particular answer or way of looking at things—the teacher both defines the educational agenda and mak[es] decisions in a self-conscious, directed manner.

Third, revealing the teacher's understanding of the supervisory process can be an important part of supervision. Although the teacher actively defines the educational project, the students have access to that process of definition. Demystification can either advance discussion of a particular issue or enable students to question or challenge the teacher's project....

Fourth, supervision requires the teacher to engage in different kinds of dialogue. In some instances, the dialogue is directive with the teacher raising issues and structuring discussion. Sometimes, she may even seek to achieve a particular result. In other instances, the dialogue is open-ended, designed to explore different possibilities or provide opportunities for students to develop their own interpretations of events.

...

Fifth, the students' actions on cases and the knowledge gained from those activities form the organizing principle for the intellectual inquiry in supervision. Students [can] examine lawyering theories, skills, social theories, institutional critique, and personal feelings within the framework of their cases. The material presented in the other components of the course is tested and modified through case experiences. Casework reveals the students' characteristics and capacities. The relationship between the students and clients takes shape through the case. Supervisory inquiry focuses upon the case.

Sixth, the student-client relationship mediates the teacher's concern for the client. Therefore, the teacher expresses her responsibility for and commitment to the client in two ways. First, the teacher intervenes in the students' construction of a relationship with a client. The intervention may be minor or major, exploratory or directive, but the students have the opportunity to construct a relationship with the client. The teacher does not become the lawyer. Rather, the teacher acts to ensure that the students adequately fulfill their responsibility to the client. Through intervention, the teacher discharges her duty to protect the client from harm. Second, the teacher repeatedly directs the students to examine their actions in relationship to the client.

...

Seventh, supervision requires an inquiry into the institutional structures within which a case arises and the social and political forces that shape the development of the case.... [E]xploring the court system's structure for handling cases shapes the litigation strategy.... Teaching students to be lawyers includes analyzing the meaning of [systemic issues] in the client's and the students' experience, in the student-client relationship, in the court system, and in the other institutions of society.

Eighth, all supervisory action is intervention. Intervention is not just acting when something has gone wrong or is about to go wrong. The students' experience with the case and the client exists within the supervisory framework and the many different sorts of interactions with the teacher shape those experiences. Although... teacher[s often have little or no] direct contact with the client and... [almost never] take over the hearing unless the student [is] making [serious] mistakes, her participation in the planning meetings and critique sessions... can alter the students' representation of and relationship with their client.

The vision of supervision that emerges... [in any] case is a tentative one. Because neither the decisions nor the contexts are fixed, the particular characteristics of the vision constantly shift. By looking at other decisions within the same contexts and by identifying other contexts that matter in our decision making we can further enrich our understanding of supervision.

Beryl Blaustone, *Reflection on Supervision in Feedback Interactions: Reinforcement of Some Fundamental Themes**

Appearing in TRANSFORMING THE EDUCATION OF LAWYERS: THE THEORY AND PRACTICE OF CLINICAL PEDAGOGY (Susan J. Bryant, Elliott S. Milstein & Ann Shalleck eds., 2014)

Introduction: Revisiting the Use of the Six-Step Feedback Model

...

In this ... article, I described a six-step feedback model, detailing my training methods for imbedding reflection habits necessary for professional clinical judgment as lawyers.... The six-step model contains six distinct steps that together implement fundamental theories of autonomy, intrinsic motivation, a mastery mindset, creativity, and life-long learning illustrated by the masters of different professions, crafts, arts, contemplative practices, and sports.

* Excerpts are reprinted with the permission of the author and Carolina Academic Press.

In the dissemination of this model, inadequate attention has been given to how a critically aware supervisor flexibly works with the model over time and with different students. In the beginning, effective utilization requires repeated use of the steps with all students to instill the habits that support student ownership of their professional development. That practice does not mean that every student-teacher conversation is a six-step conversation. The teacher selects the work segments that merit this focused discussion. This discussion can take a few minutes or a much lengthier time period, occurring immediately after the work performance or scheduled for a later date. Over time, any teacher can develop sufficient mastery over the model allowing for flexibly in choice of how to use the model. A teacher can have conversations that are a variety of combinations of the six-step feedback model because she has integrated the theory, is comfortable with the method, and has built a trusting relationship with all of her students that is premised upon student ownership of their professional development.

...

Step One: The Student Identifies Strengths of the Performance

The performing student first identifies those aspects of the work that s/he feels were done well or with which s/he is satisfied. The student's statement should include an identification of what the performance accomplished. Here the teacher expects the student to search for areas of satisfactory work in as much detail as possible. The teacher or peer participant/observer does not accept summary or superficial references. Nor does the teacher permit the student's likely rush to discuss errors or difficulties. The teacher understands that this call for careful identification of what worked and why is not an "ice breaker" for the real conversation. Rather, this is the real conversation. Because learning to accurately recognize and identify one's strength is an important goal, the teacher creates space for the student's discomfort with silence and prompts the student to state the satisfactory platform of the work that was done.

Step Two: The Peer or Supervisor Responds Solely to Those Items Raised by the Feedback Recipient

In this step, the peer or supervisor confines his or her remarks to the points that were raised by the student. No new items are raised here. The point is to reinforce the validity of the student's observations and to add more content to those observations. Only positive feedback should be given at this point and any reservation about the student's positive assessment is saved for later in the conversation. Often, if the student lawyer is allowed to navigate these steps, he or she will return to this point later and offer his or her own qualifying observations on how this aspect could have been improved as the student becomes more comfortable with this conversation.

Step Three: The Peer or Supervisor Identifies Other Strengths of the Performance

Peers or the supervisor now add additional points that the law student did well with a wide-open discussion exploring all facets of the performance that were satisfactorily done. The conversation also identifies aspects that show a potential for success, with specific illustrations of why these aspects were executed successfully. This fuller discussion of additional demonstrated skills reinforces the lesson that the student has a range of abilities that support growth into being an effective practicing lawyer.

Step Four: The Student Identifies Difficulties and/or Changes to Be Made

In this step, students take the initiative in identifying those areas that need improvement and those points where they struggled or sensed they made mistakes. The student is expected to come forward with specific comments and is given the time and silence necessary to formulate these thoughts. As with step one, the student is not interrupted except where s/he moves away from this task and then only to be refocused upon this task. The lesson reinforced here and in step one is that the student is leading the skills assessment.

Step Five: The Peer or Supervisor Responds to the Identified Difficulties

The peer or supervisor confines remarks at this point exclusively to those issues raised by the student. The comments should indicate how the issue could be handled differently next time. Students should be encouraged to explore the meaning of their colleagues' comments and should be discouraged from justifying why they did what they did.

Step Six: The Peer or Supervisor Indicates Additional Difficulties

This final stage involves another wide-open exploration of all facets of the performance. This time, the discussion focuses on additional aspects that were not satisfactorily accomplished, again with specific illustrations and concrete analyses. The supervisor and peers identify important areas of weakness or omission not identified by the student. Most of the time, the student will have previously identified the most egregious or alarming weaknesses of his or her work in step four. And if the student has not done so, then it finally becomes necessary to identify the unspoken "elephant in the room." Even in this situation, most often the students are more receptive to this input because they have set the agenda, experienced professionally supportive attention to their efforts, and recognize the purpose of this scrutiny is to improve their performance next time.

The student experiences this conversation as routine support and not as an impulsive negative judgment that his or her lawyering is unworthy or that the supervisor disapproves of the student. S/he learns that the supervisor or peer is focused on correction and thus believes the student is capable of continuous professional improvement. The student also has the experience of providing this exact same engagement to others when participating in their peers' feedback discussions. A sense of normalcy is created when everyone is participating in the same structure. Thus, all students gain understanding that no performance is entirely perfect or entirely a failure. This insight is especially important for the perfectionist as the process shows the difference between striving for excellence and the need to always be right.

Developing greater thresholds for this fuller balanced assessment of our work generates more intrinsic motivation to achieve mastery. This is the mindset of the practicing lawyer as life-long learner of a craft.

Five Principles Supporting the Model

...

A Structured Approach Focuses the Supervisor on Building the Student's Ability to Self-Critique

When we follow a structured approach to feedback, we reduce our unintentional negative influence on the student's ability to self-critique by minimizing our propensity to interfere with the student's reflection process. A structured approach to feedback encourages us to train ourselves to see all of our communication and action as a system within which the law student is learning. This focus on the communication process eliminates unconscious mistakes and reinforces behaviors that promote learning.... [W]e underestimate the huge influence of the implicit messages in our behaviors towards our students. Our tone, impatience, misunderstanding, spontaneous reactions, and use of judging language have a very large impact on how our students interpret our interactions with them.

...

All of our proclivities for ill-managing our own stress as clinical teachers work against our goal of teaching how to avoid premature professional conclusions. Too often with this behavior we model a lack of self-awareness or inadequate professional self-regulation while telling our students that they need to develop such awareness in their own lawyering.

By using the structured approach to see the communication and interaction as part of a system, a teacher remembers that we continually influence how student attorneys construct understanding. We are sending messages about our assessment of them whether intentionally or not. Our choice in tone and language contributes to or diminishes the law student's professional levels of reflection and self-regulation.

...

The law student's subjective experience creates the context within which students interpret events and distill insights for future application. When we appreciate the centrality of this observation, we are more open to performing in ways that promote insight by the student rather than predominately focusing on our transmission of knowledge to the student. This does not mean that we place less emphasis on imparting knowledge but that we know that solely imparting knowledge does not produce insights by the student.

Reinforcing Genuine Student Ownership of the Feedback Is Necessary to Promote Professional Identity

We increase the novice practitioner's motivation to act as an autonomous professional when we give students genuine ownership of the feedback agenda. Embedding a personal sense of accountability for reflecting on the sufficiency of one's work occurs when we consistently require student-initiated conversations. I premise this assertion on the established observation that self-generated observations deepen the individual's internalization of lessons and increase the individual's effort in incorporating the lessons into a framework that will be applied in future performance. These thoughts are tremendously significant to us as clinical supervisors because we must choose what substance gets covered in feedback discussions and we must choose our means of delivery. If we reinforce student ownership, we may lose some time to cover our own observations and yet we meet our overall goal of student ownership. All of this discussion is driven by the basic principle that mastery in lawyering cannot be achieved without competent levels of self-assessment skills.

...

Shifting to Full-Balanced Examination of Performance Promotes the Beginning of Professional Mastery More than Favoring Attention to Weak Performance or Mistakes

Recent studies confirm that at least for novice practitioners, recognizing specific areas of competency aids the student in learning from practice. A competent legal practitioner must be able to identify effective choices and replicate them when appropriate. In addition, the legal practitioner must be able to identify ineffective choices and take appropriate corrective action. However, the student does an ineffective job of embedding the learning from mistakes when not working from a solid comprehension of strengths. Building scaffolding necessary for doing a lawyering task requires a full assessment of the entire task rather than building scaffolding based solely on weaknesses that need strengthening. Solid areas of work need reinforcement if they are to be consciously used again in the further construction of the scaffolding for any lawyering activity. Validating capacity reinforces the student's ability to learn the undertaking of professional role. Validating capacity also increases the individual's motivation to repeat the long, and often painful, sustained effort to achieve professional competency. This challenge to forge ahead and try again, also known as "mastery as a mindset," should not be made more difficult by a teacher adding counter-productive negative experiences to the discomfort of pushing oneself past previous boundaries. A whole-performance assessment helps the student deal with the emotions sparked by "not getting it" as quickly as the student wishes.

...

Imbedding New Methods of Inquiry Requires Transparency and Repeated Articulation

Transparency has become a common buzzword to describe a solution to failures to disclose important information and key decisions. With reference to supervision in the feedback interaction, I refer to the need to articulate the framework and to consistently repeat the same framework when engaging in feedback. Reinforcing structure by explicit repetition may not be a natural tendency for the clinical supervisor nor may it be the conscious choice when juggling the many demands of supervising students and cases. However, the human mind does not readily synthesize and imbed new methods for future problem solving in deep memory. For students to acquire these new methods, the process requires repeated review and practice.

...

Peer Participation in Feedback Interaction Improves the Quality of the Student's Formative Assessment

Student-to-student peer discussions in structured feedback give students multiple perspectives on the work they have produced.... They are able to view each other as relatively safe sounding boards for feedback on their work. As they continue student-to-student peer discussions, they are increasingly able to unpack the work more precisely and thoroughly. They accumulate more experience during the semester and they initiate more discussions on their own.

...

Timothy Casey, *Reflective Practice in Legal Education: The Stages of Reflection* *

20 Clinical Law Review (2014)

...

Part I. Defining Reflective Practice

Reflective practice is the integration of intentional thought and specific action within a professional context. Reflective practice includes consideration of ethical rules and norms in a given field and offers guidance for the skillful application of professional ethics. Reflective practice is not the same as occasional review or reflection about a past professional experience, rather, it is the ingrained habit of constant reflection.

One scholar has described reflective practice as the process that produces praxis—informed, committed action. Another has described reflection as "a basic mental

* Excerpts are reprinted with the permission of the author and the Clinical Law Review.

process with a purpose, an outcome, or both, applied in situations in which material is unstructured or uncertain and where there is no obvious solution."

In the mid-1980s, Professor Donald Schon described the virtues of reflective practice, and the reflective practitioner emerged as a new vision of professional master. Reflective practice became a critical learning outcome in many programs of professional education.

...

Part III. The Stages of Reflection

The Stages of Reflection are consistent with the models from other disciplines described above. A staged approach has been widely adopted since Piaget and continues to be the preferred method of categorization. Although some researchers (for example, the Neo-Kohlbergians) prefer a model where individuals do not advance lock-step from one stage to another, all of the prevalent models include some form of movement from foundational levels to higher-order levels.

In the Stages of Reflection model described below, the first two stages assist the student with the transition away from a dualistic relationship with knowledge. For example, the first stage asks the student to compare her performance to a relatively objective standard. The second stage asks the student to describe difference and choice—the different ways the assignment could have been completed and the choices the student made in the completion of the assignment. After the first two stages, the student is ready to analyze the reasons she made specific choices.

In the third stage of reflection, the student must identify the internal factors that affected her professional decision-making process. Often the experience of practicing law forces the student to confront deep-seated and very personal issues. Frequently, the student encounters a moment of self-realization. Everything from the student's style of communication to manner of dress is open for analysis. The student should develop awareness about his internal preferences, experiences, biases, and characteristics. These internal factors shape his individual perspective and exert an influence over his decision making process. These personal factors form a personal, internal context.

In stage four, the student must move from an internal, individualistic perspective to an external perspective. The student must describe the external context of the lawyering performance. The student is not acting in a vacuum, and must be aware of the preferences, experiences, biases, and characteristics of the other people involved in the representation. These factors form the external context of the representation.

In the fifth stage, the student should develop an awareness of a broader societal context. The lens of examination becomes much wider and includes more than the individual lawyer or the specific representation. The student focuses on social structures and political institutions, on economic realities, and on human tendencies.

At the final stage, we ask the student to turn her attention back on herself. However, the object of the reflection is not the action of the lawyering process, but rather the effect of reflection on the student's thought process. We want the student to be aware of her own reflective process and the effect of reflection on her actions. At this sixth, meta-cognitive stage, the student is reflecting about reflection.

The central idea of the Stages of Reflection model is that the teacher can guide the student to the higher stages of reflection by passing through the earlier stages. Reflective assignments should ask the student to consider progressively more complex factors that affect the lawyering performance. Students should advance along a continuum by developing increasingly complex modes of reflection. The early stages of reflection meet the student on terms consistent with early levels of cognitive and moral development. The process of moving from one level to the next in the Stages of Reflection is consistent with the movement from one level to the next in cognitive or moral development....

Kris Henning,
*Combating Decision Fatigue in Supervision**

Appearing in TRANSFORMING THE EDUCATION OF LAWYERS:
THE THEORY AND PRACTICE OF CLINICAL PEDAGOGY
(Susan J. Bryant, Elliott S. Milstein & Ann Shalleck eds., 2014)

...

As John Tierney wrote in the byline of his 2011 New York Times Magazine article, "The very act of making decisions depletes our ability to make them well." Making decisions with other people in time-sensitive and sometimes life-altering contexts is even more debilitating. For a clinical teacher, decision making with students is further complicated by below-the-surface decisions about whether to give a quick answer now and follow up later or whether to help the students "unpack" the question themselves and find the answer on their own.

At times, the mental exhaustion of supervision gets the best of me. I make decisions and offer advice that I later regret. In moments of reflection, I wonder if we could make better decisions if I had more time or if my students were more self-sufficient. I have experienced "decision fatigue."

In recent years, I have been more honest with myself—and with my students—about my own limitations. I admit that I cannot always give the best answer now, in the heat of the moment. I try to buy time. When the luxury of time permits, I defer questions until we can find the space and energy we need to process them. When time is limited, I take a deep breath and do the best I can with the resources I have.

---

* Excerpts are reprinted with the permission of the author and Carolina Academic Press.

In the best circumstances, I equip my students with the analytical tools they need to make decisions on their own. I give them a framework for unpacking the problem. But even that "tooling" process has its own costs as I find myself asking students the same set of questions time and time again: *What are your options? What are the advantages and disadvantages of each option? What are the legal and ethical considerations that affect your decision? Where can you go to get more information about each option? What do you think you should do? And why?* At times I just want to write these questions on a t-shirt or print them out on a note card. While not quite as succinct, this essay might serve a similar purpose. My goal here is to refine and memorialize the decision-making framework I share with my students. As students internalize the model, they become more self-sufficient and reduce their own fatigue, as well as the teacher's. For context, I will also briefly examine the concept of decision fatigue, discuss the need for transparency in articulating and enforcing the decision-making framework, and identify the benefits of the model.

Decision Fatigue

Decision fatigue refers to the deteriorating quality of decisions made by an individual after an extended period of decision making. It permeates all facets of clinic legal education and explains why we get frustrated with students who ask questions we think they should figure out on their own, why we ignore emails we know we should answer, and how we let our emotions drive decisions we need to make with careful, methodical analysis.

An emerging body of research, most recently led by social psychologist Roy F. Baumeister, has demonstrated that each of us has a finite amount of mental energy and willpower to make decisions throughout the day. When that energy is depleted, making even simple decisions can be difficult. Decision fatigue often follows the continuous weighing of alternatives and choosing among options.

...

When we are drained, our brains look for shortcuts in decision making. Some of us become reckless and impulsive in our decisions instead of thinking through the options and potential consequences. Others try to conserve energy by looking at only one dimension of a problem and ignoring other important variables that might affect our response. Still others do nothing at all or remain passive while others make decisions for them. Decision fatigue may also reduce our ability to negotiate and compromise with others or cause decision paralysis at a time when we cannot afford to delay or avoid the decision. Even more troubling, decision fatigue might impair our ability to self-regulate and avoid obviously poor decisions.

Decision fatigue likely affects clinical teachers, students, and the clients we serve to different degrees. Lawyers often meet clients at one of the most difficult times in their lives—a time when the clients are struggling with decisions they hoped they would never have to make. Those decisions are often exacerbated by concerns about the financial and emotional burden the legal matter imposes on the client and his family.

To make matters worse, lawyers often ask clients to make decisions that are little more than a "Hobson Choice" between two relative evils, such as whether to litigate unfavorable facts at trial or accept an unfavorable plea.

Students experience some form of decision fatigue as well.... [C]linical students likely experience decision fatigue from fear of the unknown and concerns about their own ability to make decisions that have a profound impact on their clients. Students face considerable anxiety as they take on greater responsibilities in their new role as lawyer in a clinical setting. Students who are unfamiliar with the law and practice doubt their ability to predict judicial outcomes, anticipate the collateral consequences of any given choice, and identify and weigh the strategic considerations they must factor into each decision. These insecurities are often amplified when the student recognizes the impact of each decision on the client's financial and liberty interests and questions her own ability to evaluate the options within the client's unique socio-economic and cultural context. Thus, even when students have relatively few decisions to make in comparison to their supervisor or client, each new decision is mentally and emotionally exhausting.

...

Refining the Decision-Making Process

Clinical teachers should also try to minimize fatigue by reducing the number of decisions they need to make each day. Teachers should empower students with the tools they need to make good decisions on their own. Thus begins my effort to memorialize an effective decision-making framework for new lawyers. Recognizing that checklists for common routines may reduce decision fatigue and that graphic aids may help us visualize, compare, and rank various options in order of preference, I propose a series of questions that will guide students through a range of new and recurring legal decisions. The framework not only provides students with a method for answering legal questions, but also encourages them to account for the many moral, ethical, and strategic factors they must consider. As an important added benefit, the framework also helps students complete the basic case analysis before they come to supervision, preserving the preciously limited time of supervision for the more complex and vexing questions in the case.

A. Framework

The framework I adopt is one that many of us use but often take for granted. It is a framework with several components that we assume but rarely put to paper. This essay attempts to surface and analyze each component. This essay also assumes that our students have already identified some questions to be answered. At times we will need to help our students identify the *right* issues and refine the questions, but this framework presumes that a student has come to supervision with some questions in mind.

...

Early in the semester when my students are new to the clinical method, I walk them through the decision-making framework with prompts that help them analyze the problem. As the student evolves, I expect them to employ the framework on their own and come to the supervision session with a proposed plan of action, not an open-ended question.

1. Identify the Options

The first stage of effective decision making is understanding what all of the options are in response to a given question. Thus, when a student poses a question, my first prompt is always: *What are our options at this point*? In the scenario described above, the student unfamiliar with suspected child abuse may be paralyzed, but with a little encouragement and common sense, the student can develop a list of alternatives. As the lawyer, we can (a) do nothing, (b) ask the police or child protective agency to intervene, (c) notify our client's relatives, teacher, or other non-law enforcement entity of the suspected abuse, (d) attempt to secure treatment services for our client's mother outside of the legal system, (e) attempt to secure counseling and other services for the entire family, or (f) encourage our *client* to call the child protective agency, a relative, or some other non-law enforcement resources to get help for himself. With a little creativity, this list is arguably endless.

When students have a hard time generating ideas or face legal decisions that require more extensive research, I direct them to the appropriate resources. Many of the issues will be addressed in the clinic course materials or in legal resources such as code books, jury instructions, bar opinions, and rules of professional conduct. Over time, the students should look to these resources before coming to supervision.

2. Identify the Legal, Ethical, Personal, and Strategic Implications of Each Option

Effective decision making is rarely driven by the law alone. Reviewing the relevant statutes, rules, and judicial opinions may prevent us from violating the black letter of the law, but it may not help us choose between competing legal options when the law is subject to multiple interpretations and the facts and social implications are variable and ever-evolving. The law clearly works in tandem with a range of personal, practical, and ethical considerations. Thus, I often propose to my students a second question: *What are the legal, ethical, strategic, and personal considerations that we (and our client) must weigh in making this decision?* Because lawyers are bound to pursue the stated interests of their clients, the lawyer must always understand the client's personal goals and desired outcomes. Those goals are, in turn, constrained by the law and the lawyer's ethical obligations. Individual decisions within the case are further constrained by the strategic implications those decisions may have on other aspects of the case.

...

If we have provided students with enough resources in the course materials, students should be able to identify the relevant statutory provision and ethical rules with some ease. If not, we can help the student locate relevant resources in the supervision session. When the lawyer's ethical obligations appear to conflict with the law …, the student may add new options to the list of alternatives.

…

3. Identify the Advantages and Disadvantages of Every Option

Only after we have identified all the options and examined all the ethical, personal, and strategic considerations can we begin to compare the alternatives. We compare alternatives by weighing the advantages and disadvantages of each. The questions I ask to advance the students' analysis include: *What are the consequences that might flow from any choice we make? What is the likelihood that those consequences will occur? What are the advantages of each alternative?* and *What is the likelihood that those advantages will be realized?*

…

These lists [of consequences] can be expanded and replicated for each of the alternatives identified. Ideally, students will come to supervision with some predictions about the likelihood that any potential advantage or consequence will be realized, but experience suggests that students need the most help with these assessments.

…

4. Select the Best (or a Best) Option and Rank the Others if Need Be

After we walk through the decision-making framework, students often want to know what I would do. I try to be disciplined in encouraging students to share their own views and rank the options they prefer first before I offer my own opinion. Assuming students will be more willing to share if they believe they will not be judged, I offer the clinic as a safe space for students to meaningfully explore their preferences, share unpopular views, and even articulate their personal and moral discomfort with a client's choice. Creating a safe space does not mean that we will condone racist or classist views or allow our students to violate the law or code of professional responsibility, but it does mean that our students will have the space to learn and grow through an honest exchange of ideas.

Obviously, a decision-making framework as structured as the one I discuss here will not eliminate decision fatigue all together. It may even increase fatigue at the beginning of the semester when students are first learning how to use the method. Those students who are used to thinking about problems and questions as one-dimensional will be stretched as they begin to identify and unpack additional layers. The framework might also increase fatigue if it is overused on simple or unresolvable problems. New lawyers often have a hard time figuring out which issues require careful consideration of the advantages and disadvantages of each option and which ones simply cannot be "fixed," even with a labored analysis. Good judgment and experience over time will help students focus on those problems that will benefit most from the decision-making framework.

...

Sometimes all of the options are undesirable, and the student faces a "Hobson's Choice." In supervision, she must grapple with this question: *Which is the least bad choice*? Students must learn to be "comfortable" with that reality and be prepared to advise clients under these circumstances. Unfortunately, our student's effort to ensure justice and fairness for her client will often be undermined by bias and differential treatment based on the client's race, class, and immigration status. Although students should always think expansively about how to right these wrongs and should never be comfortable with the injustices they see in the system, lawyers and clients must also learn to operate immediately and productively within the confines of an unjust system. Lawyers must help clients decide whether to accept an unfavorable plea, choose the best defense in the face of a skeptical fact-finder, and think about whether to encourage clients to comply with court-imposed conditions they deem unfair. Thus, students must continue to develop and exercise effective decision-making skills even as their evolving professional identity encourages them to challenge the broader systemic injustice.

5. Advise the Client: Visual Aids and Client Counseling

Good decision making in the legal context is an important component of client-centered lawyering. Clients look to lawyers for expertise, predictions, and judgment on how to identify and analyze the options they have. A structured decision-making framework not only helps students make good decisions regarding the "means" by which to achieve the client's ultimate goals and outcomes, but it also helps students counsel their clients on the "ends" to be achieved. In the latter context, the lawyer must do more than identify the best course of action. The lawyer must present all the options objectively and provide advice to help the client evaluate the advantages and disadvantages of each option and choose the best alternative.

Unfortunately, new lawyers often make the mistake of subtly manipulating their clients to pursue the lawyer's recommended course of action. Lawyers may unduly influence client decisions by controlling the content and sequence of information shared with the client, interrupting or ignoring the client's questions, framing decisions in a narrow or one-dimensional lens, withholding information altogether, or strategically arranging the list of options to exaggerate or emphasize negative or positive outcomes. To guard against the manipulative power of client counseling, effective decision-making skills must be paired with good client counseling. Students may create charts and other aids to help the client visualize and evaluate the range of alternatives, consequences, and likely advantages.

Importance of Transparency and Consistency

Of course, the proposed decision-making framework is only as good as the faculty who teach and enforce it. As clinicians, we may introduce and reinforce the framework throughout the clinic curriculum. Transparency at the beginning of the semester helps students understand the importance of the method. We may incorporate "decision making" into our written evaluation criteria by spelling out the components of the framework and letting students know they will be evaluated on each component of the analysis. As with all evaluation criteria, we hope students will recognize good decision making as important not only to their grade, but also as a fundamental skill for good lawyering.

Students should know that although "our door is always open" for questions, we expect them to use the resources available to them and come to supervision with their own ideas. We expect them to identify the options and reason through the possibilities before they meet with us, reserving the scarce time of supervision for the more difficult questions that often implicate values, judgment, lawyer-client dynamics, the meaning of social justice, the student's professional identity, and the emotional complexity of any legal decision.

...

Decision making is a learned skill, and like any effective learning method, the decision-making framework takes time and commitment. With experience and encouragement, students should become more thorough in their identification of the available options, ethical considerations, and the strategic advantages and disadvantages of each alternative. By the end the semester, I hope students will not only learn the mechanics of good decision making that save time in supervision, but also learn to exercise wisdom and good judgment in choosing the best option.

...

Endnotes

1. This quote is often attributed to Aristotle, but Will Durant might have written it in 1936 when discussing Aristotle in his book, THE STORY OF PHILOSOPHY. *See* Caelan Huntress, *My Favourite Quote of All Time Is a Misattribution*, MEDIUM (Aug. 24, 2017), https://medium.com/the-mission/my-favourite-quote-of-all-time-is-a-misattribution-66356f22843d.

2. Phyllis Goldfarb, *A Theory-Practice Spiral: The Ethics of Feminism and Clinical Education*, 75 MINN. L. REV. 1599 (1991).

3. *See generally* Ann Shalleck, *Clinical Contexts: Theory and Practice in Law and Supervision*, 21 N.Y.U. REV. L. & SOC. CHANGE 109 (1993) (discussing the various places in which supervision can take place and the need for efficiency in choosing the appropriate venue to transmit learning).

4. *See generally id.*

5. Robert Dinerstein, *Report of the Committee on the Future of the In-House Clinic*, 42 J. LEGAL EDUC. 511, 516 (1992).

6. Judith Taack Lanier, *Redefining the Role of the Teacher: It's a Multifaceted Profession*, GEORGE LUCAS EDUC. FOUND.: EDUTOPIA (July 1, 1997), https://www.edutopia.org/redefining-role-teacher.

7. *Cf.* William P. Quigley, *Introduction to Clinical Teaching for the New Clinical Law Professor: A View from the First Floor*, 28 AKRON L. REV. 463, 471 (1995) (describing twin goals of clinical education as "educat[ing] students in a new way of learning" and "provid[ing] legal services to the indigent").

8. *See, e.g., id.* at 474 ("Clinical education, at its essence, is a process of learning how to learn from experience.").

9. *Intervention*, Merriam-Webster Dictionary, https://www.merriam-webster.com/dictionary/intervention.

10. All state student practice rules make clinic supervisors responsible for their students' actions. *See* Wallace J. Mlyniec & Haley D. Etchison, *Conceptualizing Student Practice for the 21st Century: Educational and Ethical Considerations in Modernizing the District of Columbia Student Practice Rules*, 28 GEO. J. LEGAL ETHICS 207 (2015).

11. James H. Stark, Jon Bauer & James Papillo, *Directiveness in Clinical Supervision*, 3 B.U. PUB. INT. L.J. 35 (1993).

12. Anna E. Carpenter, *The Project Model of Clinical Education: Eight Principles to Maximize Student Learning and Social Justice Impact*, 20 CLINICAL. L. REV. 39, 67 (2013).

13. *Id.* at 69 ("A troublesome aspect of the directiveness dichotomy is that it presents a technocratic view of supervision, suggesting that supervision involves only discrete and individual reactions, isolated from context, and that certain supervision choices are always wrong or always right.").

14. Stephen D. Brookfield, THE SKILLFUL TEACHER: ON TECHNIQUE, TRUST, AND RESPONSIVENESS IN THE CLASSROOM 169 (2d ed. 2006). Brookfield adopted the phrase from Ira Shore & Paulo Freire, A PEDAGOGY FOR LIBERATION: DIALOGUES ON TRANSFORMING EDUCATION (1987).

15. Saul McLeod, *Vygotsky's Zone of Proximal Development and Scaffolding Theory*, SIMPLY PSYCHOLOGY, https://www.simplypsychology.org/zone-of-proximal-development.html.

16. I was first made aware of the Zone of Proximal Development theory during a presentation by Professors Deborah Epstein and Rachel Camp at the 2nd Mid-Atlantic Clinical Conference at the University Of Maryland Carey School Of Law in 2024.

17. McLoed, *supra* note 15.

18. *Cf.* Sherri Lee Keene, *Teaching Dissents*, 107 MINN. L. REV. 2619, 2621 (2023) ("The very presence of dissents challenges the myth of legal decision-making as objective and straightforward; in speaking back to court opinions, dissents lay bare the complexities and reveal points of ambiguity in cases.... The inability to talk about law in a deeper and more hopeful way in the law school setting is

not hard to understand given law schools' traditional approach of teaching law primarily through the reading of appellate legal opinions.").

19. *Id.*

20. Peter Toll Hoffman, *The Stages of the Clinical Supervisory Relationship*, 4 ANTIOCH L.J. 301, 302 (1986).

21. *Id.* at 302.

22. Quigley, *supra* note 7, at 485.

23. *See generally* Hoffman, *supra* note 20.

24. *Id.* at 302–03.

25. *See id.* at 303.

26. *Id.* at 303–05.

27. *Id.*

28. *Id.* at 306.

29. *Id.* at 305–06.

30. *Id.* at 309.

31. *Id.* at 307.

32. *See id.*

33. *Id.*

34. *Id.*; *see also* Donna Lee, *Supervision Stories: Identifying and Engaging Professional Identity Issues*, *in* TRANSFORMING THE EDUCATION OF LAWYERS: THE THEORY AND PRACTICE OF CLINICAL PEDAGOGY (Susan J. Bryant, Elliott S. Milstein & Ann Shalleck, eds., 2014); Shalleck, *supra* note 3, at 140 ("Students in clinical courses have a unique opportunity to combine analysis of their own experience with critical, systemic analysis. Seeing, participating in, and, most importantly, reflecting upon the law in action provides the student with an opportunity for engaging in self-conscious critical analysis of legal institutions, rules, and procedures that is rooted in, yet transcends, the student's own experience.").

35. Hoffman, *supra* note 20, at 309.

36. *Id.* Readers should keep this concept—the importance of supervisors recognizing when students are in the ballpark of reasonable choices about which practitioners may disagree and deferring to the student's reasonable selection among those choices—in mind in the next chapter, Chapter 5, which addresses supervising student writing in clinics. In choosing among multiple acceptable options of case strategy, just as with writing style, it can be easy for supervisors to unnecessarily impose their own ideals onto the student. However, proper clinical pedagogy requires supervisors to make more intentional decisions about whether, when, and how to show or tell the student how the supervisor would do things. *See infra*, Chapter 5; Angela J. Campbell, *Teaching Advanced Legal Writing in a Law School Clinic*, 24 SETON HALL L. REV. 653, 688 (1993) (discussing how teachers should "avoid imposing their 'ideal text' on students" (quoting C.H. Knoblauch & Lil Brannon, THE RHETORICAL TRADITIONS AND THE TEACHING OF WRITING 120 (1984))).

37. Hoffman, *supra* note 20, at 309.

38. This five-question concept is adapted from a similar four-question concept taught to Georgetown's clinical fellows by Professors Rachel Camp and Kristin Henning.

39. The purpose of formal formative assessment sessions is described in a Chapter 13.

40. *See generally* Fran Quigley, *Seizing the Disorienting Moment*, 2 CLINICAL. L. REV. 37 (1995).

41. Anne D. Gordon, *Better Than Our Biases: Using Psychological Research to Inform Our Approach to Inclusive, Effective Feedback*, 27 CLINICAL. L. REV. 195, 197–216 (2021).

42. *Id.* at 227–36.

43. Kristin Henning, *Combating Decision Fatigue in Supervision, in* Bryant et al., eds., *supra* note 344, at 233.

44. This four-stage structure is taught to Georgetown's clinical fellows by Professors John Copacino and Deborah Epstein.

45. The *Paper Chase* is a 1973 American comedy-drama film starring Timothy Bottoms, Lindsay Wagner, and John Houseman still popular with current law students. It is based on 1971 novel John Jay Osborn Jr.'s telling the story of a first-year law student experience with a draconian professor at Harvard Law School. For critiques of the Socratic Method—or, at least, critiques of it as it is often applied in the traditional law school classroom taught by podium faculty—see, e.g., Judith A. Gunderson, *Leaving Langdell Behind: Reimagining Legal Education for a New Era*, 107 MINN. L. REV. 2407, 2418–20 (2023) (critiquing the Socratic Method's focus on legal education as a vehicle for training students to start "thinking like" a lawyer rather than "*doing* or *being*" a lawyer in a more skills-based way); Dev A. Patel, *In HLS Classes, Women Fall Behind*, THE CRIMSON (May 8, 2013), https://www.thecrimson.com/article/2013/5/8/law-school-gender-classroom/?page=single (discussing disparate impact of Socratic Method on women's classroom participation and experience in law school; "Harvard Law student Jessica R. Jensen hates the Socratic method. 'It's the worst thing in the world,' she said. 'It forces you to talk like a man.'"); *see also* Jeannie Suk Gersen, *The Socratic Method in the Age of Trauma*, 130 HARV. L. REV. 2320 (2017); Beth Hirschfelder Wilensky, *Dethroning Langdell*, 107 MINN. L. REV. 2701 (2023). For a contrary view, see, e.g., *Teaching Tips, The Socratic Method: Fostering Critical Thinking*, COLORADO STATE UNIVERSITY, THE INSTITUTE FOR LEARNING AND TEACHING, https://tilt.colostate.edu/the-socratic-method/.

46. Anthony S. Niedwiecki, *Lawyers and Learning: A Metacognitive Approach to Legal Education*, 13 WIDENER L. REV. 33, 42 (2006) [hereinafter, Niedwiecki, *Lawyers and Learning*].

47. *Id.* at 43.

48. *Id.* at 35.

49. *Id.* at 35 (defining metacognition as "awareness and control over one's learning and thinking"); John H. Flavell, *Metacognitive Aspects of Problem Solving*, in THE NATURE OF INTELLIGENCE 231 (Lauren B. Resnick ed., 1976) (defining metacognition as "one's knowledge concerning one's own cognitive processes and products, or anything related to them").

50. *Id.* at 43; E. Scott Fruehwald, *How to Help Students from Disadvantaged Backgrounds Succeed in Law School*, 1 TEX. A&M L. REV. 83, 106 (2013); Anthony Niedwiecki, *Teaching for Lifelong Learning: Improving the Metacognitive Skills of Law Students Through More Effective Formative Assessment Techniques*, 40 CAP. U.L. REV. 149, 159 (2012) [hereinafter, Niedwiecki, *Teaching for Lifelong Learning*].

51. Niedwiecki, *Teaching for Lifelong Learning*, *supra* note 50, at 159.

52. *Id.* at 161.

53. Fruehwald, *supra* note 50, at 106.

54. *Id.*

55. *Id.*

56. Gregory Schraw, *Promoting General Metacognitive Awareness*, 26 INSTRUCTIONAL SCI. 113, 114 (1998).

57. Fruehwald, *supra* note 50, at 106.

58. Schraw, *supra* note 56, at 114.

59. Fruehwald, *supra* note 50, at 106–07.

60. Schraw, *supra* note 56, at 114.

61. Fruehwald, *supra* note 50, at 107.

62. Schraw, *supra* note 56, at 114.

63. Goldfarb, *supra* note 2.

64. Deborah Epstein, Jane Aiken & Wallace Mlyniec, TEACHING THE CLINIC SEMINAR 7 (2014) (citing Morris L. Bigge & S. Samuel Shermis, LEARNING THEORIES FOR TEACHERS (1992)).

65. *Id.* (Grant Wiggins, *Granted,and . . . Thoughts on Education A Clarification of the Goal of Transfer and How It Relates to Testing*, AUTHENTIC EDUCATION, (Oct. 3, 2012), https://authenticeducation.org/a-clarification-of-the-goal-of-transfer-and-how-it-relates-to-testing/.

66. *Id.* at 8.

67. *Id.* (citing Grant Wiggins, Founder and President, Authentic Education, Presentation at the Georgetown Summer Institute on Clinical Teaching (June 18, 2008)).

68. *Id.* at 3–4.

69. *See* Ruth Vance & Susan Stuart, *Of Moby Dick and Tartar Sauce: The Academically Underprepared Law Student and the Curse of Overconfidence*, 53 DUQ. L. REV. 133, 148 (2015).

70. Niedwiecki, *Teaching for Lifelong Learning*, *supra* note 50, at 155.

71. *See* Craig Chappelow & Cindy McCauley, *What Good Feedback Really Looks Like*, HARV. BUS. REV. (May 13, 2019), https://hbr.org/2019/05/what-good-feedback-really-looks-like.

72. *See id.*

73. *See* Beryl Blaustone, *Teaching Law Students to Self-Critique and to Develop Critical Clinical Self Awareness in Performance*, 13 CLINICAL. L. REV. 143, 148 (2002).

74. Victor D. Quintanilla & Sam Erman, *Mindsets in Legal Education*, 69 J. LEGAL EDUC. 412, 419 (2020); *see also* Peter G. Glenn, *Lessons from Psychology for Law Practice Management*, 126 DICK. L. REV. 575 (2022); Kaci Bishop, *Framing Failure in the Legal Classroom: Techniques for Encouraging Growth and Resilience*, 70 U. ARK L. REV. 959, 966 (2018) (explaining "how law professors can teach their students how to respond productively when facing failure").

75. *See infra*, Chapter 6 for a discussion of case rounds.

76. *See infra*, Chapters 7 and 8 (Values and Assumption), 9 (Ethics), and 10 (Supervising Issues Relating to Race Cultural Difference).

77. Quigley, *supra* note 40, at 51.

78. Schemas are broad, pervasive themes regarding oneself and one's relationship with others, developed during childhood and elaborated throughout one's lifetime, and are often dysfunctional to a significant degree. *See, e.g.*, Shohreh Rahimian & Tooraj Ghaffary, *Schema Therapy as a Treatment for Chronic Disorders*, 4 INDIAN J. SCI. RES. 437, 438–39 (2014); Ella Salgó, Bettina Bajzát & Zsolt Unoka, *Schema Modes and Their Associations with Emotion Regulation, Mindfulness, and Self-Compassion Among Patients with Personality Disorders*, 8 BORDERLINE PERSONALITY DISORDER AND EMOTION DYSREGULATION 19 (2021).

79. *See generally* Donald Schön, *The Reflective Practitioner, and the Comparative Failures of Legal Education*, 6 CLINICAL. L. REV. 401 (2000).

80. *See* Bishop, *supra* note 74, at 960.

81. Some of my thinking about failure was enhanced by a discussion about failure at the 2nd Mid-Atlantic Clinical Conference in 2024 led by Associate Dean Lori Kohn from George Washington Law School, Professor Brad Colbert from Mitchell-Hamline Law School, and Professor Mira Edmonds from the University of Michigan Law School.

82. *See* Bishop, *supra* note 74, at 961–63.

83. *Id.* at 961–62.

84. *See* Huntress, *supra* note 1.

85. *See generally*, Bishop, *supra* note 74.

86. Lanier, *supra* note 6.

87. *See* Chapter 13 *infra*, for a discussion of formative assessment, and Chapter 14 *infra*, for a discussion of summative assessment or grading.

88. *See generally,* Bishop, *supra* note 74.

89. *See, e.g.*, Karen Sloan, *Stress and Overwork Linked to Lawyers' Suicidal Thoughts, Study Says*, Reuters (Feb. 14, 2023, 9:50 AM), https://www.reuters.com/legal/litigation/stress-overwork-linked-lawyers-suicidal-thoughts-study-says-2023-02-13/ ("Lawyers facing high stress, overwork and loneliness are more likely to contemplate suicide, a new study has found, adding to a growing body of research on mental health challenges facing the legal profession."); Amanda Robert, *Mental Health Initiatives Aren't Curbing Lawyer Stress and Anxiety, New Study Shows*, ABA Journal (May 19, 2023), https://www.abajournal.com/news/article/mental-health-initiatives-arent-curbing-lawyer-stress-and-anxiety-new-study-shows ("Despite increasing focus on mental health and well-being in the legal profession, lawyers are reportedly dealing with more stress, anxiety and depression[.] ... About 71% of the nearly 3,000 lawyers surveyed this year said they had anxiety, which represents a 5% increase from 2022[.]").

90. *See, e.g.*, *New Study on Lawyer Well-Being Reveals Serious Concerns for Legal Profession*, Am. Bar Ass'n (Dec. 2017), https://www.americanbar.org/news/abanews/publications/youraba/2017/december-2017/secrecy-and-fear-of-stigma-among-the-barriers-to-lawyer-well-bei/ (noting that recent research showed that "25 percent of law students are at risk for alcoholism," "17 percent of law students suffer from depression," "37 percent of law students report mild to severe anxiety," and "6 percent of law students report having suicidal thoughts in the last year") (citing Jerome M. Organ, David B. Jaffe & Katherine M. Bender, *Suffering in Silence: The Survey of Law Student Well-Being and the Reluctance of Law Students to Seek Help for Substance Use and Mental Health Concerns*, 66 J. Legal Educ. 116 (2016)).

91. *See, e.g.*, Ronald Tyler, *The First Thing We Do, Let's Heal All the Law Students: Incorporating Self-Care into a Criminal Defense Clinic*, 21 Berkeley J. Crim. L. 1, 7–9 (2016).

92. Supervision Rounds resemble the Case Rounds sessions described in Chapter 7. Clinical teachers use when working with students on a troublesome issue related to their case or project. Supervisors use the same process among themselves when discussing difficult supervision issues.

93. *E.g.*, Tyler, *supra* note 91, at 3–9.

94. This issue is more broadly discussed in Chapter 10.

95. Professor Colleen F. Shanahan and Emily A. Benfer refer to the Adaptive Supervision method in their article, *Adaptive Clinical Teaching*, 19 Clinical L. Rev. 517 (20120. Robert Rando, Director of the Center for Psychological Services and an Associate Professor at Wright State University, describes the "adaptive" approach to supervision of social work, https://ubwp.buffalo.edu/ccvillage/wp-content/uploads/sites/74/2017/06/AdaptiveSupervision-Rando.pdf.

96. *See, e.g.*, Karen Sloan, *"Our Law Students Need Help." Study Finds Higher Rates of Mental Health Problems*, Reuters (July 13, 2022, 2:55 PM), https://www.reuters.com/legal/legalindustry/our-law-students-need-help-study-finds-higher-rates-mental-health-problems-2022-07-13/ ("Today's law students are dealing with mental health challenges including anxiety and depression at a higher rate than their predecessors in 2014, a new study has found. Nearly 69% of respondents from 39 law schools surveyed in 2021 reported that they needed help for emotional or mental health problems in the past year. That's up from 42% from the 2014 version of the same survey [.]"); *cf.* Tyler, *supra* note 91, at 9–14.

97. *See, e.g.*, Sarah Brown & Alexander C. Kafka, *Covid-19 has Worsened the Student Mental-Health Crisis. Can Resilience Training Fix It?*, Chron. Higher Educ. (May 11, 2020),), https://www.chronicle.com/article/covid-19-has-worsened-the-student-mental-health-crisis-can-resilience-training-fix-it/; Karen Sloan, *Law Students Report Exhaustion, Anxiety, Food Insecurity Amid Pandemic*, Reuters (Nov. 1, 2021, 5:22 PM), https://www.reuters.com/legal/legalindustry/law-students-report-exhaustion-anxiety-food-insecurity-amid-pandemic-2021-11-01/; Michael Fore & Erin Stevenson, *The Impact of Covid-19 Pandemic on Overall Well-Being of Practicing Lawyers*, 18 PLOS One 1 (2023).

98. *See generally, e.g.*, Alfredo Córdova, Alberto Caballero-García, Franchek Drobnic, Enrique Roche & David C. Noriega, *Influence of Stress and Emotions in the Learning Process: The Example of COVID-19 on University Students: A Narrative Review*, 11 Healthcare 1787 (2023).

99. *See, e.g.*, Minna J. Kotkin, *Reconsidering Role Assumption in Clinical Education*, 19 New Mex. L. R. 187, 194–95 (1989) (describing how different student learning styles mesh—or clash—with aspects of clinical pedagogy).

100. Donald A. Schön, The Reflective Practitioner: How Professionals Think In Action 68, 275–83 (1983); *see also* Richard K. Neumann, Jr., *Donald Schön,* The Reflective Practitioner, *and the Comparative Failures of Legal Education*, 6 Clinical. L. Rev. 401 (2000) (surveying Schön's work, summarizing its insights, and suggesting ways to expand upon it).

101. *See* Schön, *supra* note 100, at 69.

Five

SPECIAL CONSIDERATION FOR SUPERVISING WRITING PROJECTS

Different Clinics, Different Tasks

Some teachers believe that supervising a clinical student's writing project is completely different from supervising other lawyering activities that typically happen live, in real time, and in person. Investigations, client and witness interviews, client counseling, oral advocacy at hearings before courts and other judicial tribunals, and presentations to clients, committee staff, or legislators all may generate outlines, or even drafts of what the students will say aloud. But supervising those actions takes place, for the most part, in face-to-face conversations with the student. Some teachers believe that writing only happens on the student's own time and outside the presence of the supervisor. Therefore, they mistakenly think of the student's writing as a clinic lawyering activity in which the teacher intervenes only after the student has "finished" the document and submits it for review by the supervisor. The supervisors then comment and make suggestions throughout the draft and then send the document back to the student for additional work. As explained more fully below, clinical teachers need to develop a more nuanced understanding of supervision and intervention with student writing projects and convey that understanding to the student before any writing or research takes place.

Although differences in the intervention modalities used to supervise writing projects may exist, the same questions about strategies arise whether one supervises a writing project or a non-writing project. The intervention differences arise less from the lawyering tasks associated with producing written documents than from the context in which the students are performing the tasks or the posture of the case or project. That said, there are differences in both the nature of the teacher's intervention and in the modalities they use to bring the student's final product to completion. For example, clinicians often say they intervene more robustly into writing projects than they do when supervising non-writing tasks. There are several reasons why this occurs.[1] As Professor Angela Campbell notes, collaboration is logistically easier for writing projects than speaking-based projects. Additionally, "the line between the planning and performance stages is blurred" within the sphere of writing through multiple rounds of revisions.[2] Meanwhile, one of the main reasons *not* to intervene in other settings—the risk of harming the student-client relationship by appearing to correct or undercut the student's performance in front of the client—is less likely to occur with writing projects. The client either "expect[s] such intervention or will be unaware of it" entirely, because it happens behind the scenes, before the client sees the document and before it is filed.[3] More fundamentally, a shift in the pedagogy of writing that now "view[s] writing as a process rather than a product" also makes intervention more likely.[4]

On a more generalized note, modern law practice is extremely collaborative,[5] unless one is a solo practitioner.[6] Even when practicing alone, however, many if not most, lawyers seek out advice from other lawyers they know and trust. This is especially true when it comes to writing trial or appellate briefs or policy documents. Lawyers almost always prepare multiple drafts of the document and subject them to critique by other lawyers in their firm or public interest organization before the final product is submitted. Indeed, briefs and policy papers are often collaboratively written. Certain sections are assigned to several different lawyers, who then submit their sections to a member of the team to organize the various sections into a coherent document. Even simpler documents like emails, letters, retainer agreements, straightforward wills, and pleadings are often the product of multiple lawyers.

This kind of collaboration has always been a hallmark of clinical education. This is true irrespective of the subject matter of the clinic course. Although most early clinical courses were devoted to cases litigated in trial courts and administrative agencies,[7] modern clinical courses have expanded their subject matter to a wide range of legislative, transactional, regulatory, human rights, and agency work where students litigate matters and advise clients using written documents, rather than (only) on-your-feet oral advocacy.[8] Despite this growth in nonlitigation clinics, law school clinics remain predominantly focused on litigation or dispute resolution. In the 2022–2023 Center for the Study of Applied Legal Education (CSALE)] survey, schools reported that "49% of overall clinic work is primarily focused on litigation, 7% alternative dispute resolution, 18% transactional, 13% legislative or policy work, 8% regulatory/ administrative law, and 5% other legal types."[9]

Appellate clinics, which combine both oral and written advocacy, have been a staple of clinical education for a long time.[10] Even students in traditional trial-court clinics will probably draft at least some letters to clients and opposing counsel, pleadings or motions for various types of relief, or jury instructions and bench briefs during their clinic semester. Some of these documents will not be read by their audience in the same ways that a typical brief or motion would be. Instead, the client's legal position will be read or argued aloud by the student from a written document. For example, a student may write an opening statement or closing argument and then deliver it orally at a hearing, No matter how the writing is ultimately used, the same principles of supervision discussed in this chapter will apply.

In a typical clinic course, a student's or team's emails, letters, memos, pleadings, briefs, and policy papers will likely be scrutinized several times by a supervisor to both improve the students' writing, and to ensure that clients' interests and confidentiality are preserved. In the end, like Theseus' ship, the changes from the first draft to the final draft may ultimately alter the identity of the document.[11] It may also be difficult to decipher what the work of each student on the team is or even what the faculty supervisor's contribution is. That is the nature of the collaborative process that occurs as the writing project moves from early discussions of its goals, audience, strategy, and tone to the final written product.

The nature of the product creates other reasons why some supervisors view a student's writing differently from what occurs in the typical face-to-face supervision session. The supervision of non-writing lawyering activities usually, but not always, begins with a face-to-face conversation with the faculty supervisor. Multiple supervision sessions will continue using various modalities, like those previously described in Chapter Four, to intervene in the students' work. Supervisors use Socratic inquiry, role plays, and moots of the performance to guide the student through the planning process to the final moot before the actual hearing takes place. These face-to-face interventions unfold iteratively in a give-and-take fashion. Although planning and preparing is essential, ultimately the execution of the task, whether it is a conversation or negotiation with opposing counsel, a witness interview in the field, or a cross-examination at a hearing, is the final lawyering act. Although the supervisor may be sitting next to the student as the act is performed, the execution is often out of the supervisor's complete control.

Students sometime execute the final lawyering act without a supervisor present. Supervisors seldom accompany students on investigations or sit in on every phone call. Many even permit students to conduct witness interviews and client counseling sessions alone. Depending on the forum, teachers are sometimes prohibited by tribunal rules or judicial idiosyncrasies from speaking at a hearing. As a result, students will sometimes be on their own, figuratively or literally, as they execute the lawyering task. In that space, unplanned scenarios sometimes arise during those culminating acts. Indeed, unpredictability is as much a hallmark of lawyering (both in and out of court) as it is everyday human behavior. Those realities are front and center in clinic.[12] So while supervisors help students prepare for every possible contingency and to expect the unexpected, situations for which students are unprepared can and do arise. They are then discussed after the hearing or task is completed during a reflective post-performance critique session.

In writing-focused clinics, however, the final lawyering act is the completion of the brief, policy paper, proposed statute, letter, or any other document sent to another person. The document will not be filed until the supervisor is satisfied that all contingencies have been explored in advance and accounted for. There will be no unexpected or unprepared-for experiences, and the post-performance critique will have occurred before the document is filed. Of course, opposition motions and reply briefs from opposing counsel may follow. But those developments will spawn an entirely new writing project.

Stages of the Writing Process

For the reasons noted above and others noted below, the supervision process for a writing project is different from other clinical activities. Students and supervisors in clinics where writing is the primary lawyering task usually have more time for the development of the final written document than students have in trial clinics. In trial-based clinics, there are many different lawyering tasks that have to be performed between client intake and the final hearing. When students in those clinics do get the chance to engage in writing tasks, the writing often takes place on a compressed timeline and with contextually defined expectations for what constitutes sufficient preparation and performance. Conversely, there are fewer discrete lawyering acts in a primarily writing-based clinic. Moreover, the work of a writing-focused clinic does not involve the number of personal interactions with other people that a student lawyer in a trial clinic undertakes before getting to the final hearing.

Writing-focused clinics require that students analyze the problem and potential solutions, conduct the research, develop a strategy, advise the client, and write the brief. Of course, those are not simple tasks, and several require many intricate steps as students navigate facts, law, and strategy. But for the most part, the facts are usually static (especially in an appellate clinic), client interactions may be fewer and are more controlled than in trial clinics, and the final activity—the production of the document—is for the most part controlled by the student and supervisor, rather than opposing counsel, judge, or other actors in the case or project. In addition, time limits governing the filing of documents in many writing-focused clinics are longer than the time limits in trial-based clinics. Thus, there is more time to plan for, and critique the execution of, both the mechanics and substance of the writing task.

Another difference is that unlike supervision for a non-writing task, written assignments are usually first reviewed and critiqued by the teacher outside the presence of the student and prior to a face-to-face conversation about the work product. To be sure, students begin to write after a series of supervision sessions to define the purpose of the document; assess strategy, necessary research, and document audience; and the plan for the production of the document. But then the student goes off and writes the *first* first draft of the document and submits it to the teacher when it is "finished." Students often assume that the first document they submit to a supervisor is their "first draft." But the true first draft usually is finished only after a series of drafts and interventions, where the faculty member guides the student to ensure that the purpose of the document reflects the client's interests and needs, the student's strategy for achieving them, the organization of the argument, and the audience to whom the document is addressed. Each of these multiple interventions may involve reorganizing the arguments of the document and new drafts of portions of the document that ultimately become the student's first full draft.

Once the student submits any draft, the supervisor usually reviews it alone and makes comments on the document. When this intervention is complete, the document is returned to the student who schedules an in-person supervision session. When reviewing the document alone during that first intervention, most faculty include some questions and comments in the margins or summary paragraphs for students to consider before the face-to-face meeting.[13] Given the context, supervisors might state outright that the draft seems to be addressing the wrong audience or may instead ask questions about the target audience. The supervisor might also ask the student to discuss the document's main arguments in the upcoming supervision session. In some cases, supervisors may even redraft portions of the argument. The written critique is then sent to the student for review in advance of a future in-person discussion, leaving the student to interpret it alone, on their own time.

Teachers in writing-focused clinics suggest that there are specific stages through which all writing projects should be processed. Most writers define their styles and process over time, but new writers seldom consider the stages that advance most writing projects. Students often think that writing begins after they have an idea and do some research to prepare the first draft. They often think that a first draft is just that: their first attempt to type up a completed document and press "send." On the other hand, teachers supervising student writing projects have developed a number of stages that are needed to produce the document, each with a specific purpose. In a five- or six-stage process,[14] the stage where students most likely think of as "writing," that is, the pen-to-paper or fingers-to-keyboards composition of sentences and paragraphs, actually happens somewhere in the middle.

The first stage of proper supervision of student writing begins with one or more sessions where the supervisor and student discuss the purpose of the document, the audience, and the client's goals and then define the process for achieving them. New students in writing-focused clinics often assume that they will be the sole author of the document, but that is seldom the case. Students in many writing-focused clinics co-author briefs in pairs or trios. Indeed, writing is a collaborative process in many clinics and law practices. This collaboration is not just between the novice writers and their supervisor who must sign off on the document. Multiple peers and colleagues can be involved in the collaboration. That is why it is critical to define the process and the responsibilities of the students and the supervisor in the first stage supervision before any writing actually takes place. Without this first stage, the other stages of the process may collapse.

Professor Robert Stumberg developed a five-stage process for developing a final written document: (1) Define the work and process; (2) Organize; (3) Compose; (4) Edit; and (5) Summarize.[15] I have collapsed his final two stages, Edit and Summarize, into one stage that I call the Final Document. Those stages are discussed below.

The First Stage: Define the Work and Process

There are many things to discuss in this first stage. Lawyers write many documents in the course of their practice. Some will be informative to explain a proposition to a client or to a decision-maker. Some will be persuasive to convince a judge, legislator, or other decision-maker to accept the client's position in a case or project. Some will be conclusive and legally binding documents like contracts or settlement agreements. The early supervision sessions during this first stage of the process seek to clarify the purpose, nature, audience, scope, and tone of the document with the student. Otherwise, the student's *first* first draft will likely be unresponsive to the clients' needs.

The time period required to prepare the final document should also be determined in the first stage. Time and other case-related needs create the context for the preparation and are critical factors for the document's completion. The time available between the first stage of the process to the required delivery of the document often controls both its length and the amount of research needed for an adequate explanation and argument. Timing also determines the number of drafts that can be prepared, and a determination of who and how many people will be involved in the writing project. If not already clear from the clinic orientation sessions, the student must understand role of the supervisor in the process. Deadlines for the completion of the separate drafts leading to the final document have to be set. Of course, planning is not infallible, and various aspects determined in the first stage will be subject to alteration as the supervision process evolves. But even the very act of building in "buffer time" so the timeline can accommodate unexpected contingencies is itself part of this initial planning stage.

The Second Stage: Organization

Once students understand the document's purpose, nature, scope, tone, and audience, they enter the second stage of the process: organization. Students often believe they intuitively understand what the document will look like when completed and begin composing prose sentences and paragraphs right away. This approach, however, seldom works. Ideas evolve while writing and additional information is discovered. That is because writing itself is a learning modality.[16] Through writing comes learning, and students often learn through writing that they have been on the wrong track. Arguments they once thought were solid may begin to evaporate and ideas thought to be sufficient may not lead to where a writer believes they would take them. The student may pursue a legal argument that ultimately cannot be supported by the facts that are currently known or the facts that can actually be proven. As a result, "[t]he very process of writing" in and of itself is a source and site of learning: it "exposes weaknesses in reasoning and authority and forces the [writer] to delve ever deeper into the problem to find root causes and their solutions."[17] There are many reasons a document may go off-track. One major cause is that the writer has not organized the argument properly in advance. That is why most writing teachers, clinical supervisors, and many writers themselves develop outlines before they begin to compose. Their own writing experiences lead many clinical supervisors to require outlines whether the students like them or not.

Outlines help to determine the flow of the argument or information, assess the necessity and order of various sections and subsections, and provide a road map to guide the student to a proper conclusion for the intended purpose. One function of an outline is to capture and organize the essential frame of analysis.

> What are the elements of a crime, a tort, a contract?... If the outline does not organize these elements, then the writing that follows will be inefficient if not wrong. Crucially, outlines require the student to make intentional choices in the planning and organizational process, and to make those choices in a way that is visible to the supervisor.[18]

Once the student submits the outline, the supervisor should provide comments that will themselves become the subject of another supervision session to both reflect on the student's choices and to determine the outline's efficacy.[19]

The Third Stage: Composition

Once the outline is completed, the third stage, composition, can begin. The process of supervising a writing project at this stage is not much different from supervising any element of any other case or project. The supervisor's goal is to strengthen the student's work without taking over the work itself. In trial-based clinics, supervisors discuss whether the action taken is directed toward the client's goals and whether the interview, direct- or cross-examination, or argument is sufficiently articulated to achieve them. Supervisors in writing-focused clinics take similar actions by reviewing multiple drafts of the document to ensure that it reflects the scope and purpose that they and the student identified at the first stage. The teacher and student will discuss the state of the outline to determine whether the document follows it appropriately, or if the outline itself requires an alteration. If the outline is appropriate and the document adheres to it, they will discuss whether the argument is supported by the research. If so, they will determine whether the student followed the outline so that the information or argument flows logically from one section or subsection to another, and whether the conclusion is properly related to the introduction. They will also review the tone of the explanation or argument and alter the language if it does not reflect the document's purpose as informational or persuasive, or if the tone of the document is not effective for its intended audience.

The Final Stage: The Final Document[20]

Students will submit many drafts during the third stage before the document is completed and ready to file. Questions about structure, organization of ideas, strength of analysis, the relationship between the audience and the style of a document, and the student's choice of content are far more important in early drafts than grammatical precision, word choice, and the minutiae of blue-book citations.[21] Students seldom come to the clinic understanding the concept of writing towards a goal, or how to marshal raw facts into a legal argument framed in an advocacy document. Teachers must lead the students to that understanding. Once a nearly final draft is completed, the fine-grained editing stage begins.[22] Supervisors comment on deletions, transitions, and necessary organizational changes. Clarity, grammar, punctuation, proper legal format, and culturally appropriate language and rules are fine-tuned.[23] When these are settled, student and faculty determine the need for a summary.[24]

Not all documents require a summary. The need for a summary depends on the nature, purpose, and audience. Clients may be less interested in all the steps the author used to support their position and more interested in the most important conclusions. In that case, an executive summary or an abstract will be necessary. Those may be especially important for policy-focused clinics, where legislative members often need talking points to precede the document itself. On the litigation side, however, judges and their clerks may be more inclined to read the entire document, paying attention to the logic, legal support, and the specific facts upon which a decision will rest. In that case, conclusions that are clear, concise, and precise will generally be sufficient.[25] These are strategic decisions rather than content decisions in the writing process. Nonetheless, they are critical to the proper completion of the document.

Commenting on Students' Documents

As noted earlier, these supervision sessions will occur in person, as they would in any kind of clinic. But supervising by commenting on drafts before a supervision session is a prominent form of supervision in clinics where writing is the primary skill performed. This is a critical difference between clinical settings where writing is the primary focus of the student's work and those where courtroom litigation is the focus of the student's work. "Fortunately, providing effective feedback [on a student's legal writing] is a skill that can be learned and over the years the legal writing academy has provided support for new teachers to develop successful critiquing strategies."[26] This learnable skill transfers seamlessly to writing-focused and trial-based clinics alike.

A growing body of literature has begun to discuss how legal-writing and clinical educators can collaborate to share teaching methods and support each other's professional status."[27] As noted earlier, once the clinic's mission has been defined and the nature and type of projects have been selected to further that mission, faculty must teach "students to pay attention to the rhetorical situation [i.e. the purpose, audience, topic, writer, and context they face when engaged in writing], clearly defining and communicating the clinician's and student's role, and providing feedback on drafts that is tailored to the writing process and the student's needs."[28] In assigning tasks to be completed by specific people on specific timelines, face-to-face supervision meetings that define the purpose, audience, and stance of the document, and explain the supervision method used in the clinic, are critical not only for the project but also for the ongoing relationship between supervisor and student.[29] Understanding the rhetorical situation paves the way for a clear understanding of the collaborative methods used to supervise writing projects, how the supervisor will provide comments, and how the student should interpret them. Although assigning particular tasks might be construed as a heavy-handed way to intervene, it is a necessary, intentional intervention *in context.* It reflects the supervisor's use of the full spectrum of intervention techniques, rather than using one categorically distinct version of intervention. Rather than diminishing the student's role in the development and ownership of the project, it reflects the collaborative nature of law practice generally, and experiential learning more specifically.

The number, nature, placement, subject, and tone of the supervisor's comments on a document are especially critical because they set the context for this particular assignment and establish the nature of the future relationship between student and teacher. Choosing what to comment on requires supervisors to make intentional choices about what to address and when. This approach has been called a "triage"[30] or a "feedback funnel."[31] The point is that, "[j]ust like the writing process itself, the supervisor's feedback can move like an upside down funnel from the broad to the narrow,"[32] with the focus shifting from big-picture analytical and organizational problems to fine-grained stylistic tweaks.[33] "Major flaws in the student's understanding of the substantive legal ideas and how those misunderstandings affect organizational choices in the student's paper need to be corrected before writing and stylistic problems can be effectively addressed. This is just another way of saying that 'good writing comes from good thinking.'"[34]

Once supervisors identify *what* in the student's writing warrants their attention at a particular stage of the process, they must then decide—once again, intentionally—*where* to comment on those issues. Different teachers use different methods when commenting. Asking probing questions in the margin is better than rewriting sentences or cut-and-paste reorganizing the draft. Some supervisors use long-form introductory comments at the start of the draft or conclusory comments at the end to give the questions posed in the margins some further context. Just as rewording or rewriting portions of the document merely changes the language on a particular page, reorganizing entire sections tells the student little more than that the supervisor likes things arranged that way. Neither intervention, by itself, helps the students understand *why* the changes were made. Nor do they help the student achieve the goals for the document itself. More importantly, they are not useful for building transferable skills. They do not lead the student to a greater understanding of document preparation process used for the current document or create knowledge that is transferable to other areas of legal practice. Granted, some students might benefit from reading the faculty member's rewrite. "Read lots of good writing" is a common maxim for how to improve oneself as a writer. But rewriting the student's document should not be undertaken precipitously, or without a prior discussion with the student about why that course of action is beneficial to the client and the student. Too much intervention may subtly prime the student to disengage from the iterative learning-by-writing process required for the rest of the assignment and for the remainder of clinic. If that occurs, students will not only miss valuable and necessary learning experiences, but the ownership of the entire project can move from the student to the supervisor. Referring back to Theseus' ship, it should not belong to Theseus. Theseus (and other collaborators) must belong to the ship.

Commenting Techniques

There are several ways to comment on student writing, and supervisors should use a mix of them to serve different purposes as needed. One tool is to provide line-by-line feedback, whether through "interlinear comments ... [meaning those] woven into the student's text and margin comments [meaning those] ... written on the side or bottom of the paper").[35] If supervisors comment directly into the student's Microsoft Word document electronically, they can use the Track Changes and Comments features to recreate handwritten interlinear or margin comments. On the other hand, a "narrative comment ... [meaning one] drafted in paragraph form separately from the student's paper"[36] provides a more holistic form of feedback that can complement line-by-line comments. Narrative comments, whether inserted at the beginning of a document as a preface or at the end as a summative conclusion, will allow a longer explanation of the supervisor's thoughts than will fit in an interlinear or margin comment. The latter should be shorter and crisper to avoid overwhelming the student visually. Moreover, the global nature of a longer-form narrative comment permits a synthesis of individual margin comments or interlinear comments that appear throughout the document, highlighting common themes in the feedback and helping students see both the forest and the trees.[37] Even still, specificity in referring students to particular portions of the document (or specific margin or interlinear comments) is helpful and necessary even in a summative narrative comment at the beginning or end of a piece.[38] For example, a narrative comment alerting students that their language is too casual for the formality of the document could pinpoint specific places in the document, flagged by margin comments where that problem appears.

Once the supervisor has intentionally determined through triage and funneling what to address in a particular round of comments and where and in what form the comments should appear in the student's document, the supervisor must intentionally decide how to calibrate the level of specificity and directiveness of the comment. Professor Daniel Barnett captures the considerations that must go into this calibration:

> Open-ended Socratic comments in which the teacher poses leading questions to help guide the student in finding the analytical solutions without providing the answer can be very effective because they help give the student the confidence to face complicated legal issues. Often, one or two well-designed questions will help many of the pieces of the analysis fall into place for the student. The key with Socratic comments is crafting questions that are open-ended but designed to lead the student to find the analytical solution on her own. A Socratic comment will fail if it simply poses vague questions just because the teacher does not want to "give the answer." At other times, more directed comments are required because the student has hit a substantive roadblock, and the only way to move forward is to get the student over that barrier. In those situations, open-ended, Socratic-type comments would not be helpful, and the teacher should be more directive. For example, there are times when the teacher should be as directive as saying something like, "I know the court seems to say 'x and y,' but does it really mean that? Or does the court really mean 'y and z?'" Other times, the teacher may be able to send the student back to a particular piece of authority to help guide the student through the issue without laying out the answer.[39]

Professor Barnett's advice again demonstrates the fluidity of the intervention process, showing how context determines its level of specificity and reminds us of the zone of proximal development discussed in earlier chapters. The common thread running through all of these commenting techniques, however, is intentionality. Every ounce of ink a supervisor adds to a student's written work in providing feedback must be the product of a thoughtful, intentional choice. This is true whether the comments are directive or indirective, phrased as a question or a statement, handwritten or typed, or produced as margin comments or longer summative notes.

The Audience of Me

Writing is often a personal expression of one's identity. Even when students say they enrolled in a clinic to improve their writing, they come with a sense of what they think they do well, and what they think needs improvement. Given that reality, faculty should be mindful of their tone, word choice, and empathy when making comments of any sort and in any place. Moreover, most writers' first drafts of books, articles, and documents are often written to oneself, for the "audience of me,"[40] rather than to an external audience. Students may have this tendency even more than experienced writers. This is true even though the student knows, at some level, that an external audience will be the ultimate reader of the document. By this, I mean that the writer is trying primarily to get the words out of their brain and onto the page.[41] As a result, the student is not just writing to "communicat[e] between person and person"—meaning between oneself and another person reading the document. Instead, the student is trying to communicate "between different parts of [one's own] mind."[42] Professor Donald Murray encapsulates the process of writing to, and with, oneself with this helpful visual:

> The act of writing might be described as a conversation between two workmen muttering to each other at the workbench. The self speaks, the other self listens and responds. The self proposes, the other self considers. The self makes, the other self evaluates. The two selves collaborate: a problem is spotted, discussed, defined; solutions are proposed, rejected, suggested, attempted, tested, discarded, accepted.[43]

This phenomenon is common to both novice and experienced writers. Often, one will hear experienced writers say, "It is time to kill your darlings."[44] By that, they mean that most writers are writing to themselves in early drafts but will later resolve to remove the parts that do not resonate with their readers or are either extraneous or inconsistent with the purpose of the document. New writers are especially hesitant to take this admittedly difficult but assuredly necessary step. As a result, the teacher's critique may take the student by surprise.

This also makes it especially important for supervisors to assume that students made their best effort, even when it may seem like the document is not actually the student's best work.[45] That best-effort assumption may or may not come naturally to faculty. Even an individual teacher's gut reaction about how hard they think a student worked on a particular piece of writing will vary from student to student, based on the teacher's preexisting knowledge of the student's capabilities and the professor's expectations for that student. But the point remains: teachers have to intentionally shape their own thought process when approaching student writing. This includes making the best-effort assumption, even though it may not come naturally in particular cases.

As noted earlier, students will most likely be alone when they first read the teacher's comments on a draft. As they read the comments, they will perceive these interventions either positively or negatively. How they interpret them, and their emotional reactions, may affect the upcoming face-to-face supervision session and may taint the interpersonal relationship between the teacher and the student going forward. That interpersonal disconnect can impede the student's learning and the development of the case or project. That is why early supervision sessions setting both the assignment of tasks and the scope and nature of the collaboration and supervision are critical to moving a project to a successful conclusion and establishing the trust relationship between student and faculty. Teachers have to be conscious of the student's sensibilities and need to learn how to convey the information to students in rigorous but not personally threatening ways.

All writers can be protective of the words they write, so teachers need to tailor the tone of their language and their choice of the words they use in their comments so that students understand that the critique is not personal. This is especially true when teachers suggest "killing their darlings." The critique should be directed toward achieving the client's interests and the student's learning goals. Such positive interventions with clear purpose and unambiguous language will produce more knowledgeable students who will ultimately be able to take more ownership of the document as the future drafts are developed. They will also result in better supervision sessions, provide the students with a greater understanding of the purpose of the intervention, and better prepare the student for transferring those skills to subsequent projects.

Hierarchy and Ownership

Aside from the purely personal interactions, the nature of the intervention and the language used may create a misunderstanding about clinic hierarchy and project ownership.[46] Even though clinical teachers attempt to minimize hierarchies in their clinic courses, hierarchies are inevitable. Professor David Gooblar aptly sums up the inherently hierarchical nature of supervising student writing.

> Students are behaving rationally when they are surprised to be asked for their opinions about their own writing. Part of that is relational, institutional, hierarchical. They wrote the draft because I, their instructor, assigned it, and because I, their instructor, will assess them for it with a grade that will, in part, determine whether they pass the course and get [academic] credit. Likewise, they attended our one-on-one conference because I invited them with the express purpose of giving them my presumably expert feedback. I am the expert;

> they are the novice. I have all the authority—within the institution and the discipline—and they have none. So I realize that my questions are not as harmless as they seem, and it's no surprise that students don't have ready answers.[47]

Although Professor Gooblar was writing about college-level students' writing, the hierarchies persist at the same level in law school and are even stronger in the clinic setting. Indeed, hierarchies are to some extent, ethically required in clinics, at least insofar as the teacher must assume the role of a superior in *supervising* the student.[48] Additionally, students see supervisors as "the expert" not only in writing, but also in the specific lawyering task at hand, and lawyering generally. That is true whether the lawyering task is cross-examination, negotiating with opposing counsel, or writing a brief or legislation. Nonetheless, the goal of a clinical course is to place the student in the role of a lawyer rather than that of a student, helping them become independent lifelong learners. That requires teachers to decenter themselves, shifting their focus away from exactly what they would do if they were managing the case or writing the document by themselves. Improperly focused comments can lead a student to believe that the finish line of the project is just emulating the faculty member's subjective, unique, or idiosyncratic notions about how the document should be written. That should not be the goal of the intervention, nor is it a goal of clinical education writ large. Instead, the comments on the paper and the conversations during the supervision sessions should be designed to guide the student's understanding of the drafting process and the strategy behind it, and to advance the student's own personal growth as a writer and a lawyer. Then the student can transfer those skills to other contexts later in the clinic and in their careers. Nonetheless, faculty cannot permit a less-than-exemplary piece of writing to be submitted on behalf of a client. The loose talk among some clinical faculty about student "ownership" of a work product is a goal, but the concept can become flawed if not handled properly. Although this is true in all clinics, it is especially true in writing clinics since the final document is the advocacy that the judge or legislator will consider.[49]

Moreover, students, like most people, are possessive and protective of their writing style. They are defensive when their written work is critiqued as imprecise, or worse, contains inappropriate or legally inaccurate arguments. This is especially true during the early interventions, when students are still unsure of the clinical method and interpret those comments as a personal attack. Negative experiences at the early stages of supervision can have ripple effects on students' confidence, their willingness to be vulnerable during the iterative writing-and-rewriting process going forward, and in their engagement in clinic. Faculty mismanagement of the commenting process may also lead students to feel like they are unlikely to become a successful lawyer.

There are several reasons for the crisis in confidence, but two in particular stand out here. First, students may blame themselves for the comments' imprecision or inappropriateness. They may think that a "better" student would have gotten either clearer or more appropriate comments in the first place or at least have more success deciphering the comments. Thus, they may feel that something must be wrong with them to get such comments or to not understand them. For example, if a teacher wrote "only label-like comments such as 'conclusory,' 'vague,' 'awkward,' 'no topic sentence,' etcetera, the teacher would not have provided enough information to help the student understand the flaw or the way to remedy it. Obviously, students do not think they are being 'conclusory' or 'vague' when they put the words on the page of the draft."[50] Second, students may think that because they are feeling hurt or dejected by the comments, they lack the "thick skin" that they imagine is required for practicing law out in the "real world." Both scenarios are perfectly natural and understandable responses by the students, and both are ultimately the faculty member's fault for not providing clearer or more appropriate comments in the first place.[51]

Simply put, much hangs in the balance when supervising student writing. Faculty members must ensure that their language does not result in an empathic breakdown, both when giving the comments in the first place and when working through the comments (and the student's reactions to them) during subsequent supervision sessions. Of course, such reactions can occur during supervision sessions in litigation clinics, as well as those where writing is the main lawyering task. But receiving comments on the paper while one cannot immediately ask clarifying questions, having a misguided understanding of the writing process, or experiencing the possessiveness that most new writers feel about their words can all intensify a student's reaction to the supervisor's written comments on a draft. As noted in Chapter Two, supervision must start from a place of generosity.

Supervision and Submission of the Document

A major difference between supervising written work and supervising oral hearings, negotiations, interviews, depositions, investigations, and other live lawyering tasks is that submitting the motion, brief, letter, or other document is the final act of both the legal task and the supervision sequence. In non-writing-focused clinics, many of the legal tasks take place orally after the supervision sessions end. In some cases, the task takes place without the presence of the supervisor or while the supervisor sits near but apart from the student when the questioning, negotiation, or argument takes place. Suggestions may be offered to the students as they present their case, but the critique of the final product takes place after the task is performed. In writing-focused clinics, however, all of the critique takes place in advance of the final performance—the submission of the document—and students never execute the final act alone. The performance and the post-performance critique of a student's written products are actually inseparable parts of the pre-performance planning and critique.[52] Thus, the teacher has more control over the execution of the end product. Indeed, many clinicians often express a greater desire and need for control over student writing than other aspects of students' work in clinic.[53] And the fact that the teacher's signature must go on the document means that mistakes in the final performance (the prepared written document as filed with the court or sent to a client, co-counsel, or other party) will seldom occur.

That said, errors and missteps can happen in clinic writing projects—both as accidents and as a result of intentional choices that do not land as well as the supervisor and student had expected. These developments are often revealed when an outside party engages with the student's writing. Opposing counsel filing an opposition to the motion may challenge the research or persuasiveness of the arguments. Judicial rulings on the issue presented in the submission may be rejected as non-persuasive, illogical, or simply incorrect. Those developments may reveal mistakes and missteps in the student's and supervisor's analysis and strategic choices made during the writing process. These adverse results warrant time and reflection in post-event supervision sessions. Often, these "postmortem" sessions can wait until the dust settles and work slows down on the case. Again, context will control. Indeed, the opposing party's response to the motion often sets in place a quick turnaround for a reply brief. Judges may require additional briefing about an issue, or their ruling may set up further proceedings in the case. There will always be time for reflecting on why these writing-related choices went wrong. Because of the collaborative nature of writing supervision, supervisors may have to candidly acknowledge their own strategic misjudgments, and students may have to face a negative result from their work. Choosing the right time for the postmortem becomes yet another intentional decision.

Faculty Reflection on the Writing Process

The pitfalls in supervising writing projects and commenting on documents as described above can and should be avoided. Supervisors should always be intentional and transparent in advance about the nature of the supervisory process and about their methods of intervention. However, doing so is even more important with writing projects because of the differences between supervising writing and supervising other legal tasks. Faculty supervisors need to be able to convey to students the methods and purposes of intervening into a writing task before the first written assignment and first set of comments. That helps the student understand the collaborative nature of clinic writing and that both the supervisor and student have some degree of ownership of the final product.[54]

From the beginning, teachers need to demonstrate that students don't have to reinvent the wheel to produce good legal writing. Certain conventions like citation form, the use of authority, and the prevalence of analogical reasoning differentiate a legal document from other forms of written communications. Students are likely more familiar with different forms and structures for writing from their pre-law school days. Nonetheless, good legal writing, at its core, is simply good writing in a different context. Students often forget this and become confused searching for ways to "formalize" a legal document or write "like a lawyer." This bogs down the prose in cumbersome legalese and frustrates students by focusing their time and energy on the wrong parts of the task at hand. Students seldom recognize that the skills they have as writers, or the conventions they already learned in their first-year legal research and writing courses, can be transferred to other writing projects they pursue in a clinic. Instead, they "*need to be taught* how to connect their clinical legal writing experiences to their previous legal writing instruction."[55] Moreover, teachers need to adapt their intervention techniques so that students learn these concepts and maximize their talents as they produce persuasive written documents. This involves, among other techniques, "more explicitly discussing *expectations* for the writing project before and during the writing process," using the same or similar terminology to describe the building blocks of legal writing and analysis, and modeling "appropriate solutions to real-world writing problems" when they inevitably arise.[56]

Much of this chapter involved mixing and matching concepts and theories from clinical pedagogy, on the one hand, and writing and legal-writing pedagogy on the other. But surprisingly little has been written about the intersection between basic legal-writing courses and supervising writing in the context of a clinical course. This chapter has attempted to make clear, and the accompanying readings will demonstrate, that although the same questions about intervention strategies arise when supervising writing projects and non-writing projects, the different contexts in which they occur demand differences in the nature of the teacher's response. Teachers must be aware of the discrete differences in modes and timing of intervention techniques when supervising writing projects. That knowledge will allow them to adapt the techniques used in general supervision sessions to writing projects when necessary to advance both client goals and student learning. The techniques described in the articles that follow have proven to be effective in helping clinic students and teachers gain knowledge about the process of writing. The articles also discuss learning substance through the process of writing, and suggest methods for reflection about the writing process.

Other Voices

Daniel L. Barnett, *Triage in the Trenches of the Legal Writing Course: The Theory and Methodology of Analytical Critique**

38 U. Tol. L. Rev. 651 (2007)

I. Introduction

...

Critiquing student work is also one of the most demanding elements of teaching legal writing because it is time consuming and intellectually challenging.... Commenting on student assignments is challenging because the teacher attempts to "get inside the head" of each student through the student's writing to help clarify complex legal analysis.

...

Critiquing student papers also is challenging because it requires the teacher to face the successes and failures of the teacher's own teaching. Each set of papers provides instant feedback about what worked or did not work in classes that were designed to help the students prepare the assignment.... Fortunately, providing effective feedback is a skill that can be learned and over the years the legal writing academy has provided support for new teachers to develop successful critiquing strategies.

...

Nevertheless, most legal writing professors learn how to comment on their students' papers by simply doing it. Over time, each teacher develops a method to help students refine the difficult reasoning and presentational skills that are required to effectively analyze and explain complex legal issues in writing.

...

II. Triage: Focus on Analysis First

Although legal writing teachers have many opinions about the best way to critique student work, one idea is critical: Legal writing teachers must learn to prioritize when commenting on student assignments. No teacher can, and no teacher should, attempt to deal with every problem when providing feedback on a student's paper. Limiting feedback is difficult for most novice writing teachers because new teachers feel like they are doing an inadequate job unless they comment on every problem they iden-

* Excerpts are reprinted with the permission of the author and the University of Toledo Law Review.

tify. But here is the problem: If the teacher is unable to prioritize the problems when critiquing the paper, the student will be unable to prioritize the issues that need to be addressed when rewriting the paper. The student will become overwhelmed. Typically, when overwhelmed, the student will focus on the smallest details when rewriting the assignment, ignoring the larger, more complex issues that should be corrected. Furthermore, if the teacher attempts to address every problem in most student papers, the teacher also will be overwhelmed and quickly become exhausted.

So, what is the answer? Triage. Just as a medical doctor must first treat the most life-threatening problems of a patient, the legal writing professor must focus on the most important issues when critiquing a student's paper. Therefore, the teacher must focus on analytical problems first. Major flaws in the student's understanding of the substantive legal ideas and how those misunderstandings affect organizational choices in the student's paper must be corrected before writing and stylistic problems can be effectively addressed.

The "process theory" of writing convinced most legal writing teachers that new methods were necessary to improve legal writing. At its core, "process theory" recognizes that writing is "not a smooth linear progression ... but instead is 'messy, recursive, convoluted, and uneven.'" Effective writers use writing and revision as a process to work out and develop the ideas that they are trying to explain. If writing is seen only as a final product, the process of working through the underlying ideas to clarify the concepts that the writer is describing is shortchanged or ignored altogether.

...

For feedback on draft assignments to help law students understand the importance of using the writing process to develop legal analysis, comments must assist students with the foundational reasoning skills that are necessary to prepare legal documents. Therefore, analytical and organizational issues should be the focus of the critique of the draft and comments on basic writing should be made on the final paper.

...

The teacher must provide students with comments that help students identify and correct substantive problems in these areas so the students understand the underlying analysis and the organization that flows from that analysis. Focusing feedback on substantive and related organizational challenges will help the students understand the ideas they are trying to express and, in the process, assist them in becoming more proficient legal thinkers.

...

III. Effective Analytical Critique

Recognizing that the teacher must prioritize his comments by focusing on analytical concerns on first drafts is an important step to becoming effective at critiquing assignments.... Then the true challenge begins: Providing feedback on analysis that will be useful to the students and efficient for the teacher.

...

A. Tailor Critique to Your Course

Analytical feedback must be tailored to the teacher's teaching and the curricular sequence of the course. The critique employed by the teacher should be connected to the analytical discussions that take place during class sessions and individual meetings with students. When working on legal reasoning skills in class, the teacher and students develop a shared vocabulary and experience that will help the students learn the ideas that should be the focus of the specific assignments. The teacher's feedback on student writing should reflect that focus and use the shared vocabulary and experiences from the course.

...

B. Develop In-Depth Understanding of Analysis of Each Assignment

To provide useful analytical comments on a draft, the legal writing teacher must have a more intimate understanding of the analysis than would be required to simply write the assignment as a practitioner. The teacher must not only know how he would explain the analysis of the problem, he must also anticipate all the other ways one might write the problem, and he must anticipate every wrong turn students can make so he can guide the students back.

...

C. Adapt Feedback to Analytical Needs of Each Student

...

To begin, the teacher should diagnose the analytical struggles and successes of the student's draft. Based on that diagnosis, the teacher needs to determine the best method for feedback. When beginning to critique an individual paper, the major substantive problems should be identified before providing any feedback. Accordingly, before writing any comments, the teacher should quickly read the entire memorandum or, if the analysis is divided into several sub-issues, the teacher could read the portion of the draft dealing with a particular sub-issue.

...

The diagnostic reading should be only a quick assessment because the goal is very focused: To get an overall sense of the student's paper to determine the type of critique that will best help the particular student.

Based on this diagnostic review of the paper, the teacher must decide what type of comments will be most effective for that student. There are two basic critiquing approaches that can be used when commenting on analysis: ... In a sequential critique, comments are inserted at the particular place in the draft where the problem appears. In this article, comments are called "interlinear comments" if woven into the student's text and "margin comments" if written on the side or bottom of the paper. By contrast, a narrative comment is usually drafted in paragraph form separately from the student's paper and describes the various problems the teacher encountered in the section.

The advantage of providing sequential, line-by-line feedback is that the student has the benefit of the teacher's reaction as he is reading the section.... Reacting sequentially to the paper often helps the teacher, too, because for many teachers, the critiquing process is like the writing process.... By providing comments while working through the student's paper, the teacher helps himself identify where the student has done well and the level of importance of the analytical issues and, therefore, the teacher will provide better comments to the student. After providing the specific comments, the teacher has a better sense of the student's depth of understanding of the issue.

Using a narrative comment also has benefits. A narrative can lead the student through the problems from the most critical to the less important. Thus, a separate narrative comment can provide the student with the necessary guidance without filling the margins with too many comments.

...

D. Determine Appropriate Detail for Comments

After choosing an approach to commenting, the teacher must then determine the appropriate level of detail for the student's paper. The comments should include sufficient detail to help the student progress with the analysis while not providing the answer to the student.

...

Providing sufficient assistance is ... necessary when providing feedback on student papers. If a teacher provides only label-like comments such as "conclusory," "vague," "awkward," "no topic sentence," etcetera, the teacher is not providing enough information to help the student.

...

Open-ended Socratic comments in which the teacher poses leading questions to help guide the student in finding the analytical solutions without providing the answer can be very effective because they help give the student the confidence to face complicated legal issues. Often, one or two well-designed questions will help many of the pieces of the analysis fall into place for the student. The key with Socratic comments is crafting questions that are open-ended, but designed to lead the student to find the analytical solution on her own. A Socratic comment will fail if it simply poses vague questions just because the teacher does not want to "give the answer."

At other times, more directed comments are required because the student has hit a substantive roadblock, and the only way to move forward is to get the student over that barrier. In those situations, open-ended, Socratic-type comments would not be helpful, and the teacher should be more directive.

...

E. Include Summary Comments

Whether the comments are sequential or narrative, open-ended or more directed, a student should always receive a summary of the critique placed at the beginning of the feedback. The summary should provide an overall assessment of the paper and an approach for the student to rewrite it. The summary also should explain the teacher's general impression of the analysis in the draft, including the major strengths and weaknesses.

...

In addition to providing a general impression that outlines the priority of the substantive problems, the overall comment should provide the student with a strategy to begin the rewriting process because the most difficult part of revising a paper that has received a thorough analytical critique is determining where to begin. Therefore, the summary comment must explain to the student how she should begin reworking the draft, including which analytical problems should be handled in which order.

...

F. Explain Strengths of Paper

...

Providing positive comments is often the most challenging part of giving analytical feedback because it forces the teacher to clearly separate the problem areas from the places where the student was successful.

...

The teacher should summarize the strengths of the analysis in the overall comment at the beginning of the critique and, in addition, the teacher should identify in the individual comments the specific places in the draft where the student successfully explains her ideas.... The positive feedback needs to fully explain why the student is doing something well analytically so the student will understand how that success can be repeated when revising the assignment.

G. Reinforce Ideas Throughout the Feedback

Many students benefit from seeing how the same analytical problem creates difficulties for the reader in different parts of the draft.

...

To help avoid overwhelming the student, the explanations in the later comments should not be extensive. The teacher should quickly refer to other comments that deal with the same problem without repeating the details.

H. Use Student's Own Writing as Examples

...

When commenting in one place on a draft where the student is having a hard time, referring to another part of the student's own writing where the student was more successful with the same idea can be effective.

...

I. Refer to Class Discussion and Course Materials

When possible, refer to class discussion and materials used in class to connect the assignment and the critique to the course overall.

...

2. Placement of Comments

The decision of where to put the comments physically on a student's paper is important. Students may like to see the teacher's immediate reaction on the page when the teacher writes a comment in the margin next to a section that needs the student's attention. Furthermore, circling parts of sentences or using arrows can be an efficient and effective method to help students see a better way to express their ideas. However, too many comments on the paper can be discouraging. A large number of comments and markings on the student's paper can destroy the integrity of the student's work because the comments themselves overpower the student's ideas physically on the page and give the impression that the student has failed, even when the substance of the comments is constructive and supportive....

By using a combination of interlinear, margin comments, and summary remarks at the end of sections, the teacher can focus on a specific problem right where the problems are located in the paper, while developing more complex, informative ideas in the summary remarks.

...

K. Be Sensitive to the Tone of the Critique

The tone of comments is important because it affects how the student will process the information provided in the feedback. Even when identifying serious analytical flaws, comments should stay positive so the student remains engaged in the process and feels like the end result is attainable. However, when providing comments on a paper that has many problems, even though the teacher may want to be as positive as possible, the teacher must be clear that there are serious issues so the student does not have a false impression about the overall quality of the paper.

...

L. Assume Good Faith

...

Although it may appear that the student was not fully trying, there are many demands on a law student's time and psyche, and the student may have done her best even though the paper seems deficient. Therefore, the teacher should set his frustration aside, assume good faith on the part of the student, and comment on the paper accordingly.

M. Explain Feedback Methods to Students

...

The most important message to convey when explaining the method of critique is that the teacher has not attempted to rework the analysis and rewrite the assignment for the student. Teachers must explain that the students have ownership of the revision process because the students need to understand that, to use the teacher's feedback effectively, they must internalize the teacher's comments rather than mechanically make changes.... Accordingly, the student herself must make the final determination of how to fix the analytical problems that the teacher has identified.

...

Nancy Soonpaa, *Using Composition Theory and Scholarship to Teach Legal Writing More Effectively**

3 Legal Writing: J. Legal Writing Inst. 81 (1997)

...

What Teachers Should Know

...

Understanding how views about the composing process and the nature of writing have developed since the 1960s can help legal writing educators anticipate the attitudes toward writing and the skill levels that their students bring to the legal writing class-

---

* Excerpts are reprinted with the permission of the author and Legal Writing: The Journal of the Legal Writing Institute. https://www.legalwritingjournal.org/article/24704-using-composition-theory-and-scholarship-to-teach-legal-writing-more-effectively.

room. Some practical implications suggested by the research include the following ideas:

1. The writing background the students bring to the legal writing classroom can provide great insight into their present attitudes about writing, as well as explain their written product.
2. Teachers can read about teaching writing and learn the language and techniques that professionals use and how they "translate" that knowledge for their students.
3. Depending upon students' previous writing education, concerns such as structure, argument development, and organization may initially be secondary for them.... They may not have trouble developing a legal analysis because of the complexity of the law, but rather because they had never written any kind of structured and supported argumentation before the first law school assignment.

...

What Students Do

The difficulty of researching and analyzing writers in the process of writing is that the features of turning thought into written word are hidden in each writer's mind. While one may identify a process leading to thought, followed by a post-thought analysis, one struggles to describe the actual moment of thought's genesis. Hence, research on the act of writing—not what leads to it, not what follows it, not how scholars comment on and analyze it—tends to focus on identifying real-life processes, examining product, facilitating production, and drawing inferences from those activities.

In contrast to the complex and increasingly refined theories about the intricate, multi-level process of writing is the reality of how ... students actually write. In a study that sought to determine students' actual writing process rather than some idealized writing process, researchers found that most students not only followed a strictly linear process but demonstrated one with severely truncated pre-writing and re-writing stages. Students tended to perform minimal research, re-copy and make mechanical corrections rather than re-write, and fail to consider their audience as other than the teacher. Other studies have found similar patterns and group writers into two variously named categories that generally correlate with those writers who follow something like the idealized writing process model (Experienced Writers, Reader-based Writers) and those who follow something akin to the students' process mentioned above (Basic Writers, Writer-based Writers).

...

Writer-based prose is characterized as under-transformed verbal expression, with its focus of expression on the process of thought. Writer-based prose in a legal memorandum, for example, may lecture the reader on basic legal analysis or hierarchy of authority—a concept that the student writer may have needed to think through, but that a practicing attorney long since would have internalized. Reader-based prose, however, is a deliberate attempt to communicate to a reader, with its focus of expression on the purpose of the thought or idea.

Writer-based prose, then, is not without logic and structure, nor without function. However, that logic and structure are tied to a writer's efforts in thinking about a new or complex subject. It serves as a problem-solving medium for thinking and allows the writer to manipulate stored information into acceptable patterns of meaning.

The implications of writer-based prose begin by an understanding that it does not simply indicate a problematic piece of writing, but rather a functional stage in the composing process and a powerful intermediate, though not end, strategy. But while experienced writers are able to transform and constantly re-examine their writing to fit the demands of the writing situation, inexperienced writers get stuck. Poor planning, an inability to view writing from the audience's perspective, and sometimes simple confusion about what the writing situation demands stymie inexperienced writers from sorting wheat from chaff. But rather than approaching a draft as a hopeless mess, teachers can help students to find the "good parts" in their drafts and then build on them, thereby boosting confidence.

...

As writers developing their own writing, teachers can model for students their writing processes and thus foster students' awareness of their own process—as well as the teachers' greater awareness of process.... Seeing that process through, though, can be difficult for student writers, for it requires revision. Not only are inexperienced writers uncomfortable with the idea of revision; the very term "revising" is distasteful. Their changes are mostly surface level: they eliminate repetition, improve word choice, and copy-edit.

Experienced writers see revision as a recursive process with different emphases in different revision cycles. They use revision to rework content, including finding the shape or form of an argument; they reassess and revise in light of their audience's needs. While these strategies are part of discovering meaning for experienced writers, basic writers predefine meaning, and if they alter their drafts at all, they alter them to match that meaning. The essential difference is that inexperienced writers do not see writing as discovery, but as reporting, and revision not as "just begun," but "almost done." This is not to say that all experienced writers revise similarly or revise copiously; however, unlike inexperienced writers' alterations, their revisions do tend to improve their texts.

...

When the Two Meet

Writing teachers spend so much time on an activity that is little understood: what is thoughtful commentary and what comments actually help. By viewing errors as occasions for learning, teachers can start to develop effective methods of responding.

...

One way to distinguish comments is to divide them into two categories, formative and summative evaluation, which serve two different functions. Formative evaluation tries to assist in improvement of writing. It identifies problems and possibilities; its focus is ongoing and developing. Such comments help to create motivation for revision and fit in nicely with a process-oriented method of teaching. Summative evaluation measures ranking, grading, [and] measuring up to expectations. It looks at text as a final product and assesses the writer's skills at a specific point in time.

Formative responses can be grouped into seven categories: correcting, emoting, describing, suggesting, questioning, reminding, and assigning. The importance, however, is not so much in specific labels as it is in a writing teacher's thoughtful analysis of what a comment does towards helping students to improve their own writing.

These categories suggest that teachers' roles change with different types of commentary. For instance, a teacher as commentator may variously fill the roles of editor, average reader, more experienced writer, summative evaluator, and motivator/friend. Knowing which role one is trying to fill with a particular assignment, drafting stage, or student helps to focus the job of commenting and to make the comments on a particular paper more consistent. Responding to text as in-process helps students to follow the behavior of skilled writers.

...

While some commenting styles may be unique to a particular teacher or to a particular assignment, one study showed that most comments are essentially interchangeable from one paper to another (e.g., "good statement of issue" or "argument needs development"). But teachers should comment just as they ask students to write clearly, specifically, with an audience orientation.... And those student-recipients like text-specificity—comments related to a specific assignment, rather than fungible writing comments. They also like student-specificity—comments that are both specific and directed to that particular writer, not simply the group of writers with similar problems. They like clear explanations, not just labels, codes, or descriptive comments. (e.g., "gd ts" or "this topic sentence works well to set up your paragraph" is less well received than "this topic sentence is effective because it clearly explains the relationship between the two analogous cases that you go on to discuss in this paragraph."). Effective comments should also have "transfer value," the utility to help the student's writing beyond the boundaries of a particular assignment. So, while comments should be specific to the written work being evaluated, they should also advance the student's understanding of how to write effectively in order to foster improvement in the next piece of writing.

...

Research into the characteristics of commentary and the effectiveness of different kinds of commentary provides some useful guidelines to make a time-consuming activity more productive. Those implications include the following:

1. Teachers need to consider audience as they comment on student papers. Relevant inquiries include asking questions such as these: What will the student understand? What are the limits of the student's revision potential at that stage? What is the likely reaction that an overly critical comment might elicit? Is that productive? Teachers need to be as sensitive to the needs of their readers—students—as they exhort students to be.
2. Teachers need to identify goals for their students at every stage of the writing process. If they are focusing on large-scale organization or analysis, then commenting on sentence-level concerns might be counter-productive. And teachers should identify their role in a particular or with a particular assignment: Senior partner, writing coach, grammar maven? The inquiry continues: Are the teacher's comments consistent with that role, is that role appropriate, and are the students aware of that role?
3. When deciding how to address correctness, teachers should first look at student work to determine whether the problem is surface error in otherwise decent prose, structural error, a jumble of correct and incorrect usages that seem to follow a mysterious pattern, etc.

...

4. At all times, a writing teacher must remember who owns the piece of writing that the teacher has temporary custody of for commenting purposes. Ultimately, the owner/writer has responsibility for revising and improving the written work. The teacher's responsibility is to provide the tools and techniques that enable the student to carry out a writer's responsibility and privilege.

...

Tonya Kowalski, *Toward a Pedagogy for Teaching Legal Writing in Law School Clinics**

17 Clinical L. Rev. 285 (2010)

...

It is sometimes said that most lawyers spend more time engaged in legal writing than in almost any other lawyering skill. Because law clinics are designed to train their students in the realities of law practice, it should be no surprise that students and their

* Excerpts are reprinted with the permission of the author and the Clinical Law Review.

supervising attorneys spend a great deal of time planning to write, writing, talking about writing, and then writing some more.

...

At the same time, some barriers do exist, in the sense that legal writing methods are often perceived as being very formalistic, and clinics are characterized by their dynamism. Thus, for busy clinicians, descending down the rabbit hole of legal writing instruction may feel like going among mad people. But it need not be so. A growing body of literature has begun to discuss how legal writing and clinical educators can collaborate to share teaching methods and support each other's professional status.

...

2. Theoretical Bases: Composition Theory and the New Rhetoric

The state of the art in legal writing pedagogy is solidly rooted in the New Rhetoric, a school of undergraduate composition theory developed in the 1970s and 1980s.... The New Rhetoricians perceived that writing is not separate from thinking: it is thinking.... It is the very process of writing that exposes weaknesses in reasoning and authority and forces the lawyer to delve ever deeper into the problem to find the root causes and their solutions.... Based on this perception that writing is really just a way of thinking and reasoning through a problem, New Rhetoricians focused their attention on the thinking/writing process. For this reason, contemporary pedagogical models are sometimes called the process-oriented approach.

In the field of composition theory, the process-oriented approach developed to include multiple drafts with professor "intervention" at various points along the way, including the planning, drafting, and polishing stages.

...

V. Transfer-Friendly Curriculum and Teaching Tools for Clinical Legal Writing

Based on the similarities and differences between clinic and legal writing pedagogies, a pedagogy for clinical legal writing should consider a graduated approach to independence from directive to collaborative to nondirective depending on the student's growth stage and the urgency of the task at hand; a feedback prioritization plan that increases the emphasis on creative analysis in addition to formal structures; a legal writing lexicon for clinic that may consist of an "Esperanto" that is also introduced at some point in that law school's legal writing program; a method for bridging legal analysis tools from the first-year experience to the present; a modular, deadline-driven approach to early faculty intervention in the planning and drafting stages; and, when time permits, built-in opportunities for critical reflection before, during, and after a major writing experience.

...

In their groundbreaking work on transfer theory, Dr. David Perkins and his colleagues developed a number of strategies for "teaching for transfer." The strategies to be employed depend on how far removed the new context is from the previous learning environment. When the contexts are far apart, it is harder for the brain to recognize that learning stored in an earlier schema is appropriate for recall and application in the new situation.

...

B. Simulating, Modeling, and Matching Through Exemplars and Terminology

1. Teaching with Exemplars Through Annotated Sample Banks

One important aspect of teaching for both near and far transfer is that the instructor provides exemplars of the expected work product and sometimes even models the approach to the assignment. How much clinicians model writing for students may depend in large part on whether the clinic has adopted a stricter form of either non-directive supervision or collaborative supervision. There will be more opportunities for modeling in the latter, but potentially less opportunity for the student to become immersed in creating a whole product.

...

Some concerns about using forms and checklists arise from the common experience that students—and even novice attorneys—sometimes lack the judgment to use forms effectively. In extreme cases, they may even abdicate their responsibilities as advocates, parroting the sample rather mindlessly in many places rather than critically evaluating the material to adapt and improve it for the client's needs. Sometimes students' inability to use samples and forms effectively results from stress management or motivational problems, but more often, they likely result from a lack of work experience or a misunderstanding of the teacher's expectations. A frank discussion about the dangers of using forms and samples uncritically can help to inspire greater care. Such discussions have value pedagogically, because the reality is that in law offices, attorneys must learn to recycle and adapt previous research and writing in order to increase efficiency and save client money.

In any event, because students must be able to work independently, a good bank of sample memos, motions, briefs, and other pleadings or contracts are key to avoiding wasting a great deal of client, student, and professor time on needless beginner's confusion. It is mostly fruitless for a student to waste a week of research and writing time trying to understand what content is required in a routine motion, when formal aspects of motion composition can be explained and modeled through a brief discussion and a few good, annotated samples, leaving the student to focus instead on developing unique content.

...

C. Metacognitive Reflection and Exercises

Connecting clinical experiences to past and future applications requires some time for reflection. In simple terms, metacognition means "thinking about thinking." Mindfulness of one's own thinking and learning process can bring an almost meditative quality to education that allows the mind to forge the connections necessary to foster transfer. Like any other learning strategy, educators can help students to train in metacognitive awareness by encouraging them to discuss their learning and even to work on exercises that prompt them to connect their experiences to their learning.

...

Some ideas for written metacognitive reflection relevant to the clinical setting are the transfer exercise, the private memo, and the journal, which roughly fall along a spectrum from most structured (the tailored exercise) to least structured (the reflective journal). Journaling is already popular in some clinic and externship programs. Private memos have been recommended to clinical programs before, but I suspect that they remain underused. Perhaps the most novel and underexplored form in the clinic is the tailored exercise, and it may be the tool most amenable to inter-program collaboration.

1. Transfer Exercises

Guided and structured metacognitive reflection is no longer new to legal education, but it does not appear to be in wide use yet.

...

Structured exercises prompt students to assess their current strengths and weaknesses based on feedback from first year professors, legal employers, and clinic supervisors. They also stimulate students to recall specific skills, knowledge, and resources acquired in previous contexts and to bring then into the present experience. Exercises can be generic or tailored to a specific type of work product or even an individual assignment. Whether generic or tailored, these exercises or questionnaires create the opportunity to foster recall and to create associations with previous contexts before the project gets underway, and thus before substantial student and professor resources are invested in creating a document. They also allow student and professor to spend more time building upon previous skills, rather than re-learning them.

2. Private Memos

Other authors have already extolled the virtues of the reflective memorandum in helping to illuminate a student's thought process to the professor. This tool has been coined the "private memo," and was originally designed to help legal writing professors understand their students' strategic thinking during the writing process. In a private memo, the student describes her struggles and decisions with myriad tasks in legal analysis, including litigation strategies like issue framing or how to tell a good story in a fact statement; critical reading problems like understanding the holding and reasoning in a complex but binding case; organizational challenges such as where to include the standard of review in an appellate brief; and even logistical concerns that often feel like mountains to law students, such as how to align a signature block along the right-hand margin.

The private memo helps to shortcut the triage process for the professor and helps her to target her feedback to the issues that most troubled the student, in addition to finding new points that the student may not have considered. It also has a promising side-effect, which is to encourage the student to engage in metacognition before submitting her final draft.

...

3. Journaling

Even more than the private memo, journaling has been lauded as a key learning tool across many disciplines. In fact, journaling has such a powerful effect on the psyche that it is used in many psychiatric therapies and has been associated with stress reduction and better immunity. For these and many other reasons, journaling is already in widespread use within clinical programs.

...

VI. New Rhetoric-Based Approaches to Supervising Clinical Legal Writing

As discussed earlier, legal writing pedagogy is solidly founded in the New Rhetoric, which views writing as a manifold, recursive process of thinking, researching, writing, and revising. In both college and law school classrooms, educators who teach written analysis "intervene" in the student's process, scaffolding their learning throughout all the different stages. They do this through tools like written critique and selective interlineations, one-on-one verbal conferences, modeling, exemplars, and so on. Clinicians can use earlier and more frequent intervention to encourage better initial drafts and significantly evolved subsequent drafts. Tools that are well-suited to the busy, unpredictable clinical environment are those that put the most emphasis on well-planned independent preparation by the student. By learning how better to plan their research and writing and prepare for conferences, students can make much better use of precious one-on-one supervision time. To achieve this end, clinical professors can intervene early by using tools like research plans, annotated outlines, and modular drafts. During the revision process, professors can also use even more tools that empower students to become better self-directed in their use of equally precious written feedback. They can include self-critique, peer critique, prioritized written and verbal feedback, and the metacognitive exercises discussed in the previous section. These flexible tools can adapt to time constraints as the time for revising grows shorter. Accordingly, during the final drafting process, professors can make judicious use of intervention through modeling, collaboration, and journaling.

A. Early Intervention: The Planning and Research Stage

...

Clinics can enhance their teaching by providing more advance instruction for assignments, perhaps with more general rules and points provided in writing at the beginning of the semester, and by intervening in the planning stages of writing as well as in later drafts.

1. Research Plans

Students often feel overwhelmed when beginning a new research project, and even more importantly, often overlook major sources of law, particularly when the institution's first-year curriculum fails to emphasize statutes as primary, binding sources second only to the federal, state, and tribal constitutions. The programs can collaborate to create a flexible model research template or templates for use in both programs.

...

2. Annotated Outlines

An annotated outline is a linear outline that is organized by recognizable legal components from broad to narrow, such as causes of action, then elements or factors, then parts of the analytical paradigm, such as IRAC or CREAC.... Because students are trained to think of legal analysis in analytical layers, they should easily be able to structure their outlines in the customary order and even to label the different layers for the professor, in order to expose the student's structural thinking.

Annotated outlines allow the professor to triage organization and reasoning before the student makes a tremendous investment in time and energy and well ahead of the filing deadline, leaving more time for meaningful revision and critique. Ideally, the outline should at least reflect the structure and planned content of the discussion or argument section, but can also include earlier sections like the facts.

...

Such outlines also teach the student the value of planning a project before beginning, and can give the student a sense of grounding and accomplishment before facing the dreaded "blank page" of a major writing assignment. In fact, if the outline is sufficiently detailed, it has the power to greatly reduce writer's anxiety for most students, as does the supervisor's feedback gained through the triage of the outline draft.

...

B. Mid-Point Intervention: The Recursive Drafting Stages

1. Modular Approach to Document Production with Calendared Deadlines

Due to stress and transfer problems, students sometimes flounder when faced with the "cognitive overload" of a new writing assignment, particularly if it involves an unfamiliar doctrinal legal area or type of work product. In addition to the transfer-friendly teaching techniques discussed in this article, students and professors often benefit from approaching the writing project in a modular fashion, one small segment at a time, and having the opportunity to rewrite multiple times.... In this tighter, but more paced manner, both professor and student can ensure an adequate understanding of the question presented and avoid excessive "red herring" issues and wasted research trails.

...

Of course, in the clinic, multiple and/or modular drafts are practical only when the filing deadline permits the luxury of time for a series of revisions and supervisory meetings. Moreover, individual professors' busy caseloads and schedules may create impediments to using a more frequent and routine system of drafting.

...

The modular approach lends itself well to a series of smaller, calendared assignments that build toward a whole document, and teaches students to schedule ample time for the planning, outlining, and recursive research and writing phases of the drafting process. Today's law students are well-suited to a segmented drafting cycle due to the very pedagogy employed in first year legal writing, where classes learn their "scales" through deconstructing and re-assembling legal analysis through analytical formulas, methodical organizational hierarchies, checklists, and a section-by-section approach to document assembly. A modular approach can also help to identify early those students who struggle with motivation or time management—even their early product will tend to be late and/or underdeveloped.

To put this segmented approach into practice when time allows, the professor can ask the student to take responsibility for proposing a drafting schedule that works back from the filing deadline[.]

...

2. Self-Critique and Peer Critique

In their supervision, clinicians can help students learn to become more effective evaluators of their own writing by encouraging them to use exercises for self- and peer-critique.

...

In the self-graded draft, students learn to mark up and color-code different parts of their analysis. This approach may sound rudimentary, but its simplicity belies its power to teach good structure, and even good technique. Generally speaking, students begin by labeling the layers in each separate analytical unit. Thus if a cause of action contains four disputed elements, the student would label the parts for the introductory, "umbrella" paragraphs that describe, define, and explain the cause of action, and then for the separate analyses of each of the four elements. Further steps require students to identify the focal point of each issue's analysis, to locate defining terms from the governing test, to mark citation placement and frequency, to illustrate the appropriate and sufficient use of facts from the client's matter, and so on.

In the clinic, it could be useful to revisit the self-graded draft technique in a refresher session on legal writing and to have students practice it on a very short memo of four to five pages during the class. After the refresher, the instructions for the self-grading method should be accessible by handout, twen posting, or clinic handbook. Professors who like this tool can then elect to ask students to submit their draft work products with self-graded markup for memos and briefs, illuminating the structure in advance for both professor and student. It is often a good idea to require markup to be turned in a day or two before the draft is due. Doing so can help to avoid last-minute writing and can also signal structural danger to the student while he still has time to make meaningful changes before the professor must invest time in critique.

...

As for peer critique, that tool has a love-hate reputation among the faculty and students who have used it, but the benefits promise to tip the scale even more in clinic than they do in legal writing. Proponents find peer critique tremendously enlightening as a teaching tool for both the critiquing student and the writing student, and thus a nearly indispensable aspect of legal writing pedagogy.

...

As for training, some synergy and efficiency can be achieved by combining the peer feedback training and methods provided by Professor Davis with Professor Beazley's self-graded draft technique described above. Because both approaches aim to help students teach analytical organization to themselves and each other, they combine very well.

...

3. Prioritized and Instructive Feedback

...

Fortunately, legal writing scholars have produced prolific scholarship about efficient critiquing methods. While the survey reveals that many clinicians have already developed feedback methods that they consider to be effective, some basic principles warrant summarizing here. Basic feedback methodology may be unfamiliar to newer clinicians, to those without experience in teaching legal writing, and for those who have developed a good instinctive approach, but who are interested in improving their methods or correlating them to the styles students experience in legal writing. Three of those basic feedback techniques could be categorized as prioritization, specificity, and tone.

First, because students can only effectively process a certain amount and variety of critique at one time, each professor should adopt selective feedback priorities based on whether the student's work represents a very early, middle, or late draft. In early drafts, the emphasis usually is on overall organization and large-scale analysis, for example, has the student stated a legal rule, and is it the correct rule for the jurisdiction? As the drafts progress and the analysis becomes more rigorous, professors can focus on finer points, such as strategy, nuanced argument, and smaller-scale organization such as paragraph order. Only in the final drafting stages is it usually valuable to focus on grammar and style, even though they can be very distracting—almost compulsively so—to the skeptical expert reader in early drafts.

...

Second, comments should be specific, not vague. If the student's analysis is difficult to follow, the generic "difficult to follow here" should be replaced with a diagnosis and remedy, for example, "this section does a good job of setting forth what it means to be 'demoted' under the law of constructive discharge, but then makes a very conclusory assertion that the client was demoted without significant discussion of the facts or how they can be analogized or distinguished to the binding cases and those persuasive cases that are relatively square with our facts."

...

Third, because motivation is so crucial to performance and to successful transfer of learning, professors may want to consider the emotional effect of feedback on some students' motivation as important to their professional growth and success. This is not to say that student attorneys should be coddled, but rather that the professor should aim to present some positive feedback when possible, and to frame critical feedback in terms of an opportunity to improve, rather than as a personal fault.

...

Although feedback methodology is a large topic, employing these three principles can help to make clinical legal writing more efficient and effective for both teacher and student. It also makes sense to disclose the priorities to students in the beginning so that, for example, they understand that style and grammar remain crucial, but will be explored in more depth at a later time. Nevertheless, students should also be trained to understand that legal employers expect professional-looking work even during the drafting stage, and that a distracting level of gross errors, such as incomplete sentences or a lack of citations, is unacceptable in a professional environment.

C. Late Intervention: The Final Draft and Post-Writing Stages

...

While some late interventions can be avoided through better planning, time management, and early intervention in the recursive thinking/writing process, there will be times when clinical supervisors simply must step in and intervene to protect the client when a student is unable to acquit a particular task, for example, finishing a brief in time to meet the filing deadline. This "failure" can of course be transformed into a learning experience by shifting mindfully and transparently to more directive pedagogical techniques, including modeling, and collaborative learning, and by concluding the project with post-writing metacognitive reflection. Choices should take into account various factors like the student's relationship with the client, the client's understanding of the risks involved, the teacher's relationship with the student, the teacher's ability to competently assume the task within the current parameters, and the burdens placed on the client and the system.

...

Endnotes

1. *E.g.*, Angela J. Campbell, *Teaching Advanced Legal Writing in a Law School Clinic*, 24 Seton Hall L. Rev. 653, 680–84 (1993); Tamar Ezer, *Teaching Written Advocacy in a Law Clinic Setting*, 27 Clinical L. Rev. 167, 168–69 (2021) ("Written advocacy, in particular, brings this tension [about whether and how much to intervene in student writing] to the forefront. Written products are 'memorialized,' subject to revision, and presented under the clinic's and clinician's name. Consequently, clinicians tend to be more 'interventionist' than for other aspects of the clinic work.").

2. Campbell, *supra* note 1, at 681–82.

3. *Id.* at 682.

4. *Id.*

5. For an overview of "collaborative lawyering," *see generally* William H. Schwab, *Collaborative Lawyering: A Closer Look at an Emerging Practice*, 4 Pepp. Disp. Resol. L.J. 351 (2004). *See also* Susan Bryant, *Collaboration in Law Practice: A Satisfying and Productive Process for a Diverse Profession*, 17 Vt. L. Rev. 459 (1993). And for explanations of the concrete benefits of collaboration in today's legal-practice landscape, *see, e.g.*, Mitt Regan & Lisa Rohrer, *Money and Meaning in the Modern Law Firm*, Harv. L. School, Ctr. on the Legal Profession (July/Aug. 2021), https://clp.law.harvard.edu/knowledge-hub/magazine/issues/money-and-meaning/money-and-meaning-in-the-modern-law-firm/ (empirically, "collaboration 'enhances a professional firm's client loyalty and retention. The more partners serve a client, the longer that client remains with the firm, even when an important partner leaves.' This collaboration also is a source of nonfinancial professional satisfaction for many lawyers."); *Meaningful Collaborations within Law Firms*, Thomson Reuters (Dec. 14, 2022), https://www.thomsonreuters.com/en-us/posts/legal/podcast-law-firm-collaborations/ (empirically, "the lost opportunity cost from failing to deliver collaborative legal services appears substantial"); *Building the Modern Legal Practice: The Pressures Forcing Law Firms to Modernize*, Law.com: Legal Week (Mar. 28, 2017, 8:22 AM), https://www.law.com/international-edition/2017/03/28/building-the-modern-legal-practice-the-pressures-forcing-law-firms-to-modernise/ ("Tomorrow's business and consumer world will also enable collaboration at every node of decision making. Law firms are not immune to this trend, and there is room for improvement in smoothing the edges of collaboration.").

6. The number of new law graduates hanging up their own shingle—that is, entering solo practice—has been steadily declining lately. *See* Am. Bar Ass'n, ABA Profile of the Legal Profession 46 (2022), available online at https://www.americanbar.org/content/dam/aba/administrative/news/2022/07/profile-report-2022.pdf ("Meanwhile, the number of graduates who went into solo practice straight out of law school continued to decline. Less than 1% of all 2021 grads (0.7%) took the solo route. A decade ago, 2.3% of the Class of 2012 practiced solo—a small number but triple the current rate.") Those low-and-getting-lower numbers of solo-practitioner recent graduates is dwarfed by the number of law graduates who work in more collaborative professional settings. *See id.* at 47 (among law school graduates in the classes of 2012–2021, within ten months of graduation, 50.6% worked at non-solo-practice "law firms," 10.4% worked in "government," 10% worked in "business," 9.6% held judicial clerkships, and 7.7% worked in "public interest").

7. "In the 1950s, there was no single vision of clinical legal education and the concept of a law school 'legal aid clinic' encompassed any 'law school sponsored program for law student work on legal aid cases.'" Margaret Martin Barry, Jon C. Dubin & Peter A. Joy, *Clinical Education for this Millennium: The Third Wave*, 7 Clinical L. Rev. 1, 9 (2000) (quoting Quintin Johnstone, *Law School Clinics*, 3 J. Legal Educ. 535, 535 (1951)). In the twenty-eight law school clinics identified in a study from 1951, students' clinical experience "typically included client and witness interviews, drafting pleadings, and preparation of legal documents," while a minority of early clinical programs—just under one-third, or nine of twenty-eight—"provided opportunities for trials and other court appearances." *Id.* at 9–10 (citation omitted). The subject matter of these early clinics was widely regarded as involving only run-of-the-mill "legal aid" type work. *Cf. id.* at 9–10. As the twentieth century wore on and faculty continued experimenting and revolutionizing clinics, the 1960s and 1970s saw clinics expanding "to demystify

law for students and to represent client communities with claims that thrust clinical programs into the civil rights, consumer rights, environmental rights, and poverty rights movements." *Id.* at 12–13.

8. Robert R. Kuehn & David A. Santacroce, *An Empirical Analysis of Clinical Legal Education at Middle* Age, 71 J. Legal Educ 622 (2022) at 655. also available at available at https://papers.ssrn.com/sol3/papers.cfm?abstract_id=4369708 ("What did change between 1992 and 2002 were 'dramatic increases in the number of law schools offering specialized, non-litigation clinics'—transactional clinics rose by 400% and alternative dispute resolution (ADR) clinics by over 200%.").

9. Robert R. Kuehn & David A. Santacroce, Margaret Reuter, June T. Tai, G.S. Hans, Center for the Study of Applied Legal Education (CSALE) 2022–23 Survey of Applied Legal Education, at 25, (2023), https://cdn.prod.websitefiles.com/5d8cde48c96867b8ea8c6720/660d6e828aac87a8826df928_Report%20on%202022-23%20CSALE%20Survey%20rev.4.3.24.pdf.

10. *Cf., e.g.*, Amy D. Ronner, *Real Students, Real Appeals, Real Courts: The In-House Appellate Litigation Clinic at St. Thomas University School of Law,* II The Record: J. Appellate Prac. & Advoc. Sec. Fla. B. 13 (1994); Amy D. Ronner, *Some In-House Appellate Litigation Clinic's Lessons in Professional Responsibility: Musical Stories of Candor and the Sandbag,* 45 Am. U.L. Rev. 859, 866 (1996) ("Coterminous with the movement to bring more clinics into law schools was support for improving education in particular areas like appellate advocacy and professional responsibility.").

11. *See Ship of Theseus*, Encyc. Britannica, "In the history of western philosophy, an ancient paradox regarding identity and change across time." https://www.britannica.com/topic/ship-of-Theseus-philosophy. If the planks of Theseus' ship were replaced over time, does it become a new ship or does it remain the old ship.

12. *See, e.g.*, Tonya Kowalski, *Toward a Pedagogy for Teaching Legal Writing in Law School Clinics,* 17 Clinical L. Rev. 285, 286 (2010) ("Clinicians excel at turning all sorts of unpredictable, disparate events that occur during the life of a case into teachable moments.").

13. *See, e.g.*, Daniel L. Barnett, *Triage in the Trenches of the Legal Writing Course: The Theory and Methodology of Analytical Critique*, 38 U. Tol. L. Rev. 651, 666–67, 670–72 (2007) (explaining how to effectively use a combination of margin comments, summary comments, and overall comments).

14. Another version of this process, split into five stages, is as follows: (1) prewriting, (2) writing, (3) rewriting, (4) revising, and (5) polishing. *See, e.g.*, Campbell, *supra* note 1, at 684–85.

15. I owe many of the ideas presented here to my Georgetown colleagues, Professors Robert Stumberg and Vicki Girard who, in addition to their other clinic duties, teach our clinical fellows how to supervise students' writing projects. As part the three-class-unit they describe the stages of the writing process as the students prepare the many drafts needed to complete a document. They also teach various ways to comment on the drafts without making students feel like failures.

16. *See generally* Kowalski, *supra* note 12.

17. *See id.* at 312.

18. Conversation between Professor Stumberg and the author. January 27, 2025.

19. Depending on how one slices the various stages, the creation of the outline could also be viewed as the end of the first of Campbell's five stages, titled "prewriting." *See* Campbell, *supra* note 1, at 685 ("[T]he first stage typically concludes with an outline. The next four stages [i.e., writing, rewriting, revising, and polishing] should result in the first, second, third and final drafts. In practice, however, more drafts are often required due to the recursive nature of the writing process.").

20. Professor Stumberg believes what I call the final stage is comprised of two distinct stage—editing and summary. Professor Robert Stumberg, *supra*, note 18.

21. *See* Barnett, *supra* note 13, at 654–59 (explaining the importance of "triage" in supervising student legal writing).

22. For more on the difference between higher-level "revision" and more fine-grained "editing," see, e.g., Tamar Ezer, *supra* note 1, at 173–76.

23. According to Professor Stumberg, "For a clinical program, the division of labor for final editing is important for ethical and psychological reasons. Ethically, clinics should not submit a student's B- work as the final product, especially to a tribunal in litigation. There often is not time for reflective rounds of feedback, and so the editing role should shift to a supervisor. Psychologically, students should not be led to expect autonomy over the final stage of editing—be it academic or on the job.... If supervisors "edit" grammar, syntax, punctuation, clarity, then the students are grateful and learn little about editing. Yet spotting these style issues and holding students to learning the language conventions and fixing poor usage takes time. This is an important stage of learning, but it has to be negotiated when deadlines don't allow more than a few drafts. Professor Robert Stumberg, *supra*, note 18.

24. Professor Stumberg believes the summary is a separate stage from the editing. *Id.*

25. *See, e.g.*, Brian Wolfman, *How to Conclude a Brief*, 20 Legal Commc'n & Rhetoric 117 (2023) (explaining the importance of clarity and precision in the conclusion section of a brief).

26. Barnett, *supra* note 13, at 653.

27. Kowalski, *supra* note 12, at 286; *see also id.* at 286–87 n. 3 (citing Tracy Bach, *Cooperation, Not Collision: A Response to When Worlds Collide*, 4 J. Ass'n Legal Writing Directors 62 (2007); Darby Dickerson, *Building Bridges: A Call for Greater Collaboration Between Legal Writing and Clinical Professors*, 4 J. Ass'n Legal Writing Directors 45 (2007); Phyllis Goldfarb, *So Near and Yet So Far: Dreams of Collaboration Between Clinical and Legal Writing Programs*, 4 J. Ass'n Legal Writing Directors 35 (2007); Phillip N. Meyer, *When Worlds Collide: Exploring Intersections Between Legal Writing and Clinical Pedagogy, Scholarship, and Practice*, 4 J. Ass'n Legal Writing Directors 1 (2007); Michael A. Millemann, *Using Actual Legal Work to Teach Legal Research and Writing*, 4 J. Ass'n Legal Writing Directors 9 (2007); Kate O'Neill, *But Who Will Teach Legal Reasoning and Synthesis?*, 4 J. Ass'n Legal Writing Directors 21 (2007); and Sarah E. Ricks & Susan C. Wawrose, *Comment: Survey of Cooperation Among Clinical, Pro Bono, Externship, and Legal Writing Faculty*, 4 J. Ass'n Legal Writing Directors 56 (2007)). Our classes in the Elements of Clinical Pedagogy course at Georgetown are team-taught by clinical faculty and legal-writing faculty.

28. Campbell, *supra* note 1, at 694.

29. *See id.* at 677–78, 694.

30. *See generally* Barnett, *supra* note 13.

31. *See* Ezer, *supra* note 1, at 176–78.

32. *Id.* at 176.

33. *See id.*; Barnett, *supra* note 13, at 654–55.

34. Barnett, *supra* note 13, at 654–55.

35. *Id.* at 662.

36. *Id.* at 662–63.

37. *Id.* at 662–63.

38. *Id.* at 663.

39. *Id.* at 665.

40. Donald M. Murray, *Teaching the Other Self: The Writer's First Reader*, 33 Coll. Composition & Commc'n 140, 140 (1982).

41. Campbell, *supra* note 1, at 685.

42. Murray, *supra* note 40, at 140.

43. *Id.*

44. For a helpful summary on the history of the "kill your darlings" aphorism *see, e.g.*, *What Does It Mean to Kill Your Darlings*, MasterClass (Sept. 7, 2021), https://www.masterclass.com/articles/what-does-it-mean-to-kill-your-darlings (tracing historical origins of the phrase).

45. Barnett, *supra* note 13, at 672–73.

46. *E.g.*, Ezer, *supra* note 1, at 169 (highlighting tension between clinicians' increased "interventionist" tendencies on writing projects and the need to intervene "in a way that retains student ownership and accountability"); Barnett, *supra* note 13, at 673 (discussing the importance of reinforcing student "ownership of the revision process").

47. David Gooblar, *I'm Not Ready to Quit Grading*, CHRON. HIGHER EDUC. (Mar. 21, 2018), https://www.chronicle.com/article/im-not-ready-to-quit-grading/.

48. *See generally* MODEL CODE OF PRO. CONDUCT r. 5.1 (general duties of supervisors in law practice); D.C. CT. APP. R. 48 (laying out the ground rules for supervising law student practice in Washington, D.C., under which Georgetown clinic students practice).

49. Stumberg Mlyniec conversation, *supra*, note 18.

50. Barnett, *supra* note 13, at 664.

51. *See id.* at 652 ("Critiquing student papers is challenging because it requires the teacher to face the successes and failures of the teacher's own teaching. Each set of papers provides instant feedback about what worked or did not work in classes that were designed to help the students prepare the assignment.... This is a very humbling experience.")

52. *See* Campbell, *supra* note 1, at 680–81.

53. Kowalski, *supra* note 12, at 285.

54. *See* Ezer, *supra* note 1, at 168 (observing that "the law clinic setting provides the opportunity for practical analysis, an advocacy lens, and collaborative writing typical of legal practice").

55. *See* Kowalski, *supra* note 12, at 285 (emphasis added).

56. *See id.* at 323.

Six

CASE ROUNDS

Case Rounds Defined

The concept of Case Rounds used in clinical pedagogy has deep roots that stretch back over a century and into a different professional field. Medical education pioneered the concept, and clinical legal education absorbed many of its features. In the early 20th century, William Osler "pioneered medical education reform" with what would transform into the modern method of case-based rounds.[1] Over time, medical case-based rounds evolved from a quality-control measure, which bore incidental fruit in educating new physicians, into a "purely educational" method and a "core element of training" in the medical field.[2] In medical education, participating in rounds (or "rounding on" patients) referred to the time students practice diagnosing and treating patients while being monitored by a supervising physician. It eventually became "the focus and primary method of clinical learning by future physicians [that would] be performed at the bedside with an attending physician."[3]

The pioneers of law school clinical and other experiential courses were aware of this model of medical training and adapted it to legal education. Strictly speaking, however, participating in rounds in medical schools resembles the concept of what law school clinical and experiential faculty call case or project supervision and feedback. And what law school clinical faculty now call "case rounds" (or "client rounds,") perhaps more closely resembles the medical school concept of Grand Rounds: "the principal education conference offered by virtually all departments of medicine."[4] Grand Rounds arose when the medical faculty's patient-by-patient explanations of diagnoses, treatments, and other medical procedures "moved from the bedside," next to the patient, "to an auditorium," where a larger number of medical residents and faculty alike could attend and learn.[5] Grand rounds today are an integral component of medical education. They present clinical problems in medicine by focusing on current or interesting cases.

Case Rounds as Supervision

Clinical faculty readily admit case rounds sessions can be hard to conduct. They sometimes "confess to dreading" them.[6] That dread and the frustration they sometimes feel after the session reflect genuine realities of how case rounds classes can fail. Low levels of student participation, surface level rather than in-depth discussions, and a tendency by students to accept relatively pat solutions to complex problems can all be par for the course.[7] Faculty "also confide that many of their students comment negatively on rounds classes in year-end course evaluations."[8] Additionally, every rounds session seemingly generates an "almost endless" set of possible interventions, concerns about whether to intervene at all, and when, if, and how to intervene.[9] Although all of these attitudes and concerns are understandable, they are most often rooted in the unfortunate fact that case rounds sessions are seldom well-planned. The lack of planning began to change after Professors Susan Bryant and Elliott Milstein published their 2007 article, "Rounds: A 'Signature Pedagogy' For Clinical Education?"[10] The Bryant and Milstein article grew out of a semester of collaboration among clinicians aimed at giving meaningful pedagogical structure to students' discussion of casework.[11] It succeeded in providing that theoretical structure and a soundness to a technique that many faculty had "executed with faith that [it] work[s] but without having identified the theory or mechanism for their success (or failure)[.]"[12] Since its publication, the "Signature Pedagogy" article has spurred significant developments in the field of clinical education in addition to subsequent scholarship on clinical pedagogy that implements and builds on their work.[13] Because newer teachers may not be familiar with the now nineteen-year-old article, they may struggle to conduct worthwhile case rounds sessions.

Today, case rounds are an integral part of the supervision process conducted by experienced clinical teachers. A rounds session can be designed to discuss a specific aspect of a student's case or project with the entire class participating. In that instance, it more closely resembles the attending rounds of medical school. Rounds can also be used to explore a variety of other issues. For example, a student who is having difficulty with a particular prosecutor, opposing counsel in a civil case or transactional matter, or a judge may seek suggestions about how best to approach them from fellow students who have already dealt with that other person. A student team having a disagreement about the best theory on which to develop their case may seek fellow students' assessments about which theory is stronger. Rounds are also an ideal place for students to put unusual or unorthodox case theories or legal arguments to the commonsense "laugh test." Students may want to practice witness examinations, interviews, or their delivery of a trial closing argument or appellate oral argument. Any issue that can arise in a case or project can benefit from additional input from clinic student colleagues when the primary students on the case seek to clarify their thinking. Moreover, since collaboration has become a hallmark of modern law practice, rounds sessions expose students to the benefits of collaborative analysis and provide a structure in which to have those experiences.

Rounds sessions can also be based on a specific aspect of the clinic's work that is likely to arise or is arising frequently in many of the students' cases or projects. These sessions resemble medical school Grand Rounds where information about a topic affecting the class or profession as a whole can be discussed to discover and disseminate knowledge and enhance the reasoning skills of a large numbers of students or professionals at one time. Many difficult issues reoccur in clinic cases or projects every year. For example, as Chapter Seven (The Interrelationship of Values, Moral, Ethics, and Cultural Difference) of this book explains, values issues arise in most clinic cases. The life experiences students bring to their clinic work are often quite different from those of their clients. Difficult conversations about the significance of immigration and deportation, the experiences of poverty and homelessness, or the need for racial or cultural understanding are often better discussed in case rounds to normalize those conversations before they arise during a particular student's case. Students are likely to encounter similar ethics issues in their clinic cases and can benefit from a joint conversation about how they should be resolved. In addition, most students will encounter boundary issues in their personal and professional lives that they must resolve as they seek to create their own professional identity.

Because learning and supervision can occur in various situations,[14] teachers need not wait for an issue to occur in an individual case before addressing it. Indeed, addressing issues in the group setting of rounds also helps remind students that they are not alone when they encounter difficult issues in their clinic. Most students will wonder whether their obligations to their client require more than just addressing the current legal issues in the case. For example, almost every criminal defense or domestic violence clinic student walking out of court with an unhoused client has wondered whether they can or should buy their client lunch at the sandwich shop across the street from the courthouse, knowing that client would otherwise go hungry. They wonder if they have an obligation to find housing for their homeless clients. On one level, these are questions about practical human issues. But these actions also raise issues about the boundaries of lawyer-client relationships. By proactively raising common issues, whether they arise from the substance or procedure of the law, ethics, values, morals, strategy, or even just the everyday human interactions of the profession, rounds offer an efficient and effective way to provide supervision even before a problem arises in individual clinic cases.

Some teachers choose to conduct case rounds early in the semester, so that the some of these conversations can occur before the press of other clinic work overwhelms a student facing the complicated values question. The same can be said of recurring ethics questions. Case rounds, using facts from prior clinic cases about client confidentiality, relations with opposing parties and opposing counsel, candor toward the tribunal, and other issues that can arise in every student's case all help prepare students to manage the issue when it actually arises. Addressing these issues early is not only efficient but also contributes to the scaffolding of learning. By contrast, holding case rounds later in the semester can address issues such as negotiating pleas of guilty in criminal clinics, settlements in landlord tenant clinics, or civil protection orders in domestic violence clinics can eliminate a knowledge overload that can occur in the first part of the clinic experience. It also permits better scaffolding and reduces the stress that often occurs in the early part of the semester. Other clinicians structure a semester-long "arc" of rounds based on the state of the students learning level at a particular time in the arc of the semester. For example, the first early-semester rounds session may focus on bolstering students' knowledge about their project areas, while the final end-of-semester rounds session provides an opportunity to reflect on an entire semester of learning.[15] As with all facets of clinical pedagogy, the decision of whether, when, and on what topics to hold case rounds must be an intentional choice, the product of backwards design, and tailored to achieving the clinic's learning goals.[16]

Rounds as a Teaching Method

Given its roots in patient-rounding from the medical sphere, rounds appear to be a case-by-case method of teaching. Its methodology, however, is not restricted to issues arising in individual cases or projects. The North Star for every rounds session is answering "a fundamental question: 'What did you learn about lawyering from this conversation?'"[17] As such, aspects of personal learning are also a valid subject of a rounds session. One of the most important lessons students can learn in a clinic or other experiential course is to challenge the assumptions they make when approaching decisions. Indulging in assumptions and acting upon them often lead students to make judgments and decisions that are not accurate. The assumption might cause a student to misidentify an issue, in turn leading them to find a solution to the wrong problem. Even when the problem is correctly identified, an incorrect solution may be advanced because an assumption led the student to misidentify its cause.

A necessary precondition to challenging assumptions is to recognize that assumptions are being made in the first place. Rounds provide an ideal crucible in which the self-reflection and growth that happens in clinic can lead to a deep understanding of the power, both good and bad, that assumptions can exert.[18] In a properly structured rounds session, students learn to avoid moving straight from identifying what they believe is a problem to proposing solutions for it. Rounds sessions slow this process down, forcing students to gather all possible facts that have bearing on the issue and to identify and isolate the plausible causes before deciding on a solution.[19] Most people rely on assumptions as a shorthand for understanding simple or even complex events and quandaries. We use those assumptions because they are often correct and allow us to move quickly from issue to resolution. But even minor decisions are subject to a challenge of the assumptions that led to the decision. Rounds seek to not only resolve an issue, but to make students aware of the power of assumptions and provide a method for assessing those assumptions before they are acted upon. So even when faculty are being "judicious" about speaking during rounds, they give students an opportunity to question their own assumptions.[20] By "asking perspective questions" and digging into assumptions, faculty can also "model curiosity in rounds."[21]

The rounds methodology does more than help students reach better answers for the concrete situations confronting them. It also reinforces the deeper learning concepts of independence, reflection, metacognition, and transference going forward, both in clinic and in their future careers as lawyers.[22] Put differently, rounds "are meaningful, in part, because the process highlights the grey; it shows there are many possible paths one can take when lawyering."[23] Although faculty set out the ground rules for the rounds sessions, "the learning space is largely ceded to the students. They are responsible for the substantive focus of the class and, in large part, for contributing the ideas and insights that move the learning process forward."[24] The class is driven by the student presenting the issue for discussion while the other clinic students contribute to the analysis. As a result, any issue presented for discussion is likely to generate supporting and contrary views that will challenge the initiating student's assumptions about the issue and its resolution.

When properly structured, students also learn to avoid moving straight from a problem to proposing solutions.[25] Only after all the facts are revealed to the group, and all the plausible causes for an action are discussed and weighed, should possible solutions be proposed. Indeed, the airing of all the known facts and their sources and the evidentiary bases for proving the known facts will give the students a better sense of what they do not know. That in itself can be as illuminating as reaching a solution based on a complete set of facts. During the rounds conversations with the teacher and members of the entire class, students are exposed to a range of situations where similar plausible causes, diagnoses, and resolutions arose. Watching that information emerge and seeing the value of contrary understandings of the same events or issues reinforces the notion that many things that one believes are based on their own life experiences. It also reveals how some of those assumptions are not always valid and may not be valid for everyone or in every circumstance.

At the end of a rounds session, students are asked to reflect on the conversation and the process they just underwent. In doing so, they learn the value of reflecting on the work they do and see how solutions in one area of practice resonate in others, thereby experiencing the value of teaching for transfer. "Successful rounds classes can have a powerful effect on the entire clinic experience by pushing students away from dependence on the professor toward greater independence and ownership of their own learning."[26]

The Formal Rounds Process

The rounds process has evolved over time, but certain stages are now employed by most experiential teachers who use it as a pedagogical tool. Typical conversations among students about their cases and projects involve "chat[ting] about work, nursing wounds, puzzling over problems, [and] reliving triumphs."[27] The formal structure helps transform those ordinary group discussions and "infuse[s]" the "process with productivity."[28] As explained in more detail in Chapter Five on supervising student writing in clinics, the decision to label a part of a structured process a separate "stage" or "step" is, in some sense, academic and semantic. Even still, structure matters. So, while others may use slightly different terminology or pick slightly different steps as the important ones to highlight,[29] the process laid out below best captures the essence of the stages of the rounds process.

Stage Zero—Pre-Class Preparation

Prior to the class, students are asked to submit the details about a challenge they are confronting that has yet to be resolved. The faculty member chooses one of the submissions and asks the student to present the issue to the entire class for discussion.

Stage One—Fact-Gathering

In the first stage, the fact-gathering stage, the initiating student describes the challenge with as much detail as possible. When the student has finished describing the challenge, the other students begin to ask questions to fill in information that they believe needs elaboration to address the issues in their proper context and with full understanding of the relevant facts. The teacher's role is to make sure the students are asking questions to expand the factual basis for the challenge. If statements or questions suggest a diagnosis of or a resolution to the challenge, the teacher suggests holding the thought for later, thus minimizing the use of assumptions and avoiding premature diagnoses or solutions. This allows the students to better understand the initiating student's goals, provides a richer understanding of the context, and fosters a better analysis based on complete information. The teacher can facilitate digging deeper on the facts with questions like, "What information do you still need?", or "Do we have a clear sense of the initiating student's goals?"[30]

Stage Two—Problem Diagnosis

Once the students have completed gathering the facts they consider pertinent, the faculty member encourages the students to begin considering whether the challenge has been properly defined and what the plausible causes of the defined challenge could be. As with stage one, students are asked *not* to jump to a resolution until all the possible diagnoses and causes have been explored. During stage two, students begin to identify the existence of assumptions to determine whether the initiating student has based their definition of the challenge on accurate or false assumptions. Multiple diagnoses are likely to arise because the students will bring their own life experiences and knowledge to the analysis. Students may experience the Rashomon effect at this point; that is, the malleability of truth when filtered through knowledge, biases, and emotions of multiple viewers of the same events.[31] They begin to understand the value of seeing how different people interpret the same events in different and contradictory ways based on their own life experiences. As a result, they learn the value of slowing down diagnoses, judgments, and resolutions until all the facts are clear and the possible "parallel universes"[32] of their clients' lives and those of other actors in the system are explored.

Stage Three—Question Flooding

Stage three, question flooding, is not universally used in the rounds process. When used, students are asked to pose one more question about any of the facts, issues, or unanswered questions that occur to them after experiencing the first two stages. Without responding to the question, students merely lay out other lingering questions as they move to the next stage.[33] The initiating student should be considering these questions as possible solutions emerge in the next phase.

Stage Four—Problem-Solving

The diagnosis stage will often yield more than one possible cause of a problem, each of which may be accurate. At this point, the initiating student is asked to choose the one that seems most likely to be correct and to lead the discussion on the path to possible resolution. Of course, further discussion with the client may indicate that the cause chosen, and thus the possible resolution, might be incorrect or undesirable. If so, the rounds process will likely have surfaced alternate diagnoses that may lead to the appropriate resolution.

Once the diagnosis is chosen, students enter stage four and begin to suggest ways to solve the problem. As viable solutions are suggested, each is evaluated to see if it could be effective. Some possible methods of resolving the problem will be rejected because their effectiveness is suspect or will be minimally effective and have little value. Others may seem beneficial but need additional refinement. At this stage, the students' job is more nuanced. In the earlier fact-gathering and question-flooding stages, students focused exclusively on just the task at hand. They are either gathering facts or asking questions. But now in the problem-solving stage, the boundary between diagnosing the problem and proposing solutions to that problem become "more porous."[34] This shift can be quite palpable in the room. Whereas the turn from fact-gathering to question-flooding can feel rather distinct, students may drift from problem diagnosis and problem-solving more naturally and seamlessly.

One way to evaluate the conversations that lead to a successful resolution is to use a role play, with the student proposing the resolution acting as the student attorney and the initiator of the round session acting as the client.[35] Taking the role of the client serves two purposes. The first is that the rounds initiator has a better sense of what might be on the client's mind than the other students in the class. The second is that it provides the initiator with an opportunity to operate in the parallel universe of the client. If more than one worthy solution arises in the rounds session, a second role play can be initiated to assess solutions and evaluate which might be more successful. Another alternative activity in the rounds sessions that can also be effective is "opponents rounds," where students play the role of the opposing party rather than that of their own client.[36]

A rounds session may not ultimately lead to a satisfactory resolution of a student's problem, let alone the specific one for which they had hoped to find a solution. Even still, all the students will have learned the model for exploring difficult issues before approaching the supervisor for assistance. The mere fact of the conversation can therefore expand the initiator's understanding of how the problem arose in this case, how it might arise in others, and how they might go about spotting and addressing the issue independently going forward. And the collaborative nature of the rounds conversation ensures that all of the clinic students are exposed to the benefits of that process, no matter which of them happens to be the initiator for any particular session.

Stage Five—Check-In

Stage five, the check-in, is simply that. The teacher needs to know whether the initiating student has benefitted from the experience. Supervisors need to know whether the student's thinking about the challenge was broadened by the conversation, whether the diagnoses and possible resolutions were realistic, and whether they are likely to be effective. They also need to know whether the initiating student believes more work needs to be done before determining the correct path to resolving the challenge. These and other related questions are designed to ensure the student has derived enough benefit from the process to move the case forward.[37]

The student's responses to the rounds exercise will often provide an entry point to the conversations during the next supervision session. The teacher can see whether the guidance offered by the group has influenced the student's assessment of the challenge and test again whether it will be effective. Thus, the rounds process becomes an integral part of the supervisory process of the case going forward.

Stage Six—Reflection

Stage six turns the faculty member's attention away from the individual student to the class as a whole.[38] Since a typical clinic class seldom lasts more than two hours, it is difficult to schedule rounds on more than one student's challenge in any one class. Nor is it possible to schedule many rounds sessions in one semester given the demands of other clinic cases, client meetings, clinic seminars, supervision meetings, and the other tasks that students and faculty have to perform for this case or project and the other cases or projects assigned to the student. Consequently, it is important to understand what the rest of the class has learned from any particular rounds session. The final stage's reflection exercise serves two purposes. The first is to highlight the broader lessons that have been learned in this particular session. The second is to help students understand the value of a rounds session, the methods used, and the knowledge that they can schedule sessions on their own with their clinic colleagues before coming to a supervisor for assistance. The results of those student-conducted rounds sessions can be just as productive as those facilitated by the faculty because the rounds process gives a structure to what would otherwise just be a conversation. Moreover, rounds can instill independence and collaborative learning methods in students that will benefit them their entire career.

Collaboration

An obvious element of any rounds session is a collaborative effort in which all students work together to resolve an issue in a case or project. Collaboration can be defined in many ways. Students, however, often have little understanding of the collaboration process because it is not regularly taught in most law school classes. "They often assume that collaboration means no more than parallel play: identify tasks, divide them up, and then work independently."[39] But it is more than that. In an early article on the clinical method, Professor Frank Bloch wrote, "Probably the most important element of the andragogical sound model for clinical supervision is the establishment of a co-counsel relationship between student and teacher."[40] This is undoubtedly true, but not all co-counsel relationships result in true collaboration. Some students and some faculty might think collaboration is just working together on a project or co-counselling a case. However, collaboration is more than networking, dividing up work and sharing tasks, and coordinating or cooperating on a project.

> Collaboration is a partnership; a union; the act of producing or making something together. Collaboration can take place between two people or many people, strangers or best friends. To collaborate is to commit to the possibility of producing an outcome greater than one that would be developed in a silo.[41]

That union is based on the notion that multiple perspectives and contributions from many people will generate better solutions to most problems.

Collaboration imbues all aspects of clinical pedagogy. Because faculty attempt to break down teaching and learning hierarchies, the best supervision sessions are actually a collaboration between the student and the faculty member. In the initial stages of a case, the teacher will have more understanding of the case goals and the pedagogical method and will function as a guide. During this stage, a student begins to understand the clinical method, the nature of the clinic's cases and projects, and the interests of its clients.[42] However, that does not mean that the student is a vessel for faculty members to pour their knowledge and experience into. Nor does it mean that the student and teacher are doing discrete tasks without considering how the work comes together to produce a result better than that which each person could produce alone.

In many clinics, students interview clients and witnesses, review documents, and engage in site investigations without the supervisor being present. Thus, they bring to the student-faculty collaboration information to complement the teacher's knowledge which they then jointly weave together. Clinical teachers also encourage students to become independent thinkers in the pedagogical dialog. As that skill develops over time, the nature of the collaborative effort changes. As the students' capacities evolve to a higher level and the teacher's trust in the students' knowledge and judgment grows stronger, the collaboration begins to take place on a more equal and stronger footing.[43]

Collaboration among clinic students is not just a facet of case rounds and individual supervision sessions. Students in many clinics work on cases and projects in teams in which all actions, judgments, and decisions are arrived at through a collaborative process.[44] Collaboration may even be a specific learning goal of the clinic.[45] In those clinics, students not only develop effective collaborative techniques, they also learn to recognize different styles and approaches to collaboration and to identify challenges to the process before the process is negatively affected.[46] This, in turn, "provides students with valuable insights into clinical judgment and the attorney client relationship."[47] Even when students work alone on their cases, they are encouraged to share their theories, strategies, and judgments with their team partner to other students before they come to a supervision session. Simulations and role plays also require a certain amount of collaboration to ensure that they are successfully conducted. Supervisors will experience immense joy when they walk into a clinic workroom and see the students deeply engaged in each other's work.

There are good reasons for collaboration to be an integral part of the rounds methodology and clinical pedagogy generally. Studies have shown that students and lawyers arrive at better judgment and decisions when collaborating with others.[48] Working in teams gives students an opportunity to better understand a client's life experiences because each student can provide different and sometimes unique perspectives.[49] "By providing students with an opportunity to work in teams, student attorneys can filter client life experiences through multiple personal life experiences and thereby potentially develop richer and more accurate understandings of their clients."[50] If clinical students have a more robust understanding of a client's personal and legal needs, they will make better strategic judgments and decisions which lead to better outcomes for the client. It is similarly important to capitalize on the opportunity to collaborate in a professional legal setting. Professor Clifford Zimmerman asserts it is essential to collaborate and think beyond one's own interpretation of an issue.[51] He points out that "Input from colleagues is typically received at three critical stages in a professional setting: (1) idea development, (2) outline or information sorting, and (3) draft review and revision."[52] These stages are so critical that the absence of input from colleagues results in an opportunity loss.[53]

Although some of these studies regarding the positive effects of collaboration come from outside the legal profession, there is no doubt that most lawyers will spend a significant amount of their career working in teams. This is not a new realization. Years ago, both the Crampton Report[54] and the MacCrate Report[55] found this to be true whether lawyers work in large or small firms, corporations as general counsel, public interest organizations, or government offices.[56] Law firms typically have litigation teams or transaction teams that work together on large cases or projects.[57] Due to the increasingly complex nature of the work at law firms, collaboration is now unavoidable.[58] There is a growing demand for lawyers with a technical specialty who can collaborate well with others.[59] Similarly, public interest firms also rely on interdisciplinary teams to resolve complex legal issues.[60] It is not only important that a public interest lawyer can work well in a team, but to identify when a specialist should be added to a team and how to recruit the necessary specialists.[61] Many public interest organizations have clients who struggle with more than just their legal matters. For example, a public defender may turn to a social worker or a mental health specialist to address an indigent defendant's underlying social needs. A team of lawyers and non-lawyers then work together towards the best possible outcome for the client—an outcome that would be extremely difficult to achieve without collaboration and teamwork. Additionally, in all sectors of the legal profession, cases are often tried in teams. In these cases, investigation, trial preparation, pre-trial motions, and the trial itself will be done in collaboration with another lawyer. The ability to collaborate well with others is invaluable no matter what sector of the legal profession one works in. Law school clinics and other experiential courses provide a fertile ground to study and practice collaborative learning and lawyering,[62] and the rounds process is the primary modality for teaching the value and method of collaboration.

Supervision Rounds

Clinical teachers realized the value of structured case rounds quickly after the process was introduced. Not long after that, a group of clinicians from several schools in New York and Washington, DC began meeting to explore the use of rounds to discuss difficult issues arising during supervision sessions with students.[63] What began as localized efforts in a few pockets of law schools in the Northeast soon acquired nationwide reach, thanks in part to Georgetown's Summer Institute on Clinical Teaching, where supervision rounds were a "central component of the Institute's small group work."[64] The structure remained the same as that of case rounds except that the issues discussed arose between the supervisors and students, rather than between the students and their clients. Now known as "supervision rounds," these sessions are productive when they adhere to the stages of rounds discussed above.

The rounds structure adapts rather seamlessly to conducting supervision rounds.[65] The need for this structure, even among faculty, makes sense. Rounds help faculty address the same dynamics that rounds help students address—whether they are reaching a solution too quickly or making assumptions that are not valid.[66] Although supervision rounds sessions can be conducted within one's school's clinical program, there is value to sharing ideas with clinical faculty from other schools. The cross-pollination of ideas that occur in supervision rounds is especially valuable given the day-to-day reality of the professional isolation that exists for many clinicians. That isolation can result from their colleagues' lack of availability or interest in a deeper reflection and understanding of clinical pedagogy, a lack of time or resources, or the limited number of clinical faculty at one's own law school.[67]

As experienced teachers have observed, supervision rounds

> accomplish two important goals: (1) to build a learning community through which a group of faculty from different law schools can come together and increase faculty collaboration around a shared enterprise of teaching, and (2) to improve our supervision and teaching. During rounds meetings, professors talk about events in their classrooms and supervisions, present "problems" to be probed and re-conceptualized, get ideas about what and how to teach, as well as innovative assessment tools. Professors reflect with supportive colleagues about the relationship between what they have done and their teaching goals, and plan with the benefit of the insights of others. Rounds conversations explore assumptions embedded in teaching decisions as well as naming potential strategies for improving teaching.[68]

Various topics can be explored during a supervision rounds session. Common ones are student productivity, role issues, a student's cognitive ability, relationships between clients and students, students and supervisors, or among student team members, and the effect of emotional and health issues on student learning. While engaging in supervision rounds, faculty discuss and identify the behaviors contributing to their own teaching challenges, analyze the contributing factors leading to a potential diagnosis, propose possible ways to adapt supervision methods or their clinic design to resolve the challenges, and engage in role plays to test possible solutions.[69]

Even faculty well-versed in foundational pedagogical texts and attuned to all the issues that can arise in a group discussion in clinic will find that well-structured supervision rounds can have some shortcomings but can be improved. First, some of the anecdotes giving rise to a supervision rounds discussion require that one really needs to have participated in the supervision to understand the issue affecting the student's learning. Thus, the condensed stories required in rounds may not work as well in the "highly contextualized" rounds environment.[70] Second, a "common barrier" to fully addressing issues pertaining to difference such as race in supervision rounds is that "we feel we lack expertise and/or fear that we will get it wrong."[71] (The "we" in that phrase is often, but not always, referring to white faculty members.) Overall, though, these supervision rounds sessions have proven to be invaluable as faculty explore the range of viable solutions to common and sometimes complex supervision events, thus expanding teachers' understanding of clinical pedagogy. And for fellows and newer clinical faculty, in particular, supervision rounds are valuable in developing their emerging talents as clinical teachers.[72]

Other Voices

Susan Bryant & Elliott S. Milstein, *Rounds: A "Signature Pedagogy" for Clinical Education* *

14 CLINICAL L. REV. 195 (2007)

INTRODUCTION

In almost every small group of clinicians at clinical conferences, someone raises the subject of "improving rounds." Heads nod with near consensus that clinical rounds present challenging teaching moments. Yet clinical teachers persist in engaging their students in rounds conversation because, when the conversations go well, they are precious sources of learning. In these facilitated classroom conversations in which they discuss with each other their cases or projects, students apply and test lawyering theory in the real world as well as extract theory from their and their classmates' experiences. At this start of their practice as lawyers, students engage with peers in a professional dialogue that reinforces professional reasoning and ethical decision-making. Students learn that the support from a group of other professionals engaged in honest and supportive dialogue can lighten the stresses of law practice. Finally, students develop skills that will enable them to learn from their experience and from other professionals both in the clinic and in their future practices.

...

I. TEACHING GOALS & LEARNING THEORY SUPPORTING ROUNDS

In supervision, seminars, and rounds, clinical teachers help students increase their capacity to function as independent professionals with the requisite knowledge, skill and ethical values that being a lawyer demands. While the learning goals for all three modes of instruction overlap, each offers particular opportunities to help students make the transition from being students to being professionals.

In rounds conversations, students hear about their colleagues' cases, and their colleagues' relationships with clients and others; they come to have a detailed understanding of the legal work their classmates perform. Although supervision uses the same case experience for conversation as does rounds, supervision is focused more narrowly on the individual learning of the students handling a case and upon the concrete needs of the case. In contrast, rounds conversations can be more fluid and located in the experience of the entire group. As a result, students broaden the knowledge base from which to assess and draw meaning from their own legal work. Critical perspectives emerge from the patterns they see in their own as well as their colleagues' cases.

Rounds conversations are more determined by students and more focused on cases than is the seminar component of the clinic. Typically, seminars are built around a

---

* Excerpts are reprinted with the permission of the authors and the Clinical Law Review.

syllabus that has clear, teacher-defined learning goals for each session. Clinical seminars tend to focus primarily on client-centered lawyering, theory-driven lawyering and social justice practice. To ensure that students grapple with a broader range of skills, knowledge and perspectives than those needed for their individual cases, seminars often use simulations to increase students' experiences of being a lawyer beyond those available from the limited number of cases that each student can handle. The combination of rounds, seminar and supervision allows teachers to tailor learning that draws upon both staged (simulated) and real experiences and addresses simultaneously the personal and professional dimensions of that experience.

Rounds conversations build upon learning that occurs in clinical seminars and the rest of law school. Students regularly apply the lawyering skills of planning, decision-making and collaboration taught in seminar as well as get feedback on the many other skills used in their cases. Students' experiences as lawyers also create rounds conversations that explore the norms of the profession and both the fit and the tension between the student and the norms. Finally, and importantly, rounds can be used to explore broader social justice issues that arise in the cases. Whether students talk about law, lawyering or the demands of the lawyer's role, students engage in the types of professional conversations that can enrich their lives and careers as lawyers. They consult peers for support, seek challenge to their own ideas and judgment and discover how dialogue promotes life-long professional learning.

...

Three premises ... underlie learning in rounds. (1) Rounds learning is "in-time;" students can immediately see relevance to their work. (2) Through collaborative learning, students develop insights for contextual thinking, explore professional identity, and find support for stressful work. (3) Dialogue with peers is an important method for engaging reflective practice; reflection in rounds helps students to apply, test, and refine lawyering theory while simultaneously developing professional norms.

...

A. "Just In-Time" vs. "Just-In-Case" Learning

Unlike any other classroom conversation, the ideas and thoughts that students have in rounds matter to the work each student is doing. Because students talk about topics they need to and want to address, they engage in "in-time" learning.... Other students catch the urgency of the task. Much of what students have learned in law school and in the law school clinical seminar, by contrast, is "just in-case" learning. Teachers identify what students are likely to need to know "just in case" it comes up during representation or later in their work as lawyers. In rounds, students often identify topics or, as here, teachers recognize a learning moment arising from an immediate, timely issue in a student's on-going lawyering.

Because the rounds conversation has no fixed agenda, students can shape it to serve their "in-time" learning as the conversation progresses. Adult learning theorists tell us that adults learn through education that integrates what students know with new experiences. In the example above, the students help their colleagues find answers about the consequences of bankruptcy by integrating what they know about research methods with the clients' experiences. In rounds, students explicitly build on one another's knowledge. Learning located in experience is powerful; once students integrate learning into prior experiences they recall it more readily and can use it effectively.

Rounds conversations grounded in "in-time" learning for the group work best. In the connections between what the presenting students are doing and their own work, students find relevance in the conversation.

. . .

B. Collaborative Learning

Through collaborative learning, students think about legal issues contextually and see themselves as an important part of that context. Working together they often identify a range of options, and in that process, they learn another important lesson: that professional work involves exercising practical judgments under conditions of uncertainty. Collaborative learning allows students to develop new ideas through dialogue with others. Finally, collaborative learning provides support to lessen the stress of practice.

Students build skills of contextual thinking by developing the capacity to see situations through the perspectives of others. In subjecting their decision-making to exploration by their peers, student lawyers get a window in rounds into how and why others may see different choices. They begin to identify which contexts matter in problem definition and how they shape solutions.

. . .

By engaging in personal narratives about their work, students can begin to see how they are an important part of the context that needs to be explored. When students tell their case stories, they explain themselves to their colleagues and also to themselves. Narrative about clients allows the listeners and speakers to position the storyteller; what is told and how it is told identifies the frame of reference of the narrator and reveals the perspective of the storyteller.

. . .

These same perspective conversations help students learn deeply about themselves. As they justify their beliefs and test them against those of others, students who are engaged in a supportive and challenging collaborative environment can learn how their perspectives shape their judgments.

When colleagues identify new choices supported by different assumptions, students become aware of many unexamined choices. Collaborative conversations help students lose more quickly the "either-or-analysis" of novice thinking. As novices, they look for 'the' answer and are uncomfortable with the ambiguity that collaborative exploration often reveals. However, by offering a supportive environment while identifying these many more options, students can both share the common frustrations that beginners face of acting without knowing all they want to know as well as ways of managing that uncertainty by exploring together the significant contexts of the particular case.

Much of legal education, including clinical education, can be viewed as transmission-oriented education; however, rounds conversations are often sites of dialogic learning in which "emergent knowledge" develops. Through conversation, as students reflect together, they often gain new insights and develop new ideas about what works. As students try to reconcile or assess divergent views, they produce co-constructed knowledge through a dialogue where ideas are shared and built upon.

...

Rounds conversations also help build a sense of peer cohesion and support. Lawyering is stressful work, especially for beginners. Novice bankruptcy lawyers, unsure of what they knew and needed to know, engaged their classmates in an inquiry that answered many of their questions; the group together improved the counseling to be provided by each team. Their colleagues who have more distance may have greater clarity than the new lawyers in any given case, who can be overwhelmed by ambiguity and indecision. The more that students work on each other's cases, the more they build a sense of being in a group with a common purpose. By encouraging students to share their feelings and reactions, teachers help group members learn that they are not alone in feeling stress and uncertainty; the pain of client stories overwhelms others too.

Seeing that their problems are not unique, students personalize their problems or reactions less: they do not feel "abnormal." Sharing this kind of information facilitates mutual aid.

...

Finally, professional identity is inherently a group identity. Law faculty and lawyers transmit explicitly and implicitly what it means to be a lawyer. As new lawyers, students practice using transmitted knowledge even as they reinvent their identities as lawyers through practice. Creating space while still in school for the group and the individual to adopt and adapt professional norms enables students to make that process explicit and to negotiate their way through it with their professional peers.

C. Reflection

All professionals learn through the process of reflection, a process frequently taught in clinical programs. Through rounds conversations, students learn reflective practice as well as important lessons about lawyering. We teach reflection by focusing students on past events and on events as they occur and shape each other's cases. Reflective conversations address specific events in particular contexts that allow students to give concrete meaning to theories about lawyering and legal systems that they are learning in seminar. At the same time, they explore when those theories need refining. By explicitly naming the process, teachers improve students' learning of reflective practice while building substantive knowledge about lawyering.

As in supervision, in round conversations students reflect on actions, but with a broader base of experience and multiple viewpoints that provide additional insights about why the case progressed the way it did or how another approach might be more effective.... As it does in all problem solving, problem definition influence[s] solutions.

...

Could these process and substantive lessons have been learned in supervision? Perhaps, but peer conversations often trigger reflection and they almost always improve the lessons to be drawn from the reflection. An important aspect of reflection involves surfacing tacit norms or assumptions that underlie a judgment made to take a case in a particular direction. Those norms or assumptions often remain hidden until someone in the group articulates a different approach or, as here, the teacher brings client perspectives into the mix. New ideas and points of view generate surprise, causing the student to wonder why somebody else sees it differently. Rounds conversations encourage reflection because even if the individual student sees no surprises, his or her classmates often do. Through this collective process, students can identify and evaluate the strategies or theories that were implicit in a pattern of behavior or the feeling for a situation that has led them to adopt a particular action.

Learning through reflection on experience requires that novice professionals begin to practice before they know everything. A difficult and scary process that requires an honest and searching inquiry about paths taken and mistakes, rounds conversations reinforce the value of these inquiries and make the process less intimidating by drawing on the support of the group.

Reflective, collaborative and adult learning theories help explain why rounds provide students with meaningful opportunities for professional development. The next sections explore what students learn as well as suggest how teachers can plan for and participate in rounds.

II. Professional Reasoning and Ethical Decision Making

Rounds provide each student a rich context for learning that extends beyond the particular slice of a lawyer's work that each experiences alone. This broader and more varied context allows the teacher to introduce and reinforce habits of "thinking like a lawyer," such as moving from the particular to the general, contextualized thinking, and parallel universe thinking. In professional dialogues focused on their colleagues' cases and projects, students practice repeatedly these habits of mind, through which they develop professional skills while shaping their professional identity and accompanying values.

A. Moving from the Particular to the General

One of the core competencies of the reflective lawyer that rounds teach is developing, applying and testing theory in the context of the real world. Rounds utilize the experiences of a few to illuminate something of use to all, focusing conversation on a particular moment in one case that takes others to a more general understanding of the meaning of similar moments. Working with the group, on the one hand, to both identify and shape their insights, and on the other, to make visible a process for developing and testing their theories, the teacher helps the students learn how to use clusters of particular experiences to reshape lawyering theory over a lifetime of professional practice. In addition to using this process to understand lawyering activity, this process also is essential for exploring the complexities of lawyering for social justice.

Teaching in rounds, like all clinical teaching, involves a series of judgments about how to get from the practical questions and descriptions that students often bring to the discussion to identifying, naming and developing theories that will inform not only particular questions but practice itself. Sometimes, rounds rely upon those theories that have been taught in another clinic context, such as the seminar with its readings or in supervision. Since students must apply these theories in practice and test their strengths and limitations, rounds examines from the perspective of many students' experiences whether a theory informs reality or how reality informs understanding of a theory.

At other times, students construct theories from the empirical observations of the group. Starting with a report from a team on an occurrence, such as a trial, a negotiation, or a counseling session, the group looks back at what has happened and organically moves (or the teacher moves it) from a description of a particular event to an analysis of the relationship between that event and a decision or action by the team. By doing so, students develop tentative hypotheses about lawyering that other students test through the prism of similar experiences and insights. They can see the validity and limits of their hypotheses. Teachers help the students see connections that might not otherwise be apparent between their experiences and those of others, often including those of the teacher.

The thrill of victory and the agony of defeat are enduring moments in rounds conversations. Through reflection, lawyers find meaning in both instances by exploring not only results but also the decisions and actions that define the lawyer's work on behalf of clients.

...

B. Contextualized Thinking

Thinking like a lawyer also requires thinking contextually. While we encourage students to move from the particular to the general, generalizations may be useful or problematic depending upon the particulars that define a problem. In rounds, students learn that the answer "it depends" is not an evasion but a call to the critical inquiry of analyzing what factors make a difference. By saying that contexts matter, we teach students to identify what variables matter in applying or revising a theory. Multiple experiences help students develop sophisticated thinking about the categories that alter a generalization.

...

C. Parallel Universe Thinking

In other work, Sue and Jean Koh Peters developed and described the process of "Parallel Universe" thinking, an essential habit to building cultural competence in practice. Parallel Universe thinking involves identifying multiple explanations for the same behavior, a core cross-cultural habit in recognition of the role that culture plays in the interpretation we give to behavior. Rounds are ideal conversations to develop the students' skill in parallel universe thinking. When identifying alternative explanations for behavior, especially when they feel judgmental or negative about client behavior, students can help each other see alternative explanations. Often other students who have had experiences similar to the client or to the student can see other explanations based on their experiences.

...

D. Connecting Skills to Role and Values

Clients and cases that test students' conceptions about the lawyer-client relationship raise good topics for rounds. (Should I go to the client's home to meet with him? Should I accept a gift from my client? Should I help my client find a place to live? Should I tell my client that her clothes are inappropriate for court?) The Rules of Professional Conduct rarely provide answers. In the midst of defining themselves as lawyers, students encounter questions like these daily. Rounds help students spot attorney-client role issues. For example, when one student asks, "Should I give my cell phone number to my client?" other students realize they gave their cell phone numbers without thinking. Having identified the choice, students can evaluate the pros and cons of giving the number, connecting this choice to the kind of relationship they want to have with the client.

This conversation leads naturally to questions of appropriate boundaries and power dynamics in the attorney-client relationship. For example, what if the lawyer has the client's cell number but the client does not have the lawyer's. Should the relationship be symmetrical? Should a lawyer or client expect immediate contact or should "office hours" be used for communication between lawyer and client? This conversation, like many others, takes the students' experiences and allows them to shape professional boundaries within a modern communication context.

By examining these questions with colleagues, students can question their preconceptions about the attorney-client relationship and see opportunities to reconstruct this relationship differently with every client. They can begin to understand the connections between the goals and values of both lawyer and client and the decisions and actions available to them.

...

III. Generating Conversations: Rounds Structures, Topics & Expectations

Faculty members shape rounds conversations by setting ground rules; selecting topics, structures and preparation requirements; or by asking students to make these decisions. Each clinical program's faculty and students will shape rounds differently, depending on learning goals. For example, in all rounds, students learn how to move from the particular to the general, but a clinic's lawyering priorities often dictate the selection of lawyering theories for focused inquiry. The following section discusses the choice points for setting up the conversations and identifies the unique perspectives that students and faculty contribute to the choices.

...

C. Addressing Impediments to Successful Rounds

Some frustrated students believe their questions have answers that the teacher knows or should know and that teachers withhold these answers because of the inherent perversity of law professors or failure of preparation. This search for expert answers has a potential corollary: skepticism that their peers, as inexperienced as they are, have anything useful to say. Sometimes faculty do not have answers; more often, faculty are interested in seeing what develops in the conversation either because new ideas may emerge or because learning how to think through the answers together is an important goal.

Facing this same student impulse in supervision, typical faculty responses identify the faculty's reluctance to offer an answer. "It sounds as if you think I (should) know the answer to this and that my failure to provide it to you is upsetting." "Would my providing the answer help you learn how to find solutions yourself?" "How can an experienced lawyer be helpful to you?" In rounds, the teacher has other opportunities to teach these points. By engaging the group in thinking about how the frustrated team can find answers to its question, the teacher demonstrates the process: "How will research or investigation help?" "Does anyone have any leads or suggestions?" "If you think that there is an experienced person or expert who can help, how will you find him or her, what do the rest of you think is the best way to prepare for talking with the expert? What question(s) will you ask, and how will you use the information you get?" To the extent that students participate in answering these kinds of questions, their answers can be more persuasive to their reluctant colleagues than any attempt to directly defend the clinical method of maximizing student responsibility for professional work.

...

Megan Bess, Nira Geevargis & June T. Tai, *Case Rounds Redefined: Multidisciplinary Perspectives in Reflective Practice**

75 Wash. U. J. L. & Pol'y 71 (2024)

...

III. Why a More Reflective Practice?

Rounds support lawyer development, including professional identity formation, autonomy, community, collaboration, curiosity, and listening. These skills foster the development of judgment, which, in turn, forms the core of the expertise that clients require from lawyers. "Legal professionals face complex and unpredictable situations, and therefore, they require a reflective framework which allows them greater empathy with their clients. The [case study method] ... does not equip law clinic students ... with a suitable methodology to deal with complex legal and human issues encountered in professional practice." Legal education is not unique here—in nearly all professions, resources are over-allocated to technical rationality (substantive knowledge) and under-allocated to dealing with the uncertainty that professionals face in practice. Furthermore, in all professions, uncertain situations occur where technical rationality does not apply and the professional must experiment and see how the situation plays out. During this experimentation, the professional is reflecting-in-action.

Reflective practice itself is a framework for turning thoughtful practice into potential learning, with the possibility to modify approaches to practice. Professionals learn more from reflection-in-action if they study it and treat it as an art. Kurtz defines reflective practice as "a form of in-depth thinking about work activity with the aim of developing as a practitioner." The increase of technology has "raised expectations as to how quickly work can be done and answers can be found to our questions." Reflective practice works to correct this fast pace, helping practitioners generate new questions and reframe thinking about questions with no easy answers. Historically, reflective practice has linked the integration of theory and practice to developing professional expertise. But reflection has many other benefits for student learning, including reducing stress and anxiety, improving communication and interpersonal skills, fostering problem solving, and increasing resiliency. Reflective practice "is synonymous with experiential, self-directed, and action learning."

...

Reflective practice in legal education can integrate knowledge, skills, and values in students and humanize legal education amid documented high rates of stress, depression, and substance abuse in the profession. Furthermore, reflective practice can

* Excerpts are reprinted with the permission of the authors and the Washington University Journal of Law and Policy.

support psychological needs and autonomy, two areas Lawrence Krieger and Kennon Sheldon identified as important in helping to ease the negative effects of legal education on student well-being.

Michelle Leering's model for an integrated reflective practitioner includes reflection on technique (skills), critical reflection (knowledge), and self-reflection (values). Critical reflection includes the need to practice unpacking assumptions or automatic frames of reference. A self-reflective practitioner considers who they are and the purpose of the work they are doing. Self-reflection supports the integration of personal and professional identities and develops a capacity for self-awareness that supports ethical development.

A. Support for Professional Identity Formation During Transitions

Calls for increased reflection in legal education take place against the backdrop of incorporating professional identity formation into law school curricular and extracurricular programming. In February 2022, the American Bar Association adopted revisions to the Standards for Approval of Law Schools that require schools to provide "substantial opportunities" for students to develop a professional identity.... [R]eflection ... provides key opportunities for the development of professional identity.

Professional identity formation is a process through which new entrants into the profession develop and internalize the values of the legal profession. It involves staged socialization through which students gradually transition to members of the profession. The qualities that comprise professional identity formation include deep engagement with the profession's purpose, a sense of meaning grounded in work, the conception of self as a member of the profession, interpretation of situations and response to clients through the profession's standards, and a desire to contribute to the profession. To support this process, legal educators need to provide experiences that help students develop their professional identities.

i. Major Transitions in Legal Education

As part of any professional student's path to becoming a member of their chosen profession, they will experience significant transitions—critically intense learning periods during which students reexamine and reform their sense of self and identity. Professional identity formation consists of a series of identity transformations that often occur during transitions and can provoke uncertainty as students reflect on their fit within the profession. Periods of transitions, particularly those in which students are in the settings they will experience as lawyers, are focal points for legal education to support students in professional identity formation. Neil Hamilton studied students at his law school to determine which experiences in the first year were major transitions and found summer employment that follows a student's first year to be a "singularly important authentic transition." This research supports what many legal educators have perceived—that real-world experiences are major milestones on the path from student to lawyer.

ii. Transitions in Other Disciplines

Other professions have more thoroughly examined how transitions shape professional identity. Medical educators found that transformational learning most often happens in everyday workplace settings. Subsets of medicine have also investigated and acknowledged the link between transitions and professional identity formation. Other professions, including social work, teaching, music, and counseling acknowledged this relationship as well.

Transitions are most consequential when students struggle, reflect on their work, and shift their sense of self. Medical education provides support for transitions that accompany authentic professional experiences. The focus of medical education is on helping students make it through these experiences with an enhanced sense of agency and meaning. Reflection is a key component of professional identity formation as students perform real-world work. Rounds offer opportunities for students to examine their real-world lawyering work and reflect on their reactions to it, thus furthering professional identity formation. [Case and project supervision, along with [r]ounds allow students to engage as a group in the reflective and self-critical thinking required to explore the norms of the profession.

B. Attorney Well-Being

Rounds emphasize autonomy and autonomy-supportive supervision, along with relatedness to others—all factors that are strong predictors of attorney well-being. Much of the literature on well-being, satisfaction, and happiness in the legal profession focuses on the amount of control that lawyers exercise in their jobs. This desire for control relates to a sense of mattering and believing that one's contribution matters. Students with autonomy-supportive teachers demonstrate increased classroom engagement, intrinsic motivation, and well-being. Autonomy-supportive teaching focuses on providing as much choice as possible. In situations where choice cannot be provided, the teacher provides an explanation. Finally, the teacher communicates that they are considering the students' point of view.

This autonomy is seemingly rare in law school. In in-house clinics, students experience autonomy in their fieldwork, supervision, and rounds. Moreover, both clinic and externship rounds provide law students with autonomy by offering choice within a structure. When conducting rounds, the instructor relinquishes a fair amount of control. Students choose the topic for rounds; the presenter controls what to share; and participants choose the questions to ask and solutions to suggest. Students assess whether the rounds sessions were helpful and consider lessons that impact future practice. The class engages in lawyering skills such as fact gathering and problem solving and chooses how to accomplish these goals. Given the importance of student choice to autonomy and autonomy-support, we believe conducting … rounds [as a supplement to actual supervision] in a safe and supported environment and allowing the students in the seminar to dictate the terms of their engagement furthers well-being.

Also implicit in the use of rounds is the emphasis on collaboration and building community. The increasingly complex nature of legal practice demands that attorneys and other professionals work seamlessly in teams to deliver high-quality legal services. Although effective teamwork is critical to working in law firms, much of legal training focuses on the individual. Relatedness to others, however, like autonomy, is a predictor of well-being. Building community and creating opportunities to work with others, therefore, fosters happiness.

Case rounds are one way clinical programs have created opportunities for building community and encouraging collaboration among students. At its heart, effective collaboration requires trust, including "a willingness to make oneself vulnerable to another person." As demonstrated in our opening anecdote, discussing experiences creates "emotional bonds that connect co-workers and develop through shared experiences, reciprocal disclosure, and demonstrations that individuals will not take advantage of each other."

C. Curiosity

As work evolves it will be important for employees to continuously explore and adapt to their surroundings. Thus, the importance of curiosity will increase in the workplace. Curious employees approach difficult situations more creatively and perform better on the job.

Researchers have found stimulating curiosity can enhance learning success. Curiosity also plays an important role in creative problem solving. Most problems are ill-defined, making it difficult for people to know early in the process of solving them what information is important to crafting high-quality solutions. A commitment to seeking more information can prevent an overly narrow focus too early in the problem-solving process. Curiosity is especially valuable when solving ambiguous and complex problems, since seeking out a wide range of information can bolster the problem-solving process.

Additionally, curious employees are more open to feedback and innovation. Professor Francesca Gino conducted a study that asked employees what they were curious about at the start of their workday and encouraged them to ask "why questions" throughout the day. She found that prompting workers' curiosity led to higher measures of innovative behaviors at work. Another study found that curiosity also influences how people receive feedback. Creative workers high in curiosity asked for feedback on their work in a more open manner than those lower in curiosity. Workers higher in curiosity were also more likely to make changes, resulting in overall improved design.

Case rounds help students understand the importance of sustained curiosity when addressing problems. As students engage in rounds, problems and potential solutions evolve, and students learn the value of not jumping too quickly to give advice. Both Geevargis and Tai encourage students to spend more time on the clarification stage-where students ask about the context of the situation—as opposed to the solutions stage. And, by asking students to compare their problem presentation as originally formulated in Stage 2 to their problem definition in Stage 4 they better understand the value of staying open-minded and refraining from rushing to conclusions. Staying curious long enough to gain a deeper and clearer picture of the issue presented not only enables students to provide more useful advice, but also gives the presenter space to better process and define the problem.

D. Listening

Most people assess themselves as being good listeners. In reality, many studies show that adults are not good listeners. Distractions abound in modern workplaces and most professionals admit to multitasking when listening.

"The primary challenge or barrier to skilled listening is internal." When listening to clients, many lawyers start questioning and seeking to analyze information and, thus, their attention wanders. A lawyer's internal voice prevents them from noticing the way the client tells the story, which provides clues about what matters to that client. Good listening, however, helps the attorney build trust and gather the information needed to help the client. Yet, educators and practitioners alike note the lack of intentional training on listening skills in lawyer education.

Jack Zenger and Joseph Folkman researched top listeners and made four conclusions about the behaviors and characteristics of good listeners. First, the best listeners ask questions. Second, they make the experience positive for the other party by supporting them and creating a safe environment for the conversation. Third, neither participant becomes defensive. Fourth, the listeners provide feedback and suggestions. Zenger and Folkman describe levels of listening that build on each other, including an environment free of distractions, seeking to understand through questions, picking up on non-verbal cues, developing an increased understanding of the problems or issues, and asking questions to clarify assumptions. These findings parallel cognitive theory, which suggests that developing listening skills should include (1) modeling listening techniques, then (2) trying the technique and receiving coaching through feedback and assessment, (3) followed by an opportunity for reflection.

Reflective practice groups encourage exactly this kind of active listening, modeling and feedback, and learning through dialogue with others.... [R]ounds sessions create a safe and distraction-free environment and encourage increased understanding through questions. The focus on sustained curiosity and accompanying emotions also develops listening skills. This is amplified in rounds where students are encouraged to work collaboratively, stop and assess the presenter's initial definition of the problem, and take time to see how the problem evolved over time as a result of their conversation.

...

Deborah Epstein,
Beyond the Classroom: Applying the Stages of Rounds Structure to Analysis of Clinical Supervision *

Appearing in TRANSFORMING THE EDUCATION OF LAWYERS: THE THEORY AND PRACTICE OF CLINICAL PEDAGOGY (Susan J. Bryant, Elliott S. Milstein & Ann Shalleck eds., Carolina Academic Press 2014)

Clinicians across the country confess to dreading the case rounds classes they teach. They express frustration with low levels of student participation, discussions that remain at surface-level, and a tendency to accept relatively pat solutions to complex problems. And they confide that many of their students comment negatively on rounds classes in year-end course evaluations.

In recent years, many of these same clinicians have experimented with the "stages of rounds" structure. They are uniformly enthusiastic in their feedback: the structure has transformed their teaching experiences in litigation, mediation, policy, legislation, and transactional clinics. The structure reliably deepens and enriches student rounds discussions; there is no question that the method serves as an incredibly important teaching tool.

And part of its power stems from how easily the structure can be successfully applied in contexts well beyond that of the clinic seminar. In fact, the stages of rounds method itself evolved out of a series of workshops with clinical faculty, focused on challenges arising out of student supervision experiences.

...

Evolution of the Stages of Rounds Structure

What we now call the "stages of rounds" structure evolved organically out of a series of programs designed to help experienced and junior clinical faculty explore challenges in student supervision. Both American University Washington College of Law and Georgetown University Law Center have developed structured training programs for entry-level clinical teachers.... In the fall of 2007, Elliott Milstein, Ann Shalleck (American), and I convened a similar series of rounds discussions for senior clinicians at Georgetown and American University. We held these sessions fairly regularly over a three-year period, adding Jane Aiken (Georgetown) as a fourth facilitator and expanding the group by inviting clinicians from all of the DC-area law schools.

Starting in 2008, Georgetown inaugurated its Summer Institute on Clinical Teaching, a conference for experienced clinical faculty members from around the country. Rounds sessions on supervision was a central component of the Institute's small group

* Excerpts are reprinted with the permission of the author and Carolina Academic Press.

work. Most of the Institute facilitators had experience in running rounds sessions in other contexts: Jane Aiken, Sue Bryant, Catherine Klein (Catholic), Wally Mlyniec (Georgetown), Ann Shalleck, and myself.... Participants have now organized supervision rounds at their home institutions in California, Delaware, Georgia, Michigan, Minnesota, and elsewhere.

All of these rounds sessions on clinical supervision have met with an enthusiastic response, regardless of participants' level of experience, subject-matter focus, or the size of their schools' clinical program.... But as our collective experience in facilitating these conversations deepened, we developed a basic, five-part "stages of rounds" structure which we believe to be maximally effective. Although each of us prefers a slightly different set of stages, the models are simply variations on an essential theme.... [T]his model imposes five stages on a rounds discussion: (1) Description; (2) Problem Diagnosis; (3) Goals; (4) Problem Solving; and (5) Lessons Learned.

Why Stages of Rounds Enhances Analysis of Clinical Supervision Challenges

Why is the rounds structure so useful in the context of analyzing student supervision experiences? The elegant, five-stage simplicity of this method is deceptive; its success derives from the way it forces participants to move past the imperfect instincts which often limit our problem-solving capacity.

First, just like our students, clinicians often leap too rapidly to problem diagnosis. We make assumptions based on perceived similarities between past experiences and the issue under discussion; these shortcuts cause us to miss important distinguishing data points. The stages of rounds structure create space for a full exploration of the factual context and curbs the tendency to jump prematurely to potential solutions.

Second, for most clinicians, supervision typically occurs in the context of professional isolation; many teach at schools where they are the only full-time clinical faculty member, or one of a small handful. If a clinician's only opportunity to reflect on her supervision performance is individual in nature, she will inevitably miss the rich complexity that arises from generating ideas and input from a group of engaged colleagues. The structural focus on multiple diagnoses of a challenging situation is particularly important here. This process promotes far more complex analysis than is possible when only a single theory is explored.

Third, even those of us fortunate enough to have a sizable community of clinical colleagues still struggle with numerous demands on our time. The day-to-day demands of teaching students, representing clients, and administering a small law office can crowd out time to reflect on our own performance. Consulting with others about a particular incident or relationship can appear to be an unrealistic luxury. And our colleagues face similar demands; they too may be forced to sacrifice some degree of quality for efficiency in collaborative conversations. The stages of rounds structure force all of us to slow down, to immerse ourselves fully in the facts and the larger context.

...

Finally, these obstacles to focused, rigorous reflection are compounded by the complex intimacy of the supervisory relationship. Even in the most straightforward situations, the student-teacher dynamic is sufficiently complex that it can be difficult for even the most experienced supervisor to fully grasp the nature and contours of a problem, or to come up with a meaningful range of strategic responses.... In these situations, where the most significant challenges are most likely to arise, it can be particularly difficult to maintain a professional perspective and obtain clarity and insight into one's work.

Essential Prerequisites for a Productive Clinical Supervision Rounds Session

Experience teaches that detailed problem definition and description, thoughtful problem selection, and clear ground rules are essential foundations for a successful rounds session on supervision challenges. Each of these facilitation challenges is explored briefly below.

1. Problem Definition and Description

When I first began facilitating supervision rounds, my colleagues and I asked participants to submit, in advance, "a description of a difficult problem you have encountered as a clinical supervisor." This bare-bones call for submissions resulted in few of the type we were hoping for. Several participants sent in a one- or two-sentence problem description -too brief for the facilitators to get a real sense of the issues presented. Others sent in descriptions of problems which they already had resolved with complete success; by definition, these problems no longer lent themselves to meaningful group discussion.

...

Without solid submissions, a facilitator is obviously handicapped in her ability to select the best possible challenge for group discussion. Accordingly, careful attention must be paid to defining the kind of submissions being requested.

...

Below is one successful example of a first-time call for submissions:

> Please send us a written description of a supervision challenge you've encountered as a clinician. The most useful challenges for rounds discussions tend to be those where you perceived the choices available to you as significantly difficult or risky, and where the issues are either still pending or where the resolution was, in your view, less than successful. The challenge should be one for which you believe that your own thinking might benefit from group input. Once you have a challenge in mind, please describe it in as much detail as possible, so that we can get a concrete feel for the issues as you experienced them. Please consider the following issues:

- What is the context of the supervision challenge you'd like to discuss? What background information should the group have about the student, the case, the client, the clinic structure, etc., so that we can understand the issues raised?
- What is your diagnosis of the challenge, both in terms of the issue itself as well as its underlying causes (e.g., if the issue involves a student who froze up in court, what is your theory of what happened and why it happened in this particular instance, with this particular student)?
- How does your diagnosis relate to the supervisory approach you used?
- Why did you decide to approach the issue as you did?
- Why did your interaction with this student or about this issue feel so challenging?

This request for submissions works because it fully and explicitly defines what constitutes a useful challenge for group discussion. By prompting participants to provide information about issues that are likely to be explored in a rounds conversation, it helps surface information from which a facilitator can assess the utility of a challenge for rounds and simultaneously primes participants in advance for discussion of these issues.

2. Problem Selection

Once a rounds facilitator has collected several detailed submissions, she must select the one which best lends itself to productive group analysis. A number of considerations can contribute to the analysis here:

- Does the clinician appear to recall sufficient factual details so that a thorough exploration of the situation, as well as the larger context, is realistic?
- Is the challenge sufficiently complex so that it can support a rich analysis and multiple potential diagnoses?
- Does the challenge present predictable points of connection with the experiences of other group participants, so that the group can both draw on past experiences for insight and can learn lessons transferable to situations likely to arise in their own clinics?
- Does the challenge raise a thematic issue that commonly arises in the supervision context (professionalism, client centeredness, making assumptions, maintaining boundaries, etc.)?
- Is this challenge sufficiently different from others the group has previously discussed? Does it appear to build in an interesting way on previous group discussions?

Once a group of regular participants has engaged in several sessions of rounds on supervision, they may begin to develop an interest in focusing on particular kinds of issues.

3. Ground Rules

Setting ground rules at the outset is no less important in rounds sessions for clinical faculty than it is for students. Perhaps the two most important of these are: (1) confidentiality of discussions; and (2) regular participation by group members. Confidentiality is, of course, essential to the establishment of trust. Regular participation, however, is another key component of trust building. As the same group meets regularly over time, sharing stories and insights, participants come to know each other and are less likely to engage in self-censorship.

Trust is critical to the success of a rounds project. We routinely ask our students to make themselves vulnerable; we require them to perform simulated lawyering tasks in front of their colleagues, to request and absorb critique, or to share their reflections on what they might have done differently after a lawyering "performance." But as teachers, we ourselves are rarely called upon to do the same.... Because the basic purpose of rounds on clinical supervision is to share and examine stories involving problematic choices, failed techniques, or unresolved frustrations, ensuring that participants can trust each other matters a great deal.

Lessons Learned From Rounds on Supervision

Those who have participated in clinical supervision rounds have found that when the proper foundation is set and the stages of rounds structure are imposed, the discussion is almost always a productive one.

...

Several clinicians noted that rounds discussions helped them obtain clarity about their own tendency to see supervision issues in terms of "problem students." They would typically focus on the student's capacity, attitude, and behavior in analyzing a supervision challenge, often failing to apply the same degree of focus on either the larger situational context or their own contributions to the dynamic. They left rounds with clarity about the need to rethink their approach and to find ways to methodically ensure that multiple and complex contributing factors are included in the problem diagnosis.

...

Many participants gained insight into their own tendency to avoid focused discussions about issues involving race. Whether conscious or unconscious, this tendency resulted in supervision conversations that started out including race as a factor but quickly shifted to less politically charged ground. Clinicians noted that they (and many of their students) often felt more comfortable discussing other categories of "difference," such as gender and class, and supervision conversations would either lump multiple issues together, blurring the focus, or would concentrate entirely on the easier issues. The rounds discussion helped them see the critical importance of making an intentional effort to focus directly on race when it arises, both to enhance substantive student learning and to model and normalize such conversations for our students.

Clinicians mentioned rounds discussions centered on when and how to intervene when problems arise in a student team's working relationship. Participants recognized that they often apply a different standard to interventions in such situations, taking far more control, and doing so far earlier than they otherwise would. They also realized how frequently they tend to make hasty assumptions based on the gender and race of the students on the team in question. The rounds conversation highlighted that, when intervening in response to a student team's interpersonal tensions, the supervisor's actions must reinforce the overall clinic pedagogy, where students are assuming the role of professionals, and are expected to be capable of strategically resolving their own lawyering challenges.

Some clinicians noted that rounds helped expose unexamined assumptions about the appropriate role of a supervisor's own emotional and psychological responses to student behavior. Several participants realized that they automatically assumed that they must "park" their own reactions outside of the supervision dynamic, and that there could be no productive way to share these with a student. Participants were able to gain insight about when and how a supervisor's personal reactions can provide useful fodder for student learning. They also had the opportunity to think through ways in which a choice to avoid a supervision discussion, even about issues ostensibly distinct from client representation, can substantially impede a student's opportunity to learn.

...

Endnotes

1. Jed D. Gonzalo, Philip A. Masters, Richard J. Simons & Cynthia H. Chuang, *Attending Rounds and Bedside Case Presentations: Medical Student and Medicine Resident Experiences and Attitudes*, 21 Teaching and Learning in Med. 105 (2009). Indeed, "[l]earning medicine at the bedside through patient interaction with physician guidance" began as early as the mid-17th century. *Id.*

2. Colm R. Breatnach, Alejandro Floh, Melanie Hamilton & Briseida Mema, *Case-Based Education Rounds—The Eternal Heart of an International Training Program*, 12 Frontiers in Pediatrics 1, 2 (2024).

3. Gonzalo et al., *supra* note 1, at 105.

4. Jack Ende, Editorial, *Rounding Alone: Assessing the Value of Grand Rounds in Contemporary Departments of Medicine*, 78 Mayo Clinic Proceedings 547 (2003).

5. *See* Shaifali Sandal, Michael C. Iannuzzi & Stephen J. Knohl, *Can We Make Grand Rounds "Grand" Again?*, 5 J. Graduate Med. Educ. 560 (2013); Perla J. Marang-van de Mheen, John P. Browne, Eric J. Thomas & Bryony Dean Franklin, Editorial, *Grand Rounds in Methodology: A New Series to Contribute to Continuous Improvement of Methodology and Scientific Rigour in Quality and Safety*, 32 BMJ Quality & Safety 13 (2022).

6. Deborah Epstein, Jane H. Aiken & Wallace J. Mlyniec, Teaching the Clinic Seminar 531 (2014).

7. *Id.*

8. *Id.*

9. Susan Bryant & Elliott Milstein, *Generating Conversations: Planning and Facilitating Rounds*, *in* Susan Bryant, Elliott S. Milstein & Ann C. Shalleck, Transforming the Education of Lawyers: The Theory and Practice of Clinical Pedagogy 131 (2014).

10. Bryant & Milstein, *Rounds: A "Signature Pedagogy" for Clinical Education?*, 14 Clinical L. Rev. 195 (2007).

11. Robert D. Dinerstein, Elliott S. Milstein & Ann C. Shalleck, *Fifty Years of Clinical Legal Education at American University Washington College of Law: The Evolution of a Movement in Theory, Practice, and People*, 31 Am. U. J. Gender Soc. Pol'y & L. 257, 287–88 (2023).

12. Elizabeth C. Cooper, *The Case for Structured Rounds*, *in* Bryant, Milstein & Shalleck, *supra* note 9, at 151.

13. *See, e.g.*, Rebecca B. Rosenfeld, *The Examined Externship Is Worth Doing: Critical Self-Reflection and Externship Pedagogy*, 21 Clinical L. Rev. 127, 147 (2014) (describing Bryant and Milstein's article as the "definitive article" in the "rich" area of "curricular development" on clinical rounds); Dinerstein et al., *supra* note 12, at 288 (discussing the groundbreaking nature of Bryant and Milstein's article). For an example of a recent advances in clinical pedagogy incorporating the case rounds format, see, e.g., Eduardo R. Ferrer & Kristin N. Henning, *Critical Clinical Frames: Centering Adolescence, Race, Trauma, and Gender in Practice-Based Pedagogy*, 30 Clinical L. Rev. 113, 146 (2023).

14. *See generally* Ann Shalleck, *Clinical Contexts: Theory and Practice in Law and Supervision*, 21 N.Y.U. Rev. L. & Soc. Change 109 (1993) (discussing the various places in which supervision can take place and the need for efficiency in choosing the appropriate venue to transmit learning).

15. *See* Cooper, *supra* note 11, at 153.

16. *See* Bryant & Milstein, *supra* note 9, at 131.

17. Bryant & Milstein, *supra* note 10, at 250 (citation omitted).

18. *See, e.g.*, Nicole Smith Futrell, *The Practice and Pedagogy of Carceral Abolition in a Criminal Defense Clinic*, 45 N.Y.U. Rev. L. & Soc. Change 159, 193–95 (2021).

19. *See, e.g.*, Bryan L. Adamson, Bradford Colbert, Kathy Hessler, Katherine Kruse, Robert Kuehn, Mary Helen McNeal, Calvin Pang & David Santacroce, *The Status of Clinical Faculty in the Legal*

Academy: Report of the Task Force on the Status of Clinicians in the Legal Academy, 36 J. Leg. Prof. 353, 365 (2012) ("Case rounds demand thoughtful preparation and distillation of factual, legal, ethical, or procedural themes, and careful development of classroom methods through which students may illuminate those themes.")

20. Susan Bennett, Binny Miller, Michelle Assad, Maria Dooner, Mariam Hinds, Jessica Millward, Citlalli Ochoa, Charles Ross, Anne Schaufele & Caroline Wick, *Building a Culture of Scholarship with New Clinical Teachers by Writing About Social Justice Lawyering*, 31 Am. U. J. Gender Soc. Pol'y & L. 311, 344 (2023).

21. Becky L. Jacobs, *Cultivating Purposeful Curiosity in a Clinical Setting: Extrapolating from Case to Social Justice*, 21 Clinical L. Rev. 371, 388 (2015).

22. *See, e.g.*, Megan Bess, *Transitions Unexplored: A Proposal for Professional Identity Formation Following the First Year*, 29 Clinical L. Rev. 1, 20, 30–31 (2022). Rounds also helps develop leadership skills. *See* Paul Radvany, *Experiential Leadership: Teaching Collaboration through a Shared Leadership Model*, 27 Clinical L. Rev. 309, 357–58 (2021).

23. Megan Bess, Nira Geevargis & June T. Tai, *Case Rounds Redefined: Multidisciplinary Perspectives in Reflective Practice*, 74 Wash. U. J. L. & Pol'y 71, 112 (2024).

24. Epstein, Aiken & Mlyniec, *supra* note 6, at 521.

25. *See* Epstein, Aiken & Mlyniec, *supra* note 6, at 523; Brian Reichart, *Tunnel Vision: Causes, Effects, and Mitigation Strategies*, 45 Hofstra L. Rev. 451, 465–66 (2016) (citing Bryant & Milstein, *supra* note 10, at 195, 200–01.

26. Epstein, Aiken & Mlyniec, *supra* note 6, at 523.

27. Rosenfeld, *supra* note 13, at 147.

28. *Id.*

29. *See, e.g.*, Bryant & Milstein, *supra* note 9, at 132–35 (describing a five-step process: "description of event(s)," "problem identification or clarification," "goals," "lawyering strategies," and "lawyering lessons"); Carolyn Grose, *Uncovering and Deconstructing the Binary: Teaching (and Learning) Critical Reflection Clinic and Beyond*, 22 Clinical L. Rev. 301, 308–14 (2016) (explaining the transactional clinic's four-step process: "fact gathering, diagnosis, problem-solving, and evaluation"); Bess, Geevargis & Tai, *supra* note 23, at 76 (explaining the seven-step process: "issue selection; presentation of the issue without interruption; clarifying questions to get a full picture of the issue; problem definition; presentation of the goals; advice, next steps, and solution; and reflections on lessons learned").

30. Epstein, Aiken & Mlyniec, *supra* note 6, at 527.

31. The effect derives its name from the 1950 film *Rashomon*, directed by Akira Kurosawa. *See, e.g.*, Karl G. Heider, *The Rashomon Effect: When Ethnographers Disagree*, 90 Am. Anthropologist 73, 74 (1988).

32. For a fuller discussion of parallel-universe thinking, see Susan J. Bryant & Jean Koh Peters, *Six Practices for Connecting with Clients Across Culture: Habit Four, Working with Interpreters and Other Mindful Approaches*, *in* The Affective Assistance of Counsel: The Law as a Healing Profession 183 (Marjorie A. Silver ed., 2006).

33. Epstein, Aiken & Mlyniec, *supra* note 6, at 528; *see also* Reichart, *supra* note 25, at 465–66 (citing Bryant & Milstein, *supra* note 10, at 232–33).

34. Epstein, Aiken & Mlyniec, *supra* note 6, at 528.

35. *Id.* at 529.

36. *See generally* Helen H. Kang, *Use of Role Play and Interview Modes in Law Clinic Case Rounds to Teach Essential Legal Skills and to Maximize Meaningful Participation*, 19 Clinical L. Rev. 207 (2012).

37. Epstein, Aiken & Mlyniec, *supra* note 6, at 530.

38. *Id.*

39. *Id.* at 254.

40. Frank S. Bloch, *The Andragogical Basis of Clinical Legal Education*, 35 Vand. L. Rev. 321, 348 (1982).

41. Caitlyn Ultimo, *Defining Collaboration | Types of Collaboration and How to Improve Them*, Webex Blog, https://blog.webex.com/collaboration/what-is-collaboration/.

42. Peter Toll Hoffman, *The Stages of the Clinical Supervisory Relationship*, 4 ANTIOCH L.J. 301, 302 (1986).

43. *Id.*

44. *See* Hilary E. Cameron, *The E-Team Project: A Teamwork Approach to Clinical Legal Education*, 23 J. L. & Soc. Pol'y 30 (2014) (arguing that the University of Toronto's Emergency Team was a success in part due to their collaborative approach); *see also* Sameer M. Ashar, *Law Clinics and Collective Mobilization*, 14 Clinical L. Rev. 355 (2008) (referencing the work accomplished by teams of clinical students throughout the article).

45. Robert Dinerstein, *Report of the Committee on the Future of the In-House Clinic*, 42 J. Legal Educ. 511, 515 (1992); Cassandra L. Hill, *Peer Editing: A Comprehensive Pedagogical Approach to Maximize Opportunities, Integrate Collaborative Learning, and Achieve Desired Outcomes*, 11 Nev. L.J. 667 (2011); Jeffrey A. Van Detta, *Collaborative Problem-Solving Responsive to Diverse Learning Styles: Labor Law as an Active Learning Experience*, 24 N.C. Cent. L.J. 46 (2001).

46. Epstein, Aiken & Mlyniec *supra* note 6, at 521.

47. Susan J. Bryant, *Collaboration in Law and Practice: A Satisfying and Productive Process for a Diverse Profession*, 17 Vt. L. Rev. 459, 485 (1993).

48. *See* David F. Chavkin, *Matchmaker, Matchmaker: Student Collaboration in Clinical Programs*, 1 Clinical L. Rev. 199 (1994); *see also* Clifford S. Zimmerman, *Thinking Beyond My Own Experience: Reflections on Collaborative and Cooperative Learning Theory in the Law School Curriculum*, 31 Ariz. St. L.J. 957 (1999) (asserting that collaboration leads to more effective learning and better work product); *see also* Barbara Gabbert, David W. Johnson & Roger T. Johnson, *Cooperative Learning, Group-to-Individual Transfer, Process Gain, and the Acquisition of Cognitive Reasoning Strategies*, 120 J. Psychol 265 (1986) (finding that cooperation among first graders led to improved outcomes).

49. *See* Chavkin, note 48 at 213.

50. *Id.*

51. Zimmerman, *supra* note 48 at 963.

52. *Id.*

53. *Id.*

54. American Bar Association Section of Legal Education and Admissions to the Bar, *Report and Recommendations of the Task Force on Lawyer Competency: The Role of Law Schools*, (1979).

55. American Bar Association Section of Legal Education and Admissions to the Bar, *Task Force on Law Schools and the Profession: Narrowing the Gap*, (1972).

56. *See* Janet Weinstein, Linda Morton, Howard Taras & Vivian Reznik, *Teaching Teamwork to Law Students*, 63 J. J. Legal Educ. 36, 40 (2013) (arguing that collaboration should be part of the law school curriculum in part because "[e]ffective teamwork is critical to law firms"); *see also* James R. Whitaker, *Interdisciplinary Collaboration in Public Interest Law*, 13 Ariz. L. Rev. 909 (1971) (suggesting that "[i]nterdisciplinary collaboration may offer a workable methodology for investigating and solving complex public interest issues that frequently transcend the traditional boundaries of a lawyer's expertise").

57. *See* Weinstein, note 56 at 41.

58. Heidi K. Gardner, *Collaboration in Law Firms*, in The Practice Niche Practices, (Sept./Oct. 2024).

59. *Id.*

60. Whitaker, *supra* note 56, at 909.

61. *Id* at 909–915.

62. *See*, Melinda A. Healey, *Opening Up The In-House: A Model For Collaborative Holistic Services And Education In Law School Clinical Programs*, 75 Wash. J. of Law & Pol. 152 (2024). Collaboration also has a positive effect on leadership ability. *See generally*, Paul Radvany, *Experiential Leadership: Teaching Collaboration through a Shared Leadership Model*, 27 Clinical L. Rev. 309 (2021)

63. Deborah Epstein, *Beyond the Classroom: Applying the Stages of Rounds Structure*, *in* Bryant, Milstein & Shalleck, *supra* note 9 at 162, Epstein credits Elliot Milstein and Sue Bryant with running the first Supervision Rounds in 2007 at New York Law School, featuring a few dozen New York-area clinicians.

64. *Id.* at 162–63.

65. *Id.* at 162.

66. *Id.* at 163.

67. *Id.* at 163–64.

68. AALS Clinical Section: Teaching Methodologies Committee; *Online In-House Clinic Supervision /Teaching Rounds Application*, (2025) https://www.aals.org/sections/list/clinical-legal-education/.

69. For an example of how faculty role-plays can work in Supervision Rounds sessions (albeit in the externship context), see Rosenfeld, *supra* note 13, at 158–65.

70. Epstein, *supra* note 63, at 166.

71. Laura Moy, *Tech Support: Wiring Technology Law Clinics to Serve Racial justice*, 30 Clinical L. Rev. 205, 221 (2023) (citing Epstein, *supra* note 63, at 162, 166).

72. *Cf.* Bryan L. Adamson, Bradford Colbert, Kathy Hessler, Katherine Kruse, Robert Kuehn, Mary Helen McNeal, Calvin Pang, & David Santacroce, *Clinical Faculty in the Legal Academy: Hiring, Promotion and Retention*, 62 J. Legal Educ. 115, 160 (2012).

Seven

THE INTERRELATIONSHIP OF VALUES, MORALS, ETHICS, AND CULTURAL DIFFERENCE

In a well-structured clinic or other experiential course, issues involving personal values, legal ethics, philosophical morals, tested and untested assumptions, and cultural differences can and should be explored in classroom discussions, supervision sessions, and case rounds. All states have rules that govern the ethics of the legal profession. In addition, local customs within the bar guide the profession's "idealized conception of the lawyer's vocation ... that we are in the service of justice and the protection of the oppressed, including oppressed corporate clients. Without such an idealization, the work often would be too tedious and frustrating."[1] Law students practicing in clinical courses are bound by the same rules and customs. Most states' student practice rules permit students to represent only clients who are either indigent or who are unable to afford private lawyers because of their financial circumstances.[2] Consequently, clinic clients are likely to be poor, and often of a racial or ethnic group different from that of most of the students, and from cultural backgrounds that most law students have not experienced.

Ethics, values, morals, and cultural differences are all separate concepts. Nonetheless, they are related and often united given the types of cases clinic students undertake and the clients they represent. They will be separately addressed in subsequent chapters. This chapter is an introduction to their interrelatedness and a glance at how these concepts may play out in experiential courses.

Values permeate all of our lives. They form the basis for our internal moral code, our assumptions, and our sense of ethics. However, they are formed from our own life experiences, which are often different from many of the life experiences of clients and others they encounter while working on their cases or projects. Personal values and assumptions that lead to their creation influence our teaching, learning, and practice as well as those of our students. Because student's, teacher's, and client's values, assumptions, and differences affect legal representation, professional responsibility, and pedagogical integrity, a clinical supervisor cannot passively ignore—let alone actively avoid—conversations about these issues.

More often than not, value conversations will arise during supervision sessions regarding client needs or wishes or the legal theories supporting the claims raised in a case or project. They can affect relationships between the student lawyers and their clients and the development of the strategy and tactics that the students or teachers consider as they advance a client's claims. In addition, client claims arise in fora that are frequently alien to a client. Clinic clients seldom visit courts voluntarily and almost never visit legislative halls. They seldom know the actual procedures necessary to secure their interests or may be openly hostile to the system where their claims will be decided. For all of these reasons, teachers must focus on how issues concerning values, ethics, morals, assumptions, and cultural differences arise, and how they sometimes clash during legal representation.

Conflicts during representation may be rooted in either the students' professional or personal lives or the personal lives of clients. When they arise in a case or project, supervisors must help students recognize those issues, confront the underlying assumptions, and resolve them to the satisfaction of both their personal and professional lives. In order to work through conflicts involving personal values, ethics, client interests, and assumptions, faculty members must focus on teaching and learning strategies that enable students to explore the issues during supervision sessions, in class, or during case rounds. Their goal is to ensure the lessons learned are instilled in their students throughout their clinical experience and then throughout their professional lives.

Ethics, Morals, and Values

Ethics, morals, and values are distinct, albeit related, concepts that either create or are the basis of assumptions that affect the judgments and choices lawyers make concerning their clients and their clients' interests. They also affect the students' many relationships within the clinic. Students and teachers may have different values. Differences in values may exist among clinic partners. Students' values may clash with those of opposing lawyers and their clients, or with those who will rule on the issues that arise in cases or projects. These challenges arise from the different life schemas that students, clients, and other people involved in a case or project have experienced. They arise in policy debates, negotiation strategies with opposing lawyers, litigation strategies before judges, and presentation strategies in legislative fora. If students lack the knowledge and an understanding of another person's life experiences, inaccurate assumptions affecting the behavior of everyone involved in a case may arise. Students may also fail to distinguish between the concepts of morals, values, and ethics, which can alter case strategies and lead to poor outcomes for the clients.

The legal profession defines ethics as the rules of conduct that circumscribe the actions of lawyers in the course of their work. These rules are explicitly stated in the Rules of Professional Responsibility that are enacted by states to control the behavior of lawyers as they practice their trade. Despite some speaker's and writer's interchangeable use of the words ethics and morals, they are not synonymous.[3] Indeed, the demoralization of ethics rules can be traced through the progression of different codes regulating lawyer behavior, beginning with the Canon of Professional Ethics through the Model Rules of Professional Conduct.[4] Morals are states of mind that people use to categorize conduct as intrinsically good or bad, or right or wrong. They arise from either religious or secular philosophical underpinnings that guide judgments about one's own or other people's actions.[5] Values, on the other hand, are a collection of guiding principles. They are what one deems to be correct and desirable in life, especially regarding personal conduct.[6] Put differently, values can be characterized as the ideals and customs of a societal group about which the group has an affective or emotional regard. Nonetheless, values are more malleable than morals. They reflect desirable traits or actions within a homogenous group but do not necessarily fall into rigid categories of "right" and "wrong" in the same way that morals do. Rather, they state preferences—rather than strict rules—for a kind of behavior that one chooses to guide one's own actions. Because they are personal choices, they do not always involve negative judgments concerning those who do not share one's values and who choose to act in ways another may disfavor.

An inherent ambiguity in these terms exists, especially since expanded definitions of each often encompass references to the others. Certain legal ethics or personal values need not be related to moral principles. For example, the ethical rules of the legal profession require that lawyers zealously represent a client. That remains true even in the case of a person who has confessed to a crime. However, there are some limits that are consonant with certain moral precepts. Lawyers cannot fabricate evidence[7] or lie to a judge in the course of representation.[8] Notwithstanding these ethical proscriptions, a lawyer is permitted to argue inferences from the evidence presented by the government that would lead to the conclusion that the government has not met its burden of proof. In doing so, a lawyer may use a line of cross-examination and argument that gives the impression that an otherwise-guilty person is not guilty.[9] In such a case, the thrust of the defense's argument has little to do with whether the client has, in fact, committed the illegal action. Instead, it focuses on holding the government to meet its burden of proof based on the evidence presented and argues that the evidence presented is insufficient to prove guilt beyond a reasonable doubt. Indeed, lawyers who fail to use such tactics may run afoul of their ethical duty.[10]

Non-lawyers within our society, however, may place a lesser value on the notion of zealously representing guilty people; but because they are not lawyers, they suffer no consequences if they choose to reject that value. Nor can they seek sanctions against lawyers for "immoral" or "unethical" conduct even if they abhor tactics that consciously diverge from the truth of guilt or innocence. Lay critics can apply their disdain to a lawyer's action, but they cannot apply their personal values to sanction a lawyer's actions because lawyers' ethics, as defined by the relevant rules of the profession, require such conduct.

Although lawyers operate in the world of professional ethics, they also have values that guide their personal actions. Those values may be the same or different from those of laypeople. But even when a lawyer's personal values resemble those of lay people rather than the code of ethics, it is their professional ethics, not their personal values, that must control their actions. Lawyers are bound by the rules of the profession when practicing law, not by their own values or those of the larger lay society. Thus, both prosecutors and defense attorneys must abide by the rules of professional conduct that permit defense lawyers to attack the evidence presented. The legal profession will not condemn an attorney who provides representation for guilty people in that manner, because the lawyer's action stands on firm ethical and constitutional grounds. Even more fundamentally, someone has to shoulder that responsibility in American democracy. Defense lawyers assume that obligation even when it may conflict with some of their own personal values, because the values required for upholding a constitutional democracy are paramount. Similarly, prosecutors may oppose drug laws or harsh sentencing schemes personally but still believe laws must be enforced to uphold the rule of law in a democratic society.

Beyond the notion of personal values, some people might believe that such behavior is morally wrong based on religious or secular philosophical beliefs about truth telling. In their view, no one should be able to create a false impression of the truth. Nor should they suggest that honest people wrongly perceived an event or are lying. Those who do may wish to change the ethical rules of the profession because they believe such behavior is morally wrong and that a zealous lawyer is morally guilty for distorting the truth. Our founders, however, were aware that citizens of the emerging republic would not always ascribe to the same religious or philosophical beliefs. They understood that the criminal power of the government should only be exercised when there was a high degree of certainty. Thus, they chose to write the Constitution as they did. Certainly, those who disagree may seek to change the ethical rules, but such changes cannot override the constitutional rights of all citizens.

Application to the Clinical Setting

All students, like all lawyers, come to the practice of law with a set of values and personal morals. Students, however, have seldom encountered to what extent their morals and values are endorsed or contradicted by professional ethical rules. While participating in a clinic, they need to determine for themselves how they can practice law when their values and morals do not coincide with the ethical rules of the legal profession. Some students find balance by cabining off the personal from the professional. They put on their lawyer hat in the clinic and take it off at home, without internalizing their conduct in one sphere as defining their "self" in the other. Others find moral congruence, a symbiotic harmony, in aligning the personal and the professional by carrying out the professional value of zealous representation, realizing that it might be the best way to actualize their personal values. In either case, a student's willingness and capacity for deep, uncomfortable, indeterminate, and contradictory self-reflection is critical in a clinical course. Students need to learn how to think about these issues in their own right and must also learn to assess their own thinking about those topics. This phenomenon, metacognition, is the lifeblood of a mentally healthy, morally sound, and intellectually rigorous career in law. It is also a hallmark of clinical legal education pedagogy. Indeed, it may be necessary to become a fully actualized human being.

The complexity of conversations about the distinctions among issues of ethics, values, and morals only increases when students represent clients from other cultures. Most law students, and perhaps most clients, are not cross-culturally competent.[11] Like most of us, they make assumptions about unfamiliar cultures. Experiences shape the way people see the world. People from diverse cultures or life experiences do not always perceive or understand the same events in the same way.[12] For example, non-immigrant law students and immigrant clients with different life experiences may each have their own assumptions that don't align with one another. The same may also be true for law students and clients hailing from a single nation. People who live in cities experience life differently from those who live in rural areas, and people from different neighborhoods in the same city may have very divergent perceptions of life around them. Cultural differences based on race, ethnicity, education, age, and poverty affect every aspect of our lives. Moreover, the effects of those differences often produce assumptions that can be very damaging to the representation of a client. The strength and trust necessary for the student-client relationship can also be affected. Our different life schemas further complicate political differences. Failure to address these differences has implications for our clients' cases, and thus, our clinical teaching as well.

The experiences teachers bring to and from every facet of their lives can create clashes of values and morals that can affect our students' representation of their clients. Lawyers, especially those representing poor clients, clients of a different race or culture, or clients whose life experiences are dramatically different from their own, must develop a high degree of cultural competence. Lawyers must learn to question their assumptions about those differences and be able to separate moral and value dilemmas from ethical rules in order to serve their clients while acting in accordance with the rules of our profession. Students have the opportunity to learn these lessons in any of their experiential courses as long as their teachers choose to help them understand the effects of values, morals, assumptions, and differences on the practice of law. How well those lessons are transmitted depends on how the clinical teacher chooses to address them.

Conversations among lawyers about these issues are often complex and difficult. Conversations between clinical supervisors and students are even more complicated because of the hierarchy built into the relationship. Students know their grades are based on how the teacher perceives their actions. Because values are so personal, they may decline to express them when they do not seem to coincide with those of their supervisor. Moreover, the clinic experience will probably be the first time students will have responsibility for someone else's freedom or well-being. The nature of a case or project, and the values or morals of a client or team member, sometimes force students to confront and perhaps alter their own beliefs and their own world views. They must do so while remaining true to themselves, in good standing with their profession, and loyal to their clients. Clinical teachers may also experience these same tensions when confronting their own assumptions, morals, values, and ethics. Understanding cultural differences, and learning how to recognize the interaction of values, morals, and ethics and to act upon them in the context of a clinic case, is not always easy. However, it is critical to the role teachers undertake with law students in all experiential courses.

The three chapters that follow—Supervising Issues Concerning Values, Assumptions, and Justice; Supervising Ethical Dilemmas; and Supervising Issues Relating to Race and Cultural Difference—and the readings that accompany them, seek to further delineate and differentiate among these concepts while offering suggestions to teachers who will undoubtedly confront them in the classroom, in supervision sessions, and in case rounds. Indeed, at countless points in their career, teachers may worry about knowing the right words to say to a student or to direct the student to the right resources that can help them resolve these difficult and recurring issues. Yet teachers are the most effective when they realize that their role, ultimately, is to equip students with tools to work through these problems themselves. Clearly, a teacher's advice, guidance, questioning, and redirection are important parts of the learning experience. And students should work through at least some of those problems with others aloud, whether with their teacher or fellow clinic students. But in the end, only the students can do their own internal work—work that is simultaneously academic, professional, personal, ethical, moral, spiritual, and more—to grapple with these questions themselves. The chapters and readings that follow aim to help teachers conceptualize their role in that process.

Other Voices

Geoffrey C. Hazard, Jr., *Personal Values and Professional Ethics**

40 Clev. St. L. Rev. 133 (1992)

My purpose on this occasion is to urge reexamination of personal values as a fundamental resource of professional ethics. The essential point is that rules of ethics, such as those embodied in the profession's ethical codes, are insufficient guides to making the choices of action that a professional must make in practice. I will suggest that the same is true of professional tradition and conventional ways of practice. This is not to say that rules of ethics and traditions are irrelevant. Rules of professional ethics frame the ethical problems that are encountered in a lawyer's life throughout practice. Moreover, professional tradition provides an idealized portrait of a professional that serves as a model for action in real world situations. However, framing an ethical problem is one thing, resolving such a problem is something else. Oliver Wendell Holmes remarked about the judicial function that "[g]eneral propositions do not decide concrete cases." The same point supports ethical choices that must be made by lawyers in conducting their practice. So also an idealized conception of what a professional should be, as portrayed in professional tradition, does not determine what a professional should do in the nonideal world of actual practice.

I. Professional Ethics

The term "professional ethics" can be understood to refer to at least three different but related normative sources: first, the profession's rules of ethics; second, ethical tradition including professional myths, lore and narrative; and, third, the standards of conduct that an observing anthropologist would describe as the profession's conventions of actual practice. The last source may also be captured by the term "habit" which at one time was used to describe a group's regular pattern of conduct. The term "professional" simply denotes that these normative sources function within a specific subgroup in society, in our case the American legal profession.

II. Rules, Traditions and Practice

The rules of ethics of the American legal profession are constituted in the Rules of Professional Conduct, previously in the Code of Professional Responsibility and before that in the American Bar Association Canons of Professional Ethics. Various subsections of these codes incorporate rules of general law that govern the citizenry at large.

...

Our professional tradition is another source of ethical guidance. That tradition includes such articles of faith as "equal justice under law," "a lawyer knows no duty other than to his client," "every client with a just cause has a right to a lawyer's assistance,"

* Excerpt reprinted with the permission of Cleveland State Law Review.

and "due process of law is a fundamental right." In contemporary discourse about the legal profession, the profession's espoused tradition or mythology (I use the term in the anthropological sense) is often referred to as its narrative.

The legal profession's practice conventions or "habits"—its ways of actually doing things as observable by an anthropologist—are what we learn after we get out of law school. One example is the practice of using a form book whenever possible even when the specific form is not completely appropriate to the task. A legal form embodies precedent and precedent usually produces better results for a busy practitioner, rather than thinking a problem through de novo. Another professional "habit" consists of putting off any less urgent matter in favor of a more urgent matter. In general, this is a sensible scheduling principle in our work, which mostly consists of dealing with one emergency after another. However, in practice this habit often translates into doing all tasks at the last minute.

The relationship among these normative sources—rules, traditions and "habits of practice" is dynamic and complex. Lawyers are ever mindful of the central principles in the rules of ethics even if most lawyers do not know the letter of the ethical codes, let alone follow the rules to the letter. Our profession's traditions hover in the back of every lawyer's mind, helping us to interpret, justify and give higher meaning to our work. The idealized conception of the lawyer's vocation is that we are in the service of justice and the protection of the oppressed, including oppressed corporate clients. Without such an idealization the work often would be too tedious and frustrating.

The habits of lawyers' work, as observed by an anthropologist, tend to contradict the idealized version expressed in professional narrative. Moreover, some conventions of practice violate the rules prescribed in the ethical codes. Lawyers violate the rules and fail to fulfill their own professional ideals because, like everyone else, they are subject to the constraints of economics, politics and human frailty. The contradiction between the ideal and the legal, on the one hand, and actual practice, on the other, does not prove that lawyers are indifferent to their ethical obligations. It proves only that practicing law according to the rules, let alone according to idealization, is not easy.

III. Objectivity and Subjectivity

Practice as it is actually performed is an outward and observable activity that is guided by inner and invisible norms. These norms are given expression in our codes and the traditions about our profession. The codes are promulgated as public law. The traditions are transmitted by recitations, for example, in the form of stories about lawyers such as *Anatomy of a Murder* and *To Kill a Mockingbird*. We also hold periodic recitations in the form of bar association speeches and of lectures given to law students by professional elders. In these forms the codes and traditions take on shared meaning.

Because the rules of professional ethics and professional narratives can be shared in this way, they are "objective" in an important sense. The rules are objective in the same sense that all legal rules are objective in an important way. The professional narratives similarly convey a commonly understood meaning within the legal community. Thus, "we" lawyers are able to say such things to each other as "during cross examination, never ask a question unless you already know the answer," and "there is nothing as insecure as an unsecured creditor."

The codes and the narratives are objective in the further sense that they refer to patterns of conduct that can be observed and proved through evidence. For example, the rules prohibiting conflict of interest refer to specific observable situations where a lawyer has more than one client. Accordingly, it is possible to observe in a specific case whether a lawyer in fact has more than one client and whether the relationships are such that there is an adverse interest among the clients as defined in the rules.

...

The same is true, in a less rigorous sense, of professional tradition. A narrative or tradition is a story shared among a group in terms of which the group defines its place in the world and proclaims its identity to itself and others. We tell these stories to make vivid in our minds the ways we are supposed to act. Thus, the tradition that a lawyer knows no duty other than to his client is the counterpart of the rule that a lawyer must avoid impermissible conflicts of interest. The image projected in such a story can then be compared to practice in a real world situation. Professional narratives, myths, ideals—call them what we will—are media of interpersonal communication. In this sense they too are objective like the codes or rules.

And, of course, actual practice is objective in the sense that it can be observed, described and compared with other kinds of activity. To be sure, the help of an external observer is often necessary to see what a group actually does as distinct from what it professes to do. However, the most acute observers of law practice are those newly admitted young lawyers who are learning their trade. No learning curve is as steep as that in the first few months of practice. Every beginning lawyer is something of an on-the-job anthropologist.

...

But what is going on in the minds of the people who engage in this thing called the practice of law?

IV. The Lawyer's Subjective World

From the outside, a lawyer's thoughts, her state of mind at any given moment, cannot be observed. The observer can only make inferences, perhaps nothing more than guesses, about the mental pathway by which a lawyer gets from dilemma to resolution every day and every moment of actual practice. That pathway runs through the realm of the individual lawyer's subjective reality. The pathway actually chosen is not revealed to others except through circumstantial evidence. It is the silent world of personal consciousness. Yet this is the world in which each of us as lawyers must make decisions about what to do in concrete situations encountered in practice. This is the realm that I now want to address.

Lawyers do many different kinds of things. Most of these tasks are variations of three basic functions: first, interviewing and giving advice to clients; second, negotiating contracts, settlements and other arrangements with third parties; and third, presenting evidence and legal argument before the courts. In each of these tasks the lawyer confronts an external reality, consisting of the client, the opposing parties, the court, and the world at large. But the lawyer experiences this world through the process of her own consciousness.

...

It is a familiar rule of ethics that a lawyer may not offer false evidence such as perjured testimony. How does a lawyer go about determining whether a specific item of evidence falls within this prohibited category? Awareness and interpretation is required in order to apply this rule.

...

The point ... is that the precise knowledge upon which the lawyer must proceed is known only to the lawyer. This is because the lawyer's private knowledge is by necessity the lawyer's personal, subjective awareness and interpretation of the situation before him. The lawyer cannot seek a declaratory ruling from the court as to what the facts are and what ethical judgment should be made in light of the facts. Shortage of time and urgency of circumstances will not permit the lawyer to obtain such authoritative determination of reality. Indeed shortage of time and urgency of circumstances may not even permit consultation with a colleague or seeking an answer from an ethics committee or a bar association "hot line." Solo practitioners usually have to resolve these problems without anyone to consult, and law firm lawyers often must proceed in the same isolation. Even a lawyer who has taken consultation ultimately has to make a personal decision as to what to do.

V. Personal Values in Professional Ethics

It is in this lonely subjective world that a lawyer is required to "call the shots" in ethical dilemmas. In this lonely world the rules of ethics usually appear as merely vacuous generalizations. The rules say that evidence may not be offered if the lawyer knows it is fabricated, but of what avail is that guidance? The rules do not and cannot say whether specific evidence is fabricated. A court may eventually make a finding on the issue one way or another, but such a finding will be long after the event and even then the court might be wrong. Before that event comes about the lawyer has to resolve the question through irreversible action by deciding whether to use the evidence. Similarly, the rules say that nondisclosure of a material fact in a financial transaction may constitute fraud, but so what? The rules do not and cannot say whether a specific financial datum is material or even whether it is a fact. Perhaps the datum is merely the figment of some anxious accountant's hypercautiousness. Perhaps, however, it is a fact. The lawyer has to resolve the question, sometimes in an instant.

How does a lawyer decide such issues? None of our standard professional techniques are of much help in such situations. Professional technique in the interpretation of rules would permit us to determine whether the rules prohibit introduction of fabricated evidence in litigation or require disclosure of material facts in a transaction. The difficult ethical problem in such cases is not, however, what the rule says but whether the factual conditions have arisen that call the rule into operation. The technique for interpreting the rules therefore has no application unless merely for the purpose of reaching the self-deceptive conclusion that the rule does not mean what it says. Professional technique in the proof of facts would enable us to make an evidentiary showing to someone else as to whether the evidence is fabricated or whether the facts are material. But the professional techniques for proving facts to others are insufficient for the purpose of deciding facts for ourselves. Surely it is nonsense to speak of establishing a prima facie case to one's self.

Likewise, professional narrative and tradition do not provide means of resolving issues of this kind. Professional narrative speaks in terms of concrete cases, not in the abstract generalizations of the ethical codes. However, the concrete cases incorporated in professional tradition are either historical or apocryphal. Either way, they do not replicate the concrete case that the lawyer must resolve. An example is the story of Abe Lincoln's successful use of the Farmer's Almanac to demolish the testimony of a lying witness. Such a concrete case presents a model for action in a present ethical dilemma, but only if the facts of the present dilemma correspond to those in the model case. If there are differences in the facts, the model indeed can be misleading.

...

The limited utility of professional narrative resembles the limited utility of the case method of judicial reasoning. A prior case that is on point may indeed be a binding authority. However, it is always an open question whether a prior case is on point. A prior decision becomes binding when we conclude that it is on point, but there is nothing about a prior decision that binds us to first test the prior case on point.

Conventions of practice have similar limited utility in the lawyer's subject realm. Studying what lawyers do in their practice does not tell us what is going on in their minds. As to that we can only make educated guesses. Indeed, on this matter Yogi Berra may have further wisdom from which we can benefit. He said that "You can't think and hit at the same time." A successful batter is in some sense unconscious in the moment of choice when he swings the bat. I also believe that a lawyer is in some sense unconscious in the moment of choice when he resolves an ethical dilemma.

In the literature of professional ethics, remarkably little attention is given to this matter. The rules of professional ethics differentiate various states of mind as the predicates of various kinds of ethical decisions. Thus, the rules differentiate between "believing," "knowing" and "reasonably believing." However, these rules are designed to guide decision-makers such as grievance committees in resolving issues of circumstantial evidence as to a particular lawyer's state of mind on a particular occasion. By extension, these rules also tell a lawyer how a tribunal may be inclined to assess the lawyer's conduct after the fact. At most, therefore, these rules inform the lawyer how others in the future will think about what the lawyer is now thinking. The rules governing others in assessing a lawyer's state of mind do not provide insight to the lawyer about his own state of mind.

VI. Conclusion

There is of course more to be said on this problem. When all has been said, however, the fact will remain that a lawyer's ethical deliberations are a process of personal thought and action. That process is guided by the rules of the ethical codes, by professional tradition, and by prevailing standards of practice.

...

The practical judgments necessary to these tasks are essentially the same as those made by people in ordinary life. They are personal judgments. As such, they incorporate an unavoidable element of personal value, just as an element of value is incorporated in how we treat our friends, members of our family, professional colleagues, rivals, and the people who live across the street. Thus, it is not true—no matter what they say—that in becoming a lawyer one ceases to be a person.

The question remains of what kind of person one wants to be.

Stephen Wizner, *Beyond Skills Training**

7 Clinical L. Rev. 327 (2001)

...

It has been a basic assumption of clinical legal education that students are motivated to learn by being given the responsibility for assisting real clients with their legal problems. As students come to realize the reality of their clients' legal situation, and how important legal representation is to the resolution of their clients' problems, they become ever more conscious of their responsibility to the clients.

The student's feeling of personal responsibility in representing an individual client can grow into a feeling of social responsibility for the provision of legal services to the poor. When the student realizes that, in all likelihood, the client would not have access to legal assistance but for the law student and the clinic, her consciousness is raised. This awakening to a sense of social responsibility, occurs when students represent low-income clients who are seeking—or seeking to defend—basic benefits, liberty, or fairness. Therefore, providing legal representation to low income clients, both individually and through group representation, should be the basis of clinical practice

* Excerpts are reprinted with the permission of the author and the Clinical Law Review.

and teaching. There are important lessons about the role of law and lawyers, and about social justice, to be learned from working on such cases.

...

Regardless of whether they are representing individual clients in resolving time-limited legal problems or are working on law reform cases or class actions that extend over several semesters, many students don't really believe that what they are doing has a moral purpose. They see themselves as acquiring skills that they will need when they go out to practice law, and not as participating in a struggle for social justice.

If there is a real flaw in our clinical pedagogy it is that we have failed to sustain and to pass on to our students the passion for social justice that many of us had when we first started practicing and teaching. My worry is that today's law students have become cynical about the potential usefulness of law as a means for pursuing and achieving social justice.

...

Frank Askin may be correct in suggesting that excessive concern with the teaching of lawyering skills and the nuances of attorney-client relationships have distracted our attention and that of our students from the social and political functions of law. I believe that the emphasis in clinical teaching on what I would call "micro-lawyering" risks shortchanging both our students and our clients by narrowing students' vision and stifling their passion and creativity. Focusing exclusively, or primarily, on client-centered interviewing, counseling, fact investigation, negotiation, and written and oral advocacy can fail to nurture students' capacity for moral indignation at injustice in the world, or to challenge and inspire them as lawyers to use what they have learned to work for social justice.

...

As clinical teachers we should engage with our students on a deeper level than simply teaching them the craft of practicing law. Our teaching must go beyond skills training. It is not enough for clinical teachers to instruct students in the legal skills that are essential to competent representation of clients. Nor is it sufficient to teach them that they have an ethical duty to provide competent representation to clients.

We need to profess a social, political and moral agenda in our teaching, an agenda that exposes students to the maldistribution of wealth, power and rights in society, and that seeks to inculcate in them a sense of their own ability and responsibility for using law to challenge injustice by assisting the poor and the powerless.

In professing such an agenda in teaching the representation of low-income clients, we as clinical teachers would not be doing anything new. We would be returning to our roots.

...

The question we as clinical educators need to address is, what is that overriding purpose? If it is, as I believe, teaching law students about the ability and responsibility of lawyers to work for justice and to challenge injustice through the supervised representation of low-income clients, then we as teachers must infuse the skills we teach with that overriding purpose.

…

Over the years I have often said: "We don't teach skills, we teach legal theory." What I have sought to express by that admittedly tendentious statement is my deep belief that the primary purpose of clinical legal education is to teach students that law is not an end in itself, but a mechanism for pursuing social objectives. Clinical education should not be limited to teaching interviewing and counseling, negotiation and courtroom advocacy, drafting and brief-writing. Doing law cannot, and should not, be reduced to a repertoire of technical skills. The goal of our teaching should be to teach students to use law on behalf of clients as a means for pursuing justice and working for social change.

The goal of faculty-supervised law practice should be to provide professional education in the public interest, not simply "skills training." Its overarching pedagogical objectives should be to teach students to employ legal skills and legal theory to meet social needs, to expose students to the ways in which law can work either to advance or subvert public welfare and social justice, and to inculcate in students a professional commitment to using law to address important social, economic and political issues that affect the rights and legitimate interests of the poor, oppressed and disenfranchised among us.

…

[Milner] Ball says that the goal of his clinical teaching is not to provide "skills training," but to press students to ask, "as appropriately jurisprudential questions.… 'Who am I as a lawyer?' and 'What am I doing when I do law?'"

Legal education—and especially clinical legal education—properly understood, should have a political and moral purpose that informs its intellectual and skills-training functions. It should not be limited to the acquisition of legal knowledge and the development of professional skills, although both of those are essential.

…

We who are clinical teachers must be our own sentries and continually ask ourselves, paraphrasing Milner Ball, "Who am I as a law teacher? What am I doing when I teach law?"

Susan A. McMahon,
What We Teach When We Teach Legal Analysis *

107 MINN. L. REV. 2511 (2023)

INTRODUCTION

...

Our new law student learns to identify rules from cases and apply them to new sets of facts, but is rarely asked whether the rule furthers justice, or whether biases are embedded within it, or what the rule *should* be. She is trained in the tactics of legal reasoning, can see where doctrine might be inconsistent or where an exception might swallow a rule, but cannot explain why a law is good or bad, just or unjust. She doesn't understand the forces that birthed the law or the imprints those forces have left on its surface. She is not trained to question the legal system itself.

All this leaves her with the impression that law and legal reasoning are neutral and objective, and her job, as a lawyer, is to read cases, pull out rules or general principles, and sift new facts into those categories.

...

This training contributes to a student's sense that law is natural and normal, and "*usually* OK and just," instead of invigorating her imagination as to law's possibilities and giving her the tools to push for legal change. The result is a collective of elites who have a vested interest in preserving this system they have mastered, who tend to accept things as they are instead of pushing for stark departures from the status quo.

Legal scholars have long taken aim at these methods and pushed for reform. Some of these professors seek to contextualize students' legal training with theoretical perspectives or pedagogical techniques designed to de-reify legal rules and opinions; others hope to expose students to rhetorical theory and practices—both those of the West and of other cultures—to help students understand that law is constituted by human beings in a particular social and cultural context; still others aim to de-center litigation and lawyering in favor of working alongside social justice movements to achieve change. These strategies disrupt. They aim to expose the bias embedded in legal reasoning, to create a more fair and just system, by critiquing traditional analytical tools and pursuing other methods for achieving legal objectives. This is essential work. Without adopting an outsider's gaze and a disruptor's stance, lawyers using the basic tools of legal analysis tend to replicate what has come before.

* Excerpts are reprinted with the permission of the author and the University of Minnesota Law Review.

But disruption alone is not enough. Such an approach helps students see the problems in law, but gives them little training in how to fix it. This approach can easily lead a young law student to a nihilistic, despairing view, for if all rules "lead us anywhere and nowhere, why have any?"

Thus, to be successful, students must be taught not only to disrupt, but also to create. They should learn how to use the traditional tools of legal reasoning to achieve change. This approach accepts the rhetoric, structure, and go-to moves of legal thinking as it exists, acknowledges their failures and weaknesses, and aims to arm students with the skills to work within that system to birth new rules, cement new baselines, and create new approaches to legal problem

Teaching with both strategies in mind will help the scales drop from students' eyes—they will be clear-eyed about the system's flaws—while still preparing them to operate within it and change it from the inside. As Mari Matsuda once noted,

> There are times to stand outside the courtroom door and say 'this procedure is a farce, the legal system is corrupt, justice will never prevail in this land as long as privilege rules in the courtroom.' There are times to stand inside the courtroom and say 'This is a nation of laws, laws recognizing fundamental values of rights, equality, and personhood.' Sometimes ... there is a need to make both speeches in one day.

Students who want to change the world need training in both modes of law practice.

...

II. Critiques Of Legal Analysis Pedagogy

While [learning rule-based reasoning and analogical reasoning] is necessary—any young lawyer must know how to use and apply legal rules or construct an effective analogy—it also comes with costs. First, this training implicitly presents a view of legal decision-making as rational and objective, rather than suffused with values and personal or political preferences. Second, it freezes students' imaginations about how to solve problems by indoctrinating them in the way things are rather than helping them imagine the way things could be. Third, it sidelines considerations about justice or morality. Fourth, it provides little, if any, training for students to pursue fundamental change or achieve a more just world.

...

B. The Frozen Imagination Problem

Not only does this legal reasoning training place a veneer of logical neutrality on a system filled with moral, political, and policy-based choices, but it also tends to deaden a student's imagination as to what is possible. The continuous practice of legal analysis, of identifying and applying rules, of determining the boundaries of likeness between cases, gives a legitimacy to the existing legal ordering of the world that drowns out alternatives. Students become mired in the technicalities of legal categories rather than considering a wholesale shift in foundational legal principles.

Without pairing the rituals of legal reasoning with a sustained critique of that process, students develop a sense that things are the way they are and a fear that to change them may just make it all worse. Moreover, this work, day in and day out, helps to structure students' perceptions of reality "so as to systematically exclude or repress alternate visions of social life, both as it is and as it might be."

...

C. The Justice Problem

The invisibility of alternatives—the freezing-the-imagination problem—has a particularly nasty side effect: it can make existing power imbalances, bias, or injustice embedded within the law invisible. Students trained in putting facts in this legal category or that, sandwich or not, contract breach or not, are rarely asked to assess the rule's normative value. What are the values embedded in this rule? Whom does it advantage? Whom does it disadvantage? Is that the right call? Why?

Without that assessment, students rarely see how the latticework of legal rules can incorporate injustice and bias in hidden ways. They also fail to see the law as a power-distributing mechanism. This is a problem; every law gives power to some parties and takes it away from others, and those power dynamics often advantage the already-powerful and harm the already marginalized.

...

In large part, this blind spot in legal training is because the two basic legal reasoning strategies taught and tested in the first year—rules-based reasoning and analogical reasoning—are consistently backward-looking. The resolution to a problem depends not on a theory of justice, economics, or societal well-being; the first, and often only, question, is what have past decisionmakers (judges, legislators, etc.) told us about what to do now?

...

But this consistent nod to the law as-it-is atrophies students' abilities to argue for law as-it-should-be, especially when the strategies for achieving law as-it-should-be may be radically different from maintaining law as it exists.

...

But law school rarely gives students training in tactics for bringing that new rule into being. It generally doesn't give students tools for breaking free from old categories and modes of thought. It doesn't give students practice in making novel arguments to courts, perhaps using sources outside of traditional legal authority. It doesn't ask students to explore the limits of what courts can do or think through how to solve problems by turning to legislative, regulatory, or grassroots solutions instead. Which is not to say it is never done—clinical education, in particular, has done creative work in helping students bring a critical lens into their skill sets.

...

[This]approach creates. This skills-based teaching trains students in using the tools of legal analysis to bring change about. This is the practice that stands inside the courthouse and argues for an outcome based on principles of equality and justice.

...

1. Practice-Readiness

A law school that does not train its students in how to operate within the legal system—how to engage in the recognized forms of legal discourse and use established methods of legal reasoning—has failed them.

...

Movement Lawyering clinics and courses embrace a similar pedagogy that collaborates with social justice movements with the express goal of "build[ing] power" to achieve lasting social change through both legal and political means. Its practitioners require knowledge of not only the typical legal argument tactics taught in the first year, but also other modes of advocacy—"policy reform, transactional work, organizing support, media relations, and community education"—with the goal not necessarily of winning cases, but of "maximiz[ing] political pressure and transform[ing] public opinion."

And clinics, Movement Lawyering or otherwise, have been the bastion of creative reasoning, immersing students in real problems posed by clients and requiring them to find solutions. Students in clinics both experience the indeterminacy of law in action—witnessing how decisionmakers can reach results that seem contrary to the rules—and need to make arguments to a decisionmaker in the face of that indeterminacy, often reaching for creative, context-driven solutions that draw on "the dynamics of law and lawyering."

Endnotes

1. Geoffrey C. Hazard, *Personal Values and Professional Ethics*, 40 CLEV. ST, L. REV. 133, 134–135 (1992)

2. Wallace Mlyniec & Haley D. Etchison, *Conceptualizing Student Practice for the 21st Century: Educational and Ethical Considerations in Modernizing the District of Columbia Student Practice Rules*, 28 GEO. J. LEGAL ETHICS, 207 (2015).

3. Not all teachers would agree with this distinction. Some would separate the Rules into a distinct category and discuss ethics, morals, and values as more interrelated concepts. The literature is replete with examples where the terms are used interchangeably.

4. David Luban & Michael Milleman, *Good Judgment, Ethics Teaching in Dark Times*, 9 GEO. J. LEGAL ETHICS 31, 41–53 (1995).

5. Paul J. Cain, *Doing the Right Thing: An Analytic Model of Examining the Interplay Ethical Professio nal Conduct, Morality, and Justice*, 10 T.M. COOLEY J. PRAC. & CLINICAL. L. 149, 149–50 (2008).

6. *See, e.g., Values*, YOUR DICTIONARY, *https://www.yourdictionary.com/values.*

7. MODEL RULES OF PRO. CONDUCT (Am. Bar Ass'n 2020) [hereinafter A.B.A./R.P.C.], r.3.3 ("... requires that the lawyer refuse to offer evidence that the lawyer knows to be false, regardless of the client's wishes.").

8. *Id.* ("... the lawyer must not allow the tribunal to be misled by false statements of law or fact or evidence that the lawyer knows to be false.").

9. For example, cross examining a complaining witness in a robbery case about the circumstances surrounding an identification of the defendant to suggest that it is unreliable is ethical even when there is no doubt that the defendant did commit the crime.

10. *See* A.B.A./R.P.C., Preamble ("As advocate, a lawyer zealously asserts the client's position under the rules of the adversary system.").

11. *See* Susan Bryant, *The Five Habits: Building Cross-Cultural Competence in Lawyers*, 8 CLINICAL. L. REV. 33, 41–42 (2001) (illustrating how cultural differences can lead to misunderstandings in the lawyer-client relationship).

12. Mahzarin R. Banaji, Kristi M. Lemm & Siri J. Carpenter, *The Social Unconscious, in* BLACKWELL HANDBOOK OF SOCIAL PSYCHOLOGY: INTRAINDIVIDUAL PROCESSES 134–58 (A. Tesser & N. Schwarz eds., 2001); Anthony G. Greenwald & Mahzarin R. Banaji, *Implicit Social Cognition: Attitudes, Self-Esteem, and Stereotypes*, 102 PSYCH. REV. 4 (1995).

Eight

SUPERVISING ISSUES CONCERNING VALUES, ASSUMPTIONS, AND JUSTICE

Many students and most clinical teachers come to clinical education with some sense of social justice, and some ideas about how justice can or should be achieved within the larger society. Because social justice and other personal and professional values affect the lawyer-client relationship and the quality of legal representation, teachers should not wonder whether teaching values is a proper endeavor in a clinical course. Instead, they should expect those issues to arise as students confront the demands of client representation and should address which values are a proper subject for discussion with each student.

Values-based education sometimes comes under attack as political indoctrination. These attacks have only increased as the country became more politically polarized. Even in the absence of such attacks, the nature of clinic work makes maintaining value neutrality difficult. Clinical education grew out of social justice advocacy and consciousness, and it remains a significant aspect of experiential courses today. Nonetheless, as clinical education becomes either mandatory for students, or is considered a résumé enhancer, some students in the clinic may not be sympathetic to discussions about values until they realize that values are embedded in the rules and traditions of the legal profession.

The legal profession is imbued with many values not included in the rules of professional ethics. Professor Geoffrey Hazard called them the profession's traditions and conventions of actual practice[1] Loyalty to one's firm or public interest organization; honesty, civility, and respect for our political and civic traditions, such as equal justice under the law; the right to a lawyer; non-discrimination; and respect for the other lawyers and judges working in the system have generally been espoused as values of the profession that were not always reflected in the states' codes of professional responsibility.[2]

Historical View on Teaching Values

Because the legal profession is based on values, legal education is, at least to some extent, value-laden, and therefore cannot be truly described as value-neutral. The American Bar Association, Section on Legal Education and Admissions and the Bar delineated the values of the profession in its report, LEGAL EDUCATION AND PROFESSIONAL DEVELOPMENT—AN EDUCATIONAL CONTINUUM.[3] The MacCrate Report, as it came to be known, described the values of the profession as competency, justice, fairness, and morality. The values also included improving the profession and self-development.[4] The MacCrate Commission merged concepts of ethics, morals, and values, and the Report cites various ethical considerations and disciplinary rules from the ABA Code of Professional Responsibility. Nonetheless, the MacCrate Report promotes the practice of law as a learned profession bound by the "qualities of truth-speaking, of a high sense of honor, of granite discretion, [and] of the strictest observance of fiduciary responsibility that have throughout the centuries been compendiously described as 'moral character.'"[5] Accordingly, not only should the practice of law incorporate these professional values, but law schools have an obligation to teach them.[6] The MacCrate Report did not specifically address the need to teach social justice. However, the need to do so is implicit in teaching all of the other justice-based values embraced by the profession.

Of course, this was not new. Decades ago, American legal educator Karl Llewellyn "saw teaching 'as primarily a moral enterprise.'"[7] Indeed, he "believed that the goal of legal education was not merely to create craftsmen, but also to hone a 'sense of responsibility to self and society.'"[8] This sense was especially valuable to future lawyers who were expected to become not just "decent citizens" but "officer[s]"[9] of the law. With this imprimatur given by early scholars, in concert with the MacCrate Report, clinical teachers can easily conclude that teaching the values of the legal profession and the broader values that underpin them is a valid and necessary undertaking. These important historical and contemporary endorsements for clinical pedagogy are critical since social justice movements were at the heart of the founding of the clinical education movement and remain firmly embedded there today.

Challenges to teaching value-laden education have arisen on many college campuses, especially as the political beliefs in the nation have become more polarized. Universities are places of civic learning, not just job preparation. They are places where knowledge is to be pursued and ideas explored without pre-existing ideology. Max Weber was an early proponent of value neutrality or, as he called it, "value freedom."[10] Weber believed that the pursuit of truth required that scholars eschew teaching beliefs and ideals, reasoning that only such value freedom could serve as both "a buffer against the meddling of state, church, and popular opinion" in academia and "a constraint that gives rise to an area of limited but genuine [academic] freedom."[11]

Although that notion of education seems to be weakening in the face of difficult moral and legal challenges to the norms of our universities and from the corporatization of universities, many professors and critics of values-based education still believe that ideology should not drive teachers' motives.[12] Those who maintain a strict belief in neutrality have attacked clinical professors and clinical pedagogy for their alleged attempts to inculcate a leftist political ideology that, in their view, has no place in a university dedicated to the neutral exploration of ideas.[13] Although we all have our own social values, many faculty members continue to believe that our job is to present both sides of issues, pointing out strengths, shortcomings, and fallacies embedded within intellectual and political positions with hope that students will learn a method of judgment that leaves them on the side of civic virtue.[14] But clinical teachers raise value issues to complement our purpose of providing zealous advocacy to our clients within the confines of the rules of professional responsibility.

It is dubious whether this professed neutrality ever truly existed.[15] Even if it has, understanding neutrality in the context of legal education is different from contemplating it in traditional undergraduate education, because law schools occupy a distinct place in a university. One cannot become an ethical and competent attorney without also exploring the various values that control the profession. Indeed, as critical scholars emphasized decades ago, a supposedly value-free legal education can stunt students' imagination for reforming or reinventing legal systems, lulling them into a sort of complacent conformity.

> Students are struggling for cognitive mastery and against the sneaking depression of the preprofessional. The actual intellectual content of the law seems to consist of learning rules, what they are and why they have to be the way they are, while rooting for the occasional judge who seems willing to make them marginally more humane. The basic experience is of double surrender: to a passivizing classroom experience and to a passive attitude toward the content of the legal system.[16]

This dynamic can even instill and reinforce in students the sense that they do not belong in the legal profession at all.[17] Such imposter syndrome, of course, has an outsized effect on students from underrepresented backgrounds.[18]

Teaching about values in clinic can serve as a sorely needed reminder for students, especially those from diverse backgrounds, that they too belong; that they too can and should be lawyers; and that there is nothing inherently non-lawyerly about their passion and their values. On the contrary, their values are inextricably intertwined with both learning and practicing law. On this view, the key goal in a clinic that teaches about values turns to situating students' passion and values amidst the constellation of other considerations lawyers must have for things like ethics, morals, values, and strategy.

The values of the profession that the MacCrate Report drafters believed needed to be taught, however, tended to be general rather than specific. The authors focused on practice issues, writing that "training in professional responsibility" should involve more than "just the specifics of the Code of Professional Responsibility and the Model Rules of Professional Conduct." Instead, it should encompass "the values of the profession," including "the obligations and accountability of a professional dealing with the lives and affairs of clients."[19] When doing so today, students and teachers need to look deeper into the "lives and affairs of clients" in order to understand their world views as well as our own. Most of the legal claims that poor or underserved clients bring into a courtroom involve our professional values, especially the values of equal access to justice for all and the absence of discrimination. That is equally true in administrative tribunals and legislative chambers. Moreover, they are at the heart of legal practice. So, too is the value of the rule of law as opposed to autocracy, and the values of due process and other principles of justice and fairness that are embodied in the United States Constitution. Those who cannot adhere to the basic values of fairness and due process should not be entrusted with a law degree. All of these professional values espouse the notion of social justice, whether or not they are truly followed every day or framed as such.[20] Presenting both sides of a values issue is academically essential but asserting the values our clients espouse is a primary ethical tenet of the profession.

Teaching Social Justice Is Essential

More recently, the American Bar Association again endorsed the need to expose students to ethical rules and the values embedded within them. Law School Accreditation Standard 303 now requires law schools to provide substantial opportunities for students to develop a professional identity.[21] Interpretation 5 of Rule 303 provides:

> Professional identity focuses on what it means to be a lawyer and the special obligations lawyers have to their clients and society. The development of professional identity should involve an intentional exploration of the values, guiding principles, and well-being practices considered foundational to successful legal practice. Because developing a professional identity requires reflection and growth over time, students should have frequent opportunities for such development during each year of law school and in a variety of courses and co-curricular and professional development activities.[22]

Put differently, an ethical professional identity requires students to answer for themselves questions like, "Who am I as a member of this profession? What am I like, and what do I want to be like in my professional role? And what place do ethical-social values have in my core sense of professional identity?"[23] Consequently, the teaching of values embedded in social justice is a legitimate concern of both clinical and non-clinical faculty in the legal academy.

Although clinical teachers must remain academics who explore and critique historical, societal, and professional mores, the ethical codes that guide our actions as advocates add a dimension that may not exist for the non-clinical faculty in a law school or exist at all for undergraduate educators in a standard liberal arts education. Clinical faculty and students are ethically bound to be loyal to their clients. Because most states' student practice rules limit student representation to indigent or underserved populations, and because university law school clinical faculty members generally choose to represent people from those communities, clinics frequently have clients seeking some form of social justice. Our ethical obligation of zealous advocacy requires that we seek that social justice for them. Our legal system is, in theory, based on all of the values discussed above. However, it is also based on a legal order that has, since its creation, disadvantaged non-wealthy, non-male, and non-white citizens, depriving them of equal access and fair justice.[24] Decades, if not centuries, of political historians have recorded how racism, classism, sexism, and the power of wealth permeate the United States' legal systems. That history makes it impossible to have a truly neutral discussion about our political and professional institutions. Clinic clients' circumstances and the absence of theoretical neutrality make value-based discussions of social justice inescapable in our clinical courses.

Clinical education, with the necessary espousal of social justice values, also serves a historical and fundamental purpose of university education. Colleges and universities were created in part to instill civic or moral virtue in their students. That tradition continues to exist in law schools as well.[25] That said, why shouldn't university faculty members be "forceful advocates for the principles, policies, and processes that truly serve the common good in a free society?"[26] The infusion of "moral character" and "civic virtue" teachings can be achieved in ways that are related to more than just the letter of professional ethics rules. For example, zealous advocacy is a value in which all lawyers engage as they seek fairness, honor, discretion, and fiduciary responsibility. But zealous advocacy, especially if one practices client-centered representation[27] or therapeutic jurisprudence,[28] invokes other values that teachers, students, clients, and society at large possess and bring to that representation. Seeking social justice for our clients involves values that may differ when, in a criminal case, for example, they are viewed from a victim's or a defendant's perspective. Some lawyers treat their clients as partners and even friends in the process of seeking justice, becoming more than just a lawyer to the client. Others, however, represent their clients with tighter boundaries and a more detached level of professionalism.[29] Is one way better than another? Should students be trained to adopt their teacher's view on client-centeredness and boundaries, or should students merely be guided to act in a manner most comfortable to them and most consistent with their fledgling professional identities as lawyers?[30] Some students, for religious or even secular reasons, object to same-sex unions. How should this value issue be discussed when a student is assigned to represent a client suffering from AIDS or a same-sex couple seeking to adopt a child? How do the students' personal values relate to their professional values and when does one trump the other? Some of these discussions must involve professional ethics, but more often than not, they also involve students' personal values or moral precepts.

Confronting values that diminish the autonomy, respect, and power of disadvantaged groups in society is a commonly stated goal of most clinics. Hence, value differences inevitably emerge between students and clients, among students in the clinic, and between students and their clinical professors. Value clashes become apparent as clinical professors confront the propriety of teaching values that are not directly related to professional ethics. Given a clinic's work and the circumstances of our clients, confronting social injustice is also inevitable even when social-justice education is not a stated goal of a clinic. Values and moral differences between law students and clients can affect the quality of the representation that a student provides. Echoing Llewellyn again, values, ethics, and professionalism cannot be separated. Teaching and learning legal ethics and values matter. An ethical practice that recognizes value differences and incorporates them into legal representation improves legal advocacy.[31]

Recognizing Values

Irrespective of a clinic's goal, students will have to confront situations where the assumptions they bring to their work, based on the values that form the center of their world view, are bound to be challenged. Many clinic clients are poor and are people of color; the demographics of law school students are often the opposite. Most student practice rules permit students to represent only indigent clients, or clients and organizations that cannot otherwise obtain legal counsel.[32] Students generally come to our clinics with the assumption that the law provides fair and equal access to the paths where justice is administered and that all people will obtain fair results. That assumption will be shaken when meeting their clients, they encounter an absence of access to justice or witness unfair results because of poverty or the taint of some form of discrimination. It will not take many hours in landlord-tenant, criminal, or domestic-violence courts to begin to notice—indeed, to feel totally overwhelmed and discouraged by—the inequality built into the system. It will take just a few conversations with people seeking legal immigration status or political asylum for a student to begin to wonder about the values that underlie protection of national borders.[33] It will take only a few hours in a legislative committee hearing about environmental issues or public-school funding to see how the power of wealth drives legislative policy.

Although these experiences will arise in the course of their client representation, they are often analyzed purely within the students' worldview. When that occurs, students may experience what Professor Fran Quigley denominated as a "Disorienting Moment."[34] It is a remarkable learning experience when they recognize the disconnect between their assumptions about the legal system and its reality on their own and begin to process it. But it takes considerable planning and a delicate execution of a conversation when they do not see the disconnect between what they are experiencing and what they believe. Faculty members help the student work through the source of this disconnect in the context of a clinic case or project, or in the context of their own view of how the world works. That is not political indoctrination. Rather, it is the essence of learning civic virtue, a core function of university education.[35]

Establishing the legitimacy and necessity of teaching social justice, however, is often easier than actually teaching it, Both students and teachers are often hesitant to begin a conversation about values. This is not surprising since we all make assumptions to help us navigate the world. Recognizing the conflict between what we "know" and what we have now experienced forces a person to alter one's view. To overcome this hesitancy, teachers must identify, long before our first classes and supervision sessions occur, which student and client values are likely to emerge during a student's term in the clinic. Once the potential values issues are identified, the source of the values in conflict and the assumptions that underlie them must be explored as soon as classes and supervision sessions begin.

New teachers seldom have had to confront these issues before they came to academia. They and their prior work colleagues already shared similar social justice values when they joined their organizations, so values conversations with supervisees were generally unnecessary. Similarly, students seldom engage in such conversations. Clinic students are still creating, refining, and reckoning with their fledgling professional identities. Some may come to the clinic because they subscribe to its goals, but others may not. They may have joined the clinic merely for practical experience. Moreover, no matter how familiar teachers and students may be with their clients and cases, new values issues may arise at any time.

In addition, there are institutional disincentives for both students and faculty to confront values issues. The discomfort faculty may feel is exacerbated when their non-clinical colleagues believe that universities and their subsidiary law schools should present ideas to students in a neutral fashion. Even experienced teachers may shy away from these discussions if they can find some way to achieve a client's goals without having to delve into the complexity of personal value disconnects or disorientation. Students are no different. Students may hold back or not see the importance of certain facts that implicate their or their clients' values. They seldom study that interconnectedness in their other classes. When that internal resistance occurs, faculty members may avoid the conversation. Doing so, however, risks missing a valuable teaching opportunity. Discussing the client's interests in an ostensibly value-neutral class session or case rounds may make students and faculty more comfortable. But safe spaces also need to be brave spaces. Students need to know how their own personal values coincide or conflict with their clients' interests and to what extent value conflict can affect the actions they take to pursue the client's goals.

Effective student supervision requires a teacher to anticipate the issue, drawing out the facts needed to inform the supervision. Teachers must also be aware that since these issues will arise often in most students' cases or projects, they should anticipate them and address them in advance. To do so, they need to have tools ready to address them. Discussing values in terms of a client's needs and explaining the sensitivity a lawyer must show towards a client's values is often a safe entry point for this conversation. Lawyers must show respect for a client's experiences and values if communication is to remain open and trust is to be maintained while they advocate for the client's goals.

Critical theorists provide a tool for exploring these social justice issues and their intersections with the complicated nature of pursuing change through lawyering.

> Lawyering which attempts to further social justice alongside impacted communities have alternatively and sometimes interchangeably been referred to as collaborative, rebellious, community, progressive, third-dimensional, border-

> lands, political, poverty, and movement lawyering. No perfect consensus exists on the contours of these models of lawyering, and there are nuanced differences in priorities and strategies.[36]

Once a model is chosen, there are many opportunities in a clinic for such conversations to occur. In classical clinical parlance, clinical teaching is about planning, doing, and reflecting. Those three phases of learning occur in multiple lawyering acts throughout the life of the case or project. Students learn during client and witness interviews, while developing case theory, researching, writing, investigating, counseling, and negotiating, and during court, administrative, and legislative proceedings. They learn in supervision sessions between the teacher and student and as students work collaboratively with their clinic partners. And they learn in the classroom seminar or during case rounds.

Clinical teachers use multiple teaching modalities throughout the semester. They may suggest that students read articles and books. They conduct seminar classes and simulations and engage in pre-event and post-event supervision sessions. They use videos, role plays, and moots to prepare for various lawyering tasks. They know the importance of case rounds, and they, more than non-clinical teachers, encounter students in various individual and group contexts. All of these situations present opportunities to use the full range of teaching tools to conduct these often-difficult conversations.

Addressing Value Clashes

Value clashes manifest themselves in diverse ways. A client may experience some level of kinship with a law student of the same gender or race, while another may be wary of students with different characteristics. On the other hand, clients may assume that students with traits that resemble their opponents may hold more authority or stature with a judge. Addressing the issue of value clashes should not wait until they occur. Role-plays of client-lawyer interviews or counseling sessions based on past cases can be used in orientation sessions or case rounds to explore the issues before they ever arise. Videos showing examples of clients being discriminated against because of racial, ethnic, wealth, or gender identification often provide good vehicles to explore the topics. These same tools can be used to raise questions about how the race, wealth, gender, or other characteristics of a student or a complaining witness might affect a client. Teachers can explore other value-clash issues in classes or supervision sessions to demonstrate the potential for clashes arising when sorting out the client's, the student's, and supervisor's goals as they formulate a strategy for a case. Issues of client autonomy and cultural practices may arise, especially when family members participate in lawyer-client conversations. Confronting these clashes shows the interplay of personal values, ethics, and assumptions when race, gender, sexual orientation, poverty, and political identification influence the choices lawyers make. Special techniques, described in an earlier chapter, have been developed to help demonstrate how inaccurate assumptions by any of the people involved in the case or project can affect the client's ability to obtain a successful resolution of their legal problem and the lawyer's ability to advance the client's interest.

After watching such role-plays or discussing the issues using other techniques, students can be asked to perform a quick-write to identify the issues they observed. This allows them to brainstorm about the source of ethical and value issues, how the conflict arose, and finally identify actions that either adhere to or deviate from existing strategies. All value conflicts provide opportunities for teaching moments.[37] The insights gained help students embed an awareness about the importance of recognizing and identifying the clinic's values, those of the client, and their own values. Moreover, these exercises and conversations lead to an understanding of the way assumptions can create the value disconnects, and how they can affect client representation. Such conversations also lead to a greater awareness of how a student's own values can influence a case or project and their personal growth.

Even though there are many opportunities to have conversations about the place of values and assumptions in client representation, they are seldom easy to have. They require an even greater sensitivity when the conversation involves a client's or the student's intended, unintended, or implicit racism, sexism, homophobia, or other culture-based behaviors. Like most of our teaching goals, resolving these conflicts will seldom be attained in one session. They are, for the most part, too complex for a single one-hour supervision session or a two-hour seminar class. Moreover, a semester or even a year in a clinic is just a small part of a student's life. Teachers should not be surprised if a recognition of the value-disconnect, let alone a change in behavior, is not immediate. They should be happy enough if they planted ideas that continue to take root and blossom as the students move on to their careers.

Like all aspects of clinical pedagogy, conversations about values need to have specific goals. This requires that we begin with a shared definition of what a value actually is and how it differs from morals and ethics. As discussed earlier, ethics are the rules that a state or bar association creates to govern the behavior of lawyers. Morals involve notions of right or wrong that are, at least to the subscriber of that moral, immutable. A value, on the other hand, is a principle or standard of behavior by which one guides their own life, but which carries no moral disapproval toward those who disagree. Values may stem from morals and may be consistent with legal ethics, but they are not necessarily aligned. The value under discussion may be personal, institutional, societal, or professional. The conversation may involve an abstract principle or be based on the reality of the case.

The first goal of any session on values is to reinforce that values, morals, and ethics are different and discrete, and therefore require different responses when they arise in a case or project. The second goal is to advance the notion that clinical education involves teaching students more than just doctrine and skills. Jurisprudence and social justice are equally valid pursuits of a clinical course when teachers make them a pedagogical choice. The third goal is to illuminate how morals and assumptions may underlie values and how those values and assumptions affect client representation.

Teachers whose clinic goals specifically include social justice must acquire the sensitivity needed to engage in these complex conversations and develop appropriate techniques for doing so.[38] Those who do not include value-inquiry as a specific pedagogical goal will nevertheless need to develop similar skills because there is no way to avoid the conversation in the context of client representation.

Values and Client Representation

Professor Stephen Wizner concludes his article, "Beyond Skills Training," with the questions, "Who am I as a law teacher? What am I doing when I teach law?"[39] Most clinic professors believe they should teach the law and also advance their students' understanding of justice.[40] As noted above, social justice issues cannot be ignored. The issues, however, do not solely arise in lawyer client relations. Faculty must also address how legal and political systems contribute to the clients' legal problems and whether those systems are weighted against them. A large number of law students come from privileged backgrounds. As a result, many students' first exposure to people marginalized within our legal system may come from participating in a clinic.[41] They also have been taught that our democracy is one that provides equal opportunity and fair treatment for all. A clinic student's earliest challenge may be realizing that many of their assumptions about how our society works do not apply to their clients.[42] For some, the clinic experience will call into question the fairness of the legal system and the students' role in it. Hence, issues concerning values and justice will arise from the disorienting moment that occurs when the student sees how the application of law applies to clients in ways that might not apply to them.

Teaching values in a clinic course is more difficult today than ever before. Because an individual clinic itself may have values defining its mission, one might expect that the enrolled students will sympathize with that mission and share those values with others in the clinic. While many students come to the clinic with values that are the same as their teacher, at least some students are likely to adhere to values that are different from and perhaps clash with those of their fellow students and their faculty members. For example, students and faculty today often define themselves as members of one or more identity groups. Members with strong identity affiliations to race, gender, religious denominations, socio-economic status, or political philosophy may expect others in the class to share some of those identity-defining traits with them. But some other students may not share the same values or may actively oppose them. These value differences foretell some possibility of value clashes.

Identity affiliation is not the only reason the values of students in a clinic may differ. A clinic class as a whole can consist of people with disparate personal and professional values because students enroll in a clinic for varied reasons. Not all students join a clinic because of its value orientation. Some students enroll in a clinic because it is the only one that exists in a particular subject matter. For example, few schools maintain an in-house prosecution clinic because creating an arm of the government within the law school is complicated. Thus, students favoring strict criminal law enforcement and those who want to be prosecutors may have to take a criminal-defense clinic to learn criminal law and practice. Students in a social-enterprise clinic might not want to work on non-profit or micro-enterprise projects for poor people but have to enroll in such a clinic to get the corporate skills they need to secure their positions in Big Law. Some students might join an appellate clinic for a résumé credential to obtain a judicial clerkship or Big Law job, even though they may have little concern for the overall welfare of the clients they may represent.

Clients also come to the student/lawyer-client relationship with their own values. Their values may be deeply personal, like honesty, fairness, empathy, and altruism. Some of their values, like equality, diversity, equity, and inclusiveness, may arise from the political, ethnic, racial, cultural, or economic segment of society that they inhabit. Most students in a clinic want to help their clients, either because they are trying on their lawyer role, or because they are incipient "movement lawyers" seeking to help the people they see as oppressed or at least disfavored by the way power and wealth are distributed in the society.[43] But that is not always the case. Some clinics involve their students in case selection. Although the intake process often involves only a paper review, sometimes it includes a preliminary client interview. In that case, students may resist taking on a client's case because of the client's real or perceived personal values despite the apparent legitimacy of the claim. Clinic capacity is limited, and although lawyers need not take every client who comes to their door, the ethics rules of the profession encourage lawyers to take unpopular causes or unsavory clients.[44] A teacher whose clinic has a social justice teaching goal may decide to raise that issue at intake or case selection. Even if social justice is not a goal of the clinic, a values clash will have to be resolved when a student refuses to represent a client, or a client asks for a new student lawyer, based on perceived value differences or judgments.

Although the values discussion may arise from a specific case, it often emerges earlier in conversations about who our clients are or will be, how they seem to consistently have limited access to health care, suffer from housing discrimination or disparate education opportunities, and seem to be caught in a widening wealth gap. Students may notice that those who do endure those indignities seem to consistently come from a specific racial, ethnic, or socio-economic groups. In our current era of social and political polarization, most of those conversations will likely be tied to racial dominance and subjugation or identity politics. The conversation may also arise in general discussions about the fora in which the clinic practices or where the power resides in those fora. Again, as noted earlier, the legal profession as a whole is based on certain values that give rise to its ethical rules and other norms and values of the profession. Those traditions are based on a power structure that long favored European and colonial traditions, providing little room for the traditions of non-European cultures. While some contend that some of those principles are immutable and apply to all, recent scholarship has taught us that many of our traditions are based on concepts developed prior to the Civil War and during the Jim Crow era. Hence, traditions and customs of a formerly enslaved population and those of other immigrants of color were ignored as those legal principles developed. As Professor Russell G. Pearce writes, "white lawyers ... have a tendency to treat whiteness as a neutral norm or baseline and not a racial identity, and tend to view racial issues as belonging primarily to people of color."[45]

There are many points of entry into these conversations depending upon the context in which they arise. The choice of an entry point and the unfolding of the knowledge that the teacher wants to convey must be planned, informed, and intentional. Conversations about justice and the values that each participant brings to a clinic project, whether in class or in a supervision session, require serious advance planning. Law schools are becoming more diverse, creating classrooms and clinics filled with students from multiple ethnic, social, and racial backgrounds. The current reckoning concerning the continued effects of slavery and of Euro-American primacy may engender emotions of pain, anger, misunderstanding, imposter syndrome, and sometimes outrage. These conversations in today's law school clinics may include faculty and students of the same or varied racial, ethnic, political, or interest groups. Teachers have learned that minority students should not carry the burden of leading such conversations alone; no student should be expected to speak for an entire racial ethnic, economic, gendered group. No matter the composition of the various groups, an individual's values may reflect values commonly associated with their identity group or diverge from the values shared by others in that cohort. Thus, teachers cannot begin the dialogue with any assumptions about the values an individual student brings to the conversation. Supervisors must know more than a little bit about who a student is before they plunge into these discussions. Most importantly, the conversation cannot be forced on a student who is not ready for it. Personal narratives are powerful, and no one has a single-story narrative. Teachers must guard against defining a person only by what they see.

Once a value is defined and the clash is identified, the discussion needs to focus on how some values are based on ethical rules, while others are based on moral, social, or political precepts. Assumptions must be unraveled during the conversation as the distinctions between ethics, values, and morals become more apparent. It can be disorienting for a student to determine that the ethical codes require a course of action that is inconsistent with the student's own values. If well-planned, the discussion enables students to begin to see how their announcement that "I can't do that because it is unethical or immoral," confuses concepts which, if not distinguished, may lead to ineffective client representation, or even to acts or omissions that can result in bar sanctions.

Conversely, faculty should carefully monitor students who closely identify with a client because they share a similar values system. Particularly liking or having affection for a client is not an inherent cause for concern. Client-centered lawyering often results in elastic boundaries between a lawyer's personal and professional roles. However, role confusion also poses a risk that the student lawyer will "assume their own assessment of a given situation is naturally the same as their client's."[46] The ability to step back, self-analyze, and appreciate how one's biases, culture, and history may affect client relationships are essential skills to build to ensure effective client representation.[47]

Values are inherently malleable, and a person's values may change over time. They are based on one's life experiences and assumptions about those experiences. Values to which some students adhere may be seen by others as forms of oppression that must be defeated. One's personal values may clash with those of their clinic partner, their faculty member, the court, their adversary, or even their client—and may even clash with legal ethics. When those clashes occur regarding the representation of a client, supervisors must intervene. The clinic experience is one of those life events in which values evolve. Some values are strengthened, while others are abandoned during a student's time in the clinic. Clinic faculty often discuss the power of clinic participation to alter a student's understanding of how the law operates in a democratic society and even change their prior sense of self.

Values, unlike ethics (which are shared by all members of the profession) or morals (which are shared by adherents of a particular religious of philosophical code), are ultimately personal and dynamic. As such, they can be changed by new life experiences. Universities and law schools are places where students recognize and confront ideas and learn new ways of seeing the world before they move into their professional lives. Faculty need to help students identify how values influence not only their legal obligations to their clients and to the court but affect the choices they make when selecting strategies to secure a client's interests. But supervisors must tread carefully to ensure the student is developing their own sense of self rather than merely emulating the supervisor's preferences. Teachers should always approach these conversations with the student's learning and personal development in mind.

Recognizing the Teacher's Responsibility

At some point, a personal value change might be possible during a conversation about the importance of realigning a student's values to the demands of the law or the strategy. Before addressing, identifying, and unpacking student assumptions regarding the values encountered in client representation, faculty need to know how their own values influence their teaching. Supervisors, like students, need to engage in self-reflection to determine the scope of their own values and what values they bring to the clinic. Students generally have great respect for their clinic supervisors, and a clinical course can be a life-changing event for them. For that reason, supervisors need to be transparent about their own values at some point in the conversation, as well as clear about the goals of the supervision session or class.

There are several reasons for this transparency. Students need to know that faculty members have specific values that imbue their own client representation and teaching methodology. When students understand that values discussions are at the heart of client representation and know the values faculty members bring to their work, they will not view such conversations as unwarranted intrusions into their personal privacy. Instead, they will see them as part and parcel of the clinic's work, and something they must grapple with themselves. Moreover, it will make them more willing to reveal their values and their assumptions as they work through a case. The second reason for revealing one's values is that it makes it easier to explain to a student how clients' interests are better protected when representation is consistent with legal ethics and not a lawyer's personal goals. Students need to see that checking one's own blind spots and assumptions is geared toward providing good client representation and helping students become the best lawyers they can be. It is easier for them to accept the process if they know their supervisor does the same thing they are being asked to do. The third reason is that teaching social justice remains controversial today. We should not hide that reality from the students. Indeed, students should be given notice of all of a clinic's goals before they even apply for the course. If we create an expectation early in the clinic semester that understanding values and assumptions are at the heart of good client representation, students will be better prepared to face these challenging conversations. Finally, teachers need to model the values that they teach. We cannot just talk about them in the abstract. We have to live them in our actions with students and clients and demonstrate them in all of our interventions.

These teaching moments cannot happen haphazardly or serendipitously. Teachers should not make premature assumptions about the student if the conversations are to be productive. They need to possess a good understanding of who the student is and whether they are ready for that kind of conversation. Faculty need to understand the choices they want to make when supervising students regarding values issues and have a sense of how their choices might lead to specific outcomes. Only then can they devise interventions that help students develop the skills to challenge their own assumptions when they make case related choices. These conversations are necessary not to change a student's values, although that may occur, but to produce better client service.

These are often hard conversations. Teachers need to create a safe environment in the clinic where difficult conversations about values can occur. But the safe spaces must also be brave spaces where teachers and students can be honest and grow as people and as professionals. Every aspect of the clinic structure, from its goals to its architecture, must be designed to create that safe and brave space. Growth necessarily requires stepping outside one's comfort zone. Most students will seek clinical courses to grow as professionals. Good teachers see clinical courses as places where students, in what is probably their final years of academic education, can form personal characteristics of civic virtue as well as the skills they will need in their profession. Clinical teachers, knowing their students well, will have to determine whether formal classes, case rounds, or supervision sessions provide the best space for the conversations. That is why clinic design is so important. Each aspect of the pedagogy must contribute to that safe and brave space. This is where students can learn to recognize the importance of personal values and assumptions when advising clients and making decisions. They will learn that these lessons apply not only during their time in the clinic but during a lifetime of practicing law.

Clinical teaching is a calling, not just a job. Helping students form the characteristics of civic virtue is a heavy responsibility. Understanding the nature of values education and identifying the values that students, faculty, clients, and others bring to a client's case is critical to providing effective legal assistance during the student's time in the clinic and afterwards. It is also critical to situating clinical education into a law school curriculum. If we are to serve both the values of the profession and the academic dedication to the civic imperatives of higher education, we must make it clear that social justice values are at the root of good clinical pedagogy and the legal profession. Understanding how values affect legal representation is, in turn, a major lesson in the task of lifelong learning.

The articles following this chapter and chapters 7, 9 and 10 explore how teachers in a law clinic setting can do more than teach doctrine and improve students' legal skills. These articles demonstrate how teachers can also take advantage of opportunities to teach about (in)justice and (un)fairness in the legal system. Each of these articles addresses disorienting moments—the moments when a student is presented with a situation that challenges his or her fundamental beliefs or assumptions.[48] The articles also examine the fundamental reasons people choose to pursue social justice in their legal careers and how law schools can help facilitate this interest.[49]

Other Voices

Jane H. Aiken, *Provocateurs for Justice**

7 Clinical L. Rev. 287 (2001)

...

I aspire to be a provocateur for justice. A provocateur is one who instigates, a person who inspires others to action. A provocateur for justice actively imbues her students with a lifelong learning about justice, prompts them to name injustice, to recognize the role they may play in the perpetuation of injustice and to work toward a legal solution to that injustice.

...

"Justice Readiness": A Developmental Approach

The first step in moving our students toward a commitment to justice is for teachers to understand that the ability to recognize injustice and participate in creative solutions involves a developmental process that usually occurs in sequence. First, a student must develop effective critical thinking skills. Critical thinking in the law is the ability to see that law is constructed rather than discovered. The law does not exist "out there" to be found; rather it is a reflection of a complex interplay of information, expertise, and value choice. Being "justice ready" takes critical thinking one step further: the student sees that she can play an active role in exposing the inherent biases in law. She can use that understanding to construct legal challenges that will enhance human dignity and move toward a more just society. As teachers we can become competent diagnosticians of where our students fall within the developmental sequence and foster movement toward "justice readiness."

Students come to us at varying stages in the development of critical thinking skills that require different interventions. Educational theorists have identified several developmental stages for adult learners, which I present in a legal context. First, the learner manifests right-wrong dualist thinking. At this stage, students still hang on to the idea that there is a right and wrong answer to every legal problem. The lawyer's job is to find that answer. In the second stage of development, critical thinking, the learner recognizes that there are very few or no absolute answers to legal problems. Law students at this stage believe that there is absolutely no certainty in the law. The lawyer's job is to figure out what the decision-maker wants and pitch legal arguments that appeal to the decision-maker. These students understand the important developmental step that the law is "constructed," but they feel powerless in their ability to make change. In the final stage of a lawyer's development toward "justice readiness," the lawyer demonstrates an appreciation for context, understands that legal decision-making reflects the value

* Excerpts are reprinted with the permission of the author and the Clinical Law Review.

system in which it operates, and can adapt, evaluate, and support her own analysis. At this stage, the "justice ready" lawyer can become proactive in shaping legal disputes with an eye toward social justice.

...

Teaching Tools for Provocateurs for Justice

We have many tools to help our students focus on justice. Clinical legal education has long valued reflection as a key to effective teaching. Our supervisory questions should be directed to fostering reflection rather than eliciting information. As teachers, we must deviate from system-reinforcing behaviors and challenge the students to examine and reflect upon the prevailing social, political, and cultural realities that affect their own and their clients' lives. Provocateurs for justice encourage students to engage in this kind of "critical reflection." Critical reflection has at its root an attempt to tease out or hunt down assumptions. Perhaps the most powerful tool for lawyers dedicated to social justice is the ability to identify assumptions and expose them. There are essentially three kinds of assumptions that we want our students to be good at identifying: paradigmatic, prescriptive, and causal assumptions.

Paradigmatic assumptions are perhaps the most difficult to pin down because they are the very structural assumptions we use to put our experience into fundamental categories. Many times we see these assumptions as merely facts, the way things are. These assumptions are the most difficult to examine critically because they seem as if they are the bedrock of our understanding. For example, students often believe that if a person is actually innocent, he cannot be legally held in prison. Clinics that do post-conviction work provide eye-opening experiences for students who learn that actual innocence often is not a ground for a habeas petition. Grappling with that offers students the opportunity to explore how the criminal justice system works and the degree to which a defendant's lack of resources at trial is treated as irrelevant in an assessment of post-conviction remedies.

Identifying paradigmatic assumptions can remedy resistance to clients and assist in developing case theories.

...

Prescriptive assumptions are what we think ought to be happening in a given situation. For example, if you take for granted that people are always able to make it on time to pre-arranged appointments if they are sufficiently organized, then you may believe that a client is disorganized and unmotivated if she fails to arrive on time. That prescriptive assumption incorporates an assumption about the availability of transportation and childcare that may not be true for our clients. As provocateurs for justice, we can assist our students in uncovering that prescriptive assumption. Bryant and Peters describe a very effective method for getting at these kinds of assumptions by challenging the students to imagine parallel universes. The teacher asks the student to generate alternative interpretations of a client's behavior. This process allows the student to understand how little the student knows about the client's life, helps forestall a rush to judgment and fosters open-mindedness. It is also a useful device for examining the assumptions that the student was making that contributed to her initial assessment of the client's behavior.

...

The third kind of assumption is causal. These assumptions help us understand how the world works and how we can effectuate change. For example, a clinical student acted as guardian ad litem representing a child whose mother was drug addicted. In a supervision session, the student proposed that we should recommend to the court that the mother's visitation should be conditioned on her active participation in a drug treatment program. If she dropped out, she lost visitation. The student justified this proposal by stating that the mother needed the incentive, and it was in the best interest of the child to have a drug-free mother. No drug treatment, no visits. We then shifted to talking about whether this would be best for our client, the child. The student asserted her causal assumption: the reason the mother was a bad parent was because she used drugs.

Causal assumptions are easy to miss in the rush of supervision. It is important to slow the analysis down and identify each step in the assumed chain of cause and effect. The first question in our case was: "What behaviors are you aware of that make this woman a bad mother?" This required the student to evaluate how much factual information she had about the particulars of the client's relationship with her child. In this case, the student had very little information. She had done what anyone operating under a causal assumption does: sees the behavior (using drugs) and attributes behavioral consequences that "necessarily" flow. Our next step was to identify what parenting behaviors we associate with drug addiction. After listing those, we developed a plan to determine if this mother actually engaged in those deficient parenting behaviors. By exploring the underlying assumptions about the causal connection between being a drug addict and being a bad parent, the student understood how little she actually knew about the cause of the mother's instability. This process improved her ability to do comprehensive fact investigation and be a more effective advocate for the child, who wanted to continue having regular contact with her mother.

Generally, we uncover these assumptions through reflecting with our students on their experiences. We can increase the probability that our students will engage in critical reflection if we mediate that experience through effective questions. The questions should be specific, work from the particular to the general and be conversational. It is not enough to ask the student, "what did you think of your performance?" That only elicits a certain kind of reflection. We need to encourage our students to reflect upon the content (what), process (how), and premise (why) of our work. Our questions should be directed toward encouraging the student to think about a situation in a new way, thus creating some kind of disorientation and opening the way for new meaning schemes.

Questions can focus on the discrepancies between the experience and the theoretical positions related to that experience. For example, in a domestic violence clinic, students learn that a victim of violence can procure an order of protection to keep her abuser away. It does not take long for students to learn that the order of protection is merely a piece of paper and provides little peace of mind for a woman subsequently stalked by her abuser. The clinical teacher can mine that experience for its "justice insight." We can start with the "what" questions, moving from the specific to the general: "What assumptions did the student make about the usefulness of the order of protection?" "What assumptions are implicit about the role of law in this situation?" Next, we move to the "how" questions: "How did we arrive at the decision to seek an order of protection?" "How does the legal system respond to the deficiencies in the protection remedy?" Finally, we can move to the "why" questions: "Why is an order of protection ineffective in this case?" "Why did we believe that this was the most appropriate solution for this client?" Of course, assisting the student in gaining insight into the legal system's failure to address the needs of women who are victims of violence is not enough if we want to be provocateurs for justice. Our next questions must focus on action planning and critical self-reflection: "What would you do next time in this situation?" "How have your assumptions about the efficacy of the legal system affected your ability to address the larger problems you have identified?" "What role can you play in dismantling the structure of this injustice?"

If discussions are slow to start, we can assist by identifying an engaging event, assigning a provocative reading, or creating an activity in which the students must use these critical assessment skills. One method is using "critical incident" exercises. The instructor asks the student to identify an event that for some reason is of particular significance to the student. Usually the instructor identifies some criteria for choosing the incident. I have found that asking students to identify events that have occurred with clients or the legal system that surprised them, because things were not as they expected, reap meaningful events for reflecting upon justice issues. First, the students are asked to write a short (one or, at most, two paragraph) description of the event. The description should be as specific as possible, focusing on the particular action rather than abstract concepts. I use these reports to develop hunches about what assumptions the student is making. I then can ask the student to reflect on their assumptions when I give the student feedback. Because these incidents are written, the student retains some privacy. Discussion of internal biases is often difficult in front of peers. The critical incident exercise is best used in one on one discussions about justice.

...

Another technique to assist students in understanding their assumptions and the assumptions that underlie the law is "criteria analysis." Criteria are the bases on which we evaluate worth and merit. They are necessarily value-laden.... Criteria often appear objective but they are inevitably subjective and thus offer rich fodder for students to examine assumptions, norms, and values. When we ask students to engage in criteria analysis, we are asking them to make explicit those judgments that underlie the criteria. A key component of criteria analysis is to ask them to identify the behavioral indicators that show that the criteria have been met. For example, in child protection cases, it is often helpful to have students identify the criteria they will be using to distinguish poverty from neglect, when assessing whether the parent in question has been neglectful. This analysis requires the student to think about the behavioral consequences of poverty, the standards that child protection has for what it means to be a good parent and how much those standards and judgments assume access to money and resources.

Other techniques include role-playing in which the student is encouraged to play the role of the client. After simulating an interview or counseling session, participants can discuss the experience. Questions that are likely to lead to insight about alternative perspectives include, "When you were the client, what were you thinking or feeling?" "How did you come to that reaction?" "Why is this important?" Some clinicians begin the clinic as many of us do with an exercise in which the students interview one another and then "introduce" that student to the class. This exercise offers a beginning opportunity to teach the student about interviewing. We do not need to stop there, however. We can use this exercise as an opportunity to discuss how each person felt about not speaking for him or herself. I probe whether they felt as if an accurate picture was provided and whether they felt "present." I remind them that this is what happens with clients when we speak for them in court. This exercise, offered on the first day of class, begins the process of having the students step into the client's shoes. This beginning exercise opens the door for future experiential exercises in which the client's reaction to the lawyering, not just the lawyering skill, is treated as an important part of being an effective lawyer.

It is not enough to look at each individual case for its possibilities for teaching about justice. We need to look at the bigger picture as well. We should encourage our students to evaluate whether the legal options that we offer our clients are merely designed to reduce the intensity of the injustice or whether they assist in a long-term strategy of social transformation. If our legal work is merely a short term solution to our clients' problems, our discussion should move on to activities in which we can work toward the elimination of the structures of injustice. We need to create occasions for discourse on the essential attributes of just societies. By making that space, we communicate the importance of social justice, the opportunity to make a difference that their law degree creates, and the responsibility that they bear as lawyers for the delivery of justice in our society.

Conclusion

As educators in a professional school, we are in the business of providing credentials to the elite and thereby reinforcing the ideological justification for oppressive social orders. We need not fulfill that role. Instead, we can transform our practices so that we can be provocateurs for justice. It is not enough to use our legal skills and our students to fight for justice. As clinicians, we have made a commitment to justice through our role as educators, not front-line lawyers. This means that we must hone our skills as educators to ensure that the future lawyers we are training have an appreciation for justice and work to inspire them to use their legal skills to bring about a more just society.

Willow Tracy, *Values-Ambiguous Clinics**

31 CLINICAL L. REV. 379 (2025)

...

B. Terms and Trends

This Article argues that the emergence and growth of values- ambiguous clinics (again, meaning clinics that are commonly perceived as not having foundational social justice goals) has been disruptive to the clinical community and that, in trying to come to terms with the professional integration of these clinics, we encounter some very challenging questions. I will thus begin by locating this inquiry in a particular part of the experiential/clinical universe, providing additional discussion about what I mean by values-ambiguous clinics and why I believe this new terminology is necessary, and summarizing some trends surrounding the growth of these clinics.

1. Locating the Inquiry: In-house Clinics

In this article I am primarily discussing "in-house" law school clinics, rather than externships, simulation courses, or other experiential opportunities. This focus is not because I think these issues do not come up in other settings; on the contrary, the ongoing debates about corporate counsel externships and private law firm externship placements are rich sources for this inquiry, and I will at least tangentially reference some of this discussion. However, I will be primarily discussing in-house clinics—for a few reasons. Most of the existing literature on related subjects is also carried out in terms of in-house clinics, and this is the literature I wish to engage with. I also believe it matters that more law school resources are typically required for in-house clinics than other experiential opportunities and that in-house clinics are seen as setting standards for the broader category of experiential legal education. Finally, in-house clinics are what I have the most firsthand experience with and what I personally find most compelling. I founded an in-house business law clinic in 2011 that I would describe as a values-ambiguous clinic, and I continue to serve as the director of that clinic. My experience teaching an in-house clinic and interacting with the broader clinical community in this capacity in part motivates the inquiry.

2. Defining Values-Ambiguous Clinics

I propose the new terminology of "values-ambiguous" clinics because I do not believe there is an existing term that describes the group of clinics that I am interested in, and I also believe we have been stymied in our conversations by this lack of terminology. I am aware that in suggesting new terminology I am inviting challenges, not least of which is the difficulty of engaging with existing literature in a consistent way. I am also aware that the specific term I have chosen is imperfect.

When I began thinking about this subject my focus was initially more simply on transactional clinics, and this would have been consistent with common usage and

* Excerpts are reprinted with the permission of the author and the Clinical Law Review.

with most of the scholarship on related subjects. Although there is no universal method of referring to clinics, authors have found it to be a useful shorthand to (implicitly or explicitly) split clinics into two rough groups. One group is "transactional clinics" where the lawyering activity involves "the development of organizations, businesses, and structures for clients to own and use." The second group is "traditional" or "litigation legal services" clinics that engage in advocacy, litigation, or dispute resolution.

Here, where our concern is perception of values commitments, using transactional—a word that generally describes a type of law practice—to communicate about the presence of clinics that are perceived to not have social justice values commitments, is clearly problematic. Drawing a line around transactional clinics is both over- and under-inclusive for the current inquiry and, more importantly, somewhat misses the point. Transactional clinics certainly are frequently values-ambiguous, in the sense that it frequently isn't apparent whether a transactional clinic has a foundational values commitment. But transactional clinics are also often *not* values-ambiguous and, conversely, non-transactional clinics may also be values-ambiguous.

To give an example of the over-inclusivity of a focus on transactional clinics, consider two transactional clinics, a Community Economic Development (CED) Clinic and a Business Law Clinic. The two clinics might do a similar or even identical set of transactional legal tasks—for instance, forming businesses or drafting contracts—and they might perform these tasks for a similar or identical type of clients—for instance micro-entrepreneurs within a certain city. But despite these similarities the CED Clinic would be more likely to be presumed to be carrying out this work for a social justice purpose, while the Business Law Clinic's underlying values-commitments might be seen as ambiguous. It may be the case that in fact the Business Law Clinic had the same social justice orientation as the CED Clinic, or a different but equally foundational values commitment, or no social justice orientation at all. But whatever the case may be, we would likely not presume, absent additional information, that the Business Law Clinic had a foundational social justice commitment. I would therefore describe the Business Law Clinic, but not the CED Clinic, as values-ambiguous. Tellingly, although CED clinics usually are transactional, CED clinics are often excluded from values-based critiques of transactional clinics.

The category of transactional clinics can also be under-inclusive for purposes of the current inquiry. For instance, advocacy- and litigation-based intellectual property and technology clinics or securities arbitration clinics also tend to share this quality of being perceived as having an ambiguous commitment to social justice, even though they are often grounded in a non-transactional advocacy or dispute resolution practice.

Commentators writing about clinics with unclear values commitments, many of which are transactional, address the over-/under-inclusivity of terminology in a few ways. For instance, some specify that by transactional they mean just those transactional clinics that are not community lawyering or CED clinics. Similarly, others specify that when they say transactional they primarily mean startup and entrepreneurship clinics or clinics that are "market-based." Some suggest or state that clinics, even if they have what we would typically call a transactional practice area, are actually not transactional clinics if they are focused on "community outcomes" rather than "deals." Many others do not bother to make additional distinctions at all or, understandably, use terms inconsistently—sometimes using transactional clinics to describe a practice type that is in contrast with litigation or advocacy and other times using the term to describe a specific subset of that practice area that does not appear to be mission- or values-driven. Others deal with a narrower subject area subset, such as intellectual property clinics, regardless of whether the clinics are transactional or not. Still others paint with a broader brush, describing the clinics of interest as "business oriented" or "specialty" clinics.

None of the above descriptors quite capture the concept that I believe to be at the heart of the current discussion. Perhaps the descriptor in the existing literature that comes closest to the group of clinics I mean to be discussing is Minna Kotkin's refreshingly direct description of "business-oriented clinics with questionable social utility." I depart from this description, not only in terms of the embedded critique but also in the focus on perception of values alone, rather than a combination of business orientation and uncertain values. While it is again true that business-orientation, like a transactional practice style, is a very common feature of these clinics, I believe business orientation is perceived as problematic only insofar as it is paired with values-ambiguity.

Having defended the need for a new category and provided a rationale for the specific choice of term, I now address some of the possible concerns with "values-ambiguous" as a descriptor. The first of these is that the words value and values have dual meanings. They can refer to a commitment to an ideal or principle, as in social justice values, and this is the meaning I am trying to evoke. They can also refer to an assessment of worth or importance, as in an assessment that a clinic contributes nothing of value. While I do not mean to be evoking the latter usage, there is potential for confusion, particularly when I am separately discussing the ways in which we might evaluate the relative "worth" of clinics. A second issue with the word values is that it may be overbroad. When I say values, I do not mean all possible ideals one might be committed to, for instance the ideal of loyalty. I mean the subset of values that might be termed "social justice values" as they are imagined within the clinical community.

Concerns may also be raised by the word ambiguous. As noted above, when I discuss the ambiguity of a clinic's values commitments, I mean to be specifically highlighting the tendency toward uncertainty in the perception of a values commitment, rather than making any sort of assessment of the actual underlying reality of a values commitment. In other words, the ambiguity I assign to a clinic is describing the likelihood of an observer of the clinic having the experience of being uncertain as to whether the clinic is oriented to social justice values, rather than describing an inherent quality of the clinic itself. Put more simply, I mean to be highlighting the fact that some clinics are likely to be presumed to be operating for social justice purposes, while others are not.

...

It is also worth noting that I am generally treating values-ambiguity as a binary quality of a clinic, in the sense that I am suggesting any given clinic either is or is not values-ambiguous. We could, and perhaps should, instead think of a clinic's values-ambiguity as being a matter of degree, type, or audience. For instance, we might say that a CED clinic, particularly one that focuses on individual entrepreneurs, might be more values-ambiguous than a general civil legal services clinic, in the sense that we might be less sure of its values commitments. Or, a First Amendment Clinic that does work for a wealthy conservative politician might leave some in doubt of its values-commitments, even though the clinic is obviously fundamentally concerned with protecting rights. Or, a tax clinic might be considered values-ambiguous by a member of the general public—but when the legal academy is the audience it is generally understood that most tax clinics serve low income tax payers in a way that is presumed to be in furtherance of social justice.

...

Another difficulty of using the term values-ambiguous is that it doesn't lend itself easily to a counterpart or a term to describe those clinics that are not values-ambiguous. For that I will use the term values-presumed, although it is not an exact opposite to values-ambiguous. By values-presumed, again, I do not mean that the clinic necessarily does have a values commitment. Nor do I mean that we presume we know which specific version of social justice values the clinic might be advancing. I simply mean that, absent information to the contrary, we generally will presume that these clinics operate in service of social justice values.

...

3. The Growth of Values-Ambiguous Clinics

This Article asserts that there has been a trend toward values-ambiguous clinics, in the sense that they have grown in number more rapidly than other types of clinics. Insofar as the values-ambiguous category overlaps with transactional, entrepreneurial or IP/T clinics, a growth trend has been well documented in the existing literature. While authors are not always in exact agreement about numbers, there is widespread agreement that transactional and IP/T clinics have "grown exponentially." Relatedly, there is an abundance of scholarship declaring a more general trend away from certain types of clinics that are presumed to be very strongly identified with a social justice mission. Authors have noted, for instance, the proliferation of clinical "programs that replicate the more elite elements of private and public practice" rather than "classic legal services style practice" and the rise of "special and distinct areas of practice clinics" rather than "classic legal aid or general practice style legal services in-house clinics."

...

B. The Divide

While I suspect that some aspects of the above vignette segments will be recognizable to readers of this article, and many are indeed based on trends documented in existing literature, division or tension between values-ambiguous (by any name) clinicians and other clinicians is rarely explicitly discussed in academic literature in any sustained fashion. There are a few exceptions to this phenomenon, but perhaps even more telling are the ways in which the literature does not directly or thoroughly explore this subject. In particular, very little scholarship that is written by non-transactional or IP/T clinicians describes a division or expresses concern about growth trends regarding values-ambiguous clinics.

On the other hand, a large body of writing from transactional and IP/T clinicians either explicitly references a divide or writes in response to an assumed or perceived divide. In other words, most of the discussion of the existence of an issue comes from transactional or IP/T clinicians themselves. These expressions range from mild observations that someone else has a concern, to more explicit warnings in the face of a perceived issue. Transactional clinician Paul Tremblay for instance gently notes "the uneasy relationship between teaching small business law in a clinical setting and the social justice mission of clinical teaching generally" and "the not-infrequent curiosity about whether [small business and startup] practice has any, or any significant, social justice value." Transactional clinician Patience A. Crowder similarly describes the "perennial question chasing transactional legal clinics: whether transactional law clinics are truly grounded in public service, social justice goals, and service delivery."

Cynthia Dahl and Victoria Phillips, directors of intellectual property clinics, more directly note that, because of increasing numbers of transactional and IP/T clinics "some commentators are expressing concern about the future of clinical education … and its underlying social justice values." They are specifically writing to reassure those who have these concerns, but despite the fact that these concerns are understood by them to be (and I believe are) quite pervasive, they weren't at that time able to cite any commentators that explicitly expressed concern about the effect of growing numbers of certain types of clinics on the future of clinical legal education. Even when transactional clinicians occasionally have written in defense of not having a traditional social justice mission in certain types of clinics, they are writing with an understanding that this stance is controversial, but can't cite much by way of direct criticism. Perhaps unsurprisingly then, this scholarship has also not subsequently garnered much explicit push-back in scholarship.

It is possible that this relative lack of scholarship can all simply be explained by the plentiful nature of a different type of scholarship. There is of course a tremendous body of scholarship discussing the primary importance of social justice to clinical education generally, some of which describes or decries an apparent general trend toward placing pedagogical goals and skills development above progressive values-based missions in all types of clinics. Even when these articles do not directly mention transactional, IP/T, or other frequently values-ambiguous clinic practice-types (and they usually do not), the inference that a values-ambiguous clinic would be frowned upon according to the criteria is abundantly clear.

Turning to the exceptions, the authors who do explicitly decry the trends of what I am calling values-ambiguous clinics, their concerns are often expressed strongly. For instance, Etienne C. Toussaint, notes "the dangers of neoliberalism are visible in the growing popularity of transactional law clinics that prepare law students for venture capital and start-up law practice ... such clinics can undermine the *public* purpose of law school if they fail to engage the experiences of historically marginalized populations differentiated across racial and class divides." In the only article I am aware of where concern regarding the rise of values-ambiguous clinics is expressed in any direct or sustained way, Minna Kotkin makes a powerful argument that the growth trend in transactional clinics is problematic because it replicates hierarchies found within the practice of law and further erodes "the poverty law foundation of clinical education, and its emphasis on values—local community empowerment, social justice and law reform."

That criticisms exist does not necessarily mean that a division does, but despite the relative dearth of writing directly addressing this issue, I believe the existence of a division is an open secret—one that scholars who direct values-ambiguous clinics are most likely to indicate in scholarship. Transactional Clinician Praveen Kosuri explicitly describes a division between clinicians, wondering if the friction between clinics that are and are not seen as mission driven has reached the point that "the clinical community has outgrown a single house" and stating that if clinical programs do not proactively reconcile this, they "risk a schism" brought about by outside pressure from law school administrators. Kosuri further notes his belief that the clinicians who founded the modern legal movement are threatening to destroy clinics by trying to exclude clinics that don't share their version of social justice. Similarly, transactional clinician Steve Reed opines of a divide and its significance:

> The differences in opinion manifest in small ways: a conversation after a clinical faculty meeting where someone quickly changes the subject to avoid unpleasantness, a public email exchange that flames briefly and then is forgotten, a conference planning committee meeting that strikes an "everyone is equal" compromise. But we must make no mistake: when the current generation overseeing legal clinics retires, the most powerful advocates of the public interest agenda will be gone.

Spoken or not, explicit or implied, confronted or ignored, some sort of division between values-ambiguous and values-presumed clinics appears to be alive and well. While the division appears to be pervasive and persistent, I believe it is not inevitable, and need not be permanent. The tendency in existing scholarship, discussed in the next section of this Article, has been to imagine solutions in terms of suggesting that transactional or IP/T clinics can or should operate or communicate differently to resolve this ambiguity. While I think this is an extremely important body of work, and while I am hopeful about a more unified and integrated future in clinical education, I argue that persisting in this manner is unlikely to lead to the desired outcome. Rather, I think we need to collectively grapple with some of the broader definitional and purpose-related questions that values-ambiguous clinics implicate.

...

A. Values-ambiguous Clinics and Social Justice

To the extent that values-ambiguous clinics are comprised of clinics that are transactional, a relevant argument could be and has been made that transactional law is fundamentally, necessarily, and foundationally at odds with social justice. The essence of this argument is: to the extent one believes that capitalism is fundamentally flawed as an economic system, for instance because it is racist or otherwise "incompatible with oppressed people's welfare," then transactional lawyering "must go down with it" because "some affirmation of capitalism is an unavoidable aspect of transactional lawyering." By extension, many other values-ambiguous clinics that could be said to have the tendency to affirm capitalism—for instance by assisting a wealth-seeking business with securing its legal right to exclusively profit from its intellectual property—could also fall into this category. While most would stop short of making the claim that transactional law or IP/T practices are, as an absolute matter, incompatible with social justice, the tendency to assume that transactional lawyering or IP/T law generally and social justice do not go hand in hand is prevalent. It is not surprising then that assumptions that the clinics that practice and teach these types of law are also frequently assumed to be fundamentally less compatible, if not completely incompatible, with social justice goals.

Against this backdrop, a substantial amount of careful scholarly attention has been paid to advancing some version of the claim that although certain clinics engage in a type of law that is not obviously associated with social justice or the public interest, those clinics are in fact best understood as social justice or public interest clinics. This group of scholarship is concerned with what I will call "unmasking." The essence of the argument it contains is that although a clinic might have a practice area that is not commonly associated with the public good, at least in this case, it would be a misunderstanding to not identify them with "the good fight," as they are in fact so aligned. In other words, the issue with values-ambiguous clinics is not one of fundamental values alignment, the issue is one of optics, which can be resolved by an unmasking that reveals the true nature of the clinic as having been social justice oriented all along. Some unmasking literature makes a broader claim that most transactional or IP/T clinics are social justice aligned, some makes a narrow claim that just an individual clinic is social justice aligned, and some makes a middle ground claim that a subset of clinics with a certain mission or that employ certain methodology are social justice aligned.

...

A. Concluding Thoughts

This Article has argued that the rise of values-ambiguous clinics has been a disruptive force in clinical legal education and that there is currently a largely unacknowledged divide between different types of clinicians. It seems clear that values-ambiguous clinics are here to stay, and their persistent presence forces us to confront a series of challenging but difficult questions about clinical education, and about legal education more broadly. While these questions may not have clear answers, identifying and exploring them in an intentional and reflective manner is critical. They are important both for our scholarly conversations, for our practical understandings, and for our ability to work together toward the shared goals of the clinical community, our students, and our institutions. Productive conversation will necessarily entail some exploration of what we mean by certain terms, and grappling with the intersection of several thorny juxtapositions that are implicated by clinical legal education. This Article has suggested several possible avenues for conversation.

Endnotes

1. Geoffrey C. Hazard Jr., *Personal Values and Professional Ethics*, 40 Clev. St. L. Rev. 133, 134–135 (1992).

2. *Id.*

3. Am. Bar Ass'n, Section of Legal Edu. and Admissions to the Bar, Legal Educ. and Pr of. Dev.—An Educational Continuum Report of the Task Force on Law Schools and the Profession: Narrowing the Gap (1992), *available at* http://www.abanet.org/legaled/publications/onlinepubs/maccrate.html [hereinafter, MacCrate].

4. *Id., See also* Hazard, *supra* note 1, at 140–41.

5. *MacCrate, supra* note 3 at 213–14 (citing Schware v. Bd. of Bar Examiners, 353 U.S. 232, 247 (1957) (Frankfurter, J., concurring)).

6. *Id.*

7. Justin Simard, *The Recurrent Current Crisis in Legal Education*, 56 Willamette L. Rev. 407, 417 (2020) (quoting Alfred F. Konefsky, *Karl's Law School, or the Oven Bird in Buffalo, in* Revisiting the Oven Bird's Song 56 (Mary Nell Trautner, ed. 2018)).

8. *Id.* at 417 (quoting Karl Llewellyn, *Adventures of Rollo*, U. Chi. L. Sch. Rec. 1, 22 (1952).

9. *Id.* at 417 (quoting Llewellyn, *supra* note 8, at 22).

10. *See, e.g.*, Allan N. Sharlin, *Max Weber and the Origins of the Idea of Value-Free Social Science*, 15 Eur. J. Socio. 337, 337 (1974) ("No single person seems to have been individually responsible for [value-free social science's] genesis, but Max Weber wrote the most extensively on the subject and during his lifetime became the idea's leading exponent."); Len Gutkin, *Yes, Academe is a Calling. No, That's Not an Argument Against Unions*, Chron. Higher Educ. (Nov. 7, 2022, https://www.chronicle.com/newsletter/the-review/2022-11-07 (discussing Weber's conception of value-freedom as "a methodological injunction that scholars stay in their lane, lest they transgress beyond the boundaries of scholarship by proffering beliefs and ideals) (internal quotation marks omitted).

11. Gutkin, *supra* note 10.

12. *See, e.g.*, J. Peter Byrne, *Academic Freedom and Political Neutrality in Law Schools: An Essay on Structure and Ideology in Professional Education*, 43 J. Legal Educ. 315, 316 n. 1, 331–32 & n. 32–38 (1993) (collecting sources lodging such a critique). Notably, even clinicians who advocate that "universities and law clinics should live by their values" still recognize the pragmatic reality that having academic freedom to provide values-based education does not mean clinicians must "ignore all institutional ramifications when accepting cases." *See* Adam Babich, *Controversy, Conflicts, and Law School Clinics*, 17 Clinical L. Rev. 469, 470, 483–87, 513 (2011). In other words, defending values-based education does not require ignoring the pragmatic realities of a clinic being housed within a larger university, or (for clinics at public universities) funded by the state, and the limitations that may arise in such a setting. *See id.*

13. *See* Byrne, *supra* note 12, at 316 n. 1, 331–32 & n. 32–38 (collecting sources making that critique). For more cultural commentary on the matter, see Heather Mac Donald, *This Is the Legal Mainstream? Law School Clinics are Stuck in the Sixties*, City Journal (Winter 2006), https://www.city-journal.org/html/legal-mainstream-12913.html, and John O. McGinnis, *The Law Is a Class*, Wall St. J., (March 21, 2011), https://www.wsj.com/articles/SB10001424052748704261504576205431659088782 (reviewing Walter Olson, Schools for Misrule (2011)) (critiquing clinics as "defined by a rather predictable liberal agenda"). And for a more measured take on the nature, importance, possibility, and practice of "neutrality" in law school teaching than what Mac Donald and McGinnis offer in cultural critique, see Susan Herman, *Balancing the Five Hundred Hats: On Being a Legal Educator/Scholar/Activist*, 41 Tulsa L. Rev. 637, 640–46 (2006). *But cf.* Kimberlé Williams Crenshaw, *This Is Not A Drill: The War Against Antiracist Teaching in America*, 68 UCLA L. Rev. 1702, 1706–07 (2022) (condemning the "pronounced backlash against antiracist ideas that has taken hold since the racial reckoning of 2020" and "affirm[ing] the value of this [antiracist] work and the academic freedom that we have enjoyed to pursue it").

14. *See* David Barnhizer, *Freedom to Do What: Institutional Neutrality, Academic Freedom, and Academic Responsibility*, 43 J. Legal Educ. 346, 356 (1993) ("As teachers we must challenge and be open to challenge—open to law students questioning our unstated premises and saying, 'Explain your politics. Justify your politics. Why did you make that statement? Show us why you were able to reach that conclusion.'"); Gutkin, *supra* note 10 ("'Weber is right ... to demand self-consciousness and care with regard to our own political views, and restraint in offering them in the classroom, even if this cannot be fulfilled in the way he demanded because, from Kant to evolution, climate change to genocide, gender equality to the Constitution, there are never facts or texts apart from our interpretation of them.'") (quoting Wendy Brown, Nihilistic Times: Thinking with Max Weber (2023).

15. *See, e.g.*, *id.*; Brian Rosenberg, *Should Universities Take Political Stands? In Theory, Institutions Stay Out of Political and Cultural Debates. But That's Never Been True*, Chron. Higher Educ. (March 31, 2022), https://www.chronicle.com/article/should-universities-take-political-stands; Gutkin, *supra* note 10 ("[Wendy] Brown, like others before her, criticizes Weber's categorical dichotomies (between fact and value, between politics and knowledge, and so on). '[Weber's] purism,' she says, 'is impossible.'") (quoting Brown, *supra* note 14).

16. Duncan Kennedy, *Legal Education and the Reproduction of Hierarchy*, 32 J. Legal Educ. 591, 594 (1982); *see generally* Sherri Lee Keene, *Teaching Dissents*, 107 U. Minn. L. Rev. 2619 (2023) (explaining how the traditional, value-neutral methods of law school teaching can "demoralize law students, rather than empower them").

17. *Id.* at 594–95 ("The point of the class discussion will be that your initial reaction of outrage is naïve, nonlegal, irrelevant to what you're supposed to be learning, and maybe substantively wrong.... There are 'good reasons' for the awful result, when you take a legal and logical 'large' view, as opposed to a knee-jerk passionate view, and if you can't muster those reasons, maybe you aren't cut out to be a lawyer."); Sherri Lee Keene, *The Contextual Case Method: Moving Beyond Opinions to Spark Students' Legal Imaginations*, 108 Va. L. Rev. Online 72, 74 (2022) ("A student's legal imagination is not trained to see new possibilities; a radical reimagination of the world seems either impossible or inadvisable. Students ... are instead subtly encouraged to replicate the status quo.").

18. *Cf.* Eun Hee Han, *What to Learn from Pandemic Teaching? Our Students' Names*, 69 J. Legal Educ. 816, 821 (2020) (discussing alienation and exclusion imposed on diverse students when professors fail to "create an inclusive environment" in the classroom).

19. MacCrate Report, *supra* note 3, at 135 (citing Robert B. McKay, *What Law Schools Can and Should Do (and Sometimes Do)*, 30 N.Y.L. Sch. Rev. 491, 509–10 (1985)).

20. Roy Stuckey, et al., Best Practices in Legal Education: A Vision and A Road Map, 84–85 (2007).

21. The A.B.A. accreditation rule states, "A law school shall provide substantial opportunities to students for: (1) law clinics or field placement(s); (2) student participation in pro bono legal services, including law-related public service activities; and (3) the development of a professional identity." Am. Bar Ass'n Section of Legal Educ. and Admissions to the Bar, ABA Standards and Rules of Procedure for Approval of Law Schools, 2024–2025 (2025).https://www.americanbar.org/content/dam/aba/administrative/legal_education_and_admissions_to_the_bar/standards/2024-2025/2024-2025-standards-and-rules-for-approval-of-law-schools.pdf

22. Am. Bar Ass'n Section of Legal Educ. and Admissions to the Bar, *Report to the House of Delegates* (adopted Feb. 14, 2022), https://www.americanbar.org/content/dam/aba/administrative/news/2022/02/midyear-hod-resolutions/300.pdf, at 7.

23. Heather M. Field, *Fostering Ethical Professional Identity in Tax: Using the Traditional Tax Classroom*, 8 Colum. J. Tax L. 215, 222–23 (2017).

24. *See, e.g.*, K-Sue Park, *The History Wars and Property Law: Conquest and Slavery as Foundational to the Field*, 131 Yale L.J. 1062, 1068 (2022) ("But the histories of conquest and slavery constitute more than addenda to traditional doctrines and present more than an opportunity to apologize or condemn a regrettable chapter of the past. They comprise the train's track and are essential to explaining what American property is and how it has been constructed by law.")

25. *See, e.g.*, Benjamin V. Madison, III & Larry O. Natt Gantt, II, *Morals and Mentors: What the First American Law Schools Can Teach Us About Developing Law Students' Professional Identity*, 31 REGENT U.L. REV. 161, 167–82 (2019) (discussing the role of moral and ethical formation in law school education in America).

26. Patricia McGuire, *Colleges Share the Blame for Assault on Democracy: For Four Years, Trump Unleashed a Tsunami of Lies. Higher Education Responded with Silence*, CHRON. HIGHER EDUC. (Jan. 8, 2021), https://www.chronicle.com/article/colleges-share-the-blame-for-assault-on-democracy; *see also* Ellen Condliffe Lagemann and Harry R. Lewis *Renewing Civic Virtue*, HARV. MAG. (March Aril 2012), https://www.harvardmagazine.com/2012/03/renewing-civic-education; Madison & Gantt, *supra* note 25, at 194–200.

27. *See, e.g.*, Robert D. Dinerstein, *Client-Centered Counseling: Reappraisal and Refinement*, 32 ARIZ. L. REV. 501 (1990).

28. *See, e.g.*, Susan L. Brooks, *Using Therapeutic Jurisprudence to Build Effective Relationships with Students, Clients and Communities*, 13 CLINICAL L. REV. 1501 (2006); Susan L. Brooks, *Practicing (And Teaching) Therapeutic Jurisprudence: Importing Social Work Principles and Techniques into Clinical Legal Education*, 17 ST. THOMAS L. REV. 513 (2005).

29. *Compare* Abbe Smith, *Too Much Heart and Not Enough Heat: The Short Life and Fractured Ego of the Empathetic, Heroic Public Defender*, 37 U.C. DAVIS L. REV. 1203 (2004) (arguing that essential characteristics of a great public defender could be respect for clients, honing one's craft, and a sense of outrage) *with* Charles J. Ogletree, Jr., *Beyond Justifications: Seeking Motivations to Sustain Public Defenders*, 106 HARV. L. REV. 1239 (1993) (arguing that public defenders will be able to sustain their careers if they have empathy for their clients and a feeling of heroism, meaning a desire to take on the "system" in the face of terrible odds).

30. Madison & Gantt, *supra* note 25, at 194–200 (faculty need not create and teach some "agreed-upon list" of what is right and what is wrong but rather must lead students to "grow in their 'moral insight'").

31. *See* Simard, *supra* note 7, at 415.

32. *See generally* Wallace Mlyniec & Haley D. Etchison, *Conceptualizing Student Practice for the 21st Century: Educational and Ethical Considerations in Modernizing the District of Columbia Student Practice Rules*, 28 GEO. J. LEGAL ETHICS 207 (2015).

33. *See generally* HARSHA WALIA, BORDER & RULE: GLOBAL MIGRATION, CAPITALISM, AND THE RISE OF RACIST NATIONALISM (2021).

34. Fran Quigley, *Seizing the Disorienting Moment*, 2 CLINICAL L. REV. 37, 51 (1995).

35. *See, e.g.*, Madison & Gantt, *supra* note 25, at 169–74 (tracing origins of instilling civic virtue in law students as a central theme of law schools' mission), *id.* at 194–205 (arguing that law schools should return to focusing on developing civic and other virtues in their students).

36. Laila L. Hlass & Lindsay M. Harris, *Critical Lawyering*, 21 UTAH L. REV. 683, 685–86 (2021) (internal footnotes omitted).

37. *See* Ann Shalleck, *Clinical Contexts: Theory and Practice in Law and Supervision*, 21 N.Y.U. REV. L. & SOC. CHANGE, 109 (1993).

38. *See, e.g.*, Spencer Rand, *Social Justice as a Professional Duty: Effectively Meeting Law Student Demand for Social Justice by Teaching Social Justice as a Professional Competency*, 87 U. CIN. L. REV. 77, 93–105 (2018) (stressing importance of intentionality in incorporating social justice focus).

39. Stephen Wizner, *Beyond Skills Training*, 7 CLINICAL L. REV. 327, 340 (2000).

40. *Id.* at 330. Many founders of clinical education had been active in the civil rights movements of the 1960s and wanted law schools to increase their focus on social justice issues and to present law students with opportunities to work with poor and marginalized individuals. *Id.* at 331–32. Though many law school clinics now emphasize skills building rather than social justice, clinics still typically serve poor clients, presenting law students with exposure to social justice issues to which they may not have been exposed in the past. *Id.* at 332–33.

41. Jane H. Aiken, *Striving to Teach Justice, Fairness, and Morality*, 4 Clinical L. Rev. 1, 38–39 (1997).

42. *Id.* at 30.

43. *See* Carrie Menkel-Meadow, *The Causes of Cause Lawyering*, *in* Cause Lawyering: Political Commitments and Professional Responsibilities 31, 38 (Austin Sarat & Stuart Scheingold eds., 1998); Amna A. Akbar, Sameer M. Ashar & Jocelyn Simonson, *Movement Law*, 73 Stan. L. Rev. 821, 826 (2021).

44. *See, e.g.*, Model Rules of Pro. Conduct (Am. Bar Ass'n 2020) [hereinafter A.B.A./R.P.C.], r. 6.2 cmt. para. 1 ("All lawyers have a responsibility to assist in providing pro bono publico service. An individual lawyer fulfills this responsibility by accepting a fair share of unpopular matters or indigent or unpopular clients.") (internal citation omitted).

45. Russell G. Pearce, *White Lawyering: Rethinking Race, Lawyer Identity, and Rule of Law*, 73 Fordham L. Rev. 2081, 2083 (2005). To see this concept of white normativity applied to a particular body of law (here, evidence law), see Jasmine B. Gonzales Rose, *Toward a Critical Race Theory of Evidence*, 101 Minn. L. Rev. 2243 (2017); *see also id.* at 2252 (defining "white normativity" as the "implicit belief that white ideas, practices, and experiences are inherently normal, natural, and right").

46. Claire P. Donohue, *Client, Self, Systems: A Framework for Integrated Skills-Justice Education*, 29 Geo. J. Legal Ethics 439, 459 (2016).

47. *Id.*

48. *See* Wizner, *supra* note 39, at 338–39; Aiken, *supra* note 41, at 23.

49. Menkel-Meadow, *supra* note 43, at 31–32.

Nine

SUPERVISING ETHICAL DILEMMAS

Introduction

Most legal academics believe that clinical courses are ideal venues for teaching professional ethics to law students. Unlike traditional ethics courses, clinics challenge students to consider issues concerning the American Bar Association (ABA) Model Rules of Professional Conduct (RPC)[1] and state variations of the ABA rules in the context of actual client claims. The competing claims of opponents, the uncertainty concerning the meaning of some of the rules and comments, and the vagaries of human behavior complicate the application of the rules in real cases. State ethics rules and law student practice rules[2] place similar, but not always identical, duties upon clinical supervisors.[3] It is safe to say that clinical teachers are already familiar with the general ethical rules that guide their professional behavior as individual lawyers. Clinics, however, are hybrid organizations. They reflect aspects of both academia and a law firm.

Court student practice rules and state ethical rules place certain obligations on lawyers who supervise other lawyers and law firm staff.[4] New clinical teachers may not initially be familiar with the separate ethical rules placed upon them as faculty supervisors by state bar ethic rules regarding student practice. In addition, not all students coming into a clinic have taken an ethics course before enrolling in a clinic. Moreover, those who have taken a traditional ethics course will not have had to grapple with the nuances of those rules when attempting to apply them in actual cases. Nor will they necessarily be familiar with the ethical dimensions of the state student practice rules.

Some clinical teachers believe they have academic freedom to choose whatever clients and cases they please and receive support from the school to pursue the clients' claims.[5] They view efforts by university presidents, deans, alumni, legislatures, and other governmental officials to withhold funding from clinics or to criticize a clinic's decision to serve certain clients or causes as "compromis[ing]" their "academic freedom."[6] But academic freedom is usually about thoughts, ideas, and speech. It is not about institutional financial support for advocacy. As a result, some clinical teachers report that university pressure causes them to self-censor when making decisions about undertaking representation of certain clients.[7]

Because education is the primary function of the law school itself, the American Bar Association has determined that law schools are lay organizations and therefore cannot control the legal work of the clinic.[8] Thus, the relationship between the clinic's academic mission and professional mission can be complicated. For example, law schools may not require clinics to obtain pre-approval by the school administration before bringing cases against government officials[9] or otherwise institute a preemptive review process where the law school can veto clinical representation.[10] But law schools may subject clinics' activities to review by an advisory committee of lawyers without a school-administration veto.[11] Perhaps most notably, the law school may not disrupt the ongoing attorney-client relationship between a clinic and a client it has already begun representing. In addition to the accreditation standards, the ABA and the AALS have issued several guidance-memos, statements, and resolutions affirming that academic freedom extends to clinical activities, and the AALS has filed amicus briefs in support of the academic freedom of clinical faculty. These statements and other declarations supporting academic freedom have been compiled by Professors Robert Kuehn and Peter Joy in AN ANTHOLOGY OF INTERFERENCE IN LAW SCHOOL CLINICS.[12]

It seems clear that the law school cannot interfere with ongoing litigation.[13] At the same time, clinical teachers are employees of the universities, not partners in a clinical law firm. Clinics seldom have 501(c)(3) status separate from their parent law school or university and can, in some sense, be said to speak for the university. Universities only speak through their boards of directors and presidents. Thus, a clinic probably cannot bring a case in its own name without the approval of the board of directors. Many clinical professors sign documents stating that they are speaking in their own name and not on behalf of the law school or university.

Unlike lawyers in private practice or public interest offices, clinical teachers are employees of the law school. As such, they have a duty not to harm the university. Thus, they have fiduciary relationships with the law school, their university, and their clinic clients. This tripartite role can sometimes create conflicts in both private and public law schools. Private law schools need to be somewhat solicitous of their major donors. Litigating against the interest of a major donor can create an uneasy relationship between the clinic, the university board and president, the dean, and the donor. The same may be true if the clinic seeks to sue government officials or agencies. A similar uneasiness may arise in public law schools when the litigant is a government agency or a wealthy donor to the university and to the public official's election campaign. Indeed, funding cutoffs or government regulations restricting activities may have a direct impact on the clinic's ability to exist. It would be a sad case if a state student practice rule was withdrawn because of litigation brought by the clinic.

Faculty Duty to Students, Clients, and the Law School

Duty to the Institution

Bar ethics committees have provided guidance regarding these issues. It is clear that once the case is filed, a law school dean cannot interfere in the pursuit of the claim.[14] Moreover, the ABA's Council on the Section of Legal Education and Admissions to the Bar has warned against interfering with or intimidating clinics.[15] Yet the choice of a clinic's subject matter as a course, or for that matter any course, is usually a university prerogative. Thus, a law school is not required to create a clinic in a subject matter a faculty member believes is necessary. But once a law school creates a specific type of clinical course, the dual fiduciary duties can spawn conflicts that the standards of academic freedom did not originally contemplate.

Client claims that are contrary to a law school's or university's interests can create complex ethical issues with no easy solution. For example, when I was the Associate Dean for Clinical Education at Georgetown (a Catholic University) a group asked our civil rights clinic to sue the university over its gay rights policies. We decided that there were many other civil rights cases with academic value the clinic could undertake and declined to represent the plaintiff in that case. Law schools often rely on alumni donations to pay for many of their law schools' clinical initiatives. If an environmental clinic brings claims against an oil company or an executive that donates to the university, the university's interests can conflict with a clinic client's interests. Similarly, if a public university clinic files class action against the state agency or state laws regarding voting rights, the clinic's clients will be in conflict with public officials who have oversight of public universities.

These are not simple issues easily resolved by ethics rules or academic freedom rules. Responsible clinical teachers should remain aware of the university's interests and discuss the ramifications of the conflict before the clinic takes on representation. Similarly, university presidents and law school deans must remember the state bar's ethical rules bind their clinical faculty members once a case is accepted for representation. Reason must prevail to ensure that the various fiduciary duties are maintained.

Avoiding conflicts of interest before they occur is a better course of action. A clinic teacher should be aware of the potential for conflicts arising between the client's interests and the law school's interests, and this should inform their decision to choose or forego cases where conflicts might arise. Because university-based and independent law schools are part of the schools' corporation, clinical directors and clinical deans and directors should have protocols that recognize university interests before a client's case is accepted to resolve these potential conflicts before they actually occur. If the conflict is real, it should be avoided. Besides, most clinics have any number of cases they can take to provide a substantial lawyering experience within the existing subject matter of the clinic.

Duty to Students and Clients

Aside from these institutional issues, clinical teachers should have a strong familiarity with the various ethical rules that govern their conduct as supervisors of law students and staff in the clinic. The ethical rules regarding the organization of law firms apply equally to clinics. Teachers have an ethical duty to guide students as they identify and confront the ethical issues that arise in their cases and projects. They also need to help students distinguish true ethical issues from moral and values issues, and to understand the ethical issues that may arise from the tactical or strategic choices they make while representing a client. Supervisors also need to demonstrate the tools that students can use to guide their behavior as they resolve immediate and future ethical issues in their clinic cases and projects. Thus, clinic students must learn not only the substantive law governing a case, but also the blackletter ethical rules that are implicated whenever they make choices pursuing a client's case. Students also need to understand the broader philosophical theories upon which ethical rules exist. In addition, students need to turn their attention inward, attending to their own thought processes. This metacognitive inquiry encapsulates both metacognitive knowledge, what students know about strategies that affect their thinking, and metacognitive regulation, how the students control and adjust their thinking in order to learn.[16] If students learn to use those tools and strategies well, they will continue to use them to guide their actions once they enter the legal profession.

Conversations about ethics often involve broader conversations about the student's and the supervisor's personal values. They conversations can be difficult for students and teachers alike. The techniques developed to conduct the difficult conversations about values that are described in earlier chapters of this book are equally useful in conversations about ethics. As noted previously, teachers often avoid conversations about the students' personal values when they appear too difficult to confront. Instead, they discuss an issue merely in terms of the Rules of Professional Conduct (RPC) and ignore the broader social context of a value-based ethical or strategic choice. Similarly, they may avoid conversations about the student's personal values because they view those conversations as too difficult or because the students resist them. Conversations about ethical rules are much easier to have because the principles contained in the RPC are formalistic rules that lend themselves to purely legal discussions. When discussing the issues as purely legal constructs, teachers avoid the broader considerations of morals or values that a particular ethical issue might present. Teachers who are uncomfortable discussing the broader context and those who have not engaged in such conversations may simply ask a single question—what does the RPC require? They then ignore the richer academic and personal discussions that surround the narrow question of the appropriate compliance with ethics rule. Notwithstanding these temptations, teachers should engage students in the broader conversations to demonstrate how ethics and values differ, how they affect client's needs, how lawyers make decisions in furtherance of those needs in ways that comply with the ethics rules, and how effective lawyering is enhanced by a broad and deep understanding of the interplay between ethics and values. The same can be said about strategic choices that implicate ethical rules. In doing so, teachers will also expose students to the nature and boundaries of a lawyer's role.[17]

The demands of a case or project are great and time-consuming. Conversations about values in relation to ethics can slow down the process. But, as stated before, clinical education is not designed to be efficient. Clinics are part of an academic community; they should not be viewed solely as an active law firm or public interest organization. Conversations about ethics and values not only move the case along, they also serve to test the very values and principles that support a democratic society. The guiding principle of our jurisprudence is the "rule of law." We are guided by statutes and by the constitutions of the various states and the United States to avoid arbitrary decision-making and achieve justice for all people. It is easy to say that all people deserve access to justice and due process of law. It is more difficult to test the assumptions that underly those principles when they do not seem to apply to a typical clinic client. A day litigating cases in state criminal, housing, or domestic relations courts, especially those where the right to counsel is not guaranteed, will severely test the notions of fairness and justice within the boundaries of the ethical rules. If students leave the clinic and the law school without questioning the legal system to which they will dedicate their lives, we as teachers will have failed in our academic responsibilities even as we fulfill our lawyering duties.

Duty to the Bar

All supervisors and students must abide by their state's RPC during their interactions with their clients, witnesses, other lawyers, and judges. But those same Rules of Professional Conduct also place specific obligations on lawyers who supervise other lawyers beyond their own personal conduct. Lawyers in firms and legal organizations who supervise subordinates must ensure that those subject to their supervision conform to the state's ethics code. The codes also make the supervisory lawyer responsible for ethical violations committed by other lawyers under certain circumstances.[18] The codes impose that responsibility when the direct supervisor "knows of the conduct at a time when its consequences can be avoided or mitigated but fails to take reasonable action."[19] The obligations flowing from the ethical rules governing supervisory lawyers apply to clinical faculty as well. In addition, student practice rules usually place the same supervisory responsibility on clinic faculty. Moreover, specific rules governing student practice commonly make clinical supervisors responsible for all of their students' actions.[20]

These rules place a heavy burden on clinical supervisors. Both students and their supervisors may be subject to bar sanctions if students engage in intentional, or even unknowing, ethical lapses. Indeed, the soundness of the supervisor's judgment implicates more than their own exposure for ethical violations. It also colors the viability of a student's defenses to ethical challenges to their conduct.[21] The stakes are high, and not just while the student is in the clinic and practicing under a student practice license. Of course, the student's limited license can be revoked for ethical violations.[22]

Because students and faculty must report those violations to bar associations of the states wherein the student later applies, ethical lapses by a student or the supervisor can affect the student's ability to pass the Bar character and fitness investigation and the supervisor's ability to teach or practice.

Common Ethical Issues within the Clinic

Confidentiality

The range of ethical issues that might arise during a student's term in the clinic is broad, and new clinic students generally have little sense of how the ethical rules interact with the role of a practicing lawyer. Clinic is exciting and students often want to share their experiences with the friends, partners, and roommates. They may forget, or not realize, that they may not share the rich stories about their clients with any members of the public. Those stories, fascinating as they are, may be shared only with fellow members of the clinic.[23] A client's trust that their lawyer will not disclose information relating to their representation without consent is the lifeblood of the attorney-client relationship. It promotes effective representation by fostering open and honest communication—even (and especially) about embarrassing or sensitive topics.[24] Because clinic supervisors' confidentiality duties extend beyond themselves, they are also responsible for preventing unauthorized disclosures of confidential information by their clinic students and staff.[25]

Conflicts

Law school is expensive, and students may have part-time jobs that might conflict with their clients' interests.[26] For example, the RPC generally prohibits the use of information relating to the representation of one client to the client's disadvantage absent informed consent. Consequently, students cannot use the sensitive information they learned about a client in their part-time job to that client's detriment.[27] Indeed, information about clients should not be shared with anyone for any reason without prior discussions with the case or project supervisor and the client. Nor should those employed as law clerks in firms work on issues where the firm client's position is adverse to that of the clinic client.

Clinic students working in part-time government jobs are subject to additional conflicts rules. Absent consent from their government employer, students may not represent a clinic client in connection with a matter in which they personally participated substantially in their government job.[28] The RPC's conflict rules—generally and for government work specifically—also have implications for the work others in the clinic can take on.[29] Federal law also imposes criminal sanctions on government employees who bring cases against the United States.[30] States may have similar conflict laws.

Client Loyalty

Clear rules like those regarding conflicts and confidentiality are not the only issues upon which students may inadvertently stumble. Students sometimes misjudge their clients' actions, inactions, and motives because they are unfamiliar with the lives of their clients and the environments in which their clients live. When they do, their loyalty is weakened, their zeal may suffer, and their judgment may become impaired. Students often assume clients are uninterested in the outcome of a case because they do not arrive for appointments or show up late. When this occurs, they may not have considered the impediments poor people must overcome to simply arrive on time. Distance, poor transportation options, work responsibilities, and poor childcare options constantly drive the choices poor people make. When the client offers these explanations for their nonappearance or tardiness, students often decide too early that a client is lying. They do so because they have not analyzed the reasons why the client's narrative could be true, even when it seems unlikely. The same may occur when the stories told by witnesses or facts discovered during investigation in a case appear to be at odds with their client's story. Again, students will often assume their clients are lying to them. Divergent stories, however, are what make a legal conflict. The late Justice John Paul Stevens perfectly encapsulated the difference between the difficulty of determining what the "facts" are as a case unfolds in real time and the seeming clarity that solidifies only with hindsight:

> From the perspective of an appellate judge, after a case has been tried and the evidence has been sifted by another judge, a particular fact may be as clear and certain as a piece of crystal or a small diamond. A trial lawyer, however, must often deal with mixtures of sand and clay. Even a pebble that seems clear enough at first glance may take on a different hue in a handful of gravel.[31]

Confidentiality requirements and evidentiary privilege rules are not always treated the same under ethical rules.[32] Rules regarding candor to the court may seemingly conflict with ethical rules regarding confidential communications or secrets[33] and zealous representation. Ultimately, the student's loyalty to the client is subject to very few rare exceptions. Exceptions typically apply when evidence about dishonesty or criminality arises. Loyalty to the client must yield where the student learns that they, their client, or a witness they called offers material evidence that is false.[34] The same may be true where a client intends to engage, has engaged, or is engaging in criminal or fraudulent conduct regarding an adjudicatory proceeding,[35] and perhaps even when failing to disclose a material fact would assist a client's criminal or fraudulent act.[36] But even those situations must be evaluated with Justice Stevens' admonitions in mind. They must be evaluated in the context of confidentiality and the truth of the statements which lead a lawyer to believe fraud or lying exists. Only when no doubt exists does the student have to take remedial measures that might include disclosure to the tribunal or third parties.[37]

Overzealous Representation

Students often are passionate about client relationships and seek to protect their clients in ways that might violate ethical rules. This can occur in cases involving immigration and political asylum when students are vehemently opposed to laws regarding the exclusion of migrants. It can also occur in landlord-tenant disputes where property is held by a corporation or slumlord, and in criminal cases in which governmental overreaching is apparent. In the last example, students may acquire tangible evidence because they believe they are helping their client but are unaware of the ethical complications of doing so.[38] They may also have a deep political aversion to police practices and take inappropriate actions because of their beliefs. Ethical issues can arise in cases of domestic strife or other cases where a child is the client. Students may attempt to protect the battered spouse or child from harm without thinking about ethical rules. They may seek to protect children they believe to be neglected by their client, even when state statutes have eliminated mandatory abuse reporting requirements for lawyers who gain information in the course of legal representation.[39]

Students can also be passionate about the subject matter of a clinical course. These passions are often broad and deep. Students often join environmental clinics or political asylum clinics not just to protect their clients but to advance the "cause." This desire to help a cause may lead students to stray from what is ethically permissible in a case or project. Their passion and zealousness may make them lose perspective about client interests and push resolutions that coincide more with their own passion for an issue than with their client's interests. Even when a client's interests in the subject matter coincide with student interests in the cause, students may forget that other ethical or court rules may prohibit some courses of action.[40] Extremely complicated ethical issues arise when they do.

A student's interest in systemic change might also suggest forgoing a client's interest in the pursuit of effecting greater systemic change. Students may also believe the cause is more important than, and at times even at odds with, a client's individual interest. The clashing personal values can create tension between the actual duty to a client and the perceived duty to a broader cause. It may cause a student to hesitate or avoid doing things for their client that they ethically must pursue.[41] Yet this tension is not something that only affects students. Nor is it solely attributable to their age or lack of professional experience, though the perspective and wisdom that comes with years of practice surely helps counteract it. Instead, this tension may well be inherent in practicing law where the representation overlaps with an area about which the supervisor has strongly held ideological beliefs. As Professor Derrick Bell wrote, "[I]t is [sometimes] difficult to provide standards for the attorney and protection for the client where the source of the conflict is the attorney's ideals."[42]

Bell's examination of the tension within the lawyer-client relationship in school desegregation cases is an excellent case study. On the one hand, the national NAACP's civil rights lawyers "would not settle for anything less than a desegregated [public schools] system," and "it was generally made clear to potential plaintiffs that the NAACP was not interested in settling the litigation in return for school board promises to provide better segregated schools."[43] Their goal was "integrated schools without regard to the educational effect of such assignments."[44] But local counsel and plaintiff class members—Black children attending segregated schools and their parents—were also concerned about the quality of education they would receive, leading them to be more open to compromise solutions that the national NAACP's leadership and litigators refused to settle for and actively fought against.[45] While Bell writes about this tension, "[th]is malady," in the class-action context,[46] the conflict between a student's or supervisor's ideals and the client's best interests can also arise in individual-representation relationships, as discussed above.

Clinical educators play a vital role in mediating these ethical conflicts in two ways. First, they help students identify, appropriately process, and move through the conflict.[47] But they can also structure the clinic so as to find creative ways, working within the system, to incorporate big-picture values into their individual client's representation, all while still serving the client's interests.[48] For example, Professor Nicole Smith Futrell, the Co-Director of CUNY School of Law's Defenders Clinic, has written about harmonizing abolitionist beliefs with student practice in clinics. She writes, "Law students must be taught how not to just be passive observers who reinforce the system, or mere critics who fail to meaningfully challenge it; rather, they can pursue their work as 'fellow travelers' operating in solidarity to support abolition without co-opting its values."[49] And as always, case rounds provide especially fertile ground for these sorts of discussions and reflections.[50]

Working with Coalition Clients

Faculty in legislative and policy clinics create related but different learning goals and experiences than small case clinics[51] and teach several different lawyering skills that are difficult to replicate in individual-representation clinics.[52] Nonetheless, they are not immune from complex ethical challenges.[53] Students in those clinics often represent coalitions or organizations, rather than individuals. The client groups are often composed of a large number of individual members, each with different opinions. The members can also be other groups that collaborate with each other as a coalition. The personal interests of individual members or membership groups concerning strategy, tactics, and the interpretation of facts often diverge from the leadership of the group.[54] Determining who the client is in those circumstances and to whom loyalty is due can become a complicated issue.[55] Even when the leadership position is clear, individual members of the client group may still seek out clinic students to try to persuade them to take a different approach. Although individual constituents of organizational clients are also covered by client-lawyer confidentiality rules, they are not themselves the client. Accordingly, students may not disclose to them information regarding the organizational client's representation without the organizational client's explicit or implicit authorization.[56] Understanding the constraints and working productively and ethically can take students down difficult paths as they sort out how to manage the conflicting opinions within the group and still practice according to the ethical rules. Such legislative lawyering straddles the lines of "the often disparate worlds of law, policy, and politics,"[57] and requires the intra-group coordination of several distinct but related roles.[58] Legislative clinics also pose the issue of whether the student is acting as a lawyer or acting as a representative of a group asserting its First Amendment rights.[59] Tracking whose interests the clinic represents, and carrying out the client's wishes through tangible advocacy, becomes even more complicated when clinics follow a grassroots approach to policy advocacy.[60]

Resolving Ethical Questions

As noted in an earlier chapter of this book, ethical issues sometimes arise in a case or a project not because of a rule but because of the students' personal feeling about their or their client's anticipated behavior. The student's personal or moral values, or lack of cultural sensitivity, can exacerbate already complex ethical issues. What must lawyers do when their loyalty to the client is tested because the alleged act is repugnant to a lawyer or student, or when the client's personal values shock the lawyer or student? How should the student respond when the clinic is asked by a court to take on an unpopular cause? Must the student take it if the case is assigned to them by the supervisor, or may the student ethically withdraw or academically refuse the case without suffering harm to a grade? The RPC acknowledges a lawyer's (qualified) freedom to choose their clients.[61] Yet lawyers are also encouraged to take on their "fair share" of unpopular cases and clients, including court appointed cases, as part of discharging their pro bono obligations.[62] The bar for refusing a judge's request is a high one. The client must be "so repugnant to the lawyer as to be likely to impair the client-lawyer relationship or the lawyer's ability to represent the client."[63] These issues are more likely to arise today given the hardening of political and cultural positions within American society. All of the events mentioned above require the teacher to help the student sort out conflicting ethical rules, the laws that seem to contradict ethical rules, and events or clients that challenge a lawyer's personal values.

The timing of a supervisory intervention and finding an appropriate teaching moment in a clinical course is always a critical issue. Supervisors often spot the ethical issue before a student is aware of it. As such, the supervisor needs to make very quick judgments about the need for immediate action to resolve the ethical issue, or whether action can wait while the student gathers more information. Clinical teaching is based on intentionality rather than haphazard intervention into the students' analyses of issues, strategy, and tactics. Supervisors should always consider when intervention should occur, and why it should occur at a specific time. If the issue is related solely to a particular case or project, the intervention can occur during the planning stage, the performance stage, or the reflection stage of the case. If it arises in other current projects or has general applicability to lawyering ethics, it could be raised in a student-led case rounds or in a general seminar class structured around that particular ethical issue. Unlike teachers in non-clinical ethics courses, supervisors cannot think about ethics issues solely in the abstract as they arise in a typical law school ethics course. The context in which the issue arises in a clinic case or project and how the intervention might change depending on the context is what controls the intervention decision.

Most clinical teachers intersperse ethical considerations throughout the clinic seminar and during supervisions sessions. However, if a clinic takes the same kind of cases from semester to semester, teachers can avoid many ethical issues by anticipating them before they occur and addressing them in class, case rounds, or in supervision sessions. Despite the teacher's power to address the issue preemptively, students perform many tasks during the course of their client representation outside of the supervisor's presence. Consequently, ethical issues can arise without the supervisor's knowledge. Despite the intensity of student oversight during the supervisory relationship, a potentially unethical act may have already taken place before the faculty member even learns about it. Faculty members must remember that context determines both the kind of teaching intervention that will take place and when it will take place. Some ethical issues that arise must be resolved quickly to ensure that the case, the client, the student, and the teacher are not compromised. The supervisor might choose to resolve the issue with an intervention that requires the student to perform a specific act immediately followed by a reflective supervisory session after the ethical issue is resolved. At other times, potential ethical issues arise during the planning stages of the case, providing a different atmosphere in which to contemplate whether an issue is truly one of ethics or values, or of tactical choices that do not involve values or ethics.

No matter how or when the ethical issue arises, its mere resolution is insufficient in a clinical course. Students must learn to identify potential ethical issues and identify them before they occur. The lessons learned in clinics will be critical later in their careers when they may not have a supervisor to advise them.[64] Even when law firms or public interest organization supervisors are available, the advice might come too late or may be compromised by other factors. Indeed, new lawyers face significant difficulties in developing their own fledgling professional identity that aligns with the profession's ethical rules amidst the top-down, conformist, employer-first-and-client-second culture of law firms.[65] This puts new lawyers at risk of falling into "groupthink"[66] at best and "wrongful obedience" at worst.[67] To be sure, after-the-fact corrections and debriefs can be beneficial.[68] Nevertheless, the pervasiveness of unconscious biases and motivators also requires careful planning and reflection before, during, and after each lawyering activity undertaken, whether by clinical students or by newly minted lawyers.[69] The planning and reflection may not occur with new lawyers, but must occur with clinic students. Moreover, personal values and professional values are embedded in most actions students take when representing clients, especially when representing clients for the first time. It is essential that students confront those value-ethics disconnects in order to become successful professionals.

Teaching Ethical Awareness

Because ethics is at the root of appropriate lawyering, teachers must help students determine how to quickly assess the scope of an ethical issue, whether the source of the problem involves the ethical code or personal values, and how to ameliorate the danger of or damage from an ethical breach. In addition, students must learn how to confront ethical lapses when they see them committed by other members of their legal team and develop the courage to report them to their supervisor. "Snitch rules" exist in some state bar ethical rules.[70] When they do, complicated ethical issues are raised within the team. Our goal is to teach students, not to penalize them for mistakes. Moreover, if the student has had an ethical lapse, the supervisor is as culpable under the rules, as are the students. Similar complex issues arise when students see unethical behavior on the part of other lawyers. Even in the absence of a "snitch rule," complicated but necessary conversations about professionalism have to be addressed.

Resolving an ethical issue is not the only goal of a clinical course. An adequate resolution may solve the particular ethical issue, but resolution alone does not serve the profession or the student. The clinic's goals are to instill the profession's interest and the student's personal commitment to social justice. Another goal is to demonstrate how an awareness of one's personal values affects good representation. No matter which goal is in play, supervisors need to develop techniques to engage in the ambitious task of helping students identify and question the source of the assumptions that underlie the values that surfaced as they attempted to identify an ethical violation and the proper response to the possible breach.

An abundant literature exists concerning professional ethics that helps prepare teachers to recognize legal ethics as they arise in clinical cases. Some articles exist that specifically discuss methods for teaching students about the interplay between ethics and values. In order to prepare students for these ethical challenges, teacher should consider assigning excerpts from the MacCrate Report on Legal Education,[71] as well as articles by Geoffrey Hazard,[72] David Luban and Michael Milleman,[73] Peter Joy and Robert Kuehn,[74] and Catherne O'Grady. These readings discuss the foundations of the ethical rules and explore the respective duties of clinical supervisors and their students.[75] They emphasize the discipline that students may face if they commit misconduct, either through their own acts or because of bad advice from their supervisors.[76] Other articles specifically discuss the Rules of Professional Conduct in the context of student practice. Excerpts from some of the articles follow this chapter. The readings further encourage supervisors to be mindful of the structural differences between the collaborative clinical setting and the often hierarchical nature of most law firms and organizations where students will practice after completing their studies.[77]

A series of case studies follows that teachers can use to sharpen their understanding of how ethical and value issues arise in the context of litigation, legislative advocacy, or transactional representation. They also can be used as a study for a case rounds session with the students during Orientation or during the course of year. Reviewing these examples and the analysis that accompanies them can help new teachers develop an approach to supervisory interventions. Using them in a case rounds session helps alert students to the kinds of ethical quandaries that may arise in their cases or projects during the semester.

Scenarios to Explore Ethics and Values in a Clinical Course

The following are a series of exercises exploring the kinds of ethics and values issues that might arise in a clinical course. I created the original to help the fellows in Georgetown's Elements of Clinical Pedagogy class. Many of the Georgetown faculty contributed to this document as it evolved. As with many ideas in clinical teaching, it is very difficult to determine which of my colleagues wrote or revised which aspects of each problem. I am grateful to all of them for their contributions.

1. Bill, a student in your clinic asks to meet with you privately. Bill reports that at a Happy Hour for public interest students, he overheard a fellow student, Josh, talking about one of his clients. The client had been a handful and was constantly complaining about his case and the handling of the case. Josh was talking about the client by name and referred to him as the "client from Hell." Josh also said that the client had called him at home and complained about the production of a document in discovery that Josh believed was clearly discoverable. Bill said none of that really bothered him, but he overheard Josh say, "I am not sure if he is telling the truth about what happened in his apartment." Bill asks if Josh's comments were OK and how he or you should manage it if it is not.

   What do you do?
2. Your clinic represents D.C. Tenants United. The clinic helped organize United into a limited partnership and has helped the organization negotiate leases and purchase agreements. The head of United is Arthur Williams. The clinic has worked with Arthur for 5 years now. A team of two students, who are working with Mr. Williams and United to purchase a building for the tenants come to you to discuss the case. During the discussion, one of the students said that she had received a disturbing call from an accountant who had been hired to help put together the financial papers to make the lease/purchase agreement. The accountant had told her that he thought someone was "cooking the books." The money was still in the partnership but since Mr. Williams was the head of the partnership, he had access. The accountant said that it looked like Mr. Williams had set up his own private slush fund and was hiding money from the tenant members of United. The students ask you what to do about this.

   What do you do?
3. Your clinic represents children in juvenile proceedings. The clinic has accepted the case of a 14-year-old boy who has been accused of assaulting his classmate. Your students have been very proactive with the case. They have learned that their client has no previous record but that he has a history of minor incidents which suggest that he has some undiagnosed psychological and learning dis-

orders. They got their client to agree to talk with a psychiatrist. The psychiatrist recommends intensive therapy for your client and suggests that without it his antisocial acts will continue to escalate. The students contested the case but at the hearing the court found the client guilty. The prosecutor wants the boy committed to a secure juvenile facility where there is very little if any psychiatric support. Your students have contacted the probation officer. They now think that they might be able to help the client avoid incarceration if he will go to a therapeutic group home where he will receive intensive psychiatric counseling. The client has told the students that there is no way he is going to a nut house and that he will just take his time. One student says to you, "This is really stupid. I want to talk with his parents and see if we can put some pressure on him to take this deal." The other student says, "That would be really wrong. He gets to make up his own mind, right?" They seek your assistance in resolving their different approaches about next steps.

What do you do?

4. Your clinic represents women who have been victims of domestic violence. Your students come to you because they have just met with their client, a woman who is a Bosnian immigrant. She is now separated from her husband and is living in a shelter with her two children. She has told the students about horrendous violence perpetrated by her husband. She also mentioned that he beats the children. When the students started to talk with her about filing for a civil protection order and about asking the prosecutor to bring charges against her husband for assault, she said absolutely not. She told the students that her husband has said that if she goes forward with a protection order or even seeks custody in the divorce, he will kill her and make sure her family in Bosnia suffers as well. One student says to you, "I think we need to explain how safe the order of protection is and encourage her to change her mind. We cannot let this go on." The other student says, "Are you crazy? Orders of protection are just pieces of paper. We need to send her on her way." The other student says, "At least we need to call the department of Child Protective Services to let them know about the children."

   What do you say/do?

5. You work in an environmental clinic. One of your clients is a community group seeking to stop industrial development in their neighborhood, which is already overburdened with polluting sources. The community group wants to try to stop a trash transfer facility from being built in the neighborhood. The project would subject residents to nuisance odors, pests, and diesel exhaust from garbage trucks. However, the city has already approved the project. An enthusiastic student assigned to the case comes to supervision telling you she has "good news and bad news." She states that the good news is that she researched the developer financing the facility and determined that the company is in a shaky

financial position. They need this project to proceed quickly to survive. The student suggests that the community group sue to stop the project. She reasons that, "it doesn't matter whether we win, it will tie up the developer and may kill the project or, at least, force the developer into bankruptcy. I mentioned this to the client. They think it is a great idea." The bad news she relays is that in emailing the client contact, Dorothy Eberson, the student mistakenly sent the email to Dorothy *Edgerson*, a random Georgetown community member not associated with the clinic. The email outlined the student's understanding of the project, set an agenda for the meeting, and included questions about the current legal landscape.

What do you do?

6. The Clinic's client is a women's rights group advocating enactment of S. 1952, a bill pending in Congress that would strengthen federal laws against sexual harassment in the workplace. A student in the clinic has accepted a summer job at the U.S. Chamber of Commerce, which generally opposes expanding the rights of workers but hasn't taken a position on this particular bill. In her clinic work, the student gained a great deal of knowledge about why the bill was drafted as it was, what intra-coalition tensions among civil rights groups existed on how narrow or broad the law should be, and about strategies for moving the bill forward. The student comes to you in a supervision session asking whether there are any restrictions on her working on this issue at the Chamber over the summer, and if not, how she should manage the situation.

   What do you do?

7. The Clinic's client is a non-profit organization seeking to eliminate mandatory minimum sentences in the U.S. Criminal Code. The client wants to remove mandatory minimum sentences from all categories of federal criminal offenses, including child pornography. A student in the clinic has a very strong revulsion to child pornography, based on something in her past. She comes to you and says she cannot work in support of the client's position with respect to that category of offenses and wants to be reassigned to another project. However, the student informs you that she just had a meeting with a friend from college who currently works as a Legislative Assistant for a Senator. The meeting was supposed to be "just a friendly chat," but the conversation turned to this issue. The student decided to inform the staffer that he was currently drafting a model bill on elimination of mandatory minimum sentences. The staffer thought that was a great idea and said his office might even consider sponsoring that kind of legislation. The student feels like they have just won a victory for the clinic even though they personally do not want to work on the project. Unfortunately, it is too late in the semester for the student to switch projects.

   What do you do and how do you respond to the suggestion regarding the Legislative Assistant?

Other Voices

Roel Sneider & Qin Zhu, *Connecting to the Heart: Teaching Value-Based Professional Ethics**

26 Sci. & Eng'g Ethics 2235 (2020)

Introduction

...

The main point of this paper is that ethics education can be an essential component of the broader development of students, and that ethics education needs to go beyond a depersonalized approach that focuses on teaching only the professional (e.g., what should be done by following codes of ethics), intellectual or philosophical (e.g., ethics as a purely intellectual or philosophical exercise) aspects of morality.... To achieve this goal, ethics education needs to help students develop capacity for self-refection in the process of "personal analysis of one's beliefs, actions, and outcomes of those actions[.]"

...

Dominant Approaches to Professional Ethics Education: Professional and Philosophical

In practice, the goals of ethics education vary among institutions, the scopes of classes, and even instructors. One prevalent method is the professional approach, which is often concerned with teaching professional ethical standards and how to contextualize and comply with these standards in professional practices.

...

Before students receive any ... ethics education, they have a set of preexisting values.

...

These prior values may be deep or shallow, and they may or may not be connected to ... practice. Similarly, codes of ethics ... have been informed by values that the ... community holds. Yet in presenting these codes of ethics to students, these underlying values may not be explicitly articulated.

The second dominant approach to professional ethics education is the philosophical approach, which teaches students the historical, social, or philosophical viewpoints of ethics [the theory of ethics].... In this approach, students gain a broader and deeper understanding of the ethical issues and of the ways to think about these issues.... [E]thical theories are also informed by values. For example, social values (e.g., making

---

* Excerpts are reprinted with the permission of the authors and the Journal of Science & Engineering Ethics in accordance with the Open Access under a Creative Commons Attribution 4.0 International License, http://creativecommons.org/licenses/by/4.0/.

a better world) may drive consequentialism; historical and/or religious values (e.g., moral duties derived from historical and religious traditions) may drive duty ethics; virtuous values drive virtue ethics; and the values of compassion drive the ethics of care. Yet these underlying values are often not made explicit and the conversation centers on philosophical argumentations.

Both approaches—professional and philosophical—serve a purpose of professional ethics education and may enrich students' learning experience. However, they also have limitations that may prevent students from committing to a lifelong project of moral learning and development.

...

Nevertheless, there are some caveats to be made with regards to the functionality of... codes of ethics. First, in order for codes of ethics to be efficacious they often require: (1) collective commitment (e.g., a code of ethics is a convention that a group ... agree[s] on); and (2) personal commitment (e.g., joining a professional ... society means that one promises to comply with its code of ethics and implicitly commit in certain ways required by the code of ethics).... In order to make codes of ethics really work, we need more than just the written articles included in them. We need [professionals] to commit themselves to the values ... that support the formulation and implementation of these codes of ethics.

Second, students may raise questions that challenge ethics codes.... We, as instructors, have been challenged when teaching the code of ethics to students in an authentic, reflective, and meaningful way, as we are sympathetic to the challenging questions raised and their struggle to internalize and harmonize the code of ethics with their own personal values.

Third, ethics codes may not always be sufficient to resolve dilemmas that arise in practical situations. As noticed by Lyes, ... "ethics, in the sense of a code of ethics, is not a complete guide in decisionmaking, since our more difficult choices are among alternatives that arise when we cannot act strictly according to our professional code or when we are not sure how to apply the code to the immediate situation."

It is widely acknowledged that codes of ethics often have limitations that may affect their practical effectiveness in guiding ethical decision-making in engineering: (1) most codes are written in general wording and contain substantial areas of vagueness; and (2) codes of ethics can be misused or abused if not taken seriously, e.g., treated as "sacred documents" rather than documents open to public criticism (Martin and Schinzinger 2005).

...

The second approach to ethics education is based on the philosophy of ethics and the historical development of ethical thinking. The history of philosophical ethics is rich, and the distinction between utilitarian, deontological, and virtue ethics helps students understand the different drivers for ethical decision making. Yet, this approach to ethics teaching may reduce ethics to an intellectual exercise that focuses on the nuanced differences between different ethical theories.

...

Moral psychologists, such as James Rest, argue that there are multiple elements that contribute to ethical action: moral sensitivity (or recognition), moral judgment (or reasoning), moral motivation, and moral character (Rest et al. 1999). Arguably, teaching ethical theories might be able to improve students' moral judgment (and maybe also their moral sensitivity). However, moral motivation and moral character are too complicated to be shaped exclusively by the knowledge of ethical theories.

...

In other words, knowing what is right and wrong does not necessarily lead to ethical action. People need to be personally committed to the moral judgment they have made.... What we caution against is that ethical theories are taught in a purely skill-based way: students use the ethical theories to solve a hypothetical dilemma and then set the theories aside and return to their technical decision.

...

Teaching ethics based on the codes of ethics helps students be aware of general ethical issues they may encounter in their professional life, while teaching the philosophy of ethics and ethical theory helps expand their ethical perspective. Both approaches are worthwhile, but as argued above, they both have their limitations.

...

Toward Value-Based Professional Ethics Education

What do we value? That which we deem to be important. We are more likely to make choices that support that which we value. Our values are shaped by factors such as our history, upbringing, past experiences, faith, and education. Values come both from within and from outside whereas rules are externally imposed (e.g., codes of ethics were developed by professional societies). In general, we are more likely to break rules when they are not aligned with our values.

Ideally, rules are based on values. If we embrace the value that supports a rule, then we are like to follow the rule, but adherence to rules, whose value we question or simply don't understand, leads to actions governed by fear of punishment.... We often fail to tell students what values this rule seeks to support[.]

...

Real-life situations are more complicated, as values may often conflict.... Dilemmas ... don't have easy answers, but without knowing how to value the different alternatives, one has no map to navigate by for making wise decisions. Incorporating values into decision-making thus does not solve the problem of dealing with conflicting considerations—as we noted earlier with codes of ethics or with ethical theories—but incorporating values into such conflicting considerations assists our choices to be driven by what we consider to be most important.

...

Peter A. Joy and Robert R. Kuehn, *Conflict of Interest and Competency Issues in Law Clinic Practice**

9 Clinical L. Rev. 943 (2002)

...

I. Understanding the Ethical Obligations of Law Clinic Students and Supervising Faculty

Clinical legal education has always embraced "the dual goals of hands-on training in lawyering skills and provision of access to justice. These two goals are explicitly stated in the ABA's 1969 Model Student Practice Rule, which established a model for state high courts to give law students the authority as certified students under student practice rules to represent clients, provided the student-lawyers work under the close supervision of a licensed attorney. Since the promulgation in 1969 of the Model Student Practice Rule, all fifty states, the District of Columbia, and most federal courts have adopted similar student practice rules. Clinic law students certified under a student practice rule are granted a limited license to practice law and can actually provide legal advice and represent clients in role as a lawyer—something that nonlawyers such as paralegals, law clerks, legal assistants, or law students in clinical programs who are not certified under a student practice rule may not do.

The ethical obligations of law students and their supervising faculty in clinical programs are defined by the student practice rules and the ethical rules in the various jurisdictions. While there are some general points of agreement among the ethics rules in the different jurisdictions, the following discussion demonstrates that there are a number of significant differences among state student practice rules and in the application of state ethics rules to students admitted to practice under student practice rules. With very few exceptions, almost all the ethics rules treat lawyers in public interest/legal services offices the same as private lawyers representing private clients. Thus, except for these few exceptions, there are no special ethics rules that apply to lawyers providing legal services in public interest law clinic programs.

A. Obligations of Clinic Students

The ABA's Model Student Practice Rule does not directly address the ethical obligations clinic students certified and admitted to the limited practice of law under the

---

* Excerpts are reprinted with the permission of the authors and the Clinical Law Review.

rule owe their clients, though there is language in the rule indicating that it seeks to facilitate the provision of competent legal services. For example, the Model Student Practice Rule mentions in its statement of purpose the bar's responsibility for providing "competent legal services for all persons, including those unable to pay for these services." In the requirements section, the rule requires a certification from the dean of the law school attesting to the student's "good character and competent legal ability, and as being adequately trained to perform as a legal intern." Finally, the supervision portion of the rule requires the supervising attorney to "[a]ssume personal professional responsibility for the student's guidance in any work undertaken and for supervising the quality of the student's work."

Although the Model Student Practice Rule is generally silent concerning the ethical duties certified clinic students owe their clients, the student practice rules in many states require students to certify in writing that they have read and are familiar with the state rules of professional conduct. Additionally, a number of states require law students to certify in writing that they will follow the prevailing ethical rules. Some states also require students to complete their law school ethics course prior to certification under a student practice rule, some require students to file a written oath similar to an attorney's oath pledging to follow the rules of professional conduct in the state, and at least one requires law students to take a special professional responsibility exam prior to certification under its student practice rule. Finally, New York's student practice rule is silent with respect to a certified student's ethical duties but does require each law school clinic to seek an order from the presiding justice of the appellate division of the Supreme Court of New York authorizing the student practice. In some of the resulting orders, courts require the lawyers supervising law student activities to ensure that the students have had "adequate instruction as to the professional responsibilities, obligations and ethics of an attorney licensed to practice in New York."

Most state student practice rules do not explicitly require students to face professional discipline if they violate the applicable rules of professional conduct, though some do. Thus, the penalty against a certified clinic student for unprofessional conduct while practicing law under a student practice rule is usually revocation of the right to practice law under the student practice rule, which can take place without any hearing and without the showing of any cause. At least one state—Arizona—explicitly provides that the procedures "governing the discipline of lawyers shall not be applicable to the termination" of a student's certification under the rule, and termination of the certification "shall be without prejudice to the privilege of the ... student to make application for admission to the practice of law if he is in other respects qualified for such admission."

Additionally, students practicing law pursuant to student practice rules may find some insulation from professional discipline for alleged ethical violations as a "subordinate lawyer," under ABA Model Rule 5.2(b) or, if students are considered nonlawyer assistants, under Model Rule 5.3. Model Rule 5.2(b) provides: "A subordinate lawyer does not violate the rules of professional conduct if that lawyer acts in accordance with a supervisory lawyer's reasonable resolution of an arguable question of professional duty." Although Model Rule 5.2(b) does not define subordinate lawyer, a comment to the rule refers to "lawyers in a supervisor-subordinate relationship." The Restatement of the Law Governing Lawyers provision closely parallels the Model Rule approach, and it refers to "a lawyer under the direct supervisory authority of another lawyer."

Although neither Model Rule 5.2 nor the Restatement specifically refer to law students practicing law under student practice rules, it is most likely that the level of supervision most certified clinic students receive would make certified clinic students the functional equivalent of a subordinate lawyer—a lawyer under the supervision of another lawyer. This conclusion would be subject to the structure of the clinical program, the requirements of the student practice rule, and the actual relationship among clinic client, certified clinic student, and the supervising clinical faculty member in any given clinical program. Even if the certified clinic student is treated as a supervised or subordinate lawyer, the clinic student has an independent duty to act ethically, and a "'following orders' defense depends on the reasonableness of the order." and cases exploring this relationship usually focus upon associates working If the clinic students are considered nonlawyer assistants, then Model Rule 5.3 places all of the professional responsibility on the supervising lawyer to ensure that the nonlawyer assistant's conduct "is compatible with the professional obligations of the lawyer," and makes the lawyer responsible for the nonlawyer assistant's conduct.

In addition to facing the possibility of professional discipline in some states, clinic students in every jurisdiction face the effect that ethical misconduct as clinic students may have on their application to the bar. Every jurisdiction requires good moral character for admission to the bar, and professional misconduct as a clinic student is likely to raise the red flag of faulty moral character.

...

C. Obligations of Supervising Faculty

There are many different types of clinical models, and the various models also implicate different supervisory relationships between students and their supervisors. For example, some clinics enroll students who are not certified under student practice rules. In these clinics, the students may function solely as lawyer assistants or clerks for supervising faculty in an in-house law clinic, or for field supervisors in externship programs, and work on briefs and legal documents without establishing their own lawyer relationship with clients. Other clinical programs enroll only students certified to represent clients pursuant to a student-practice rule. Still other clinics may enroll both students certified under student practice rules and those who are not, and the students may have varying degrees of responsibilities for clients depending on whether or not they are certified as student-lawyers. Finally, some clinics focus on work that may be performed by a nonlawyer, such as representing clients in administrative hearings that permit nonlawyer client representatives. All of these different structures have some impact on the supervisory obligations of the supervising faculty and the nature of the ethical obligations students owe law clinic clients.

Supervising faculty in law clinics have ethical obligations defined by both the student practice rules—when supervising student-lawyers—and by the ethics rules in the jurisdictions where they practice—whether the law clinic faculty are supervising student-lawyers or law clinic students who are not certified under student practice rules. Many state student practice rules track the ABA Model Student Practice Rule and require supervising faculty and other supervising lawyers to assume "personal professional responsibility for the student's guidance in any work undertaken and for supervising the quality of the student's work." Student practice rules in most other states require supervising faculty and lawyers to undertake "personal responsibility" or "full responsibility" for the student's work or conduct. Even in the minority of states where the student practice rules do not explicitly characterize the supervising faculty and lawyers as "responsible," the student practice rules require students to work "under the supervision" or "with approval" of the supervising faculty.

In addition to the requirements of the student practice rules for lawyers supervising student-lawyers, most state ethics rules track Rule 5.1 of the ABA Model Rules of Professional Conduct which requires that "[a] lawyer having direct supervisory authority over another lawyer shall make reasonable efforts to ensure that the other lawyer conforms to the Rules of Professional Conduct." Student-lawyers' limited licenses to practice law, their ethical obligations under student practice rules, and the supervisory responsibilities of clinical faculty are factors leading one commentator to conclude that "the relationship between clinical supervisor and student attorney approximates the senior attorney-junior attorney relationship [under Rule 5.1]."

The ethical obligations of law clinic faculty and field supervisors in programs with clinic students who are not certified as student lawyers are framed differently by Model Rule 5.3, which requires that "a lawyer having direct supervisory authority over the nonlawyer [assistant] shall make reasonable efforts to ensure that the person's conduct is compatible with the professional obligations of the lawyer." The difference between the Rule 5.3 obligation to ensure that a nonlawyer's conduct is "compatible" with the ethics rules as compared to the Rule 5.1 supervisory obligation to ensure that subordinate lawyer "conforms" to the ethics rules reflects that ethics rule are not directly applicable to nonlawyer legal assistants—the status which clinic students who are not admitted under student practice rules occupy. But in either case, the supervising lawyer is responsible to ensure that law clinic students act consistently with the ethical obligations of the lawyer.

Thus, both student practice rules and prevailing ethical rules impose ethical responsibilities on clinical faculty to provide adequate supervision of law clinic students' work. This requires sufficient supervision to ensure students follow applicable ethical rules including the ethical requirement that clinic students avoid conflicts of interest and that student-lawyers provide competent representation to clinic clients.

...

II. Conflicts Of Interest

In many ways, conflicts of interest are like tips of icebergs for law clinic programs—the visible parts of conflicts issues representing small pieces of the potentially huge problems lying below the surface. The reason for this may be, as some clinical faculty have observed, that the pedagogical use of cases creates a tension with obligations of client confidentiality and conflicts of interest leading clinical faculty "to take contradictory positions on conflicts of interest, sometimes defining our [clinic] 'law firm' broadly and sometimes narrowly to accommodate our teaching and supervision needs." These same commentators also have identified client confidentiality and conflict of interest rules as "problematic for many clinics," but rather than directly discussing the issues they "recommended further study in those areas." As the following material suggests, clinical faculty who fail to confront and resolve conflict problems may be like the sleeping captain of the Titanic.

...

B. *Defining the Clinic Law Firm, Understanding Imputed Conflicts, and Considering the Availability of Ethical Screens for Removing Imputed Conflicts*

1. *Defining the Clinic Law Firm*

Defining the clinic law firm is essential to understanding how conflicts of interest rules, particularly the rule imputing conflicts of interest from one lawyer to another, apply to law school clinic students and faculty.

The Model Rules defines "firm" as including lawyers in "law partnership, professional corporation, sole proprietorship or other association authorized to practice law; or lawyers employed in a legal services organization or the legal department of a corporation or other organization." A comment to the Model Rules further states that if lawyers "present themselves to the public" or "conduct themselves as a firm, they should be regarded as a firm for the purposes of the Rules." Although the Model Code does not explicitly define the term "firm," it does discuss lawyers who are "affiliated," thereby referring to lawyers who are associated with one another in practice settings other than law firms. Additionally, the Restatement states that lawyers may practice as a solo practitioner, an employee of another lawyer or law firm ("constituted as a partnership, professional corporation, or similar entity"), as lawyer-employees of governmental and non-governmental entities, or as "of-counsel."

In considering conflict issues in law clinics, particularly imputed disqualification issues, Professor James Moliterno notes that the analyses of the issues largely turn on how the clinical program is structured. Imagining a clinical program with four components—a criminal defense clinic, a general civil practice clinic, a domestic violence clinic, and a housing issues clinic—Moliterno observes that a program may take steps, "treating each clinic as its own law office entity, or as part of the larger law school clinic law office, or broader still as if the clinics were all a part of the law school's law office." Further, the Model Rules state that even if lawyers are loosely associated with one another and not structured as a firm but "present themselves to the public in a way suggesting that they are a firm or conduct themselves as firm, they should be regarded as a firm for purposes of the Rules."

Thus, how the clinical program is structured and held out to the public will determine whether or not for conflicts purposes each individual clinic will be considered a separate law firm or all of the clinics in the entire clinical program will be treated as one law firm. For example, if the faculty structures a clinical program so that each of the four components described by Moliterno is held out to the public as a separate law office entity with separate support staff, separate filing systems, separate computer systems, and other adequate measures to assure that confidential information from clients in one clinic will not be shared among the students and faculty in the other clinics, then the four clinics will be treated as four separate law firms.

It is unlikely, however, that many clinical programs take all of the steps necessary to create separate law office entities for each subject matter clinic. No one has surveyed how all of the clinical programs in the United States are organized, but visits to clinical program websites, samples of law school clinic brochures and magazines, and other anecdotal observations demonstrate that law schools often portray their clinics to the public as components of a single law school clinical program and many consist of several subject matter specific clinics sharing some office space, personnel, or equipment. Thus, by holding its clinics out to the public as components of a single program or law office, or by having its clinics share common space, a law school's clinical program may be considered a single "law firm" for conflict of interest purposes.

...

Catherine Gage O'Grady, *Preparing Students for the Profession: Clinical Education, Collaborative Pedagogy, and the Realities of Practice for the New Lawyer*[*]

4 Clinical L. Rev. 485

...

I. The Development of the Individual Lawyer in Practice

"Then, all of a sudden, the issue is not whether we agree with what we have heard and read and studied.... The issue is us, and what we have become."

—R. Coles, Erik H. Erikson: The Growth of His Work 39 (1970) (Cited in Bellow & Moulton, The Lawyering Process (1978).)

A. Individual Lawyers and Individual Lawyering

Numerous lawyering choices exist for every practitioner, all of which contribute to the development of the lawyer as a professional. While the uniform bar continues to

---

* Excerpts are reprinted with the permission of the author and the Clinical Law Review.

advance the fiction of a "unitary profession, "and hence perhaps a "unitary professional," some scholars are acknowledging the existence of a variety of unique "styles" of lawyering and numerous opportunities for "individual choice" in lawyering. Similarly, although a lawyer's approach to any lawyering activity or decision will be guided by standard rules, codes of conduct, and discernible traditions, it will also, quite naturally, be shaped by the individual lawyer's own unique fundamental values. The suggestion in this Article that lawyers should value and maintain "autonomy" in lawyering refers to an individual attorney's power to make his or her own lawyering choices, among the broad spectrum of opportunities for choice, rather than having the choices made by someone else.

The opportunities for individual choice in each lawyer's professional development are nearly unlimited. In her article Styles of Lawyering, Professor Naomi Cahn argues that many different styles of lawyering exist, and that there is no one right way to practice law effectively. To illustrate her point, Professor Cahn identifies and analyzes one component of a lawyer's "ethic of care"—"connection" in the attorney-client relationship—as an important lawyering attribute that may help redefine the traditional attorney role. Recasting Professor Cahn's analysis somewhat to reflect the role of individual choice on professional development, it might be said that some lawyers will remain true to their sense of self and be comfortable in their professional role only if they are permitted to establish and maintain a "connection" with their clients that is based on mutual trust, knowledge, and understanding. Other lawyers, on the other hand, might be uncomfortable with a deeply "connected" client relationship, choosing instead to adopt a more traditional neutral or "detached" posture with a client. The detached lawyer views herself as not responsible for the client's moral or political beliefs and not "accountable" for the client's actions with respect to third parties. Regardless of whether it is more desirable for a lawyer to be connected to or neutrally detached from her client, the individual choice an attorney makes regarding her approach to clients can affect an entire spectrum of the attorney's work, from the initial selection of cases and clients to the processes selected to resolve disputes. Whether to respond to clients with empathetic connection or detached neutrality is a lawyering choice, one among many, about which attorneys will legitimately differ and, if they are to find satisfaction in their profession, should be permitted to differ.

The spectrum of different choices that reflect different styles of lawyering runs from general visions of lawyering to specific lawyering activities. A lawyer has a range of choices in her overall vision of herself "from civic republicanism to political and social activist to entrepreneur to power broker." Similarly, lawyers may have very different views about their own role or the role of law in the judicial process. Some may view lawyering as a "combative and potentially effective vehicle for acting on feelings of outrage." Others may prefer a less combative style of advocacy—an approach that more closely resembles "conversations with fact finders instead of persuasive intimidation. "Some may view the law as a means of holding individuals responsible for their antisocial acts in order to preserve social order. Still others may see the bottom line as "less important than the person the lawyer seeks to help."

An individual attorney's overall viewpoint and perspective on lawyering will shape lawyering conduct at virtually every stage. At a broad level, an attorney's unique perspective affects numerous core areas of lawyering that may call for choice, including such "fundamental lawyering skills" as problem solving, formulating legal theories, investigating facts, communicating, counseling clients, negotiating, participating in litigation or other dispute resolution procedures, organizing work, and balancing professional responsibilities with personal responsibilities. Similarly, it may affect the way an individual attorney evaluates fundamental professional values, such as providing competent and zealous representation, and reconciling such goals with the professional obligation to "promote justice, fairness, and morality."

Specifically, individual lawyering choice may directly affect an attorney's relationship with her client, and thereby, the ways in which the attorney selects clients, communicates with them, and counsels them about solutions. In a trial, an individual attorney's distinctive viewpoint may shape a decision on what approach to take in cross-examining a truthful witness. In addition, it may determine a lawyer's willingness to engage in hurtful conduct in the name of zealous client representation. Moreover, it may provide the framework for decisions regarding the full and good faith disclosure of information under recent state or federal rules mandating disclosure of information in litigation. Even choices individual lawyers must make to balance their personal and professional responsibilities factor into the picture of the whole person as professional attorney.

Thus, the wide spectrum of discrete choices a lawyer makes when practicing law may profoundly affect the professional development of the individual lawyer. A lawyer's failure to participate in her own professional development may result, at best, in a vague sense of uneasiness or unhappiness with herself as a professional, and at worst, in seemingly unexplainable unprofessional conduct. New lawyers stand a better chance of finding happiness in the profession, and the profession stands a better chance of benefiting from the fresh insights of its newest members, if new lawyers recognize and accept the challenges presented by the various opportunities to make individual choices in lawyering. Moreover, all lawyers, regardless of their practice setting, benefit from a foundation in maintaining autonomy and exercising independent choice in lawyering. Sole practitioners and lawyers who work with peers in small firms obviously need to be able to rely on their own instincts in their practice. Even associates in medium or large law firms ultimately have to rely on their own judgment to make some decisions and their own personal values to resolve ethical problems.

Within the collaborative work environment adopted by many lawyers in the practice of law, it is singularly challenging for new lawyers to engage in the process of consciously influencing their own development. Participating in the development of one's own identity as a lawyer is a uniquely personal process. Yet, it is a process that must co-exist within the common collaborative work structures adopted in the profession.

...

C. Conformance Pressures and Realistic Hierarchical Collaborations in the Practice of Law

To some extent, the existence of conformance pressures within professional working collaborations is understandable and noncontroversial. Without some level of conformity, organizations would likely fail to operate effectively. Increasingly, law firms appear to be adopting a bureaucratic form of governance, apparently due to a growing acceptance of the view that a bureaucratic structure is more efficient than the traditional form of individual partner control. Thus, conformance pressures and hierarchical working collaborations are woven into the existing institutional framework of the practice of law.

If practitioners "over-conform" to practice norms, however, especially if they do so unthinkingly, the result will be reduced creativity in lawyering, diminished opportunities for deliberate autonomous input in individual professional growth, and a reduced likelihood of improvement or change in the profession from within. This section suggests that pressures to conform confront the new professional immediately and are at their highest influential peak in the early years of a lawyer's career. The new lawyer is subject to numerous pressures to conform to "norms of conduct" advanced by others. Indeed, the tendency to conform to the expectations of others is a component of moral development and an integral part of human nature in certain developmental stages, especially when those imposing conformance expectations are in positions of authority. Moreover, the pressures to conform are not entirely external: A new attorney's initial view of his or her own role in practice will influence the attorney's response to the existing structure of the profession and the conformance pressures within it.

1. The Potential Impact of the Early Workplace Experience in Shaping the Lawyer

Clinical educators and proponents of clinical education have long appreciated the significance of work experiences to student learning and growth. There now seems to be a "growing appreciation" among legal educators in general that "it is workplace experiences that have the greatest impact on shaping professional behavior." When viewing the entire career of a seasoned lawyer, the significance of the workplace experience on the development of the individual professional is obvious. The experiential nature of clinical education provides an optimal environment within law school for promoting the development of the individual professional lawyer; however, it is just a beginning step in an ongoing process.

The relative impact of an attorney's early or initial workplace experiences is less obvious, but there is some anecdotal support for and a pragmatic acceptance among some scholars of the view that early experiences in the workplace are likely to have an extraordinary impact on the shaping of the individual lawyer. After all, new lawyers "do not yet know themselves as lawyers;" thus, early work with senior lawyers, who serve as role models, is an "important professional training ground" for the new lawyer. Even the MacCrate Report, while focusing on law school as the primary forum for instilling professional values in the new lawyer, recognized the possibility that early workplace experiences might wholly override law school experiences, especially if workplace lessons conflict with the lessons learned in law school.

A recent study purports to "demonstrate that a student's practice environment quickly supersedes law school as a source of reference for demarcating professionally acceptable behavior.... Professor Lawrence Hellman analyzed student entries from 81 journals, prepared by students participating in his "Professional Responsibility in the Legal Intern Experience" course at the Oklahoma City University School of Law. The students in Professor Hellman's class were placed as legal interns in positions at law firms, working with attorney supervisors. The students were instructed to work with and observe the lawyers in the firm and to maintain journals identifying and discussing "issues of professional responsibility that arose in their work environments." Although the results of the study produced a few examples of exemplary attorney supervision and professionalism, the student interns generally were exposed to shocking portrayals of attorney misconduct and inadequate supervision. As noted by Professor Hellman, "[f]orty-seven different journals reported 103 separate instances where a supervisor or another lawyer in an intern's office gave instructions to an intern or followed a course of conduct which was directly contrary to a provision in the Model Code, which was in force at the time." The character and range of the unethical attorney conduct observed by the student interns was "truly startling." Examples of the misconduct observed by student interns included senior attorneys destroying evidence, knowingly assisting a client to set up an illegal business operation, commingling funds, using client funds, lying to a client about the status of a case to delay reimbursement, instructing the intern on how to lie to the court clerk to obtain a case file under pretext, failing to consult with a client regarding terms of a settlement offer, instructing the intern to misrepresent his or her identity to a third person, refusing to correct a client's false deposition testimony, directly contacting adverse parties known to be represented by counsel, and ignoring conflicts of interest.

...

As Professor Hellman notes, students in their early work experiences are "at a turning point in the formation of their personal concepts of the legal profession's values." After evaluating the students' journal entries to gauge the effect of the students' exposure to professional misconduct, Professor Hellman concluded that the "real world" took its toll on students by fostering disillusionment and eroding idealism. Moreover, a number of journal entries indicated that these early work experiences caused some students to "consciously lower their expectations of themselves with regard to their level of conformity to professional ideals." Thus, early work experiences have the potential of dramatically shaping and impacting a new attorney's professional development.

...

3. Collaborating With Power: The Associate and the Senior Lawyer

Both the influence of the early workplace and the new lawyer's tendency to see herself as an "employee" in the workplace enhance the impact of a commonly experienced early lawyering collaboration—the "basic teamwork unit" formed between an associate and a senior lawyer. Even in non-hierarchical teams of co-equal peer attorneys, successfully working collaboratively is difficult, often because communication in the team breaks down. For the new lawyer, working collaboratively brings unique stresses and conflicts.

Consider, for example, the following well-publicized account of an associate's conduct while immersed in a working collaboration with a senior lawyer. During the deposition of defendant's key expert witness, a senior defense lawyer told plaintiff's counsel that certain documents previously written by the expert witness and requested by both the court and the plaintiff had been inadvertently destroyed. An associate on the defense team, who had been primarily responsible for the defense's discovery and document work, heard the senior lawyer make this statement and knew it to be untrue. The documents in question were damaging to the defense because they indicated that the expert witness's initial position on the case was equivocal. The associate whispered to the senior lawyer that the documents had not been destroyed and were in fact back at their law firm. The senior lawyer, however, ignored the associate and eventually signed an affidavit attesting to the documents' destruction. Upon returning to the law firm, the associate located the documents and stored them away in a locked closet. The associate told the senior lawyer what he had done and then never discussed the incident again with anyone. Later in the litigation, through cross-examination of the expert witness at trial, the existence of the documents was dramatically revealed.

...

Understanding why the associate chose the path he did requires some appreciation of the difficulties of collaboration for the new lawyer. The hierarchical structure and power differentials in the early collaborative working relationships reinforce new lawyers' tendency to view themselves as "employees" with little autonomy. By definition, an associate is an employee who works within a hierarchical, and often bureaucratic, organization.

...

Indeed, the demands on an associate are varied and sometimes confusing or conflicting. Like the law firm partner and the sole practitioner, the associate is an attorney and therefore has ethical and fiduciary duties to clients, the legal profession, and the general public. Unlike other attorneys, however, the law firm associate is subject to a senior lawyer's right to control and thus is arguably an "agent" of the law firm with the duties of "good care and skill," "loyalty," and "obedience" to the law firm. The "duty of obedience" to the firm has been interpreted by one commentator as requiring associates to obey all reasonable and ethical instructions regarding their job performance. The associate simultaneously has an independent duty to ensure that the directions of the senior lawyer do not lead the associate into unethical conduct.

...

In his study of professional ethics, Professor Jerome Carlin suggested that associates in hierarchically structured firms are frequently given work tasks which require arguably questionable behavior for successful completion. According to Professor Carlin, such unpleasant tasks are delegated to the subordinates on the team, and an attorney can look forward to receiving less questionable work only after achieving some level of status in the hierarchy.

For a new associate, the very process of collaborating with a senior lawyer or a team of senior lawyers invites conformance to a "group identity" because law-work collaborations require an associate to have an almost intuitive understanding of typically unspoken, implicit "rules" of the team.... Most lawyer work teams have neither the time nor the opportunity to communicate fully with all members on every detail of the work. As Professor Twitchell explained, to prevent "information overload," associates must reduce the amount of information they share with senior lawyers. However, almost any legal decision is based on ambiguities that, once a discussion is initiated, would likely require complex, lengthy explanations. Thus, for the team to work most effectively, senior lawyers may refrain from developing a communications system for junior lawyers and for the team; rather, they may simply strive to create a team "whose members share the same values, know each other well, and trust one another to make similar decisions under the same set of circumstances."

...

Professor Hellman's observations regarding his student placement program indicate that communication within senior lawyer/associate collaborations can be strained and that senior lawyers may be extremely uncomfortable with a junior lawyer's initiating a discussion of ethical issues. In concluding that his study provides "reason to worry" about the openness of communication within law firms, Professor Hellman noted that only six of the 81 journals indicated an "open and informative channel of communication in place," while 16% of the sample encountered law office environments "which appeared to the students to be clearly hostile to the discussion of ethical limitations on the practice of law." It is especially difficult for the new associate, the "lowest status class in the professional hierarchy," to raise sensitive or difficult matters with a senior lawyer. The associate's conduct in the Kodak example illustrates the difficulties of communication for the law firm associate. Once his initial attempts to communicate were ignored by the senior lawyer, the associate chose to remain silent. He did not attempt to discuss the senior partner's lie with the partner himself or other partners in the firm. His loyalty to the senior member of his team and the difficulties of talking about such matters within a firm that had no process in place for such discussions curtailed the associate's ability to communicate.

Finally, associates cannot help but be affected by their own self interest in attaining promotion within the law firm. The associate in the Kodak case, for example, may have allowed his desire for security and attainment of partnership to govern his decision to cover up the senior lawyer's fraud. As Professor Twitchell noted in her analysis of the associate's conduct in Kodak; his "immediate self-interest lay in preserving [the senior lawyer's] ethical reputation and his own, be cause partnership promotion probably depended on [the senior lawyer's] sponsorship."

Thus, immediately upon entering the profession, new lawyers confront conformance pressures. New lawyers' image of themselves as employees in a volatile market make them particularly susceptible to such pressures. At a minimum, new professionals must be aware of the dynamics that create pressures to conform before they can recognize viable lawyering choice opportunities. The challenge for the new associate is to maintain a sense of professional identity and some autonomous control over professional development, while working successfully within the realities of law practice collaborations.

...

B. Preserving Autonomy Within Collaborations

As previously noted, clinical educators should not, and need not, sacrifice an optimal learning atmosphere by introducing explicit hierarchy into clinical collaborations simply to prepare their students for realistic practice collaborations. Instead, clinical supervisors should acknowledge the times when inherent elements of hierarchy seem to factor into a student's case work and classroom performance and use these opportunities as springboards for discussion about conformance to authority.

1. Lessons on Autonomy Within Case Work Collaborations

Opportunities often arise in clinical supervision when the supervisor realizes that a student is willing or even eager to do whatever the supervisor desires. In an article on clinical supervision, Professor Margaret Martin Barry presents an example of such an opportunity. I will borrow this clinical supervision vignette to illustrate how the clinical supervisor could have taken advantage of a difficult supervisory session to teach the student a lesson on maintaining autonomy in the face of pressures to conform.

In this scenario, a student and supervisor have been working on a motion that is due in a few days. After opening the supervisory session with some praise of the student's draft, the clinical supervisor (denoted as "J.A.") begins to question the student (denoted as "D.J.") on his treatment of a pivotal precedent:

> J.A.: *** [O]n Hodari, you just say it doesn't apply, and leave it kind of hanging out here in the end.
>
> D.J.: Well, I dunno. I mean you said you wanted Hodari in there. I read Hodari and it doesn't seem to me like we really have a case. They seemed to be saying that even if the guy threw out the dope because the cop was chasing him, it's not a seizure and they won't suppress the stuff.
>
> J.A.: So you're not convinced, yourself.
>
> D.J.: Well I know we've gotta say something.

J.A.: Right, but it's hard to say things unless you're on board yourself first. The problem is we can't just rely on these nice older cases, if Hodari changes the test, and the judge knows it's the Supreme Court's big news on what constitutes an "arrest."

D.J.: Yes ma'am. (Pause)

J.A.: I agree, it's not a great case for us, but I thought we were going to focus on that "submit to an assertion of authority" language and argue that's what Mr. Brown was doing when he slowed down the jeep in response to the flashing lights.

D.J.: (Reflexively) Yes ma'am. Well. O.K. I'll, uh ... I'll add it in.

J.A.: I get the feeling I'm kind of pushing you into this and you'll go along with it cause I'm saying to. What do you think about it?

D.J.: (Slight shrug, with shake of head) I don't know really. I mean I'll do it.

J.A.: But what I'm saying is, if you are not into the argument, I think it will be hard to write. Can you tell me your reservations about it, or why it's not working? You've probably read the case more recently than I have.

D.J.: I don't really have reservations.

J.A.: Do you want to go over the case together?

D.J.: If you want. I underlined it last time when we talked about it.

J.A.: Would you rather try re-working it from that then?

D.J.: That's fine. [Discussion then turns to deadline for the next draft and student leaves to revise the motion.]

The clinical supervisor in this vignette seems to be concerned about her student's willingness to conform to her will, and she spends at least some time attempting to talk to him about the need to be individually committed to an argument. Professor Barry explains in the article, however, that the supervisor could have better served the student by helping him participate in the critique of his work so he could learn from the process instead of simply conforming to her request. For example, the supervisor could have had the student role play an oral argument on the motion, and then asked the student questions that would have forced him to reconcile the precedent with the facts of the case. Professor Barry also commented that the supervisor should have insisted on more thoughtful input from the student, refusing to accept the student's "if you want" attitude and pressing him further on what was inhibiting his discussion of the case.

I would add that the supervisor in this vignette should have used this opportunity to challenge directly the student's willingness to conform to authority unthinkingly. This vignette presents a picture of a student who, as a young lawyer, is likely to acquiesce uncritically to the demands of an authority figure. Ideally, the supervisor would, perhaps through role play, strive to impress upon the student the importance to his own professional development of having input in the process that produces lawyering decisions. For example, the supervisor might have taken some time to back away from the specific discussion of the motion and asked this student to consider what he would do if she asked him to make what he considered to be a frivolous argument. Such a hypothetical would, at a minimum, permit the supervisor and student to explore the independent professional responsibilities of junior lawyers when confronted with inappropriate or unwise demands from a senior lawyer. The student might then return to the immediate issue at hand with a fuller appreciation of the importance of making independent lawyering decisions. Admittedly, the supervisor was under time constraints imposed by the case, and deadline pressure was likely the primary cause of the supervisor's directiveness in her interaction with the student. However, as discussed earlier, most key teaching opportunities occur in case supervision; thus, super visors need to be able to step back from pressing deadlines to teach important, albeit secondary, lessons. Unfortunately, this hypothetical student would leave his law school clinic no more knowledgeable about the contours of conformance pressures than when he started and no more willing to challenge authority at times when it is appropriate for him to do so.

In addition, supervisors should look for opportunities to use the work of other lawyers the students encounter in their clinical practice to discuss individual lawyering styles and choices. For example, if in the course of their case work the students observe a lawyer who is particularly aggressive in her deposition style, the supervisor should not pass up the chance to discuss with the students whether they thought the lawyer's aggressive tone was a successful approach and whether that choice would be appropriate for all lawyers. Moreover, clinical educators are often presented with unique opportunities in their supervisory work to model an active involvement in self-development by sharing more of their own professional development with their students. If a professor strives to share the various ways her own identity has informed her development as a lawyer, her students can perhaps better understand the role they themselves should play in their own development. Thus, observing an assertive lawyer in action might spark a professor-student discussion· of their respective visions of themselves in the lawyering world and what they want to do as lawyers.

Student collaborations on case work also present opportunities for faculty supervisors to teach lessons on maintaining· autonomy while working collaboratively. Initially, one of the most important things clinical educators can do to enhance autonomy and independent thinking within student collaborations is to ensure that, as a matter of clinical policy and objectives, such attributes are valued and students understand that they are valued. Most students, and perhaps many supervisors, likely perceive a successful collaboration simply as one in which the students "get along with each other" and "work well" together. Although it is obviously important to encourage collegiality, supervisors should avoid creating environments in which students are more prone simply to concur with a teammate's plans and proposals rather than to think independently and challenge each other when it is appropriate to do so.... Thus, clinical educators will promote more valuable collaborations by conveying to students that independent thought and critical assessment are important and valued by the faculty.

...

Endnotes

1. *See generally* Model Rules of Pro. Conduct (Am. Bar Ass'n 2024) https://www.americanbar.org/groups/professional_responsibility/publications/model_rules_of_professional_conduct/model_rules_of_professional_conduct_table_of_contents [hereinafter R.P.C.].

2. For a discussion of student practice rules, *see generally* Wallace Mlyniec & Haley D. Etchison, *Conceptualizing Student Practice for the 21st Century: Educational and Ethical Considerations in Modernizing the District of Columbia Student Practice Rules*, 28 Geo. J. Legal Ethics 207 (2015).

3. Most student practice rules place the ultimate responsibility for the case on the supervisor. *See, e.g.*, D.C. Ct. App. R. 48(e)(2).

4. R.P.C., *supra* note 1, r. 5.1, 5.2.

5. *See generally* Kuehn & McCormack, *Lessons from Forty Years of Interference in Law School Clinics*, 24 Geo. J. Legal Ethics 59, 62 (2011) at 60–62, 67, 83–84, 89 (presenting university, industry, and government interference in or objection to clinic work as threat to academic freedom); *see also* Babich, *supra* note 9, at 480–81 ("University administrators are accustomed to the concept of academic freedom and few of them could realistically expect to regulate the content of their academic employees' professional activities.")

6. *Id.* at 60. For a "typology of interference," documenting the multitude of ways in which universities, governments, and others have pushed back against clinics' decisions over client representation and litigation strategy, *see id.* at 60–74.

7. *See id.* at 74–80 (empirical survey results).

8. ABA Comm. On Ethics and Prof'l Responsibility, Informal Op. 1208 (1972) [hereinafter ABA Informal Op. 1208].

9. *See, e.g.*, Robert R. Kuehn & Bridget M. McCormack, *supra* note 5 (citing ABA Informal Op. 1208; Adam Babich, *Controversy, Conflicts, and Law School Clinics*, 17 Clinical L. Rev. 469, 484 n. 57 (2011) (same; also citing ABA Comm. On Ethics and Prof'l Responsibility, Formal Op. 334 (1974) [hereinafter ABA Formal Op. 334]). For a more comprehensive taxonomy of ethical opinions on this matter, *see* Robert R. Kuehn, *Undermining Justice: The Legal Profession's Role in Restricting Access to Legal Representation*, 2006 Utah L. Rev. 1039, 1067 (2006) (detailing ethics opinions "condemn[ing] efforts to restrict the clients or causes that legal assistance programs may represent.")

10. *See* ABA Formal Op. 334, *supra* note 9.

11. *See id.*

12. Robert Kuehn and Peter Joy, An Anthology of Interference in Law School Clinics, https://sites.wustl.edu/anthologyofinterferenceinlawclinics/ (September 2025).

13. *See* Kuehn & McCormack, *supra* note 5, at 60 (the "clinic attorney's professional loyalty to the client" in "the middle of ongoing representation" makes any "attempt to direct or regulate the lawyer's professional judgment ethically improper"); *id.* at 86 (citing R.P.C., *supra* note 1, r. 1.8(f), 5.4(c); Restatement (Third) of Law Governing Lawyers § 134 (2000)).

14. *See, e.g.*, R.P.C., *supra* note 1, r. 5.4(c) ("A lawyer shall not permit a person who recommends, employs, or pays the lawyer to render legal services for another to direct or regulate the lawyer's professional judgment in rendering such services."); *see also* Babich, *supra* note 9, at 470 n. 3 (collecting R.P.C. rules supporting clinic's duty to client as trumping any university interference in the course of the litigation); Kuehn & McCormack, *supra* note 5, at 86 & n.136 (discussing ethical impropriety of interfering in ongoing litigation and collecting ethical rules to that effect); *cf.* Polk Cnty. v. Dodson, 454 U.S. 312, 321 (1981) ("Administrative and legislative decisions undoubtedly influence the way a public defender does his work.... But a defense lawyer is not, and by the nature of his function cannot be, the servant of an administrative superior.").

15. *See* Kuehn & McCormack, *supra* note 5, at 67 (citing Memorandum D8383-25 from James P. White, Consultant on Legal Educ., ABA, to Deans of ABA Approved Law Schools (Feb. 21, 1983),

reprinted in ABA, Standards and Rules of Procedure for Approval of Law Schools 146 (2009–10)); *id.* at 85.

16. Jennifer A. Gundlach & Jessica R. Santangelo, *Teaching and Assessing Metacognition in Law School*, 69 J. Legal Educ. 156, 159–63 (2019).

17. American Bar Association, Section of Legal Education and Admissions to the Bar, Legal Education and Professional Development—An Educational Continuum Report of the Task Force on Law Schools and the Profession: Narrowing the Gap (1992), *available at* http://www.abanet.org/legaled/publications/onlinepubs/maccrate.html [hereinafter MacCrate Report], at "Chapter 7A. The Law Schools' Role in Professional Development."

18. R.P.C., *supra* note 1, r. 5.1(b) and (c).

19. *Id.*, r. 5.1(c)(2).

20. *See, e.g.*, D.C. Ct. App. R., *supra* note 3, r. 48(d) and (e) (2).

21. *See* R.P.C., *supra* note 1, r. 5.1(b) ("A subordinate lawyer does not violate the Rules of Professional Conduct if that lawyer acts in accordance with a supervisory lawyer's reasonable resolution of an arguable question of professional duty.")

22. *See, e.g.*, Alaska Bar Rules, r. 44 § 7 (authorizing revocation of intern permit for, *inter alia*, violations of Alaska Rules of Professional Conduct); Idaho Bar Comm. Rules, r. 226(c)(2) (application for student license requires disclosing whether—and if so, why—a prior student license was revoked); Okla. Stat. Ann. INTERN 6.3 (West 2022) (authorizing revocation of limited license for "good cause"), Miss. Code. Ann. § 73-3-207 (West 2011) (similar "good cause" standard).

23. *See* R.P.C., *supra* note 1, r. 1.6 (describing duties of confidentiality); *id.*, r. 1.6 cmt. para. 5 (permitting intra-law firm disclosures of information "in the course of the firm's practice," unless the client has instructed that certain information remain confined to only certain lawyers); *see also id.* r. 1.9(c)(2) (confidentiality rules apply to former clients); *id.*, r. 1.6 cmt. para. 20 (same).

24. *See id.*, r. 1.6 cmt. para. 2.

25. *See id.*, r. 1.6 cmt. para. 18.

26. *See id.*, r. 1.7 (conflicts of interest rules for current clients); r. 1.8 (specific rules for current clients); r. 1.11 (special conflicts rules for current and prior government work)

27. *See id.*, r. 1.8(b).

28. *See id.*, r. 1.11(a) and (d).

29. *See id.*, r. 1.10 (imputing conflicts from one lawyer in a firm to all others in the firm, with limited exceptions); *id.*, r. 1.11(b) (prohibiting any lawyer in a firm in which a lawyer is disqualified from representation for prior government work under r. 1.11(a) from undertaking or continuing to represent a client in the disqualifying matter unless the conflicted lawyer is screened out and the government agency receives written notice); *id.*, r. 1.8(k) (conflict-of-interest prohibitions that apply to one lawyer in a firm also apply to all other lawyers in the firm).

30. *See* 18 U.S.C. § 205 (imposing prohibitions); 18 U.S.C. § 216 (describing applicable penalties, including fines and imprisonment of up to one year).

31. Nix v. Whiteside, 475 U.S. 157, 190 (1986) (Stevens, J., concurring in the judgment).

32. *See, e.g.*, D.C. Rules of Pro. Conduct (D.C. Bar Ass'n 2022) [hereinafter D.C./R.P.C.], r. 1.6 cmt. para. 6–8 (discussing interplay of confidentiality rules, attorney-client evidentiary privilege, and work-product doctrine); R.P.C., *supra* note 1, r. 1.6 cmt. para. 3 (similar).

33. *Compare* D.C./R.P.C., *supra* note 32, r. 1.6 (explaining requirements of, and exceptions to, duty of confidentiality) *and* D.C./R.P.C., *supra* note 32, r. 3.3 (candor toward the tribunal) with R.P.C., *supra* note 1, r. 1.6 (confidentiality) *and* R.P.C., *supra* note 1, r. 3.3 (candor toward the tribunal).

34. *See* R.P.C., *supra* note 1, r. 3.3(a) (3).

35. *See id.*, r. 3.3(b).

36. *See id.*, r. 4.1. *But see id.*, r. 4.1(b) (disclosure is hemmed in by R.P.C. r. 1.6, *supra* note 1, regarding confidentiality).

37. *See id.*, r. 3.3(a)(3) and (b); r. 4.1(b).

38. *See, e.g.*, In re Ryder, 263 F. Supp. 360, 361–66 (E.D. Va. 1967), *aff'd*, 381 F.2d 713 (4th Cir. 1967) (finding "experienced criminal attorney" violated professional ethics rules by knowingly moving stolen cash and sawed-off shotgun that his client used in armed robbery from the client's safe deposit box to safe deposit box in his own name in order to protect his client).

39. *See* D.C. Code § 4–1321.02 (b) ("Such persons are not required to report when employed by a lawyer who is providing representation in a criminal, civil, including family law, or delinquency matter and the basis for the suspicion arises solely in the course of that representation.")

40. Even when the student and client interests converge on a particular course of action, ethical rules may counsel against, or prohibit, pursuing that option. *See, e.g.* R.P.C., *supra* note 1, r. 3.1 (setting requirements for meritorious claims; prohibiting frivolous arguments); *id.*, r. 3.4 (imposing obligations rooted in fairness to opposing party and counsel); *id.*, r. 3.6 (restricting avenues for trial publicity, with limited exceptions). *But see id.*, r. 2.1 (permitting lawyers to advise clients with reference to considerations that transcend the legal sphere, including "moral, economic, social [,] and political factors"). And state law also provides important guardrails, perhaps most notably with "anti-SLAPP" laws. So-called "SLAPP" suits—Strategic Lawsuit Against Public Participation—are intended to retaliate against, or threaten into silence, people who speak out, whether in public commentary on litigation, in legislative testimony, or in other fora. *See, e.g.*, Reporters' Comm. for Freedom of the Press, https://www.rcfp.org/resources/anti-slapp-laws Dan Greenberg & David Keating, *Anti-SLAPP Statutes: A Report Card*, Institute for Free Speech (Feb. 28, 2022), https://www.ifs.org/anti-slapp-report/. To stem the chill of these retaliatory lawsuits and protect the First Amendment rights of their citizens to speak out on matters of public concern, many states have implemented "anti-SLAPP" laws. Some help courts dispose of frivolous SLAPP suits more quickly (e.g., filing an anti-SLAPP motion immediately suspends court proceedings, and defendants filing an anti-SLAPP motion are entitled to an immediate appeal), while others punish parties filing SLAPP suits and serve as a deterrent (e.g., awarding costs and attorneys' fees). *See, e.g.*, Public Participation Project, https://anti-slapp.org/your-states-free-speech-protection#reference-chart (chart comparing states' anti-SLAPP protections).

41. *See, e.g.*, Nicole Smith Futrell, *The Practice and Pedagogy of Carceral Abolition in A Criminal Defense Clinic*, 45 N.Y.U. Rev. L. & Soc. Change 159, 161–62 (2021) (describing exchange between public defender teaching cross-examination strategy of using witness's prior conviction against them and student who found that practice perpetuated the same racist tropes that hurt their clients for having prior convictions).

42. Derrick A. Bell, Jr., *Serving Two Masters: Integration Ideals and Client Interests in School Desegregation Litigation*, 85 Yale L.J. 470, 472 (1976).

43. *Id.* at 476.

44. *Id.* at 480.

45. *Id.* at 470–73, 482–83. *See also id.* at 485–87 (describing a compromise settlement in Atlanta that local NAACP counsel and several thousand members of the plaintiff class agreed to, but that "horrified" the "national NAACP office and LDF lawyers," leading to the "oust[ing of] the Atlanta branch president who had supported the compromise" and multiple attempts to litigate out of the compromise).

46. *Id.* at 493. For an alternative vision of the lawyer-client relationship, and the role of lawyers more generally in effectuating systemic change, as exemplified in the practice of "movement lawyering," see What We Can Do: Movement Lawyering in Moments of Crisis, LAW 4 BLACK LIVES, http://www.law4blacklives.org/respond (last accessed Apr. 17, 2023) ("Movement lawyering means taking direction from directly impacted communities and from organizers, as opposed to imposing our leadership or expertise as legal advocates. It means building the power of the people, not the power of the law.... It requires being part of a team and following direction from organizers."); Statement on Movement Legal Work, Collective Defense, and the Role of Law, Nat'l Lawyers Guild (Aug. 15, 2022),

https://www.nlg.org/nlg-statement-on-movement-legal-work-collective-defense-and-the-role-of-law/ (citing, inter alia, LAW 4 BLACK LIVES, *supra*) (similar); Betty Huang, Movement Lawyering as Rebellious Lawyering: Advocating with Humility, Love and Courage, 23 Clinical L. Rev. 663, 664 (2017) ("[Movement lawyering is lawyering that supports and advances social movements, defined as the building and exercise of collective power, led by the most directly impacted, to achieve systemic institutional and cultural change.").

47. *See* Futrell, *supra* note 41, at 161–62 (describing a public defender's commitment to differentiating between "effectively defend[ing] my client ... us[ing] any means I have available to do so" and "leav[ing] taking the system down to the activists and the organizers") (internal quotation marks omitted); *id.* at 195–96 (internal citation omitted) ("Clinicians can prepare students to engage in an abolition-inspired practice, which calls for attorneys to actively shield clients from the power of the carceral state while also supporting the work of organizers who are seeking to transform how we deal with social problems."); Raymond H. Brescia, *Creative Lawyering for Social Change*, 35 GA. ST. U. L. REV. 529, 553–55 (2019) (discussing complexity for social-change lawyering in differentiating between client as an individual and client as representative of a broader community).

48. *See, e.g.*, Futrell, *supra* note 41, at 192–93 (discussing concrete ways to weave abolitionist principles into criminal defense clinic without sacrificing duty to client, including learning trauma-informed interview practices, incorporating systemic factors that affected client's life into sentencing and post-conviction advocacy, and subtle shifts in language that better humanize clients); *cf.* Herbert A. Eastman, *Speaking Truth to Power: The Language of Civil Rights Litigators*, 104 YALE L.J. 763 (1995) ("A thin, sterile complaint reflects the thin, sterile professional who slices away her fully human role. Written differently [i.e., as a "thick pleading"], the complaint can serve as a way of integrating the two parts of the lawyers—the personal and the professional."). *But see* Eastman, *supra*, at 855–62 (discussing practical, ethical, and strategic limits on "thicker pleading" to consider).

49. *Id.* at 196.

50. *Id.* at 193–95.

51. *See, e.g.*, Katherine R. Kruse, *Biting Off What They Can Chew: Strategies for Involving Students in Problem Solving Beyond Individual Client Representation*, 8 CLINICAL L. REV. 405, 407–08 (2001–2002).

52. *See, e.g.*, Katherine R. Kruse, *Biting Off What They Can Chew: Strategies for Involving Students in Problem Solving Beyond Individual Client Representation*, 8 CLINICAL L. REV. 405, 407–08 (2001–2002).

53. *See, e.g.*, R.P.C., *supra* note 1, r. 3.9 (requiring that lawyers representing clients before legislative bodies or administrative agencies in nonadjudicative proceedings conform to the RPC's ethical rules regarding candor to the tribunal, fairness to opposing party and counsel, and impartiality and decorum of the tribunal); *id.*, r. 1.13 (organization as client); *cf.* Rachel Dunn, Lyndsey Bengtsson & Siobhan McConnell, *The Policy Clinic at Northumbria University: Influencing Policy/Law Reform as an Effective Educational Tool for Students*, 27 INT'L J. CLINICAL LEGAL EDUC. 68, 69 n.4 (2020) (noting global spread of "policy and law reform clinics"); *id.* at 90–91 (assessing potential for policy clinics to fill curricular gap on ethics training).

54. For example, recall the sharp divergence in strategy and ideology between the national NAACP lawyers in the school desegregation cases on the one hand, and the local NAACP chapters and the community members they served on the other. *See* Derrick A. Bell, Jr. *supra* notes 42–46 and accompanying text.

55. *Compare* R.P.C., *supra* note 1, r. 1.13(a)–(f) (explaining nature and ethical obligations of client-lawyer relationship where the client is an organization) *and* R.P.C., *supra* note 1, r. 1.13(g) (permitting dual representation of organizational client and any of its individual directors, officers, employees, members, shareholders, or other constituents, subject to conflict-of-interest rules for current clients) *with* R.P.C., *supra* note 1, r. 1.13 cmt. para. 3 (requiring that lawyers prioritize best interests of organizational client when they "know [] that the organization is likely to be substantially injured by action of an officer or other constituent that violates a legal obligation to the organization or is in violation of law

that might be imputed to the organization"). *But see* R.P.C., *supra* note 1, r. 6.4 cmt. para. 1 (explaining, with analogy to bar associations, that lawyers merely "involved in organizations seeking law reform generally do not have a client-lawyer relationship with the organization).

56. *See* R.P.C., *supra* note 1, r. 1.13 cmt. para. 2 (distinguishing between organizational client and its constituents for confidentiality and disclosure purposes); *id.*, r. 1.6 (confidentiality rules).

57. *See* Chai R. Feldblum, *The Art of Legislative Lawyering and the Six Circles Theory of Advocacy*, 34 McGeorge L. Rev. 785–850, 786 (2003).

58. *See id.* at 791–801 (explaining theory of six circles of advocacy, which requires triangulating efforts among various parties performing different roles in support of the same legislative cause); *id.* at 788–91 (illustrating that theory playing out in the passage of the Americans with Disabilities Act); Hina Shah, *Notes from the Field: The Role of Lawyer in Grassroots Policy Advocacy*, 21 Clinical L. Rev. 393, 406–12 (2015) (same, for California's Domestic Worker Bill of Rights); Alexander T. Holtzman, *Misery Acquaints A Man with Strange Bedfellows: A Plan to Pass Immigration Reform*, 34 Chicana/o-Latina/o L. Rev. 67, 90–100 (2016) (arguing that Feldblum's six-circles theory is an effective blueprint for passing comprehensive immigration reform, and mapping six-circles-theory's role responsibility onto immigration reform stakeholders to that end).

59. *See, e.g.*, Feldblum, *supra* note 57, at 806 n.27 (discussing perceived incongruity between Model RPCs and the self-conception of lobbyists and legislative lawyers, who often do not see themselves as "practicing law" and whose work involves an unusual calculus for who their "client" actually is).

60. *See, e.g.*, Shah, *supra* note 58, at 409 (recounting "time consuming" but worthwhile process of resolving minute policy details when clinic was legislative lawyer to a coalition of grassroots organizations all committed to democratic decision-making).

61. *See* R.P.C., *supra* note 1, r. 6.2 cmt. para. 1 (acknowledging, but qualifying, lawyer's freedom to choose clients and ordinary lack of obligation to represent repugnant clients or causes).

62. *Id.*

63. *See id.*; *id.*, r. 6.2; *id.*, r. 6.1 (pro bono obligations). *But see generally id.*, r. 1.7-1.11 (conflicts of interest).

64. *See* Catherine O'Grady, *Preparing Students for the Profession: Clinical Education, Collaborative Pedagogy, and the Realities of Practice for the New Lawyer*, 4 Clinical L. Rev. 485, 485 (1998) [hereinafter O'Grady, *Preparing Students for the Profession*].

65. *See id.* at 486–89.

66. *See id.* at 493–94, 494 n.34 (collecting sources describing groupthink).

67. *See* Catherine O'Grady, *Wrongful Obedience and the Professional Practice of Law*, 19 J.L., Bus. & Ethics 9, 21 (2013) [hereinafter O'Grady, *Wrongful Obedience*].

68. *See* Wallace J. Mlyniec, *Lawyering Practice: Uncovering Unconscious Influences Before Rather Than After Errors Occur*, 51 New Eng. L. Rev. 81, 87 (2017) (discussing, *inter alia*, Catherine O'Grady, *Behavioral Legal Ethics, Decision Making, and the New Attorney's Unique Perspective*, 15 Nev. L.J. 671, 672 (2015) [hereinafter, O'Grady, *Behavioral Legal Ethics*]).

69. *See id.* at 90–92, 94.

70. *See* O'Grady, *supra* note 64 at 507; *see also* R.P.C., *supra* note 1, r. 8.3 (imposing an affirmative requirement upon lawyers to report conduct of other lawyers that "raises a substantial question as to that lawyer's honesty, trustworthiness, or fitness as a lawyer" to the appropriate authority).

71. MacCrate Report, *supra* note 17.

72. Geoffrey Hazard, *Personal Values and Professional Ethics*, 40 Clev. St. L. Rev. 133 (1992).

73. David Luban & Michael Millemann, *Good Judgment: Ethics Teaching in Dark Times*, 9 Geo J. Legal Ethics 31, 41–53 (1995).

74. Peter A. Joy & Robert R. Kuehn, *Conflict of Interest and Competency Issues in Law Clinic Practice*, 9 Clinical L. Rev. 493 (2003).

75. *Id.* at 499–503.

76. *Id.* at 502–03.

77. *See, e.g.*, O'Grady, *supra* note 64, at 508.

Ten

SUPERVISING ISSUES RELATING TO RACE AND CULTURAL DIFFERENCE

The modern-day reckoning about race in America that emerged after the death of George Floyd in 2020 brought issues of racial inequity back to the forefront of American consciousness.[1] Similarly, advances and reversals regarding lesbian, gay, bisexual, and transgender rights have amplified the discussion of those issues in public and private commentary.[2] After the onset of the COVID-19 pandemic, irresponsible criticism regarding the origin of the disease correlated with an increase in assaults on Asian Americans.[3] Muslim Americans have borne the brunt of citizens' and officials' anger since the unprovoked September 11th attacks on America in 2001, and have increased since the U.S. attack on Iran.[4] Similarly, Hamas' attacks against Israel and the Israeli response have awakened long-dormant anti-Semitism as well as renewed antipathy toward Islam.[5] While debates regarding immigration issues are not new, their intensity has risen in the United States as thousands of South and Central Americans and Haitians crossed the Rio Grande to escape wars, gang activity, poverty, and political unrest in their home countries.[6] At the time of this publication, the Trump administration's policy of cultural revanchism is undermining the progress toward equality in the American society. Gains in societal tolerance and acceptance of disparate cultures achieved during the last six decades are being wiped out daily.

Intense and acrimonious political battles about these issues are entrenched in American society and will continue to plague the nation for years to come. Students and faculty are also immersed in these debates on both college and law school campuses.[7] The positions students have taken about them often become a basis for the personal and cultural identity many of them adopt.[8] As a result, students who support or oppose specific cultural and political solutions to these societal problems are often likely to end up in the same clinic. Clinical pedagogy cannot ignore these and other issues concerning "Difference"[9] because so much of the work taking place in experiential programs involves clients who are members of groups that do not possess social, economic, or political power in the American society. It is understandable when students and clients see their identity tied to their cultural status and feel a sense of "otherness" because of the treatment those without power or wealth have historically endured.

Clinic students usually represent clients who are members of groups that are often under-represented and outside of the main structures of power and wealth in America.

The clients are also frequently members of groups which have suffered discrimination and subordination throughout America history. As noted elsewhere in this book, student practice rules generally permit students to represent only indigent individuals or public interest groups that cannot easily find lawyers to represent them. As a result, clinic students represent low-income tenants and people without homes; adults and children who are charged with criminal offenses or are incarcerated; adult and child survivors of domestic and sexual abuse; immigrants and asylum seekers with little or no proficiency in the English language; members of the LGBTQ community; low-income workers and people out of work; people of color; and people who are sick or disabled. In representing them, discussions concerning issues of Difference, along with case strategies and tactics that recognize those differences, will inevitably implicate the personal morals, values, ethics, biases, and assumptions that students, faculty, clients, other lawyers, judges, and witnesses bring to the clinic's work. This is not to say that our identities totally define who we are. There is often great disparity of thought within an identity group. Nor is it to say that people in one group will never understand the feelings, interest, desires, and experiences of people from dissimilar backgrounds. But it does mean that unless students become culturally curious and work to truly comprehend perspectives that may be unknown to them, their lives will be less rich, and their practice less successful.

Some law students are members of the same disadvantaged groups as their clients and will share some of the same values and life experiences as their clients. Others will not. More often than not, however, white or wealthy law students share few similar life experiences with their clients. Nor have they had substantial exposure to individuals who are similar to their clients or their clients' cultures. Conversely, members of the same identity group may share some, but sometimes only a few, similar cultural traits or values. Despite students' efforts to relate to their clients and provide client-centered representation, uncertainty may arise when the students are completely unfamiliar with various Differences such as English language fluency, cognitive ability, age, mental illness, and extreme poverty when they are expected to provide representation. A client's appearance or demeanor may not fit an expectation. It may be unsettling to meet a client who appears to be physically or emotionally traumatized or mentally ill. The uncertainty can occur even when the Differences are common and apparent, such as age, gender, physical disability, or race.[10]

Because we are generally unfamiliar with the lives of people who come from different life experiences or who are perceived to be not like us, students and teachers can make unwarranted assumptions about clients' abilities, values, experiences, wishes, and motives. The same can be said of clients who view their lawyers with some skepticism because they perceive their lawyer to be different or part of the system that they believe is oppressing them. When that occurs, they may begin to believe their lawyers are not even capable of understanding their issues and needs. And of course, clinic clients may have even more reason to be skeptical when they learn that the person representing them is not even a full-fledged or licensed lawyer, but rather a student who has not even completed their legal studies. Clients may also make other assumptions about lawyers or students assigned to represent them. Because most clinic clients have little choice regarding who represents them, they may assume that their counsel is more aligned with the court than with them. Some clients may get to choose their lawyer, but because of the economics of law practice, that choice may be limited.[11]

Difference may exist beyond the student lawyer-client dyad. Issues regarding Difference may also emerge among students in the clinic, especially between student partners who have been assigned to work together on a case or project. The issues may emerge between the clinic director and the other supervisors in the clinic, and they arise between students and the supervisors. Not all Difference issues will involve race. Politics, gender, identity, age, ethnicity, religion, class, and economic differences can emerge just as easily among any of the participants in the clinic. Hierarchical issues may exist among faculty and support staff as well. Navigating them will have similarities but each may call for different strategic choices. Whenever personal disconnects occur, they create impediments to learning, clinic collegiality, and legal practice.

Clinic Goals and Difference

The goal of all experiential educators is to train their students to confront and analyze the legal issues that arise in their cases and projects and perform the legal tasks necessary to achieve their clients' goals. Understanding and acting in the role of a lawyer is also a goal of every clinic and experiential course. Faculty try to achieve those goals by creating substantive classes and forensic exercises that prepare students to represent their clients with a high level of skill and knowledge. For example, most clinical courses include classes on interviewing and counseling. Questions implicating those tasks regularly arise in supervision sessions and are at the core of how a case or project will proceed. It is during the initial interviews and subsequent meetings where a relationship based on trust between a lawyer and a client begins to develop. In addition, students begin to understand their client's interests, develop case theories, discuss strategies, and develop plans of action to secure their client's interest. Whether students admit it or not, their assumptions affect the way they see the world. Perceptions about people and their actions or inactions that do not take into consideration the effect of Difference and how assumptions about Difference operate, can undermine a lawyer's understanding of a client's interests in a case. Consequently, an awareness of personal and professional values regarding the differences that students perceive between them and their clients, and an awareness of the assumptions arising from those differences, are critical to understanding clients' needs and interests and performing successfully in the role of a lawyer.

For example, students may assume that clients who fail to come to an appointment or those who are constantly tardy for meetings are disinterested in their cases. A client's failure to appear in court can generate even more odious assumptions. Most lawyers who work with economically stressed clients know that such behavior is not always caused by a disinterest in the case or client irresponsibility. It is more likely, or at least just as likely, caused by health reasons, poor transportation corridors, an inability to pay for taxis or ride-share cars, fear of losing a job by choosing the meeting rather than showing up for work, or an inability to arrange for childcare. Communication between lawyers, courts and clients may also affect attendance at meetings and court dates. In fact, research has shown that failure-to-appear rates in court, which judges often treat as intentional and thus deserving of a bench warrant or a severe sentence, can be reduced with a behavioral nudge as simple as a text message reminder.[12]

Complicating life events happen—for everybody, but especially for poor clients. Economic stress may also be the reason clients surprise their student lawyers when clients say they would rather spend a couple of nights in jail than pay a fine. Clients may also choose to plead guilty when innocent to avoid a lengthy trial or jail time or to avoid missing their next work shift and losing their job. There are multiple reasons why a battered spouse may choose not to testify about her abuser despite a pattern of prior harm and a likelihood of future abuse absent a protection order. A lack of trust based on a client's prior experiences with lawyers may make the information flow from client to lawyer slow, halting, deceptive, or nonexistent. If a student fails to understand that their response to a client's behavior is based on false assumptions, the necessary trust between them will be damaged. The inaccurate conclusions described above are generally based on what the students expect from people who find themselves involved in those and similar situations. Those assumptions, however, are often ill-informed or based on the students' belief that people they know personally would not behave that way in similar situations.[13] Supervisors need to help their students understand and challenge their cultural assumptions even before they represent their first client. If they do not, an emotional disconnect or breach of trust in the student lawyer-client relationship is likely to result.

Differences and the assumptions about clients will arise and sometimes become topics of conversation even when they do not directly affect a student's project. Students often meet their clients in their own homes and neighborhoods which are often quite different from a student's life experiences. Students, like many other people, may have many assumptions about so called "bad neighborhoods" and the people who live in them. However, many of those assumptions about the "bad neighborhoods" and the people who live there are exaggerated and often false. Even when assumptions have some validity, they are seldom true about everyone living there. We all create life schemas as we grow because our brains structure knowledge based on our prior experiences. When students find that the reality they now perceive is different from what they assumed it would be, confusion can set in. When a student confronts an assumption about Difference that no longer seems accurate, they may experience what Professor Fran Quigly named a "disorienting moment."[14] Students may choose to confront the assumptions on their own. When we learn during a supervision session that the student confronted it on their own and determined its false premise, it provides a learning moment to celebrate.

Just as often, however, students will come to a supervision session where an inaccurate assumption has colored their perception of the neighborhood, their client or a witness, or the validity of the client's claim. When that occurs, teachers must be attuned to how issues of Difference affect the student's relationship with the client and the development of the theory of the case. They then must develop strategies and techniques to address the issues so that they do not affect the outcome of the case. Faculty do this not to indoctrinate students to a particular ideology, but to help them understand how their assumptions may be affecting their assessment of the clients' needs. When understood, students can then discard the false assumption and develop appropriate case plans and strategies or to remedy any harm that their misunderstanding has caused to the attorney-client relationship. If this understanding results in a learning transfer, it will bring an improved perspective to the next client and case. Faculty do this not just to help the student learn during their clinic experience, but to create a life lesson that alters the way students see the world in which they live.

Aside from case planning and strategy, the supervisor may also choose to address how the student's own personal values and incorrect assumptions affect their personal lives. Like all other aspects of clinical teaching, supervisors need to tread a fine line between indoctrination and discussions about how an assumption rejected in the current case resonates through other aspects of the practice of law and the practice of life. If managed poorly or with personal judgment, the student may walk away angry. But if managed appropriately and in the spirit of generosity, it can become a moment of personal and professional growth for the student. Finding the correct entry point for the conversation is not easy. People do not easily alter assumptions that seem to have served them well for many years.[15] These conversations are hard to begin and are often met with resistance from the student. This is especially true if the assumption is based on a person's internalized life schema. Clinical faculty members try to design clinical courses as safe places to make mistakes and have hard conversations. But they must also be "brave places"[16] and honest places or these hard and necessary conversations will not occur.

Incorporating Cultural Proficiency into the Curriculum

Implementing cultural curiosity and understanding into the practice of law is not easy even for seasoned lawyers. Nor is multicultural competency easy to teach. Culture is defined as "the systems of values, beliefs, and ways of knowing that guide communities of people in their daily lives."[17] Put differently, culture "is the pillar on which we stand when we experience the world."[18] Because clients and lawyers in public interest practices seldom share a similar culture or life experiences, acquiring multicultural humility, curiosity, and competence are necessary for anyone who wants to be a public interest lawyer or a clinical teacher. Of course, cross-cultural understanding is not limited to poverty law. Effective lawyering in any context requires that the lawyers familiarize themselves with the communities they serve, educating themselves about the values, morals, language, and the larger cultural and economic conditions of their clients.[19] This is especially true, however, in the context of experiential teaching.

Lawyers who possess multicultural competence are conscious of the Differences that may exist between themselves and their clients. Those who have this consciousness can challenge their assumptions regarding a client's culture or behavior and adjust their own behavior and approach to effectively represent their clients. Doing so helps them better understand a client's individual background, needs, and expectations in order to secure their client's interests. Faculty may face similar assumption challenges while teaching and supervising students whose life experiences differ from their own. Similarly, a clinic student's project partner may experience a similar feeling of otherness within the class or within the partnership. That is when those safe, brave, and honest places are most important to clinical teachers.

There are many ways to incorporate cultural proficiency into a clinic curriculum. One way is to intentionally include the works of authors from underrepresented groups in the clinic syllabus.[20] Doing so raises the issue from the first day of the clinic. Centering the clinic work with diverse intellectual contributions helps to provide exposure to and establish trust in the abilities of underrepresented scholars and lay people.[21] At the same time, teachers must be careful to avoid the expectation that faculty and students of minority groups should be responsible for teaching cultural proficiency to everyone else in the class.[22] Nor should professors or students be expected to speak for everyone in their shared culture. Placing the onus on members of the minority group to foster cultural proficiency in others can degrade a minority student's law school experience, result in minority faculty bearing a disproportionate share of the work to make law school environments more inclusive, and reaffirm and entrench the existing power dynamic between those with privilege and those without.[23] Moreover, doing so only reinforces the notion that only members of an identity group can understand what are truly universal human characteristics.

Aside from introducing the issues of Difference though the syllabus, clinical teachers should identify the issues at every stage of our teaching, supervision, and representation. We also need to plan how to demonstrate that understanding Difference is relevant to almost every aspect of a clinic case or project and foresee the kinds of issues students will encounter because of cultural misunderstanding. Framing the work students do within the concept of race or other Difference characteristics of the client group helps students to understand how the law operates within the client community. Students need to explore and learn techniques to confront the issues when they arise obviously or latently. Faculty need to develop, or borrow from the work of others, techniques that enable deeper conversations about Difference if they or their students choose to do so. In some sense, doing so may not even be a choice. It is inevitable that issues of Difference will arise in clinic cases, so faculty and students need to reflect on them throughout their time in the clinic.

Issues of Difference permeate all aspects of modern life because a truly post-racial American society does not yet exist. Indeed, all people whose characteristics are not consonant with those of the majority population suffer some form of inequity on some occasions. Since almost all of our clients are outside of the predominant culture, aspects of Difference will appear in almost every case or project undertaken in a clinic. Because our clients tend to have little power, they will experience that inequity in multiple aspects of their lives. Contemporary studies show that people whose characteristics are at odds with the predominant culture fare poorly within our legal systems.[24] Some clients may have multiple marginalized identities and experience those inequities and lack of power along multiple, intersecting axes. Consequently, teachers will also need to develop an intersectional approach to their work.[25]

Why Clinical Teachers Should Care about Difference

There are many reasons clinical teachers should care about Difference. First and foremost, it's an irreducible imperative in fully seeing and treating our clients and our students with the fundamental dignity and respect that everyone deserves, simply by virtue of being human beings.[26] Practically speaking, another reason clinical teachers need to care is because many student-lawyers have not thoughtfully or carefully considered the significance of interacting with clients from diverse backgrounds.[27] Ethical lawyers must, of course, put the client's interests at the heart of their representation.[28] Doing so, however, requires that a lawyer be able to understand and appreciate what matters to their clients.

In many cases and projects, particularly among those handled by public interest lawyers and law school clinics, clients come from racial minority communities, immigrant communities, and lower-income communities. Clients sometimes do not speak the same language as the students, often interpret words in dissimilar ways, or speak with a different regional or generational vocabulary. They may not have the same level of education as a law student. Lawyers most effectively gain information when they are culturally aware of how they perceive a client and how a client perceives them. Lawyers and teachers must be aware of nuances in language so that they actually understand what a client is saying. Similarly, students need to ensure that clients understand what they are saying. If they are not making themselves understood, teachers, lawyers, and student lawyers need to improve their communication skills accordingly in order to maximize client service.[29]

Our job as teachers is to increase our students' ability to situate clients in their cultural context, to be aware of the students' own cultural context, and to challenge the assumptions others in the system might have about clients. Faculty do this to ensure that everyone views a client as an individual, not as a stereotype reflecting false assumptions. A client-centered lawyering approach more easily adapts to cultural differences than other forms of lawyer-client relationships. Because each person has pre-existing biases and prejudices, often unacknowledged or unrecognized, it is important to become aware of the differences that exist between student and client. These unrecognized biases can be disconcerting and affect client trust, zealousness, and sense of fairness. Only when students and teachers recognize these biases can they determine whether their assumptions about the differences are affecting their work. This heightened attention to assumptions can help move students and supervisors alike from so-called "unconscious incompetence" that leads to the formation of stereotypes to a state of "unconscious competence" in which each individual is able to appreciate the cultural dynamic between teachers, students, and clients and act accordingly. When that occurs, teachers and students can communicate more effectively across those Differences.[30] Thus, clinical teachers must learn to account for the Differences across clients and help students to develop a deeper understanding and awareness of the world that surrounds them.

Another reason to understand the power of Difference is because clients care about how they are treated.[31] They come to attorneys from individualized backgrounds within their communities and with unique personal traits, experiences, and issues that carry significant emotional importance. Many also come with a wariness and skepticism about the legal system that developed from their past experiences with the law and the courts.[32] Clients' perceptions of competence depend on the cultural sensitivity that they are shown, not by culture-blind behavior.[33] Since personal boundaries may be disparately defined, even relatively tiny variations in communication style such as shaking versus not shaking hands, the degree of eye contact, and using first names rather than titles and last names can lead to widely disparate reactions depending on the cultural background of the client.[34] Students will not always be aware of these differences and interact with their clients in ways that reflect the student's and not the client's culture. Consequently, clinical teachers must learn to create an environment where students are comfortable discussing this critical feature of lawyering. Psychologically healthy environments for communication and education occur when there is a "spirit of mutuality" and each party feels respected, accepted, and supported.[35] Teachers must learn to adapt their actions and attitudes in their classroom and supervision sessions to each individual in order to foster similar environments and communication patterns between clients and students.

Clinical supervisors have told stories over the years about how their students must balance their role as a legal authority figure and advice-giver in a clinic project with their role as a listener and one who appreciates the cultural context of their client.[36] Those students who have difficulty empathizing with their clients' situations may find their clinical experience frustrating.[37] Thus, teachers must be able to clarify these cross-cultural issues as they arise,[38] addressing, rather than avoiding, issues of Difference. Doing so can help to broaden understandings of fairness and justice in society[39] and inspire students to strive for successful and rewarding careers in public service.[40] As voices of authority and teachers of culturally different practices, clinical supervisors must be competent and aware that their own values are likely to influence those of their students.[41] Unless clinical teachers are prepared to guide students through these conversations, the conversations will be stilted, difficult, and may even not occur.

External Considerations and Educational Necessity

A separate reason to care about Difference issues is that there is significant resistance in our society to discuss those issues, especially race, honestly. Most new and many seasoned teachers share this resistance. Unless we can overcome this resistance, we are left with silence and a lost educational opportunity. Education is meant to open the minds of our students and to inspire a search for knowledge and truth.[42] Even still, these conversations are admittedly hard.[43] Faculty come to discussions about Difference from diverse backgrounds and from various levels of prior engagement with these issues. We are all creatures of what social psychologist Arlie Hochschild has called our own "deep story."[44] All clinical teachers recognize that pedagogy is importantly situational and that each different class, case, or supervision session is a complex, living, and multiheaded entity that demands careful, continual, contextually-aware stewarding. This is especially true in a clinic where clients' interests intersect with faculty educational goals and students' personal learning goals, all of which create a higher level of complexity. Students also come to their legal education with varied backgrounds. Many come from places of great privilege. Some already understand the urgency of recognizing and interrogating their own social advantages; others are resistant, and still others are not sure what to make of it all. On the other hand, students coming from societally marginalized groups now seek more explicit recognition of and reckoning with expressions of systemic racism, gender bias, and other negative assessments based on Difference. These students are right to want and demand more searching explanations of the way legal education generally and legal institutions specifically, wittingly or unwittingly, reproduce and reinforce systemic bias and injustice. Often the conversations, from both sides, begin and end with frustration, disappointment, or outrage. If teachers do not have the courage to address the issues in a nonthreatening fashion in an academic environment, and to tolerate the justifiably broad range of thoughts and emotions that students bring to the matter, who else will? And where else will those conversations take place?

What Are the Steps?

Clinical faculty will have to address a few questions at this juncture. The first question is where and how cultural competence training fits into the clinic, relative to its goals and structure. Professor Susan Bryant, whose writings provide a framework for teaching cultural competence, points out that this has both micro- and macrolevel dimensions. "On the microlevel," she explains, "a clinic may teach cross-cultural lawyering to improve representation of clients and to introduce students to cross-cultural theory that they will be able to apply to practice in an ever increasingly diverse legal profession."[45] And at the macrolevel, the clinic might "teach cross-cultural perspectives and skills to enable students to help build a more just legal system" writ large.[46]

The next question is, once a teacher decides to incorporate cultural competency into their clinic and has found time and places in the clinic to address it, where do we look to find help in learning how to navigate these difficult issues? Clinical teachers have several sources from which to learn and to use as guideposts. In addition to the writings of Professor Susan Bryant noted above, Professor Shahrokh Falati offers two different frameworks that may be used to measure the stages of cultural competency and to identify what habits, skills, and ideas are needed to better develop cross-cultural skills.[47] The first is Dr. Milton Bennett's Developmental Model of Intercultural Sensitivity (DMIS), a six-stage framework that describes the way in which people transition into a stronger state of cultural awareness.[48] This model conceptualizes cultural competency as a linear journey and explains how to guide people through each of the six stages, which include Denial, Defense Reversal, Minimization, Acceptance, Adaption, and Integration.[49] While first three stages—Denial, Defense Reversal, and Minimization—are all "ethno*centric*, meaning the individual's experience of his/her own culture is central to his/her reality,"[50] the last three stages—Acceptance, Adaptation, and Integration—"are more ethno*relative*, meaning the individual's experience of his/her own culture is in the context of other cultures."[51] The second model proposed by Professors Kikanza Nuri-Robins, Dolores B. Lindsey, Randall B. Lindsey and Raymond D. Terrell focuses on the unique challenges that a person in each stage would have to overcome in order to gain cultural competency.[52] Yet another model comes from Professor Bryant and her colleague, Professor Jean Koh Peters. They describe a "Five Habits" model of building cross-cultural competence.[53] The Five Habits, in turn, rest on a foundational belief about "good lawyering and learning." They suggest that "all lawyering is cross cultural;" that remaining "non-judgmental ... towards yourself and [your] client promotes learning and good lawyering;" that cross-cultural competence requires "remaining present with the individual client;" and that the process of "knowing yourself as a cultural being" is both "ongoing and necessary."[54] These authors offer these methods, but they are not the only ways to teach about cultural difference and how it can affect good lawyering. By adopting a framework like any of those described above, teachers can create a stronger strategy to assess and intentionally cultivate cultural awareness and competency in their students.[55]

Facilitating Successful Conversations

It is not uncommon to sense resistance among some teachers to such discussions in class or supervision sessions. The source of that resistance for faculty may be internal (flowing from each teacher's own views), relational (among the teachers within a faculty), or wholly external (cultural and political forces outside the school entirely).[56] The social justice mission of most clinics, however, and the nature of our clientele make these conversations not just inevitable, but undeniably necessary. An overarching goal of a clinical course, and indeed any course in a law school, is to foster a more widespread understanding of the necessary entanglements between law and systemic bias and injustice.[57] We do so to help our graduates emerge equipped to build a better legal system and a better society. As such, teachers need to plan the conversations in ways that attempt to reduce and manage the anxiety students feel, without promising total elimination of the inherent discomfort of deconstructing social advantage. They must also demonstrate that it is vitally necessary to have these hard conversations if the students want to achieve the goals we set for our clinics and the learning goals students set for themselves.

Fear of Being Judged and the Power of Words

Even if we as teachers gain our own comfort with discussion about Difference, we find that the conversations are easier to have in the abstract than when Difference issues actually arise during a student's case or project. Conversations about hypothetical situations and about the inability of other people to recognize Difference issues are generally nonthreatening to teacher and student alike. They become harder when those conversations involve our own perceptions and assumptions or those that we see in our students. Misunderstanding can even occur by merely starting a discussion about a potential incident of bias. Of course, the use of unkind and inappropriate words—words with deep meaning to those who are part of minority groups—during the underlying incidents themselves, may cause misunderstandings and personal discomfort even if protected by free speech values. Indeed, those targeted may experience their own free speech being negatively affected by the hurtful speech of others. These conversations can easily carry the suggestion or accusation of racism, sexism, classism, homophobia, ableism, ageism, entitlement, or some other sensitive issue related to identity, whether or not it is intended. They may also be seen as some sort of indelible trait inherent in the student's character. Expressing those sentiments may unleash accusations of "white privilege" in return.

Indeed, the word privilege carries its own baggage of opprobrium. Students from majority cultures often resent the accusation. They misinterpret the meaning of the word in the context of social justice because they see the systemic issues as ones of historical vintage rather than of current reality. Or they may not feel privileged because of their own societal standing, given intersecting identities along the lines of class, gender, sexual orientation disability, or otherwise. In addition, they may feel unjustly attacked because they consider themselves allies of the cause rather than an enemy. Words can be so powerful on both sides, and the speakers may not be fully aware of the meaning they convey to a listener, especially in the heat of a debate, which can quickly turn, or at least feel, personal.

Because students of both the majority and minority groups may struggle to engage in deep discussions of Difference out of fear of being judged or losing the respect of their friends, colleagues, or professors, teachers need to distinguish between intent and impact when having these conversations.[58] These conversations are tough to navigate and require both active listening skills and articulate and precise speaking skills. Those who have not yet refined these abilities may find that when given the choice between speaking one's mind or facing public pushback and criticism or the ostracization by one's peers, it is easier to stay silent. That is another of the reasons why such conversations are difficult to have. They challenge one's worldview, assumptions, and value system—their "deep story"[59]—in ways that other conversations in the clinic do not.[60]

Students' cultures, like those of all of us, are at the center of their identity. Their cultures are based on experiences which have influenced their development and decision-making throughout their lives. As a result, conversations about culture and difference are sometimes difficult and emotional.[61] Members of minority groups in particular may be skeptical when presented with assistance or advice from members of majority cultural groups, especially when the conversation or decision-making involves cultural issues. They may wonder what makes the advice-giver any different from other members of the majority group who have oppressed them or discriminated against them previously.[62] While such generalizing attitudes may be harmful, the sense of oppression and discrimination listeners feel are based on their prior experiences and therefore may arouse deep sentiments and feelings of harm.

Navigating the Pitfalls

For all of these reasons, it is no surprise that conversations about Difference are often extremely sensitive, can be raw, and require skill and tact to initiate, lead, and sustain. They are difficult to conduct because they force students who actually engage in biases or prejudices, and those with implicit bias resulting from unexamined assumptions, to confront them. When this occurs, students often feel threatened. That threat is both intellectual and emotional. Students worry about how the teacher may be judging them personally, or how their answers to questions may affect their grade. They may not know the answer to a hard question and may not realize the answers are too complex for a simple response. For teachers, the question itself may be more important than the answer because it forces the student into a self-examination rather than any quick and easy response. For many students, this will be the first time that they thoroughly interrogate how their assumptions developed and whether they are simply unexamined by-products of their life experiences or whether they are signals of actual prejudice that need to be deeply examined and hopefully retrained. For students from both advantaged and disadvantaged backgrounds, the possibility of "stereotype threat"—the unconscious fear that one's actions will confirm a negative stereotype about the group to which they belong—looms large.[63] For starters, Black and Latine students experience stereotype threat as "the norm in academic environments."[64] The awareness of a negative stereotype, often about a minority student's skill or competence ("ability-relevant stereotype threat") affects the brain, mind, and body in several ways. They "divert cognitive resources that could otherwise be used to maximize task performance" and result in physiological, cognitive, and affective changes.[65] On the other hand, white students also experience another form of stereotype threat ("character-relevant stereotype threat") stemming from a general social stigma against being racist and being perceived or thought of as such.[66] For example, in one study involving discussions of racially sensitive topics like racial profiling, white participants physically distanced themselves from Black participants when discussing their own views, but did not do so when discussing an "openly assigned" position (i.e., not their own), regardless of the white participants' levels of implicit bias—all suggesting that "their levels of concern about *being seen as racist* predicted their actions."[67] Even though there are complicated dynamics at play on all sides of these already-difficult conversations, teachers should still keep in mind that these situations can be especially taxing to students from minority groups.

Teachers must anticipate and employ strategies to reduce the anxiety experienced during inter-cultural interactions regardless of their students' backgrounds.[68] If students are successfully guided though a factual analysis of observed behaviors and the effect of those behaviors on their interactions with others, they may learn more about themselves.[69] In order to gain multicultural competence, one must "break" preexisting assumptions and develop habits of communication that serve to more effectively engage with others.[70] Teachers must learn to introduce dissonance into the ways students currently think of things to help them contemplate differing perspectives.[71]

An active process to facilitate cross-cultural competency is one that encourages students to contemplate and answer questions like: "What is the Difference I observed or perceived? Why did it draw my attention? How did I react? Why did I react the way I did?"[72] Through discussions in class and in supervision sessions, and through self-reflection exercises, students can develop tolerance and a more mature understanding of issues of Difference and their assumptions and reactions to it, all in service of better serving their clients' interests. They may evolve not only as lawyers, but as more enlightened citizens too.

Even when the goal may be clear, teachers need to understand that there are reasons why it takes time to truly break down the biases, prejudices, and false assumptions that affect good lawyering. Students may say little or nothing at all about these issues when talking among themselves, with clients, or with supervisors, fearing they might expose their own stereotypical thinking or be accused of being anti-something. Clinical students refrain from these conversations out of fear that they will lose favor with their peers and colleagues or negatively affect their grades if they say what they are really thinking or feeling. Teachers and students who choose to engage in these thoughtful discussions must necessarily reveal their individuality by drawing upon their own experiences and identities. These often result in painful, personal disclosures. Teachers may also experience student resistance to learning cultural competency at the expense of what may be perceived as more "important" matters like the substantive law of the clinic's focus.[73]

As human beings who live in the world we inhabit, all of us have inherent biases and prejudices. As a result, people often do not even realize when their reactions to someone different can have a negative effect. When they come to realize it, they may berate themselves not just for that one action or comment, but for an internalized sense of *being* prejudiced. To reframe, teachers need to acknowledge these stereotypes as reflections of us being merely human.[74] That acknowledgment neither excuses nor condemns the existence of the unrecognized assumption. Instead, it helps the student better understand, alter, and grow beyond it. "[U]nconscious biases can be transformed... [but] they must be acknowledged."[75] Over time, we are all capable of habituation; that is, of noticing differences less and evaluating them in a more sensitive and capable manner.[76]

Some of these conversations will involve the progress of a case or project and must take place if the client's goals are to be achieved. Others may occur because the teacher wants to expand a student's understanding of the world, believes that the student is ready for the conversation, and feels that it can happen in a non-threatening fashion. Such discussions may lead to arguments, hostile comments, and hurt feelings between students or between students and teachers. While such episodes can be difficult to manage, they can take place in a well-structured clinic. Teachers need to learn how to strike a balance between intervening in the moment when comments exceed intellectual boundaries and become insensitive,[77] and following up later when the moment is less heated. There is urgent work to be done reconciling the demands of the social justice paradigm with the equally justified demands of a law school environment for reasoned analysis and argument.

Teachers will inevitably have conversations about cultural attributes in their classes and supervision sessions as values, ethics, and morals collide with the reality of Difference. In doing so, teachers should remember that the methods of teaching described in the earlier chapters on supervision and the chapter on clinical pedagogy should be integrated into the intentional planning needed for these conversations. The conversations about Difference must be "normalized" so that they become an expected and valued part of the clinical experience, rather than an emotionally charged and unwelcome aberration. Being explicit about Difference and why it matters to client representation is important. It should be introduced in Clinic Orientations sessions or in the first few classes of the semester and revisited throughout the semester in different contexts. For example, classes on interviewing or counseling clients should explore the importance of recognizing Difference during these early conversations and revisited when discussing other interactions between students and clients. Introducing the conversations early in the semester and frequently revisiting them will help students begin to adjust their assumptions which will help them to better understand their clients' interests. For some students, these conversations may lead to life-changing experiences. Some teachers cherish these moments and may build their clinic goals around such experiences. Others may choose to minimize the deeper conversations and concentrate only on those discussions that move the case along. Teachers who choose the latter course may nonetheless find that merely moving the case along will still require some complicated conversations about the students' assumptions about Difference in order to achieve the client's goals.

Although many of the issues will be client-based, others will be related to the teachers themselves. Faculty of color may worry about how an all- or mostly-white group of students will perceive them as the leader of the clinic. Female, gay, trans, and nonbinary teachers may wonder how cisgender male students will relate to and respect them as supervisors. Many young teachers worry about how students will relate to a teacher who is just a few years older than they are. Sexual orientation and viewpoint differences may also arise. Majority culture faculty may worry about saying something wrong or how they will walk the line between the several Differences that exist in the clinic. These hierarchical issues may be better addressed in case or project rounds or in role-plays rather than supervision sessions to reduce the emotional and personal discomfort the conversation produces. No matter what path we take, the issues and the conversations are not going away. We have to determine how to navigate them.

There have been hundreds of articles written exploring the issues touched on in this chapter. Many are cited in the endnotes to the chapter. They provide the background for a teacher to explore these issues themselves and to enable discussions with students that confront the issues of class, race, ethnicity, gender, sexual orientation, disability, and age as they arise in supervision sessions, classes, and client work. But while these seem to be the dominant issues that arise, others such as political, religious, cultural, educational, geographical, language, and economic differences can just as easily become part of the conversation. The article by Professors Susan Bryant[78] describing her work with Professor Jean Koh Peters has been cited consistently by clinical teachers so I would suggest you go beyond the excerpt and read the entire article.

Other Voices

Neil Hamilton & Jeff Maleska, *Helping Students Develop Affirmative Evidence of Cross-Cultural Competency**

19 The Scholar: St. Mary's L. Rev. on Race & Soc. Justice 187 (2017)

I. Introduction

...

Cultural competence can be broadly defined as the ability to "relate to others comfortably, respectfully, and productively." In the context of legal education, however, cultural competence is defined as a lawyer's "ability to develop knowledge, skills, and values to enable effective representation and communication with individuals from a different race, ethnicity, gender, sexual orientation, age or cultural background." Indeed, cultural competence is necessary to improve intercultural communication between lawyers and their clients. Accordingly, it is necessary for a lawyer to first identify the various cultures to which he or she belongs in order to understand which cultures are different than the lawyer's own.

Culture is defined in this context as "the body of customary beliefs, social forms and material traits constituting a distinct tradition of a racial, religious or social group." Further, culture can include a person's age, gender, race, ethnicity, sexual orientation, physical ability, nationality, religion, or socio-economic group. Even if a lawyer shares all of those categories with another person, different regions of the same country may have different cultures. Different organizations may also have different cultures. Indeed, "[a] broad definition of culture recognizes that no two people have had the exact same experiences and thus, no two people will interpret or predict [culture] in precisely the same way."

For a lawyer to truly provide competent representation to his or her clients, the lawyer must not only understand the law, but also understand the culture of: (1) the client; (2) the groups with whom the lawyer works to advance the client's interests; and (3) the adversaries and decisionmakers whom the lawyer seeks to influence. Without awareness of the various cultures of these stakeholders in a lawyer's work, a lawyer cannot see how it affects the representation. And, if a lawyer chooses to ignore the cultural differences between the lawyer and his or her clients, it is likely that the representation will not be as effective as it should be. For example, not considering a client's culture could cause a misunderstanding of the client's goals, needs, and personal preferences. The inability to understand a client's culture can also make it more difficult for the lawyer to build a trusting relationship.

---

* Excerpts reprinted with permission of the authors and The Scholar: St. Mary's Law Review on Race & Social Justice.

...

In our view, empathy is at the heart of developing cross-cultural competency for students and lawyers. Empathy is the ability to understand someone else's experiences and perspectives combined with an ability to communicate this understanding and an intention to help. In simpler terms, empathy is the ability to walk in another person's shoes, to view life from his or her perspective, and to communicate that understanding and an intention to help.

There is an existing literature on engaging law students in a critical examination of how race, ethnicity, sexual identity, socio-economic class, and other cultural factors have influenced both the law and the student's own sub-conscious biases. Engaging students in such a way can generate varying degrees of student resistance that presents a significant barrier to their learning. This article assumes that students want meaningful employment. The premise is, if students understand that legal employers value affirmative evidence of cross-cultural competency, a greater proportion of students—motivated by enlightened self-interest—will seek to develop evidence that the student has created and implemented a plan to develop this competency.

...

II. The Effects of Cross-Cultural "Incompetence

A good starting point for a discussion on why it is important to develop cross-cultural competence is to examine the negative effects of being cross-culturally "incompetent." A lawyer is most commonly culturally incompetent because the lawyer fails to recognize that a need for cultural competence exists in a given situation.

...

For example, one major problem that a cross-culturally incompetent attorney may encounter is difficulty establishing trust in the attorney-client relationship. Without trust, a relationship between the lawyer and client cannot work well. Trust is not established simply because the client chose the lawyer to represent them; rather, the lawyer must work to establish trust in the relationship. Cross-cultural competence can help lawyers signal that they accurately understand the client's goals and behavior, thus building trust.

A cross-culturally incompetent attorney will also likely miss important information because of failed or misunderstood communication. Communication failures can have a detrimental effect on the attorney-client relationship. In fact, a client's satisfaction often depends on how lawyers communicate with them.

When lawyers interpret a client's messages solely through the lawyer's own cultural lens, communication can easily break down. Moreover, a lawyer's failure to recognize the inherent differences and nuances of each culture can lead them to make decisions their client may not have made. In fact, "[s]tudies show that client satisfaction often relates as much to how lawyers communicate as to actual results achieved in a given case." To be effective, lawyers must "recognize, and appropriately respond to, their own and others' cultural perceptions and beliefs because these often play a central role in lawyer-client communications."

Cross-cultural incompetence also "may impede lawyers' abilities to effectively interview, investigate, counsel, negotiate, litigate, and resolve conflicts." Not recognizing the impact culture plays on a lawyer's interactions with others can lead the lawyer to ask the wrong questions, suggest an unfavorable course of action, take a bad settlement offer, or even lead to an inability to resolve a conflict.

III. Developmental Stages of Cross-Cultural Competence

Scholars have attempted to classify the various "stages" a person may fit into on a spectrum of cross-cultural competence. While not every model can perfectly describe the nuances of the process of developing cross-cultural competence, the models provide useful guideposts that allow a person to self-reflect and gauge where they fall on the spectrum. In addition, although we do not view any one of the models discussed as "best" or complete, each model provides insight into the process of developing cross-cultural competence.

With respect to the stages of development of cross-cultural competency, one challenge is that it is unclear whether such competency is specific to a culture other than that of the student or lawyer, or whether it is generalizable and transferable. Milton Bennett emphasizes that "intercultural learning refers to the acquisition of generalizable (transferable) intercultural competence; that is, competence that can be applied to dealing with cross-cultural contact in general, not just skills useful for dealing with a particular other culture." It makes common sense that one's overarching paradigmatic assumptions about (and skills relating to) other cultures are generalizable; however, one also needs to come up to speed, so to speak, within the context of each specific other culture. In other words, while a student or lawyer can develop later stages of cross-cultural competency regarding specific other cultures, and could thus claim generalizable and transferable competency, they should acknowledge that obtaining such cross-cultural competency takes time and effort.

...

D. A Synthesis Model of Cross-Cultural Competency

Looking at ... [other] models, we synthesized our own developmental model of cross-cultural competency to define stages of cross-cultural competency such that a law student or practitioner could demonstrate affirmative evidence of the competency. Our model also recognizes that it is possible to be at a later stage of cross-cultural competence in a particular area, like gender, while also being at an earlier stage in another area like age or race. Thus, our model first asks the law student or lawyer to identify which cross-cultural area is the focus of the self-assessment.

There are four stages in our alternative model: (1) lack of awareness, (2) recognition, (3) conscious implementation, and (4) proficiency. In the first stage, lack of awareness, one does not recognize that they lack cross-cultural competency. Someone in this stage may stereotype people in other cultures or feel uncomfortable interacting with others different from them. In general, this stage reflects ignorance of the role that culture plays in one's interactions with others. At the second stage, recognition, one acknowledges their lack of cross-cultural competency, but may be unsure of how to develop it. Indeed, someone at this stage may notice the role culture plays, reflect on how their own culture affects decisions and begin to see the need to develop cross-cultural competency. At the third stage, conscious implementation, one takes an initial affirmative step toward developing cross-cultural competency in a specific area by refraining from making on-the-spot judgments in unfamiliar situations. In addition, someone at this stage proactively seeks culturally diverse experiences and feedback from those from a different culture. Moreover, while there may be some initial difficulty or discomfort in these interactions, such a person reflects on the difficulties, discomfort and feedback and seeks greater understanding. What is important are the affirmative steps one takes to become more cross-culturally competent. At the final stage, proficiency, a person has become educated in the particular culture and could fairly be considered as cross-culturally competent in that area. A person at this stage is able to interact freely and genuinely within another culture and understands that culture's differing viewpoints and customs. They may have genuine respect and appreciation for the other culture, although they need not wholeheartedly agree with every facet of it.

Susan Bryant, *The Five Habits: Building Cross-Cultural Competence in Lawyers**

8 Clinical L. Rev. 33 (2001)

This article describes a process called "the Habits" that was developed by Professors Bryant and Jean Koh Peters that can be used by lawyers to increase their cross-cultural competence. [The article is based on a series of conversations that Professors Bryant and Peters had to develop classes and materials to create "Habits" to develop cross-cultural lawyering.]

...

IV. Teaching The Habits To Develop Cross-Cultural Competence

In planning a cross-cultural class, a teacher should strive to develop awareness, knowledge, skill and motivation for learning in her students. The Habits are a way to gain greater knowledge and awareness as well as develop skills essential to cross-cultural lawyering. They raise our awareness by causing us to pay attention to the significance of differences and similarities and increase knowledge by gathering culture-specific information. The Habits also encourage the development of skills that are needed to gather and process information about clients and their culture. The selection of Habits

* Excerpts are reprinted with the permission of the author and the Clinical Law Review.

on which a teacher focuses and the manner in which a teacher develops the concepts of cross-cultural lawyering are highly dependent on the teacher's background and skills and her students' background and skills.

...

A. Developing Motivation

Whether the teacher's goal is developing awareness of the impact of culture or skill in cross-cultural interactions, a lawyering focus will increase the likelihood of student receptivity to the material. If the teacher uses primarily materials that contain examples of lawyering issues, students will be less likely to think that they are simply being asked to be a different (better) person. If the students see these skills as important to good lawyering, they will be more open to including them in their repertoire of skills. As I discussed earlier, resistance to this subject is to be expected and may arise for different reasons. Identifying the potential resistance and ways to address it are important aspects of planning classes and supervision.

...

Hostility can be expected from some of the students, especially if they feel targeted and judged by the instruction. I recall early teaching experiences in which I tried to raise issues of racism and privilege and white male students felt targeted and reacted with hostility. These early classes accomplished few of the goals that I had for them. They did not help all students prepare for the racism they would face in the legal profession; they did not help students relate better to clients; and they reinforced what some students already understood about the world without really teaching skills for translating their knowledge.

...

B. Raising Awareness of the Significance of Culture

Introducing the Habits through classes and using supervision to encourage students to use the Habits will help students appreciate the significance of cultural similarities and difference for lawyering. Even after one class on the Habits, most students report an increased awareness of how culture might influence their lawyering. Teaching Habit One is a good starting place for raising awareness about the influence of culture because it asks students to articulate similarities and differences between lawyers and clients and begins a conversation about the effects of these factors on lawyering.

In class, we have used a variety of starting points to teach Habit One, including commencing with a focus on the cultural identity of the student or by asking students to apply Habit One to themselves and a student with whom they are paired or to themselves and their client. When students apply Habit One, we ask them to do both the Venn Diagrams and lists in less than five minutes.

...

In other classes, we asked students to apply Habit One to each other in pairs, listing all of the differences and similarities and then categorizing the differences and comparing the resulting roster with the list in the materials. In response to a "what did you learn?" question, one pair offered an example from their exchange. The first student listed economic differences because the other student was using an expensive pen. When the second student revealed that she had found the pen in the subway on her way to school that day, the students recognized the basic lesson that assumptions of similarity and difference can be inaccurate if based on unexplored facts.

After identifying differences and similarities between students, we ask students to apply Habit One to their relationship with a client. This application of the Habit serves to illustrate that we have different identities depending on the individual with whom we are interacting and that we notice different things about ourselves when the reference point changes. Clients may also have different identities depending on the interaction and players.

In focusing on the client-student circles and lists, we often ask questions that are directed yet open-ended. Are there large or small overlaps? What are the relative lengths of the lists of similarities or differences? What's the connection between these two? We have asked students to compare the lists in the materials with the lists they have created and to consider whether there are differences. Students sometimes recognize that they have omitted something. For example, occasionally white students have noted that they omitted race as a difference when dealing with a client of color. Often, students have listed commonalties that are very specific to the case.

With open-ended discussion, we ask the students to begin to analyze the lists and diagrams and consider how these might affect their lawyering. Did they learn anything new or gain a useful insight into the case or client by making the lists? What might cause us to omit a characteristic like race that another lawyer or the client might list? Inevitably, we get a few good examples that foster awareness of the importance of culture to the attorney-client relationship. Since our ultimate goal is to build awareness, a wide range of examples can be used to convey the lessons the session is designed to teach.

C. Developing Knowledge—Specific and General

One way to acquire general knowledge about the nature of culture is to identify the ways in which the law itself is a culture.... Students come to realize that law has its own language, values, ways of thinking, hierarchy, categories, rules and professional norms. The culture of argument and competition predominate, and time is measured in precise terms.

We have asked students to identify examples of the changes in thinking, communicating, and valuing that they have experienced over the course of two years of law school. Even if students did not themselves detect transformations of the content and style of their communications, undoubtedly friends and family did, and we ask students to talk about those reactions. This discussion facilitates an exploration of students' reactions to the legal culture and the existence of any culture clashes.

We ask students to think about the stress they feel upon entering a courtroom to represent clients and to connect this experience to the stress of entering a culture in which the cultural rules are hidden and one does not know how to predict the responses of others. For example, the introductory rituals of the courtroom are not clear and comfortable for the students. Because the legal culture is not quite as hidden to students as the cultures in which they have been raised, exploring the legal culture presents an opportunity for them to learn about culture generally.

Other ways to teach the general topic of culture is to look at the chart of cross-cultural themes in the materials and to ask students to identify how the particular theme might play out in law practice. By telling a story about their own client interaction or other lawyering they have observed, or by using examples from the material, students can explore cultural themes and their relationship to lawyering.

...

Conversations with clients are often a good way to develop or test culture-specific information. In simulated interviews and planning for client interviews, students should be encouraged to identify the ways they have or will gather culture-specific information. A series of questions that can be used for this purpose are described in Habit Four in the materials.

Because culture is very complex, students should be encouraged to gingerly use the new knowledge they are acquiring. When we learn "specific cultural rules," we have to be careful to apply them correctly and to guard against substituting them for information about the client. Significantly, the client may or may not follow the "rules." Thus, the student who has worked with two or three clients from a particular group should scrupulously avoid generalizing from this experience to conclude that all people from this group are ______ (you can fill in the blank).

What is the proper use of the student's knowledge about the specific cultures and about culture-general themes? The student can use this new information to develop different hypotheses about client behavior based on greater cultural awareness and can explore these with the clients. The more the student knows, the more the student's antennae to difference and similarity will be raised. Being attuned in this way is a critical cross-cultural skill.

...

D. Developing Cross-Cultural Skills

The Habits are designed to help develop analytical and interaction skills. Many of these skills have been taught in the context of other legal work. By furnishing a cross-cultural context, we enhance the students' capacity to employ the skills by focusing attention on why the skills are needed and how they might be used to address potential problems in client interaction.

1. *Raising Antennae to Recognize Ethnocentric Thinking*

a. Habit One: Similarities and Differences

The evolution from being able to talk the talk of "cross-cultural" to walking the walk of "cross-cultural" requires a capacity to recognize when we are making assumptions and judgments about our clients that grow out of our own cultural blinders. If students can attain this heightened awareness, they can begin to develop competence. Habits One and Two encourage students to focus on difference and similarity and their effects on lawyering. By using these habits, students will begin asking themselves questions such as: Why am I judging this client negatively? Is it because we have different values, experiences, or opportunities? Sometimes, as teachers, we have difficulty raising these questions. Students can also use Habit One to reflect on interviews and identify areas that are left unexplored because of assumed similarities.

b. Habit Two: The Three Rings

Habit Two develops skills of analyzing the effects of similarities and differences among the client, legal system and the lawyer.

...

Because students need the practice of applying the framework of culture to analyze a case, Habit Two is one that we also often teach and reinforce in supervision. We have found it especially useful when we or the students are troubled by a case. Often, it helps the lawyer move away from irrelevant facts or issues about the client or the case that are bothering the lawyer and to focus instead on facts and issues that will be relevant to the fact finder.

Habit Two analysis can help the student spot weaknesses and brainstorm possible ways to explain the client's behavior or statements to a court that may be unfamiliar with the client's culture. The student may identify similarities between the court and client and build an explicit connection to the fact finder with these similarities. If the client is resisting the attorney's advice, the lawyer should try to identify the reasons for the client's behavior. Is there something in the client's background or culture that causes this resistance? The student should consider whether she is asking the client to do something that violates the client's norms and, if so, whether there are other possible approaches that might resolve the case. As Kimberly O'Leary recognizes, the identification of difference is a starting point for creative legal thinking; so too is the recognition of similarities between client and court and lawyer.

Like the conversations suggested by Habit One, a regular dialogue between supervisor and student on issues of difference and similarity can make the conversations less loaded because they are not limited to occasions when the student has done or said something that is ethnocentric.

c. Habit Five: The Camel's Back

In classroom teaching of Habit One, a teacher can also introduce Habit Five. Habit Five depends on the analysis of similarities and differences from Habit One and on recognizing some of the more pernicious effects of bias and stereotyped thinking. Once the framework for Habit Five is laid in the classroom, Habit Five conversations are more insightful for students when they are applied to the student's fieldwork. This exploration might be accomplished by discussing whether the student's behavior or thinking would be different if the characteristics of the client changed. The challenge here is to strike the right balance of support and challenge in the conversation with the student. The goal is to provide the students with sufficient support and information so that they can challenge themselves. One way to do so is to acknowledge our own assumptions and biases when they occur.

2. Remaining Flexible and Making Isomorphic Attributions

a. Habit Three: Parallel Universes

Teaching Habit Three is easy. Students grasp the concept readily and its use reinforces the critical skill of remaining flexible and making isomorphic attributions. We usually introduce the Habit by connecting it to the concept of attribution, explaining that cross-cultural interactions often result in lawyer and client ascribing different meaning to the same behaviors. Habit Three invites students to imagine alternative explanations for the client's behavior.

...

By interpreting the behavior and responding to it, students can begin to appreciate that they are substituting their own cultural explanations and norms for the behavior and are making lawyering choices based on these explanations. We usually end with a suggestion that parallel universe thinking alerts us to the possibility that we need additional information to develop a culturally appropriate response.

Including a cautionary note in teaching Habit One and the other Habits allows a teacher to identify the limitations of lists and charts and of culture-centered training. In addition to understanding that we are constantly changing identities, we also need to acknowledge that we may move quickly to sort and order to lessen ambiguity. This may result in our ignoring the complexity of the situation and the relationship, and perhaps contributing to a different kind of misunderstanding. Thus, such situations require flexibility and the ability to be comfortable with not knowing or changing the lists and diagrams to incorporate more and different information.

3. Remaining Non-Judgmental

In our classes, we explicitly address the importance of remaining non-judgmental towards clients and ourselves as learners. We talk about the highly judgmental nature of the legal culture and the special difficulty that lawyers may experience in cross-cultural encounters as a result of our training. To teach the skill of remaining non-judgmental, we use Habits Three, One and Five.

a. Habit Three

In one class, we asked the students to recall a negative judgment that they made about a client's behavior. We asked them to write down the behavior and their interpretation of the behavior. Then, we asked them to use parallel universe thinking to identify at least three other possible explanations of the behavior. When we asked for volunteers, one student identified an instance in which she assumed that her client was no longer interested in a housing eviction case because the client did not respond to the student's phone call and letter. We wrote the behavior on the board and asked the student and her classmates for alternative explanations. We stopped after approximately twenty different interpretations had surfaced. Then, we asked about the sources of the interpretations and how they connected to our experiences and culture.

This technique of exploring alternative explanations is commonly used in clinical teaching to expose students to the limitations of relying on their own experiences to interpret client behavior. By teaching the technique as a cross-cultural lawyering skill, students learn the importance of searching for alternative explanations. They learn to hold off making judgments until they have considered what additional information may be needed to make sense of the behavior.

b. Habit One

In addition to Habit Three reasoning, students can learn to use Habit One thinking when they are feeling judgmental towards a client or client's behavior. Searching for similarities, an integral part of Habit One, is another useful way to counter negative judgments about clients.

c. Habit Five

An essential component of Habit Five is to address one's bias and stereotyping in a non-judgmental way. In teaching the Habits, a teacher needs to set a similarly non-judgmental tone in the classroom.

...

4. Cross-Cultural Communication Skills

The practice of Habit Four increases students' skills at cross-cultural communication. We have taught Habit Four primarily through watching and interpreting videotapes, conducting simulated role plays in class and engaging in reflection in supervision of meetings with clients. These methods of teaching mirror the ones I use to teach interviewing skills. I design short exercises, simulations or videos to focus on parts of an interview for demonstration and analysis. For example, focusing on the beginning of the interview, we can identify the different introductory rituals that cultures use and we can role play the integration of these into the attorney-client interview.

To help students acquire the deep listening skills that cross-cultural interaction requires, we expose students to exercises that help the student become mindful of the interviewing process. Deep listening is difficult for students to master because many western cultures undervalue listening. Most students who were encouraged in their childhood to pursue a legal career probably received this advice because they displayed a tendency to argue, not because they were good listeners.

In watching videotapes or reflecting on case interviewing, we ask whether we are correctly interpreting the client and she us. Especially when we are using translators or working cross-culturally, the lawyer must prepare for the possibility of some misunderstanding. We ask questions designed to surface the cues the students are using to understand the client. These include: What evidence do we have for our interpretation? What non-verbal cues are we using and is our interpretation correct? Is the client's style different from our own and can we separate content from style when the style is so different from our own? What other steps could we take to confirm that our interpretation is the correct one? How many times did we change the topic and what was the result?

Learning deep listening skills proves difficult for students because they are trying to put together many different tasks and sub-tasks in client interactions. Thus, one key piece of the deep listening of Habit Four is to alert students to look for red flags—clues that something is going wrong in the interview. By teaching students this, we implicitly acknowledge that these interviews are difficult and that we often can make mistakes. Recognizing and responding to red flags, which is a complicated task in any interview, requires even greater attention and skill in a cross-cultural interview.

...

Professor Jacobs encourages students to reflect on their role in the interview and the non-verbal cues they may be sending if they find themselves labeling the client as difficult or uncooperative. Reflection on the means available to improve the communication may also allow the student to consider how their clients' experiences with other lawyers or others from the lawyer's cultural group may complicate the interviewing process.

As part of developing the skill of debriefing an interview, students should be asked to examine what they followed up on and what they left unexplored.

...

Conclusion

If we can make the subject of cross-cultural lawyering one that our students and we can talk about, our collective capacity to practice law in non-discriminatory and culturally-sensitive ways will increase access and substantive justice for our clients. By developing a framework and vocabulary for cross-cultural lawyering, Jean and I hope to increase our students' and our own capacities to talk and think about difference and similarities in a more complex manner. If we lessen the anxiety of interacting with others whom we perceive as different, we promote an openness to learning more about our clients and ourselves.

By thinking about this work as creating Habits, we enable students and ourselves to explore issues of difference in a routine way that, we hope, makes conversations less loaded. This spares the teacher the difficulty of figuring out how and when to raise issues like race or gender, stereotyping, bias or others. Instead, the conversation takes place on a regular basis within the framework of the Habits.

Our work on the Habits and learning about cross-cultural teaching in other fields has been among the most stimulating work I have done as a clinical teacher. There are many good resources out there from which we can learn, and we need to continue to create paths to greater cultural competence for ourselves and our students. I agree with Professors Montoya and Harrison that [c]ross-cultural learning is possible only in tandem with others. It is a journey that cannot be taken alone. The borderlands are places of collaboration, of interactivity, of shared as well as opposing values, of exposed and juxtaposed weakness, and of ignorance, unmasked and remasked. Borderlands beckon to risk takers, meaning awakers, and vision makers.

Thus, I end where I began: by thanking colleagues, staff, students and Jean, who have been learners and teachers and who have made this project an enriching journey. As clinical teachers, we have an enormous contribution to make to our profession and the clients it serves if we can build cross-cultural competence in our students and in ourselves. By using the multi-cultural resources and starting the conversations, we start or continue an important journey for ourselves and our students.

...

Endnotes

1. *See* Kimberlé Williams Crenshaw, *This Is Not A Drill: The War Against Antiracist Teaching in America*, 68 UCLA L. Rev. 1702, 1712 n. 17 (2022) (citing, *inter alia*, Alicia Garza, Robin D.G. Kelley, Devon Carbado, Maria Moore, AG Keith Ellison & Kimberlé Crenshaw, *Under the Blacklight: The Fire This Time*, Intersectionality Matters! (June 10, 2020), https://podcasts.apple.com/us/podcast/19-under-the-blacklight-the-fire-this-time/id1441348908?; Angela Onwuachi-Willig, *The Trauma of Awakening to Racism: Did the Tragic Killing of George Floyd Result in Cultural Trauma for Whites?*, 58 Hous. L. Rev. 817 (2021)).

2. *See* Emily Bazelon, *Can North Carolina Get Away With Rolling Back L.G.B.T. Rights?*, N.Y. Times (Mar. 25, 2016) https://www.nytimes.com/2016/03/25/magazine/can-north-carolina-get-away-with-rolling-back-lgbt-rights.html; Pete Williams, *In Landmark Case, Supreme Court Rules LGBTQ Workers Are Protected from Job Discrimination*, NBC News (June 15, 2020), https://www.nbcnews.com/politics/supreme-court/supreme-court-rules-existing-civil-rights-law-protects-gay-lesbian-n1231018 (discussing Bostock v. Clayton County, 140 S. Ct. 1731 (2020); Jo Yurcaba, *Transgender People in 'Survival Mode' as Violence Rises, Anti-Trans Bills Become Law*, NBC News (Nov. 19, 2021), https://www.nbcnews.com/politics/supreme-court/supreme-court-rules-existing-civil-rights-law-protects-gay-lesbian-n1231018/; Anne Branigin & N. Kirpatrick, *Anti-Trans Laws Are on the Rise. Here's a Look at Where—And What Kind*, Wash. Post (Oct. 14, 2022, 8:00 AM), https://www.washingtonpost.com/lifestyle/2022/10/14/anti-trans-bills/.

3. *See, e.g.*, Jill Cowan, *Looking at the Rise of Anti-Asian Racism in the Pandemic*, N.Y. Times (Mar. 15, 2021), https://www.nytimes.com/2021/03/19/us/anti-asian-racism-pandemic.html; Jack Healy, *For Asian Americans Wary of Attacks, Reopening Is Not an Option*, N.Y. Times (June 8, 2021), https://www.nytimes.com/2021/06/08/us/asian-american-attacks.html.

4. *See, e.g.*, Shibley Telhami, *Islamophobia: Making Muslims the Enemy*, N.Y. Times (Jan. 6, 2008), https://www.nytimes.com/2008/01/06/books/review/Telhami-t.html; Erik Bleich & A. Maurits van der Veen, *Newspaper Coverage of Muslims Is Negative. And It's Not Because of Terrorism*, Wash. Post (Dec. 20, 2018), https://www.washingtonpost.com/news/monkey-cage/wp/2018/12/20/newspaper-coverage-of-muslims-is-negative-and-its-not-because-of-terrorism/.

5. See, e.g., Maya Yang, Islamophobia and Antisemitism on Rise in US Amid Israel-Hamas War, Guardian (Nov. 10, 2023, 4:55 PM); Emily Mae Czachor, 'Unprecedented Surge' in Anti-Arab, Anti-Muslim Bias Incidents Reported in U.S. Since Israel-Hamas War, Advocacy Group Says, CBS News (Nov. 9, 2023, 3:42 PM).

6. *See, e.g.*, James Dobbins, Eileen Sullivan & Edgar Sandoval, *Thousands of Migrants Huddle in Squalid Conditions Under Texas Bridge*, N.Y. Times (Oct. 19, 2021), https://www.nytimes.com/2021/09/16/us/texas-migrants-del-rio.html; Bill Chappell, *U.S. Border Agents Chased Migrants on Horseback. A Photographer Explains What He Saw*, NPR (Sept. 21, 2021), https://www.npr.org/2021/09/21/1039230310/u-s-border-agents-haiti-migrants-horses-photographer-del-rio; Sandra Cuffe, *Fleeing the Pandemic and Two Hurricanes, Thousands of Migrants Walk Toward the U.S.*, L.A. Times (Jan. 16, 2021), https://www.latimes.com/world-nation/story/2021-01-16/fleeing-the-pandemic-and-two-hurricanes-thousands-of-migrants-walk-toward-the-united-states.

7. *See, e.g.*, Greta Reich, *Judge Kyle Duncan's Visit to Stanford and the Aftermath, Explained*, Stan. Daily (Apr. 5, 2023, 11:39 PM), https://stanforddaily.com/2023/04/05/judge-duncan-stanford-law-school-explained/; Mark Joseph Stern, *A Trump Judge's Tantrum at Stanford Law Was Part of a Bigger Plan*, Slate (Mar. 13, 2023, 4:53 PM), https://slate.com/news-and-politics/2023/03/trump-judge-kyle-duncan-stanford-law-scotus-audition.html; Eda Aker & Philip Mousavizadeh, *Yale Law Students Protest Anti-LGBTQ Speaker, Armed Police Presence Triggers Backlash*, Yale Daily News (Mar. 15, 2022, 2:14 AM), https://yaledailynews.com/blog/2022/03/15/yale-law-students-protest-anti-lgbtq-speaker-armed-police-presence-triggers-backlash/; Mark Joseph Stern, *The Truth About the Yale Law Protest That Prompted a Federal Judge to Threaten a Clerkship Blacklist*, Slate (Mar. 18, 2022, 1:38 PM), https://slate.com/news-and-politics/2022/03/yale-law-school-laurence-silberman-free-speech-blacklist.html; Francie Diep, *After Academic-Freedom Controversy, Hamline University's*

President Will Step Down, CHRON. HIGHER EDUC. (Apr. 3, 2023), https://www.chronicle.com/article/after-academic-freedom-controversy-hamline-universitys-president-will-step-down; Vimal Patel, *After Lecturer Sues, Hamline University Walks Back Its "Islamophobic" Comments*, N.Y. TIMES (Jan. 17, 2023), https://www.nytimes.com/2023/01/17/us/hamline-lawsuit-prophet-muhammad-religion.html; Vimal Patel & Anemona Hartocollis, N.Y.U. Law Student Sends Anti-Israel Message and Loses a Job Offer, N.Y. TIMES (Oct. 11, 2023), https://www.nytimes.com/2023/10/11/us/nyu-law-harvard-hamas-israel.html ("The actions were part of a wave of fallout on campuses for students, who are deeply polarized over the fighting."); Eren Orbey, The Anguished Fallout from a Pro-Palestinian Letter at Harvard, NEW YORKER (Oct. 20, 2023), https://www.newyorker.com/news/dispatch/the-anguished-fallout-from-a-pro-palestinian-letter-at-harvard; Andrew Hay, US Professors Suspended, Probed Over Gaza War Comments, Reuters (Nov. 17, 2023, 5:22 PM), https://www.reuters.com/world/us/us-professors-suspended-probed-over-gaza-war-comments-2023-11-17/; Collin Binkley, Columbia, Cornell and Other Colleges Face US Inquiries Over Alleged Antisemitism and Islamophobia, AP NEWS (Nov. 17, 2023, 3:32 PM), https://apnews.com/article/israel-hamas-colleges-civil-rights-investigation-discrimination-f93aa9355f4c2d97b188df8546cc5131 ("The federal government has opened civil rights investigations into seven schools and universities over allegations of antisemitism or Islamophobia since the outbreak of the Israel-Hamas war.")

8. *Cf., e.g.*, Milenko Martinovich, *Americans' Partisan Identities are Stronger than Race and Ethnicity, Stanford Scholar Finds*, Stan. News (Aug. 31, 2017), https://news.stanford.edu/2017/08/31/political-party-identities-stronger-race-religion/ ("[T]he strongest attachment, according to recent research from a Stanford scholar, is Americans' connection to their political party. And the strength of that partisan bond—stronger than race, religion, or ethnicity, has amplified the level of political polarization in the U.S., the researcher said."); Jean Guerrero, Opinion, *Gen Z Has Good Reason to be Angry. Will They Burn it all Down?*, L.A. Times (Apr. 3, 2023, 3:01 AM), https://www.latimes.com/opinion/story/2023-04-03/genz-young-voters-polarization-republicans-politics ("[Generation Z] share[s] millennials' progressive ideas on social issues, but are more likely to support radical policies, such as reparations for descendants of enslaved people. They're more likely to believe the government should do more to help people. They believe in advocating for the Other, except when the Other is a bully. 'You either have sensitivity to people or you don't,' Mariah Allen, an 18-year-old Black student at Loyola Marymount University, told me ahead of her class on Bad Bunny's activism. 'If you don't, you're kind of being excluded.'").

9. I choose to capitalize Difference when writing about it as a concept that includes the many ways clients and others are or appear different from a student or a client. "Difference" is capitalized in this chapter when I write about it as a concept that refers to the diverse range of identities, backgrounds, and experiences that affect the unique perspectives, priorities, and relationships among clients, students, teachers, and others involved in a legal case or project. Other scholars of clinical pedagogy have taken a similar approach. *See, e.g.*, Margaret E. Montoya, Comment, *Voicing Difference*, 4 CLINL L. REV. 147 (1997).

10. *See, e.g.*, Nancy B. Miller & Catherine C. Sammons, EVERYBODY'S DIFFERENT: UNDERSTANDING AND CHANGING OUR REACTIONS TO DISABILITIES 3 (1999).

11. *See, e.g.*, Joanna C. Schwartz, *Civil Rights Without Representation*, 64 WM. & MARY L. REV. 641 (2023).

12. *E.g.*, Dimarie Alicea-Lozada, *Text Message Reminders Reduce Failure to Appear Rates and Backlogs*, NAT'L CTR. FOR STATE CTS. (Sept. 7, 2022), https://www.ncsc.org/information-and-resources/trending-topics/trending-topics-landing-pg/text-reminders-reduce-failure-to-appear-rates-and-backlogs.

13. *Cf. generally* Jasmine B. Gonzales Rose, *Towards a Critical Race Theory of Evidence*, 101 MINN. L. REV. 2243 (2017) (deconstructing how the legal system's seemingly neutral or natural assumptions about certain behaviors, like fleeing from police, often actually reflect white normative views rather than some set-in-stone, natural truth).

14. *See generally* Fran Quigley, *Seizing the Disorienting Moment: Adult Learning Theory and the Teaching of Social Justice in Law School Clinics*, 2 CLINICAL L. REV. 37 (1995).

15. *See, e.g.*, Elizabeth Kolbert, *Why Facts Don't Change Our Minds*, New Yorker (Feb. 19, 2017), https://www.newyorker.com/magazine/2017/02/27/why-facts-dont-change-our-minds; Kegan Lahey & Lisa Lahey, *The Real Reason People Won't Change*, Harv. Bus. Rev. Mag. (Nov. 2001), https://hbr.org/2001/11/the-real-reason-people-wont-change ("People rarely realize they hold big assumptions because, quite simply, they accept them as reality. Often formed long ago and seldom, if ever, critically examined, big assumptions are woven into the very fabric of people's existence.... [A]dmitting to big assumptions makes people uncomfortable.").

16. I learned of the concept of "brave places" to Georgetown Law Professor Janel George, speaking during a class on difficult supervision issues. For more on the concept of "brave places," *see* Brian Arao & Kristi Clemens, *From Safe Spaces to Brave Spaces: A New Way to Frame Dialogue Around Diversity and Social Justice*, *in* The Art of Effective Facilitation: Reflections from Social Justice Educations 135–50 (Lisa M. Landreman ed., 2013), available online at https://static1.squarespace.com/static/5b6af3b236099ba883a28b1e/t/5dcc5b2ae2b90a3c5af08fc5/1573673770842/From+Safe+Spaces+to+Brave+Spaces_2013.pdf.

17. Carrie Rothstein-Fisch & Elise Trumbull, Managing Diverse Classrooms: How to Build on Students' Cultural Strengths 35 (2008).

18. Shahrokh Falati, *The Makings of a Culturally Savvy Lawyer: Novel Approaches for Teaching and Assessing Cross-Cultural Skills in Law School*, 49 J.L. & Educ. 627, 637 (2020).

19. Bill Ong Hing, *Raising Personal Identification Issues of Class, Race, Ethnicity, Gender, Sexual Orientation, Physical Disability, and Age in Lawyering Courses*, 45 Stan. L. Rev. 1807 (1993).

20. *See* Norrinda Brown Hayat, *Freedom Pedagogy: Toward Teaching Antiracist Clinics*, Clinical L. Rev. 149, 160 (2021) (discussing the Cite Black Women movement to center the experiences and knowledge of Black scholars in academic spaces).

21. *See id.*

22. *See, e.g.*, Anastasia M. Boles, *The Culturally Proficient Law Professor: Beginning the Journey*, 48 N.M. L. Rev 145, 146 (2018).

23. *See id.*

24. *See generally* Michelle Alexander, The New Jim Crow: Mass Incarceration in the Age of Colorblindness (2010); David Cole, No Equal Justice: Race and Class in the American Criminal Justice System (1999); Policing the Black Man: Arrest, Prosecution, and Imprisonment (Angela J. Davis ed., 2017); Dean Spade, Normal Life: Administrative Violence, Critical Trans Politics, & The Limits of Law ix–xv (2015).

25. *See, e.g.*, Kimberlé Williams Crenshaw, *Mapping the Margins: Intersectionality, Identity Politics and Violence Against Women of Color*, in Critical Race Theory: The Key Writings That Formed the Movement 357–83 (Kimberlé Williams Crenshaw, Neil Gotanda, Gary Peller & Kendall Thomas eds., 1996); *see also* Jane Coaston, *The Intersectionality Wars*, Vox (May 28, 2019, 9:09 AM), https://www.vox.com/the-highlight/2019/5/20/18542843/intersectionality-conservatism-law-race-gender-discrimination (discussing contemporary political debates about Crenshaw's intersectionality thesis).

26. *See, e.g.*, Dana Brownlee, *Dear White People: When You Say You "Don't See Color," This Is What We Really Hear*, Forbes (June 19, 2022, 2:17 PM), https://www.forbes.com/sites/danabrownlee/2022/06/19/dear-white-people-when-you-say-you-dont-see-color-this-is-what-we-really-hear/?sh=79eb47ff26d6 (white people claiming not to "see color" regarding race serves only to "claim an unearned high ground that abruptly stifles and neutralizes very necessary, long overdue grappling with fundamental issues of racism and inequity"); Larry Frelazzo, *Saying "I Don't See Color" Denies the Racial Identity of Students*, Education Week (Feb. 2, 2020), https://www.edweek.org/teaching-learning/opinion-saying-i-dont-see-color-denies-the-racial-identity-of-students/2020/02; Jarrett Hill, Opinion, *Dear "White Allies," Stop Saying That You "Don't See Color,"* NBC News (Dec. 2016, 6:14 PM), https://www.nbcnews.com/news/nbcblk/opinion-dear-tomi-lahren-please-stop-saying-you-dont-see-n690801 ("The idea that you are blind to my existence as a Black man doesn't say to me that you lack a bias, or that you are somehow woke. It says to me that you ignore my reality and you choose to do it, because (save for legal blindness) there's no way that you can't actually see me and my melanin.").

27. *See* LAW SCHOOL SURVEY OF STUDENT ENGAGEMENT (LSSSE) 2008 ANNUAL SURVEY RESULTS, STUDENT ENGAGEMENT IN LAW SCHOOL: PREPARING 21ST CENTURY LAWYERS, available at http://lssse.iub.edu/2008_Annual_Report/ (finding roughly 20 percent of students at A.B.A. accredited law schools self-reported that their school did little or nothing to encourage contact and understanding with "people of other racial and ethnic backgrounds"); Marjorie A. Silver, *Emotional Competence, Multicultural Lawyering and Race*, 3 FLA. COASTAL L.J. 219, 229 (2002) (noting that almost half of the largest cities in America have fewer whites than racial groups who have historically been minorities).

28. *See generally* MODEL RULES OF PRO. CONDUCT rr. 1.1–1.6.

29. Antoinette Sedillo Lopez, *Making and Breaking Habits: Teaching (and Learning) Cultural Context, Self-Awareness, and Intercultural Communication Through Case Supervision in a Client-Service Legal Clinic*, 28 WASH. U. J. L. & POL'Y 37, 39 (2008).

30. *See* Susan Bryant, *The Five Habits: Building Cross-Culture Competence in Lawyers*, 8 CLINICAL L. REV. 33, 57–64 (2001). Unconscious incompetence is when students are unaware that they are lacking cultural awareness, while unconscious competence is when they unconsciously incorporate cross-cultural awareness into client interactions. *Id.* at 62–63.

31. The importance of feeling respected and included has been extensively studied by scholars of procedural justice. *Cf. generally* Tom R. Tyler, *Why People Cooperate with Organizations: An Identity-Based Perspective*, 21 RSCH. ORG. BEHAV. 201 (1999); Tom R. Tyler & Steven L. Blader, *The Group Engagement Model: Procedural Justice, Social Identity, and Cooperative Behavior*, 7 PERSONALITY AND SOC. PSYCH. REV. 349 (2003).

32. *See, e.g.*, Matthew Clair, *Being A Disadvantaged Criminal Defendant: Mistrust and Resistance in Attorney-Client Interactions*, SOCIAL FORCES 1 (2020) ("Given racialized and classed constraints, many disadvantaged defendants mistrust their court-appointed lawyers. Their mistrust often results in withdrawal from their lawyers and active efforts to cultivate their own legal knowledge and skills. Defendants use their lay legal expertise to work around and resist the authority of their lawyers. Defense attorneys and judges respond with silencing and coercion, given the unwritten norms and rules of the court."); Eve Brensike Primus, *Culture as a Structural Problem in Indigent Defense*, 100 MINN. L. REV. 1769, 1769 (2016) (arguing that when indigent-defense delivery systems have a culture of not fully "fight[ing] for their clients," it causes "many indigent defendants who go through the criminal justice system (as well as the friends and families of defendants who suffer through these ordeals with them) [to] feel confused, angry, and ignored."). Research has also shown that contact with the criminal legal system affects more than just how individuals interact with the criminal legal system itself but also bleeds into how they orient themselves towards other legal or political institutions and the state writ large. *See, e.g.*, Vesla M. Weaver & Amy E. Lerman, *Political Consequences of the Carceral State*, AM. POL. SCI. REV. 1, 1–2 (2010) ("The argument we make here is that the criminal justice system is a primary site of civic education. Through both interpretive and resource mechanisms, custodial interactions negatively affect the likelihood of participating in politics and carrying out the responsibilities of citizenship.... [W]e find that the effect of exposure to criminal justice dwarfs some of even the most important predictors in the resource models of participation. The robustness of the relationship, even after accounting for other factors, suggests that punitive encounters with the state foster mistrust of political institutions and a weakened attachment to the political process."); Jonathan Ben-Menachem & Kevin T. Morris, *Ticketing and Turnout: The Participatory Consequences of Low-Level Police Contact*, AM. POL. SCI. REV. 1 (2022) (empirical study finding that even "lower-level" police contacts like traffic stops "materially decrease" voting participating by both Black and non-Black individuals).

33. *See* Robert F. Cochran, John M.A. DiPippa & Martha M. Peters, THE COUNSELOR-AT-LAW: A COLLABORATIVE APPROACH TO CLIENT INTERVIEWING AND COUNSELING 205–23 (2d ed. 2006).

34. *See id.*; Tamar Jacobson, CONFRONTING OUR DISCOMFORT: CLEARING THE WAY FOR ANTI-BIAS IN EARLY CHILDHOOD 1 (2003); *see also* Rothstein-Fisch & Trumbull, *supra* note 17, at 106. In the classroom setting, Rothstein-Fisch describes a situation where an administrator believed a Latino student was lying because he did not make eye contact with his superior when talking. However, the student's teacher—who had greater familiarity with the student and his culture—knew that his looking down was a sign of respect rather than of guilt. *Id.* Professor Susan Bryant describes another

hypothetical involving potential cultural difference—a non-English speaking client brings her brother to an initial intake meeting to discuss a landlord-tenant dispute, and the lawyer must decide how to address the brother's continued presence for a further consultation—as an example of how "the lawyer's assumptions and responses to the situation [may be] based on the lawyer's experiences or culture" and how the lawyer can "correctly attribute meaning to their clients' behavior and thereby make better lawyering decisions." Bryant, *supra* note 30, at 34–35, 45.

35. *See* Malcolm S. Knowles, The Modern Practice of Adult Education 44 (1970); Frank S. Bloch, *The Andragogical Basis of Clinical Legal Education*, 35 Vand. L. Rev. 321, 330 (1982).

36. *See, e.g.*, Abbe Smith, *Rosie O'Neill Goes to Law School: The Clinical Education of the Sensitive New Age Public Defender*, 28 Harv. C.R.-C.L. L. Rev. 1 (1993); Bryant, *supra* note 30.

37. *See, e.g.*, Robert Rader, *Confessions of Guilt: A Clinic Student's Reflections on Representing Indigent Criminal Defendants*, 1 Clinical L. Rev. 299 (1994).

38. After being exposed to cultural otherness, an individual may experience the phenomenon now widely referred to as "culture shock." Within the phenomenon, first given a name by Kalvero Oberg in 1960, the person experiences four successive stages: first, an initial fascination and excitement at the newness of the encounter; second, anxiety that what that individual knows will be inadequate to fit in within such newness; third, an initial understanding of what differences are present; and fourth, complete adjustment as the individual adapts what they know to fit this initially foreign situation. *See* Kalvero Oberg, *Culture Shock and the Problem of Adjustment in New Cultural Environments*, 7 Practical Anthropology 177–82 (1960), *reprinted in* Culture, Communication and Conflict: Readings in Intercultural Relations 117–168 (Gary R. Weaver ed., 2d. ed. 1998); *see also* Delia Flanja, *Culture Shock in Intercultural Communication*, 4 Studia Europaea 107–25 (2009), available at https://www.thefreelibrary.com/Culture+shock%20+in+intercultural+communication.-a0221850915 (discussing concretely Olberg's four stages of culture shock).

39. *See* Jane Aiken, *Striving to Teach Justice*, 4 Clinical L. Rev. 1 (1997).

40. *See* Charles J. Ogletree, *Beyond Justifications: Seeking Motivations to Sustain Public Defenders*, 106 Harv. L. Rev. 1239, 1290–94 (1993).

41. *See* Jacobson, *supra* note 34, at 7–8.

42. Much of the material from the next few paragraphs originated in an email conversation between the author and Georgetown Law Professor Julie Cohen, Mark Claster Mamolen Professor of Law and Technology.

43. *See, e.g.*, Montoya, *supra* note 9, at 152 ("Engaging in public dialogue about Difference ... requires practice because we so often can, and do, get things wrong. We learn vocabularies and realize we must re-learn more accurate ones. We grapple with complex theories, only to find they have been replaced by emerging ones. We employ provisional pedagogical and interactive strategies because we are constantly in a learning mode.")

44. Arlie Russell Hochschild, Strangers in their Own Land: Anger and Mourning on the American Right (2016).

45. Bryant, *supra* note 30, at 36.

46. *Id.*

47. *See* Falati, *supra* note 18, at 637.

48. *See id.* (citing Milton J. Bennett, *A Developmental Approach to Training for Intercultural Sensitivity*, 10 Int'l J. Intercultural Rel., 179, 179–95 (1986)).

49. *See id.* at 637–38 (citing Bennett, *supra* note 48).

50. *Id.* at 637 (emphasis original) (citing Bennett, *supra* note 48, at 182).

51. *Id.* at 638 (emphasis original) (citing Bennett, *supra* note 48, at 181–82).

52. *See id.* at 640 (citing Kikanza Nuri-Robins, Dolores B. Lindsey, Randall B. Lindsey & Raymond D. Terrell, Culturally Proficient Instruction: A Guide for People Who Teach 80 (3d ed.

2012)). The Nuri-Robins *et al.* model also uses six stages. The first category describes the person who is "culturally destructive" and seeks to eliminate what is different to the dominant group. The second category focuses on a person who is "culturally incapacitated," referring to the ability to tolerate cultural differences without actually accepting it. The third category concerns people who are "culturally blind," meaning that they do not see difference at all and treat all students the same. The fourth stage is "culturally precompetent," where the person understands the importance of developing the skills to respond but lacks the ability to respond appropriately to differences. In the fifth stage, the person is culturally competent and can understand differences, while responding appropriately. In the sixth and final stage, the person is "culturally proficient" and can appreciate both the differences and similarities between the minority and majority groups. *Id.*

53. Bryant, *supra* note 30, at 64–67 ("Habit One first asks students to list and diagram similarities and differences between themselves and their clients and then to explore the significance of these similarities and differences."); *id.* at 68–70 ("Habit Two asks students to identify and analyze the possible effects of similarities and differences on the interaction between the client, the legal decision-maker, and the lawyer—the three rings."); *id.* at 70–72 ("Habit Three teaches students a method for exploring alternative explanations for clients' behaviors."); *id.* at 72–76 ("Habit Four encourages conscious attention to the process of communication—a skill and perspective that clinical teachers have used to improve interviewing skills in all attorney-client relationships."); *id.* at 76–78 ("Habit Five proposes two ways to work with bias and stereotype. First, to prevent these factors from affecting the relationship or decisions, Habit Five encourages the student to create settings in which bias and stereotype are less likely to govern. Second, the Habit promotes reflection and change of perspectives with a goal of eliminating bias."). For a concrete example of how to teach Habit Two, for example, see Hayat, *supra* note 20, at 159–60.

54. Bryant, *supra* note 30, at 49; *see also* Hayat, *supra* note 20, at 157 ("Over the course of several pieces building on the *Habits*, Bryant and Peters offer the modest clinician suggestions for 'removing the rocks and sowing the seeds of constructive conversations about race' in class and suggest a structure for holding such conversations. There is no place for racial modesty in the era of the Movement for Black Lives. We cannot merely discuss race in class, but must center Blackness in our teaching, scholarship, and practices. So doing recognizes our clients as experts in their own lived experiences, including about their own lived experiences as Black people in America, and is literally central to understanding them and their legal cases and what will make them whole. Alternately, a failure to acknowledge the centrality of race in lawyering and counseling not only breeds distrust between lawyer and client, but it also harms outcomes.") (internal citations omitted).

55. *See* Falati, *supra* note 18, at 628.

56. *Cf. generally* Crenshaw, *supra* note 1 (imploring legal institutions to confront their "historical agnosticism toward racial subordination" and to resist attacks against, and misrepresentations of, Critical Race Theory in the classroom).

57. For example, Georgetown Law in September 2021 added a school-wide Institutional Learning Outcome along those same lines: "Ability to think critically about the law's claim to neutrality and its differential effects on subordinated groups, including those identified by race, gender, indigeneity, and class." Georgetown University Law Center's Institutional Learning Outcomes, https://www.law.georgetown.edu/admissions-aid/aba-required-disclosures/institutional-learning-outcomes/.

58. Some institutions have taken the initiative to expressly offer suggestions of alternatives to language that is or may be harmful. For example, in the wake of George Floyd's murder in 2020, Stanford University's CIO Council and People of Color in Technology affinity group published an "Elimination of Harmful Language Initiative" (EHLI), originally to course-correct harmful language in the information technology space, but that later broadened into a more comprehensive language-use guide. Conservative backlash from the *Wall Street Journal* editorial page and Fox News, among other outlets, was swift, decrying "political correctness" while often misunderstanding the nature and purpose of the EHLI. It wasn't long before the EHLI was retracted and removed from Stanford's website. *See, e.g.*, Susan D'Agostino, *Amid Backlash, Stanford Pulls "Harmful Language" List*, Inside Higher Ed

(Jan. 10, 2023), https://www.insidehighered.com/news/2023/01/11/amid-backlash-stanford-removes-harmful-language-list; Mark Allen Cu, *University Removes "Harmful Language" List Following Backlash*, STAN. DAILY (Jan. 8, 2023, 11:11 PM), https://stanforddaily.com/2023/01/08/university-removes-harmful-language-list-following-backlash/; Diya Sabharwal, Opinion, *Was the "Elimination of Harmful Language Initiative" Really That Bad?*, STAN. DAILY (Jan. 11, 2023, 7:46 PM), https://stanforddaily.com/2023/01/11/sabharwal-was-the-elimination-of-harmful-language-initiative-really-that-bad/ (defending the EHLI). The EHLI is still available online in archived form at https://stanforddaily.com/wp-content/uploads/2023/01/Stanford-EHLI-Harmful-Language-List.pdf (last visited Jun. 11, 2023). For more on the intent/impact distinction, see, e.g., Melanie Tannenbaum, *"But I Didn't Mean It!" Why It's So Hard to Prioritize Impacts Over Intents*, PSYSOCIETY (Oct. 14, 2013), https://blogs.scientificamerican.com/psysociety/e2809cbut-i-didne28099t-mean-ite2809d-why-ite28099s-so-hard-to-prioritize-impacts-over-intents/.

59. *See generally* Hochschild, *supra* note 44.

60. Then-U.S. Attorney General Eric Holder found this out when he called us a "nation of cowards" when it comes to discussing the racial divide. This quote was reprinted in Charles J. Ogletree, Jr. & Johanna Wald, *After Shirley Sherrod, We All Need to Slow Down and Listen*, WASH. POST, Jul. 25, 2010, at A19.

61. *See* Jacobson, *supra* note 34, at 49.

62. *See* Silver, *supra* note 27, at 235; *see generally* Derald Wing Sue & David Sue, COUNSELING THE CULTURALLY DIFFERENT: THEORY AND PRACTICE (2d ed. 1990).

63. *See* Boles, *supra* note 22, at 165.

64. Rachel D. Godsil, Linda R. Tropp, Phillip Atiba Goff & john a. powell, *The Science of Equality, Volume 1: Addressing Implicit Bias, Racial Anxiety, and Stereotype Threat in Education and Health Care*, Perception Inst. (Nov. 2014), at 31–33, available at https://equity.ucla.edu/wp-content/uploads/2016/11/Science-of-Equality-Vol.-1-Perception-Institute-2014.pdf (quoting Gregory M. Walton, Steven J. Spencer & Sam Erman, *Affirmative Meritocracy*, 7 SOC. ISSUES AND POL'Y REV. 1 (2013)).

65. *Id.* at 31–32 (citation omitted).

66. *Id.* at 32.

67. *Id.* at 32–33 (citing Phillip Atiba Goff, Claude M. Steele & Paul G. Davies, *The Space Between Us: Stereotype Threat and Distance in Interracial Contacts*, 94 J. PERSONALITY AND SOC. PSYCH. 91 (2008)).

68. Boles, *supra* note 22, at 164 (discussing the numerous problems that racial anxiety can cause in a classroom, including depriving interpersonal interactions of the full attention and energy of the participants).

69. *See* Jacobson, *supra* note 34, at 20; Carwina Weng, *Multicultural Lawyering: Teaching Psychology to Develop Cultural Self-Awareness*, 11 CLINICAL L. REV. 369, 397–99 (2005).

70. *See* Lopez, *supra* note 29, at 45–46.

71. *See* Jacobson, *supra* note 34, at 49–51.

72. *See* Miller & Sammons, *supra* note 10, at 7.

73. See Falati, *supra* note 18, at 643.

74. *See id.*

75. Ogletree & Wald, *supra* note 60.

76. *See* Miller & Sammons, *supra* note 10, at 7.

77. *See* Okianer Christian Dark, *Incorporating Issues of Race, Gender, Class, Sexual Orientation, and Disability into Law School Teaching*, 32 WILLAMETTE L. REV. 541, 557–60 (1996).

78. Bryant, *supra* note 30, at 78–107.

Eleven

CLASSROOM TEACHING AS SUPERVISION

As early as 1980, the Association of American Law School (AALS)—ABA Committee on Guidelines for Clinical Education included classroom instruction as part of clinical methodology.[1] Notwithstanding the AALS-ABA report, not all law schools required clinics or other experiential courses to conduct classroom sessions to provide some structure and theory to practice component.[2] Even though most interactions between a student and a experiential course teacher occur in case- or project-supervision sessions, the American Bar Association (ABA) Accreditation Standards now require that every experiential course also include a classroom instructional component.[3]

The nature of the classroom instruction differs among traditional clinics, externships, and hybrid clinics. Because the ABA rules do not prescribe any specific guidance, the classroom component could be about substantive law, practical lawyering skills, learning methods, professionalism, or anything else as long as the experiential course, as a whole, puts the student in the role of a lawyer with opportunities to advise or represent clients.[4] Despite this requirement and the now-common practice of including classroom instruction, the literature about clinical teaching seldom focuses on the role and nature of the classroom component in clinical or other experiential courses. Thus, teachers sometimes struggle to determine the goals and content of their individual clinic classes, or the pedagogical techniques that best convey the knowledge they seek to impart.

Case supervision sessions and classroom teaching are different, although both relate to the concept of supervision. They are both a mix of art and science but generally have different goals. Thus, the development of a classroom session differs from the planning of a supervision session. Despite these differences, good classroom teachers and good supervisors possess similar traits. These traits may come easier to some people than others but are all fundamentally *learnable skills*. In other words, great teachers are made, not born, even if some have a head start through luck of the genetic lottery.

Rob Jenkins, an English professor at Georgia State University's Perimeter College, has outlined four key traits of teaching excellence: personality, presence, preparation, and passion.[5] Although some people have a funnier or more open personality than others, the behaviors that create one's personality are still learnable skills. For example, teachers can learn to think more creatively about their classes by using more interesting techniques proposed by pedagogical theorists or by their own colleagues.

Teachers can learn ways to be more approachable without surrendering to the notion of merely becoming the students' friend. And while hierarchies abound in the academic atmosphere, teachers can all learn to take themselves less seriously.[6] Presence, in turn, involves a charismatic command of an audience's attention. But it also means focusing on *being present*, that is being aware in the moment of the feel of the class and listening carefully and responding clearly to the students comments and questions while teaching.[7] Jenkins believes that the third trait, preparation, is the facet most in a teacher's control. Preparation takes multiple forms. Long-term preparation involves career planning, like whether to pursue an advanced degree, or (for law faculty advancement purposes) obtaining additional professional experience and training in teaching, scholarship, or the practice of law. Medium-term preparation involves maintaining one's competency through research and writing about one's legal specialty and teaching, reading the literature about teaching methodology and legal practice, and attending various clinical conferences. Short-term preparation involves what teachers do or should do every day to prepare for every class, and to critically reflect and reassess one's knowledge and methods after the class is over.[8] Finally, Jenkins highlights passion, which is also fully in a teacher's control. It involves "love for students, for your subject matter, and for your job as a teacher."[9] In addition to these concrete skills, perspective is also critical. "Good teachers are those who remember being a student," and channel that perspective into all aspects of how they teach.[10]

Ultimately, being an excellent classroom teacher is all about the work one does to *become* an excellent classroom teacher. That work is hard and often requires becoming comfortable with a high degree of discomfort. But at its core, the set of skills required to be a great teacher are fundamentally learnable and thus achievable by anyone willing to care enough about the craft and to put in the work. The goal of this chapter is to help provide the scaffolding for doing that work.

Building an Educational Model

Because experiential courses seldom enroll more than sixteen students, teachers are able to employ many techniques to convey information. Like most law school professors, clinicians sometimes deliver traditional Socratic-style lectures. But given the nature of clinical education, the Socratic method will not be effective in every class or supervision session. While that teaching method may be useful when discussing aspects of substantive law, it is seldom effective when demonstrating the relationship between substantive law and practice.[11] Moreover, law students, as adult learners, do not always respond well to the typical methods of the legal academy. Thus, many clinical teachers seek teaching strategies and methods that are effective for adult learners in other contexts and replicate them in the clinic classroom. Indeed, the notion of combining theory and practice as a learning experience came from the medical schools' grand rounds and supervised practice. Simulations and case studies have roots in business schools.[12] Recognizing their value in clinical courses, teachers have over time adapted simulations,[13] performance critiques,[14] case rounds,[15] structured discussions,[16] and problem-solving exercises[17] and added them to their classroom repertoire.

Most law professors do not receive any training as teachers before they enter the academy.[18] As a consequence, many newer teachers merely replicate the teaching strategies of their former professors.[19] Those former teachers may or may not have been good role models and seldom employed teaching techniques relevant to the needs of a clinical teacher. Moreover, new professors should be reluctant to implement large law school classroom teaching strategies in the clinical classroom unless there is a specific and goal-driven reason to do so.

The uneven performances new teachers have witnessed in the past often cause them to believe that creating and implementing proper classroom teaching techniques is based on an innate talent that one either does or does not have. Some may believe good teachers are simply born great, while the rest of us are winging it and trying in vain to catch up. Like most of life's endeavors, however, hard work and clear guidelines can improve any and every teacher's performance. Although all teachers can become better at their art, few law schools provide new law professors with training to become adequate, let alone good, classroom teachers. As a result, many new teachers, both clinical and nonclinical, plunge into their first classroom experiences with little, if any, instructions on how to ensure that the way they teach their classes relates to what students are expected to learn from the lessons. Although the ABA Accreditation Standards now require law schools to establish learning outcomes that guarantee competency in the knowledge, skills, and ethics of the profession, law schools and their faculty are still left to their own devices to establish the methodology to achieve those outcomes.[20]

Clinical pedagogy evolved to incorporate real-life experiences into the educational mission. The first generation of modern clinical teachers spent much of their time trying to define the essential elements of clinical pedagogy and to understand what teaching modalities best served experiential education. Their task was enhanced by the many national and regional conferences supported by the AALS and the Clinical Legal Education Association (CLEA). Yet few, if any, of the sessions at these conferences were devoted to classroom-teaching techniques. That remains the case today. Clinical teachers often forget that classroom sessions are part of the supervision process. As such, every action they take in the clinical classroom is, like those in a supervision session, guided by goals. Those goals are achieved by intentionally driven teaching modalities that address topics which frequently arise while supervising student cases. The work in the classroom thus makes student supervision sessions more efficient. Teachers need to learn the basics of planning and executing classroom teaching techniques and be intentional when choosing their topic and methods as they design each class and the entire curriculum. Classroom work should always complement the work students perform on their cases or projects.

All teachers, new and experienced, have concerns and anxieties about classroom teaching. Discussing those concerns and anxieties with other teachers, both new and experienced, helps them develop methods to confront and overcome substantive concerns and anxieties and to develop their own classroom teaching styles. It also enables them to experiment with techniques they glean from other faculty members that alter or complement their own methods as they grow into expert teachers.[21] Equally important, they will come to realize that classroom teaching is not intuitive, but rather a skill they can master.

The Wiggins and Brookfield Theories

The Backward Design Process

Most of the literature about classroom teaching modalities does not come from the legal academy. Instead, it comes from articles and books by college professors such as Joseph Lowman,[22] Nira Hativa,[23] Stephen Brookfield,[24] and Grant Wiggins.[25] These days, many other college professors are writing about teaching theory. Clinical teachers can also learn some helpful classroom-teaching methods from the vast array of articles written about clinical education, even though most of them do not specifically address classroom teaching.[26] In our fellows training course at Georgetown and in our national training sessions for other law professors, we especially encourage the use of techniques developed by Stephen Brookfield and Grant Wiggins. Professor Wiggins' theory of backward design begins with the premise that teachers are designers, "crafting curriculum and learning experiences to meet specified purposes."[27] He asserts that a curriculum should be designed to meet a particular end, and not originate from methods or activities. Thus, professors must first understand the goals of the curriculum and each individual class before contemplating teaching modalities and learning exercises to use and before assigning pre-class readings. Further, he believes that the entire curriculum will fail unless teachers know what they want the students to understand before the semester begins.[28] In designing a course, teachers should focus on what a student's understanding of clinic goals will "look like in terms of concrete student performance."[29] Teachers need to create observable events that demonstrate an understanding, or a lack of understanding, of the clinic goals. Without observable actions, teachers have no way to determine whether learning has taken place. Although Wiggins' theory relates to the entire clinic curriculum, it also applies to each and every individual class comprising that curriculum.[30] Indeed, teachers need to make these goal-driven decisions while they construct a syllabus[31] and plan the clinic orientation sessions.[32]

Wiggins' backward design process has three stages: (1) identifying a desired result, which involves clarifying priorities;[33] (2) determining the acceptable evidence that will establish what is necessary to demonstrate that the students understand the material;[34] and (3) planning learning experiences and instruction to formulate the most effective way to teach the material so that it will result in the observable desired outcomes.[35] The following two examples illustrate backward design in action.

First, working in the University of Denver Sturm College of Law's Movement Lawyering Lab, Professors Alexi Freeman and Lindsey Webb identified a learning goal of "develop[ing] a base level understanding and familiarity with the multi-faceted strategies employed by movement lawyers in partnership with organized communities."[36] A critical component of that goal is the decentering of lawyers *lawyering*, and instead considering strategies other than adversarial litigation to help achieve their clients' (i.e., a movement's) objectives.[37] That learning goal, in turn, created a "bucket" into which they could then sort class topics like Strategic Communications, Data Analysis, Legislative Advocacy and Drafting, and Rapid Response.[38]

Second, working in Georgetown Law's Juvenile Justice Clinic, Professors Eduardo Ferrer and Kristin Henning identified four critical "frames" for students "to consider and apply ... throughout every aspect of their client representation and coursework:" adolescence, race, trauma, and sexual orientation and gender identity.[39] Because those frames are so "pervasive" to the clinic's work, they formed "a key pillar around which [the clinic's] course is designed."[40] That goal, in turn, sets the table for the clinic's construction, from the syllabus (which introduces the themes and identifies which classes focus on them and when) to the seminars and readings (into which the frames are comprehensively "woven").[41] As the semester progresses, they add layers of complexity and nuance to the frames, expanding students' understanding of how they can use the frames with the law to challenge oppressive structures and better advocate for their clients.[42]

These examples show how Wiggins' backward design method forces teachers to focus on building students' understanding of a concept when designing a curriculum rather than merely focusing on increasing their knowledge and skills.[43] Teaching students to understand a concept entails more than just knowing the sum total of all the facts. Students who achieve understanding are able to think critically about what they know, draw conclusions, reflect on what they have learned,[44] and transfer the knowledge and skills to other circumstances This notion comports with the concepts of metacognition and transference discussed earlier in Chapter 4, Supervising Cases and Projects.[45]

The Brookfield Theory

Professor Brookfield's theory recognizes that even when adhering to the Wiggins method, teachers will sometimes be presented with often uncontrollable situations,[46] in which they have to improvise or "muddle through."[47] Brookfield suggests that practical reasoning is likely to be the best way for the teachers to get through uncommon situations.[48] Practical reasoning includes three characteristics: (1) scanning—quickly identifying and understanding the existence of the uncommon situation; (2) appraisal—interpreting the situation given previous experiences; and (3) action—taking action that one believes best fits the situation based on one's interpretations.[49] Brookfield has four core assumptions around which his theory is based: "[s]killful teaching is whatever helps students learn[;] [s]killful teachers adopt a critically reflective stance toward their practice[;][t]he most important knowledge skillful teachers need to do good work is a constant awareness of how students are experiencing their learning and perceiving teachers' actions[; and] ... students of any age should be treated as adults."[50]

Brookfield delineates a number of methods and strategies that teachers can use to implement skillful teaching in the classroom. In order to encourage student engagement in the classroom, Brookfield suggests that teachers engage students with several iterations of reflective activities, including, for example: the "one-minute paper" (clinicians call this a "quick-write") which asks students to write for one minute on some topic covered in class that day;[51] student learning journals (long used by clinical teachers to encourage students' self-reflection) in which students describe their daily or weekly difficulties and learning experiences;[52] and the Critical Incident Questionnaire (CIQ), an instrument given to students at the end of the week that asks them to reflect back on specific moments in class that week when they felt "engaged" and when they felt "distanced;" what anyone did that they found "affirming or helpful" or that they found "puzzling or confusing;" and, finally, what "surprised [them] the most."[53] Brookfield also describes methods for establishing credibility and authenticity in the classroom—methods that he believes are essential to teaching students effectively.[54] His methods generally focus on creating a relationship between the students and teacher such that the students will trust their teachers when they have to improvise or steer the class to a discussion of different and challenging issues.[55] This trust and flexibility is especially important in clinical teaching, since legal work resides in uncertainty and indeterminacy.

Using the Theories to Develop a Clinic Seminar Class

My colleagues, Professors Deborah Epstein and Jane Aiken, and I proposed an outline for planning a clinic class in our book, TEACHING THE CLINIC SEMINAR.[56] Using backward design, we proposed the following structure.

1. Why teach this class in a clinic seminar;
2. Learning goals and concrete student behaviors that demonstrate learning in relation to those goals;
3. Common student misunderstandings;
4. Reading assignment;
5. Assignment in preparation for class;
6. The Class:
    a. Introductory lecture,
    b. Set up,
    c. Exercises,
    d. Learning Prompts;
7. Wrap-up;
8. Connecting back to client representation:
    a. End-of-class learning prompts,
    b. End-of-class critical incident questionnaire,
    c. Post-class reflection memo.[57]

The first two are the obvious starting point. We included analyzing students' common misunderstandings because students may come to class with prior knowledge of a topic from social media, movies, or plays. "Even the most careful, goal-driven seminar plan can be subverted if a teacher is unaware of the misconceptions students bring with them to the topic at hand. Adult learners bring strong ideas of their own to all seminar subjects."[58] "Teachers need to pay attention to the incomplete understandings, the false beliefs, and the naïve renditions of concepts that learners bring with them to a given subject.... These preconceptions must be addressed in order for them to change their beliefs."[59] So, planning has to include what students need to unlearn as well as what they need to learn. Planning reading assignments, assignments in preparation for class, and teaching modalities are discussed later in this chapter.

We suggested that teachers create learning prompts for each class.

> Learning prompts are questions posed by a teacher and designed to support the identified student learning goals for a class. They are an essential part of promoting classroom learning, particularly in the context of a participatory exercise. Learning prompts can: (1) help students reflect on and gain insight about the choices they have made; (2) help students move past common pre-existing misconceptions; and (3) help the instructor assess student understanding. Learning prompts tend to be most effective when the teacher has clearly thought through the particular student learning goal each one best supports.[60]

Finally, we suggested that classes need some sort of formal end to the class—a wrap-up. Rather than just ending after the class when formal instruction is over, we suggest that faculty save some time at the end of each class to "to explicitly name the central lessons and "take away" points of the class. To take maximum advantage of these last few moments, a teacher could connect general learning goals with the particular issues raised and with insights gained by the students in a participatory exercise. By explicitly naming learning insights, a teacher can help students obtain clarity in their thinking, as well as encourage connections with other class sessions and clinic field work."[61]

Student Engagement and Learning Styles

Successful teachers recognize that successful classes occur when they instill an "intellectual excitement" in their students that, in turn, creates an "interpersonal rapport" between them.[62] Successful learning environments are characterized by "clarity, organization, stimulation of student interest and engagement, and a positive classroom climate."[63] Diminished student learning can occur if these elements are absent, even when the class is properly designed. Law school classroom instruction is often ineffective when visual information, written lesson plans or outlines, variation in presentation style, or a democratic classroom environment are absent.[64] Although teachers generally agree that clarity is an essential characteristic of effective teaching, engaging students with the material appropriate to varied learning styles is also necessary for successful learning.[65] Similarly, creating an environment in which students feel comfortable voicing their opinions, are encouraged to pay attention to the opinions of others, and encouraged to constructively respond to others will result in a more engaged and active classroom.[66]

Students usually come to the clinic ready to be fully engaged, and "really like to experience a relationship between the classroom component of clinic and their case work."[67] But they often minimize their attention to, and the importance of, classroom sessions as the workload on their cases increases. When this occurs, participation often falls off, readings are ignored, and pre-class assignments are not completed. Even when students have prepared, they may engage in the classroom discussions in a less than satisfactory fashion. Aside from the pressure of work, students can easily be distracted by texts on their phones, emails popping up on their computers, or by web searches about spring break vacation ideas.[68] In addition, evidence is emerging that students are stressed more than ever and that their mental health has suffered because of world events. Recent data show that 25% of law students are at risk for alcoholism, 17% of law students suffer from depression, 37% of law students report mild to severe anxiety, and 6% of law students report having suicidal thoughts in the last year.[69] Although these problems are not new, they are trending in the wrong direction and getting worse over time.[70]

Lack of engagement, no matter what its causes are, is a serious impediment to learning. Although students' mental and physical health along with the press of client work sometimes cause deficient classroom performance, faculty may also be sending unconscious signals about what efforts students should prioritize as they themselves feel the pressure of case demands. Stress can cause the faculty member's class preparation to decline and delay the teacher's return of pre-class assignments. Teachers who note a student's classroom engagement decline should first rule out their own complicity in the behavior and then look for other causes and solutions.

Clinical teachers looking for solutions to students' apparent disinterest often discuss student learning styles and how their teaching modalities respond to the varied styles students bring to the classroom. The styles identified in these conversations usually include auditory and visual learning; learning by reading, watching, or doing; and learning through abstract or concrete thinking. Recent studies have shown that no matter which learning style students prefer, students learn best when teachers use multiple teaching strategies in each class.[71] These studies suggest that teaching to a particular learning style does not necessarily lead to better outcomes in the classroom.[72] However, the research also suggests that teaching methods that seek to improve comprehension for specific types of learners often have a carryover effect to all students in the class, irrespective of their learning style.[73] Thus classroom sessions can become engaging for all students if multiple modalities are employed.[74] Moreover, the allure of phone, email, and web distractions often decreases when students find the material and the presentations challenging and interesting. Faculty can achieve this by using multiple learning modalities in each class.

Classroom sessions are always planned before students arrive in the clinic classroom. All teachers, but especially new teachers, will face great difficulty determining student learning styles before meeting their students. Over time, however, veteran teachers use their experiences with former students to predict the kinds of learning styles they will encounter. They then will consider what teaching methods, types of materials to assign, and the presentation formats they will use to convey the information so that they achieve their teaching goals and the students desire and need to learn. Indeed, "the factors that make clinical classroom teaching so challenging are also what makes this work endlessly interesting, intellectually and emotionally sustaining, and deeply inspiring."[75] Nonetheless, all teachers may have to adapt their established classroom instruction patterns when several students in a particular class are not grasping the material because of the teacher's methods of presenting it.

Although using multiple modalities will enliven the learning environment for most students, they may not work for those with mental or physical health conditions or those with overwhelming personal and family demands. Those issues will need to be addressed in another manner. Students experiencing mental health struggles may pose learning issues beyond the knowledge of the supervisor. Those problems may affect student learning in ways that affect client interests. Clinic faculty may have to engage other professionals from inside or outside the law school community to address those complex conditions.

Pre-Class and In-Class Teaching Modalities

Faculty-Led Learning

Using Wiggins' backward-design methodology, teachers identify and clarify the learning goals for the class before they begin to create the seminar plan and determine what the students are expected to learn. Even if a teacher is able to create the right classroom environment and provides information in an accessible manner, engaging the students in discussion can often be a challenging task.[76] Various in-class presentation methods[77] and pre-class exercises[78] that increase engagement are available depending upon the subject matter of the class. The teacher can implement the learning goals by lecturing, employing large- or small-group discussions on specific substantive or procedural issues, using Socratic questioning and case analysis, and creating video or film clips, role-plays, and simulations to demonstrate problem solving and strategic thinking. These methods all have value, but only if they are intentionally chosen to meet the learning goals for the clinic as a whole and for the particular class. Using techniques more common in undergraduate classes, such as having students read fiction and discuss it in class, may seem at first glance to be an unorthodox and irrelevant form of pedagogy in a law school experiential class. But it can be effective if tied to a clinic's goal. For example, in a class accompanying a Gender and the Law Clinic, Professor Beverly Balos identified disrupting the "traditional legal discourse that dominates most of their classes" as a clinic goal.[79] She then worked backward from that goal to create a classroom component that was based on readings from fictional stories. She chose the fictional stories "so students [would] gain some notion of what the lives of white women and women of color are like and to bring the students out of the distancing of traditional legal discourse that dominates most of their classes."[80] Some teachers invite clients to come to class to demonstrate narrative exploration or client-centered representation. Teachers also invite other guest lecturers, for example judges, prosecutors, social workers, and other participants in the clinic's cases or projects, who bring their perspectives into the strategic discourse. Bringing these people to clinic classes should not be just for "show and tell" sessions. These guest appearances, like all teaching events, must have a clear purpose related to clinic learning goals, be used intentionally to advance them, and have an expected outcome to be successful. Although gaining control over a classroom and building rapport with students takes time, following the techniques described in the pedagogical and clinical literature, combined with patience, can help teachers provide a positive learning environment in the clinic classroom sessions.[81]

Student-Led Learning

The in-class presentation format need not be teacher-led. Non-traditional formats can also be useful in switching the learning modality from professor-directed learning to student-directed learning. Examples include student-led class discussions of specific topics or written homework; student-led case rounds; peer critique of written documents; reports back from exercises performed prior to the classroom session or from observations of real-world performance;[82] and in-class role plays or moots of actual student cases. Student-led presentations and small group discussions allow classroom-reticent students to create experiences that enable them to gain confidence. They also demonstrate and encourage collaborative learning and address non-traditional learning styles. As Heather Dubrow, an English professor at Fordham University, describes it, allowing students to learn from each other is a valuable approach because it

> builds the skills in listening attentively that are even more valuable in a culture of multitasking and skimming. It can give our students more confidence in their own ideas when others, including peers, treat them with respect. It encourages them to consider a range of perspectives rather than believing all they should know (or need to know) comes from the teacher. And of course, the bottom line is that they can indeed learn from each other.[83]

Pre-Class Preparation

Teachers have to determine which materials students should use to prepare for the classroom experience. Various materials can be assigned in advance to prepare the students for the classroom session. Common materials assigned for pre-class preparation in clinical courses can be written reports from real-world observations of court or legislative sessions; case opinions, statutes, and legislative reports; legal and non-legal articles and books; research reports and case studies; actual transcripts of witness testimony or client interviews; and movies, videos, and television shows. All of these can provide context for the lawyering tasks that students will be asked to simulate in the classroom or perform while representing clinic clients. "Unlike classroom hypotheticals," which can feel "contrived for pedagogical purposes," these real-world materials infuse the learning environment with an authentic sense of reality that fosters deeper student engagement.[84]

These passive learning methods can also be supplemented—or even replaced—by more active forms of pre-class learning. For students to truly "become independent in the field," the classroom cannot just be the place "where the teacher 'imparts knowledge like a mother bird dropping worms into the mouths of her chicks.'"[85] For example, the faculty can create a series of reflective questions about the topic to be analyzed before the class, and then discussed in the class. Some faculty assign simulated legal tasks in advance of class to ensure that students are prepared but also to enrich the class that follows. Teachers can distribute client and witness stories (either fictionalized or with appropriate redactions and anonymizations) and ask students to write the witness examinations or legislative testimony in advance of class. They can provide synopses of witness testimonies and ask students to prepare closing arguments. They can ask students to prepare negotiation strategies based on a client's and opponent's interest. If these pre-class exercises occur, additional learning can take place if the faculty member responds to them in writing with observations about knowledge, strategy, and format.

Quick-Writes

Students usually come to a clinic class right after another law school class that has nothing to do with their clinic work, or from some non-school activities that occurred either on- or off-campus. Simply put, their minds are usually elsewhere as they walk into the classroom. Their conversations with colleagues as they walk in are seldom about the upcoming clinic class, no matter what pre-class work has been assigned. As a result, refocusing students at the beginning of the class is essential to learning. Some faculty use quick-writes to focus the students on the subject matter at hand. Sometimes they are collected and reviewed either before or after the class by the teacher. A quick-write asks the students to take a few minutes to think about the topic of the class and their pre-class preparation, and to write down questions they have about the class topic or materials. Some teachers ask students to state the difficulties they may have encountered with the assignment or concepts that they did not quite understand.

Students can be asked to consider how the topic relates to their current case or project. They can also be asked to write about moral, ethical, or values-based issues or assumptions that are embedded in the exercise they performed and the materials that they read, or whether their pre-class preparation raises value issues and assumptions they see in their cases. Indeed, the quick-write's prompt may be the first thing that unearths a realization that such issues or assumptions were actually present in the assigned materials all along. No matter what it asks, the quick-write serves to immerse the students in their learning and increases the chance that the class will help the students scaffold their learning to a higher level of understanding. They also serve as an incentive for students to actually do the pre-class work, and when collected, help determine whether the students have really done the preliminary work required for the class.

Conducting the Class

Once students are focused on the clinic class at hand and ready to learn, teachers often start a class session by identifying the goals for the class and explicitly telling the students what they want them to learn by the end of the session.[86] Because the teacher has designed the entire class to fulfill at least one of the clinic's goals, each activity can reference the goal that it seeks to advance. Doing so will not only help students understand what they are learning in the moment. It also helps them see interrelationships of the classes throughout the semester. That, in turn, benefits the teacher when students address what the class was supposed to achieve when they fill out course evaluations.

Teachers may also focus the students on the work of the class by initiating a conversation with updates about clinic cases. Doing so creates a space for students to celebrate successes and find camaraderie and support when sharing their struggles with their individual cases. These introductory remarks may help spark conversations later in the class about the substantive topic of the day or otherwise provide fodder for future case rounds sessions. In any event, they help students fully shift their mindsets from that of a regular law student who happens to be enrolled in a clinic to that of a student lawyer actively engaged in clinical learning.

Post-Class Reflections

Of course, not all classes are successful, even when they are well-planned and tailored to the clinic's goals. Teachers who use quick-writes as the class begins often invite the class to reflect on what they learned at the end of the class. They can pose questions about the class prior to its formal ending, asking students to assess the success of the class. Teachers can also send the questions after the class via email, asking students to reflect on the class and submit the responses after they have done so. Brookfield suggests using Critical Incident Questionnaires or CIQs,[87] where teachers ask the students to write down two takeaways from that day's class that will help them with their cases or projects going forward. Sometimes, the CIQs ask what questions the students still have after the class or ask for suggestions to improve the class. If the teacher collects these takeaways to gauge whether the goals they have set for the class have worked out as planned, the CIQs serve both student and faculty goals. The teacher gains insight into the effectiveness of the class, and the students understand that the class does not stand alone in the learning process. Instead, each class is an integral part of the whole clinic experience, designed to complement the full arc of the supervision process.

The CIQ is not the only way to gather this information. Some teachers end the class by asking the students to do one more quick-write setting forth two things discussed in class which clarified their thinking about identity formation, lawyering in general, a specific lawyering skill, or how the class helps them with their clinic case or project. Quick-writes and CIQs reinforce an understanding that the classroom experience is part of the supervision and learning process. When integrated with other methods of learning in the clinic, these techniques demonstrate to students how reflection and scaffolded learning actually works. They also foster independent thinking and the self-assessments they need to become lifelong learners.

Faculty Reflection on Teaching

Teachers often discuss their teaching with colleagues after specific clinic classes are designed and conducted. Indeed, they will continue to discuss teaching methods and strategies throughout their academic careers. Law, culture, strategic thinking, and technology evolve, and clinical courses must keep pace with those changes. Artificial intelligence is the latest change in teaching and learning that will have to be adapted to experiential courses in the future.

Good teachers constantly review their methods, materials, and presentations to ensure that their goals are met in each class and that students are actually learning what the teacher hopes to impart. But as Professor Jenkins explains, this "means more than just reviewing your notes or PowerPoint slides."[88] It involves constantly reassessing what one does in the classroom. It requires abandoning those teaching strategies and modalities that proved to be ineffective or outdated and replacing them with new ones. Unfortunately, teachers often assume their goals are met and their classes are well-constructed because students tend to love their clinics and write glowing course evaluations at the end of the semester or year. This general admiration for our work, however, does not always tell us how successful individual classes have been.

Teachers need to learn that there are other ways to get feedback on whether they have achieved their class session goals. Most law school student-evaluation forms are designed for traditional classroom teaching and are less than helpful for experiential courses. Even evaluation forms designed for clinic courses do not capture the effectiveness of individual classes. Evaluations by students have also been found to be popularity contests and subject to bias along several axes of identity.[89] Moreover, there seems to be "little to no correlation between how highly students rate their instructor and how well they have learned the subject."[90]

CIQs are one way to keep teaching goals and methods relevant. To get accurate feedback, however, students must know the goals for each class. Comments received right after a class are more helpful, but also more time-consuming for students and faculty alike. Student-to-teacher feedback may come from informal conversations with students after the class, but these one-off observations may reflect only one student's opinion. As previously mentioned, Brookfield suggests teachers use CIQs to help determine whether they have achieved the goals of their class.[91] He also suggests faculty give their students a CIQ at the end of a series of classes asking them to reflect back on what they learned or found challenging, and then to digest and reflect upon the students' responses.[92] Teachers can then take note of any particularly confusing aspects of the prior classes, significant differences in student perceptions of the same portion of the class, and of the general themes in student comments.[93]

Ideally, faculty-directed CIQs should be anonymous, but students' preference for electronic responses to handwritten responses will require an office manager or some other intermediary to collate the responses, especially if the teacher wants to share them with the entire group at subsequent classes[94] or with other faculty members. Faculty-directed CIQs are effective for improving the classroom experience because they alert the teacher to problems, encourage students to reflect on their learning, help improve diversity in teaching, build trust between the students and teacher, provide suggestions for development, and model critical thinking.[95] Once a teacher understands the nature of the critique, teachers can then incorporate the information gleaned to make relevant changes in future classes.[96]

Another way faculty can improve their teaching is by participating in teaching workshops at regional or national clinical conferences to test their ideas among colleagues from other schools.[97] Attending AALS national and regional clinical conferences and CLEA conferences is always helpful for improving teaching methodologies. Faculty can observe sessions conducted by more experienced teachers and informally bounce ideas off of colleagues to add new techniques to their teaching methods.[98] They will also find a supportive community willing to help each other, while contributing to the maintenance and advancement of the clinical education enterprise.[99]

Clinical faculty, especially new faculty, need to remember that teaching, like lawyering, is not always instinctive, even though some people will become better teachers than others. All teachers, however, can become very good classroom teachers if they are intentional about their work, have goals, prepare each class session with the backward design to achieve those goals, and implement methods that allow each student to attain what they need to learn from the class. Even the so-called (and sometimes self-described) "old dog" teachers, who may feel they are too deep into their careers to learn any "new tricks," stand to benefit from reflecting on their classroom methods and intentionally grounding their approach in the methods described above.[100] After all, it's never too late—whatever one's age or experience—to "finally, actually learn how to teach."[101]

Other Voices

Deborah Epstein, Jane H. Aiken & Wallace J. Mlyniec, *Introduction: Teaching the Clinic Seminar**

TEACHING THE CLINIC SEMINAR (West Academic Publishing 2014)

How to Make the Most of the Teacher's Guide

Few clinical law professors, whether new to the field or highly experienced, feel fully satisfied with the seminar component of their program. This makes sense—developing an excellent clinical seminar is a real challenge and little guidance exists for how to do it.

But the factors that make clinical classroom teaching so challenging are also what makes this work endlessly interesting, intellectually and emotionally sustaining, and deeply inspiring. Even after decades of experience, most clinicians find that there is still more to learn. There are insights to be gained from learning theory, teaching exercises to be "borrowed" from colleagues, and new understandings to be obtained from reflection on the strengths and weaknesses of one's own practices.

In a sense, the excitement inherent in clinical classroom teaching echoes the excitement students feel when they are immersed in the clinic learning experience. Clinicians teach their students that there are few "right" answers in lawyering work; instead, there are issues to be spotted and choices to be made. The best decision in one situation is not necessarily the best decision in another, because the soundness of any choice depends in large part on client goals and an understanding of the situation-specific context. And every lawyering choice involves some degree of risk. As a result, clinical teachers expect far more from their students than a successful client outcome. We tend to be proudest when our students are able to clearly identify a strategic lawyering decision point when it arises, to brainstorm a wide variety of possible options, to carefully analyze the strengths and weaknesses of each option, and—later—to reflect back on the strategic soundness of their ultimate choice and draw lessons for future lawyering challenges.

These principles apply with equal strength to the process of designing and structuring a clinic seminar. There is no one right way to teach and no foolproof approach that will ensure that students absorb a targeted lesson. Just like our students, clinical teachers are faced with a series of choices in the classroom, each of which admits to multiple solutions and each of which, in turn, involves context-dependent pros and cons. We do our best teaching when we recognize those decision points, make intentional choices in response to them, and reflect on and learn from our successes and our mistakes.

---

* Excerpts are reprinted with the permission of the authors and West Academic Publishing.

But the clinical community tends to focus heavily on the student supervision context as the site for this kind of transformative learning. Copious scholarly articles and conference presentations analyze the rich learning opportunities that arise in supervision sessions, where clinicians encourage students to assume the role of a professional, to take on responsibility for a client, to become active seekers of their own knowledge, to exercise critical professional judgment, and to learn the profound lessons that flow directly from this real-world experience.

Advice about how to design an effective seminar course, in contrast, can be hard to come by, even though the same goals can—and must—be realized in the classroom. Clinicians cannot expect their students to become independent in the field if the classroom environment is one where the teacher [, as noted by Professor Matthew Fraiden,] "imparts knowledge like a mother bird dropping worms into the mouths of her chicks." Instead, student experiences in the clinic seminar should mirror those in supervision. The seminar teacher should push her students to transition out of their traditional role of passively receiving knowledge from their teachers and assuming responsibility only for themselves, typically through an academic paper or final exam. If a clinician believes that creating an atmosphere of profound respect for, and faith in, student competence best promotes learning in the field, then she must infuse her classroom with the same atmosphere. If she believes that effective supervision necessitates subverting her own ego and sharing the learning space with students in a meaningful way, then she must adopt a similar approach to classroom teaching. To be successful, a clinician's efforts to promote student independence must permeate every component of the clinical program.

But how can a clinician structure a seminar course around independent, student-driven learning? Complex questions abound here. Some are structural in nature: What factors should guide the choice of seminar topics? What principles should guide the balance between class sessions devoted to reflections on field work and those devoted to particular substantive topics? Are some skills better or more efficiently taught in the seminar than in supervision sessions? What kinds of student learning goals best lend themselves to the seminar context? How does one design classroom teaching activities that will best support an identified student learning goal?

Other questions are more conceptual: How can a teacher truly share the learning space with the students, when all of us are so deeply conditioned to a profoundly hierarchical approach to classroom teaching? How can a teacher ensure that knowledge is imparted in the classroom and, simultaneously, ensure that the students exercise ownership of their own learning process? How do different teaching methodologies promote or undermine independent student learning? How can a teacher assess whether students are actually achieving the learning goals sought? How can a teacher convince the students that their classroom learning truly matters as much as their fieldwork?

These are difficult questions that are all the more challenging because clinicians are constantly pulled in so many different directions. The time a clinician can devote to powerful classroom teaching typically competes with client representation, community involvement, scholarship, committee work, fundraising, and the numerous day-to-day tasks inherent in administering a law office. Although many clinical teachers would welcome the opportunity to spend more time on their clinic seminar, they often end up giving short shrift to both advance planning and post-class critical reflection. New clinicians have few opportunities to learn about clinical pedagogy. When they do have opportunities to learn, it can be challenging to find the time to translate new ideas into their day-to-day classroom teaching. More experienced clinicians tend to have few occasions to revisit their initial teaching choices or to discuss them with thoughtful colleagues.

…

… [A]s novices at the outset of our teaching careers … [w]e wanted models—successful teaching exercises that we could try out in our seminar classes or use as springboards for designing exercises of our own. But we also wanted help in developing our individual teaching voices, in engaging in the challenging process of identifying and thinking through the hard questions at the heart of clinical pedagogy.

…

[To that end, e]ach class is structured according to the following … segments:

- Why teach this class in a clinic seminar?
- Learning goals and concrete student behaviors that demonstrate learning in relation to those goals
- Common student misunderstandings
- Reading assignment
- Assignment in preparation for class
- The Class
    - Introductory lecture
    - Set up
    - Exercises
    - Learning Prompts
- Wrap up
- Connecting back to client representation
    - End-of-class learning prompts
    - End-of-class critical incident questionnaire:
    - Post-class reflection memo
    - Subsequent targeted rounds class
- Teaching methods

- Opportunities for transfer of learning
    - Seminar
    - Supervision

...

Why Teach This Topic in the Clinic Seminar?

No two clinic seminar syllabi are alike. Even within a particular subject matter area, substantial differences abound. Some clinicians conduct an intensive, multi-day orientation session before the regular semester begins; others start seminar meetings during the first full week of school. Some clinicians do not touch on substantive law in the classroom; for others, substantive law is the primary focus. Some clinicians construct their seminar primarily, or even exclusively, on rounds conversations; a few do not incorporate rounds at all. Some clinics have an intensive classroom component, with seminars that meet for two hours at a time, twice a week; others meet for shorter sessions, or less frequently. Semester-long clinics cannot provide as many seminar sessions as do those that run for a full academic year. For every clinician, the decision about what to include in the seminar syllabus is a critical one.

Going Deep, Rather than Broad

Many law professors, including clinicians, feel pressure to provide broad "coverage" in the classroom. But maximizing coverage is hardly a sound principle on which to formulate a syllabus. In the context of a single course, students can learn a finite number of lessons. No teacher can possibly cover everything relevant to the overall subject matter of a course. And by trying to accomplish more than is realistic, teachers may undermine their overall effectiveness and teach everything less well.

Clinicians can have far greater impact by limiting themselves to a carefully selected set of essential topics, spending substantial time exploring each one. This approach allows teachers to focus on the particular areas of learning where they can add the greatest value.

Weighing the Utility of Various Clinical Learning Sites

Multiple learning sites exist in a clinical program. Many topics can and should be taught in the supervision context, but some are particularly well-suited to the learning opportunities afforded in a seminar class.

The topic of client-centered lawyering helps to illustrate this issue. Because an in-depth understanding of the different roles played by lawyer and client is critical to a student's ability to successfully transition to a professional lawyering role, this topic is worth prioritizing in the classroom. In addition, classroom lessons on this topic are likely to be useful as a base from which students can build when they engage in field work because this issue permeates the entire experience of client representation. Because this topic is both inherently complex and fundamental to the lawyering process, students are likely to benefit from opportunities to work through related issues with their peers in a structured format. Each student is likely to learn from a full-class collaboration, both in terms of planning for strategic challenges likely to arise in their field work, and in terms of reflecting on the meaning and significance of field work experiences after they occur.

Complementing Other Learning Opportunities

The clinic seminar also can serve to complement other student learning opportunities. Classes are particularly valuable when they focus on important lessons students are unlikely to encounter elsewhere, either during law school or in the early years of law practice. For example, few students or lawyers are likely to have meaningful, focused opportunities to examine topics such as exploring justice, collaboration or the establishment of professional boundaries. Because these skills are essential to successful lawyering but are rarely discussed either in class or in practice, they are fertile ground for the clinic seminar.

Classes included in the clinic seminar might also productively focus on topics where the realities of law practice are inconsistent with the lessons students learn in the traditional law school curriculum or in the popular culture. Informal fact investigation is just one example. A student can easily graduate from law school having read nothing but appellate court opinions, which turn on a pre-packaged factual universe, defined by the four corners of the trial court transcript. In sharp contrast, real-world facts are chaotic, incomplete, and constantly changing. In the absence of exposure to these realities, students are likely to enter the practice of law with wildly unrealistic expectations regarding both the neatness and stability of the factual universe they will regularly encounter and the critical importance of a dynamic, strategic investigation plan to successful lawyering.

Learning Goals and the Concrete Student Behaviors That Demonstrate Learning in Relation to Those Goals

Using learning goals as a starting point for class planning may sound both basic and commonsensical, but in fact few teachers begin here. It is far more typical, even for the most experienced teachers, to proceed directly from the question of "what content do I wish to cover?" to that of "what interesting classroom teaching methods can I use to help students engage with this material?" But this planning norm is problematic; it is crucial for a clinician to consider student learning goals from the outset for several reasons.

First, a clear set of student learning goals provides a useful frame for an instructor to assess student success and failure in the learning process. Such goals provide a touchstone for the inquiry: If a student understands my learning goal, what will that look like in terms of concrete student performance? If a student does *not* understand my learning goal, what will that look like in terms of concrete student performance?

This inquiry is essential to productive teaching. The greatest gains in student achievement occur when students are provided with salient and specific feedback, and when they have multiple, timely opportunities to reflect upon and implement that feedback. A focus on goals and concrete evidence of learning ensures that instructors have clarity about what "mission accomplished" looks like for their students. Teachers can then ensure that classroom learning activities are carefully designed to create meaningful opportunities to observe behaviors indicative of successful or unsuccessful learning and provide necessary individual or group feedback.

A second reason for starting with goals stems, in large part, from an idea that is often implicit, but rarely explicit, in our teaching: the most successful student learning occurs when we teach to "transfer." Transfer has been defined as the "use of knowledge and skills (acquired in an earlier context) in a new context. It occurs when a person's learning in one situation influences that person's learning and performance in other situations." A student who is able to apply a concept in new and varied settings, without being shown exactly how to do so by his teacher, has fully understood the idea in question.

... [M]ost "[e]ducators hope that students will transfer learning from one problem to another within a course, from one year in school to another, between school and home, and from school to workplace. Assumptions about transfer accompany the belief that it is better to broadly 'educate' people than simply 'train' them to perform particular tasks. In other words, a student who learns a concept in a single context may be able to apply it if the context remains constant, but may not truly understand its meaning. "Many teachers just expect transfer to happen if content is well taught. No research supports this view. Students who have not been taught for transfer overwhelmingly respond as follows to a 'novel' but do-able challenge: *We didn't cover this; I don't know what to do....*" Learning theorist Grant Wiggins illustrates the problem with an anecdote from his experience as a soccer coach. During a game, he recalls yelling out to a player, encouraging her to apply the lessons they had focused on all week in practice sessions. The player yelled back: "But the other team isn't lining up the way we did [during] the drills!"

As Wiggins puts it, we teach to transfer because, "given that there is too much for anyone to learn; given that unpredictability is inevitable; given that being flexible and adaptive with one's repertoire is key to any future success, it stands to reason that we should focus our [teaching] efforts on the goal of transfer.... The point of school is not to get good at school[,] but to effectively parlay what we learned in school in other learning and in life." We know that we have taught to transfer when students achieve understanding; are able to apply that understanding independently; and are able to apply it in a variety of different contexts.

The importance of teaching to transfer leads to a crucial insight. We need to think about and plan for student learning that can be applied beyond the parameters of a particular class. We need to identify learning goals that are sufficiently fundamental that they will arise not only in a single setting, but in multiple settings in the clinic experience.

Content alone provides insufficient guidance for the process of teaching to transfer. A content-driven class plan gives the instructor no rigorous way to develop a meaningful hierarchy of learning goals, or to assess which lessons are the most critical to cover. Planning from content alone creates a tendency to go broad, rather than deep, in an effort to try to cover all of the most salient aspects of the topic at hand.

In contrast, starting with an identified set of essential, transferable student learning goals takes a teacher in the opposite direction, emphasizing depth over breadth. The process of thinking through these goals pushes the instructor to make careful, intentional choices about what aspects of a topic deserve the greatest amount of time and attention in the seminar.

A concrete example may help illustrate the difference. Consider a class on the topic of direct examination where the instructor plans to raise the issue of question form. In a class where planning derives solely from consideration of content, the emphasis is likely to be on lessons like the following:

- Lawyers typically ask open-ended questions on direct, so that attention is focused on the witness, rather than on the lawyer.

In a class where planning derives from early consideration of fundamental and transferable learning goals, the emphasis is more likely to be on lessons such as:

- Lawyers make strategic, considered choices about language and phrasing in every aspect of their work. In the context of direct examination, where the witness' individual perspective is critical, that choice typically plays out in favor of open-ended questions.

The process of thinking through learning goals helps teachers identify the habits of mind and behaviors they hope to develop in their students. When teaching activities and prompting questions stem from clearly defined learning goals, students are far more likely to understand not only what a particular skill looks like in practice and how to implement it, but also how to think critically and make sound strategic choices about its implementation, both in clinic and beyond. Seminar then becomes a rich opportunity for facilitating the transfer of learning from classroom exercises to real-world practice. Student learning, in turn, tends to be deeper and more powerful.

...

Common Student Misunderstandings

Even the most careful, goal-driven seminar plan can be subverted if a teacher is unaware of the misconceptions students bring with them to the topic at hand. Adult learners bring strong ideas of their own to all seminar subjects. Accordingly, "[t]eachers need to pay attention to the incomplete understandings, the false beliefs, and the naïve renditions of concepts that learners bring with them to a given subject.... These preconceptions must be addressed in order for them to change their beliefs."

Over time, a teacher can predict the common misunderstandings held by clinic students that can interfere with learning about a particular seminar subject. These misunderstandings tend to be most strongly-held in areas where the realities of law practice are inconsistent with the lessons students learn in the traditional law school curriculum or in the popular culture.

...

By identifying the pre-existing misconceptions that are most likely to interfere with student learning in a particular class, a teacher can intentionally design classroom learning activities that surface such misunderstandings. Each class ... [should be] structured to provide opportunities for students to re-examine their beliefs and gain new insights. In our experience, students find these learning experiences to be extremely powerful.

...

Assignment in Preparation for Class

Pre-class assignments can provide students with a chance to jump start their thinking about a topic before class begins. Such assignments lend themselves to a wide variety of formats. Some may be designed as independent structured reflections, with no requirement of sharing the results with faculty or other students. Others might form the basis for a classroom exercise for which all students will be asked to contribute. Still others might require the drafting of a more formal memorandum, to be turned in and reviewed by the teacher in advance of class. Regardless of format, pre-class assignments are valuable in helping students feel ready to dive in and be open to learning from the outset of a seminar class.

...

Teaching Methods

Designing an effective seminar class involves the strategic consideration of a wide range of teaching methods, each of which has a particular set of strengths and limitations. This process includes both selecting the most effective teaching method for each learning activity, and sequencing learning activities and teaching methods to promote the deepest possible student engagement.

...

The teaching methods most frequently used in classes ... as well as the purposes for which each can be most effective, are described below.

Lecture

A well-organized lecture can be a highly effective way to convey conceptual information and can help students transition into a participatory exercise. For classes that are primarily centered on student participation, the lecture segment may be quite brief—an introduction to the substantive topic and a structural overview of the remainder of the class. A lecture might be more substantial for classes where more extensive exposition is needed to scaffold students' participatory work. Longer lectures can be interspersed with real-world lawyering examples, video clip demonstrations, or brief participatory brainstorming sessions, so that the students remain engaged in, and an important part of, the learning process at all times.

Warm Up

A brief warm up exercise or discussion can serve similar purposes as a pre-class assignment. These exercises can help students focus their thinking and open themselves to learning.

Individual Reflection or "Quick Write"

This teaching method involves asking students to spend two or three minutes reflecting individually on a question, or short series of questions. To help students focus, the teacher may wish to distribute index cards to the students and ask them to do a "quick write," jotting down their thoughts about the question(s) posed. Individual reflection helps students collect their thoughts in advance of group engagement. This process tends to improve subsequent student contributions to class discussion, both in terms of quantity and quality.

Because students are given only a few minutes to reflect here, assigned question(s) should be brief, clearly stated, and easy to understand. Otherwise, too much of the allotted time is spent parsing out the questions, rather than thinking through the answers.

Full Group Brainstorm

This teaching method involves posing a question, or set of questions, to which all class members are invited to respond. Students are encouraged to throw out creative ideas, regardless of their practicability. Because students are not required to limit themselves to the "correct" answer, they tend to feel more comfortable participating. Group brainstorm sessions allow an instructor to demonstrate the multiplicity of possible approaches to a particular lawyering task or challenge. These sessions can create a broad base within which to frame more focused, deeper discussion. A teacher can take full advantage of the large group brainstorm process by selecting questions or issues which are amenable to a broad set of possible responses.

Small Group Discussion

This teaching method involves breaking the class up into smaller units for focused discussion. Small groups promote student participation in several ways. First, some students feel more psychologically safe and less self-conscious in a smaller group, and therefore are more likely to contribute. Research shows that students working in small groups tend to feel more comfortable "sharing their own experiences, revealing a lack of knowledge, displaying their extensive expertise, and disagreeing with the professor." Second, working in small groups increases the likelihood that all students will contribute ideas and fully engage. Even those students who prefer to sit back and remain passive in the larger class setting tend to feel a sense of responsibility in a small group; a failure to participate is far more noticeable. In addition, research suggests that student-centered discussions are more effective than are instructor-centered discussions in terms of "retention, application, problem solving, attitude change, and motivation for future learning." The likelihood that each student will have a full opportunity to participate is greatest when small groups are truly small, such as when the group is comprised of only three or four students.

Full Group Report Back

This teaching method involves asking one "reporter" from each small group to share information about that group's discussion with the full class. This technique allows students to take advantage of the small group opportunity for extensive participation, and also learn from the wider variety of perspectives held by their colleagues. Report back sessions also allow small group members to obtain a sense of the full group's reaction to the ideas they generated.

This method is particularly effective when small group reporters are provided with a focused discussion prompt, rather than simply being asked to describe the discussion that occurred in their small group. For example, an instructor might help focus the report back process by posing such prompting question as:

What were two interesting ideas raised in the group?

What were two interesting conclusions the group arrived at?

What were two things that surprised you about the discussion?

What were two useful contributions that your group's discussion could make to the larger group's understanding?

Learning Prompts

Learning prompts are questions posed by a teacher and designed to support the identified student learning goals for a class. They are an essential part of promoting classroom learning, particularly in the context of a participatory exercise. Learning prompts can: (1) help students reflect on and gain insight about the choices they have made; (2) help students move past common preexisting misconceptions; and (3) help the instructor assess student understanding. Learning prompts tend to be most effective when the teacher has clearly thought through the particular student learning goal each one best supports.

When developing effective learning prompts, it is also important to think through when they might be most effectively posed to the students. Some questions will best facilitate focused discussion following a particular student classroom performance, or particular portion of a performance. Others will be most effective after all classroom performances have been completed, when students can focus on broader lessons to be gleaned from reviewing the full range of performances that have occurred.

Wrap Up

Few teachers intentionally create a formal "end" for a seminar class. Instead, the norm is to simply end their classes at the moment when they have finished covering the assigned topic or when the allotted class time has run out. But saving a few minutes for an intentional wrap up discussion can provide closure and deepen learning. An intentional "wrap up" gives a teacher a final opportunity to explicitly name the central lessons and "take away" points of the class. To take maximum advantage of these last few moments, a teacher may connect general learning goals with the particular issues raised and insights gained by the students in a participatory exercise. By explicitly naming learning insights, a teacher can help students obtain clarity in their thinking, as well as encourage connections with other class sessions and clinic field work.

Connecting Back to Client Representation

In some clinic classes, students can easily see the connections between their seminar learning and their work on behalf of their clients. Interviewing, informal fact investigation, direct examination, and many other skill-focused classes fall within this category. But with other classes, such as those on establishing boundaries, collaboration, and exploring justice, the connections may not be quite so clear.

Recognizing the connection between classroom learning and field work is deeply important to most clinic students and can help with the transfer of learning process (see "Opportunities for Transfer of Learning," below). A teacher can enhance lessons learned in a particular seminar class by creating concrete opportunities for students to link them with their lawyering work.

... [There are] a variety of suggestions for clinicians to help students make these connections. The methods we suggest ... tend to include:

End-of-Class Learning Prompts: where a teacher reserves the last several minutes of class for full group discussion of suggested connecting question(s).

End-of-Class "Critical Incident Questionnaires:" where a teacher distributes index cards during the last few minutes of class, and asks student to reflect on and jot down notes about suggested connecting question(s).

Post-Class Reflection Memos: where a teacher asks students to draft a more formal response to suggested connecting question(s) after class. The teacher may collect them for instructor review or distribute them to the full group.

Performance Rounds: where a teacher designs a follow-up seminar class designed specifically to apply the seminar lessons to student client representation work. For example, after teaching a class on cross examination, a clinician might devote a second, subsequent class to the topic, and assign each student who is working on a cross examination in an actual clinic case to present the cross in the rounds session. The students might tape a simulated version of their anticipated examination (with another student role playing the witness), or to be prepared to do a role play live in class, and then lead the class through a debriefing discussion, with opportunities to examine strengths, weaknesses, and ideas for change.

Opportunities for Transfer of Learning

As described more extensively above, educational research clearly demonstrates that transfer across contexts is especially difficult when a subject is taught only in a single context rather than in multiple contexts. "When a subject is taught in multiple contexts, and includes examples which demonstrate wide application of what is being taught, people are more likely to abstract the relevant features of concepts and to develop a flexible representation of knowledge." Clinicians can help their students continue to learn the lessons emphasized in a particular class by identifying other points in the clinic curriculum where the same or similar understandings apply.

Some of these related learning opportunities may involve what is often referred to as "near transfer." Near transfer occurs when two situations are sufficiently similar that the lessons learned in one are easily, almost automatically, applied to the other. Many of the lessons learned in a simulation played out in a client interviewing class, for example, are fairly easily applied to a live-client interview situation, or to an interview of a non-client witness. The contexts are similar, but not identical; the student will need to draw upon existing understandings and stretch them to apply to the new situation.

"Far" transfer, in contrast, is more challenging for students to accomplish and for teachers to facilitate. Far transfer can occur when two situations are sufficiently different and connections are difficult to see, yet lessons learned in a prior context may be useful in the new one.... For example, it might require fairly careful analysis for a student to see how lessons learned in a class on storytelling might apply to the task of developing a closing argument or the task of designing a presentation for a group meeting. A teacher can facilitate this kind of transfer by helping students stretch to see the correlations between seemingly dissimilar situations. By naming the underlying connections for students, for example, a teacher can help them see the applicability of their learning across different contexts in their clinic work. Moreover, by providing students with practice at both near and far transfer, a teacher can greatly facilitate the ease with which students approach fully independent transfer in their post-graduate professional lives, long after their clinic experience is complete.

...

Endnotes

1. Report on Clinical Legal Education (1980) Ass'n of Am. Law Schools (AALS) & Am. Bar Ass'n Comm. on Guidelines for Clinical Educ., Report on Clinical Legal Education (1980) at 21.

2. The new Standard represents a welcome change from past practice, where some clinical programs "d[id] not contain any seminar component." *See* Deborah Epstein, Jane H. Aiken & Wallace J. Mlyniec, Teaching the Clinic Seminar 4 (1st ed. 2014) (making this observation and "hop[ing to] provide[] an impetus for reconsidering that structural choice").

3. Standards and Rules of Proc. for Approval of Law Sch., 2023–2024 Standard 304(a)(5), (A. Bar Ass'n. 2023–2024) https://www.americanbar.org/groups/legal_education/resources/standards/.

4. Am. Bar Ass'n, *supra* note 1, at Standards 304 (a)–(d).

5. Rob Jenkins, *The 4 Properties of Powerful Teachers*, Chron. Higher Educ. (March 16, 2015), ht tps://www.chronicle.com/article/the-4-properties-of-powerful-teachers/.

6. *Id.*

7. *Id. accord* A.C. Grayling, *What Makes A Good Teacher?*, Chron. Higher Educ. (Dec. 6, 2015), https://www.chronicle.com/article/what-makes-a-good-teacher-234422/.

8. Jenkins, *supra* note 5.

9. *Id.*

10. Grayling, *supra* note 7.

11. For a slightly contrary view that casts a (modern, well-calibrated) form of the Socratic method as helpful preparation for participation in democratic society and real-world lawyering, see Jeannie Suk Gersen, *The Socratic Method in the Age of Trauma*, 130 Harv. L. Rev. 2320, 2345–47 (2017).

12. This type of cross-pollination—where clinical teachers import theory and techniques from other areas of teaching unrelated to law or legal academia—also appears earlier in this book. *See infra*, Chapter 5 (Special Considerations for Supervising Student Writing). Just as that Chapter explained how legal writing teachers borrow methods from teaching writing in non-law-school contexts, so too do clinical faculty. They draw on prior work in other fields of classroom teaching to further develop and hone their craft. For an example of how legal-writing pedagogy has cross-pollinated into the classroom component of a writing-focused clinic, see Sarah O'Rourke Schrup, *The Clinical Divide: Overcoming Barriers to Collaboration Between Clinics and Legal Writing Programs*, 14 Clinical L. Rev. 301, 326–34 (2007).

13. *See, e.g.*, Paul S. Ferber, *Adult Learning Theory and Simulations—Designing Simulations to Educate Lawyers*, 9 Clinical L. Rev. 417–19 (2002) (explaining that many clinics put students through one to three weeks of simulation training before students engage in actual clinic work); Philip G. Schrag, *Constructing a Clinic*, 3 Clinical L. Rev. 175, 239 (1996) (discussing usefulness of simulations); Ian Weinstein, *Teaching Reflective Lawyering in a Small Case Litigation Clinic: A Love Letter to My Clinic*, 13 Clinical L. Rev. 573, 593 (2006) ("I often play the role of prosecutor in these simulations [in a criminal-defense clinic]. Self-indulgence is generally not useful in teaching, but in this simulation, I often release my cranky and sarcastic inner lawyer. The students begin to tell me how weak my case is, and I tell them I will see them in court. Or they begin to ask for a very favorable resolution, and I flatly refuse before they finish their argument. Sometimes they persist and get me to listen. But often we break the simulation, analyze the beginning and they restart and get past my difficult initial reaction. In my mind, the key to this exercise is for them to see past the surface reactions and stick to their strategy. In other words, this simulation continues the theme of executing strategy."); Patience A. Crowder, *Designing a Transactional Law Clinic for Life-Long Learning*, 19 Lewis & Clark L. Rev. 413, 429–31 (2015) (highlighting importance of simulations in classroom component of transactional clinic).

14. *See generally* Peter Toll Hoffman, *Clinical Course Design and the Supervisory Process*, 1982 Ariz. St. L.J. 277 (1982) (describing how performance critique can help the student improve her skills in the clinic, as it fully engages the student in her learning).

15. *See generally* Susan Bryant & Elliot S. Milstein, *Rounds: A "Signature Pedagogy" for Clinical Education?*, 14 Clinical L. Rev. 195 (2007) (examining the effectiveness of case rounds at educating students in the clinical setting, why they are widely used throughout clinical programs, and how faculty can meaningfully be involved in case rounds).

16. *See, e.g.*, Anna E. Carpenter, *The Project Model of Clinical Education: Eight Principles to Maximize Student Learning and Social Justice Impact*, 20 Clinical L. Rev. 39, 92–94 (2013).

17. *See, e.g.*, Joseph Lowman, Mastering the Techniques of Teaching 168–80 (2d. ed. 1995) (providing examples of problem-solving discussions).

18. Nira Hativa, *Teaching Large Law School Classes*, 50 J. Legal Educ. 95, 98 (2000).

19. *Id.* at 101.

20. Am. Bar Ass'n, *supra* note 1, Standard 302 ("A law school shall establish learning outcomes that shall, at a minimum, include competency in the following: (a) Knowledge and understanding of substantive and procedural law; (b) Legal analysis and reasoning, legal research, problem-solving, and written and oral communication in the legal context; (c) Exercise of proper professional and ethical responsibilities to clients and the legal system; and (d) Other professional skills needed for competent and ethical participation as a member of the legal profession.").

21. *See* Epstein, Aiken & Mlyniec, *supra* note 3, at 2 (identifying the tension new clinical teachers face between "want[ing] models—successful teaching exercises that we could try out in our own seminar classes or use as springboards for designing exercises of our own[.]" but also "want[ing] help in developing our individual teaching voices").

22. Lowman, *supra* note 17.

23. Hativa, *supra* note 18, at 101.

24. Stephen D. Brookfield, The Skillful Teacher: On Technique, Trust, And Responsiveness In The Classroom (3d. ed. 2015).

25. Grant P. Wiggins & Jay McTighe, Understanding by Design 206 (2d ed. 2005).

26. *See J.P. Sandy* Ogilvy & Karen Czapanskiy, *Clinical Legal Education: An Annotated Bibliography* (3d ed.), 11 Clinical L. Rev. 1 (Special Issue No. 2) (2005).

27. Wiggins & McTighe, *supra* note 25, at 13.

28. *Id.* at 14–15.

29. Epstein, Aiken & Mlyniec, *supra* note 3, at 5.

30. *See id.* at 3.

31. *See, e.g.*, Schrag, *supra* note 13, at 190 ("Before a semester starts, the group [of faculty and clinical-teaching fellows who manage the clinic] make major decisions about the syllabus, case intake criteria, student case load, the use of class time, divisions of responsibility for developing new classroom exercises, the development of new supervisory norms, office routines or forms, and the like."); *id.* at 238–41 (discussing construction of the clinic classroom component by focusing on syllabus construction); Crowder, *supra* note 13, at 429–31 (similarly focusing on the syllabus as part of clinic's classroom component). For an in-depth discussion of syllabus writing and its relationship to designing and teaching a course, see Nancy J. Soonpaa, *The Ins and Outcomes of Writing an Effective Syllabus*, 63 J. Legal Educ. 833 (2018).

32. *See, e.g.*, Colleen F. Shanahan & Emily A. Benfer, *Adaptive Clinical Teaching*, 19 Clinical L. Rev. 517, 549 (2013) (explaining how a goal-driven decision about what information students need to perform later-in-clinic skills can inform decisions about what to cover in orientation).

33. Wiggins & McTighe, *supra* note 25, at 17–18.

34. *Id.* at 18.

35. *Id.* at 18–19.

36. Alexi Freeman & Lindsey Webb, *Yes, You Can Learn Movement Lawyering in Law School: Highlights from the Movement Lawyering Lab at Denver Law*, 5 How. Hum. & C.R. L. Rev. 55, 66 (2020).

37. *See id.* at 62–63, 68–70.

38. *Id.* at 68–70.

39. Eduardo R. Ferrer & Kristin N. Henning, *Critical Clinical Frames: Centering Adolescence, Race, Trauma, and Gender in Practice-Based Pedagogy*, 30 Clinical L. Rev. 113, 143 (2023).

40. *Id.* at 143–44.

41. *Id.* at 144–46.

42. *See id.*

43. Wiggins & McTighe, *supra* note 25, at 35; *see also* April Land & Aliza Organick, *Moving Law Schools Forward by Design: Designing Law School Curricula to Transfer Learning from Classroom Theory to Clinical Practice and Beyond*, 71 J. Legal Educ. 503, 519 (2022).

44. Wiggins & McTighe, *supra* note 25, at 39.

45. For more on the importance of teaching to transfer in the clinic classroom specifically, *see, e.g.*, Epstein, Aiken & Mlyniec, *supra* note 3, at 6–8, 12–14.

46. Brookfield, *supra* note 24, at 5–8 (comparing the unpredictability of the classroom to whitewater rafting).

47. *See id.* at 2; *see generally id.* at 1–14 (Chapter 1: "Experiencing Teaching").

48. *See id.* at 2–3, 5.

49. *Cf. id.* at 3–5.

50. *Id.* at 15. Although Brookfield's fourth core assumption, in the original, refers specifically to *college* students, *id.*, the observation is equally—and even more—important in graduate or professional schools like law school, where the student population reflects an even broader age range than most undergraduate institutions.

51. *Id.* at 28; *see also* Gerald F. Hess, Michael Hunter Schwartz & Nancy Levit, *Fifty Ways to Promote Teaching and Learning*, 67 J. Legal Educ. 696, 719 (2018).

52. Brookfield, *supra* note 24, at 28–29.

53. *Id.* at 34–36.

54. *See generally id.* at 42–53.

55. *See* Bonny L. Tavares, *Changing the Construct: Promoting Cross-Cultural Conversations in the Law School Classroom*, 67 J. Legal Educ. 211, 221 (2017) ("Students also need an opportunity to get to know their professor as someone who is fair, respectful, and supportive. These traits are essential to building the kind of rapport that students need to open up, to become willing to take risks in the classroom, and to trust the professor as 'a compassionate mentor' who will help them navigate issues of cultural diversity in the safety of the classroom, before they experience those issues in practice." (citing Charles R. Calleros, *Training A Diverse Student Body for a Multicultural Society*, 8 La Raza L.J. 140, 163 (1995)). And when it comes to trust-building, even the little things matter—like learning how to properly pronounce each student's name. *See generally* Eun Hee Han, *What to Learn from Pandemic Teaching? Our Students' Names*, 69 J. Legal Educ. 816 (2020).

56. Epstein, Aiken & Mlyniec, *supra* note 3.

57. *Id.* at 4.

58. *Id.* at 14.

59. *Id.* citing National Research Council, How People Learn: Brain, Mind, Experience, and School 39 (1999).

60. *Id.* at 14.

61. Id. at 14–15.

62. *See* Lowman, *supra* note 17, at 26–37; *accord* Gerald F. Hess, *Heads and Hearts: The Teaching and Learning Environment in Law School*, 52 J. Legal Educ. 75, 82–83 (2002).

63. Hativa, *supra* note 18, at 98; *see also* Andrele Brutus St. Val, *Survey Says—How to Engage Law Students in the Online Learning Environment*, 70 J. Legal Educ. 297, 317–18 (2021) ("The more engaged the student, the better the learning outcomes." (citing Heather J. Leslie, *Trifecta of Student Engagement: A Framework for an Online Teaching Professional Development Course for Faculty in Higher Education*, 13 J. Rsch. Innovative Teaching & Learning 149, 150 (2019)).

64. Hativa, *supra* note 18, at 101.

65. Lowman, *supra* note 17, at 23. Lowman also provides a list of suggestions for both good and bad lecturing. *Id.* at 154–56. These suggestions highlight the importance of providing clear information in an engaging manner. *Id.* at 154.

66. Hativa, *supra* note 18, at 101.

67. Schrag, *supra* note 13, at 238.

68. *See, e.g.*, Kenneth R. Swift, *Take A (Cognitive) Load Off: Using Principle of Adult Education Theory to More Effectively Integrate A Drafting Unit into A First-Year Legal Writing Course and Ensure Student Success*, 63 How. L.J. 29, 37 (2019) (collecting some sources). No wonder "many law school instructors focus their efforts on keeping students *off* of the Internet[.]" Elizabeth G. Porter, *Imagining Law: Visual Thinking Across the Law School Curriculum*, 68 J. Legal Educ. 8, 9 (2018) (emphasis original)).

69. *New Study on Lawyer Well-Being Reveals Serious Concerns for Legal Profession*, Am. Bar Ass'n (Dec. 2017), https://www.americanbar.org/news/abanews/publications/youraba/2017/december-2017/secrecy-and-fear-of-stigma-among-the-barriers-to-lawyer-well-bei/ (citing Jerome M. Organ, David B. Jaffe & Katherine M. Bender, *Suffering in Silence: The Survey of Law Student Well-Being and the Reluctance of Law Students to Seek Help for Substance Use and Mental Health Concerns*, 66 J. Legal Educ. 116 (2016)); *see also* Peter Coy, *People in Their 20s Aren't Supposed to Be This Unhappy*, N.Y. Times Newsletter (Sept. 27, 2023), https://www.nytimes.com/2023/09/27/opinion/mental-health-20s-wellness.html.

70. *See, e.g.*, Karen Sloan, *"Our Law Students Need Help." Study Finds Higher Rates of Mental Health Problems*, Reuters (July 13, 2022, 2:55 PM), https://www.reuters.com/legal/legalindustry/our-law-students-need-help-study-finds-higher-rates-mental-health-problems-2022-07-13/ ("Today's law students are dealing with mental health challenges including anxiety and depression at a higher rate than their predecessors in 2014, a new study has found. Nearly 69% of respondents from 39 law schools surveyed in 2021 reported that they needed help for emotional or mental health problems in the past year. That's up from 42% from the 2014 version of the same survey[.]").

71. Benedict Carey, *Forget What You Know about Good Study Habits*, N.Y. Times (Sept. 6, 2010), https://www.nytimes.com/2010/09/07/health/views/07mind.html.

72. *See id.*; Cindy May, *The Problem with "Learning Styles,"* Sci. Am. (May 29, 2018), https://www.scientificamerican.com/article/the-problem-with-learning-styles/ ("A recent review of the scientific literature on learning styles found scant evidence to clearly support the idea that outcomes are best when instructional techniques align with individuals' learning styles. In fact, there are several studies that contradict this belief.") (citing Harold Pashler, Mark McDaniel, Doug Rohrer & Robert Bjork, *Learning Styles: Concepts and Evidence*, 9 Psychol. Sci. in the Public Interest 105 (2009); Laura J. Massa & Richard E. Mayer, *Testing the ATI Hypothesis: Should Multimedia Instruction Accommodate Verbalizer-Visualizer Cognitive Style?*, 16 Learning and Individual Differences 321 (2006)).

73. *See id.*

74. *See, e.g.*, Avi Fleischer & B. Fleischer, *Multiple Modality Pedagogical Approach Based on High Engagement for Diverse Learners*, 9 Psychol. & Psychol. Res. Int'l J. 1 (2024); Cathal Doyle & Yi-Te Chiu, *Blending Modalities, Pedagogies, and Technologies: Redesigning an Information Systems Course to Encourage Engagement*, 53 Comms. of the Ass'n for Info Sys. 323 (2023). For a helpful primer

on how to incorporate an additional modality—here, visual learning—into law school curricula, see Porter, *supra* note 68. *See, also*, Carey, *supra* note 71

75. Epstein, Aiken & Mlyniec, *supra* note 3, at 1.

76. Lowman, *supra* note 17, at 179, 186 (explaining that while starting a discussion might not be the most difficult task a teacher faces, guiding the students through the discussion and on to the right topic can be very challenging).

77. *Id.* at 168–80 (providing several examples to promote student engagement in discussion, including breaking students up into groups, role-playing, and problem-solving discussions). Indeed, most clinical teachers use these techniques. And for good reason: they "can powerfully enrich the primary learning that emerges from handling particular cases" in clinic. *See* Schrag, *supra* note 13, at 236–37, 239–41.

78. *See, e.g.*, Epstein, Aiken & Mlyniec, *supra* note 3, at 9.

79. *See* Beverly Balos, *Learning to Teach Gender, Race, Class, and Heterosexism: Challenge in the Classroom and Clinic*, 3 Hastings Women's L.J. 161, 171–72 (1992); *cf.* Linda Morton, *Creating a Classroom Component for Field Placement Programs: Enhancing Clinical Goals with Feminist Pedagogy*, 45 Me. L. Rev. 19, 44–52 (1993) (explaining implementation of feminist methodology in the classroom component of a field-placement externship program).

80. *Id.*

81. Lowman, *supra* note 17, at 181.

82. Having students report back on their observations from real practitioners in court can often provide a much-needed confidence boost for students struggling with imposter syndrome. Many students roll their eyes when practitioners who judge mock trial or moot court competitions tell them that they are "already better than most of the lawyers I see in real practice." But it is often, sadly, true. Additionally, these observe-and-report-back exercises also help remind students about the importance of one of their biggest assets as student lawyers: their passion and earnestness in advocating for their client. For example, in a criminal-defense clinic, just watching a few attorneys "phone-in" arraignments can helpfully remind students how prepared they are because of clinic, how passionate they are about the work they're doing for clients, and how palpable a difference there is in the courtroom and for clients when an attorney—yes, even a student attorney—engages in zealous advocacy at all stages of a case.

83. Beth McMurtrie, *How to Get Your Students to Engage with One Another*, Chron. Higher Educ. (Jan. 25, 2024), https://www.chronicle.com/newsletter/teaching/2024-01-25.

84. *See* George Fisher, *Evidence by the Video Method*, 68 J. Legal Educ. 15, 15 (2018).

85. Epstein, Aiken & Mlyniec, *supra* note 3, at 2 (quoting Professor Matthew Fraidin).

86. *See* Brookfield, *supra* note 24, at 28, 71, 79–80.

87. *See id.* at 27, 34–36.

88. Jenkins, *supra* note 5; *see also, e.g.*, Shanahan & Benfer, *supra* note 32, at 549.

89. *See generally, e.g.*, Beth McMurtrie, *Teaching Evaluations Are Broken. Can They Be Fixed?*, Chron. Higher Educ. (Feb. 6, 2024), https://www.chronicle.com/article/teaching-evaluations-are-broken-can-they-be-fixed (collecting studies); Meera E. Deo, *A Better Tenure Battle: Fighting Bias in Teaching Evaluations*, 31 Colum. J. Gender and Law 7, 16 (2015) ("While faculty generally believe that excellence in teaching requires fairness in grading and the appropriate pedagogical approaches, students instead tend to emphasize whether a professor 'smiles and displays a friendly demeanor, treats students as equals, greets students encountered outside of class, [and] adjusts course material to fit student interests.'" (citation omitted)); Gregory S. Parks, *Race, Cognitive Biases, and the Power of Law Student Teaching Evaluations*, 51 U.C. Davis L. Rev. 1039, 1041–43 (2018) (collecting studies on bias related to race and gender); Pamela J. Smith, *Teaching the Retrenchment Generation: When Sapphire Meets Socrates at the Intersection of Race, Gender, and Authority*, 6 Wm. & Mary J. Women & L. 53 (1999) (focusing on the unique challenges that Black women teachers, in particular, face);

LawProfBlawg, *Making Student Evaluations More Meaningful*, ABOVE THE LAW (June 7, 2022, 4:16 PM), https://abovethelaw.com/2022/06/making-student-evaluations-more-meaningful/ ("The literature has shown that student evaluations as currently constructed are strewn with gender and racial biases. Instructor attire and weight has impacts on student evaluations, too. In short, there is a lot of noise in student evaluations that have nothing to do with teaching and everything to do with student biases." (collecting studies)). N.B.: "LawProfBlawg" is the pen name of a well-known (but anonymous) law professor who runs the eponymous LawProfBlawg. *See, e.g.*, *Mr. Miyagi's Teaching Evaluations (and firing)*, LAWPROFBLAWG (Nov. 18, 2022), https://lawprofblawg.wordpress.com/2022/11/18/mr-myagis-teaching-evaluations-and-firing/ (blogpost including a satirized letter from a fictional dean to Mr. Miyagi—the teacher from the *Karate Kid* movie franchise—regarding teaching evaluations).

90. McMurtrie, *supra* note 89; *see also* Deborah J. Merritt, *Bias, the Brain, and Student Evaluations of Teaching*, 82 ST. JOHN'S L. REV. 235, 239 (2008) ("The nonverbal mannerisms [like smiling and how a professor walks into a room] that drive teaching evaluations bear little relation to learning.").

91. *See* Brookfield, *supra* note 24, at 27, 34–36.

92. *See id.*

93. *Id.* at 35.

94. *Id.* at 35–36.

95. *See id.* at 21, 36–39.

96. *See id.*

97. *See, e.g.*, Hess, Schwartz & Levit, *supra* note 51, at 701–02 (discussing importance of conferences).

98. *Cf.* Emily Grant, *At the [Other Side of the] Lectern*, 64 J. LEGAL EDUC. 103, 104–08 (2014) (detailing several benefits to observing colleagues' teaching).

99. *See, e.g.*, Jenkins, *supra* note 5 (identifying "attending conferences and seminars, conducting and presenting your own research, and remaining a practitioner of your art or science" as key components of the "preparation" required for excellence in teaching).

100. Daniel Keating, *Finding New Classroom Tricks in a Virtual Teaching World: One "Old Dog's" Tale*, 70 J. LEGAL EDUC. 462, 472–73 (2021).

101. *See id.*

Twelve

THE INTERRELATIONSHIP OF FEEDBACK, FORMATIVE ASSESSMENT, AND SUMMATIVE ASSESSMENT

This chapter is an introduction to the next two chapters, one on formative assessment and one on summative assessment, in order to distinguish between them and provide a deeper understanding of the issues embedded within them. Both are related to and based on feedback which occurs primarily in supervision sessions but can occur at any moment in the life of a case or project. The terms supervision, feedback, assessment, evaluation, and grading often rise in conversations among clinical faculty and between faculty and students.[1] The terms also appear repeatedly within the large body of books and articles written about clinical methodology. They often overlap and are sometimes used interchangeably. For example, evaluation and feedback are often used to describe the same thing. The terms "qualitative or formative assessment" and "quantitative or summative assessments" are sometimes all used to describe grading. The term "evaluation" may often be used to mean both. As such, faculty writers and conference presenters often confuse them with each other and sometimes misuse them within clinical literature. Students also misconstrue them during teacher-student discussions because of the imprecise use of the terms.

Despite the varied and interchangeable uses of the words, the concepts are all discrete. Readers, listeners, and teachers who are new to the profession will often come away confused when the terms are used inappropriately. Worse, they may take what they have heard and incorporate the loose meanings into their own teaching without a complete understanding of the differences. When that occurs, students and newer teachers can become confused. When confusion occurs, students may come away with an incomplete understanding of their learning patterns, their accomplishments, and their shortcomings.

Feedback is the form of intervention into a student's work that occurs during the pendency of the case or the project. It is the staple of a supervision session. The essence of feedback was discussed extensively in Chapters Four and Five of this book. In short, faculty members provide feedback to offer guidance to a student about a lawyering task that will be performed in the near future with the goal of understanding the law, strategy, tactics, and elements of the execution of the task. Faculty give feedback to ensure the tasks the student undertakes will move the case or project forward in ways that maximize the student's ability to achieve the client's goals. Supervisors will provide feedback many times during the life of the case. Although much of the feedback occurs prior to the execution of a task, it can also occur after the task is completed. As such, the conversations that occurred prior to the performance of a task are revisited after the student completes a task to determine whether the execution of the task successfully enhanced the client's goal. Feedback can also occur during the execution of the lawyering task itself when the supervisor offers an in-the-moment suggestion to improve the performance as it is being executed. Whenever feedback occurs, the conversations ensure that students are learning the integration of theory and practice. These conversations can also demonstrate how lessons learned performing one task can be transferred to other lawyering tasks that students will encounter in the clinic or during their careers as lawyers.

Some teachers refer to the post-event feedback as evaluation. Doing so, however, implies, especially in the mind of students, that a grading or summative assessment of those acts is taking place. But case or project work is not like an examination. Clinic work is iterative, so "evaluating" a student's work on any one task gives an incomplete "evaluation" of a student's overall work. It also gives an incomplete formative assessment since growth throughout the student's cases or projects and from one task to another is at the heart of formative assessments.

Formative or qualitative assessments are more fully explained in Chapter Thirteen, Conducting Formative Assessments.

> Formative assessment refers to tools that identify misconceptions, struggles, and learning gaps along the way and assess how to close those gaps. It includes effective tools for helping to shape learning and can even bolster students' abilities to take ownership of their learning when they understand that the goal is to improve learning, not apply final marks.[2]

These assessments involve broader conversations about learning that are based upon a student's total body of work. They are based on the faculty's observations of a students' evolution as they execute lawyering tasks while working on cases or projects over a period of time. They are also based on a student's reflections about their work, and their growth as learners during their time in the clinic.

Formative assessments usually take place either mid-semester or mid-year when a full body of work is examined. They can occur at the completion of a single case or project, but their utility is limited because growth, reflection, and the transference of knowledge may be limited after only one case. No matter when a formative assessment occurs, it permits students to appraise their own achievements and learning success during their time in the clinic. It offers the teacher the opportunity to speak about patterns they have observed during the student's performance that are related to the student's and clinic's learning goals. Formative assessments therefore provide a forum to celebrate a student's success in reaching those goals, and to provide advice and guidance for the path to continued improvement. These formative assessments, however, are not grading sessions.

A quantitative or summative assessment is the reward a student receives, based on a law school's institutional grading system, for the work and effort they performed during the course of the clinic. Summative or quantitative assessments are more fully explained in Chapter Fourteen, Assigning Grades—Summative Assessments.

> "Summative assessments evaluate student learning, knowledge, proficiency, or success at the conclusion of an instructional period, like a unit, course, or program. [They] are almost always formally graded and often heavily weighted (though they do not need to be). Summative assessment can be used to great effect in conjunction and alignment with formative assessment, and instructors can consider a variety of ways to combine these approaches."[3]

The term refers to the traditional grades given to students based on transparent rubrics designed to measure the student's accomplishments. But the measurement is not totally idiosyncratic to the student. It is determined in relation to the clinic's and student's goals when compared to other students in the clinic. Students are also measured in the context of the institutional demands and the constraints involving comparative judgments. Accurate assessment is further complicated by grading curves mandated by the law school faculty.

Although most clinical teachers feel comfortable providing feedback and critiquing a student's performance on tasks related to their cases and projects, they acknowledge that formative and summative assessments are two of the more difficult aspects of their jobs. Correctly assessing a student's work requires a system based on the stated goals of the clinic and on rubrics which guide the process. Equally important, those goals and rubrics must be explicitly defined for the students so that they can measure their own progress during their time in the clinic. Feedback, formative assessment, and summative measurements are based on those goals and rubrics and build on one another.

The three terms, feedback, formative assessment, and summative assessment, are each discrete terms. If teachers understand the differences among all these concepts and perform each task intentionally, using criteria and language clearly understood by students during their tenure in the clinic, they will satisfy the institutional needs of the law school and the true educational goals of the student. That nuanced understanding and use of the terms will guide the way teachers conduct supervision sessions, provide feedback, conduct case rounds and seminars, offer formative assessments, and assign grades. Students will attain a grade that is fair in relation to the goals of the clinic and the requirements mandated by the law school for assigning grades. Equally and perhaps more important, when all parts of clinic methodology are integrated, students will also know whether they have achieved their own learning goals and what they need to master in the future. Moreover, they will leave the clinic with a clearer understanding of where they stand on the path to becoming a successful lawyer.

Other Voices

Nina W. Tarr, *The Skill of Evaluation as an Explicit Goal of Clinical Training**

21 McGeorge Law Review 967 (Issue 4 1990)

...

I. The Purposes for Making the Skill of Evaluation an Explicit Goal

The advantages of making the skill of evaluation an explicit goal are numerous. At the outset, assessment is a critical skill for the students' growth after they have left law school. Assessment provides insurance that lawyering standards are not compromised by unrecognized, outside pressures. Second, becoming skilled at self-evaluation forces the students to be more responsible for their own education during the period that they participate in the skills program. Third, the students frequently think the theory or planning that is discussed in law school has no application in the "real world," and teaching them to assess themselves and others in terms of the theory is the follow-through that helps them apply theory to reality. Finally, the supervisors in the skills programs will be able to give more effective feedback to the students if evaluation is seen as part of the overall program. The assessment process can facilitate grading the students who have a wide range of performances and a wide variety of cases.

A. The Skill of Evaluation Ensures Long-term Learning and Will Preserve the Learning That Has Already Taken Place

What happens in law school and in the skills program is only the beginning of the students' development as lawyers. Historically, law schools have claimed that they teach people how to "think like a lawyer." The traditional classroom courses train the students to critique cases and apply the previous case's analysis to the next case. In the traditional classroom, we pose hypotheticals so that the students can apply the analyses to a variety of situations. The students become legal problem solvers with skills to find the law they will need in the future.

In the skills setting, we teach students a broader range of a lawyer's functions.

> For example, we discuss the goals of an initial client interview and how to most effectively accomplish those goals. Unless the student is able to look back at his or her own performance and evaluate whether he or she effectively executed the desired skills, the learning has stopped. The student will only develop to a certain level while in the program. In order to facilitate continued growth when a supervisor is no longer available to critique their work, students must learn to constantly examine their own work. What makes lawyers improve rather than stagnate is the ability to examine and learn: to learn how to learn

* Excerpts are reprinted with the permission of the author and the McGeorge Law Review.

in the skills context as well as the substantive or procedural context. We owe it to our students to train them to learn for the future in this arena.

New lawyers will neither be trained in the skill of evaluation nor even necessarily be critiqued in an effective manner once they are out of law school. Training usually occurs in the various settings in which our students will work, but the dynamics of time and money control the training programs. Further, the training that will take place usually focuses on the particular type of practice the lawyer has entered. Consequently, the student/lawyer will learn the skill of evaluation only in a skills program.

The research of social scientists who have examined professional competence indicates that, even if professionals become aware of the ineffectiveness of their behavior, they are resistant to change because of existing behavior patterns and values.

> [The mode of professional] social interaction orients interpersonal relationships towards specific goals: maximizing winning and minimizing losing; acting in a rational manner; and minimizing the open expression of feelings. "Theories of action" based upon these goals result in "minimal learning, defensive and mistrustful relationships, ineffectiveness of relationships and human systems, and long-term deterioration of problem-solving processes."

Because law school relationships among students and between students and their teachers "are characterized by persuasion, intellectualizing, competition, information suppression, manipulation, and outward conformity with limited internal commitment," they particularly feed into the students' resistance to self-evaluation for the purpose of ongoing learning. Recognizing that the traditional classroom courses and methodologies undermine inclinations to self-evaluation, the skills program must undertake the responsibility to explicitly teach this skill.

Everything we teach in the skills course is a microcosm or specimen to be examined and from which to be learned. We teach such cerebral areas as how to develop a theory of a case and such mundane areas as how to compute time for billing purposes. Our hope is that every time our student, who has now become a lawyer, is faced with a new client's case, he or she will routinely develop a theory of the case that will guide their work. We also expect that our well-trained graduates will routinely keep accurate time records so they can bill their clients or document their time for their public sector employer.

We should also expect that our students will routinely pause and examine their own performances and those around them to continue to develop their skills. When they walk out of a trial and return to their office, they should stop and consider what happened and why. Most lawyers go home at the end of the day and say "I did well in that negotiation today" or "that other attorney really ruined my client's case," but the excellent lawyers ask themselves what they can learn from what happened.

The first step is to develop the habit of reflection. However, the absolutely critical aspect of this continued learning process is the ability to realistically and critically examine activities and occurrences so the lawyer can use the experience to learn. Simply stopping after the trial and saying, "I did a great closing argument," is insufficient. The question must always be, "Why?" The skill that we should explicitly be teaching the student in the skills courses is how to answer that question. We must teach them to "think like a behavioral scientist" about all of the dynamics of what happened. For example, did the closing argument go well because he or she established good eye contact with the judge so it felt like the judge was really listening? Is this something the lawyer can replicate, or is it a peculiarity of this particular judge? Was the ability to establish eye contact because the lawyer was unusually familiar with the law and facts so felt comfortable and spontaneous? If so, more preparation on cases in the future might pay off.

Was it because the argument was the first thing in the morning and the lawyer was alert and awake? Is sleep more critical to performance than the lawyer realized? Since a lawyer cannot always control the time of day a part of a case is heard, how can he or she compensate?

These are examples of the student/lawyer beginning to distinguish between that for which he or she is responsible and can control versus that which is outside his or her control. Many interns will return from a hearing and complain their client surprised them with unknown facts on the stand. Why? The student will want to shift the responsibility to the client, which is sometimes justifiable. However, more commonly, the trial preparation was superficial and the student must figure out what to do differently in the future. Alternatively, the student claims he or she lost the case because the lawyer on the other side did a great job or that the judge hates law students. These responses are evidence of classic projection and the student must learn to realistically distinguish between what is circumstantial and what is related to their lawyering abilities.

The limits of time and money not only affect the quantity and quality of training the students will get, but also put pressure on them to conform to the "normal" behavior which may not be consistent with the behavior they want. Moreover, the desire to conform undermines the student/lawyer's inclination to reflect. Without being taught evaluation, many students will begin to compromise their standards without even realizing it. Only if the students are skilled and in the habit of evaluating themselves and others will they realize what is happening.

...

C. The Skill of Evaluation Will Reinforce the Applicability of the Theories of Lawyering Skills and Lawyering Process

Skills training has developed far beyond the early days when students were thrown into situations and expected to learn by survival. Supervisors in most settings articulate expectations, theories, techniques, etc. that they expect the students to incorporate. In simulated skills courses and the classroom components of live client clinics, supervisors and faculty members are teaching students how to effectively execute various professional functions. Books and articles have been written on these subjects. Videotapes have been produced illustrating how experts would actually perform. In sum, numerous resources exist on which supervisors can rely and the students understand the components of a certain, lawyering function. Yet the students see much of what is taught as pure cerebral theory that has no application to what they will do when they are out of the school setting.

Barnhizer describes how he divided his clinical program into the initial phase of non-clinical academic learning and then the clinical stage. The division gives the students a preview of what is to come:

> participation in the introductory course is intended to develop in the students a cognitive structure or framework for the experiences they will have in the actual clinical quarters. This cognitive framework enables them more readily to perceive the relevance of the experiences they are having and to fit each of these experiences into a conception of the overall process, rather than see them as a series of isolated or unrelated events. This 'learned sense of the significant' permits the student to gain the greatest amount of understanding...

Whether the program is formally divided as described by Barnhizer, designed so that the theory and practice are taught in a concurrent seminar, or structured with individualized tutoring and no classroom component, Barnhizer's theory of learning is taking place. The students are thinking and planning with some theory in mind to facilitate the purpose and direction of the work. Barnhizer does not go far enough, however, because the "learned sense of the significant" should be reinforced in the follow up activity that constitutes evaluation. If the students are learning the skill of evaluation and understand how it incorporates the theory they have learned, the significance is heightened even further.

For example, in the classroom component of a live client clinic, or in the simulation course that is the prerequisite for the live client clinic, the students read and discuss Binder and Price's three steps for an initial client interview. The students may be involved in some in-class simulated exercises which illustrate how to apply Binder and Price's techniques. The student then faces his or her first "client," either real or simulated, and conducts an interview. Unless the student is asked for a self-critique or evaluation that uses the language of the Binder and Price, the theory remains an abstraction. If the student has read Bellow and Moulton on negotiation, the self-evaluation of him or herself and the other attorney should be in the language of the text. Even if the supervisor's instructions to the student are based on the supervisor's experience, certain "theory" is given that students will discount as academic or applicable only to the school based experiences. Again, if the self-evaluation and evaluation of others is based on the instructions given, the theory is absorbed as applicable and the "learned sense of the significant" is reinforced.

D. Explicitly Teaching Evaluation Skills Will Facilitate Critiquing and Grading the Students

Skills teachers sometimes find it difficult to effectively critique students because the supervisors are not entirely sure how to conduct the critique, because the students may be unreceptive to the critique, because the students' defense mechanisms make critiquing a struggle, or because time constrains the critiquing process. For example, after the judge rules that custody is given to the opposing party, supervisors sometimes find it hard to explain to the heartbroken student the strengths and weaknesses. The student who views himself or herself as a compassionate person who has conducted his or her first mock interview may not be receptive to the news that controlling, paternalistic behavior is inappropriate in an attorney/client relationship. Finally, when the negotiations break down the day before the hearing, the supervisor may not take the time to analyze the student's performance.

If the skill of evaluation is an explicit goal of the course, evaluation takes on a different light and the critiquing job of the supervisor becomes easier. At the outset, if the supervisor had laid out a system of how critiques will be conducted, even the student who is in an emotionally delicate condition will expect the critique. A system should be in place, and the process should be routine. Moreover, if the student is responsible for conducting the self-evaluation and evaluation of the others involved, the process can be very healing.

The student who is hostile to being supervised or at a lesser extreme, disinterested in feedback, should find a self-evaluation process easier to accept. If the students are told at the outset of the course that evaluation is one of the skills they will be expected to master as part of the course and the reasons they are expected to master this skill, these students will recognize the process as part of the bigger picture. Evaluation will be the students' job and the supervisor will be training them in how to effectively execute this function just like the supervisors are training them to do an effective closing argument. The evaluation process will become more relevant to the student.

Because the value of feedback is affected by timing, the evaluation system that is created should be simple enough so that it may be used even in rushed or stressful times. Even if a hearing is pending, a client has immediate needs, or a simulated exercise is turned in minutes before class, the idea that the skill of evaluation is an articulated part of the program will help ensure the important step in the learning process is not lost.

In addition to helping supervisors give feedback, teaching the skill of evaluation will help supervisors in grading. Whether to grade skills courses or not continues to be an issue. Evaluation skills can help in determining grades and provide a vehicle for equalizing some of the imbalances when quantities of cases, qualities of performance, and various levels of student commitment make grading so difficult. For example, the student who neglects to prepare for the case but somehow blunders through and "wins" feels they deserve a high grade. The supervisor may feel exasperated at the student's lack of preparation and not want to reinforce the simplistic, lazy approach the student took by giving him or her a high grade. In contrast, the student who works hard but cannot quite execute the good planning may also deserve some positive reinforcement by the grading system. A follow-up evaluation that reflects that the student understood what happened creates another dimension to the experience which could facilitate a "fair" result. An inability to articulate what was learned could reduce the grade and vice-versa.

...

Endnotes

1. The terms "formative assessment" and "qualitative assessment" have the same meaning and are used interchangeably throughout this book. The terms "summative assessment," "quantitative assessment," and "grades" are also roughly the same and are used interchangeably throughout.

2. *Formative and Summative Assessments*, YALE POORVU CENTER FOR TEACHING AND LEARNING, https://poorvucenter.yale.edu/Formative-Summative-Assessments (citing Elise Trumbull & Andrea A. Lash, *Understanding Formative Assessment: Insights from Learning Theory and Measurement Theory*, WESTED (Apr. 2013)).

3. *Id.*

Thirteen

CONDUCTING FORMATIVE ASSESSMENTS[1]

Clarifying the Terms of Assessment

As noted in Chapter Twelve, The Interrelationship of Feedback, Formative Assessment, and Summative Assessment, the terms feedback, assessment, evaluation, and grading often arise in conversations among clinical faculty and between faculty and students. They are used and often misused when authors or speakers use the terms in ways which suggest that they are the same thing. Each concept is discrete in clinical pedagogy, and clinical teachers should use them appropriately so that colleagues understand what they are talking about. Using the terms appropriately also allows students to understand what the faculty member is really saying, and whether they are being measured or graded when the words are used.

As noted in the various chapters on clinical supervision, feedback is the form of intervention into a student's work that occurs continuously during the pendency of the case or the project. As discussed in those chapters, these conversations are case- or project-focused and are the staple of a supervision session. While learning certainly occurs during supervision sessions, the conversations do not necessarily focus on student learning writ large. Faculty provide feedback to offer guidance to a student about a lawyering task that will be performed in the near future. As noted in various chapters, the goal of feedback is to help the student understand the law, strategy, tactics, and elements of the performance that will occur before the case or project is completed. Faculty give feedback to ensure a specific task will move the case or project forward in ways that maximize the student's ability to achieve the client's goals while increasing a student's knowledge and skill. Doing so, however, implies that an assessment, formative or summative, is occurring.[2] But few teachers actually assign grades to each lawyering activity students perform after its completion. When the feedback occurs after the fact, some clinicians refer to the conversations in those sessions as evaluations or assessments, again confusing the terms feedback, formative assessment, summative assessment, evaluation, and grading, Earlier chapters on supervision techniques relate primarily to methods of feedback. Summative assessment and grading will be discussed in a subsequent chapter. This chapter focuses on formative or qualitative assessments.

Elements of Formative Assessment

Purpose

Formative assessment refers to conversations with or written comments to students that identify learning goals that the student achieved, legal tasks successfully mastered, and professional and personal growth. Modern learning theory suggests that formative assessments enhance student learning and outcomes.[3] In education generally, formative assessments are regarded as "one of the most important interventions for promoting high performance ever studied."[4] Formative assessments, unlike summative assessments, are premised on the idea that students can and should be making mistakes.[5] When students are allowed to make mistakes, they, with the guidance of their supervisor, can analyze why the mistakes happened, receive corrective suggestions, and then continue to work on the same task with that feedback in mind.[6] By eliminating the focus on grading that is typically present in legal education, students can engage in this process more openly, which ultimately enhances learning outcomes. Formative assessment sessions then become the place where metacognition is recognized and explained, where transference occurs, and where the zone of proximal development is reestablished.[7]

Parts of the conversations during a formative assessment are sometimes similar to the feedback that occurs during a case or project supervision session. But the prior feedback conversations take on a larger purpose during the formative assessment session. This is because the formative assessment explores the basis for the actions taken and judgments made on the students' cases or projects throughout the semester. The purpose in the formative assessment is not to move any case or project forward but rather to assess "tasks and activities to provide the teacher with a window into students' cognitive processes. It is student-focused rather than case- or project-focused. Formative assessments allow students to show their thinking and allow teachers to learn and gauge students' cognitive processes."[8] It also shows the teacher how the student's thought processes evolved over time and provides a window into the student's growth as a lawyer and a learner.

Learning from clinic activities is an iterative process. "Evaluating" students' development based on any one lawyering task performed during a case or project usually provides a limited amount of data to assess a student's overall performance. A formative assessment after one case will generally be incomplete because growth as a learner develops from one's case and from one task to another. Unlike feedback in a supervision session, a faculty member in a formative assessment session describes a series of actions from multiple cases and projects that a student has taken during the semester and asks the student to reflect on those actions evolved. That permits the supervisor to assess the student's professional growth as a lawyer and personal growth as a learner.

Faculty use formative assessments to understand what a student has learned during the clinical course. The assessments involve broad conversations about learning that are based on how the student implemented the faculty member's prior supervision feedback. It is also based on the supervisor's observations of the student's individual efforts to plan and perform lawyering tasks that occurred during the period of client representation in each of the student's cases or projects. The faculty member's formative assessment also identifies patterns of recurring behavior that result in success but also those based on misconceptions. It can also note where the student still struggles, and where learning gaps still exist. More importantly, the formative assessment outlines a path to closing those performance gaps[9] and identifies how students can maintain a growth mindset even in the face of incomplete success.

The learning path is at the heart of a formative assessment for both the teacher and the student because it serves to illuminate effective tools to help shape the student's learning process. In addition, the conversations can bolster students' abilities to take ownership of their learning as they come to understand and accept that the goal of the formative assessment is to improve their learning and not to award final grades.

Self-Assessments

Successful lawyers are able to critique their own work accurately and continue to improve their skills as they mature in their practice.[10] Thus, clinical faculty are expected to assess not only the students' progress and growth, but to teach students self-assessment techniques. Faculty-led formative assessment sessions are more successful if students prepare a self-assessment[11] prior to engaging with the faculty in the formative assessment. The students' self-assessments should relate to the clinic's goals, to lawyering tasks performed, and to the students' own learning goals. Students should use the self-assessment to reflect on their body of work and assess their growth, their areas of struggle, and their educational needs. The purpose of the self-assessment is to have the students analyze the actions they took over a period of time and to understand how and why they made the judgments that led to a choice to take one action as opposed to another possible action. They can then better assess whether the judgments and the choices they made over time were successful and determine whether their successful actions and processes were replicated subsequently in similar and dissimilar circumstances.

Assumptions that can lead to less than effective client representation are always a possible subject for both the students' self-assessments and the formative assessment session. If teaching social justice is a goal of the clinic, the self-assessment enables the students to contemplate how their assumptions about justice helped or hindered their work with their clients and either advanced or detracted from the role of law and lawyers in American society. Even if social justice is not a clinical goal, a self-assessment can help students understand how personal values can distort a lawyer's understanding of their clients' interests.

The self-assessment should encourage students to become engaged in the reflective process and enables them to explore their actions more critically.[12] It also ensures that the student has reflected on his or her actions in each of the areas the supervisor has identified in the clinic goals as being essential for student progress.[13] Students' self-assessment skills might initially be weak.[14] However, students who engage in self-assessment over the course of the semester or year are better able to improve those skills, just as they improve their legal skills. Reflection and assessment sessions provide meaningful information about one's abilities and shortcomings. Requiring students to engage in self-assessments, especially when reflection is an explicit goal of the clinic, helps students acquire the habit of assessing their own work during the course of their lives.[15] They will also help students confront issues in their personal lives and in the larger issues of American society.

Conducting the Formative Assessment Session

Assessments can occur at the completion of a single case or project, but their utility at that time is limited because the evidence of growth, reflection, and the transference of knowledge will be constrained by a small amount of data. Consequently, most clinical teachers prefer to conduct formative assessments midway through the term when a sufficient body of work can be examined. While delaying the assessment until the end of the term provides a greater amount of data, doing so deprives the student of the opportunity to alter their misconceptions about their own progress or improve their performance. In addition, delaying the assessment does not help the teacher know whether the lessons of the formative assessment have been internalized. Equally important, end-of-semester assessments come too late for students to recognize their own growth as it is occurring.

Although most clinical teachers feel comfortable providing feedback and critiquing a student's performance on tasks related to their cases and projects, they acknowledge that formative assessment conversations can be difficult. Formative assessments should be based on clinic goals and rubrics. They are or should be related to one another and should be built upon one another.[16] Without clear assessment rubrics, conversations can become random and unstructured. Engaging in a successfully formative assessment requires a system based on the stated goals of the clinic and on rubrics that are known and understood by the student, to guide the process. Throughout this book, I have stressed the importance of goals, and the equal importance of conveying those goals and expectations clearly to students from their first day in the clinic. The goals and rubrics must be explicitly defined for the students so they can measure their own progress during their time in the clinic.

Supervisors will feel more comfortable conducting a formative assessments and students will be less defensive about receiving them if reflection is an explicit goal of the clinic.[17] Teachers sometimes feel uncomfortable when assessing students, especially in a clinic where the relationships between teacher and students are so personal. Reading the students' self-assessments in advance of the formative assessment session gives the supervisor some insight into the students thoughts and feelings about their work and helps the supervisor feel more comfortable when assessing their work.[18] Supervisors can then use the students' self-assessments as the starting point for the formative assessment session. Letting the students start the conversation by recalling their successes and mistakes remind them that the session is about their sense of their development. It also gives the teacher some insight into the accuracy of the students reflection on their skills and growth.[19] Self-assessments also allow the faculty and the students to determine what the students believe they actually learned from the materials studied and from the actions they and others took during the case or project. Going into the formative assessment, the teacher also will have some sense of the students' reasons for the choices they made.

No matter the strength of the trust relationship between the student and supervisor, many students will feel stress prior to the conversations. Supervisors may fail to achieve their goals for the formative assessment session unless they acknowledge that stress and have carefully planned the conversations. Like everything else in clinic, formative assessment sessions are intentional and not casual conversations. The self-assessment form will have reminded the students of the goals of the clinic and the rubrics upon which the assessments are made. It will also have given the student space to reflect on their own goals[20] and prepare to rebut assessments they believe may be inaccurate. Nonetheless, the preliminary work will not totally relieve the stress the students feel as they enter the teacher's office.

The formative assessment is to assess whether lessons students learned from classes, prior supervision sessions, and feedback on performances have been internalized and used in similar, as well as dissimilar, subsequent actions. They are objective, detailed, both retrospective and prospective, and comparative relating to transparent goals and course rubrics. Formative assessments should never be a one-way conversation. They should be planned in a way that encourages students to appraise their own achievements and learning growth. Because formative assessments concern the evolution of the student's learning and behavior, the conversation focuses on the student as well as the actions taken.

As noted earlier, the teacher should let the student begin the discussion. Once the student has opened the conversation, the teacher should praise the student both for their good work and reflections about it. Whether the student opening gambit is accurate or not, it provides the teacher with an entry point to speak about patterns of behavior they have observed during the student's performances relating to both the student's and clinic's learning goals. The faculty can continue to affirm and celebrate the student's successes in reaching those goals and provide advice and guidance for the path to continued improvement.

Social science research demonstrates that people rarely change ineffective or unproductive behavior if not pointed out with actual examples. Similarly, people seldom challenge assumptions that underpin the behavior patterns developed over the course of a lifetime in the absence of some form of intervention.[21] Hence, the assessments are not only about lawyering tasks. They are also about the student's assumptions concerning personal values as they affect client representation, the student's views about the justice of the legal system in which they will work and the roles of the various participants, and the student's understanding of how their values integrate with professional ethics.

There may be disagreements about the student's assessment. That can be an entry point for a conversation about expectations. "Statements of expected standards, curriculum objectives, or learning outcomes [can be] insufficient to convey the richness of the meaning that is wrapped up within them."[22] If so, teachers can use the formative assessment to clarify misunderstandings about the goals of the course and the standards expected of the students. Formative assessment sessions, then, can reinforce the clinic learning goals and outcomes when a student has not previously internalized them or has misinterpreted them.

Few students will have completely succeeded or failed in their clinic work. The formative assessment conversation should be designed to describe the significance, worth, and quality of a series of actions that the student has taken. Both students and teachers should use the assessment for an honest discussion. Teacher should remind the student that the formative assessment is not about a grade. It is about learning and growth. Both come from success and from mistakes. When focused on the student, however, the conversation reflects on the student's assumptions and growth as a learner. Faculty should offer observations on patterns of both successful and unsuccessful behavior, needed skills improvement, and actions to take to improve the skills so that the student's growth continues.

Overcoming Impediments to the Conversation

Assessment conversations are not always easy. One reason is that students may be beaten down after two years of traditional law school pedagogy and grading, leaving them defensive about assessments and critiques. Additionally, the fact that students, like most adults, can be fairly set in their ways increases the complexity of conducting good formative assessment sessions. Clinical education can also challenge patterns of behavior that are so deeply ingrained in a student that criticizing their performance can be interpreted as a criticism of their overall ability or character.[23] All students hope to impress their supervisors and sometimes believe their teacher's opinion of them is dependent on the value of their work. That is why the critique should be directed at the work and not at the person. Moreover, suggestions to improve student's learning and performance should always be included in the formative assessment.

Formative assessment sessions are more productive when conducted in a relaxed format. Supervisors should maintain a generous tone during the conversation. The student will have a more active role in the assessment process and get more out of those sessions if the supervisors avoids merely listing the student's shortcomings and the supervisor prescription about ways that a student can improve.[24] More importantly, successful formative assessments result when the students are able to determine on their own where the shortcomings exist and set their own path forward to growth as a lawyer and a learner.

The formative assessment conversation will be helpful only if it provides students with more than mere opinions about their work. These assessments are a collaborative endeavor by the student and the teacher. Teachers should listen to the student's perspective on the learning issue being discussed before they begin to offer their observations about the issue. Doing so may bring forth information that the teacher neglected to consider. It also signals to the supervisor how a student feels when being evaluated.[25]

A supervisor's affirmation concerning some of the work that was done is essential to help set the tone and diminish the anxiety the student might feel coming into the session. The affirmations should precede the more difficult conversations regarding student shortcomings that may have to come later. It should be easy to focus on some of the student's good work. When teachers begin their responses, it is best to start with measures of success that the student has achieved. The teacher should explain exactly which aspects of the student's work were successful and why, and how actions later in the semester demonstrated growth regarding the issue being discussed at that point in the session. Beginning with praise and maintaining empathy for the student shows that the session is not designed to attack the student, (something that they might have anticipated), but instead to be a truly reflective conversation between student and teacher. Nonetheless, unsuccessful actions, assumptions, and results need to be discussed, as well as actions, skills, and events that still require improvement.[26] The comments must be specific and identify the patterns of behavior, both strong and weak, that emerged from the student's work during the course of the clinic. A successful formative assessment session occurs when students reflect on a body of work, rather than on any one action. Moreover, most students will have successfully completed many lawyering activities. Hence it is highly unlikely that a student's performance will be substandard in every element of the clinic's practice.

Reflection

The critical part of the formative assessment involves reflection. A reflective formative assessment identifies and then analyzes the causes of both effective and ineffective behaviors. One goal is to name the ineffective behaviors and replace them with effective methods and strategies. Another goal is to analyze why successful endeavors occurred. Hence, the focus of the assessment is both on the actions and the thought processes of the student. Educational reflection has been defined in many ways. One of the better definitions is that "reflection is dialectical, putting multiple perspectives into play with each other in order to produce insight. Procedurally, reflection entails a looking forward to goals we might attain, as well as looking back to see where we have been. When we reflect, we thus project and review, often putting the projections and the reviews in dialogue with each other, working dialectically to discover what we know, what we have learned, and what we might understand."[27] "Reflection allows students to make sense of material/experience in relation to oneself, others, and the conditions that shaped it; and to reimagine material/experience for future personal or social benefit."[28] Moreover, "transformative learning can take place when, after thoughtful examination, [students] can articulate ways of making sense of disorienting moments."[29] Reflection then is the basis of the metacognition that leads to learning for transference.

"Teachers can encourage students to reflect on their accomplishments, challenges, and mistakes by asking questions that spark critical thinking: What was your task, your ultimate goal, or the desired outcome for this activity? What are some important concepts and ideas that you discovered/learned? Why are they important? How did you solve the problem or task? Did you reach your goal? Explain. Would you make changes if you had to do it again? Explain."[30] Reflection methods can vary. Professor Alex Scherr suggests asking students to consider an action taken or observation made, recall their initial responses or reactions to them, analyze the causes for that reaction or judgment, consider alternatives and articulate a theory for both the ineffective and potentially more effective responses, and then assess how the lessons learned might apply to similar or dissimilar situations in the future.[31]

Professor Amy Ziegler provides some examples of what a student's reflective response looks like in practice. While her examples describe reflection in the context of feedback on a single event rather than in formative assessment session, they provide some insight into the process. The first example she provides is about a student who fails to address relevant information in an initial client interview.[32] She asks the student to reflect on why her questioning strategy was unsuccessful and then explore alternative strategies.[33] In a second example, she describes a student who had trouble confronting a client she believed to be lying during an interview.[34] She asks the student to "discuss the contradictory information that formed the basis of the student's assumption that the client was lying and weigh it against the client's credibility. The reflection would include an evaluation of the student's reaction, which could possibly have been frustration or anger.[35] The reflection process in this example provides clinical professors with the opportunity to address the social and ethical issues that reveal themselves through the reflection process.[36] It creates opportunities to enrich the educational experience by challenging student beliefs and analyzing how they impact the client.[37]

As noted earlier, the terms feedback and assessment are often used interchangeably. The questions Professor Ziegler poses for reflection are used in her examples as part of the feedback on ongoing cases. But these same questions could be replicated during a formative assessment session when looking at patterns or comparing a performance of two similar events. The main difference is that the questions posed in the Ziegler article are based on a single event, not on a pattern. Consequently, they address the immediate problem in a case but do little in terms of metacognition. Certainly, the larger questions could be addressed here, but the issue is a one-off to move the case along. It is resolved with a quick recognition by the student of the assumptions made, and quick and lasting corrections of the error in this context. On the other hand, had the supervisors noticed a pattern of repeated similar behavior, it would suggest that the student did not move out of the zone of proximal development to a level of higher understanding. That would require a deeper conversation with more faculty support to move the student's learning to a high plane.

The student's progress should be assessed against a standard of achievement that the faculty member believes is attainable given the goals of the clinic, the content of the classroom work, the nature of the cases, the current measure of the student's knowledge and ability, and the interactions that occurred in the supervision sessions during the period of time in question.[38] Students may not be prepared to listen to honest comparisons of their work in relation to the standard of achievement prescribed by the clinic's learning goals. On the other hand, they have the ability to reach the intended lesson on their own if they can arrive at it though their own reflection guided by the teacher.

I have been consistently surprised at how students' self-assessments echo the faculty member's own observations. However, difficult conversations may still occasionally occur. Despite the difficulty, they are essential to helping students accurately judge their own progress and to help them internalize what they have learned.[39]

Maintaining Trust Relationships

The students' growth in the responsible use of their knowledge and power as professionals is facilitated by the personal relationship between student and teacher. This is what makes clinical education within the law school different from a job in a public or private legal services organization, government agency, or law firm. Teachers must remind themselves that they are no longer simply public interest lawyers. They are now members of the academy whose job is much broader than providing good representation to clients. This is where clinical education adds value to the law school curriculum. Clinicians bring not just our legal skills as lawyers, but also our critical pedagogic skills to the development of new lawyers. The formative assessment is where much of this work occurs. New teachers often lack confidence in their ability to provide assessments, but they must learn to do it. Insufficient or less than honest assessment will not give the students what they deserve from an academic experience.

Interpersonal issues may be lurking within the student-teacher relationship and may arise during the formative assessment. Clinic work is not simple or easy for either the students or the supervisors. It can produce disagreements and stress. A student and a clinic teacher may have experienced several misunderstandings and disagreements or even periods of empathic disconnect during the semester. Events such as these can color the faculty member's perception of the student's work or the student's perception of the validity of the critique. Conversely, a good student-teacher relationship may have created expectations of high praise on the part of the student or a discomfort on the part of the teacher when a less than positive critique has to be delivered. No one likes to fail, and no one wants to disappoint those who matter to them. As I have said several times throughout this book, mistakes are not always true failures. Even true failures can become moments of immense growth. They are all bumps on the long road to learning and living an honorable life.

For the most part, students have profound respect for their teachers and do not want to feel as if they have let them down. All of the learning problems mentioned throughout this book can be avoided if the clinic is well-structured. The notion of a growth mindset should permeate every conversation a supervisor has with a student throughout the experiential course. This is especially true during the formative assessment. Faculty should take students where they are and judge actions, not people. It is true that a formative assessment is an "evaluation" of sorts and is judgmental in that it assumes a certain level of quality attaches to every task. But formative assessments do not judge the person. They judge the quality of an action and offer suggestions for growth.

No one is merely the sum total of his or her work output. Moreover, the duration of the clinic is only a small part of the student's career. For the student or the teacher to assume that the budding lawyer will be an accomplished professional at the end of the clinic is unrealistic. Thus, supervisors must conduct the assessment sessions in ways that help students understand that the assessment is based on just a small period in what will be a lifelong profession. Both students and teachers should realize and accept that there can be no learning without mistakes and even failure. Failure, however, is almost never caused by a personal trait.[40]

Another reason the interpersonal relationship between the student and the professor can become strained during a formative assessment is because critique is often as hard to give as it is to receive. Most teachers want to communicate unequivocal respect and affection for their students, even when they are pointing out the students' shortcomings. Teachers usually like their students and want to be liked in return. Those emotions, however, can cloud a teacher's judgment. Sometimes teachers cannot find the precise words to describe a particular assessment. This may occur because the goals of the clinic are incomplete or unarticulated. Teachers must be precise and name concepts to create a common vocabulary and to extrapolate from one situation to another. Without such clarity, the message teachers seek to convey for future learning may not be accurately or appropriately received. When this occurs, the relationship going forward can be fractured and the ability to transfer what one learns to another situation is weakened.

A free, honest, and open formative assessment conversation is one that strengthens rather than damages the bond and trust between teacher and learner. These conversations require generosity, humility, and cross-cultural understanding.[41] Cross-cultural assessment interactions can have a negative impact on both the student and the teacher,[42] especially when implicit bias affects the assessment.[43] This outcome negatively affects students' learning experiences. One specific way implicit bias impacts student performance is when a professor's and the student's preconceived notions of the student's ability creates a self-fulfilling prophecy.[44] If a professor communicates an expectation for a high level of performance through the feedback process, it is likely to occur.[45] Conversely, low expectations can translate into low performance. This can be particularly harmful for minority students and students who are part of other marginalized groups. A self-fulfilling prophecy can have severe consequences on student performance and learning and can even lead professors to give up on students for whom they have low expectations.[46]

Choosing the correct language to use during formative assessment sessions is critical to maintaining the teacher-student trust relationship, especially in times of heightened sensitivity to emotions and identity. Respect is essential, and empathy toward students is critical throughout the clinic but especially during the formative assessment. All clinical teachers long to conduct free, honest, and open conversations. Faculty need to understand that clinical teaching is not just about moving a case along in the most advantageous manner for the client. That is what supervisors in law offices do. The privilege and responsibility of an academic is to use the case or project to explore the larger questions about the role of a lawyer, the theory of lawyering, lifetime learning, personal development and growth, and the values that support the profession. As I have written several times in other chapters of this book, our job is to educate the whole student—mind, body, and spirit—and to instill a passion for learning, reflection, service, and the greater good of humankind.[47] At their best, experiential teachers engage in the evolution of students' lives and minds, assisting in the fullest possible development of their talents as individual human beings. That is the purpose of a reflective formative assessment. But it cannot happen if teachers are unaware of all the adverse influences affecting the interpersonal relationship between student and teacher.

The Relationship Between Formative and Summative Assessments

All teachers must have some understanding about how feedback, formative assessments, and summative assessments relate to one another, how formative assessments translate into written summative assessments or grades, and how one assigns grades for the multiple accomplishments or shortcomings noted in the rubrics and goals. However, if teachers truly understand the differences among the terms feedback, formative assessment, summative assessment or grading, and if they perform each task intentionally using criteria and language clearly understood by students during their tenure in the clinic, faculty will satisfy the institutional needs of the law school and the true educational goals of the student and the clinic. That nuanced understanding will guide the way teachers conduct supervision sessions, case rounds, seminars, formative and summative assessment sessions, and grading. At the end of their clinic course, students will not only attain a grade that is fair in relation to the goals of the clinic and the grading requirements the law school mandates, but they will also know whether they have achieved their own learning goals. Moreover, when all parts of clinic methodology are integrated, students will leave the clinic with an understanding of where they currently stand on the path to becoming successful lawyers and have a clearer path to continue their growth as lawyers. They will also know a method that will help them continue to improve their skills and methods as they mature in the profession.

The assessment teachers provide at mid-semester is a reflection on the quality of the multitude of tasks that students have been asked to perform up to that date that the teacher has observed. It is reflective, retrospective, and prospective, and it identifies and analyzes the learning strategies the student has employed. It also includes the strategies the teacher has used to determine whether the student has demonstrated an increasing understanding of the role of lawyers, the tasks they perform, and the goals that supervisors expect the student to achieve in the course. Formative assessment sessions are about growth not grades. As such, it is important to avoid grade conversations because they tend to carry the sense of judgment not encouragement. Despite our desire to avoid them, students may continually return to the grade question, hence not internalizing the growth assessment.

Even with adequate preparation and planning, the formative assessment conversations can be complex and sometimes difficult for the same reasons grading is complex and difficult. Students often assume that the supervisor will announce a grade during the formative assessment because assessment also connotes the notion of "How am I doing?" Because grades are the coin of the realm in law schools and the currency for a first job, students may assume that assessment means evaluation and that translates into "What grade are you giving me?" Grades are a critical concern to the students and are the boarding pass to desired employment. Nonetheless, grades should not be a subject of the formative assessment. Once a grade is announced, the subsequent conversation will be less productive. Students may want to challenge the supervisor's determination of the grade. When that happens, the conversation will turn away from what the students have learned, how what they have learned transfers into other areas of practice and life, and what they need to do to continue learning. Formative assessments are about learning. Summative assessments are about grades.

Students will sometimes not ask directly about a grade but will instead want to hear about comparisons between their work with that of other students in the clinic. Since law school is notoriously competitive, students want to know where they stand in comparison to those whose work that they themselves may have already judged. This is especially true when students work in teams or when the case or project does not generate the same kinds of tasks that other students in the clinic are performing. Like conversations about personal grades, conversations about comparisons to other students should be avoided. Even though there is a relationship between the formative assessments teachers prepare and the summative assessments or grades they ultimately assign to all the students in the clinic, the formative assessment session is not the place for that discussion. Since most teachers conduct the sessions midway through the term, there is more time to learn and to improve student performance. Grades and the comparisons among students that play a part in the grading process have no place in sessions devoted to acknowledging and advancing learning. Hence, grade conversations and conversations about other students' performances during the semester should be avoided during formative assessment sessions. Indeed, those conversations should not occur at all until after grades are actually assigned.

Reflecting on the Process

After each formative assessment session, supervisors should reflect on the dynamics of the session, noting to themselves what went right, what went wrong, and how they felt delivering a critique. Faculty members, especially new ones, can make mistakes just like students can. Reflection on the process and its success or failure allows teachers to consider what they could have done differently to make the conversation with the student more productive. It is important that students understand the goals and expectations of the clinic. Teachers must reflect on whether the goals were clearly set forth for the students; whether the student understood the goals; and whether the student knew the assessment would be based on those goals. Teachers should consider whether their comments were based on a pattern of observable events, or merely opinions that were difficult to support. Those opinions might have been true, but without carefully taking notes about each practice event, supervision session, and classroom activity, accurate assessments of the student's work cannot be delivered. Teachers should reflect on the language they used with the student. If the tone of the conversation was negative and without sufficient praise for actions performed, the disappointment of negative critique will not be accepted easily. The same result can be expected if the negative critique was personal rather than directed at the student's actual actions. If the concepts discussed were not sufficiently named, students will easily dismiss the session as unproductive. If clinic structure or mistakes in how the teacher conducted the session were the reasons for a less-than-successful formative assessment, the fault cannot be that of the student. The reflection about an unsuccessful formative assessment has to begin by questioning whether the failure of the session was the teacher's failure. Our mistakes or "failures" are no different from those of the students; they are errors that need to be remedied. Our goals for ourselves must include a growth mindset, just as we expect to instill it in the students. Reflecting on our own actions encourages that growth as a teacher.

Other Voices

Jerry R. Foxhoven, *Beyond Grading: Assessing Student Readiness to Practice Law**

16 Clinical L. Rev. 335 (2010)

...

Introduction

When a law school professor or clinician hears the word "assessment," there is a natural assumption that it refers to tools for grading students or evaluating instructors. Of course, assessments used for grading and instructor evaluation are essential to tracking student progress and teacher success. However, law schools owe more than a course evaluation to their students. Law schools should be engaged in fully preparing their students for entry into the practice of law and erasing the "gap" between legal education and the practicing bar. Law schools cannot assume that just because a student has completed the requirements for a degree, the student possesses the requisite "skills, values and knowledge" necessary to effectively transition to the practice of law. Rather, law schools should adopt an integrative strategy for legal education, focusing on a holistic rather than an atomistic approach. In addition to assessments for grading and instructor evaluation, law schools should provide their students with an assessment of their overall readiness to begin the practice of law. Armed with this assessment, students would be able to tailor the balance of their law school experiences and extra-curricular activities to complete their preparation for a smooth transition into the legal profession. Clinical teachers are particularly well-positioned to conduct this assessment process.

This article describes a process that the Children's Rights Clinic at the Drake University Law School recently developed to assess its students' possession of the knowledge, skills and professional values needed to successfully begin the practice of law. In developing the assessment process, we drew upon established research about the successes and failures of legal education, and we aimed to make students interactive partners in their own evaluations. Our assessment process is in addition to—and separate from—the grading the Clinic has long conducted and, as such, requires additional faculty and student effort. However, we have found the additional assessment process well worth the time. It helps faculty provide a well-rounded clinical experience for each student by directly focusing on the areas where students need individualized improvement and support.

...

* Excerpts are reprinted with the permission of the author and the Clinical Law Review.

Law Schools and Preparation for the Practice of Law

...

Establishing Core Competencies

It is fundamental that instructors in clinical education clearly identify and understand the essential skills and professional characteristics that they wish to inculcate in their students.... The MacCrate Report itemized ten "Fundamental Lawyering Skills" and four "Fundamental Values" needed by every practicing attorney.

...

While these fundamental skills and values may be too comprehensive to cover in any single clinical course because they entail more than could be taught in a single semester, they provide good guidance in setting outcome measures for the entire law school experience. Using these metrics, two legal clinicians identified the following ten areas in which to evaluate the performance of clinic students: attorney-client interactions, theory of the case development and implementation, oral and written advocacy, practice management, professional relationships, professional responsibility, reflective skills development, class participation, simulation participation, and personal development. This list includes not only core competencies, but also classroom objectives such as class participation and simulation participation, which foster engaged learning. An assessment of student readiness for the practice of law examines the student's abilities in the core competencies, leaving an evaluation of class performance for the grading process.

...

Drake's Attempt to Assess the Core Competencies

...

Assessments of Student Progress

Research shows that most legal clinical teachers in the United States have not spent enough time on assessment and have failed to develop reliable tools for evaluating the development and progress of clinical students.... Both the Best Practices Report and the Carnegie Report contain full chapters dedicated to assessing student learning. The Carnegie Report explained the most basic reason for assessment of students, "From our observations, we believe that assessment should be understood as a coordinated set of formative practices that, by providing important information about the students' progress in learning to both students and faculty, can strengthen law schools' capacity to develop competent and responsible lawyers." The Best Practices Report goes a step further in stating that assessment methods may have more influence on how and what students learn than any other factor. Assessment is a powerful tool because law students uniformly desire to be prepared to become competent lawyers, but being novices in the legal profession, they are unable to identify core competencies themselves. The [Children's Right Clinic] (CRC) designed its assessment process to take account of these insights.

In developing a comprehensive assessment process, the CRC puts all students through a five-step assessment process: (1) a self-evaluation by the student of his or her accomplishments and development in the identified competencies; (2) an evaluation by the faculty supervisor of the student's accomplishments and development in the identified competencies; (3) an accumulation of a portfolio of documents representative of the student's accomplishments in clinic; (4) a case study self-assessment; and (5) the student's assessment of outside attorneys with whom they have interacted while in the clinic. Each of these steps will be discussed separately.

Self-Assessment of Competencies

As noted earlier, the CRC developed twelve "key skills and learning opportunities" for students in the clinic. Each student is asked to assess their own development of the competencies at two points—at the halfway point and at the conclusion of their clinical experience. Each student must assess their success in terms of degrees. They can choose from the following levels for each skill:

The student is familiar with the skill/practice, but not able to perform it.

The student can perform the skill/practice but requires close supervision.

The student can perform the skill/practice with minimal supervision.

The student can perform the skill/practice adequately without further training.

The student can perform the skill/practice in an outstanding manner with virtually no supervision and could provide assistance to others.

This scale of supervision requirements virtually mirrors the one used by the Law Society of England and Wales and suggested in the Best Practices Report. The use of scaled skill levels does not emphasize deficiencies; rather, it focuses on the degree of supervision required, which is more supportive of students. The CRC assessment form contains an area for narrative comment after each key learning skill.

The direct self-assessment of identified competencies is designed to implement what the Carnegie Report refers to as "intentional learning," where students are aware of the skills and professional levels they are trying to attain, rather than just trying to pass a test. The gradients of the assessment allow the student to determine the level of expertise attained; levels range from novice, advanced beginner, competent, proficient, to expert. Self-assessments help students see how they progress through the four steps of learning: experience, reflection, theory, and application. The process forces students to focus on the key competencies, engage in self-reflection, develop an awareness of their limitations, and identify a plan for improvement. Likewise, by performing the self-assessment at two points in the clinical educational process, the student is able to recognize their growth in competency that experience, reflection, planning, and repetition help develop.

Faculty Assessment of Competencies

The assessments not only give feedback to students on their progress but also help faculty members know whether or not they have given their students sufficient experience and feedback in each of the key areas identified. Attaining the skills and professional qualities necessary to become a successful practicing lawyer requires not only repeated performance and reflection, but also expert feedback.

Before reviewing the student's self-assessment, the supervising faculty member conducts an identical assessment of the core competencies. This is done independently of the student's self-assessment, so that the assessment by one does not influence the other. Afterwards, the student and the supervising faculty member meet and compare their completed assessments of the student's performance. This process is designed to accomplish several goals. The CRC aims to provide an independent, expert assessment of the student's competencies, allow an opportunity for the student and instructor to discuss skills and professional development, and provide an opportunity for the student to reflect on the accuracy of the self-assessment.

...

Student Portfolio

The Best Practices Report sets forth eleven principles and proposals for assessing student learning, including the requirement that students compile educational portfolios. That report defines student portfolios as "... compilations of materials that document a student's academic achievement and personal development." Similarly, the Carnegie Report has described the use of a student portfolio as "... a promising approach to assessing the complex of skills of practice that has been relatively underused in legal education, as compared with other domains of higher education..." Accordingly, the CRC requires students to place copies of a variety of documents in their portfolio, including case management notes... about a court hearing; a memorandum describing a home visit and at least one other case activity; a report to the court drafted by the student and filed in one of the student's assigned cases; a series of pleadings drafted and filed in court by the student; a research project completed by the student on an assigned case (such as a memo or brief); and a piece of correspondence. Throughout the clinical experience, the student must continually update the portfolio to reflect the "best example" of the student's work in each category.

...

The student portfolio is designed to meet several purposes: providing a concrete "product" for the supervising faculty to use for student assessment, allowing the student to reflect on the quality of their work by self-selecting and comparing documents for inclusion into the portfolio, and providing the student the opportunity to see growth in skills throughout the clinical experience.

...

A Case Study Self-Assessment

The Best Practices Report asserts that "[t]he entire law school experience should help students become expert in reflecting on their learning process, identifying the causes of both successes and failure, and using that knowledge to plan future efforts to learn with a goal of continuous improvement." In good clinical practice, students learn to develop theories of practice and performance, to analyze their performances, and to learn from their strengths and weaknesses.

Accordingly, at the end of each semester, students must provide a one-page narrative containing a critical analysis of their performance in one court case they handled. We ask students to critique their attorney-client relationship, their development of case strategy, and their performance in court. Students reflect on what they would have done differently, and what effect, if any, such changes might have had on the case or on the client. The student and the faculty advisor meet to discuss the case study along with the core competencies assessment at the mid-point and end of the clinical experience. This case study is designed to provide an intense reflection by the students on their performance and directly relate the skills of the student to the outcomes for the client.

...

Mentoring and Lifetime Learning

...

One legal clinician has asserted that the most important goal of a legal education should be to develop lifelong learning skills. This amounts to more than just attending continuing education classes because there is little evidence that these classes have any effect on lawyer competency. Rather, lifelong learning skills involve reflection, identification of successes and failures, and development of plans for improvement. CRC students are reminded that law school is just the first step in a lifetime of learning that is necessary to become, and to continue to be, an outstanding professional. CRC faculty encourage students to view continuing legal education as more than a requirement to remain in good standing with the state licensing authority, but as a tool for continuous development of their character and skills.

...

Evaluating the Impact of the Assessment

...

Faculty Time Expended on the Process

It should be noted that the assessment process described in this paper is not designed to measure the success of the clinical experience to the student or to provide a grade for the student. The grading process is separate and distinct from the assessment process. A grading process must, by definition, only assess the skills acquired by the student in the clinical setting. The assessment process described in this article is intended to assess the student's core competencies regardless of where those competencies were acquired. Therefore, any time expended by faculty members in this assessment process is in addition to the time expended for grading or assessment of the clinical experience itself.

...

The Value of the Process

Because the assessment process described in this article has only been used for one year, it is impossible to evaluate the long term impact of the process. Nevertheless, students and faculty alike have unanimously concluded that the process is valuable. Each student has entered the second semester with clear tools for improving their skills.... As the faculty members anticipated at the beginning of the process, law students did not have good insight into their abilities. Exceptional students routinely under-rated their abilities, while less skilled students routinely over-rated their abilities in the self-assessments. However, at the conclusion of the student-faculty meetings, there was general agreement as to the skill level of each student. The process itself, then, contributed a great deal toward student reflection and insight.

Georgetown Juvenile Justice Clinic Student Self-Assessment Form

This form was created by Professors Kris Henning and Eduardo Ferrer for the Georgetown Juvenile Justice clinic. It asks student to reflect on the various activities they performed while in the clinic. The topics listed as well as a memo regarding the grading process and rubric are distributed during the clinic orientation. The student's self-assessment is the basis for the formative assessment and is used along with subsequent work to assign a grade at the end of the academic semester for one-semester students and at the end of the year for full-year students.

Memo to the Students

Re: Mid-year reviews

Between the end of the first semester and the beginning of the second semester, we hold mid-year reviews. Mid-year reviews involve students completing a self-review memorandum and an hour-long meeting with the faculty. Please provide detailed information on each category below and reflect on your performance and any other aspect of the case that you think relevant. It is helpful to provide specific examples from your cases. We will use your memo to guide our meeting. Additionally, please sign up for a meeting and send your memo to the supervisors at least 24 hours in advance of your scheduled meeting. Feel free to ask any questions regarding the mid-year reviews before you sign up for your meeting.

1. Prepare a memo with a self-assessment of your performance in the clinic. Look at the Evaluation Criteria Memo in the Administrative Section of your Class Manual. The Evaluation Criteria Memo is also posted on Google Drive.
   a. Within each category discussed in the Evaluation Criteria Memo, please identify areas where you think you are particularly strong.
   b. Within each category discussed in the Evaluation Criteria Memo, please identify areas you think you need to work on.

   Please feel free to use bullet points if that is better for you. We are not looking for an essay or dissertation. That said, we do expect this to be a thorough reflection piece. Think critically about yourself and your clinic work. It will be helpful to draw upon concrete examples from your cases.
2. In the memo, please also let us know how we can help you.
   a. How can we help you improve in those areas you have identified above? What concrete steps do you think you should take to improve in the areas identified?
   b. What are you getting out of the clinic professionally/personally? What else would you like to get out of the clinic?
   c. Do you have any general advice/suggestions for the clinic?

      Student Name:

      Semester/Year:

      Name of Evaluator:

      Student's Investigative Partner:

Cases for which you were the student attorney and the name of the supervisor:

I. **Role Assumption**
   A. Ethical Considerations
   B. Zealous and Responsible Representation

      Putting forth effort to provide zealous representation and the best possible defense.

      Taking personal responsibility for a client's case.

      Ensuring that cases are prepared for court hearings.

      Maintaining appropriate relationships with clients, other attorneys, and court officials.

      Meeting deadlines imposed by the court, by your supervisors, and on your own initiative.

      Being punctual and attending to professional obligations, including court appearances, and meetings with clients, supervisors, witnesses, and other students.

Maintaining files accurately and precisely and complying with office procedures.

Allocating time and effort to carry out tasks responsibly.

II. **Case Planning**

A. The Planning Process

Developing a theory and strategy for each case, taking into consideration the application of evidence, statutes, regulations, and case law to develop a plan for using facts and law to the benefit of the client.

Modifying and reassessing strategy in light of subsequent developments.

Refining and improving work between planning and final draft or performance.

Considering consciously the ethical, strategic, and client specific issues in cases.

Weighing consciously the risks and benefits attendant to different strategies.

Making appropriate judgments and decisions and setting priorities given available information and resources.

Student *will come into supervision meetings having considered the various challenges you face and having identified several responses to them*. Student will be able to articulate these challenges and responses for your supervisor.

III. **Skills Development**

A. Lawyering Skills

Interviewing: Structure, rapport, obtaining information. (To be evaluated within the constraints of our decision not to have supervisors at client interviews.)

Counseling: Helping the client to understand his/her alternatives; keeping the client informed; remaining sensitive to full range of the client's needs.

Fact Investigation: Planning, thoroughness, effort, creativity.

Legal Research: Thoroughness, accuracy, appropriate analysis of relevant sources.

Writing: Organization, structure, use of language and writing techniques that are appropriate to the audience, and are concise and persuasive.

Negotiation: Executing the plan; dealing flexibly with unexpected developments.

Hearing Performance: Executing of the plan; adequately performing the skills in court; dealing flexibly with unexpected developments.

IV. **Educational Growth and Engagement**

Preparation for class.

Consistent participation in class.

Quality of class contributions including meaningful participation in discussion and analysis.

Participation in simulations and execution of assignments, while remaining in role.

Preparation for supervisory meetings.

Initiative and creativity in raising issues and planning case.

Class and supervision session attendance and punctuality.

...

Endnotes

1. The terms "formative assessment" and "qualitative assessment" have the same meaning and will be used interchangeably throughout this chapter.

2. Noted educator Mantz Yorke, former Professor of Higher Education at Liverpool John Moores University and Visiting Professor in the Department of Educational Research, Lancaster University once described informal formative assessment as an "instantaneous feedback as the student takes part in a learning activity and comments on drafts of material for inclusion in portfolios. Mantz Yorke, *Formative Assessment in Higher Education: Moves Toward Theory and the Enhancement of Pedagogic Practice*, 45 Higher Education, 477, at 479, (2003).

3. *See* Julie Ross & Diana Donahoe, *Lighting the Fires of Learning in Law School: Implementing ABA Standard 314 by Incorporating Effective Formative Assessment Techniques across the Curriculum*, 81 U. Pitt. L. Rev. 657, 663 (2020); *see also* Olympia Duhart, *The F Word: The Top Five Complaints (and Solutions) about Formative Assessment*, 67 J. Legal Educ. 531, 538(2018). See also Yorke, *supra* note 2, at 482.

4. Ross, *supra* note 3, at 663–664(quoting Org. for Econ. Co-Operation & Dev., Formative Assessment: Improving Learning in Secondary Classroom 13–17, 22 (2005).

5. *Id.* at 665.

6. *Id.*

7. *See* Chapter Four, Supervision, for a discussion of metacognition and the zone of proximal development.

8. *Formative Assessment*, Teaching Excellence in Adult Literacy (2010), https://lincs.ed.gov/sites/default/files/9_TEAL_Formative_Assess.pdf.

9. *Formative and Summative Assessments*, Yale Poorvu Center for Teaching and Learning, https://poorvucenter.yale.edu/Formative-Summative-Assessments (last visited June 17, 2023) (citing Elise Trumbull & Andrea A. Lash, *Understanding Formative Assessment: Insights from Learning Theory and Measurement Theory*, WestEd (Apr. 2013)). On the other hand, "summative assessments evaluate student learning, knowledge, proficiency, or success at the conclusion of an instructional period, like a unit, course, or program. [They] are almost always formally graded and often heavily weighted (though they do not need to be). Summative assessment can be used to great effect in conjunction and alignment with formative assessment, and instructors can consider a variety of ways to combine these approaches." *Id.* Summative assessment will be discussed in chapter fourteen.

10. *Id.* at 980, 984.

11. In the clinical literature, self-assessments are often called self-evaluations.

12. Jerry R. Foxhoven, *Beyond Grading: Assessing Student Readiness to Practice Law*, 16 Clinical. L. Rev. 335, 345 (2009).

13. *Id.*

14. *See* Nina Tarr, *The Skill of Evaluation as an Explicit Goal of Clinical Training*, 21 Pac. L.J. 967, 970 1990 (explaining that new lawyers have generally not developed the skill of self-evaluation).

15. *Id.* at 971–72.

16. The goals and rubrics we use in our Juvenile Justice Clinic can be found after this chapter.

17. *Id.*

18. *Id.* at 982.

19. *Id.* at 354.

20. Some samples are included with the articles following this chapter.

21. Nina Tarr, *supra* note 14, at 971–72 (1990) (explaining why creating the habit of self-reflection is important for long-term development as attorneys).

22. Mantz Yorke, *supra* note 2, at 480.

23. Brookfield, The Skillful Teacher (3d ed. 2015), at 174 (describing how evaluations can be personal for students and have long term consequences that professors should recognize when providing evaluations).

24. Any Zeigler, *Developing a System of Evaluation in Clinical Legal Teaching*, 42 J. Of Legal Educ. 575, 589 (2018) (explaining that "[T]he most dynamic conversations occur when the students take the lead in questioning, and my role is limited to supplying information and suggesting questions.").

25. Steven Brookfield, *supra* note 23, at 187–88.

26. *Id.* at 178.

27. *The Purpose of Reflection*, Purdue University, Department of English, College of Liberal Arts, https://cla.purdue.edu/academic/english/icap/assessment/purpose.html (citing Kathleen Blake Yancy, Reflection in the Writing Classroom 6 (1998)).

28. *Id.* citing Mary Ryan, *The Pedagogical Balancing Act* in: Teaching Reflection in Higher Education, 144, 147 (2013).

29. The quote is from an unpublished PowerPoint presentation given by and in the possession of Professor Susan Brooks. The idea expressed in the PowerPoint are more fully discussed in Susan L. Brooks, *Meeting the Professional Identity Challenge in Legal Education through a Relationship-Centered Experiential Curriculum*, 41 Balt. L. Rev. 395, 431–432 (2012).

30. Teaching Excellence, *supra* note 8.

31. The language here is an adaptation of a method used by Professor Alex Scherr. Alexander Scherr, *Evaluating Reflection*, 6 (May 6, 2015) (unpublished PowerPoint) (in possession of author).

32. Amy L. Ziegler, *Developing a System of Evaluation in Clinical Legal Teaching*, 42 J. of Legal Educ. 575, 578 (2018).

33. *Id.*

34. *Id.*

35. *Id.*

36. *Id.* at 579.

37. *Id.*

38. *See* Foxhoven, *supra* note 12, at 346 (finding that faculty evaluations, based on the same criteria as the student evaluations, provides a more objective evaluation that ensures the student has an accurate perception of the quality of his or her work).

39. Brookfield, *supra* note 23, at 174.

40. Kaci Bishop, *Framing Failure in the Legal Classroom: Techniques for Encouraging Growth and Resilience*, 70 Ark. L. Rev. 959 (2018).

41. Anne D. Gordon, *Better Than Our Biases: Using Psychological Research to Inform Our Approach to Inclusive, Effective Feedback*, 27 Clinical. L. Rev. 295, 219 (2021).

42. *Id.* at 220.

43. *Id.*

44. *Id.* at 222.

45. *Id.*

46. *Id.* at 224 (explaining that "[i]f a professor subconsciously classifies a student as less capable, every time the student under-performs, his bias is confirmed; he may be more likely to give up on the student.").

47. Georgetown University is a Jesuit institution of higher learning. "The objective of Jesuit education is to assist in the fullest possible development of all of the God-given talents of each individual

person as a member of the human community." ETHOS AND IDENTITY REVIEW FOR JESUIT-OWNED SCHOOLS AND PARTNER SCHOOLS, at 8, citing The Characteristics of Jesuit Education, #1.2, par 25, 1986, and former Fr General Peter-Hans Kolvenbach, SJ, "Jesuit education aims at joining learning and virtue and developing a faith that does justice. It means the ideal of being young men and women of competence, conscience and compassion, who know that life is only lived well when lived generously in the service of others. It means helping them to discover that what they most have to offer is who they are rather than what they have." At 13, file:///C:/Users/Wally/Downloads/Australian%20Province%20SJ%202011%20Ethos%20and%20Identity%20Review%20for%20schools.pdf.

Fourteen

ASSIGNING GRADES— QUANTITATIVE OR SUMMATIVE ASSESSMENTS

Most law schools require that the qualitative or formative assessments faculty make regarding student performances in a clinical course be translated into quantitative or summative assessments—i.e., a grade—at the end of each student's clinic experience.[1] The terms formative assessment and qualitative assessment have the same meaning and have been used interchangeably throughout this book. Similarly, the terms summative assessment, quantitative assessment, and grades also have the same meaning, so have also been used interchangeably throughout the book.

Students, parents, and some teachers believe grades have been around as long as there have been centers of learning. That is not the case. "Grades and rankings emerged gradually through the 18th and 19th centuries, with Mount Holyoke College introducing the first modern letter grades in 1897. Other institutions—including Harvard and Yale, which had experimented with their own grading schemes—followed suit. By the 1940s, the A-to-F scale became the standard."[2] "From their inception, grades were designed more for the efficiency of institutions than for the education of individuals. As student populations increased, grades were simple to calculate, easy to administer and convenient to communicate across an expanding education infrastructure... [G]rades have always reflected 'the constraints of institutional systems rather than the needs of learners,"[3] But they at least provided a common vocabulary within a particular school to think and talk about comparative assessments. Nonetheless, in some undergraduate schools and at least one law school, formative assessments have replaced the traditional grading system[4] because descriptive words are usually more precise than a single letter or number grade.

As noted in previous chapters, quantitative assessments or grades are related to, and dependent upon the many tasks that students undertake on their case or project. For example, faculty consider whether the students have a well thought-out plan prepared for the various tasks that they will perform, have mastered the law and facts of the case or project, have executed the tasks successfully, and have represented their clients zealously and ethically. Faculty also monitor and evaluate the interactions between the student and the faculty member during supervision sessions. For example, supervisors observe and record whether a student took leadership in solving the problems posed by the case or project or merely waited for the faculty member's instructions on how to proceed. Faculty determine whether the students have successfully fulfilled their personal learning goals and the clinic's learning goals, and whether the students have achieved their clients' goals or at least maximized their interests. Faculty record whether the student's performances show the ability to transfer lessons learned from one task to another. They also note whether the students demonstrated personal and professional growth or whether the students' patterns of behavior showed little or no improvement. Finally, they also assess the students' reflection about all the lawyering activities they performed, and their reflection during the self-assessment and the formative assessment session.

Of course, all the factors above are discussed in the formative assessment. Notwithstanding the thought and conversations about the student's progress, translating formative assessments into quantitative evaluations is difficult for several reasons. Indeed, some teachers and education researchers have come to believe that grading itself is an inhibitor to actual learning.[5] "Decades of research, at all levels of education, has demonstrated that grades can promote short-term performance rather than long-term understanding, encourage both superficial studying and outright cheating, and can undermine a student's intrinsic interest in the material."[6] If that is true, a case could be made to eliminate all grading in schools or at least in clinical courses where students have to disclose their shortcomings in order to move forward on the path to becoming a successful professional.

Clinical teachers use these multiple factors to assess the quality of students' work because they seek to maximize students' individual achievements rather than ranking them in relation to others in the class. Most clinical teachers tell me they would prefer to avoid giving grades because competition within the clinic can actually harm the learning capability of all of the students. Notwithstanding the preferences of clinical teachers, most law schools require the faculty to quantitatively measure a student's performance with some scale, rank it in comparison to the accomplishments of others in the class, and assign some form of a traditional grade for the student's participation in the course.

Grading systems vary from school to school today.[7] Some schools use numerical grades, often based on a familiar 100-point scale, though some schools use unusual numerical markers.[8] Some schools use adjectival descriptors with various words like high honors, honors, satisfactory, and unsatisfactory. Other schools use traditional letter grades. Though the meaning of those letters and numbers convey some sense of ranking among the students in the course, the actual meaning of the letters in terms of specific learning outcomes are seldom transparent. Indeed, letter grades, numerical scores, and adjectival words all may convey different meanings to those giving and those receiving those grade designations. They also result in widely varying interpretations by judges, employers, higher degree program admissions officers, parents, and other students after the teacher issues a grade.[9]

The relationship between the formative assessment and the summative assessment may also seem opaque. Understanding their equivalence, albeit in different forms, is seldom explained. There are also variations in the meaning of a grade from one clinic teacher to the next no matter what system is used. Teachers in different clinics and even within the same clinic may sometimes disagree about the quality of the student's class assignments and case or project performances and assess the efforts differently when determining the final grade. This is especially true if there is no clear rubric that informs the student of a specific criteria used to assign a grade. Similarly, in the absence of a rubric, faculty have no guide to what a grade means.

The Challenge of Grading Clinical Students

For reasons that will be more clearly explained later in this chapter, grading clinical students is more complex than grading a final examination or final paper. Some school administrators are aware of the complexity of clinic grading and choose to avoid the meaninglessness inherent in awarding grades by using a simple pass-fail system. That system lends itself to fairly clear interpretations of a student's performance for both the teacher awarding the grade and the student receiving it, as long as there is agreement on what constitutes a failing performance. The pass-fail system, however, tells the student nothing about whether they have achieved specific learning goals or whether they are strong or weak at performing specific lawyering tasks. In addition, the baseline for passing can also vary, making the two categories imprecise. The baseline for failure cannot be malpractice in a clinic course because allowing students to commit malpractice would be a sanctionable ethics violation for both the student and the supervisor. Nor can it be equal to the ability of the best lawyer in town or even that of the clinic supervisor because that would be too stringent and unattainable for most students. A wide range of judgments is possible for each performance and thus determining the baseline for failure is not much easier than defining the meaning of any other grade.

The relationship between administrators and faculty is somewhat perplexing when it comes to awarding grades. Some schools give faculty members complete discretion when awarding grades to members of a class. Others, however, enforce a mandatory or recommended curve which adds another complicating factor to the grading system. Law school administrators and nonclinical faculty are usually unaware of the work students do in a clinic. As a result, they often create identical grading curves that are applicable to all clinics, seminar courses, and large classes. These curves indicate the percentage of students in the clinic that can come within a specific grade category. But curves require consistency of what is being calculated, as well as a certain number of participants to be valid. Using a unified curve for disparate courses makes little sense, since they have different goals and measure different skills. Notwithstanding the complexity of grading and despite a distaste for assessing individual achievement against a group norm, clinical teachers must comply with school-wide grading curves when translating formative assessments into summative assessments. They must do so in a manner that is fair and accurate, within the mandatory curve, explainable to the student, and justifiable. The ability to explain and justify becomes especially important when students challenge the grade awarded.

Some difficulties and concerns related to the grading process are functions of the process itself and the way teachers implement it. Teachers sometimes confuse elusive high marks for a sign of genuine rigor, forgetting the distinction between challenges that support student learning and those that "are arbitrary obstacles that may well hinder it."[10] Some reform advocates believe that current grading systems are the product of industrial-age values and needs that are now over a century old.[11] Reformers also say that when used today, those systems undermine creativity and teach fixed, outdated mindsets that do not serve the values and interests commonly held today.[12] There are even calls for an end to grading as we know it. Those who make that call base their critique on evidence that grades create barriers between students and faculty, undermine student motivation, sort students for employment, maintain unfair class hierarchies,[13] and most importantly, inhibit learning.[14] Proposed replacements, however, are also imperfect and are often limited to modified implementation within traditional systems.[15]

Structural Complexity of Clinical Courses

The structure of a clinical course adds to the difficulty of complying with a universal grading system. That structural difficulty is exacerbated by the pedagogical relationship that exists between the students and the faculty member in a clinic. There are at least eight structural elements in a clinical course that make grading more difficult in a clinic than in non-clinical law school courses.

The Invalidity of Grading Curves in Clinical Courses

First, a grading curve is a statistical assessment that assumes a cross section of a population is being measured and that a sufficient number of that population will be assessed to bring out the inherent differences within the group. From its inception, clinical education pedagogy has been based on a low teacher-student ratio in order to foster individual student development and ensure that clients' interests are protected. The most common student-to-faculty ratio is eight-to-one.[16] Moreover, getting into a clinic is often extremely competitive. Faculty often select students to participate because they have a demonstrated interest or previous work experience in the clinic's subject matter. For example, students with immigration experience will gravitate to immigration or political asylum clinics. Students interested in women's rights or intra-family violence issues often enroll in domestic violence clinics. Criminal and juvenile practice clinics often seek students who have worked with a public defender or a prosecutor. Innocence or wrongful conviction clinics look for people with more than a basic knowledge of criminal and habeas corpus law. Other clinics select students who possess a talent in the core practice aspect of the clinic. For example, social enterprise clinics will attract students with some prior transactional work and intellectual property clinics may attract students who are adept at the newest technological advances. Appellate clinics often seek good writers because the nature of the client work requires more than basic writing skills. Those students will often be seeking clerkships after graduation and tend to be among the higher achievers in law school. Additionally, students who have joined and competed on moot court or mock trial teams are often preferred because they developed some basic and perhaps advanced trial or appellate advocacy skills.

The factors that provide for the statistical analysis that determine the validity of the curve are thus lacking in a clinical course. Most clinic classes usually have too few students and an insufficient disparity of talent and background among them to develop a valid statistical curve.[17] The sample—the number of students in the clinic—is usually between six and fourteen, depending on the number of supervisors in the clinic. Under the Central Limit Theorem, a valid sample for analysis must be larger than the size of a clinic class to render an accurate statistical analysis. The sample is often thought to require at least thirty people to be valid.[18] In addition, a statistically valid survey requires a cross section of population. The similarities among the students further skew the sample. The students in a clinic are usually similar to each other in both interests and talent. Try imagining grading a class of seven Nobel prize-winning economists in a basic economics course. Nonetheless, most schools continue to use curves to evaluate students, and many administrators and non-clinical faculty believe that they are appropriate for a clinical course.

Measuring Assessment

NON-CLINIC CLASSES

Second, measuring assessments in clinic classes is different from that of non-clinic classes Most non-clinical law school courses measure students' performance using final and sometimes midterm examinations. Faculty derive a measurement based on the students' ability to analyze a set of facts and laws set forth in the examination, or from a seminar paper written during the term of the course. Thus, the assessment measures, at least for the most part, only the skills of reasoning and memory in an exam course. Writing skills and research can also be assessed in a seminar course, albeit most often using only a student's final draft. Thus, teachers in non-clinical courses assess all students in terms of the same two or three lawyering skills.

In non-clinical courses, where the use of a curve might produce valid statistical results, the instruments used to measure the students are relatively consistent. All students take the same examinations or write papers related to a similar subject matter. Teachers conducting seminar courses may, but do not always, offer feedback on the quality of the work in a uniform fashion as the paper is being written so improvement in the student's writing and research can be measured. Teachers in an exam course provide feedback only after the exam is graded. Some students seek to establish a potential student-teacher relationship which can sometimes serve to improve their final grade on both seminar papers and exams. Some regularly attend office hours with faculty members teaching their course or become research assistants to a faculty member. As they meet informally with their teachers, students can gain deeper insights into the subject matter of the course. Those insights can enhance their analytical skills and their knowledge base, both of which can positively affect their performance on papers and exams. Those relationships, however, are random and seldom built into nonclinical courses. Thus, they cannot be used for a student's formative or summative assessment unless the student's increased knowledge or understanding is reflected in the exam. Moreover, unless students regularly visit their teacher during office hours, constant feedback on what they are learning will be absent.

CLINIC CLASSES

Students in a clinic are assessed with many instruments and on many tasks. Even when students enrolled in a clinic possess comparable cognitive ability, they will come with different proficiencies within the specific skill sets being measured. Some students will be more experienced or even innately more talented at some lawyering skills while possessing less skill or experience in others. In addition, clinical students are asked to perform a wide variety of lawyering tasks during the duration of the course. Lawyers must be able to write effective advocacy documents; they must be skilled researchers; and they need to develop good interviewing, negotiation, and oral advocacy skills. They also need to demonstrate good judgment and how to use that judgment to anticipate and head off as well as solve problems in their cases and projects. They need to have or develop good relational skills to communicate with people from different social and economic situations There are obviously many more skills that successful lawyers must perform over the course of a career. Students in a clinic will be asked to perform many of them and all of them will be subject to continuous assessment.

Because few students come to the clinic with experience or talent in every one of those legal practice tasks, they will be asked to reflect on their performances in order to improve. That reflection is also subject to qualitative and quantitative assessments. Moreover, there will be a mix of lawyering talents among the students within the clinic. Some will have strong organizational skills. Others will have the poise and charisma of an experienced litigator and an uncommon ability to persuade. Some students may be more introverted yet have great analytic and strategic skills. Some students will write exquisite prose, while others may have writer's blocks, learning disabilities, or grammatical challenges. Some will prefer investigating, while others enjoy researching legal issues. Some will be more empathetic toward clients and witnesses as they conduct interviews and counseling sessions than their team colleagues. Those preferences and proficiencies will result in different abilities and various levels of achievement within those tasks. But all factors and performances will be evaluated with regard to the individual student without comparison to the entire group. Both formative and summative assessments are about individual learning and growth and thus they should not be assessed comparatively. When balanced, all students in the class will be individually assessed across their total work effort, even if they possess varied strengths in different areas of practice. That is quite a contrast from grading an examination or even a seminar paper, and quite a challenge for the teacher.

It is true that the differences in an individual's mastering of lawyering skills within a group of ten or fourteen students can be expansive. As such, a faculty member must decide how to assess and evaluate a student who is exceptionally talented in most skills, but who improved only moderately throughout the course. Conversely, teachers must decide how to assess and evaluate a student who enters the clinic with less developed talents, but whose performance substantially improves throughout the course. At the end of the term, teachers must determine how to translate the formative assessment of all individual students into a summative assessment where there is little consistency in the potential outcomes. But it is the assessment of the whole, not just the individual parts of the student's performance, that give rise to the formative assessment that will be translated into the grade.

The Cumulative Effect of Multiple Lawyering Tasks

Third, students engage in multiple performances of the numerous lawyering tasks that arise as a case or project is developed throughout the semester. Representing a client from the inception of a case until its conclusion will involve many, but not necessarily all, of the tasks seasoned lawyers are asked to perform. More than memory, analysis, and writing will be involved. Clinical students receive a great deal of feedback prior to, sometimes during, and always after almost every action they take and every choice they make throughout the semester.

Faculty seldom apply a grade to these individual events as they occur. Instead, they take copious notes regarding these tasks as they are planned and executed, and also during supervision and reflection sessions about the performance. All of those notes are then qualitatively—and, ultimately, quantitatively—assessed as the parts of a complete body of work. Students are capable of improving during a clinical course and are expected to improve their planning and performance over time. First-time mistakes and single "wrong" answers hardly ever reflect a student's potential. This was recognized by cognitive psychology and learning theory years ago.[19] Evidence of the student's improvement is as important as the ability to perform a task well or make a sound choice the first time around. Moreover, analyzing the reasons for failure is as important to learning for transfer, as is analyzing successes. Thus, assessments in a clinic are not like those from an examination at the end of a semester. Each task in a clinic is like an "examination" but the formative and summative assessments in a clinic come after many "examinations." Some of the mistakes could be considered failures in isolation. When viewed together with subsequent improvement, they reflect the arc of growth and learning that the clinic is designed to produce. The failure is just the beginning of that growth process. It is the path to improvement, rather than the failure that is ultimately of most importance.[20]

The refusal to issue grades for each activity as it occurs makes sense. As mentioned earlier, students come to clinics with little understanding of the role of a lawyer and little experience with the various skills a lawyer employs on behalf of a client. In addition, faculty interventions in supervisory sessions occur more frequently in the early weeks of the course and then gradually diminish as the student learns more and begins to take more ownership of the case or project.[21] Formative assessment depends upon that growth and no single action early in the semester reflects what the student will ultimately gain from the clinic experience. Thus, quantitatively assessing an event contemporaneously with its performance makes no sense in a clinic. Students have little or no frame of reference for analyzing a lawyering skill before it occurs. It is a little like riding a bicycle.[22] One cannot understand the skill until one begins to "ride" and one cannot master it without losing one's balance and falling down a few times. Those "failures," to borrow from Harvard physics professor and education reformer Eric Mazur, should be seen as necessary. They are "learning opportunities, not negatives, ... as steppingstones to success."[23]

Different Tasks for Different Cases or Projects

Fourth, unlike traditional law school courses, the tasks students perform during their time in the clinic are not always identical to those performed by other students in the course. Each case or project in a clinic creates its own distinct tasks and responsibilities. Thus, the case or project will determine which of the many lawyering tasks a student will perform. Because not all cases require the same lawyering tasks, students in the same clinic will not necessarily be asked to perform identical tasks. Some students will write motions involving specific facts and laws and will argue their position before a judge. Others may litigate complete trials. Some students will forego trial in favor of a guilty plea in a criminal case or a negotiated settlement in a civil case which enables clients to avoid prison, retain their apartment, or otherwise resolve the dispute. Other students will conduct research and write motions, briefs, policy analyses, or white papers, but present them only to their clients. Some will draft contracts or articles of incorporation, and some will prepare for an in-person coalition meeting or a legislative hearing. All students are eager to have as many of these exciting lawyering opportunities as they can. However, the nature of the clinic case or project does not guarantee a live hearing. Nor does it guarantee the student's level of preparation for it. It is impossible to know in advance which lawyering activities the case will require. Thus, comparison grading is difficult—if not impossible—in a clinic.

Some students will spend hours counseling a client to counter their worst impulses. They may also have to discourage a client's preferred course of action because it is detrimental to their legal interests or is impossible to attain. Some organizational clients may alter their position or withdraw from providing testimony after counseling sessions. Other students working on projects may be drafting reports or comments, while their partners are preparing to deliver testimony or negotiating for a favored result.

A faculty member in a non-clinical course may make distinctions based on points allotted for certain answers and describe the differences between an A- and a B+ as a matter of points. They do so even though the point allotments in non-clinical courses are essentially arbitrary. In a clinical course, however, there is no way to ascribe points to a clinic student's performance for the multitude of tasks they must perform. To issue a fair grade, a clinical faculty member must devise a quantitative assessment system that takes all these disparate activities into account without overweighting one or undervaluing others, while avoiding comparisons among students who have performed different tasks. This is especially important in the clinical setting where the existence and frequency of certain opportunities will vary from student to student and from client to client for any particular student. The reasons for the varied tasks are often wholly outside their or the student's control. Just as no one can force a client to turn down a plea just so the student can gain the experience of trying a case, a clinical teacher cannot hold the absence of an opportunity that occurred through no fault of their own against a student.

Complying with Professional Standards

Fifth, the practice of law in and of itself requires a high and consistent level of work. Bar association codes of professional conduct and jurisdiction-specific student practice rules hold clinic students to the same exacting standards of performance as those governing members of the Bar. Students must perform the tasks according to acceptable levels of lawyerly performance while representing their clients. Moreover, Bar rules and codes of ethical practice, as well as sound pedagogical "best practices," require faculty members to supervise students in ways that ensure a professional level of practice. Indeed, a failure to do so will result in Bar sanctions for the student and the faculty member. Hence, supervisors must ensure that their students' work remains at a high degree of competence. They cannot allow students to do less than very competent work on behalf of clients.

If the clinic is well-structured, the differences among the students in terms of growth and competence are likely to be small at the end of the course. As a result, making comparisons among students is difficult and sometimes imprecise. Law students, by and large, are very talented. Most will come to law school well educated from their undergraduate experience, with academic records that tend to be high. They have also, in order to gain admission, taken the rigorous Law School Admissions Test (LSAT) or Graduate Record Examinations (GRE), which eliminate students who might not be capable of succeeding in law school. Thus, students without the requisite capability will probably never enroll in a clinic. Those who do enroll are usually in their third or at least their second year of law school. For all of these reasons, all students are likely to meet professional standards.

It is possible that a student's performance will fall below the minimum level of professional standards. In other cases, the task involved will be beyond the student's current competence. In either case, faculty may have to perform some of the needed tasks on a case or project and students may occasionally have to be removed from representing the client. Removal, however, does not always require a negative formative or summative assessment. If the lawyering activity is beyond the student's current capacity, or as explained in Chapter Four, Supervising Cases and Projects, outside of the student's zone of proximal development, removal is a learning moment rather than a "failure."

Students may experience personal issues that can interfere with their performance. Students' personal lives do not disappear during the clinic participation. When adverse personal issues arise, they may affect a student's performance on the case. Not every act of intervention caused by negligence requires harsh grading. If the cause is true negligence on the part of the student, a grade must reflect that. Not telling a supervisor about personal difficulties that are impairing the student's performance is a form of negligence. It is different, however, from ignoring a client's case to go somewhere during spring break.

Sometimes the cause of a poor performance is not student negligence. Being temporarily unable to work on a case or project because of emotional or physical disabilities is not negligence. Such events require academic accommodation to maximize the student's learning. Nonetheless, grades will still need to be issued. Rubrics may have to be altered in those circumstances because internal law school policies that comply with federal and local law and regulations may govern the process and the standards.

Although students in the clinic will have various levels of prior academic achievement and personal characteristics, a well-thought-out pedagogical plan implemented by a well-trained clinical teacher will result in fair comparative quantitative assessments that reflect professional standards. If all students in the clinic are able to demonstrate the high level of professional competence that we expect, teachers bound by institutional grading curves may have a grading problem.

Accounting for Student Collaboration

Sixth, legal work in the modern world is collegial and collaborative, not competitive. It is true that competition among lawyers does exist, at least for salary increases and partnership invitations in law firms, and for promotions and sometimes salary increases in public interest legal organizations. However, law firms and public interest organizations all work better when individuals collaborate, each lending their expertise to produce the best results for clients.[24] Law school clinics, "the most prominent site[s] of collaborative work in legal education,"[25] operate similarly, except that clinic faculty are equally interested in the individual growth of all of their students. Thus, it seems inconsistent to grade students relative to each other—the essence of curved grading—as opposed to assessing students on the basis of their collaborative contributions to the team's achievements.

Assigning an individual grade to each member of the team can be complicated. Collaboration is often a specific goal of a clinic because students will collaborate with colleagues during their careers. Students need to learn to organize the collaboration process as well as collaborate with team members to achieve the clients' goals. The problem at grading time is to sort out which part of the team effort was produced by which student, while at the same time evaluating the effectiveness of collaboration process. Teachers need to devise a supervision system that permits them to know what each student on the team has done on the case or project. It makes good sense to have supervision meetings with the team as well and with the individual members of the team to determine the extent of each member's contributions to the project.

The Effect of Mentorship

Seventh, the clinic experience creates fruitful but atypical teacher-student relationships. Most students have had little, if any, opportunity to act in the professional capacity of a lawyer before they enroll in a clinical course. Mentorship by nonclinical faculty members can occasionally substitute for that lack of opportunity, but true mentorship seldom occurs in non-clinical courses because students and teachers do not often work together on a project.

A goal of every clinic is to permit the student to experience the role of a lawyer. To do so, students must reflect upon the role, work with the supervisor to understand the strengths and contradictions within the role of a lawyer, and improve their ability to operate within the role throughout the semester. Although one hopes this takes place in all parts of the law school environment, the truth is that it does not. Students in a clinic, however, are encouraged to openly discuss their difficulty understanding case or project issues and the role-conflicts they experience when confronting those events while representing their clients. They are also expected to discuss the general organizational and learning problems they face as cases and projects develop. Educator and equity consultants "recognize that mistakes are not only important to learning but [that] learning cannot occur without mistakes."[26] Opportunities to reflect on and remediate shortcomings are rare in non-clinical courses, whereas faculty in clinical courses embrace them and work with students to overcome obstacles, cultivating true mentorships in the process.

Of course, knowing that a grade will come at the end of a course can inhibit a student's openness to suggestions for needed growth. That can create obstacles to learning and leave supervisors unaware of why the student seems to be progressing slowly or haphazardly. Although most clinical teachers decline to issue grades on individual tasks and discourage grade conversations, especially in formative assessment sessions, grades always linger in a student's consciousness. The mentorship relationship can minimize the preoccupation with grades and ease students' reluctance to reveal their doubts and challenges. Experienced teachers strive to break down those barriers by reminding students that the purpose of a clinic is to improve one's capability to practice law and to understand that failure produces progress when it is recognized, acknowledged, and remedied. That openness between student and teacher as mentor is a hallmark of clinical courses, one that usually brings warm feelings between teachers and students. Empathy opens avenues for conversation and generosity of spirit, but it can complicate the grading process. Those warm feelings that are established in the relationship must be compartmentalized when the summative assessment begins.

Not all personal relationships between a student and faculty members in a clinic are personally positive. The pedagogical intimacy of a clinic setting allows for substantive mentoring and unique collaborative learning opportunities. However, the daily opportunities for personal encounters between supervisors and students that create mentorship relationships are sometimes absent with some students. Personality differences and perceived insufficient student engagement in clinic case work or in the pedagogical process can sometimes "press supervisors' buttons" in ways that create an empathic disconnection that can amplify biases in assessments.[27]

Faculty members in non-clinical teaching settings assign grades based on anonymous, end-of-semester exams that have delineated and relatively objective metrics based in black-letter law. Clinical settings incorporate personal relationships and subjective opinions to a much higher degree. Both empathic regard and empathic disconnection that can result from relationships and the personal opinions can affect learning as well as grading in a clinical setting. Strong personal relationships can be a strength, especially when a student is undergoing personal or family stress. It is beneficial when students are having difficulty understanding issues concerning their professional role or the substantive nature of the case or project. It can also help when the student cannot understand the nuanced lawyer and client interactions because they cannot yet see or understand what experienced lawyers recognize. All these issues are more easily addressed when a strong mentorship relation exists.

On the other hand, if an empathic disconnect exists between the student and teacher, because of personality differences or perceived insufficient student effort that remains unrecognized or unresolved, it can result in subtle biases that discourage learning and alter honest assessments.[28] Empathic disconnects can be devastating. They can alter students' learning growth. If a disconnect exists, supervisors should look inward before analyzing the deficiencies in terms of the student's shortcomings or assign personal fault to the student.

When the relationship between student and teaching is good, it may actually enhance learning or the teacher's perception of the students achievements. However, the empathic regard accompanied by the lack of anonymity at clinic grading time requires that personal feelings become compartmentalized so that they do not result in unconscious favoritism. When an empathic disconnect exists, the lack of anonymity and negative personal feelings require the same compartmentalization to avoid assigning an inaccurate and unfair grades. Both require that teachers have a heightened sensitivity and self-awareness when appraising students' performance and before assigning grades.

Credit Allocations Affect the Grading Process

Eighth, aside from the problems inherent to curve grading and structural issues within the clinic, law school credit allocation complicate the grading process. Students work hard in their clinical courses; most students report that they work harder than they ever did in their non-clinical courses. That effort often exceeds the credit allocation that the entire faculty has approved for the clinic course.

Deciding how to reward a student's effort in relation to the credit given complicates the translation of a qualitative assessment into a quantitative assessment. But hard work is expected and is a baseline in law practice and in clinical courses. In the Juvenile Justice Clinic that I co-taught at Georgetown, we include the following statement about hard work. The rubric reads:

> Participation in this clinic requires hard work. Ethical obligations of competence and zeal require that attorneys work hard for their clients. It is expected that every student in the clinic will fulfill this obligation. It is likely that every student will work harder while participating in this course than they have in any other course in law school. Even if that happens, not every student will get an "A" or "A-." Simply put, hard work is a minimum requirement of this course. It puts you in position to receive a passing grade. It does not guarantee an "A" or "A-."

Credit allocations for clinical courses vary among law schools.[29] Some schools award a large number of credits, some as many as fourteen or sixteen, and others a small number, as low as three or four.[30] The number of credits and how they are allocated contributes to the difficulty of translating formative assessments into summative assessment. Ten or fourteen credits of an A or a C can have a large effect on students' grade point averages which then affects their eligibility honors and award designations as well as future job possibilities. Awarding a single grade for such a large number of credits is not easy. Nor is it easier in clinics with a small number of credits given the amount of work students do.

Grading requires combining assessments arising from many different lawyering and academic tasks into a unitary quantitative assessment that most likely does not reflect reality. Some students perform consistently in all areas that are assessed and graded. More often than not, however, a student will do A level work on some tasks, A- or B+ level work in others, and maybe occasionally C level work in yet another. How does one balance superior performance in one set of tasks with less than stellar work in another when only a single grade is awarded? What weight is appropriate for each? Why is one weightier than another? And how does that allocation of weight work when not all students have performed the same tasks? These weight allocation choices are cumbersome no matter what number of credits is assigned.

Translating formative assessments about multiple and disparate tasks fairly into a single grade is nearly impossible, especially in clinics that give a large number of credits. A fairer and more accurate method of translating qualitative assessments into quantitative assessments is to split students' clinic grades into three or more separate categories and then grade each category separately. There are diverse ways to do this. Most clinics have both a classroom component and a case or project component. A simple and seemingly intuitive method of creating multiple grades would be to give a classroom grade and a case or project grade. But students often give short shrift to classroom work because they see their field work as more important. Faculty will sometimes grudgingly admit that they do as well.

While it may sound easy to separate classroom grades from experiential grades, doing so is not as neat in practice. Moreover, seeing classroom work and case work as separate is a lost opportunity. The work that students prepare and perform in the classroom should be integrated directly into the case or project supervision sessions, and into the actual performance of the lawyering tasks. Learning the integration of theory and practice is an essential feature of clinical pedagogy. The students' work in the classroom is necessarily reflected in the tasks they will perform in their cases and projects and leads to more sophisticated supervision sessions. This is true about the performance of lawyering skills whether students are creating trial or appellate strategy or analyzing a complex legal or policy option.

As noted in Chapter Eleven, Classroom Instruction as Supervision, supervision takes place as much in the classroom as it does in a supervision session. Supervising the entire group of students in the classroom is often more efficient since it reduces teaching the same thing to each student individually.[31] Consider interviewing, for example. Students often misperceive the differences between a client or witness interview and a conversation with a friend or stranger. Teaching the theory of interviewing in a classroom session, discussing the differing goals of each interview, the various facilitators and impediments to conducting the conversations, and then viewing and critiquing demonstrations conveys a great deal of critical information before the case or project supervision session that precedes the actual execution of a real interview. Moreover, the information is provided to all students at one time, thereby eliminating the need for repeating conversation of the theory behind the skill to each student individually. In addition, subsequent supervision sessions will begin at a higher level of conversation. Hence, separating classroom performance from case or project performance for grading purposes is artificial. Doing so demonstrates a misunderstanding of the importance of learning the integration of theory and practice and is unhelpful when grading field work and assessing student learning. All clinic activities require engagement of a high order to master the material and learn lawyering skills and to represent the clients in a highly professional manner. Integrating classroom and field work drives that process. Thus, separating the grades is artificial.

Assessing the value of a student's work in the classroom poses its own challenges. The structure of the class created by the faculty member is critical to understanding how the student relates to the material that is presented in the class. Many ideas about designing productive class sessions are presented in the chapter on classroom teaching. Faculty often rely on class participation to assess whether the students are grasping the material presented. As noted above, class participation may be the basis of an entire grade when faculty award separate grades for classroom work and field work. But raising one's hand and talking does not always indicate true engagement. Conversely, remaining quiet in class does not necessarily reflect the absence of engagement. We can only know whether class participation creates learning if it is reflected in the students' approach to their clinic work and in their post-project reflection of their own performances.[32] A key feature of assessing in-class performances is distinguishing between performative speaking and true engagement. Most teachers will recognize whether a student is engaging with the material to advance their own or their colleagues learning or just talking for personal recognition. Engagement includes preparation, focus, presence, asking questions, listening, commenting with specificity, and synthesizing.[33] All of these can be demonstrated by talking in the classroom if the student has prepared. However, they can also be demonstrated in other ways by those who, for one reason or another, are reluctant to speak in the classroom. Modern technology provides many different ways for students to engage in the material with the supervisors and classmates. A student's supervision sessions and their performance on cases and projects will reflect the extent of their engagement, whether it occurred inside the classroom or in other ways outside the classroom. It is engagement, not merely class participation as measured by number of times raising one's hand or talking, that reflects learning and growth.

Recognizing that classroom and case or project work are integrated still leaves the grading problem unresolved. Even when students know that classroom work is integrated into their work in case rounds, supervision sessions, reflection meetings, planning, performance, and self-assessment, and know that all lawyering tasks are assessed in all learning venues, students often place less emphasis on their classroom preparation and performance as the semester draws to a close. The demands of their cases and projects make the classroom sessions seem less important.

Faculty members know that devoting more time to case and project preparation at the expense of classroom activities can diminish rather than enhance field performance. Nonetheless, supervisors also often see actual outcomes for clients as more important than class work. As a result, teachers overlook low classroom effort in comparison to case and project work when awarding grades. When they do, students can receive an unwarranted final grade of A or A-. Conversely, superior classroom performance may sometimes enhance a single grade for students who finish their clinic with lesser practice-related skills. Although giving undue weight to field work in grading will benefit some students, doing so is unfair to those who maintain a high-quality classroom performance. Therefore, understanding the purpose of classroom work in clinical pedagogy and assessing it properly underscores the importance of unifying classroom and case and project engagement when grades are assigned.

Benefits Derived from Grading

Despite all the difficulty in translating qualitative assessments into quantitative assessments, teachers must comply with the law school's mandatory or recommended curve requirements. Failure to do so will result in the grade not being accepted by the registrar, or a trip to the dean's office to explain the deviation. Despite some teachers' desires to do away with grades, they continue to exist in most clinical courses. When assessed and awarded properly, they may provide some institutional benefits for the law school and some benefits to students, notwithstanding the constraints that exist in any grading system.

One reason to grade students in the clinic is that most law schools give academic awards and use grades to recognize students who do outstanding work. Many schools have dean's lists and give award designations, monetary prizes, and sometimes scholarships based on class grades. Schools attach variations of *cum laude* designations to diplomas and nominate students for membership in the Order of the Coif. Clinic students work hard, arguably harder than students in non-clinical courses. They also continuously exert intellectual energy every day as they analyze the law and learn the symbiotic relationship between theory and practice. Moreover, they learn the law and the relationship between theory and practice more deeply in clinical courses than they do in non-clinical courses. For these reasons, it would be unfair to deprive clinic students of an opportunity to receive awards just because the faculty member's teaching and learning methods and the students' work in a clinical course differ from actions of faculty and students in non-clinical courses.

Assuming that grades are given, receiving a fair grade and determining its precise meaning is important to each student, to the students in the clinic as a whole, and to the faculty member who has to assign the grades. Grades are important to an individual student because they have real effects on students' lives no matter how often teachers try to minimize their importance. "Grades play a gatekeeping role, helping to sort students into ... graduate programs and jobs. They can shape the way students see themselves. Heck, they can get them a discount on their car insurance."[34]

Grades are the "coin of the realm" in law schools whether teachers like it or not. The grades students receive may actually determine their future. Law firms are notorious for excluding students with lower grades from opportunities to even interview for a position in their firms. Public defenders and other public interest organizations, especially those considered to be among the elite organizations around the country, will seldom take anyone whose clinic grades are not among the highest. Judges rely on grades to sort through the numerous applications they receive for clerkships. Most employers view clinical experience as a plus and sometimes require applicants for a legal position to have taken a clinical course and received a high grade. A clear and well-defined grade to a student in a clinic course sometimes carries more value to employers than grades in non-clinic courses. Students seeking those kinds of opportunities will strive mightily to get that good grade, and when they do excellent work, they should be commensurately rewarded.

Grades are important to the class as a whole if the law school administration requires that grades be awarded to students on some form of comparative basis. Students will compare grades no matter what teachers tell them. No matter how often faculty try to diminish the importance of grades when compared to personal growth and accomplishment, students will compare their grades and want explanations for why they received a grade that is different from their partner, other students in the clinic, or their own expectations. Moreover, they will justifiably demand that teachers assess their performance fairly among the members of the class. Although the grade itself may not meet a student's expectation, the grading system must be transparent and understandable so that the class as a whole believes that grade is fair within the required institutional system.

Grading is important to the faculty because they owe it to their students and our universities to be honest, fair, and clear when developing our grading practices and to be as objective as possible when quantitatively assessing our students. Grading may also send a message to current and future students that clinic courses should be taken just as seriously as classroom courses. This is seldom necessary, but occasionally, some students inaccurately imagine that clinic is a route to an easy A grade. They know that they will do a lot of work but assume that the amount of work will automatically translate into a high grade.

Because non-clinical law school courses often do not discuss the practice of law, students may mistakenly believe that doing things on a case or project in a clinic is easier than remembering black-letter law, taking exams, or authoring research papers. Students may have also taken a prior externship where the supervision is less rigorous than it is in the clinic and assume that a limited level of guidance will occur, and a limited amount of responsibility will be expected of them. Honest grading discourages those kinds of mistaken notions. In addition, grades still serve to motivate some clinic students to do their best work or at least keep them from doing only the bare minimum amount of work needed on a case or project.

Warning students about deficient performance during a formative assessment and the potential for an unfavorable grade should not be a primary tool in a clinic. It can, however, in some very limited circumstances reinforce the message that a student's work needs improvement if they expect to get a coveted legal position after graduation.[35] Doing so should not be done regularly because the existence of grades in an academic setting carries the notion of threat. Clinical teachers' goals are to meet their students where they find them and do their best to enhance the students' ability in the clinic and create a method for lifelong learning. Threats are an impediment to that kind of growth. They should be reserved for students who are underperforming intentionally.

A tangential benefit of grading is that students will be evaluated by their supervisors throughout their professional lives in the more public arena of their law firms or public interest organizations. Experiencing a personal evaluation in the less competitive and more supportive environment of a law school clinic will help make that transition a little bit easier.

The Benefits of a Multi-Category Grading Rubric

Once a teacher understands the purpose of engagement in classroom and field work performance and its relation to learning the integration of theory and practice, the need for three or more separate grading categories, each with integrated features, becomes clearer. Some students will do outstanding work in some areas of performance and less than outstanding or merely adequate work in others. Oftentimes, the less-than-outstanding work in one area becomes significant when single grades are being tallied. Students who perform outstanding work in most areas may receive a lower grade than expected because of less-than-stellar work in a separate area of performance. Students, like most people, remember their successes rather than their shortcomings. Thus, they often forget those shortcomings when considering their grade. When they do, they are disappointed when they receive their grade and feel unfairly evaluated. When they come to the teacher's office to discuss the grade, faculty members often find it difficult to demonstrate why the subpar performance in one area took on so much significance in comparison to the stellar performances in others.

Faculty will find it hard to defend the amount of weight given to each of the numerous factors that lead to a single grade. It will be especially difficult if the faculty member does not have a clear grading rubric for the course that is related to the course goals and expectations. This is especially true when a large number of credits are involved. A system with multiple grading categories, accompanied by clear rubrics that situate the discrete tasks students perform in the clinic within relevant categories, helps minimize summative assessment inequities. It also helps, and indeed is essential, to eliminate bias and the intrusion of personal feelings in the process and better reflects the formative assessment that preceded it.[36]

Multiple grading category systems make a clinic grade assignment fairer and more accurate and make conversations about grade distinctions easier to explain. For example, in a four-grade system, students may receive grades for (1) role assumption, which includes recognizing and resolving ethical issues that arise in a case and assesses the level of zealous and responsible representation; (2) case or project planning, which concerns the steps a student took to move from the client's goals to the ultimate resolution of the case or project; (3) skills development, which assesses the preparation and performance of the various tasks the student undertook to achieve the client's goals, and whether growth occurred between the early performances and the final product; and (4) overall engagement and growth, as reflected in the classroom, case rounds, supervision sessions, client engagement, lawyering task performance, and reflection. Reflection and self-critique are required for each area, but can also be a separate, fifth rubric category.

Of course, there are many different variations of the categories that can reflect the work of specific clinics and their goals. Faculty members will need to deconstruct the work in their specific clinic to create the proper rubric. Once a teacher chooses the categories within the rubric, students need clear descriptions of the relevant tasks within each grading category, what the goals of the clinic are, and what they are expected to accomplish from the very first day of the course.

Even when teachers adopt the multiple-grade rubric, two additional and related yet distinct issues arise when considering how a formative assessment translates into a grade that actually has meaning. The first is what kinds of demonstrated behaviors and performances constitute a particular grade, and second, how to merge multiple assessed behaviors and performances into a single quantitative grade for the rubric category. Explaining why a student received a particular grade requires that both the faculty and the student have a similar understanding of what a letter or adjectival grade means. Creating a universal understanding of the meaning of a grade is probably not possible,[37] but it is possible to describe what a grade means within the closed cohort of a single clinic course. Teachers need to develop concrete descriptions of what a certain grade means, and articulable reasons why a student deserves their particular grade. This requires an understandable grading rubric that explains what constitutes a particular grade *and* a clear record of the various tasks a student undertook. The record should include specific examples of a student's work that demonstrates why their work falls into a particular grade level.

Replacing a single-grade system with a multiple-grade system ultimately benefits the student and the faculty member. The multiple-grade system has benefits for the student even when the cumulative effect of four grades on a student's law school grade point average may not be significantly different from that awarded in a single grade system. A student's transcript will reveal a separate grade for each of the goal/grade clusters, thereby reflecting a more accurate quantitative rating of the qualitative assessment. It permits students to celebrate their various accomplishments and to more accurately reflect where they need to improve their performance as they move to the next stage of their development. The multiple-grade system benefits teachers because they can feel more secure about the accuracy of the grade. It will also likely result in fewer grade complaints at the end of the term, especially when the grades are given in concert with intensive self- and faculty-led formative assessments prior to issuing the grade.

There are many ways to describe in words what constitutes a performance worthy of a grade. A rubric I find useful was developed by Professor John Copacino at Georgetown's Criminal Justice Clinic. It is now also used in the Georgetown's Juvenile Justice Clinic. The rubric defines the meaning of various grades as follows:[38]

> A: Consistently excellent work in all areas, with at least one outstanding piece of significant work. A student who earns an "A" in Role Assumption, for example, will take full ownership of their cases, be organized and attentive to details, and will always allocate sufficient time and effort to carry out tasks responsibly, and will recognize, consider, and appropriately resolve ethical issues. A student who earns an "A" in Case Planning will show initiative and creativity in planning and developing cases rather than merely carrying out plans encouraged by the supervisor. A student who earns an "A" in Skills Development will have mastered the various lawyering skills necessary to be a highly competent attorney. A student who earns an "A" in Engagement will actively prepare, participate, and take initiative in all class sessions, simulation exercises, supervision sessions, and case rounds, assist other students with their cases when necessary, and demonstrate greater responsibility for each area as the semester proceeds.
>
> A-: Mostly excellent work in all areas, but occasionally some less than excellent work
>
> B+: Consistently good work, or a mix of generally good work and some excellent work

B: Competent and adequate work with some particularly good work, but with some weaknesses

B-: On the whole, competent work but with some significant lapses or shortcomings

Below B-: Serious difficulties with performance; failing to make appropriate use of supervision; failing to meet responsibilities[39]

Clinic faculty members need to recognize the importance of having clear formative and summative assessment rubrics, explore the pros and cons of various forms of grading rubrics, and compare them with other systems before deciding how to translate qualitative assessments into quantitative evaluations.[40] If rubrics are to give grades meaning, faculty must share them with the students from the outset so that the meaning is transparent. Teachers will have their own way of phrasing the language and explaining the meaning of the various grades. But using language that permits the student to understand what is expected, supported by concrete examples of what the letter, number, or adjectival grade requires, gives the students a better sense of why a grade was assigned.

That said, all grading systems contain some elements of subjectivity. Rubrics are not immune to the tension between specificity and generality. They can minimize but not eliminate the inherently imperfect nature of translating a formative assessment into a summative assessment. Nor will they remove all disagreements about an assessment or wholly eliminate all unconscious bias.[41] Using a system similar to the one above, however, gives the teacher and student a distinct and mutually understandable standard from which to understand a grade and articulates paths toward future progress. Students will understand the grade even better when the faculty member bases the grade on the clinic's goals, on meaningful conversations during case and project planning and supervision sessions, and during the formal formative assessment sessions that preceded the assignment of the grade.

Detailed Record-Keeping Informs the Grading Categories

In addition to having a rubric, case and project supervisors need data that permits the assignment of an accurate grade. It is essential to keep accurate and detailed records of all faculty-student interactions and interventions about the progress on the case or project. Descriptions need to be specific. The conclusory words "good" or "poor" do not alone provide evidence of learning. Why something was good or deficient needs to be specifically explained in the notes. The notes should record at least:

the nature and quality of supervision sessions

the student's role in the planning and executing all case and project events

the nature and quality of the student's participation in classes

non-classroom examples of engagement

whether the student participates in, and sometimes leads, case rounds sessions

the quality of the student's research strategy and writing process through each of the multiple drafts of a document

the quality of the execution of all lawyering tasks and the reasons for the assessment

the extent to which the student's actions and reflections demonstrate growth

the teacher's reflections on the student's work and the reasons for that reflection

Recognizing the need for accurate notes is different from finding the time to do so. Keeping timely records of student-faculty interactions is often difficult because of the pressure from a teacher's other responsibilities at the law school, their own efforts on the path to tenure and scholarly accomplishment, and the needs of other students in the clinic. Nonetheless, formative and summative assessments will be meaningless without a collection of accurate and detailed data that was recorded soon after the events. Grades are not merely guesses about vaguely remembered actions of whether a student performed well or poorly. Proper assessments and proper grading can occur only if the teacher and students are aware of the clinic's goals and expectations from the early days of the course, and if the teacher's recorded comments about their own interventions and the students' performances are connected to them.

Finding time to produce these notes is not always easy. Teachers often schedule back-to-back supervisory sessions with students throughout the day. If supervisors delay recording the notes, they run the risk of inaccurate recording. Remembering a series of individual conversations with multiple students about multiple cases or projects is not easy. Our memory can suffer from overemphasizing first or last conversations while lumping together those that happen in between. Teachers will find that transcribing the notes of the session will be easier if they preserve at least thirty minutes between supervision sessions to organize their thoughts and record them in their student files. Those notes are not unlike the summary comments to written work described in Chapter Five, Special Considerations for Supervising Student Writing. Making decisions, especially in potentially life-altering events, reduces our ability to make good decisions.[42] Inaccurate decision-making can occur in all aspects of clinical teaching. If supervisors do not provide time between supervision sessions to relax, clarify their observations and impressions, and record them calmly and precisely, their assessments of a student's performance could inadvertently be incorrect.

The articles and rubrics that follow give examples and describe how other clinical teachers approach their grading systems.

Other Voices

Georgetown Juvenile Justice Clinic
Summative Assessment Rubric*

Memo to the Students

This memo describes what is expected of you this year and discusses the factors we will consider in grading your performance. This description is detailed, but it cannot be exhaustive. We cannot list everything you will experience this year, as we do not know just what your cases will require. You can expect to be asked to do the many things described below, and perhaps other things as well. We will try to take it all into account when assessing your work, just as we hope you will take it all into account when representing your clients.

To best appreciate the system by which grades are assigned, you should consider each of the criteria and factors we set forth in this memo. You are being trained to be a skilled and responsible practicing attorney. The center of the clinical experience is your clients and their cases; therefore, you will be graded on your ability to take responsibility for your cases and do everything necessary to provide a zealous and legally sophisticated defense for your clients. To prepare you for your cases, the clinic also includes class readings and assignments designed to develop your proficiency in both the analysis and delivery of your cases. Finally, you are expected to learn from your experiences so that you will become a better attorney—both by improving your advocacy in the clinic, and by developing habits that will serve you in your professional life.

Participation in the clinic requires that you perform a number of tasks in a wide variety of settings. You will advocate in courtrooms. You will research in the library. You will conduct interviews in the office and in the community. You will draft opening statements and deliver them before you get to court (in your supervisor's office, in the classroom, and perhaps in the student workroom for your colleagues). You will counsel your clients (in the office, at their homes, and on the phone). You will perform simulations in class. You will read cases for class and for your clients' cases. This list could go on for pages.

We will be giving you four separate and distinct grades in the clinic. Full-year students will receive one 4-credit grade for Assumption of Role, one 3-credit grade for Case Planning, one 4-credit grade for Skills Development, and one 3-credit grade for Educational Growth & Engagement. One semester (Fall Only) students will receive one 3-credit grade for Assumption of Role, one 2-credit grade for Case Planning, one 2-credit grade for Skills Development, and one 2-credit grade for Educational Growth.

* This assessment and grading rubric was created by the professors in the Georgetown Juvenile Justice Clinic. It is given to the students during Orientation. The criteria are consistent with the topics noted in the student self-assessment form.

We have tried to set forth the criteria that we will consider in assessing your performance in each of these areas. We think this is important for two reasons: 1) the criteria will help us to provide consistent assessments of all students in the clinic; 2) the criteria will let you know what is expected and what factors will be used to grade your performance. We have tried to be as thorough as possible, but you should not consider these factors to be the exclusive criteria for evaluation.

*Note: Full-year students will receive grades for the full year at the end of the academic year. One semester students will receive grades at the end of the semester.

Role Assumption Full-year students—4 credit grade
One-semester students—3 credit grade

Having students assume the role and responsibilities of a lawyer is the foundation of clinical education methodology. Students in the Juvenile Justice Clinic will assume the role of an attorney in all of its manifestations.

Ethical Considerations

Professional responsibility is an indispensable feature of good lawyering. Knowledge of, and adherence to, ethical rules is obviously necessary to practice law. You will be expected to zealously represent your clients and, of course, preserve client confidences. You will also be expected to identify the ways in which these obligations and others contained within the D.C. Rules of Professional Conduct affect your work on any case. As with any other issue, we expect that after you are familiar with the rules, you will recognize ethical concerns in your cases, consider the choices presented, develop a plan of action that will respond to the issues presented, and initiate discussion with your supervisor. The penalties for noncompliance with ethical obligations and zealous representation may include grade reduction or course failure.

Zealous and Responsible Representation

Professional responsibility is not limited to the ethical considerations of lawyering. It also includes attention to cases and to other clinic responsibilities, effort in the representation of clients, and management of one's workload. Some specific factors are:

Putting forth effort to provide zealous representation and the best possible defense.

Taking personal responsibility for a client's case.

Ensuring that cases are prepared for court hearings.

Maintaining appropriate relationships with clients, other attorneys, and court officials.

Meeting deadlines imposed by the court, your supervisors, and on your own initiative.

Being punctual and attentive to professional obligations, including court appearances and meetings with clients, supervisors, witnesses, and other students.

Maintaining files accurately and precisely and complying with office procedures.

Allocating time and effort to carry out tasks responsibly.

Making use of all resources available, including our Education Advocate and the Social Work Adjunct Faculty.

Reflection & Self-Critique

Reflection applies to all four graded areas and is discussed at length below in Part IV. B.

Case Planning Full-year students—3 credit grade

One-semester students—2 credit grade

The Planning Process

This is a broad area that encompasses the development of a case theory, deliberation about alternative strategies, and judgment exercised in the context of fluid information and uncertainty. Planning is the single most important feature of good lawyering. In the context of representing children charged with delinquency, planning must occur in several areas. First, in developing and executing your theory of the case, you must plan investigation, research, and examinations of witnesses. As you uncover new facts (or fail to uncover desired proof of expected facts), you must adjust your plan accordingly. While hoping from the outset that your client will not be found guilty, you must start right away to plan for the possible disposition hearing. In addition, you must devise a plan that will help address the various other issues affecting your client's case (e.g. school, family, substance abuse). This plan will necessarily be designed in accordance with your client's directions. Some activities in this area are:

Developing a theory and strategy for each case, taking into consideration the application of evidence, statutes, regulations, and case law to develop a plan to use facts and law to benefit our client.

Modifying and reassessing strategy in light of subsequent developments.

Refining and improving work between planning and final draft or performance.

Consciously considering the ethical, strategic, and client-specific issues in cases.

Consciously weighing the risks and benefits of different strategies.

Prioritizing work and making appropriate judgments and decisions, given the available information and resources.

Basically, we expect that, as the person chiefly responsible for the development of a case, *you will come into supervision meetings having considered the various challenges you face and having identified several responses to them.* We expect you to articulate these challenges and responses for your supervisor. We expect you to realize that rules of ethics, the law of evidence, common sense, and many other factors may favor some responses and constrain you in implementing others. We do not expect that any of this will come naturally. Nor do we expect that each of you will enter your first supervision meeting with a plan that would be developed by an experienced lawyer. We do expect that your planning will show a serious application of time and effort and that, with more time and effort, it will improve.

Reflection & Self-Critique

Reflection applies to all four graded areas and is discussed at length in Part IV. B.

Skills Development: *Full-year students—4 credit grade*
One-semester students—2 credit grade

Lawyering Skills

Work in the clinic provides the opportunity to develop a wide variety of skills. Your performance both in and out of court will be evaluated.

> Interviewing: Structure, rapport, and ability to obtain information. (To be evaluated within the constraints of our decision not to have supervisors at client or witness interviews.)
>
> Counseling: Helping the client understand their alternatives; keeping the client informed; remaining sensitive to the full range of the client's needs.
>
> Fact Investigation: Planning, execution, thoroughness, effort, and creativity.
>
> Legal Research: Thoroughness, accuracy, and appropriate analysis of relevant sources.
>
> Writing: Organization, structure, and the use of language and writing techniques that are appropriate to the audience and are concise and persuasive.
>
> Hearing Performance: Executing the plan; adequately performing skills in court; dealing efficiently with unexpected developments.
>
> Trial Skills: Mastery of fundamental trial skills (e.g., cross-examination for trial and probable cause hearings, direct examination, opening statements, closing arguments, etc.). Note: We can evaluate your trial skills through in-class performance even if none of your cases go to trial.

Reflection & Self-Critique

Reflection applies to all four graded areas and is discussed at length in Part IV. B.

Educational Growth & Engagement: Full-Year Students—3 credit grade
One-semester students—2 credit grade

We expect that students will actively engage in the learning process both inside and outside of the classroom. The learning curve will be steep for most of you, even those of you who have interned in criminal justice and youth justice spaces. To serve your clients most effectively and maximize your own professional development, we expect that all of you will be eager to learn, willing to try out new skills and techniques, and open to feedback.

Classroom Work & Supervision Sessions

Classroom work is an important aspect of your work in the clinic. Your thoughtful contributions will be essential to the success of the clinic. You are expected to be prepared for all classes and to participate in all discussions, supervision sessions, and simulations. We do not want you to talk for the sake of talking any more than we would expect you to cross-examine a witness just for the sake of saying something. However, we choose the topics for class carefully, with an eye toward having the group learn with, and from, each other. We expect the same sort of preparation, participation, and engagement from you in the classroom, group and individual email exchanges, and supervision sessions.

Some specific factors are:

Preparation for class.

Consistent participation in class.

Quality of class contributions, including meaningful participation in discussion and analysis.

Participation in simulations and execution of assignments, while remaining in role.

Preparation for supervisory meetings.

Initiative and creativity in raising issues and planning cases.

Attendance and punctuality to class and supervision sessions.

Reflection & Self-Assessment

Reflection will factor into all four of the graded areas. Reflection is a critical feature of clinical learning. You should be reflecting during and after every task you perform in the clinic. Reflection is not simply reviewing what happened. Instead, we want you to engage in critical analysis of your work so that you can learn how to improve your advocacy in the future. We expect that you will ask yourselves questions, such as those listed below, and be prepared to discuss the answers with your supervisor. ***Then, when you are engaged in your next task, we expect you will use what you learned through reflection to decide what to do.***

Some questions to ask yourself while reflecting are:

What went well? Why do you think those things went well?

What didn't go as well as you would have liked? Why do you think those things didn't go as well as you would have liked?

What judgments and decisions did you make in advance of the event (i.e., in advance of the hearing, the argument, the interview, the negotiation with the prosecutor, etc.)?

How did you come to make the decisions that you made (e.g., Why did you choose to call one defense witness and not another? or Why did you choose one defense theory over another?)

How did you determine the choices you thought were available?

Why didn't you see other choices?

What led other people (clients, judges, opposing counsel) to act as they did?

How do the cases we read and the exercises we do in class affect your actual case work?

How will the answers to these questions affect the way you approach your work in the future?

Clinic can also be a challenging year for students on a personal level. As you transition from student to attorney, it can be difficult to learn to manage your caseload in the midst of all your other personal and academic responsibilities. Additionally, because we often represent indigent clients during a particularly challenging period in their lives, it can be challenging to learn both how to be a lawyer in that context and how to manage the emotional impact of the work on us as individuals. We encourage reflection and discussion during supervision about these aspects of the work as well.

Some questions to ask yourself while reflecting are:

How are my clients responding (or not responding) to me? How are my clients responding (or not responding) to other actors in the system?

Why were those responses forthcoming?

How can I put myself in my clients' shoes to better understand how they may be experiencing this case and how they may perceive the different actors in the system, including myself?

What assumptions am I making about the behavior of my client? My client's parent? The probation officer? The prosecutor? The judge?

What lessons can be drawn from these experiences about the way the legal system actually works?

How do those lessons align or conflict with your ideals of how the system ought to work?

What have I learned about personal values and legal ethics?

The Grading Process

The following is a rough description of the quality of work which corresponds to the various grades. These are necessarily general and limited descriptions, but ones which we hope will be useful in helping you understand our grading criteria.

A: Consistently excellent work in all areas, with at least one outstanding piece of significant work.

Role Assumption: Student takes full ownership of his/her cases, is organized and attentive to details, and always allocates sufficient time and effort to carry out tasks responsibly and recognizes, considers, and appropriately resolves ethical issues.

Case Planning: Student shows initiative and creativity in planning and developing cases, rather than merely carrying out plans encouraged by the supervisor.

Skills Development: Student mastered the various lawyering skills necessary to be a highly competent attorney.

Educational Growth and Engagement: Student actively prepares, participates, and takes initiative in all class sessions, simulation exercises, team meetings, and supervisory sessions.

A-: Mostly excellent work in all areas, and some occasionally very good work.

B+: Consistently very good work, or a mix of generally very good work, occasional excellent work, and some competent work.

B: Competent and adequate work with some very good work, but with some weaknesses.

B-: On the whole, competent work but with some significant lapses or shortcomings.

Below B-: Serious difficulties with performance; failing to make appropriate use of supervision; failing to meet responsibilities.

A Note on Effort

Participation in this clinic requires hard work. Ethical obligations of competence and zeal require attorneys to work hard. It is expected that every student in the clinic will fulfill this obligation. It is likely that every student will work harder in this course than in any other course in law school. Even if that happens, not every student will get an "A" or "A-". Simply put, hard work is a minimum requirement of this course. It puts you in a position to receive a passing grade. It does not guarantee an "A" or "A-."

Melina A. Healey, *Sharing the Tuna Platter: A Uniform System of Assessment or Clinical Education**

31 Clinical Law Review 275 (2025)

...

I. Program-Wide Standardized Assessment of Students: A Tool for Improving Clinical Education and Illustrating Its Essential Role

Clinicians resist standardized assessment of student performance, yet most will ultimately assign a final grade to all students at the semester's end. Unlike most law school courses, which involve prepared simulations, doctrinal multiple choice and es-

* Excerpts are reprinted with the permission of the author and the Clinical Law Review.

say exams, or final papers, the majority of a student's work in clinic is based on a real client's present needs and goals. This work is commonly regarded as too subjective and "idiosyncratic" to permit uniform evaluation of performances. Complicating matters, clinicians, and law faculty generally, receive no systematic training on how to provide feedback and grade. Moreover, there are no national standards against which clinical competence in lawyering is assessed that can be used as a template for clinic assessment.

Clinicians can remedy these deficiencies at the program level, and by doing so lead the way toward more effective assessment and licensing systems that better measure a lawyer's competency for practice. The adoption of uniform clinical program-wide rubrics to evaluate students is a valuable first step. Uniform and universal clinical program student assessments facilitate consensus among the program's clinicians about the basic learning outcomes that all clinics should achieve. The use of any assessment scheme in turn influences what is taught and how much value students and institutions attribute to the various types of work the students engage in. In acknowledgment that clinical teaching is intended "for transfer," student achievement of lawyering skills can benefit from our collaboration across practice areas to develop these uniform program-wide assessment tools. This collaboration also helps ensure that, in addition to basic lawyering skills, core clinical principles such as lawyering, and cross-cultural competence, among other "relational competencies," are presented universally in clinical programs. At the program level, uniform assessments can also identify where the program suffers from gaps in providing students with exposure to or ability to achieve those commonly accepted learning outcomes. This gives clinical programs actionable information to ensure they are providing quality education. It also helps clinicians participate more fully in the important task of school-wide development of institutional learning outcomes and curriculum mapping.

Inter-clinic faculty assessment also improves the quality of the assessment of individual students. Multiple assessors enhance the reliability of assessments and reduce the effect of bias. Finally, clinicians can turn to these universal assessments, with common learning outcomes and measurements, to underscore the critically important role clinic plays in the development of professionals and perhaps even contribute to necessary reforms in attorney licensure.

Working together as a clinical faculty to develop learning goals and rubrics, and then complete the rubrics, is critical to the valid and reliable assessment of clinic students.

...

A. Collectively Developing Clearly Defined Learning Objectives and Standardized Program-Wide, Criteria-Based Rubric Assessments

Experiential learning, like all programs of legal education, must identify (1) clear learning objectives and (2) how students' achievement of these objectives will be measured. To accomplish this, "both faculty and students must be aware of and share a common set of instructional goals and objectives, which should be explicit, published, and widely disseminated." However, clinicians have historically experienced difficulty coming to a consensus on the goals of clinical education. Clinicians also have not developed uniform systems for assessing student competence against learning objectives. Clinical faculty can reverse this trend by working together at the program level to develop standardized clinical rubrics for student assessment.

... Rubrics are "detailed written grading criteria, which describe both what students should learn and how they will be evaluated." Clinic rubrics transparently announce to students how they are being assessed, what constitutes different levels of performance in practice, and what they can expect to engage in during their course experience. Rubrics also reduce the effects of bias, enhance learning, and are of particular importance to younger generations of learners.

The explicit criteria of a rubric provide a formal context in which to name and reward good performances by students. Unfortunately, students who perform well in a busy law practice often have their performances dismissed as simply an unqualified "good job." The use of a standardized rubric assessment requires that the instructor instead name the specific ways that the student was successful. This increases faculty accountability for helpful and rigorous feedback.

While difficult to develop at the program level due to the number of faculty voices involved, clinical programs benefit from criteria-referenced standard rubrics rather than norm referenced assessments. Criteria-referenced rubrics increase the reliability of the assessment. Norm referenced assessments are based on how students perform compared to each other or compared to an elusive and unarticulated standard of competence. Norm-referenced rubrics "do not help students understand the degree to which they achieved the educational objectives of the course." By contrast, criteria-referenced assessments "rely on detailed, explicit criteria that identify the abilities students should be demonstrating [...] and the bases on which the instructor will distinguish among good, competent, or incompetent performance." This allows clinicians to be explicit about what they are looking for and avoid ambiguous feedback. Moreover, a standardized rubric used across clinics within a program signals to clinic students that the competencies they gain in their clinic are transferable even if their case work experiences and practice areas appear distinct.

Collaboration among the clinic faculty to build these explicit rubric assessments benefits students because it improves the feedback they receive. It is also helpful for individual clinicians and for the program. Developing common learning outcomes and identifying how a specific clinical course aligns with those outcomes allows clinical faculty and leaders of experiential learning programs to identify where there are gaps in students achieving learning outcomes across the clinical program and make necessary reforms or curricular additions. Creation of common programmatic-level rubrics further enables rigorous assessment of program effectiveness, in turn contributing to the ABA's outcome assessment accreditation mandates. Faculty dialogue over learning outcomes and measurements itself yields benefits, which may explain other new proposed imperatives from the ABA to align the minimum learning outcomes of required courses.

B. Collaborating Across Clinics to Overcome Siloed Programs

Genuine collaboration among the faculty to create uniform assessment tools is critical. At Touro, when I became Director of Clinical Programs, I convened our clinical faculty over the course of an initial year to meet regularly and collect and review all of the student assessment and feedback tools used in each clinic. Our clinical faculty then gathered and reviewed hundreds of other tools used in clinical law programs, externship programs, and other professions' clinical practice settings, identifying and coding the most common learning outcomes and criteria enumerated in those tools. We reviewed the tools and findings as a clinical faculty and worked together to identify the ones we collectively agreed were most important to measure for our students. I then created our uniform tool. Each year, we review the tool and analyze patterns in our assessment and refine the tool. Ongoing collaboration at least annually by the clinical faculty to refine assessment tools is critical to ensure that the faculty buy into the tool's relevance rather than to ignore it or regard it as a burden.

...

The dialogue over what is included in a standard program-wide assessment is not easy. It poses particular challenges to clinicians who are often so busy with so many responsibilities to clients, students, and their institution, or when there are differences of opinion within programs about what we expect of our students. The process of collaborative assessment requires that clinicians commit to working across perceived differences and the inherent barriers resulting from commitment to academic freedom. But the enterprise has value in that it forces a conversation. It also helps set standard expectations for in-house clinics that share law practices and office space.

...

E. Including Rigorous and Explicit Self-Evaluation Metrics in Rubrics to Invite Student Collaboration in Assessments

Clinics are commonly referred to as "skills" (or worse, "soft skills") courses. The term implies that there is some basic set of tools that can be reduced to a list of criteria against which to judge each individual student. Unfortunately, the "skills" label obscures the more abstract, yet critical, learning goals of clinic education, for students to "learn how to learn from experience." In other words, clinic should help students develop capacity for self-reflection. The ABA has recently formalized the importance of self-reflection and growth in legal education through mandating instruction on "professional identity formation" in new accreditation Standard 303(b)(3).

The goal of self-reflection is achieved if a student is able to plan when confronted with a novel situation, execute their plan, and meaningfully reflect on the plan and performance. Self-reflection is necessary to a professional's ability to be "metacognitive" about their practice, meaning "aware of what it takes to become competent in their chosen domain and to equip them with the reflective capacity and motivation to pursue genuine expertise." To achieve the learning outcome of self-reflection, the student must develop a methodology in which they learn from their own experiences and "ask themselves appropriate questions that will give them an understanding of their own lawyering processes." If clinic works, the student will be able to confront novel situations with recognition of the biases, cultural contexts, and assumptions that affect the relevant relationships and perceptions, strategize creatively in problem solving, and build a professional identity that they can apply to their careers. They will also be able to continue learning from experience, "an important life-long skill for lawyers to acquire."

Performance of this learning outcome is difficult to standardize and scale. Can a rubric measure how deeply and genuinely the student has examined their own biases, context, and role in legal systems while performing legal work? While challenging, metrics for self-reflection (and other "relational competencies") should be intentionally and explicitly built into clinic learning outcomes and assessments so that students are aware that their ability to be self-reflective is a key learning outcome for their experience in clinic. Clinicians have developed a number of methodologies to evaluate self-reflection. Rubrics can be designed to measure the quality of self-reflection. The inclusion of self-reflection in a rubric makes explicit that this is an important goal of the course and contributes to the more interactive dialogue the clinician and student should have as follow up after a scored assessment. Assessment tools are often important not as much for the written information they contain, but because they are springboards for rich conversations about the student's experience in clinic and provide a foundation for further self-reflection. It is also useful to include a space for students to articulate specific moments when they have had opportunities for self- reflection during clinic.

A student's ability to self-critique is important for their professional lives after law school because graduates "will not always be able to depend on others to provide critique and feedback." Self-assessment provides a formalized opportunity for students to practice self-critique and facilitates feedback from peers and faculty for how effective the student's self-critique is as well.

...

Jodi S. Balsam, Susan L. Brooks, and Margaret Reuter, *Assessing Law Students as Reflective Practitioners**

62 N.Y.L. Sch. L. Rev. 49 (2017–2018)

...

III. Developing and Workshopping Our Rubric

A rubric, simply put, is an expression of the learning goals a teacher has laid out for her students. It anchors the students' expectations and performance as well as sets the teacher's agenda. It is up to the teacher to plan instruction, discussion, activities, and assignments that will reasonably lead the students to achieve those goals, for example, an emerging skillfulness in reflective practice about their work and their profession. The goals are necessarily supported and constrained by situational factors, such as credit load, grading, and student-teacher ratios, among others. In supervised practice classes (clinic and externship), reflective writing assignments generally direct students to write about activities and experiences occurring in their legal work-whether their own work, or interactions or observations involving clients, supervisors, judges, or others. Depending on the teaching goals, the reflective writing assignment or prompt might specify a particular aspect of the student legal work to reflect upon, for example, self-critique, challenges to developing client trust, or exercise of prosecutorial restraint, or it might be open-ended, allowing for the student to choose the topic. Each of these aspects of reflective writing impacts the scope of the students' performance of the skill and the teacher's ability to be part of the coaching and evaluation of the skill.

Each of the authors has conceived, introduced, and assigned reflective writing in diverse ways, aligned with their larger teaching goals. In her graded, one-credit externship seminar for first-time student externs, Balsam assigns four guided reflective essays throughout the semester, between 750 and 1,250 words each. Students are expected to prepare a critical essay, as opposed to an informal journal entry, that closely analyzes a valuable learning experience at their field placement. They receive detailed instructions on the format and structure of the critical essay, prompts for self-interrogation about their fieldwork experiences, and a grading rubric. Rubrics that Balsam used previously were presented as a traditional grid, with three levels of proficiency (excellent, competent, and needs work) along seven factors, each with specific point ranges. The factors included multiple aspects of reflection and the quality of the writing.

...

In the two-credit, graded externship seminar she formerly taught, Reuter required seven bi-weekly journals, totaling fifteen to twenty pages by semester's end. The journals were graded as a body of work rather than individually. Reuter's comments on

* Excerpts are reprinted with the permission of the author and the New York Law School Law Review.

each journal were largely designed to push the students toward further reflection on the particular observations, suggest thought experiments, and address the struggles identified. She set out a rubric in bullet form with three levels of reflective writing skill (A, B, and C grades), with criteria that focused on professional growth and connections to readings and doctrinal coursework. In the first weeks of the semester, students read a number of exemplars of previous students' reflective essays, and in small groups the students dissected an essay to discern what it demonstrated about the student's experience and personal growth. Reuter moderated the class discussion to illuminate the power of reflection to root and propel one's learning.

In Brooks's two-credit, graded Justice Lawyering Seminar, she generally assigns two essays, each about 2,000 words. One of the essays is on a focused topic and the other is open-ended. The reflective writing assignments are previewed at the outset of the semester, yet are due closer to its end to allow time for students to acquire experience that invariably leads to disorienting moments, alongside building understanding of and engagement with various social justice issues. Brooks provides a four-page assignment memo with specific points and dimensions students need to cover, including the grading criteria. Brooks's original rubric lays out the factors and dimensions important to reflective writing, for example, consideration of alternative perspectives and evidence of movement from previously held beliefs, though it does not offer delineations of levels of proficiency. Brooks grades and comments via an emailed paragraph on the first essay, sent before the second essay is due.

We were impressed with the significant overlap in our approaches and the shared qualities-we hoped our student writings would demonstrate, despite the different routes to our teaching of the skill of reflective practice. In some form or another, we each value reflective writing that shows:

careful description of the object of reflection (experience, observation), such that it demonstrates the capacity of close observation;

both cognitive analytical treatment and emotional engagement;

personal reaction and evidence how the student has changed or intends to change;

appreciation for the perspectives of others; and

quality writing and compliance with requirements as to form and deadlines.

Brooks has explicitly required students to consider and describe the perspectives of others. This aspect of reflective practice is similar to parallel universe thinking that Jean Koh Peters and Susan Bryant have described in Five Habits for Cross-Cultural Lawyering. In parallel universe thinking, lawyers explore multiple alternative interpretations of client behavior, not just as it relates to the lawyer, but also as it concerns the client herself.

Neither Balsam's nor Reuter's original rubrics included such a grading factor. Very quickly, though, the two professors realized that the reflective journals that resonated most were written by students who showed an ability to see through the eyes of others and to adapt their understanding accordingly. Both then added "Perspective-taking" as a grading criterion and thereby made explicit to the students a grading factor that had been present, yet unstated.

This kind of group dialectic has led us to develop our mash-up rubric with six characteristics or grading factors presented directly to the students. Four factors address specific elements of reflection. They are: 1. Object of your reflection; 2. Personal engagement; 3. Lessons learned; and 4. Perspective-taking. Two additional factors cover writing attributes: 5. Overall quality and 6. Writing mechanics. These two additional factors are included to reinforce the professional habit of clear writing that conforms to format standards. Each of the criteria includes explanations at three proficiency levels: (1) First-year attorney work, (2) Effective law student work, and (3) Undeveloped. Labeling the most proficient student efforts as "first-year attorney work" is a way to communicate to students that reflective practice is not merely an academic exercise. Their path to becoming effective practitioners depends on continued reflection and self-evaluation.

Here, we lay out the four reflection-based criteria described at the highest level of proficiency, first-year attorney work.

Object of your reflection

Writing articulates clearly the topic chosen and reason for choosing it.

Topic setup provides clear and appropriately detailed background information.

Perspective-taking

Writing addresses multiple perspectives, including writer's personal perspective.

Each perspective is supported by appropriate, valid evidence (for example, direct observation, information learned from others, factual background, and/or additional research, as appropriate).

Personal engagement

Writing shows the writer engaged in deep, analytical self-reflection.

Writing shows meaningful personal reaction or struggle on the intellectual-cognitive level and on the emotional level.

Writing shows self-awareness and writer's assessment of her strengths and weaknesses and contemplates what she still needs to learn.

Lessons learned

Writing explores insights gained and developments in writer's knowledge, values, or beliefs.

Writing anticipates and projects future actions the writer will take toward personal change, or other relevant development.

Psychologists and learning theorists note that "[b]efore transferring information or ideas from a class to a new situation, [the student] must first anchor the concept in the mind. To do this, the student must attach the new information to the existing scaffolding in the student's memory." Reflective writing that explicitly seeks to envision how the new learning might be applied in future contexts has far greater likelihood of use and adaptation.

We decided to bring our unified rubric to faculty workshops to elicit reactions from other faculty with the aim of learning about their teaching goals and discovering commonalities and differences. The first workshop, which took place in March of 2016, was led by Brooks and Reuter and was attended by faculty members who teach across the curriculum at the Drexel University Thomas R. Kline School of Law. In an informal discussion, the group generated a list of the kinds of criteria they saw as critical to reflective writing. Brooks and Reuter chose not to share their rubric first; rather, they began by inviting participants to offer their suggestions freely. Fortunately, though perhaps not surprisingly, the group found much common ground in the kinds of characteristics that mark meaningful reflective writing. Brooks and Reuter then asked the participants to work in small groups to review and evaluate two students' reflective essays to test their emerging ideas of assessing reflective skills. Both essays were well written, but differed in how well each demonstrated the student's introspection on the chosen topic. In the dialogue that ensued, participants showed some range in their assessment of different factors. At the same time, they showed considerable congruence and intuitive ease in applying these grading criteria.

A few months later, at the Alliance for Experiential Learning in Law conference at New York Law School in June of 2016, Brooks and Balsam proceeded in a similar fashion with a group of faculty across multiple schools, disciplines, and teaching modalities. They first briefly introduced the context of their work on assessing reflection and engaged workshop participants in a wide-ranging discussion about whether and how they assign reflective writing in their courses. The diverse faculty present-both doctrinal and clinical-described similarly diverse reflection assignments, including externship fieldwork journals, post-performance self evaluations, post-collaboration teamwork assessments, court observations, reflections on the attorney-client relationship in a professional responsibility course, unit summaries in torts and remedies courses, and first-year student reflections on adjustment to law school. Participants' goals for their reflective writing assignments also varied considerably, including verifying that a student performed an assigned task, improving student writing, sharpening insights for higher quality class participation, transferring learning to an upcoming course unit, and cultivating professional identity and discernment. The discussion focused next on developing criteria for assessing reflective writing to serve all these contexts and goals, including the quality of the writing, analysis, and insight.

. . .

V. Observations, Benefits, and Challenges

As noted earlier, our thinking regarding this rubric has benefited from exchanges with faculty and administrators across the curriculum. The discussions have been rich, yielding several illuminating observations, preliminary understandings, and questions. First, it is clear that many faculty assign one or more reflective essays in their courses. While such assignments are quite typical in supervised live practice courses, faculty teaching doctrinal or skills courses also use reflective writing in their classes. Across these different audiences, faculty members have been eager for discussion and peer learning about this particular teaching enterprise. It encourages us that there is fertile ground for our pursuit. And yet, we have faced skepticism and resistance as well.

Some audience members at our workshops have asserted that assessing reflective writing is inherently subjective and cannot be performed fairly. These critics seem generally to believe or assume that final exams in doctrinal courses can be and are assessed in a manner that is suitably objective. Our deep belief is that assessment of any work that requires critical thinking is inherently and fundamentally subjective. If we accept that premise, then the question becomes, how we can work with any given assessment to maximize clarity, transparency, coherence, and accountability? We are committed to developing a rubric for assessment of reflective writing precisely to meet this challenge.

An examination of the benefits of the rubric helps to answer such critics. One of the greatest benefits of a well-drawn rubric provided in advance to students is its instructional value in teaching the meaning and utility of reflective practice. Reflective writing offers more than a vehicle to provide a record of student activities or a chance to improve their writing. It can also heighten students' self-awareness and observational skills; sharpen their insights; improve their ability to integrate doctrine, theory, and practice; activate the examination of multiple perspectives; and develop the habit of self-inquiry. Class time spent examining the rubric and its constituent parts is instructional time well spent.

Using this type of rubric compels the faculty member to link her grading assessment to concrete and specific criteria that provide transparency—for both students and teachers. The simple exercise of creating a rubric requires law teachers to identify the specific characteristics that reflective writing must exhibit at its highest and lowest levels of proficiency.

The rubric reduces idiosyncrasy by articulating identifiable and coherent elements of reflective practice, rather than an opaque feeling that reflective practice is personality-driven. Our experience of discussing the rubric in class has enabled us to see how quickly students grasp the advantages of assessment that is clear, consistent, and criterion-based. The rubric provides accountability. It functions to keep the evaluator "honest" and enforces even-handedness. Students perceive the transparency of a rubric as an antidote to subjectivity of essay-graders, whether in the context of a final exam or a reflection assignment.

Few of us are innately skillful at reflective practice. Thus, multiple opportunities for performance of the skill of reflection coupled with formative assessment is a vital element of building this skillset. When a rubric is used to assess a series of similar assignments, such as multiple essays reflecting on student live-practice experience, it allows students to chart their individual progress. Ideally, a rubric like ours is used in conjunction with written comments on a reflection paper. Narrative feedback helps avoid mechanical application of the criteria and prompts further self-inquiry by students. The goal of efficient and timely feedback on student writing is always in tension with the level of individualized feedback an instructor has the bandwidth to provide. Obviously, student-teacher ratios, length of writing, and other situational factors significantly impact how an instructor achieves this balance.

One potential challenge presented by use of this rubric is also a potential strength—striking the proper balance of specificity and generality to give students both direction and freedom. We have described the value of specificity above, but generality is vital too. Students need freedom to write creatively, especially in this area. Reflective writing is nothing like brief writing. It should not be formulaic. When we give students the breathing room to write from the heart and gut, the results can be amazing and authentic. Similarly, law teachers need flexibility to assure quality writing, and deep reflection can be encouraged and recognized as achieving the highest proficiency level. In the process of testing out this reflective writing rubric among faculty, we hope to elicit feedback about whether the rubric includes the essential factors, without constricting student reflection.

...

Endnotes

1. "Formative assessment refers to tools that identify misconceptions, struggles, and learning gaps along the way and assess how to close those gaps. It includes effective tools for helping to shape learning and can even bolster students' abilities to take ownership of their learning when they understand that the goal is to improve learning, not apply final marks." *Formative and Summative Assessments*, YALE POORVU CENTER FOR TEACHING AND LEARNING, https://poorvucenter.yale.edu/Formative-Summative-Assessments (last visited June 17, 2023) (citing Elise Trumbull & Andrea A. Lash, *Understanding Formative Assessment: Insights from Learning Theory and Measurement Theory*, WEST ED (Apr. 2013)). On the other hand, "summative assessments evaluate student learning, knowledge, proficiency, or success at the conclusion of an instructional period, like a unit, course, or program. [They] are almost always formally graded and often heavily weighted (though they do not need to be). Summative assessment can be used to great effect in conjunction and alignment with formative assessment, and instructors can consider a variety of ways to combine these approaches." *Id.*

2. Daniel Pink, *Why not get rid of grades? When the goal is an A, real learning gets lost.* WASHINGTON POST, (May 3, 2025), https://www.washingtonpost.com/opinions/2025/03/03/grade-inflation-why-not/?utm_campaign=wp_post_most&utm_medium=email&utm_source=newsletter&carta-url=https%3A%2F%2Fs2.washingtonpost.com%2Fcar-ln-tr%2F4166566%2F67c5e362b0f46b08f8e5b242%2F5d32dd04ae7e8a7c4f4da70e%2F38%2F56%2F67c5e362b0f46b08f8e5b242.

3. Pink, *supra* note 2, quoting Jeffrey Schinske and Kimberly Tanner.

4. Pink, *supra* note 2. Northeastern Law School in Massachusetts uses formative assessments rather than grades. Northeastern University School of Law, https://law.northeastern.edu/academics/programs/jd/degree-requirements/

5. Alfie Kohn, *The Case Against Grades*, 69 EDUC. LEADERSHIP, 28–33; Joe Feldman, GRADING FOR EQUITY: WHAT IT IS, WHY IT MATTERS, AND HOW IT CAN TRANSFORM SCHOOLS AND CLASSROOMS 27–64 (2019); Beckie Supiano, *Grades Can Hinder Learning: What Should Professors Use Instead?*, CHRON. HIGHER EDUC. (July 19, 2019), https://www.chronicle.com/article/grades-can-hinder-learning-what-should-professors-use-instead/?cid2=gen_login_refresh&cid=gen_sign_in.

6. Daniel Pink, *supra* note 2.

7. See Robert R. Kuehn & David A. Santacroce, Margaret Reuter, June T. Tai, G.S. Hans, CENTER FOR THE STUDY OF APPLIED LEGAL EDUCATION (CSALE) 2022-23 SURVEY OF APPLIED LEGAL EDUCATION at 31 (2023), describing the percentages of schools using the various grading systems.

8. *Compare* e.g., *Grading*, UNIV. OF CHICAGO LAW SCHOOL, 4.16, https://www.law.uchicago.edu/students/handbook/academicmatters/grading (explaining the University of Chicago's 155 to 186 point scale) with Georgetown University Law Center, https://www.law.georgetown.edu/wp-content/uploads/2021/02/Explanation-of-Grading-System_09-01-20.pdf.

9. *See* Beckie Supiano, *What Does an A Really Mean? We asked professors, students, and high-school counselors.*, CHRON. HIGHER EDUC. (April 10, 2024).

10. Beckie Supiano, *The Redefinition of Rigor: The Pandemic Has Amplified the Debate Over How Professors Should Challenge Their Students. What's Really to be Done About It?*, CHRON. HIGHER EDUC. (March 29, 2022), https://www.chronicle.com/article/the-redefinition-of-rigor.

11. Feldman, *supra* note 5, at 17–24. Feldman, a former public-school teacher, principal, and district administrator who now works as a consultant helping schools and districts establish more equitable grading and assessment practices, traces contemporary grading practices to their origins in the late nineteenth and early twentieth century. At that time, as the American economy shifted from agriculture to manufacturing, student enrollment exploded, theories of natural intelligence took hold, and behaviorism drove policy, narrative grading was replaced by today's norm-referenced letter grading. The latter better matched the logistical and philosophical needs of the time, quickly and seemingly-scientifically sorting students. *See generally* FELDMAN, *supra* note 5.

12. *Id.* at 27–37.

13. M.H. Hoeflich, *The Craft of the Law: An Essay After Forty Years as a Law Teacher*, 70 U. KAN. L. REV. 483 (2022).

14. Supiano, *supra* note 9.

15. Beckie Supiano, *The Unintended Consequences of 'Ungrading' Does Getting Rid of Grades Make Things Worse for Disadvantaged Students?*, CHRON. HIGHER EDUC. (April 29, 2022), https://www.chronicle.com/article/the-unintended-consequences-of-ungrading.

16. The maximum student-to-faculty ratio should be no more than ten-to-one depending on other institutional responsibilities of the clinic teacher. *See* Association of American Law Schools, Section on Clinical Legal Education, *Report on the Future of the In-House Clinic*, 42 J. LEGAL EDUC. 511, 565–68 (1992). "The most common student-teacher ratio for case/legal work supervision is 8 to 1, the same as the four prior surveys. Over 80% of clinics have casework ratios of 8 to 1 or fewer." See Kuehn. Santacroce, Reuter, Tai, & Hans, supra note 7, at 28.

17. *Id.*

18. Joshua M. Silverstein, *In Defense of Mandatory Curves*, 34 U. ARK. LITTLE ROCK L. REV. 253, 309–10 (2012) ("A mandatory curve must be adjusted when applied to classes in which the pupils are not representative of the overall student population. Under the Central Limit Theorem, the danger of this happening becomes statistically significant when the course enrollment falls under roughly thirty students. In other words, in classes with fewer than thirty members, there is a statistically significant likelihood that the registered students will be above or below average when compared to the student body as a whole.").

19. *See generally* Beth A. Brennan, *Explicit Instruction in Legal Education: Boon or Spoon?*, 52 U. MEM. L. REV. 1 (2021). It is worth noting that although Brennan emphasizes the application of cognitive psychology and learning theory to improve upon traditional inquiry-based learning, her conclusion implicates discrete learning exercises more than broad clinical goals. To increase understanding and transferability, clinical students engage not just the *how* but also the *why* of their work. To reach the *why*, students must personally engage murky and tension-filled subject areas, making some amount of indirect teaching essential.

20. Kaci Bishop, *Framing Failure in the Legal Classroom: Techniques for Encouraging Growth and Resilience*, 70 U. ARK L. REV. 959 (2018).

21. Peter Toll Hoffman, *The Stages of the Clinical Supervisory Relationship*, 4 ANTIOCH L.J. 301, 303–12 (1986).

22. Donald A. Schön, Ford Professor of Urban Studies and Education, Mass. Inst. of Tech., Address at Iowa State University (April 28, 1989), (transcript available at https://hiredthought.com/2021/02/24/donald-a-schon-at-iowa-state-university-talk-transcript/); *see also* Donald A. Schön, EDUCATING THE REFLECTIVE PRACTITIONER, (1987). Schön's work has influenced many clinical teachers. *See, e.g.*, Richard K. Neumann, Jr., *Donald Schön, The Reflective Practitioner, and the Comparative Failures of Legal Education*, 6 CLINICAL L. REV. 401, 1–2 (2000).

23. Dan Berrett, *The Making of a Teaching Evangelist*, CHRON. HIGHER EDUC. (June 5, 2016), https://www.chronicle.com/article/the-making-of-a-teaching-evangelist/ (internal quotations omitted) (quoting Professor Mazur's then-current syllabus).

24. *See* Heidi K. Gardner, *The Collaboration Imperative for Today's Law Firms: Leading High-Performance Teamwork for Maximum Benefit*, *in* MANAGING TALENT FOR SUCCESS: TALENT DEVELOPMENT IN LAW FIRMS (Rebecca Normand-Hochman ed., 2013).

25. Clifford S. Zimmerman, *"Thinking Beyond My Own Interpretation": Reflections on Collaborative and Cooperative Learning Theory in the Law School Curriculum*, 31 ARIZ. ST. L.J. 957, 1002 (1999).

26. Feldman, *supra* note 5, at 30. *See also* Kaci Bishop, *Framing Failure in the Legal Classroom: Techniques for Encouraging Growth and Resilience*, 70 U. ARK. L. REV. 959 (2017).

27. I was introduced to the concept of empathic disconnects by Professors Deborah Epstein and Rachel Camp.

28. *See* Anne D. Gordon, Better Than Our Biases: Using Psychological Research to Inform Our Approach to Inclusive, Effective Feedback, 27 CLINICAL L. REV. 195, 236–48 (2021).

29. See Robert R. Kuehn et.al., supra note 7, at 17.

30. Students at Georgetown can receive between eight and twelve credits in one-semester clinic courses and up to fourteen credits in yearlong courses.

31. See Ann Shalleck, *Clinical Contexts: Theory and Practice in Law and Supervision*, 21 N.Y.U. REV. L. & SOC. CHANGE, 109, 110–13 (1995).

32. Beth McMurtrie, *Is It Time to Redefine Class Participation?*; CHRON. HIGHER EDUC. (Sept. 8, 2022), https://www.chronicle.com/newsletter/teaching/2022-09-08.

33. *Id.* (citing Professor Mark Sample's syllabus).

34. Supiano, *supra* note 9.

35. As noted earlier, grade conversations should not routinely be part of a qualitative assessment. Nonetheless, it may be necessary in some rare cases.

36. *See supra* Gordon note 28.

37. *See* Supiano, *supra* note 9.

38. This rubric was first used at Georgetown by Professor John Copacino and has been revised for the Juvenile Justice Clinic by Professor Kris Henning.

39. Only students who are intentionally shirking their responsibilities will receive a B- grade. Very few do. Almost no one receives grades below B- because the faculty's sense of professional responsibility will not let this happen.

40. *See generally* DANNELLE D. STEVEN & ANTONIA J. LEVI, INTRODUCTION TO RUBRICS: AN ASSESSMENT TOOL TO SAVE GRADING TIME, CONVEY EFFECTIVE FEEDBACK, AND PROMOTE STUDENT LEARNERS (2004) ("At its most basic, a rubric is a scoring tool that lays out specific expectations for an assignment.").

41. Jodi S. Balsam, Susan L. Brooks & Margaret Reuter, *Assessing Law Students as Reflective Practitioners*, 62 N.Y.L. SCH. L. REV. 49, 68–70 (2017/2018).

42. See generally, Kristin Henning, *Combatting Decision Fatigue in Supervision*, in Susan Bryant, Elliott S. Milstein, and Ann Shalleck, TRANSFORMING THE EDUCATION OF LAWYERS: THE THEORY AND PRACTICE OF CLINICAL PEDAGOGY, (Carolina Academic Press 2014)

Fifteen

THE ROLE OF SCHOLARSHIP IN CLINICAL PEDAGOGY

Early Attitudes about Scholarship in Law Schools

The debate about the role of scholarship by clinical faculty is as old as the modern clinical movement itself. The first cohort of clinical teachers came from civil and criminal public interest offices. As explained in Chapter 3, A Short History Of Clinical Pedagogy, their goal was to move public interest practice into the law school curriculum. Many clinical teachers in that generation, either by choice or by happenstance, were good lawyers but did not possess the traditional qualifications required by law school appointments committees. As a tenured professor at Georgetown once said during the early debates about the value of clinics in the law school curriculum, "They, they just don't look like us, they are not like us."

Others of the founding generation, however, possessed the credentials then associated with traditional law school faculty members. They had attended prestigious law schools where they excelled as test takers, served on law journals, and even became members of the Order of the Coif. They then went on to serve as judicial clerks, usually in federal circuits or state supreme courts after graduation and ultimately took jobs in civil legal services or public defender organizations. Despite their academic pedigree, their interests were the same as their non-credentialed colleagues—to teach legal skills and social justice lawyering in law schools to the next generation of lawyers.[1] They had little or no interest in becoming traditional legal scholars.

Although law schools claim to be professional schools within a university, the driving force of the school's curriculum, the pre-teaching credentials of its faculty, and a teacher's career advancement opportunities all rely on traditional scholarship and not on practice. Academic legal education in many countries around the world was established according to the Germanic or Humboldtian model of higher education that featured the integration of teaching and research.[2] Initially reliant on the faculty of philosophy, it later incorporated the arts and sciences into its teaching and research mission.[3] This Germanic model of higher education was also prevalent in 19th century universities in the United States.[4] When universities began to create law schools toward the turn of that century, the Germanic model became the foundation of the Langdellian (named after Harvard law Professor Christopher Columbus Langdell) method of academic legal education in the United States. The research led to the proliferation of theoretical scholarship as the basis for teaching and faculty advancement. It also spurred the growth of law journals and law reviews in the United States. The University of Pennsylvania Law Review, originally published in 1852 as The American Law Register, is the oldest law review in American legal education.[5] Today, more than 1,500 law reviews and journals exist.[6]

Early Attitudes about Scholarship in Clinical Education

When William Pincus began to provide grants to establish law clinics in American law schools, he did not list traditional scholarship as a necessary qualification of a clinical teacher.[7] In fact, he specifically called on law schools to move away from scholarship. He wrote, "A priority item here is for law faculties to get over the 'hang-up' about being 'scholars' like others in the academic community."[8] Nor was it one of the goals of clinical courses set by the Association of American Law Schools (AALS) in its report on the future of the in-house clinic.[9] The Report of the AALS and ABA Committee on the Guidelines for Clinical Education[10] did suggest that clinical teachers on a tenure track should be required to "contribute to and promote a body of permanent knowledge"[11] and that law schools should "expect individuals to [give] evidence [of] research ability" if tenure is awarded.[12] The Committee also indicated that when law schools assessed a clinical law teacher's research ability, "judgment may start from bases traditionally used, but should be broadened to reflect the relationship between clinical legal studies and the teacher's own development."[13]

Notwithstanding this tepid acceptance of some clinical teachers' desires or ability to produce scholarship, early clinical teachers were writing for law reviews and journals. The AALS-ABA Committee report itself indicated that at the time of publication, 17% of full-time clinical teachers were eligible for tenure.[14] As early as 1974, the Council on Legal Education for Professional Responsibility (CLEPR) published a bibliography of articles written between the 1920s and 1970s about clinical education.[15] Most of the very early articles, as well as those in the 1950s, focused on the value of adding clinical courses to the law school curriculum. Despite these arguments, true clinical courses remained outside of the law school curriculum in those early years.[16] While that debate continued, some clinical teachers entering academia in the 1960s and 1970s began to write law journal articles and books arguing that clinical classes and cases could be used to enhance not just the practice of law but the theory supporting practice. Others, however, began to write more traditional academic scholarship.

What Is Clinical Scholarship?

The university's commitments to the pursuit of knowledge and its revelation of truth guides its scholarly mission.[17] Law schools are usually part of a university, so they share that mission. Even independent law schools expound similar sentiments.[18] Law schools are a training ground for the legal profession. As such, the pursuit of knowledge must be embedded in that training. In addition, the revelation of truth is committed to, and is even defined by, the ideal of justice.[19] Consequently, all legal scholarship, traditional and clinical, should reflect this dual mission.[20] Yet since the beginning of the modern clinical education era, traditional law teachers have believed that there was a difference between their exploration of theory as the search for truth and the exploration of whatever it was that clinical teachers were writing about.

Perhaps the most significant early clinician writing and speaking about the theoretical value of clinical education in the 1970s was Professor Gary Bellow. In a paper delivered in 1973 at the Council on Legal Education for Professional Responsibility's Buck Hill Conference, Professor Bellow attempted to "sort out the implications and assumptions of experience-based teaching, [by] making use of the general literature of learning."[21] Soon thereafter, he and Professor Bea Moulton published THE LAWYERING PROCESS: MATERIALS FOR CLINICAL INSTRUCTION IN ADVOCACY,[22] a foundational piece of scholarship in the clinical education canon.

A second major influence on clinical scholarship was the creation of the CLINICAL LAW REVIEW. The idea of a law journal dedicated to clinical legal scholarship was first raised in 1986 in the AALS Clinical Education Section Newsletter[23] by Professor Gary Palm, then the chair of the Section, Several years later, Professor Robert Dinerstein, the 1992 chair of the AALS Section on Clinical Education, raised the issue again.[24] In that Newsletter, Professor Dinerstein tried to define clinical scholarship. He wrote that not all writing by clinicians was clinical scholarship; but "[w]hen a clinical scholar writes about clinical themes, he or she is speaking (or writing) in the clinical voice."[25] He also set out goals for clinical scholarship. Those goals were:

1. Inform one's understanding of the lawyering skills one seeks to teach; [and] develop a practice-oriented scholarship;
2. Allow us to see connections between our experiences and those of others;
3. Sharpen and require us to defend our ideas;
4. Permit the advancement of knowledge in the field;
5. Describe and analyze critically the phenomenon of role-based learning—the insights and distortions it can produce;
6. Analyze critically the pros and cons of different forms of clinical education-simulation, externship, in-house clinic beyond mere description; and
7. Examine the relationship between theory and practice.[26]

He added that he thought that clinical scholarship was distinct from most other legal scholarship, because clinical legal scholarship

1. Uses the lawyer's or client's actual experiences as a point of departure for analyzing legal or social problems; it is contextual and grounded in the real experiences of real people;
2. Is more likely to consider what happens in trial courts than in appellate courts;
3. Is likely to focus on issues of poverty, under-represented people, and public interest issues;
4. Can be concerned with the clinical law student's learning process and pedagogy more generally; and
5. Can evaluate different ways of teaching students to learn how to learn from experience and engage in self-evaluation.[27]

In a separate article, he added that scholars writing with the clinical legal scholarship perspective could be expected to:

1. Study the settings in which lawyers provide representation to clients;
2. Examine lawyer-client relationships—client-centeredness, lawyer domination of clients, etc.;
3. Address issues of professional responsibility and provide a critique of professionalism;
4. Incorporate interdisciplinary and multi-disciplinary perspectives;
5. Include empirical studies of lawyering;
6. Make use of clinicians' outsider status within the academy; and
7. Explore theories of justice.[28]

A final component of his description of clinical scholarship was included in his message in the Newsletter. He stated that clinical scholarship could also address "structural barriers clinicians face in producing clinical scholarship; present brief case reports and discussions of pedagogical techniques that could help clinicians in their daily work; and deal with the seemingly mundane aspects of clinical teaching—for example, examining inconsistent approaches to student empowerment—that could inform our daily clinical practice and approaches."[29]

The CLINICAL LAW REVIEW was launched in 1994. The first three editors of the law review, Professors Stephen Ellmann, Isabelle Gunning, and Randy Hertz, added to Dinerstein's conception of clinical scholarship. Dinerstein later described the editors contribution to the understanding of clinical scholarship. He wrote,

> They noted that clinical pedagogy was such a new discipline that "[c]linicians still are debating fundamental questions concerning the nature and potential of the teaching enterprise." They expressed the hope that the CLR could reflect in print the "intellectual challenge and emotional responsiveness of the best of our clinical conferences." They stressed the importance of multi-cultural, multi-racial, and gender concerns, as well as issues of difference more generally.' They anticipated that there would be articles about the different locations

of clinical legal education—in-house clinics, externships, and simulation courses—and articles about non-clinical courses. They stated that they sought a diverse range of formats, welcomed letters to the editor, and noted that, "[W]e welcome shorter pieces that seek to advance inquiry in a more discrete fashion through the clarity of their observations, the questions they raise, and the areas they identify as deserving of exploration."[30]

It was not long before an explosion of books and articles were published adhering to the definitions of clinical scholarship set forth by Dinerstein and the editors of the Clinical Law Review. Indeed, in 2001, the first iteration of *Clinical Legal Education: An Annotated Bibliography* was published.[31] The bibliography contained forty-five pages of articles.

The Legal Academy's Reaction to Clinical Scholarship

In 1997, Professors Alex Hurder, Frank Block, Susan Brooks, and Susan Kay published the first edition of CLINICAL ANTHOLOGY, READINGS FOR A LIVE CLIENT CLINIC containing various articles on the many facets of clinical teaching.[32] The articles published were consciously directed to teaching. As reported in the first edition of the book, it grew out of the authors' "search for readings to use in the classroom component of a live client clinic."[33] Those articles reflected the growing body of scholarship about issues and dilemmas that lawyers confront in practice."[34] These articles were denominated by the book authors as "a new body of clinical scholarship."[35] However, the book did not have a section on how traditional theoretical scholarship could improve clinical teaching or why it was important for clinical teachers to write scholarly articles.

The legal academy did not initially recognize the value of clinical scholarship. Indeed, many disparaged it, characterizing it as "both un- and anti-intellectual."[36] Professor Carrie Menkel-Meadow once described this perspective as, "the false dualism of so-called intellectual rigor in legal ideas and 'science' and the presumed 'weakness' of skills training."[37] Others believed that professional training was "best performed in an environment in which the ideals of scholarship are paramount."[38] Those espousing the importance of scholarship believed that "Theoretical knowledge has lasting and permanent value ... [which develops] among students theoretical understanding, critical judgment, and discipline."[39] To a large extent, this commitment to theoretical scholarship defined traditional legal scholars. Their self-identity—their "education, hiring and promotion, social prominence, and economic well-being were all based on [traditional legal] scholarship."[40] That is why my unnamed colleague at Georgetown who I referenced earlier in this chapter, was able to note this disconnect between clinical faculty and non-clinical faculty saying, "They are different from us." Understanding this disconnect, Professor Mark Spiegel, criticizing this antipathy toward clinical education and its scholarship, once wrote, "... to allow clinical education into the main tent would threaten the self-identity of law teachers because it would threaten the centrality of doctrine."[41]

Notwithstanding the expansion of clinical education and the emergence of clinical scholarship in the 1970s and 1980s, there also seemed to be a growing rift between the legal academy and the legal profession. A prominent critic, United States Circuit Judge for the District of Columbia and New York University Law School Professor Harry Edwards, authored several articles noting that the work of legal academics was becoming less and less helpful for the practicing bar.[42] In his robust critiques about the disjunction between legal education and the legal profession, he divided legal scholarship into two categories: "impractical scholarship" that is abstract and with little relevance to concrete issues and "practical scholarship" that is used to criticize doctrine and resolve problems that the doctrine fails to address.[43] Edwards argued that an inordinate amount of legal scholarship fell into the first bucket and no longer served to positively influence the practice of law.[44]

The disconnect described by Judge Edwards echoed the same arguments between clinical and traditional law professors who debated the value of clinical courses. John Elson captures that symmetry in his article, *The Case Against Legal-Scholarship or, If the Professor Must Publish, Must the Profession Perish?*

> Most law faculty would not willingly slacken their scholarly efforts to satisfy demands for more emphasis on education for professional competence. Indeed, the advocates of practical training through clinical methods have been characterized by some law faculty as both un- and anti-intellectual and, at the very least, insensitive to the role of legal scholarship in promoting social welfare and law student development.[45]

Elson's critique was taken by many early clinical faculty as an indictment of all scholarship. Moreover, they read the article to condemn even clinical scholarship as a distraction from what they saw as the core purpose of law school—the training of students for the practice of law. This criticism still finds support today.

During the same period, traditional legal scholarship was moving away from doctrinal analysis. In the 1970s and 1980s, scholarly debates at the theoretical level were occurring about Critical Legal Studies, Feminist Critique, Law and Economics, and Critical Race Theory led by a new cadre of legal academics with Ph.D. degrees.[46] Although these scholars often had little legal practice experience, their analyses could lead practicing lawyers to a more perspective-based understanding about how the law operated and its place in society. As Martha Minow and Susannah Barton Tobin described in *Archetypal Legal Scholarship: A Field Guide*, these new academics sought to expose unstated assumptions and internally inconsistent structures, and to highlight tensions, contradictions, or paradoxes behind the surface of legal practices.[47] With the emergence of articles about new methods of analysis, fewer examples of doctrinal scholarship appeared in law journals and clinical scholarship, as defined by Dinerstein and others, was seen as marginal and out of the new mainstream of legal scholarship. In addition, articles about teaching methods, often a staple of early clinical scholarship, continued to be dismissed as something other than legal scholarship. Thus, the worth of articles written about clinical pedagogy was seen as irrelevant or negligible when clinical teachers applied for tenure.

Scholarship and Tenure— The Debate within the Clinical Community

As mentioned earlier, the debate about the need for clinical teachers to produce scholarship is as old as the clinical education movement. One of the earliest attacks on scholarship by a clinician, Professor Elson's *The Case Against Legal-Scholarship or, If the Professor Must Publish, Must the Profession Perish?*,[48] was less about whether clinicians should participate in scholarly activities than about the value of theoretical scholarship as the foundational focus for training lawyers in an academic setting. In that article, Professor Elson deconstructed both traditional doctrinal scholarship and the emerging perspective scholarship. His purpose was to show that there was no empirical proof that traditional legal scholarship was a valuable primary source for training professionals, and that the legal scholars did not even achieve their own purported goals.[49] His article, however, did not spur other articles by the clinicians about the purpose and need for scholarship by clinical teachers. The arguments among clinicians themselves about the need to produce scholarship generally occurred in oral debates and conversations at the various clinical conferences and in email exchanges, rather than in law journals. The email debates continue to resonate today.[50]

The arguments for and against the value of scholarship were also integral to the debates occurring within the community of clinical teachers about their faculty status and the requirement that clinical teachers publish scholarly articles to gain tenure. Grants funded by CLEPR required schools receiving money to employ full-time teachers, but the grants did not require that those teachers be tenured.[51] The absence of tenure status, however, prevented clinical teachers from participating in faculty governance and having a voice in how the financial and other resources of the law school should be allocated. Many, if not most, traditional legal academics viewed clinical education as a marginal aspect of legal academia. Although most clinicians believed that the entire clinical education enterprise could not be maintained and expanded without a role in faculty governance, many did not believe legal scholarship should be required to gain tenure.

Because of the general animosity that deans and traditional law teachers had toward the clinical method and its proponents, clinical teachers had to look elsewhere for allies in the battle for job security, pay parity, similar work conditions, and most of all, the right to participate in faculty governance. Professor Elliot Milstein noted that,

> ... law schools treat clinicians with something approaching disdain ... [T]he law schools withhold the symbols and perquisites of the profession from us. They deny us promotions and titles. They deny us voting rights and salaries of other faculty members. This leads to the myth that teaching lawyering skills is beneath the law schools.[52]

Over time, clinical faculty found those allies in the American Bar Association. Practicing lawyers generally supported the clinical movement. Moreover, the ABA was the accrediting body for American law schools. "Long before the ABA first adopted an accreditation standard on the status of law school faculty teaching clinical courses, leaders of the legal profession and reports on legal education repeatedly expressed concerns over what they considered the unfair treatment of clinical faculty and its negative effects on the development of clinical legal education."[53] Despite continued opposition from Deans and traditional faculty, the ABA adopted Accreditation Standard 405 (e) in 1984. It stated that law schools should offer full-time faculty members whose primary responsibilities are in its professional skills program a form of security of position reasonably similar to tenure, and perquisites reasonably similar to those provided full-time faculty members. However, 405 (e) did not require that clinicians be given tenure. An interpretation accompanying the accreditation standard stated that they should be offered a type of security of position reasonably similar to tenure [which] includes a separate tenure track or a renewable long-term contract.[54]

The debate within the clinical community did not diminish after the accreditation battles. In some ways, it grew more intense. Those who favored participating in the scholarly community provided several justifications for that position. They believed it was the inevitable trade-off for gaining full tenure and governance rights. They also believed that since the gatekeepers to the faculty were traditional scholars, there would be no equivalence among clinical and non-clinical faculty without accepting traditional university values. Many who opposed that position thought there would never be an acceptance of parity. They believed that a separate clinical tenure system without a scholarship requirement was sufficient since teaching students about legal skills and the role of a lawyer in a just society was what they came to the law school to do. Others were willing to accept a long-term contract regime absent a scholarship requirement. They believed that parity would never occur anyway, since faculty status would always be based on scholarship, something which they had no interest in pursuing. Still others subscribed to John Elson's critique that traditional scholarship was in many ways the "Emperor's New Clothes." Even if it had theoretical value, they thought it offered little to the practicing bar and had little value when it came to teaching students.

Both sides recognized that the teaching demands placed on clinicians were dramatically different from those of podium faculty. Members of both camps knew that writing serious scholarship—traditional, clinical, or pedagogical—required a significant amount of time and effort. Those opposing scholarship as the cost of gaining the benefits of faculty parity believed that getting tenure based on scholarship was a nearly impossible task without seriously curtailing their supervision of student cases and projects. They argued that accepting a scholarship requirement would also minimize the number of cases for which students would be responsible and reduce the number of clients the clinic could represent. Some also feared that even if their scholarship were honestly evaluated, they might write something that could come back to haunt them while working on a client's case or project. Those ready to accept the scholarship requirement reminded their friends in opposition that clinics were now part of a university and no longer just a public interest law firm.

The Current Systems Regarding Status and Scholarship

The passage of Accreditation Standard 405 (e) and its later revisions incorporated into Standard 405 (c) solidified the existence of clinical education and better integrated experiential education into the overall curriculum. The standards guaranteed a form of status and security, academic freedom, and a right of governance for clinicians, and made life in the law school more tenable for clinical faculty. But the standards did not resolve the issues regarding the value of traditional scholarship or the need for clinicians to produce traditional scholarship to attain a long term contract or tenure. Because the ABA Standards permitted law schools to fashion their own internal standards regarding the type of faculty status and the requirements to attain it, some clinicians warned that there would be a "bloodbath" as clinical teachers applied for tenure or an increase in the number of clinical teachers being hired on a long-term contract. The bloodbath never really occurred although there were instances of clinicians being denied tenure and of others leaving the profession rather than subjecting themselves to the new standards.

There is, however, some evidence of a decline in tenure-track hiring. The Center for the Study of Applied Legal Education (CSALE)[55] has, since 2007, "collected data on applied legal education in areas including program design, capacity, administration, funding, pedagogy, and the role of applied legal education and educators in the academy."[56] The CSALE reports have become the critical source for understanding how clinical programs and clinical pedagogy are operating in American law schools. Schools take it so seriously that ninety-five percent of ABA accredited law schools participated in CSALE's most recent survey.[57]

CSALE grew out of a study by an AALS Section on Clinical Legal Education task force created in 2005.[58] The task force found that during the twenty years after the adoption of ABA Standard 405 (e), law schools had created four faculty tracks for clinical professors: 1) a unitary tenure track; 2) a clinical tenure track; 3) a long-term contract arrangement; and 4) a short-term contract arrangement.[59] Today, almost forty years after the adoption of Standard 405 (e), those four statuses still prevail. Surprisingly, the number of unified tenure track and clinical tenure track faculty has declined as a percentage of clinical faculty over the years.[60] According to the data reported in the latest CSALE report, only 21% of clinical and externship faculty were on a unified tenure track in 2019, and only 12% were on a clinical tenure track.[61] During the same year, combined short- and long-term contract appointments held steady at around 50%,[62] 17% higher than combined tenure track and clinical tenure track appointments. Moreover, those holding tenure-track positions tended to be clinicians with more than twelve years' experience.[63]

Tenure committees in most schools continue to value scholarship more than any other category of work that clinicians perform. Nonetheless, the number of clinical faculty members required to produce scholarship irrespective of their appointment status has declined. According to the latest CSALE data,

> Thirty-two percent of clinical faculty (excluding fellows) were required to produce scholarship as part of their job in the 2019 CSALE survey, compared with 38% in the 2016 survey, 42% in the 2013 survey, and 48% in the 2010 and 2007 surveys. This decline likely reflects the increased reliance by schools on contractual appointments noted above. For 48% of respondents in the 2019 survey, scholarship is beneficial to their position but not required, while for 20%, scholarship is neither required nor beneficial.[64]

The 2019–20 CSALE data also shows that as the ABA Standards require law schools to provide more experiential learning opportunities, "new clinical faculty are increasingly not being hired into tenure-track positions, traditional or clinical...."[65] Interestingly, The CSALE data from 2019–20 shows that 27% of full-time clinical teachers were on a presumptively renewable, long-term contract and 6% on a probationary contract leading to a renewable long-term. That combined percentage of 33% is equal to the percentage of clinical faculty with positions on one of the two tenure tracks.[66]

My purpose here is not to debate which type of status is best, although my personal belief is that unitary tenure with full governance rights is critical to the clinical movement. Contract faculty, whose contracts are presumptively renewable, are at significant risk. As Professor Robert Dinerstein once said, the word "presumptively" when used in a system dependent on presumptively renewable contracts "provides room for mischief when a [contract] renewal comes up."[67] They seldom have pay parity and have limited or no voting rights on critical issues.

Faculty using a clinical track may experience slights in their so-called equivalent status. They report different voting schemes for the two tracks which minimize their votes when compared to the voting rights of traditional tenure track faculty. They often have different titles and unequal pay that reinforce their less than equal status of clinical teachers.

Some faculty on both tracks also report that their scholarship is not valued in the same way as that of faculty on the traditional tenure track. Unitary tenure systems can only be trusted when tenure determinations are guided by a thorough understanding of clinical methodology and a recognition of the differences in the teaching and research responsibilities between traditional and clinical teachers. When tenure is denied because clinical scholarship is deemed insufficient, it is often because non-clinical teachers, who do not understand the different demands on clinical teachers, form the majority of the entire faculty.

Results like these solidify the belief among non-clinical faculty that clinical scholarship is, by its nature, inferior to traditional scholarship and that clinicians do not belong among a community of scholars. These attitudes and policies create a sense of second-class citizenship, which deprives clinical faculty and the clinical pedagogy movement of respect.

Why Scholarship Is Important to Clinical Pedagogy

Why then should clinical teachers value scholarly writing? The CSALE data shows that no matter what status clinical teachers hold, or what titles precede their names, scholarship remains the driving force for maintaining many clinical faculty positions and is beneficial even when not required. To my mind, that is a good thing because clinical teachers have a lot to say. Traditional scholars, even those working in an interdisciplinary milieu or with empiricists, seldom work with individual clients and thus their research remains mostly, if not completely, theoretical. If they did work with clients, they might discover that their theoretical models might not be verifiable. Theory is often developed by controlling variables that might disrupt the core of the "truth" of the theory. Rejecting an investigation of the practical application of the theory weakens its "truth."

Clinical faculty should not disparage theory when writing clinical scholarship. Indeed, clinical programs that remain purely skills-based miss incredible opportunities to foster growth and long-term learning strategies for their students. The best proponents of clinical pedagogy use the uncertainty of human behavior to unite theory with practice, rather than divide theory and practice. When they litigate, they use the "truth" of the theory in appropriate cases to support their position. When they write about the shortcomings of the theory that occur when human behavior distorts the "truth" of the theory, they challenge the theorist to reconsider their positions and evaluate the hypothesis anew. In some sense, that is what gave rise to the Critical Legal Studies movement and the other critical assessments of assumptions that exist in the law that were seldom challenged by traditional scholars.

More importantly, clinical scholarship is not just useful for scholarly inquiry. It creates better clinical teachers and case and project supervisors. Clinical teachers who write become the curious lawyers who explore the evolving theories of justice and apply them to their legislative proposals and case strategies to benefit their clinic clients. Professors Ellman, Gunning, and Hertz describe this phenomenon in their piece "Why Not a Clinical Lawyer-Journal."[68] "Like their non-clinical colleagues, clinicians have come to see scholarship as a means of disseminating information about innovative approaches and exploring ideas that grow out of clinical teaching experiences."[69] Moreover, they demonstrate to their students how to become lifelong learners who challenge assumptions before making decisions and taking actions. The knowledge they develop and disseminate to students and lawyers by writing about their new knowledge and personal impressions becomes incorporated into their teaching and is spread beyond the clinic and the law school to the entire profession and to the general citizenry as well. This is what the AALS-ABA Report on Clinical Education expected.[70]

Moreover, this is what universities are for. "The distinctive mission of the University is to serve society as a center of higher learning, providing long-term societal benefits through transmitting advanced knowledge, discovering new knowledge, and functioning as an active working repository of organized knowledge. That obligation, more specifically, includes undergraduate education, graduate and professional education, research, and other kinds of public service, which are shaped and bounded by the central pervasive mission of discovering and advancing knowledge."[71] Clinical teachers' faculty position in a university makes them privileged public interest lawyers. They practice with low cases loads, ample support services, higher salaries, and many other benefits that typical public interest lawyers do not possess. As such, they should recognize that these privileges entail responsibility not only to the university and the law center which provide them, but to all public interest lawyers. It is a responsibility to the core mission and purpose of their institutions and to the citizenry at large. Public interest lawyers' caseloads and time and support limitations prevent them from transmitting advanced knowledge to the profession. When clinical teachers accept the privileges of faculty membership, they must accept the institutional responsibilities. It is a two-way street. Moreover, as described above, participating fully in that mission will make them better teachers, better lawyers, and better contributors to the advancement of democratic principles and a more just society.

Legal Scholarship Today

Although legal scholarship is often considered steeped in high theory, actual law journal articles are quite diverse and often disparate. Renowned scholar Professor Martha Minow created a guide to help aspiring law teachers to situate their research projects within the many varieties of legal scholarship. That guide was ultimately published and a second edition of "Archetypal Legal Scholarship: A Field Guide" followed.[72] In the article, she and her co-author list nine different forms of scholarly inquiry. They are:

1) Doctrinal restatements;
2) Recasting projects;
3) Policy analysis;
4) Testing a proposition about society, the economy, technological developments, or about human beings/human behavior that is used by lawyers or assumed in legal sources;
5) Studying, explaining, and assessing legal institutions (including courts, agencies, and law schools), systems, or institutional actors (including end users—litigants, subjects of enforcement—affected by law);
6) Critical projects;
7) Comparative and historical inquiries;
8) Jurisprudence, philosophy of law, and connecting philosophy and law;

9) Combinations of the other eight topics.

Interestingly, her list of traditional scholarly inquiry encompasses many of the topics Professor Dinerstein lists in his definition of clinical scholarship.[73] To the extent differences appear, it is because Dinerstein specifically notes how the events clinical teachers experience through their work can enhance many of these traditional scholarly research motifs.

As noted in the CSALE study, whether one is appointed on a unified or clinical tenure track or appointed within a contract regime, scholarship is now a critical factor in hiring, promotion, and retention of teachers in a law school's clinical program. It remains to be seen how this will affect the future of clinical pedagogy and the clinical movement. There are potentially ominous signs in the CSALE data that show a decline in the percentages of tenure-track clinical faculty. Many clinicians have been warned to produce more traditional scholarly articles and fewer clinical or teaching articles while in their pre-tenure status and wait until after they receive tenure to expand their clinical scholarship. Some clinical teachers have abandoned writing clinical pedagogy entirely because traditional scholarly articles may be weighted more heavily in salary assignments and promotions.

All of this is worrisome, but it cannot be seen as the end of the clinical scholarly movement. Clinical teachers are generally innovative and adaptable. As schools are forced to hire more experiential teachers to satisfy the ABA accreditation standards, the numbers of clinicians on the faculty will continue to grow. Understanding and exercising the power they possess through governance and their ability to reform structures will be important going forward. Perhaps the trade-off will be adjustments in their teaching and supervision loads. But that may be a good strategy in the long game.

Other Voices

Martha Minow and Susannah Barton Tobin, *Archetypal Legal Scholarship: A Field Guide, 2d. Edition**

71 JOURNAL OF LEGAL EDUCATION 494 (2022)

"It has been my pleasure to be a sounding board and advisor to many people who consider becoming law professors and yet it has not always been easy to introduce people considering their own research projects to reflect on how their ideas connect with the varieties of legal scholarship. One day I decided to write up a 'field guide,' meant to be rather like the guides to birds that offer pictures and descriptions to assist the casual or serious birdwatcher.... The explosion of interdisciplinary research in law contributes to the variety of legal scholarships. So does the contrast between 'inside' and 'outside' thinking in law schools where we try both to equip people for practice and effectiveness within existing institutions and for roles as critics, institutional reformers, and scholars who may explain and analyze in terms quite different from those in the minds of actors operating within existing legal systems. So here with an invitation for supplements, critiques, and revisions is my Archetypal Legal Scholarship: A Field Guide."

...

I. Doctrinal restatement, e.g., Robert Clark, *Corporate Law*, Laurence Tribe, *Constitutional Law*; Yoram Dinstein, *War, Aggression and Self-Defence*; Cohen's *Handbook of Federal Indian Law* and Erwin Chemerinsky, *Federal Jurisdiction*.

a. Organize and reorganize case law into coherent elements, categories, and concepts.

b. Acknowledge distinction between settled and emerging law.

c. Identify difference between majority and "preferred" or "better" practice—ideally with some explanation for the criteria to be used.

II. Recasting project, e.g., Charles Reich, "The New Property;" L.L. Fuller & William R. Perdue, Jr., "Reliance Interest in Property;" Samuel D. Warren and Louis D. Brandeis, "The Right to Privacy;" Guido Calabresi & A. Douglas Melamed, "Property Rules, Liability Rules, and Inalienability: One View of the Cathedral;" Melissa Murray, "Marriage As Punishment;" and Michael Coenen, "Rules Against Rulification."

a. Gather more than one "line" of cases across doctrinal fields, categories, or historical developments, and show why they belong together or expose unjustified discrepancies.

---

* Excerpts reprinted with the permission of the authors and the Association of American Law Schools, which owns the copyright for articles published by the Journal of Legal Education.

b. Offer a new framework or paradigm that can recognize past, present, and future material.

III. Policy analysis, e.g., Elizabeth Bartholet, *Nobody's Children: Abuse and Neglect, Foster Drift, and the Alternative of Adoption*; Jeff Sovern, "Opting in, Opting Out, or No Options At All: The Fight for Control of Personal Information;" Russell Korobkin, "Bounded Rationality and Unconscionability: A Behavioral Approach to Policing Form Contracts;" Roderick Hills, Jr., "Is Federalism Good for Localism? The Localist Case for Federalist Regimes;" William W. Fisher III, Promises to Keep: Technology, Law, and the Future of Entertainment; and Ashley Deeks, "The Judicial Demand for Explainable Artificial Intelligence."

a. Usual structure: present a problem; canvass alternatives; propose an evaluative scheme or method; recommend preferred solution.

b. Attribute problems to: distance between goal and implementation; conflict with a powerfully competing goal; the lack of fit between legal rules or practices when compared with changing social, economic, biological, or technical circumstances; or mistaken assumptions as demonstrated by historical review, economic model, psychological research, or evidence from other fields;

c. Not a brief: include fair analysis of a range of alternatives and alternative criteria; offer useful analyses even for people who do not agree with the assumptions, methodology, or conclusion.

IV. Test a proposition about society, the economy, technological developments, or about human beings/human behavior that is used by lawyers or assumed in legal sources, e.g., Robert Ellickson, *Order Without Law: How Neighbors Settle Disputes*; Robert H. Mnookin and Lewis Kornhauser, "Bargaining in the Shadow of the Law;" Lucian Bebchuk and Alma Cohen, "The Costs of Entrenched Boards;" Andrea Roth, "Machine Testimony;" and Da Lin, "Beyond Beholden."

a. Take a widely assumed or commonly known proposition familiar to lawyers or legal theorists;

b. Undertake an empirical investigation about its validity or summarize and assess empirical work conducted by others or undertake model- building or summarize and apply model(s) developed by others;

c. Digest the findings for legal audiences.

V. Study, explain, and assess legal institutions including courts, agencies, law schools), systems, or institutional (including end users—litigants, subjects of enforcement—affected by law), e.g., Abram Chayes, "The Role of the Judge in Public Law Litigation;" Marc Galanter, "Why the 'Haves Come out Ahead;" Richard Lempert, "A Classic at Galanter's 'Haves' Article and Work It Has Inspired;" George L. Priest & Benjamin Klein, "The Selection of Disputes for Litigation;" Judith Resnik, "Managerial Judges;" Patricia Ewick & Susan Silbey, *The Common Place of Law: Stories From Everyday Life*; David B. Wilkins & Mitu G. Gulati, "Reconceiving the Tournament of Lawyers: Tracking, Seeding, and Information Control in the Internal Labor Markets of Elite Law Firms;" John F. Manning, "What Divides Textualists from Purposivists;" Muneer Ahmad, "Interpreting Communities: Lawyering Across Language Difference;" Elizabeth Mertz, "Inside the Law School Classroom: Toward a New Legal Realist Pedagogy;" D. James Greiner & Cassandra Wolos Pattanayak, "Randomized Evaluation in Legal Assistance: What Difference Does Representation (Offer and Actual Use) Make?" Anna E. Carpenter, "The Project Model of Clinical Education: Eight Principles to Maximize Student Learning and Social Justice Impact;" Jeffrey L. Fisher, "A Clinic's Place in the Supreme Court Bar," Jack Balkin, Living Originalism; Bert Huang & Tejas N. Narechania, "Judicial Priorities;" William Baude & Stephen E. Sachs, "The Law of Interpretation;" Andrew D. Bradt, "'A Radical Proposal': The Multidistrict Litigation Act Of 1968;" Issa Kohler-Hausmann, *Misdemeanorland: Criminal Courts and Social Control in an Age of Broken Windows Policing*; Donna Shestowksy, "Inside the Mind of a Client: An Analysis of Litigants' Decision Criteria for Choosing Procedures;" Richard H. Fallon, Jr., "The Statutory Interpretation Muddle;" Lauren Sudeall & Ruth Richardson, "Unfamiliar Justice: Indigent Criminal Defendants' Experiences with Civil Legal Needs;" Matthew D. Cain, Sean J. Griffith, Robert J. Jackson, Jr., & Steven Davidoff Solomon, "Does Revlon Matter: An Empirical and Theoretical Study;" Kevin Tobia, Brian G. Slocum, & Victoria Nourse, "Statutory Interpretation From the Outside;" and Nicole Summers, "Civil Probation."

a. Offer historical, anthropological, sociological, or economic analysis of the behavior of legal actors or institutions, often exposing complexity, gaps between theories and practice, dynamics, and layers of meaning and effects;

b. Use, elucidate, or assess empirical methods and/or models;

c. Offer a normative assessment or agenda for further study.

VI. Critical projects, e.g., Duncan Kennedy, "Form and Substance in Private Law Adjudication;" Robert Cover, "Supreme Court—1982 Foreword: Nomos and Narrative;" Kimberlé Crenshaw, "Race, Reform, and Retrenchment: Transformation and Legitimation in Antidiscrimination Law;" David Shapiro, Federalism: A Dialogue; Randy E. Barnett, "The Misconceived Assumption About Constitutional Assumptions;" Libby Adler, Gay Priori: A Queer Critical Legal Studies Approach to Law Reform; Benjamin Levin, "What's Wrong with Police Unions;" Jamie Abrams, "Feminism's Transformation of Legal Education and Unfinished Agenda;" and Jamelia Morgan, "Rethinking Disorderly Conduct."

a. Expose unstated assumptions, patterns, or results, internally inconsistent structures or other tensions within a body of law or legal practices or institutions;

b. Highlight the tensions, contradictions, or paradoxes behind the surface of law or legal practices; sometimes they are not resolved but instead linked to larger psychological, social, or philosophic difficulties and political or normative efforts.

VII. Comparative and historical inquiries, e.g., Mary Ann Glendon, *Abortion and Divorce in Western Law*; Bruce H. Mann, *Republic of Debtors: Bankruptcy in the Age* *of American Independence*; William Forbath, "The Shaping of the American Labor Movement;" Anne Fleming, "The Rise and Fall of Unconscionability as the 'Law of the Poor;'" Nikolas Bowie, "Why the Constitution Was Written Down;" and Jennifer M. Chacón, "Immigration and Race."

a. Offer a rich description of an earlier era or contrasting legal regime;
b. Satisfy the criteria within the fields of anthropology or history in use of sources (including archival and primary), triangulation, and contextualization;
c. Suggest how this study illuminates differences, choices, or continuities when compared with contemporary domestic practice.
d. Present insight into the interactions across legal institutions or across law and society.

VIII. Jurisprudence, philosophy of law, and connecting philosophy and law, e.g., Ronald Dworkin, *Law's Empire*; Catharine MacKinnon, "Feminism, Marxism, Method, and the State: Toward Feminist Jurisprudence;" Richard A. Posner, *The Problematics of Moral and Legal Theory*; Seanna Shiffrin, "Speech, Death, and Double Effect;" Scott. A. Hershovitz, "Tort as a Substitute for Revenge;" Deborah Hellman, "A Theory of Bribery;" and Benjamin Eidelson, "Respect, Individualism, and Colorblindness."

a. Develop or elaborate a theory that tries to explain how all of law or chief portions of it hang together;
b. Engage with alternative theories;
c. Demonstrate the contribution this theory makes to a conceptual puzzle or set of doctrinal or practical problems;
d. Advance view of justice or analysis of what norms law should pursue.

IX. Combinations. Some works combine elements from more than one category, e.g., Cass Sunstein, "Interest Groups in American Public Law;" Derrick Bell, Jr., "Brown v. Board of Education and the Interest-Convergence Dilemma;" Lani Guinier, "The Triumph of Tokenism;" Frank H. Easterbrook & Daniel R. Fischel, "Voting in Corporate Law;" Ian Haney Lopez, White by Law: The Legal Construction of Race; and Carol Sanger, About Abortion: Terminating Pregnancy in 21st Century America.

Getting Started

How do you start on a project? In advising students, we have suggested the following. First, be excited about your idea. You can't write a good paper unless you care about your research question. Spend time thinking about the question itself. What makes you mad? What needs to change? The beauty of being a legal scholar … is getting to own your own mind. Once you've identified your motivating question, write a concise paragraph about it, explaining the question as if you were talking to your grandmother. Identify the idea or the problem and explain your argument, without including a literature review or introductory wind-up. What's the elevator pitch? Share that pitch with mentors and colleagues as you begin to develop your argument and situate it in the literature.

Genre

Projects differ in scope, size, and timeliness. When writing up the one paragraph of your idea, you should consider the form that idea will ultimately take. In this guide, we have cited books and articles as exemplars of each category. With innovations in communications, scholarly debates are also taking place in new settings beyond books and journals, especially when relevant to topics of immediate concern.

...

Audiences

As a scholar, you may find that your audience includes other scholars, judges, practitioners, law students, or the public at large, or, more likely, some combination thereof. As you situate your contribution in the literature, think about whom you want to reach and use framing, vocabulary, and explanations appropriate to those audiences.

...

Methodology

Legal scholarship draws on a number of methodological influences; as you work on your piece, consider which ones make sense for you. Are you engaged in empirical work (qualitative or quantitative)? Are you working entirely or largely with judge-made doctrines? Drawing on philosophical frameworks? Using historical research methods? Some combination? Being mindful and even explicit about your chosen method can assist readers and also remind the author to consider what is left out, what counterarguments to engage, and what to acknowledge but locate outside the scope of the project.

...

Edward Rubin,
*Should Law Schools Support Faculty Research?**

17 J. Contemp. Legal Issues 139 (2008)

...

Why don't some law schools cease to support or reward faculty research? If they did so, they could cut the faculty by two-fifths to a half while offering the same number of courses, and thus charge substantially lower tuition. Or they could offer a more intensive educational program, with individualized training in specific legal skills, while maintaining the same tuition. And why don't law firms then prefer to hire the graduates of these law schools, so that they could pay lower starting salaries or pay the same salaries for students who had received superior training? Regulation may have eliminated the competition between accredited law schools and other modes of training, but it has not eliminated the possibility of competition among law schools.

* Excerpts are reprinted with the permission of the author and the Journal of Contemporary Legal Issues.

...

The answer seems to be that research output is closely connected to the law school's prestige. Prestige is often a somewhat vaporous notion, but in the case of law schools it can be defined with exceptional, if much-maligned, precision by the school's ranking in U.S. News and World Report. The U.S. News rankings have a highly circular relationship with research-related indicators. Of the various weighted factors that are used to construct a school's ranking, reputation among other law schools (determined by a survey mailed to the dean and three faculty members at each school) counts for 25%, and reputation among legal practitioners counts for 15%. Other leading factors included are: student selectivity (determined largely by LSAT scores and grade point average), counting for 25%; and employment rate, which counts for about 20%. Reputation may be partially historical, but the main factor that determines it is the scholarly output of the faculty, the only feature of the school that is externally observable by the academic and practitioner communities.

Of course, the reputation that results from faculty research output may be merely symbolic; it is not impossible to imagine an entirely different structure for a system of legal education, where prestige depended solely on the quality of teaching that each school provided. But given the present system, any law school that tried to institute such an approach would experience a severe and probably fatal first mover problem. In addition, the connection between prestige and desirability may extend beyond the boundaries of legal education. Most law schools are part of a university and their prestige is not only determined by the research output of their faculty, but by the reputation of the university in general. The university's reputation is itself determined by its research output across a variety of fields and if that is also a symbolic relationship, it is one that the system of legal education, considered as a whole, is insufficiently powerful to change.

...

Research in other academic fields, whether hard science, social science or humanities, is regarded as valuable in our society. It provides knowledge for its own sake, it sustains our cultural traditions, and it serves as the basis for pragmatic advances in technology, social services and public governance. Legal scholarship serves all of these functions. It is particularly devoted to exploring the way our society is governed and recommending improvements in that process.

...

Even more particularly, if somewhat obviously, legal scholarship is uniquely focused on the legal system. While political scientists, economists, historians and sociologists devote some of their time to studying law, legal academics are responsible for the great bulk of the scholarly work on this subject and for an even greater portion of the normative work, that is, the work devoted to critiquing current law and legal practices and framing recommendations to legal decision makers for improvement of the process....

A typical work in law is directed toward a real-world decision maker—a judge, legislator, or administrator—and proposes a new possibility for judicial doctrine, legislation or administrative regulation.

...

As a result of its normative orientation, legal scholarship produces both direct and indirect benefits for participants in the legal system, benefits that accrue to legal practitioners as well as legal decision makers. For decision makers, legal scholarship is often a source of specific new ideas, or provides a summary and critique of existing rules and practices that serves as a basis for maintaining or altering these rules and practices. For legal practitioners, such as members of large corporate law firms, scholarship provides direct benefits in its summaries and critiques. Much of the research and analysis that practitioners would need to perform on their own is provided by law review articles, treatises, casebooks and even monographs. In addition, the scholarship provides an indirect benefit to practitioners through its direct benefits to legal decision makers.... But, to take a long-term view, the better the legal system functions, and the more social values such as fairness it achieves, the more our society will rely on law to address its problems and achieve its promises.

In short, then, legal scholarship benefits legal decision makers and legal practitioners.... It cannot possibly be claimed that there is any unfairness in a teacher's assiduous study of her subject matter. Indeed, the reverse is clearly true; law teachers are expected to be knowledgeable—for the most part, deeply knowledgeable—in their area of instruction.... The law professor who fails to keep pace with these developments, who is teaching overruled cases, outdated statutes or rescinded regulations, is not serving the students very well at all.

Thus, the concern is not that faculty members are spending time studying their subject matter, rather than teaching or preparing lessons, but that they are researching subjects that are unrelated to their teaching and engaging in the time-consuming task of writing articles and monographs on those unrelated subjects to establish or improve their scholarly reputations. Research-oriented law schools, like research universities in general, may claim that the faculty member who engages in creative, path-breaking research is likely to be a better teacher, but the assertion is difficult to sustain.... Thus, while there is almost certainly a connection between knowledge and teaching ability, the connection between research and teaching ability is attenuated at best, and the great likelihood is that these two skills vary almost independently of one another.

...

B. The Possible Reintegration of Teaching and Scholarship

... As an abstract matter, a person will be more externally effective and more internally fulfilled if the two roles mutually inform each other. Moreover, this was the premise on which law schools were initially designed; when Langdell moved away from the previous model of the practitioner as part-time instructor and hired his most enthusiastic student, James Barr Ames, as a full-time academic, it was with the idea that Ames' teaching and writing would correspond. This expectation was fulfilled during the so-called formalist era, the first half century after Langdell's appointment at Harvard. As stated above, the great scholarly achievements of this era were casebooks and treatises that closely mirrored the material that was presented in class and whose organization and arguments rested on the same conceptual foundation as the pedagogic methodology.

... [I]f we want to re-integrate teaching and scholarship and thereby restore the bygone unity of the formalist era, then what should we change? Should we tell law professors to abandon their current scholarly endeavors and return to the subject matter and conceptual orientation of the first year curriculum? Should we insist that they reverse their growing interest in empirical research and stop investigating the realities of law and legal practice in the twenty-first century? Should we relinquish the legal academy's hard won familiarity and expertise with other disciplines and close legal scholarship off from a century's progress in economics, political science, sociology, anthropology, social psychology and social history? Should we ask legal scholars to return to analyzing the internal logic of judicial decisions in isolation from the spectacular intellectual developments of the last hundred years and the general interdisciplinary trend in other university departments?

Or would it be better to think about changing the content and methodology of the law school curriculum? The first year of this curriculum, which is regarded as the most important year in terms of impact and career effect, is largely devoted to common law subjects and no longer reflects the kinds of legal practice that most graduating students enter. It ignores the advent of the regulatory state, globalization, corporate law, large-firm litigation and a variety of other developments, and even ignores transactional practice, which was as common in the 1870s as it is today. The methodology of these first year courses, moreover, remains rooted in the formalist belief that close analysis of cases will reveal enduring principles of Anglo-American law, a belief that very few lawyers or law professors find credible after the repeated criticisms of virtually all of twentieth century jurisprudence. Law school then introduces its students to the twentieth century in upper class, elective courses, but these courses have no relationship to each other; they are just a collection of individual topics, typically selected by individualized negotiation between each faculty member and the school's associate dean for academic affairs. They have no methodology of their own but borrow the methodology of the first year courses, although the formalist conception of law on which this methodology is based is completely at odds with the content of these largely statutory courses. To be sure, the upper class curriculum now includes a variety of seminars, simulations and clinical courses, but these are all seen as add-ons to the basic curriculum.

Consequently, if we want to eliminate the divergence between scholarship and teaching, what should change is not the scholarship but the curriculum. The scholarship is up-to-date with both the current practice of law, in its broadest sense, and with the current theories about what law is, and what it does, in our society. The curriculum has been obsolete, on both these fronts, for close to one hundred years.

Given the reward structure of the legal academy, this is hardly surprising. As stated above, all the material rewards that faculty receive are based on the quantity and quality of their research. Faculty members are thus strongly motivated to make their research innovative, relevant and insightful. And they can do so on their own, since scholarship is essentially an individual enterprise, involving coordination with one or two collaborators at most. In fact, law professors, in their role as legal scholars, can be regarded an individual entrepreneurs, marketing their product primarily to other legal academics, and secondarily to legal practitioners and the scholarly community in general. In contrast, teaching is a generally left to the faculty member's personal sense of responsibility and the few paltry awards that are conferred for excellence do little to change this. Many law professors take this responsibility seriously, and are effective teachers, but since the students, unlike legal academics and practitioners, are generally not in contact with new developments in the legal field, they do not place demands on their teachers to update their courses. Moreover, even if they do so, it will not be sufficient.

Those who criticize legal scholarship because it has diverged from teaching often condemn legal scholars as self-indulgent, as following their own interests rather than serving the students' needs. But there is nothing self-indulgent about conducting research in new, exciting areas, nothing self-indulgent about an experienced researcher pursuing interests that have developed from years of studying a particular field. At least one philosopher of science, Imre Lakatos, has identified the research program as the essence of a rational knowledge....

Scholarship seems self-indulgent only when contrasted with the so-called service courses to which law professors have chained themselves, and which so many of them don't want to teach because the course is so remote from their research. The sensible response to this problem is not to discourage or suppress faculty research because it diverges from a curriculum which is over a hundred years old, and which faculty members have never been incentivized to change. Rather, the response should be a change in the curriculum so that it corresponds more closely to the up-to-date, intellectually stimulating research that faculty members are pursuing.

...

The obvious objection, already noted above, is that law students don't want to be, and are not being trained to be, researchers.... Lawyers need to be able to gather facts, to organize large bodies of material, and to analyze this material in accordance with some theme or purpose. They need to be able to present the material, and their analysis of it, to their colleagues in an effective manner. They need to be able to critique a colleague's work in a searching, rigorous manner, while remaining on good terms with that colleague. These are all skills that can be taught in a seminar format where students do a serious research project and present it in the class.

...

This same approach can be expanded well beyond the traditional format of a research project, that is, a written paper based on written sources. It could, for example, include clinical experiences, a common activity for third year students, and one of the few types of law school courses that continues to engage their interest at this stage. The traditional view of a clinic is that it provides a legal service, that it enables the students to learn legal skills by doing what they would do in practice on a smaller scale, and with people who are not in a position to obtain assistance from a more experienced attorney. But, without abandoning this approach in any way, clinics can also be viewed as sources of empirical data. A clinic connected to a research seminar can function as a window on the outside world. It could inform a criminal justice seminar about the operation of the courts in the community or the local prosecutor's plea bargaining practices. It could inform an administrative law seminar how state or local agencies function. It could inform a commercial law seminar about consumer or institutional behavior. Thus, students who were not so inclined would not even need to write anything to benefit from an integrated seminar and clinic where the seminar component was taught by a faculty member who is actively engaged in research. The faculty member could advance the students' education by giving them a set of questions to ask themselves, a protocol for inquiry, some themes to note in a journal and to report on orally in class. In other words, the faculty member's research agenda could thus inform the students' work, so that they would be participant observers as well as service providers.

To realize possibilities of this sort, the rigid structure of law school classes would need to be altered. In place of the three or four credit lecture class, or the three credit seminar that fits into the same temporal and conceptual slot, a research-oriented seminar would need to run all year and give the students enough credits so that they could spend a significant portion of their time on their research or clinical project and related classroom activities. If the students spent half their time on a seminar of this sort, they would need to receive ten to fifteen credits.

...

Endnotes

1. Praveen Kosuri, *Clinical Legal Education at a Generational Crossroads: X Marks the Spot*, 17 Clinical L. Rev. 205, 205–208 (2010).

2. Frank Albritton, *Humboldt's Unity of Research and Teaching: Influence on the Philosophy and Development of U.S. Higher Education*, (2006), https://ssrn.com/abstract=939811.

3. *Id.* at 6–7.

4. *Id.* at 7–8.

5. *The Law Review*, Penn Carey L., Univ. of Pennsylvania, https://www.law.upenn.edu/journals/lawreview/.

6. *Submitting Papers to Law Journals: Journal Rankings*, Mich. L. Library https://libguides.law.umich.edu/journal_submissions/rankings. (citing the Washington & Lee's Law Journal rankings).

7. William Pincus, Clinical Education For Law Students at 56–57 (1980).

8. *Id.*

9. Robert Dinerstein, *Report of the Committee on the Future of the In-House Clinic*, 42 J. Legal Educ. 511, 516 (1992).

10. Clinical Education, The Report Of The Association Of American Law Schools—American Bar Association Committee on the Guidelines for Clinical Education, (1980) (hereinafter AALS—ABA Report).

11. *Id.* at 121.

12. *Id.*

13. *Id.* at 122.

14. *Id.* at 114, n.146.

15. George S. Grossman, Clinical Education: An Annotated Bibliography, Council on Legal Education for Professional Responsibility (1974) https://repository.library.georgetown.edu/bitstream/handle/10822/1060795/CLE-An-Annotated-Bibliography.pdf?sequence=1. The bibliography listed articles by Jerome Frank, Karl Llewellyn, and other legal realist scholars advocating for practical legal training between the 1920s and 1940s, articles by Dean Edward Levi, Professor John Bradway and Erwin Griswold as the debate reemerged in the 1950s, and articles by various members of the founding generation of the new clinical teachers during the 1960s and 1970s.

16. When I say "true" clinical courses, I mean those later envisioned by William Pincus—inhouse clinical course awarding credit, taught by full-time law faculty members, with real clients represented by students with faculty supervision.

17. Robin West & Danielle Citron, *On Legal Scholarship*, at 3, https://www.aals.org/wp-content/uploads/2014/08/OnLegalScholarship-West-Citron.pdf.

18. *See*, Brooklyn Law School, *Our Mission Statement*, https://www.brooklaw.edu/About-Us/Mission.

19. West & Citroen, *supra* note 17 at 3.

20. *Id.*

21. Grossman, *supra* note 15 at 18, citing Gary Bellow, *On Teaching the Teachers: Some Preliminary Reflections on Clinical Education as Methodology*, Papers From the Buck Hills Conference 375.

22. Gary Bellow & Bea Moulton, The Lawyering Process: Materials for Clinical Instruction in Advocacy, Foundation Press (1978).

23. Gary Palm, *Message from the Chair, Scholarship and Clinical Education*, Sect. On Clinical Legal Educ. Newsletter, Ass'n Am. L. Schs. 1 (Sept. 1986).

24. Robert Dinerstein, *Message from the Chair*, Sect. On Clinical Legal Educ. Newsletter, Ass'n Am. L. Schs. 3 (Vol. 92, No. 2, Sept. 1992).

25. Robert Dinerstein, *The Clinical Law Review At 25-What Hath We Wrought?* 26 CLINICAL L. REV. 147 at 148 (2019).

26. *Id.*

27. *Id.* at 149

28. Robert D. Dinerstein, *Clinical Scholarship and the Justice Mission*, 40 CLEVE. ST. L. REV. 469, 469–74 (1992) [in Symposium, The Justice Mission of American Law Schools, 40 CLEVE. ST. L. REV. Nos. 3 & 4 (1992).

29. Dinerstein, *supra* note 25 at 149.

30. *Id.* at 150 (quoting various portions of Stephen Ellmann, Isabelle R. Gunning, and Randy Hertz, *Foreword, Why Not a Clinical Lawyer-Journal?*, 1 CLINICAL L. REV. 1 (Spring 1994)).

31. Sandy Ogilvy & Karen Czapanskiy, 7 CLINICA. LAW REV. 1, Special Issue (2001) It has since been revised several times.

32. Alex J. Hurder, Frank S. Block, Susan L. Brooks, and Susan L Kay published the first edition OF CLINICAL ANTHOLOGY, READINGS FOR A LIVE CLIENT CLINIC, (Carolina Academic Press (1997).

33. *Id.* at 7

34. *Id.*

35. *Id.*

36. See John S. Elson, *The Case Against Legal-Scholarship or, If the Professor Must Perish, Must the Profession Perish?*, 39 J. OF LEGAL EDUC. 343 at n. 2 (1989), citing articles by Francis A. Allen, Robert Stevens, and Robert Condlin.

37. Carrie Menkel-Meadow, *Narrowing the Gap by Narrowing the Field: What's Missing from the MacCrate Report—Of Skills, Legal Science and Being a Human Being*, 69 WASH. L. REV. 593, 595 (1994).

38. *See* Elson, *supra* note 36 at 343 n. 1–3, citing articles by Paul D. Carrington, Anthony T. Kronman, Roger C. Cramton, and John O. Mudd.

39. *Id.* at 350 n. 22 citing Michael J, Graetz, Charles H. Whitebread II, and Monrad Paulson.

40. *Id.* at 354.

41. See Mark Spiegel, *Theory and Practice in Legal Education: An Essay on Clinical Education*, 34 UCLA L. REV. 577, 606 (1987).

42. Harry T. Edwards, *The Growing Disjunction Between Legal Education and the Legal Profession*, 91 MICH. L. REV. 34 (1992).

43. *Id.* at 35

44. *Id.*

45. See Elson, *supra* note 36 at 343.

46. Richard Delgado & Jean Stefancic, *Critical Race Theory: Past, Present, and Future*, 51 CURRENT LEGAL PROBLEMS, 467 (1998).

47. Martha Minow & Susannah Barton Tobin, *Archetypal Legal Scholarship: A Field Guide*, 2d. Edition, 71 J. LEGAL EDUC. 494 (2022).

48. Elson *supra* note 36.

49. *Id. passim.*

50. Not so long ago an email thread on the Clinical Listserv renewed the conversation. Emails from Bruce Boyer, Robert Dinerstein, Jon Dubin, and Wallace Mlyniec in May of 2022 (on file with the author).

51. Volume V, No. 11 Council on Legal Education for Professional Responsibility, *CLEPR Invites Applications* at 45 (1973). https://www.law.edu/_media/imported-media/clepr-newsletters-jan-1973-may-19742.pdf.

52. Peter A. Joy, Robert R. Kuehn, and Beverly Owens, *The Evolution of ABA Standards for Clinical Faculty*, 75 Tenn, L. Rev. 197 (2008) citing Beverly T. Watkins, *Teachers of Clinical Law Seek Recognition, Better Treatment*, Chron. Higher Educ., Jan. 19, 1983, at 14.

53. Peter A. Joy, Robert R. Kuehn, & Beverly Owens, *The Evolution of ABA Standards for Clinical Faculty* 75 Tenn, L. Rev. 183, 190 (2008).

54. *Id.* at 205 n. 123.

55. Seed money for the original CSALE study was supplied by the Clinical Legal Education Association (CLEA).

56. The Center for the study of Applied Legal Education, https://www.csale.org/#results.

57. *Id.*

58. Bryan L. Adamson et al., *Clinical Faculty in the Legal Academy: Hiring, Promotion and Retention*, 62 J. Legal Educ. 115 (2012).

59. *Id.* at 126–131. They also included another type of status, the clinical fellowship, which was a time-limited arrangement, sometimes accompanied by an LL.M degree, designed to train people to become clinical teachers. *Id.* at 131.

60. Robert R. Kuehn & David Santacroce, *An Empirical Analysis of Clinical Education at Middle Age*, 71 J. Legal Educ 622, 641(2022).

61. *Id.*

62. *Id.*

63. *Id.* at 642.

64. *Id.* at 650.

65. *Id.* at 641.

66. *Id.* at 642.

67. *See,* Dinerstein *supra* note 24.

68. Stephen Ellmann, Isabelle R. Gunning & Randy Hertz, *Why Not a Clinical Lawyer-Journal*, 1 Clinical L. Rev. 1, 2 (Spring 1994).

69. *Id.*

70. *Id. see also* AALS—ABA Report, *supra* note 10 at 121.

71. *See* Mission statement from the University of California Academic Plan, 1974–1978, https://www.ucop.edu/about/mission/index.html.

72. Martha Minow and Susannah Barton Tobin, *Archetypal Legal Scholarship: A Field Guide*, 74 J. Legal Educ. 494 (2022).

73. *See* Dinerstein, *supra* note 25, at 27 and accompanying text.

INDEX